P9-BIX-407

MAGILL'S CINEMA ANNUAL

1982

MAGILL'S CINEMA ANNUAL

1982

A Survey of 1981 Films

Edited by

FRANK N. MAGILL

Associate Editors

PATRICIA KING HANSON

STEPHEN L. HANSON

SALEM PRESS
Englewood Cliffs, N.J.

ISBN 0-89356-400-1
ISBN 0-89356-401-X pbk.

First Printing

PRINTED IN THE UNITED STATES OF AMERICA

PUBLISHER'S NOTE

Magill's Survey of Cinema, English Language Films (First Series, four volumes; Second Series, six volumes) and Silent Films (three volumes), has provided the film industry and filmgoers with an invaluable reference tool. As an outgrowth of these projects, and of the projected foreign-language film set, *Magill's Cinema Annual* will make available the same depth of information on contemporary films. Covering the 1981 film year, this first annual volume provides the reader with a variety of articles about cinema, reviews of eighty 1981 films, reviews of twenty films of the past, and extensive indexes which make all the information readily accessible. Subsequent volumes to follow annually are planned and will adhere to the same format.

The volume begins with an article on the year's recipient of the Life Achievement Award, which is presented annually by the American Film Institute. Following this essay are personal interviews with notable figures in the film industry. Essays of general interest appear next, one of which will always be devoted to an overview of the year and another to a discussion of cinema-related books published during the same year.

The largest portion of the volume is devoted to essay-reviews of noteworthy English- and foreign-language films released in the United States during the year. Arranged alphabetically, each review follows a consistent format. First, all relevant information about the film appears in the article's top matter, which always includes a listing for production, direction, screenplay, cinematography, editing, art direction, music, MPAA rating (for all American films), and running time in minutes. Any other information pertinent to the film is also included in the top matter; for example, because *An American Werewolf in London* won the first Academy Award for "special makeup effects," a listing for that category is given. The top matter also provides a list of the film's principal characters and the names of their performers.

Should the information for any of the standard listings be unavailable, the heading is followed by the phrase "no listing." Also, all Academy Award winners appearing in the top matter are followed by the designation (AA).

The body of the essays is devoted to an analysis of the film, which discusses the plot, the artistic achievement, the film's relevance to a particular genre or artist's canon, or any other element that has contributed to the film's importance.

The next section of the volume is retrospective and covers films released prior to the year under discussion. The format of these films follows exactly that of the previous section, except the MPAA rating, which does not exist for those films released before 1956.

The final two sections of the book are listings. The first list is the "Obituaries," an extensive alphabetical presentation of "industry people" who died during the year. Second is the "List of Awards," which includes the major awards presented by the Academy of Motion Picture Arts and Sciences, the Directors Guild of America (one award given), the Writers Guild, the New York Film Critics, the Los Angeles Film Critics, the National Society of Film Critics, the National Board of Review, the Golden Globe Society, Cannes International Film Festival, and the British Academy.

Concluding the volume are nine separate indexes; the first is the Title Index, which lists all the films with an individual review, as well as those discussed in the various essays (the page references for those titles appearing in the essays are set in bold-face type to distinguish them from the regular reviews). This index is followed by an individual index for directors, screen-writers, cinematographers, editors, art directors, music directors, and performers. The final listing is a Subject Index, in which any one film can be found under several subject headings. For example, the film *Arthur* is listed under the headings "Alcoholism," "Death and Dying," "Maturing," "New York," "Prostitutes and Prostitution," "Romance," and "Weddings."

In sum, *Magill's Cinema Annual* gives the user an in-depth and accurate look at the year in film. In a single volume, it provides an up-to-date and informative source for anyone interested in the cinema.

PREFACE

MAGILL'S CINEMA ANNUAL, 1982, is the inaugural volume in a new reference service planned for yearly publication in the field of cinema. This upkeep service will be especially useful for those who have acquired *Magill's Survey of Cinema* (13 vols., 1980, 1981, 1982). The current volume, comprising one hundred essay-reviews of three to five pages each, includes eighty films released in the United States in 1981—nineteen of which are recently released foreign films—and twenty retrospective films still worthy of note. The latter selections range in time from the 1920's to 1980, with one 1923 silent film included (the delightful *Dulcy*, starring Constance Talmadge.)

In addition to one hundred films selected for this volume from the hundreds released in 1981, other features herein embrace reports of awards given, including the Life Achievement Award presented to Fred Astaire by the American Film Institute, interviews with screenwriter DeWitt Bodeen and actress Fay Wray, three critical essays on "The Cinema of 1981," "Modern Cinema and Silent Cinema," and "Cinema Books of 1981," and an extensive coverage of obituaries. Eight separate indexes at the end of the volume show Directors, Screenwriters, Cinematographers, Editors, Art Directors, Performers included in the films covered, as well as music involved, and the subject classifications. Each essay-review is headed by a listing of pertinent information giving data on production, direction, screenwriting, cinematography, editing, art direction, music, MPAA rating (when applicable), running time of the film in minutes, and a list of the principal characters with corresponding performers.

Limiting the number of films covered obviously implies a highly selective list, but an attempt has been made to deal with those films that are controversial with good reason, or representative of the societal mood of the times, or that exhibit outstanding creativity, or that seem possessed of enduring qualities beyond the norm.

Humor has always been one of the Hollywood staples, often expressed in the screwball comedy, and *Arthur*, which provided an Oscar for John Gielgud, offers a prime example. A surprise winner of four Oscars was *Chariots of Fire*, an intriguing story based on the 1924 Olympics, which won the Academy Award for Best Picture, Best Original Screenplay, Best Costume Design, and Best Original Score. Perhaps the most popular Oscar selection of the year was that of Henry Fonda as Best Actor, in *On Golden Pond*. Fonda's great career had never been recognized with this honor until his last picture. Katharine Hepburn, who won the Academy Award for Best Actress in the same film, had won three previous Oscars during her distinguished career.

Among other above-average films of the year were *Atlantic City*, critically acclaimed with five Academy Award nominations but no first places; *The*

French Lieutenant's Woman shared the same fate. *Reds* and *Raiders of the Lost Ark*, however, did much better, the first gaining Academy Awards for Direction, Supporting Actress, and Cinematography while the latter won Oscars for Editing, Art Direction, Visual Effects, and Sound. Also listed under the "Award Winners" section are the selections of the following organizations: Directors Guild of America, Writers Guild, New York Film Critics, Los Angeles Film Critics, National Society of Film Critics, National Board of Review, The Golden Globe, and the British Academy.

The twenty retrospective films reviewed in this volume include *Apache* (1954), a film that offers a sympathetic portrayal of the American Indian in contrast to the usual Hollywood insensitive depiction of native Americans; Rouben Mamoulian's *Becky Sharp* (1935), which features Miriam Hopkins as *Vanity Fair*'s grasping central character; Joseph L. Mankiewicz's *The Barefoot Contessa* (1954), featuring Humphrey Bogart and Ava Gardner; and *Napoleon*, the much admired 1927 Abel Gance film which has been rescued from oblivion by film historian Kevin Brownlow and director Francis Ford Coppola.

The nineteen films represented here which originated in foreign countries were released in the United States in 1981. Countries of origin are France (5), England, Germany, Australia, and Poland (2 each), with one each from Switzerland, Yugoslavia, Italy, Japan, Brazil, and Hungary. The German releases include the famous *Lili Marleen*, and the two Polish films are *Man of Marble* and *Man of Iron*, directed by Andrzej Wajda and dealing with political repression in that country.

The obituary section lists eighty-four figures associated with films who died in 1981, one of whom is Hoagy Carmichael, perhaps remembered best for his song "Stardust" but also known to filmgoers for roles in a number of fine films, including *The Best Years of Our Lives* (1946). Among other performers named in the 1981 list are Melvyn Douglas, Robert Montgomery, Patsy Kelly, Beulah Bondi, Ann Harding, and Vera-Ellen. Filmgoers were also especially saddened by the accidental deaths of Natalie Wood and William Holden during the year. Among the noted directors who died in 1981 are William Wyler, Norman Taurog, Allen Dwan, Brazilian director Glauber Rocha, and French director Abel Gance, whose 1927 film *Napoleon* was revived in 1981 in time for the director to be aware of its renewed impact. Other Hollywood figures who died during the year include Jules C. Stein, founder of Music Corporation of America, costume designer Edith Head, composer Harry Warren, screenwriter Anita Loos, and Karl Straus, one of Hollywood's greatest cameramen.

Two other features appear in the new *Cinema Annual*: a review of cinema-related books published in 1981, and two special essays, one on the state of the art in 1981, the other a historical sketch discussing silent cinema's influence on modern sound films. In "Cinema Books of 1981," Stephen L. Hanson applies his two academic backgrounds—Library Science and Cinema—to provide a survey of some of the outstanding books dealing with cinema that were published in 1981.

In his essay "The Cinema of 1981," Blake Lucas, in discussing the shift from the "classical" period of cinema to the contemporary version of popular film entertainment in the mid-1960's, takes note of the enormous technological developments spawned by the audience appetite for home entertainment (called by some the "video revolution") and also draws attention to "the gradual coarsening of the American cinema which began around 1964." Social upheaval has resulted in changing mores, reflected in popular entertainment which spreads instantaneously throughout the land by means of cable television and video cassettes honed for private viewing. No cultural force of such power has ever existed on this massive scale.

"Modern Cinema and Silent Cinema" pays homage to the exquisite moods developed in the days of silent cinema, whose potential is now being recognized and employed by perceptive sound filmmakers. As the essay points out, the communication of intense emotions on the screen can, on occasion, be more effective without the use of a sound track. Readers interested in film history should find this essay interesting and enjoyable.

I wish to thank the Staff and the special writers for their contribution to the development of this initial volume in a new Annual series. We trust that we have provided a useful reference service for those concerned with the growth and study of film criticism and film history.

Frank N. Magill

LIST OF CONTRIBUTORS

Irene Kahn Atkins
DeWitt Bodeen
Ronald Bowers
Pat H. Broeske
William M. Clements
Joan L. Cohen
Grant Davidson
Rob Edelman
Patricia King Hanson
Stephen L. Hanson
Thomas A. Hanson
Larry Lee Holland
Julia Johnson
Timothy W. Johnson
Judith M. Kass
Roberta Le Feuvre
Diana Lisignoli
Janet E. Lorenz
Blake Lucas
Frances M. Malpezzi
Carl J. Mir
Robert Mitchell
Anthony Slide
Ellen Jo Snyder
Betti Stone
Anna Kate Sterling
Don K Thompson
Frederick Travers
John Wilson
Marilynn Wilson
Sharon Wiseman

CONTENTS

MAGILL'S CINEMA ANNUAL

1982

Life Achievement Award
FRED ASTAIRE

The American Film Institute's Life Achievement Award in 1981 was given to Fred Astaire, the man who has appeared in more classic musical films than any other performer. Astaire has choreographed much of his own work, and has continued his career as an actor in nonmusical productions. It is arguable that he has had a greater impact upon American cinema than any other single performer; it is certainly true that he played a key role in the two eras of musical films that are most often called classic: at the RKO studio in the 1930's and at the M-G-M studio in the 1940's and 1950's.

Frederick Austerlitz was born in Omaha, Nebraska, in 1899. At the age of four, however, his mother took him and his older sister, Adele, to New York to learn dancing and to become performers. Within a few years they had begun a vaudeville career and had changed their last name to Astaire, the maiden name of their paternal grandmother. By the time Fred was seventeen, the two had progressed to Broadway and were extremely popular in such shows as *Lady Be Good*, *Funny Face*, and *The Band Wagon*. (Though Astaire much later appeared in film versions of the latter two, the films were nothing like the stage shows; they used only the titles and a few of the songs.) The Astaires were also a hit in London. Then, in 1932, Adele retired to marry Lord Charles Cavendish. Fred appeared in one more stage musical, *Gay Divorce*, and then turned to Hollywood. It was also during this time that he courted and married Phyllis Potter, to whom he remained married until her death in 1954.

Astaire's first appearance in a film, a small part in *Dancing Lady* (1933), showed no indication of what was to come; but, by the time he had made two more films, it became obvious that a new cinematic talent had emerged. Actually Astaire was both talented and fortunate. He was fortunate that he began making films at precisely the right time. The changeover from silent to sound that began in 1927 had been accomplished, and most of the technical problems of making sound films had been solved. No longer did the camera have to be enclosed in a large, unmovable booth, and no longer were microphones kept in one position for an entire shot. Obviously a static camera would be unsuitable for filming a dancer. Although much progress had been made in the technical aspects of sound filming by the time Astaire turned to Hollywood, the film musical was still being developed. Because the musical was in its infancy, Astaire was able to try his own ideas without being restricted by established rules.

Astaire was also fortunate that he signed his first contract with RKO, because that studio allowed him to have great control over the filming and editing of his musical numbers and because at that studio were two people with whom he was to work quite successfully for many years: dance director

Hermes Pan and actress Ginger Rogers.

After his small part in *Dancing Lady* for M-G-M, Astaire had a larger part in his first film for RKO, *Flying Down to Rio* (1933), but he was not the star. The film, which featured Delores del Rio and Gene Raymond, used Astaire and Rogers in supporting roles. Astaire and Rogers did, however, dance to "The Carioca." It was in his next film, *The Gay Divorcee* (1934), that Astaire moved from the background to the foreground—where he was to remain for several decades. In this film, Astaire and Rogers were the romantic costars and danced together to "Night and Day" and "The Continental." Film audiences finally were able to see the many facets of Astaire's talent: dancing, singing, choreography, and light comedy. He and Rogers went on to make seven more films together for RKO, a body of work that by itself constitutes one of the three or four classic periods of American musical cinema.

In these films, the plots were light, frivolous, or foolish, depending upon one's point of view. They often depended upon such contrivances as coincidence and mistaken identity, and the story and dialogue portions are regarded by many as merely something to be endured between the musical numbers. Compared to other comedies of the 1930's (or to the crude comedies of the late 1970's and early 1980's), however, the story element of the films is entertaining and enjoyable if not sublime. Astaire's talent for light-comedy acting is well-employed, as is that of Rogers and the expert supporting players who appear in most of the films—Edward Everett Horton, Alice Brady, Helen Broderick, and Eric Blore.

It is not the plots, of course, that make the Astaire-Rogers films the exquisite delights they are; their principal virtue is the dancing of Astaire, alone or with Rogers. In *The Gay Divorcee* are two of the best numbers of the series, numbers that established patterns that were used in many of the other films. Early in the film, Astaire dances alone to "A Needle in a Haystack," using no props except the furniture of the room and such items as a dressing gown and a tie as he gets dressed to go out. According to dance critic Arlene Croce, who has written an entire book on the Astaire-Rogers films, this is "the number that first defined the Astaire character on the screen." Later, he dances with Rogers to the Cole Porter classic "Night and Day." In this flawless number Astaire must use dance to persuade Rogers to accept him. When he begins dancing, she resists him, but finally gives in, joins him, and they dance together brilliantly. The sequence is superbly effective as dance and as drama. In many of the future Astaire-Rogers films, the plot would give Rogers some reason to dislike or resist Astaire so that he could persuade her through dance.

Though he had no experience in film before 1933, Astaire quickly developed a style of filming dancing that combined the best features of stage and screen presentation. He did not like two techniques that were (and still are) often used in filming dance: inserted shots that interrupt the flow of a dance number and close-ups that prevent the audience from seeing the dancer's whole body. As much as possible he avoided such commonly used inserted shots as someone watching the dancer, and because he knew that a dancer's performance is given with the whole body, not merely the feet, he shunned close-ups of dancing feet. Film does have at least two great advantages over the stage, however, and Astaire used them well. Not only can film show the dance from the best angle and distance, but it can also preserve the dancer's best performance. Since Astaire is a perfectionist, this latter quality appealed to him. He spent immense amounts of time preparing and rehearsing for each number and then usually filmed it over and over so that he could select the best performance. It is amazing that Astaire was able to grasp so quickly the essentials of filmmaking, and equally amazing that he was allowed to exercise such control over the early films in which he appeared.

During the time he was making films with Ginger Rogers, Astaire made only one film without her (*A Damsel in Distress*, 1937), but after *The Story of Vernon and Irene Castle* in 1939, the series of Astaire-Rogers films ended and Astaire moved on to other partners and other studios. In his first post-RKO film, he danced with Eleanor Powell in *Broadway Melody of 1940*, and then went on to share the screen with many other dancing partners—Rita Hayworth, Lucille Bremer, Judy Garland, Cyd Charisse, and Audrey Hepburn. He had announced his retirement after *Blue Skies* in 1946, having already danced professionally for more than forty years, but he returned about two years later. He continued his dancing roles through *Silk Stockings* in 1957, and from that time on has appeared only as a straight actor, except for three award-winning television specials in 1959 and 1960, in which he danced with Barrie Chase. Although he never achieved the special onscreen chemistry that he enjoyed with Rogers with any of his other partners, his post-RKO career was nearly as outstanding as the earlier one. Each of his films had at least one outstanding number and several—*Easter Parade* (1948), *The Band Wagon* (1953), *Funny Face* (1957), and *Silk Stockings*—are recognized as classics of American musical cinema. He even had an unexpected reunion with Ginger Rogers when she replaced Judy Garland just before the shooting of *The Barkleys of Broadway* (1948). Unfortunately, the result was merely an average musical rather than a return to the exciting quality of the RKO films.

Astaire did not like to repeat his old dance routines in new films, so he was continually devising inventive new dances. He danced with a hatrack as his partner (*Royal Wedding*, 1951), with disembodied shoes (*The Barkleys of Broadway*), with firecrackers (*Holiday Inn*, 1942), and in *Royal Wedding* he danced on the ceiling of a room. These sequences are often shown to demonstrate Astaire's versatility, but in most of his best numbers he dances alone or with a human partner in a fairly simple setting.

Another noteworthy aspect of Astaire's career is that of the top five American popular composers who were writing during his musical career—George Gershwin, Cole Porter, Jerome Kern, Irving Berlin, and Richard Rodgers—only Rodgers did not write any songs for Astaire. Indeed, the British critic John Russell Taylor contends that writing for Astaire brought out the best in Irving Berlin, and the numbers in such films as *Top Hat* (1935), *Follow the Fleet* (1935), and *Easter Parade* support the argument. Taylor writes that "The essence of Astaire's singing style is that he sings as he dances—lightly, swiftly, with a buoyancy which seems to defy gravity and chafe at confinement to the ground."

By the beginning of the 1950's, Fred Astaire had become such an important figure, or legend, in musical films that his own career became the basis of one of his best films. Betty Comden and Adolph Green, who had written *The Barkleys of Broadway* for him, were assigned to write another film. The only requirements were that it star Astaire and use the songs of Howard Dietz and Arthur Schwartz, who had written the songs for *The Band Wagon*, Astaire's last Broadway show with his sister Adele. The studio also stipulated that the film would be called *The Band Wagon*, even though it would bear little resemblance to the stage show. Comden and Green decided to use as part of the plot some elements of Astaire's career that any filmgoer would recognize. The film begins with a shot of a top hat and cane, Astaire's trademarks. They are being auctioned off as the "most famous top hat and stick of our generation." The plot does not, however, follow Astaire's career exactly. It gains added resonance by its concern with the themes of loneliness, failure, and the passage of time; it therefore presents Tony Hunter (the Astaire character) as having lost his popularity and trying to make a comeback on the Broadway stage. The resulting film, which Adolph Green calls "a kind of tribute to, and summing up of, the grace and charm of Fred's performing lifetime," is a masterpiece of cinema musicals and arguably the best film Astaire made after leaving RKO. At one point, Gabrielle (played by Cyd Charisse) tells Hunter that she saw his films in a revival at a museum; now *The Band Wagon* itself is shown at museums and revival theaters.

After *Silk Stockings*, Astaire made his screen debut as a dramatic actor in *On the Beach* (1959) and received quite favorable reviews. He has continued this phase of his career with film appearances every few years, even receiving an Academy Award nomination for his role in *The Towering Inferno* (1974). Astaire's success as a dramatic actor surprised some people and has been overlooked in many evaluations of his career as a whole, but it is a natural outgrowth of his musical career. After all, most of his musical films contained less than fifteen or twenty minutes of singing and dancing, so Astaire did have ample experience in straight acting in a variety of roles. Most of these roles, of course, were lighter than that of the sardonic British scientist he played in *On the Beach*, a film about the annihilation of mankind in a nuclear war.

It is impossible for one brief article to describe and evaluate all of Fred

Astaire's contributions to film; as Ephraim Katz states, "Almost single-handedly, Fred Astaire restyled the song-and-dance film, leaving his mark on all musical movies to come." When M-G-M collected numbers from its greatest musicals in *That's Entertainment* (1974) and *That's Entertainment, Part II* (1976), many Astaire numbers were included, and Astaire served as one of the on-camera narrators. In the first film, one of the other narrators, Frank Sinatra, remarks about Astaire and Eleanor Powell dancing to "Begin the Beguine," "You can wait around and hope, but I'll tell you, you'll never see the likes of this again." Strangely, Astaire has not received a regular Academy Award, but in 1949 the Academy made up for this oversight by presenting him with a special Oscar for his contributions to the technique of musical films and for his "unique artistry."

Timothy W. Johnson

An Interview with
DeWitt Bodeen

For more than forty years, DeWitt Bodeen has been making literary contributions to most of the lively arts: motion pictures, the theater, television, magazines, and books. The common denominator of all these efforts is his enjoyment of, and faithful devotion to, accurate and thorough research.

Born in Fresno, California, in 1908, he became, he says, alternately "stage-struck" and "movie-struck." His first work that brought recognition was a play, *A Thing of Beauty*, which was based on the life of John Keats. It was followed by plays about George Gordon, Lord Byron, Percy Bysshe Shelley, and the Brontë sisters; all required extensive research. His playwriting came to the attention of Gilmore Brown, production head of the Pasadena Playhouse. DeWitt Bodeen's affiliation with the Playhouse included, in addition to production of several of his plays, acting, teaching, and a book of biographical essays about several famous stage actresses.

His knowledge of the Brontës led to an assignment as research assistant on David O. Selznick's *Jane Eyre* (1944), working with Aldous Huxley. At the Selznick Studios, Bodeen met Val Lewton, who assigned the young man to script his first production, a "high class horror" film. That was the inception of *Cat People*, the subtly gripping 1942 thriller, not the blood-soaked 1982 version. Research into legends about cats of ancient Egypt and India added an intriguing touch to the mysticism of the Lewton film. Frequently revived, the 1942 film truly deserves the approbation "classic."

Bodeen's film scripts, while not numerous, include the touching *I Remember Mama* (1948), Herman Melville's *Billy Budd* (1962), and two other Lewton features. All required patient, skillful writing under demanding producers.

His interest in silent films and "the old-timers" led to his researching and writing many articles of film history, often detailing Hollywood in the 1920's, his favorite era. These essays now appear in book form, in *From Hollywood* and *More from Hollywood*.

Bodeen's knowledge of the sweethearts of the screen during the 1910's and 1920's forms the background of his entertaining mystery novel, *13 Castle Walk*. Most significant is his collaborative work on the standard reference volume on screenwriters, *Who Wrote the Movie and What Else Did He Write?*

Although DeWitt Bodeen has experienced shared screen credits and arbitrations, his complete lack of rancor toward any of his colleagues with whom a conflict had arisen was impressive. He also was scrupulously attentive to giving credit to his collaborators. One is also impressed by the idea that he is completely at ease with his own special talents and achievements, and heartened by his eagerness and enthusiasm to keep on writing about films and the Hollywood he knows so well.

Irene Kahn Atkins

Q: You were born in Fresno. Did being that close to Los Angeles and Hollywood have an influence on your life?

Bodeen: Yes, it did. My parents always went to stay in Ocean Park or someplace along the beach every summer, and I came, too. I was just a kid then, and I was movie crazy, and I loved plays, going to theaters in Los Angeles, the El Capitan and the Hollywood Playhouse. In Fresno, I went to the theater whenever it came to town, and then eventually the little theater movement came there and I was interested in that.

Q: Were there many movie theaters in Fresno when you were growing up?

Bodeen: Yes, lots of them. I was brought up on silent films, and was interested in them, but I never cared for talkies until later on. Writing for films didn't interest me at all at that time, but as the movies got better I thought, This *is* a medium, and I sort of cottoned to it.

I came down here actually to go to UCLA and because of my interest in acting. I went into acting in the theaters in Los Angeles. I also worked during the day for my uncle, who was a maker of cosmetics. I got into the studios on that and watched a lot of stuff. I got more and more movie-struck. Then I got into the Pasadena Playhouse and got stage-struck all over again.

Q: How did you happen to go to the Pasadena Playhouse?

Bodeen: I wrote a play based on the life of Keats, called *A Thing of Beauty*. It won a California State prize, and Gilmore Brown of the Playhouse called and asked me to come over and meet him. He said, "I would like to produce your play in the Playbox," which was a subsidiary of the Playhouse, for special plays. All the time I was at UCLA, I was writing plays on the side. I wrote one on Byron, one on Shelley, and one on the Brontës. Then I began writing other things, some modern stuff. After I graduated from UCLA, I had luck in a way. Edward Chodorov, the screenwriter, knew about my Brontë play and my interest in the Brontës, and he helped me get a contract at Warner Bros. to write a picture about the Brontës, called *Devotion*. I wrote it, but it didn't go into production because, I think, Kay Francis, whom they wanted for it, left the lot. They kept revising it, getting new authors to write new versions of it. By the time it came out [1944], seven or eight years had elapsed, and I was established as a writer at RKO. Warners asked me to read the script to see if I was entitled to a credit on it. When I read it, I said, "There's not only not thirty percent of what I wrote in here, but there are not thirty words." So I disclaimed all credit for what I thought was a terrible script.

At the Playhouse, Gilmore Brown had said, "We'll find a place for you here." I had appeared in some plays in Fresno, and I loved acting on the stage. I read for *Twelfth Night*, which John Craig from Castle Square Theater in Boston was going to direct. They asked me to play Orsino, the Duke. Betty Bronson played Viola. It was one of the first things Gloria Stuart did, as Olivia. From that she went into pictures. I did quite a lot of acting and writing, and the Playhouse put on most of my plays.

Q: Did you have a special arrangement with them, to do your plays?

Bodeen: No. The minute I finished one I submitted it to Gilmore. He was marvelous. The whole Playhouse was built on him, really. It was amazing that a structure should be so dependent on one person. When he died, it all went to pieces. The Playhouse started in a little place in Pasadena in the Twenties. Gilmore got money to build a new, really wonderful Playhouse. Then it became a school, too. I loved going over there. Most of my friends at that time came from the Playhouse, and I run into a lot of them occasionally now, like Robert Preston.

Q: You were doing so many things simultaneously—writing, acting, going to school.

Bodeen: Yes. I even went to New York for a while, from 1936 until 1939, doing all sorts of odd jobs to hang on. I reviewed plays for *Rob Wagner's Script* in Beverly Hills. I did lots of things like that, and I kept my foot in the door in the theater. I submitted plays all around. There was interest, but not until much later was a play produced. And it was not done well.

Q: Did your Playhouse connection have anything to do with you getting a studio job?

Bodeen: In a sense, because the play I wrote about the Brontës was done in Pasadena and at a subsidiary theater of the Playhouse in Santa Monica. The girl who played the lead, Charlotte Brontë, was Rita Piazza. Her father was casting director at RKO. He had been casting director at M-G-M, where he had discovered Robert Taylor and a number of other people. Through his help, I became a reader at RKO, first as a specialized reader, when they had something that had to be done fast, and then as a regular reader. Then Ben Piazza called me and said, "Mr. Selznick wants you to work as research assistant on his *Jane Eyre*." So I went and saw Val Lewton, Selznick's story editor. I worked with Aldous Huxley, who was doing the screenplay. Then Val was going over to RKO, and he asked me to write his first movie. He went to see Charles Koerner, who was then head of production at RKO. Mr. Koerner said, "I've had some audience research done on horror pictures. Nobody's done anything about cats. I've registered the title *Cat People*. I think it's a good title. It was proved by audience research that people are interested in it." Val was horrified. He said, "God, that I should come to this—a picture called *Cat People*!"

Q: What *did* he want to do?

Bodeen: Some literary classics, I think, like Stevenson's *Body Snatchers*, which he did later. He had a literary approach to everything. I was very fond of Val as a person, but I found I couldn't work with him as we went along. I did three pictures for him. He let me alone on *Cat People*, but on *Curse of the Cat People* [1944], I almost walked out, because I didn't like what he was doing, the changes he was making. He fancied himself as a writer and wanted to write more than anything else. He couldn't write dialogue, and yet he insisted on doing it.

I like *Cat People*, and I liked Simone Simon in it. Val was easy to work with at that time, although you had to devote yourself to him. He would come in when he wasn't shooting and say, "Let's work tonight." If you had tickets for something, you just had to call up and say, "I can't go." He'd invite me to his house for the weekend, and we'd go out on his boat on Sunday. It was pleasant—but not every weekend! I think Mr. Koerner sensed that I was not happy with Val and that I wanted to get away from the kind of picture he was doing. He arranged for me to see Herbert Wilcox, who was looking for a writer. He had an interesting story of espionage, *Yellow Canary* [1943], that he had bought from his daughter. He planned to produce it with his wife—she was his mistress then—Anna Neagle. He told me to go ahead and write a screenplay, which I did. He also told me that he wanted to get back to England very much, that he felt at a loss being away while London was being bombed. He said, "Don't be surprised by anything that happens." I finished the script, and next thing I knew he had gone to Canada and from there on to England. I learned that he was doing a revised version of the picture, so I shared credit with Miles Malleson. But it was a good espionage film, and there was a surprise in it. The story was based on Unity Mitford, a girl who actually was crazy about Hitler!

After that, Harriet Parsons came to RKO as a producer. She asked me if I would like to write *The Enchanted Cottage* [1945] for her. I said I'd love to, that it was one of my favorite silent films. I did three films for her, and we became very good friends.

There was one problem on the film, in that over a weekend we suddenly thought, they're fooling around with something, because we knew they were talking to Jean Renoir. He had an idea about doing it, and Harriet was afraid she might lose it. He wanted to do it with Ingrid Bergman, as a plain girl who had been forced into a life of prostitution. But his interest only lasted about a week, and then he realized the difficulties. I finished the script. Just before production started I was on something else. John Cromwell, who was going to direct, wanted some rewrites, and asked for Herman Mankiewicz, who had written *Citizen Kane* [1941]. Harriet still had affiliations with the Hearst organization here, and she said, "Oh, my God! I'll never dare go to the Hearst office again!" But somehow the front office convinced her that it would be all right, and she came in and wrote some special scenes.

When you see *The Enchanted Cottage* now, it's been cut, and scenes are missing from it, all Mankiewicz's ideas and scenes. It's almost back to the way I wrote it. The straight-line continuity is there.

Q: Did you and Mankiewicz ever meet during this period?

Bodeen: Yes. Harriet introduced us, and I went on the set several times when Cromwell was shooting, and to the party when the picture finished. It was all very pleasant. I'm very fond of the story. Dorothy McGuire, Robert

Young, and Herbert Marshall were all excellent in it. The reviews came out and were very flattering.

One day, some guys came to the studio and *told* her a story from a three-page synopsis. She assigned me to do a treatment and work it into a screenplay, which I did. That became *Night Song* [1947], and it was a pleasure to do. The picture was written with Dorothy McGuire in mind as the lead, but she became pregnant, and they got Loretta Young, who then backed out when Samuel Goldwyn wanted to borrow her for *The Bishop's Wife* [1947]. Then they said Merle Oberon, who had a picture commitment at RKO, would do *Night Song*. At first I thought, "Oh God," because the whole gimmick was that she was pretending to be another girl, and Merle Oberon's voice is so recognizable. But I have to take my hat off to Miss Oberon. She really understood the problem, and she changed her voice, for the other girl. She and Ethel Barrymore were the best people in the movie. I was very pleased because I created the character that Ethel Barrymore played.

Then I started work on *I Remember Mama*, for Harriet. I worked on it for two years, doing a treatment and a first draft screenplay. Then the studio sold the stage rights to the novel, which was called *Mama's Bank Account*, to Oscar Hammerstein, who produced it on Broadway, but RKO managed to buy back the movie rights. Harriet sent me to New York to see the play, and I did a screenplay based on the play as well as the book.

Q: Was your first screenplay anything like what you saw on the stage?

Bodeen: Yes. John Van Druten, whom I got to know quite well, said, "I took some ideas from your thing. I was glad you saw it as told by the girl."

The war was over, and George Stevens came back to RKO as executive producer on *I Remember Mama*. Harriet moved down to just plain producer. He wanted some script changes, so I did another screenplay for him. He was wonderful to work with. He took part in the writing, although he didn't sit down with a pencil or at a typewriter. He would tell me things that he wanted. We got along so well together that he said, "I would like you to be on the set the whole time we're making the picture." I was about to ask if I could be on the set as much as possible, so that was wonderful. Working on that was a real pleasure, and the reception of it was really worthwhile. The movie holds up very well, if you've seen it lately. I would have loved to have done something else for George Stevens, but he had his former writer for his war films, Ivan Moffat, come in and work with him, and he never asked me to do another screenplay for him.

Irene Dunne was absolutely marvelous in *I Remember Mama*. It was quite a departure for her. They got a Norwegian woman who taught her an accent, and it was very authentic. Miss Dunne got tired of wearing aprons instead of beautiful dresses in the picture, but it was actually one of the best things she ever did. She was nominated for Best Performance. She never has won an Oscar, although she's been nominated five times. But they ought to give her a special Oscar.

In the meantime, Jesse Lasky called me in. He and Walter McEwen were associated at RKO. They asked me to do some work on *Miracle of the Bells* [1948], which I did. By the way, my salary went up all through the years, from seventy-five dollars a week, the lowest you could pay a writer, to a thousand dollars a week.

Q: Did you have a special way of working, with a secretary or a dictating machine, or. . . ?

Bodeen: I can't dictate or talk a story. I have to see it appear in letters on a piece of paper. I type it all out. I had a good secretary at RKO, and I'd turn things over to a typist. But on *Miracle of the Bells*, I got Academy credit for it, but I didn't ask for screen credit, because it only had to do with Frank Sinatra's scenes. I didn't really approve of casting Frank Sinatra as a priest, but Bing Crosby had just done it, so they were going to do Sinatra. Then I did my play, *Harvest of Years*, in New York. Lasky sent me a wire saying, "We still love you."

When I came back to Hollywood, I wrote *Mrs. Mike* [1949], on which I shared writing credit, and a couple of things that have not been produced. Then I got *Billy Budd*, which was a prize one to do, the last important one. The producer was Franklin Gilbert, who was the son of the sister of the first Mrs. Jack L. Warner. I had known Franklin in New York, and I went to see the play there. I was crazy about it, and I did a screenplay for Franklin. But when he couldn't interest people in making a picture of it, he sold the rights to Gabriel Katzka, who in turn sold them to Robert Rossen, who intended to produce and direct the picture. Rossen called and asked me to come to New York to do a screenplay, which I did. I worked on it for seven weeks, this time going back to the book and using some things from the play. Rossen liked it very much, but I had a strange feeling, because he started calling me when I came back to Hollywood. He asked me to send him my copy of the screenplay, but I said, "No, I've got to keep it in case there's any credit arbitration." He said, "I've done another version. You'll have a credit arbitration, anyway." I went to Europe and was living there. Meanwhile, they were shooting the picture in England and off the coast of Spain. When I came back to Hollywood, after not quite two years, I bought a copy of the trades that had a review of *Billy Budd*. The author's credit was "screenplay by Peter Ustinov and Robert Rossen." I immediately went to the Guild. They said, "We had an arbitration on that, but you never submitted anything." I immediately submitted my script, and they called in the Board. Next day there was an article on the front page of *The Hollywood Reporter* that said, "Bodeen Bounces Rossen." He had to pay to have all the publicity and the title credits on the picture brought in. They were all changed.

Q: Weren't you active in Guild affairs at one time?

Bodeen: I was on the Board for two years. I went to all the meetings and everything, but I'm really not very good at this sort of thing.

I did a lot of television. I went to New York and was there for nearly three years, in the early days of TV. All the first shows were done in the East, for live television. When TV moved West, I moved West, too, again. At one time I was working on three different television scripts. I really did too much work in TV, and I had a heart attack. It wasn't worth it.

Q: Did writing for live television resemble writing for films or for the theater?

Bodeen: It was like working in the theater, and it was wonderful. They asked you to be present at rehearsals and make changes. They wanted you there when it was actually televised, in case they had to make some quick changes and cut from them. I loved that. But when it came out here, it was all on tape, and eventually it got to be like a lot of "B"-pictures. The writer's presence was not required on the set while they were filming. You turned in a finished teleplay to them, and they didn't even say "thank you."

Q: What about filmed television?

Bodeen: I did that too, but it began to be hack work, really, even though I was working for *Climax*, which was CBS's prestigious program then. I did seven or eight of them, and I liked doing them very much. I haven't done any television for a long time. I get residuals occasionally, and I have to scratch my head and think, What was that that I did?

Q: You're a novelist, too.

Bodeen: Yes. When I first went to Spain I had a novel, *13 Castle Walk*, all mapped out, and I did it that winter there. When I got to London I sent it to an agent in New York. She sold it to Pyramid. It came out in 1975. I got praise for it, and I got some money for it!

Q: Has it ever been optioned for a movie?

Bodeen: Harriet was going to do it, and I was going to do the screenplay. Then she called me tearfully and said, "The doctor says I can't go back to work, that it will probably kill me." She spent forty days in the hospital just recently, so it's just as well she didn't. I liked working on *13 Castle Walk*, and in the novel form. I've written three other novels, but they're all still in manuscript form.

Q: I also think of you as a very fine researcher. You must enjoy it, because I see you working at the library so often.

Bodeen: Oh, I do. I've done about seventy-five articles about motion-picture history, and I love doing things about the old-timers. I have some things on the backlog at *Films in Review*, for whom I did most of them. I like working for *Focus on Film*, too, very much.

Q: One of your greatest accomplishments is your work on *Who Wrote the Movie?*, the book of writers' screen credits. How did that come about?

Bodeen: I was working at the old Academy Library, on Melrose, one day, when the lady who was the head of it asked me if I would like to work there on research for *Who Wrote the Movie?* So I became a member of the staff at the Academy. That lasted almost exactly one year. Leonard Spigelgass was the general editor. Three other writers and I worked on it, and we all got credit. I enjoyed doing it. When I finished, Sam Brown, the Executive Director of the Academy, said, "Would you like to stay on? There's an awful lot of stuff that needs to be sorted, boxes and boxes." So I was backstage, sorting stills.

Q: Are there plans to do an update on *Who Wrote the Movie?*

Bodeen: No, partly, I think, because the book didn't sell too well. I wish there could be a new edition, because I've discovered some mistakes. You know, you never get through discovering errors. One of the maddening things is that *The Bridge of San Luis Rey* is listed as *St. Luis Rey*.

Q: But it's a wonderful book. Your "films of" books must have required extensive research, too.

Bodeen: Yes. I did one on Cecil B. De Mille, which was a big seller, and one on Chevalier, which was suggested by the head of Citadel Press soon after Chevalier died. He said, "A Chevalier book should be a winner." Well, it wasn't. After he died, all interest in him as a personality stopped. His pictures are rarely revived. But the De Mille book has gone on forever. Those books do take a lot of time and effort. Yet no matter how carefully you do them, there are errors. When my articles were put in book form, in *From Hollywood*, I caught some of the errors. But then they made *new* errors in printing in book form. I nearly died when I saw that they left out three of Constance Talmadge's pictures. I enjoy doing research, and I probably will go on doing more for magazines and books.

Q: What are you working on now?

Bodeen: Some things for Salem Press on foreign films. I just finished *Children of Paradise*. I like French films more than any others, except American ones. I thought American and English films were marvelous when they were really doing them. But now I've reached the place where it's difficult for me at the end of the year to think of ten worthy pictures.

Q: I know you didn't like the recent *Cat People* very well. What was your main objection?

Bodeen: It's the same story, but they have cheapened it so, vulgarized it. The wonderful thing about the first version was that we could not show violence of any kind, and sometimes censorship worked in your favor. And there was so much nudity in it! I just sort of laughed about it. I thought that at this late time in my life I've written a story for a pornographic picture! I read the script and thought I was entitled to credit on it. I told the producers, and there was no problem getting that credit.

Q: What about payment?

Bodeen: Nothing. RKO owned it. The only money I can hope to get from it is if it plays on television, and I don't think that will ever happen, unless they sell it on a closed channel. But there's *so* much sex. It was redolent with sex before, but it was all implied. I'm so tired of seeing two people in bed, and three people. It's not interesting. I guess younger audiences like it. It was far more interesting, I thought, when you really didn't know the whole thing about the cat people, or whether she was a cat person or not. She could have been somebody who was losing her mind.

The first *Cat People* was a joy to write, and *Enchanted Cottage* was, and *I Remember Mama* and *Billy Budd*. Those were my favorites among the pictures I worked on. They came nearest to the conception of what I had put down on paper.

Q: I know you've spoken at various screenings and retrospectives. Have you ever taught film classes?

Bodeen: William Everson at NYU has asked me to speak to his film classes, which I've done. I enjoy talking about film, but I can't talk about anything unless I've had experience myself, pictures that I've worked on. I'm glad to talk about those. I could also get up and speak about foreign films, for instance, but I'd have to map out a speech.

Q: Have you ever had any desire to direct?

Bodeen: At one time I thought about it, but then I thought that if somebody is a writer/director/producer/actor, as Orson Welles was, one of those suffers. He produced and directed *Citizen Kane* very well, but his performance wasn't all that it might have been. This is true of almost anybody, Ustinov, for instance. He wants to be everything. I think Woody Allen suffers a lot, too. I can't imagine a Woody Allen picture without Woody Allen in it, but sometimes his performances aren't anything extraordinary. But I liked directing in the theater. A few years ago I directed a play, not my own, that went on tour to four cities outside of London. I enjoyed that.

I'm glad I came into the business when I did. I sometimes wish I'd done so in the late Twenties, when I first came to Hollywood, because I love that period. But when I started, in 1941, it was an ideal way to be. You had a certain amount of security when you knew you were getting a paycheck forty out of fifty-two weeks. That was the studio system. But that kind of thing doesn't exist anymore. Writers are not under contract to a studio, and there are no week-to-week jobs, except a few in television series.

Q: So few people know anything about the Motion Picture Country House, where you live. Please tell me something about it. Who is eligible?

Bodeen: Anyone who's worked in movies or television twenty-one years. When they boiled it all down I had worked in the industry thirty-seven years, so there was no question about my being eligible. I like living here very much. It settles a lot of problems, including if I should get ill and need a doctor. The people here are very accommodating. I just let them know where I'm going to be, in case of an emergency. They're not checking up on you. For me it's ideal, because you don't have to stay here if you're ambulatory. I went to England for six weeks. I've been to New York, San Francisco, and to Fresno, where my brother still lives. I go into town quite regularly, because I find if you stay in one place, especially—I hate to say this—where there are so many old and sick people, you begin to get old and sick yourself.

Q: Do you have to pay something for your bungalow or your meals?

Bodeen: No, everything's taken care of, even haircuts, incidentals. When I came in, I didn't have a great deal of cash. I gave them all I had. I think I'm one of the ones they took for prestige value.

Q: But suppose some successful, retired director wanted to live here, someone who was wealthy?

Bodeen: He would have to turn in all his money, or would have to make some kind of arrangement that when he died it all came here. I've been in the same cottage for six years. It's very pleasant and I have a nice view. That's the John Ford Chapel over there. He had it on the back lot at Republic, and he shot everything there that had to do with a little church. And I've got some nice rose bushes. And I'm glad the Country House is functioning.

Q: Thank you, Mr. Bodeen, for this enlightening interview. I'm sure readers will find it intriguing.

An Interview with FAY WRAY

Fay Wray is a cult figure, and, as so often happens, the character responsible for the creation of the cult—in this instance, a screaming woman in the paw of King Kong—dominates the public mind, and it is all too easy to forget that one is also dealing with an actress of talent, integrity, and intelligence. Fay Wray is happy to be remembered for her performance in *King Kong* (1933), but she also deserves recognition for her roles in Merian C. Cooper and Ernest Schoedsack's *The Four Feathers* (1929), Josef von Sternberg's *Thunderbolt* (1929), Frank Capra's *Dirigible* (1931), Michael Curtiz's *The Mystery of the Wax Museum* (1933), Raoul Walsh's *The Bowery* (1933), Jack Conway's *Viva Villa!* (1934), and, above all, Erich Von Stroheim's *The Wedding March* (1928).

It was *The Wedding March* that made Fay Wray a star, and her performance as Mitzi lifted her from the ranks of leading ladies in Hal Roach two-reel comedies and Universal Westerns to international recognition as an actress capable enough to play opposite, and under the direction of, Erich Von Stroheim. Through the years, the right vehicles were not always forthcoming, but Fay Wray could be relied upon to handle the material that she was given as well as, and often better than, any other actress.

From stardom in the late 1920's and 1930's, Fay Wray enjoyed lasting marriages to two prominent screenwriters, John Monk Saunders and Robert Riskin, to end her screen career as a featured player in films as varied as *The Cobweb* (1955), *Tammy and the Bachelor* (1957), and *Summer Love* (1958). Her most recent—one hates to write last—appearance was as Henry Fonda's dowdy landlady in the made-for-television film *Gideon's Trumpet* (1980).

In 1930, Fay Wray's first husband, John Monk Saunders, created the character of Nikki, an American girl living in Paris shortly after World War I whose insouciance hides an intelligent and emotional psyche. There was a lot of Fay Wray in Nikki's character, and, indeed, Fay Wray was to star in the musical comedy of *Nikki*, which had a short Broadway run in 1931. The cultists will not forget Fay Wray's Ann Darrow in *King Kong*, but Nikki was, and is, closer to the real Fay Wray, a woman who accepted whatever came along in the way of screen roles without argument and without temperament, but, beneath the surface, never allowed Hollywood to take away her sense of reality and her intelligence, who never permitted the film industry to pry into her personal griefs and joys. Fay Wray may have been a Hollywood star, but she was also a woman apart. She was always her own person and never a Hollywood creation.

Anthony Slide

Q: You were born in Canada. Why did your family move to Los Angeles?

Wray: The idea was to get away from the extreme cold. It was as much as anything because the winters were very hard for me. I seemed to be a delicate child. First we went to Arizona, where my mother had family, and then to Utah, which was again where her family was. My father and my mother were separated before we came here.

Q: In Hollywood you attended Hollywood High School, and the obvious question is how did you come to go from Hollywood High School into films?

Wray: At that time it was like a big village. It was a very simple thing to know people who were involved in the industry. And so, through friends, I got an extra role one day and the very next time a "bit" to do at the Century Comedies. As a result of those two times I got a leading lady role in *Gasoline Love* [1923], and it was really because I was walking in front of the studio, and the owners of the studio were coming out, and I guess they remembered having seen me in the studio on those other two occasions. They asked if I would like to do this leading-lady thing, and the appropriate answer was "Yes."

Q: At that time, did you have ambitions for a film career or was it simply a matter of making money?

Wray: I'd always been in love with films. I'd been in love with acting. It was a joy doing the school plays. That was the one thing I seemed to have great pleasure from, aside from just being in school (which I loved). I knew that in time I would try earnestly to get into films, but these were just little roles that were not the result of much effort on my part.

Q: The same applies to the Westerns that you made?

Wray: No. After I did *Gasoline Love*, I did the *Pilgrimage Play*, and that was the initial impetus for me deciding I should, I could, work.

Q: What part did you perform in the *Pilgrimage Play*?

Wray: An extra, just one of the extras that trudged around the hills in bare feet. So, I had known of a man who was the head of the Hal Roach Studio, F. Richard Jones, and it seemed to be no problem to go to the studio and ask for an appointment with him. I told him I would like to work, and he said, "I think we can give you a six-month contract." Today, it seems that would be an impossibility, but it just so happened that way. I was at Hal Roach about six months and then moved on to Universal.

Q: Whom did you work with at Roach?

Wray: Charlie Chase; Leo McCarey was the director. I worked with Laurel of Laurel and Hardy.

Q: You never had any concern that it was undignified to work in comedies?

Wray: Oh no, it was a lovely thing to have that contract, to work and get a salary. It was helpful to my family. I didn't look down on comedies. I would rather have been a comedienne than a leading lady. To be a foil to a male comedian, that was a little dismaying to me. I thought that if I was going to be in comedies I could be comic, but I learned soon that leading ladies are not supposed to be funny, just decorative.

Q: Then you moved to Universal and Westerns.

Wray: Yes, I had a contract there. I worked with Art Acord, Hoot Gibson, and Al Hoxie. The thing about Universal, I think, was it was a nice family studio. All the Laemmles were very kind and very nice. I enjoyed the family feeling.

Q: I believe your first feature was *The Coast Patrol* [1925], produced and directed by Bud Barsky.

Wray: It was a "B"-minus picture—I don't think I ever saw it. That was a little independent company. I don't remember how I got that job, but it was in the summertime, and I think I was still at high school. Bud Barsky was a round little fellow who smoked cigars a lot, and wanted me to change my name to June Darling.

Q: Your first break was, of course, *The Wedding March* [1928]. How did Erich Von Stroheim come to select you?

Wray: There was a lady who lived in this town, whom I had met a year or two before in a social situation, and she was an agent. She was an agent for writers. She came into the Universal studio, and when she saw me, she spoke about Von Stroheim preparing for *The Wedding March*, and she would like to take me to see him. His was a very exciting name, and my awareness of him was very strong. We went to the studio and saw the vice-president of the company, which was formed just to make *The Wedding March*. This little man, who was French, looked at me and said it was no use for me to see Von Stroheim because I was not blond and a little too tall. It was an impasse, so I asked him if I could come back the next day, because my hair was piled up on top of my head and I thought I could take off a few inches. We did go back the next day, and he made no comment at all, except to show us where to find Von Stroheim's office. It was an extraordinary meeting. It really was quite unforgettable. He paced up and down and told me the story of *The Wedding March* and asked me if I could play Mitzi, and I told him I could. So he held out his hand and said "Goodbye Mitzi." And I thought that was firm and took it as such. I was so thrilled that I just began to cry, and from that moment on he seemed very secure about me.

Q: He had never seen you in a film?

Wray: No. Just that one meeting.

Q: You were not frightened of him as a person or as a director?

Wray: Oh, no. There was something quite different than I would have expected about him. He was very real. He had great energy. He was personable. He was dressed very casually, and there was none of that austere raiment that you might expect.

Q: Can we talk a little bit about Von Stroheim's working methods?

Wray: He had written the story, and, as you know, he played it. He did all things. He was all things. There was a total creative quality about him.

I don't remember much about his auditory direction, but he certainly talked me through the scenes. Of course, there was music on the set; it was his music, the music of Vienna. It was very stimulating.

Q: Was there any suggestion that you would continue to work for him?

Wray: There might well have been. He would have liked that. But it was really cut off at the end—the economy of the thing. The money didn't necessarily run out, but Mr. Powers (Pat Powers who was producing it) didn't want to go deeper into his capital. He was a very nice man and a good businessman, and he elected to sell his share of the film to Paramount, which was simply to have released it. He got them to take over. Production was stopped. It was a little bit ignominious for Von Stroheim. Part of the consideration was that Paramount should take over my contract.

Q: When you went under contract to Paramount, did the studio try to change your image by having you play a gangster's moll in one film, *Thunderbolt* [1929] and a Spanish girl in another, *The Texan* [1930], and so on?

Wray: No, I don't think there was any design about that. Once you got into a big studio, they had a certain number of pictures to be made, and they had a certain number of people under contract. And where there was availability, that made the casting situation as much as anything. I had no choice as to the films, and that was an uncomfortable feeling. I felt that had I done two more films with Von Stroheim or at least with a director who had a strong artistic integrity (which I think he did) . . . Who knows?

Q: You can't say that about Josef von Sternberg and *Thunderbolt*?

Wray: No. I think it was an awkward time for him because he was trying to find his way in sound films, and I didn't feel comfortable about being a gangster's moll. It just didn't feel right, and he was not the communicator that Von Stroheim was. There was a distance, as though he was a painter, painting from a distance. He was a cold person, and his wife at that time, Riza Royce, was much more articulate.

Q: You had no problem making the transition from silent films to sound? You had no stage experience.

Wray: I think that was a fallacy that you had to have been in the theater in order to be heard.

Q: Did Paramount loan you out to Columbia for *Dirigible* [1931]?

Wray: Yes. And that had as much as anything to do with the studio being in financial trouble, so they were quite happy to loan their contract players. I had no say in the matter. There was really no one to watch over me, and I do think actors need some management and someone caring. I think *Dirigible* was Frank Capra's first or second big production. He had not yet come into the flavorful time of his comedies, which I do think (of course, I am prejudiced, but I try not to be) Robert Riskin helped him to realize. Frank was not a lighthearted man at that time; he was rather heavy in his style—there was no sparkle. While he was doing *Dirigible*, it seemed to me he had something of a struggle to explain what he wanted. He was always a very intelligent man, but I think he was feeling the pressure of such a big-budget production. Also, I don't think he really wanted me in the film. He didn't say that. Paramount wanted Harry Cohn to take me for that, and I don't think Frank had any choice. Harry Cohn was very happy; we really got along very well—better than I did with Frank.

Q: In the early 1930's you seem to have gotten into a rut with the films that you were making: *Doctor X* [1932], *The Most Dangerous Game* [1932], *The Mystery of the Wax Museum* [1933], and so on.

Wray: It was just appalling. I really felt badly about it. I had done a great variety of pictures until I came to do *King Kong* [1933]. And once I came to do *King Kong* . . . even before that was released there was a kind of groundswell of wanting me for those kind of pictures. But don't forget it was Depression. A lot of people were not working. I was working too much. Yes, I felt very unhappy with that situation.

Q: What are your feelings today about *King Kong*? Looking back, would you have been happier not to have made it?

Wray: Not at all. There is nothing about *King Kong* that makes me feel unhappy.

Q: I am thinking perhaps that it has typecast you in history.

Wray: Well, I don't think I did anything as enduring. *The Wedding March*, yes. That was a beautiful film experience. And for the rest, I did a few interesting things and a lot of not so interesting things. *King Kong* has a kind of mythological character, which I respect, and its endurance has been remarkable. I guess it's because I really love the people that made it that I have a feeling for it. I had great good feeling for Ernest Schoedsack and Merian C. Cooper as people and as friends.

Q: You worked at so many different studios—Fox, Paramount, RKO, M-G-M, etcetera—was there any studio which you particularly cared for?

Wray: I enjoyed working at Columbia. It was the poorest studio, but perhaps that was one of the reasons why I liked it: it was unpretentious. The people there were very nice and unpretentious, they had to try harder and did; it was a comfortable studio to work in.

Q: Why did you go to England in 1935 to make those four films [*Bulldog Jack*, *The Clairvoyant*, *Come Out of the Pantry*, and *When Knights Were Bold*]?

Wray: When I was offered these films in England, I just leapt at the chance because now I thought I would break away from this thing that seems to have happened to me with these horror films. I was a little surprised and a little bit shocked when I got to England to find that everyone wasn't Ronald Colman. Things didn't run as smoothly as they did in the American studios. They were nebulous films; there was nothing very distinguished about them. However, I would say that *The Clairvoyant* had an interesting story and concept.

Q: Did being away in England affect your Hollywood career? The films after your return to this country are not particularly distinguished.

Wray: There were a lot of personal things developed that were difficult. My marriage with John Monk Saunders was breaking up. My career suffered much from those experiences. My first child was born, and so I took some time off. Then things just got complicated, and I did fewer films.

Q: You were married to two major screenwriters, John Monk Saunders and Robert Riskin, which leads to an obvious question: Were you naturally attracted to writers, and did you have any interest in being a writer yourself?

Wray: Yes, I do admire writing achievements, and I've always felt I'd like to write myself (and have done some few, little things). I do respond to people who are writers—except, of course, I'm married to a doctor right now! I married Robert Riskin at a time when both of us were out of the motion-picture scene. He was chief of the Overseas Motion Picture Bureau of the Office of War Information and had separated himself from Hollywood. During the war, I had been doing summer theater and some theater in New York City. To stop working was a pleasure!

Q: Why did you return to films in the 1950's?

Wray: Because he [Robert Riskin] became ill about Christmas of 1950, and after the second year of his illness came the realization that he could not improve. It just became essential for me to start working again.

Q: Of course, you starred in the ABC television series, "Pride of the Family," from 1953 through 1954. Did you enjoy that?

Wray: No. It was such a rush, and there was no time to do anything thoughtful. It was almost like a comic strip, you couldn't develop anything. It was very hard, with lots of long hours, and I never knew I had a view from the house I bought for almost six months.

Q: Of your later films, which do you like the most?

Wray: I think *Hell on Frisco Bay* [1956].

Q: To bring us up to date, I guess *Gideon's Trumpet* was your last appearance, albeit on television.

Wray: I wouldn't have done that except it was my son-in-law who wrote and produced it. When he first asked, I told him, "No," it was ridiculous. Then, almost in the same breath, I thought, why not? The thing that was different about the role was I tried to make myself look as awful and plain as I could. Unfortunately, I succeeded. Some of my friends thought I was an idiot to do that. In fact, I got a good deal of pleasure out of wearing no makeup and looking dreadful.

Q: Are you officially retired?

Wray: Well, as you know, I'm working at writing and getting a lot of things together that I find interest in doing. I don't seem to need to act. I think about it in a fantasy way. In my imagination, I'm acting on the stage, but it's all rather a pleasant fantasy. But I do love motion pictures, and I've always been very glad to have been associated with them. I don't know of any other medium that's more vital or influential.

Q: Thank you for your time; your comments have been most interesting.

THE AMERICAN CINEMA IN 1981

The cinema as we have known it is changing at a rapidly accelerating pace, and a consideration of contemporary American films requires a perspective which acknowledges that fact. Although the 1970's witnessed the beginning of a changing context for the mainstream theatrical film, by the early 1980's the nature of these changes has begun to crystallize. A swiftly evolving technology has altered the relationship of the audience to films. Cable television and video cassettes are achieving a centrality in the presentation of recorded visual entertainment to an even greater degree than had commercial television for the three preceding decades. Inevitably, this has had a significant effect on the theatrical feature film.

It is sometimes theorized that all change in art is the result of the development of technology. If this were true, American films of the last few years would be radically different from their predecessors. In fact, the American cinema changed most dramatically in the mid-1960's, well after television had become commonplace and before the so-called "video revolution." It is the nature of this change that bears directly on both the quality and the character of the films of 1981—works conceived and marketed within the context of "home box office" and video games. Thus gradual coarsening of the American cinema which began around 1964 has now coincided with a much more dramatic and readily evident change in the market for films.

The manner in which these coexisting aesthetic and technological changes relate to a change in the consciousness of American society is open to speculation. What is certain is that such a change was inevitable. All classical periods of art—classical Greece, the Italian Renaissance, Elizabethan England—experienced decline when fundamental cultural changes began to occur. It is now a widely accepted view that the American cinema enjoyed a classical period of this type. It is perhaps relevant, then, that the end of this classical period (in the mid-1960's) occurred at a time in American history when there was great social upheaval. Although this social divisiveness centered on an unpopular war, it extended to a conflict over fundamental values. Characteristically, a classical era of art is made possible by stable values. This stability should normally be strong enough to permit all manner of artistic questioning and ambivalence, because shared beliefs impart to the classical work a coherence and balance which effectively contains any disturbing undertones.

An example of a classical work of American cinema is *The Best Years of Our Lives* (1946). Although opinions of the precise merit of this film may vary, there is no disagreement as to the nature of its subject—society's readjustment to peace after a long and arduous war—and, more important, no disagreement over the numerous moral positions which the film takes. At the time of its release, the experiences of its characters were shared in some measure by most Americans. The emotional power of the work, however greatly it may have been enhanced by the skill of director William Wyler and his collaborators, derives from the shared experiences and collective perceptions of the characters. Interestingly and impressively, *The Best Years of Our Lives* is still appreciated in much the same terms by modern audiences. The sense of stable values and common ideals was so strong after World War II that it is still easily understood today.

At the opposite extreme, a recent American film dealing with the Vietnam War, *The Deer Hunter* (1978), although enjoying a great deal of critical recognition, has not known the same unanimity of response. On the very night that it won an Academy Award, a group of protesters marched outside the auditorium, declaring the film to be an imperialist work, a charge that the film's director Michael Cimino vigorously denied. Some agreed with Cimino that the film was simply a character study while others claimed that it reflected some truths about American involvement in Vietnam and still others claimed that it was not truly reflective of that experience. The meaning that emerges from this confusion should be clear. *The Deer Hunter*, whatever its merits, is not a classical work in the manner of *The Best Years of Our Lives* because it is no longer possible to create such a work. The earlier film was completely lucid in expressing its subject matter and remains so today, while the later film arouses controversy because it is ultimately a romantic statement forged from the private emotions of its creator and is comprehensible only if a viewer feels that he understands the creator's sensibility. Ironically, the personal feelings of the classical director, William Wyler, were perhaps even more relevant to the creation of *The Best Years of Our Lives* than Cimino's feelings were to *The Deer Hunter*, since Wyler had served during World War II and shared the homecoming experiences of his characters. These two contrasting examples are illuminating because of the superficial similarities between them. Both are ambitious and lengthy (running approximately three hours in each instance), the subjects parallel each other, and the films were both honored with Academy Awards for Best Picture. Further, it is a reasonable contention that both films have great artistic merit. The differences cited, however, are far more striking than the similarities.

There are, of course, more profound differences between the contemporary American cinema and the classical American cinema. It is necessary to allude to the classicism of the past in order to undertake any kind of overview of the specific year under consideration. As a popular art, the cinema has always been governed as much by commercial consideration as by artistic aspiration. In the classical era, however, the disparity between artistic integrity and commercial necessity was softened by the ability of filmmakers to keep faith with both. In 1981, the apparent callousness of the most commercially viable films is no more discouraging than the artistic and emotional impoverishment of most films of alleged serious purpose. Formerly, the virtues of the American cinema could be discerned in both light entertainments and seriously intentioned works. In 1981, the vices of a declining medium can be located in both categories. Any perspective on the American cinema in 1981 will reveal the same symptoms of decline.

The following is *Variety*'s list of the top-grossing films for 1981, twenty-one films each earning more than fifteen million dollars in film rentals. The top-grosser was *Raiders of the Lost Ark* ($90,434,000), followed by *Superman II* ($64,000,000), *Stir Crazy* ($58,408,000), *9-5* ($57,850,000), *Stripes* ($39,514,000), *Any Which Way You Can* ($39,500,000), *Cannonball Run* ($37,378,000), *Arthur* ($37,000,000), *The Four Seasons* ($26,800,000), and *For Yours Eyes Only* ($25,439,479). The eleventh highest grosser was *Seems Like Old Times* (22,068,000), followed by *The Fox and the Hound* ($18,-000,000), *Cheech and Chong's Nice Dreams* ($17,636,000), *Excalibur* ($17,-000,000), *Flash Gordon* ($16,100,000), *Time Bandits* ($16,000,000), *The Great Muppet Caper* ($16,000,000), *Tarzan, the Ape Man* ($15,642,396), *Clash of the Titans* ($15,632,341), *Bustin' Loose* ($15,300,000), and *Endless Love* ($15,100,000). The next film on the list was a reissue of *The Empire Strikes Back* (1980) so the line of 1981 commercial winners may be safely drawn at this point.

It is an extremely dispiriting list. Reasoned disagreement is possible with regard to the worth of any of the films named, but there is no question that there are prevailing patterns of subject matter and approach which confirm that theatrical films now exist primarily for a teenage audience—and, to judge by the content of the films, a teenage audience strangely disinterested in the nuances of human relationships.

Raiders of the Lost Ark, *Superman II*, *Cannonball Run*, *For Your Eyes Only*, *Excalibur*, *Flash Gordon*, *Time Bandits*, *Tarzan, the Ape Man*, and *Clash of the Titans* all have the same fantasy adventure/comic strip frame of reference. Several of these films are actually based on comic strips. Super heroes are at the center of virtually every one of these films. The most popular film of the group, *Raiders of the Lost Ark*, was cleverly publicized to exploit the fondness of producer George Lucas and director Steven Spielberg for Saturday matinee serial adventures. Pure escapism and incredible adventures in the classical era had been generally limited to those serials and to modest programmers and "B"-pictures, but *Raiders of the Lost Ark* was greeted as one of the year's major releases. Though offered in an allegedly innocent spirit by the filmmakers, it had the effect of confirming an overwhelming contemporary taste for a cinema free of formal and emotional complexity.

The prevailing comic-strip level extends to numerous other films on the list, frenetic comedies such as *Stir Crazy*, *9-5*, *Stripes*, *Any Which Way You Can*, *Cheech and Chong's Nice Dreams*, and *Bustin' Loose*. Physical comedy figured in classic screen comedy as well, but on a much less spectacular and less violent level, and the great comedies of the 1930's, 1940's, and 1950's also boasted verbal wit, characterization, and some quiet moments. By contrast, a vaguely facetious exploitation of liberal contemporary attitudes towards relationships prevails in *The Four Seasons* and *Seems Like Old Times*. *Arthur*, the comedy which seems most intent on demonstrating that it has a mind of its own, was widely hailed as a return to the screwball genre of *My Man Godfrey* (1936) but can only suffer by such a comparison. It is directed with no evidence of comic timing, and in order to honor superficially the form it emulates, it sabotages the underlying character dilemma it postulates. The hero (Dudley Moore) glibly decides to keep his money in the last few seconds of the film, although the screenplay has insisted throughout that his wealth has prevented him from growing up.

That leaves only three films among the twenty-one big rental pictures. *The Great Muppet Caper* and *The Fox and the Hound* are not live-action features and should be the "children's films" among the top grossers, but are they any more childish than the strained comic destruction of Cheech and Chong or the unreal adventures of Indiana Jones? In fact, Disney's *The Fox and the Hound* appears to have been originally devised to draw a sobering moral, which unfortunately became so diluted with misplaced sentiment by the time the film reached the screen that the potential of this animated feature to boast more maturity than the "adult" films on the list was subverted. *The Fox and the Hound* appears to have been a victim of committee thinking overruling a few venturesome creators at Disney (not to mention the steady decline of standards in animation at that studio since its best days), but in this it only emulates the impersonality of the popular live-action films. The final entry on the list, *Endless Love*, appears to have drawn its appeal from a fabricated adolescent sex symbol, Brooke Shields, and the film's poor critical reception seems to confirm that the subject of adolescent passion deserves more sobriety than this film was able to offer.

A recapitulation of the subject matter and particular appeal of these top grossers of 1981 reveals their deficiencies as fully realized works. Even if it is conceded that the American cinema has always been dominated by larger-than-life adventure and melodrama requiring a suspension of disbelief, these contemporary equivalents can be faulted for not achieving a corresponding level of moral and dramatic interest in the manner of their predecessors. Unrelentingly, they sacrifice everything else for speed and superficial effect.

It suffices to consider *Raiders of the Lost Ark*, one of the films on the list widely claimed to be a well-realized work. Steven Spielberg, the film's director, had already demonstrated considerable cinematic flair and an engaging if youthful personality in previous films (*The Sugarland Express*, 1974; *Jaws*, 1975; *Close Encounters of the Third Kind*, 1977; and even the miscalculated *1941*, 1979). His style is readily discernible in *Raiders of the Lost Ark*. After an exciting opening sequence, however, all hope of accepting the film on its own level dissipates as the sequence concludes with the hero, Indiana Jones (woodenly played by Harrison Ford), escaping from a dangerous situation in a manner too broadly comical to sustain belief. Crucially, both the character and the film itself seem to acknowledge freely this broad level (but not in the appealing, almost Pirandellian manner of, for example, *The Crimson Pirate*, 1952), and it is worth recalling that the Saturday matinee serials of the past—whose creators were surely no more innocent—presented the contrivances of their humble films with a straight face, so that the audience could readily pitch its collective sensibility to the level which those films sought. The unappealing Indiana Jones subsequently commences a series of adventures notable for their frequent unpleasantness (being caught in a cavern full of snakes), visual monotony (most of the film takes place in colorless desert locales), and lack of character interaction (the presence of an engaging heroine is no help as she is ill-served by the script after her first scene). The climax is woefully inadequate within the traditions the film evokes because the villains are destroyed not by the hero (who is rendered helpless in this sequence) but by an elaborate array of special effects. *Raiders of the Lost Ark* is a film which fails on its own terms. As an escapist matinee adventure, it is a pallid and careless imitation of the most humble models from the classical era. The attempted resurrection of this type of film—which has always held an honorable place in the American cinema—is not necessarily to be scorned. What is so discouraging about the success of *Raiders of the Lost Ark* is that 1981 audiences were so enamored of the *idea* of this type of film, as opposed to all other possible films, that they embraced a pathetically inferior example.

The emphasis on special effects in *Raiders of the Lost Ark* and other popular films of 1981 (a trend continuing at full force in 1982), provokes an ambivalent critical response. Special effects are not necessarily more imaginative than in the past (as a comparison of the 1976 *King Kong* with the 1933 original demonstrates) but there have been remarkable technical developments (exemplified by Rob Bottin's make-up effects in the otherwise negligible 1981 werewolf film *The Howling*). It has always been true that if something can be invented it will be used, so the dominance of effect-oriented films is understandable from at least one perspective. At his best, the special-effects wizard can contribute something essential to a film which would not exist without him. If this contribution is aligned to the strong creative imagination of a true artist, the result can be an extraordinary work. Perhaps the finest example of such a work is *The Birds* (1963), a visionary fable directed by Alfred Hitchcock at the peak of his powers. A considerable amount of innovative technique was required on every level—both visual and aural—to make this film work, and the team which served Hitchcock on the film accomplished prodigious effects which will always remain impressive. The ultimate value of the film, however, is not in its dazzling array of effects but in the formal and dramatic coherence that the effects helped to make possible. In the contemporary cinema, films are often characterized by an abundance of gratuitous effects, often nauseating and gruesome to behold and not aligned to any deeper artistic level. Pure visual sensation is overvalued in contemporary cinema. At its worst, it has as much relevance to life as a computer game.

The dominance of special effects is only a symptom of the deeper problems of popular films in the year under consideration. In any given year, the most popular films may or may not be the best films. In past years, however, there was usually a greater balance. The popularity of certain stars or the effectiveness of the advertising might have had a lot to do with a film's fortunes in the classical era, but the substantive content of American films in that period—weak films as well as strong ones—also had a great deal to do with a given film's success or failure. The relentless gravitation to a level of mindless comic-strip adventure, so pronounced in 1981, did not really dominate the motion picture industry until the remarkable success of *Star Wars* (1977, now the all-time box-office champion), although it is perhaps traceable to the James Bond series (which has been commercially viable since it began at just about the end of the classical era). By contrast, it is sufficient to name the single film from the classical years which still remains high on the list of all-time grossers—*Gone with the Wind* (1939). This production is far from the most subtle ever made in Hollywood. It is a very accessible romantic melodrama set against a sweeping historical background. On no level, however, is this popular film a resolutely escapist work in the manner of the comic strip/fantasy films of 1981. Its central character, Scarlett O'Hara (Vivien Leigh), is a reasonably complex creation—a woman who earns the audience's sympathy in spite of many undesirable attributes. Scarlett and the other characters in *Gone with the Wind* develop and change as the narrative progresses. The spectacular sequences, such as the burning of Atlanta, contribute to the film but do not dominate it. Psychological and emotional levels are more essential in sustaining the audience's attention.

Returning to the list of high rental films of 1981, it must be conceded that at least one of the fantasy films—*Excalibur*—is distinguished by a serious tone and a sober presentation. Unfortunately, even this rewarding film cannot claim freshness of narrative or characterization. The viewer of *Excalibur* is responding to characters (King Arthur, Lancelot, Guinevere, Perceval) who are mythic archetypes existing in narrative situations preordained by past incarnations of the same material. The major dramatic conflict in the film occurs on a magical level as two sorcerers, Merlin (Nicol Williamson) and Morgana (Helen Mirren), fight for control over the destinies of the mortal characters. Cinematography, set design, and effects combine in the brilliant compositions of John Boorman to compel interest in this abstract conflict. *Excalibur* is eloquent and forceful because of its visual realization. Its popular appeal is essentially the same as that of the more frivolous fantasy films of the same year, and it shares the same unfortunate tendency to favor expansiveness over intimate detail.

Turning to the more prestigious films of 1981, those which do not figure on the list of box-office hits but which won great critical admiration, one finds certain tendencies in contemporary cinema which are perhaps even more insidious. It should be stressed that such films are not necessarily commercial failures. Most of them were released near the end of the year, and their popular success cannot be measured by the 1981 list of top grossers. Academy Award winners such as *Reds*, *On Golden Pond*, and *Chariots of Fire* (a British film but relevant in this context) could hope for the kind of good fortune which almost invariably accompanies Academy recognition. Escapist fantasy is not the avowed intention of these films. It is their aim to treat stories closer to life and to touch the human heart.

Of the trio of films named, one is so inadequate and unpersuasive in dramatizing its story that its critical success is cause for bewilderment. The lamentable *Reds*, a three-and-one-half-hour biography of celebrated Communist author John Reed, is an oppressively literal cinematic experience characterized by a visual realization which never captures the imagination and characters which never achieve any dimension. It is a film which provokes retrospective appreciation for the visual care and dramatic intelligence which inform the later films of David Lean (notably *Lawrence of Arabia* in 1962 and *Dr. Zhivago* in 1965), films often reproached for their ponderousness. The allegedly daring subject matter of *Reds* is treated from a relentlessly safe middlebrow point of view, and the central relationship of Reed (Warren Beatty) and his wife Louise Bryant (Diane Keaton) is never given to any real development. Throughout the film, he continually neglects and devalues her. In spite of this selfishness and the ruptures it provokes, the couple continually reconciles in a manner so nakedly maudlin and conventional that it becomes difficult to concede any level of seriousness to the film whatever. An incidental result is that Diane Keaton, whose earlier roles (notably in *Annie Hall* and *Looking for Mr. Goodbar*, both 1977, and especially *Manhattan*, 1979) had shown her to be an intelligent and interesting actress, is made to be alternately petulant and teary-eyed throughout, defeating any hope that either the character or Keaton's screen presence will engage the audience. Somehow, this tedious work enjoyed enough critical praise to win awards (including an Oscar for Best Direction!). It may be inferred from this that poor narrative construction, weak characterization, and an absence of cinematic style are readily overlooked in the contemporary cinema. In the case of *Reds*, the declared seriousness of the film replaced the realized work as the primary basis for critical judgment.

On Golden Pond and *Chariots of Fire* are more problematical because they are both competently made (in fact, both boast uncommonly impressive cinematography among 1981 films). *On Golden Pond* is an intimate family drama about an aging couple and their relationship to their daughter and her future husband's son. Its screenplay is not notably sensitive or profound, but the story and characters are certainly workable. The problems of aging have rarely taken a central place in the American cinema, so that subject is a commendable one. Unfortunately, sentiment has attached itself to this film out of all proportion to its modest merits. The reason for this is the casting of Katharine Hepburn and Henry Fonda, two deservedly beloved veteran stars, as the couple. It should be emphasized that this is not the fault of Fonda or Hepburn. They give their usual excellent performances in roles which are clearly neither the greatest nor most challenging they have enjoyed in their long and exceptional careers (contrary to the short-sighted statements of some overzealous critics). It should also be emphasized that the material is not treated by director Mark Rydell in an overly sentimental manner. It is the attitude of the audience which attaches excessive sentiment to the film. Fonda and Hepburn are loved in their roles almost before they appear. They are identified as a revered couple who have grown old, and the emotions they arouse become confused with those the fictional characters are attempting honestly to earn. Ultimately, this is an extremely gentle and untroubled little comedy-drama which is successful to the extent that high expectations are not brought to it. The greatest portrait of aging in American cinema, Leo McCarey's *Make Way for Tomorrow* (1937), boasted no legendary stars and did not receive nearly as much attention in its time, but it remains beautiful and meaningful today. Character actors Beulah Bondi and Victor Moore superbly played the elderly man and his wife who are cruelly separated during their last years. The film is not soothing in the manner of *On Golden Pond*. Though more disarmingly comic at times, it is ultimately stark and compelling. The sentiment it arouses derives from its artistic conviction and is richly deserved.

Chariots of Fire is similar to *On Golden Pond* in that it aspires to instill in its audience a warm, uplifting feeling. Regrettably, this seems like the most prevalent alternative to the comic strip/fantasy film in current American cinema—human interest stories which provoke an uncomplicated and thoroughly positive empathy for the characters (*Rocky* in 1976 was perhaps the popular model). The principal characters of *Chariots of Fire* are in competition with each other, but ultimately each achieves a share in the victory the film celebrates. Although executed in a fairly interesting, visually modish style, *Chariots of Fire* is really a throwback to British films of the 1940's and 1950's which took pride in the spiritual glories of the British Empire even after history had so diminished the Empire that it remained only a set of traditions and ideals. At this late date, there is something curiously touching about such a film; at the same time, it is puzzling that the superficial cinematic qualities of such a work would apparently conceal from the collective critical and popular mind its innately old-fashioned and numbingly conventional appeal.

As in any recent year, there were a few excellent American films in 1981 and others that were at least interesting. Several of these films are especially instructive for what they reveal about the commercial difficulties faced by even the most accessible film if it lies outside the mainstream, and several other films articulate in various ways a bleak contemporary mood which has relevance to even the most slick and frivolous popular films already discussed. *Cutter's Way* and *They All Laughed* are the outstanding examples of the first type, as both encountered serious distribution problems. *Cutter's Way*, a contemporary murder mystery emphasizing character and relationships, encountered enough critical misunderstanding on its initial release under the title *Cutter and Bone* to be withdrawn from distribution (it had only played in a few cities, not including Los Angeles) for the better part of a year. Subsequently, United Artists Classics retitled it, created a new advertising campaign, and sold it as an art film, thereby permitting a general release but severely inhibiting its chances for even a modest commercial success. *They All Laughed*, a light romantic comedy reminiscent in spirit if not in texture of the classics admired by its director Peter Bogdanovich, has had an even more checkered history. Twentieth Century-Fox was to distribute the film but waited so long that the director bought the rights back and distributed it himself. This was a losing proposition for an individual, as the film would have had to be a huge success in order to return a profit in spite of its relatively modest budget. Critical and popular reception to the film was fairly positive, but again its release was very limited. Apparently, Bogdanovich is now negotiating with another distributor to handle the film in the future.

Both of these films deserved a better commercial fate, as neither was an overly difficult modern work intent on alienating the general audience. *Cutter's Way* is the more idiosyncratic of the two (not incidentally, it is the work of a European emigré, Czech director Ivan Passer). It does tell a somewhat ambiguous story, and its characters are not infallible or lovable fantasy figures who solicit ready admiration or identification. At the same time, its intriguing narrative is rich in dramatic incident and vividly presented. With any justice, a film should be able to depart from prevailing fashion to some extent and still have commercial viability. *They All Laughed* is an even more curious case. Although it can easily be argued that its underlying themes are serious, its explicit purpose is to entertain. It has a great deal of comedy, much of it physical. This comedy is placed in a sophisticated perspective and possesses a grace not present in the vulgarities of *9-5*, *Arthur*, *Any Which Way You Can*, and *Bustin' Loose*. Several stories are blended together to permit emotional contrasts, and the images and sound track conspire to create a free-flowing, almost impressionistic mood mildly reminiscent of European films. It appears that this humble effort to create a comedy in a reasonably subtle style has resulted in a film too fragile and delicate to have wide popular appeal. The restrictiveness of the contemporary American cinema is well demonstrated by the fates of these two films. Both films boasted the excellence of production values which has been so often missed since the classical era, but sadly, this was not generally appreciated.

The understated but tangible influence of European models is felt in other 1981 films of merit as well. *The French Lieutenant's Woman* suggests the relationship that a modern film might have to the classical genres. Rather than indulging in pale imitation, *The French Lieutenant's Woman* places its melodrama in a double perspective whereby a contemporary sensibility is able to redefine its relationship to Victorian melodrama. The self-consciousness of *The French Lieutenant's Woman* is not at all pretentious because it is articulated so honestly. Far from seeming overly detached and disengaged, it succeeds in offering an emotional experience roughly equivalent to that of a classic film. *The French Lieutenant's Woman* enjoyed a modest commercial success and met with a mixed critical response. It seems very unlikely that it will be taken as a positive example; its qualities are too dissimilar from those of the most popular films.

Similarly, the 1981 version of James M. Cain's *The Postman Always Rings Twice*, directed by Bob Rafelson, strips the story of the fatalism associated with classic *film noir* and brings the sexual obsession which entraps the two principal characters down to earth, where a slowly evolving relationship is described with admirable honesty and unexpected reserves of emotion. By contrast, the more commercially successful *Body Heat* is simply one more example of the insidious cannibalizing of the classics of Hollywood's past. The fatal *film noir* woman is restored (complete with the white dress worn by Jane Greer in the 1947 *Out of the Past*), but she has become a synthetic creation, there to serve the slick convolutions of a tired variation of *Double Indemnity* (1944, another Cain adaptation) rather than emerging as a compelling characterization resonant with the most troubling aspects of the psyche. *Body Heat* offers no equivalent for *Double Indemnity*'s final cathartic emotional exchange between Barbara Stanwyck and Fred MacMurray (which occurs when Walter Neff shoots Phyllis Diedrichson as they embrace). The relationship of the pseudo-*film noir* couple in *Body Heat* can only exist in a mechanical manner. Not surprisingly, it is a less erotic film than *Double Indemnity* in spite of its greater sexual explicitness. *The Postman Always Rings Twice* also overvalues the erotic potential of its explicit sex scenes, but it compensates for this by using these scenes to describe crucial character revelations which are not strictly sexual. The careless critical praise accorded to *Body Heat* (a film written and directed by Lawrence Kasdan, who scripted *Raiders of the Lost Ark*) suggests that a shallow revamping of *film noir* iconography is more likely to find favor than a genuinely personal approach to the deeper implications that are *film noir*'s true legacy to the modern cinema.

Veteran directors such as George Cukor (*Rich and Famous*), Blake Edwards (*S.O.B.*), and Billy Wilder (*Buddy Buddy*) have been much less callous in responding to a changing cinema than younger counterparts such as Kasdan, Spielberg, and Lucas. The 1981 films of these directors inevitably reflect their formative years in classical cinema, but they are not nostalgic reminiscences cast in inappropriate formal structures. The most consistently eloquent film of the three, Cukor's *Rich and Famous*, is a remake of a 1943 film (*Old Acquaintance*) but it abandons the melodramatic conventions which were effective in its predecessor in favor of a more elliptical narrative. Cukor remains theatrical enough in his approach to permit one of his two principal characters (played by Candice Bergen) to appear totally outrageous for most of the length of the film. His strategy in doing this is revealed by the film's expressive conclusion in which the Bergen character coheres with a psychological precision enjoyed throughout by the other principal character (played by Jacqueline Bisset). Superficially a story describing a bond of friendship, *Rich and Famous* suggests that the Bergen character is too limited ever to understand the Bisset character and is genuinely envious of her, but in a rather sad way is nevertheless able to give her emotional sustenance. The kind of emotions and life experiences dealt with in *Rich and Famous* are so uncommon in the context of 1981 American cinema that the film was completely misunderstood, its melancholy taken for parody. In fact, however, the allegedly old-fashioned Cukor has shown a deeper attunement to the fragile structure of modern life in this film than most of the younger and more fashionable directors have demonstrated in their entire careers.

Buddy Buddy and *S.O.B.* are more problematical films, but they possess an even more significant relationship to the deepest currents underlying virtually all contemporary American cinema. Both of these films openly scorn the present, and *S.O.B.* explicitly directs this scorn against the Hollywood of its own time. Edwards' corrosive portrait of selfishness, stupidity, and opportunism in the film world is consistently funny for its first hour, remarkably so considering that much of the humor derives from the spectacle of a hapless producer's suicide attempts in the midst of a dispassionate group of friends and associates. The third quarter of the film is interesting and disturbing, as the producer (Richard Mulligan) sabotages his own failed motion picture (an innocent musical presumably untouched by the more callous fashions of the era) by transforming it into a sleekly pretentious piece of quasi-erotica in which his wife (Julie Andrews), a beloved star of family films, exposes her breasts. This segment of the film is arguably a clever metaphor for the death of classicism and the resulting artistic conflict for the classical filmmaker who wants to go on creating. Significantly, in the ensuing plot complications, the transformed film is a hit but the producer dies a comic death.

It is possible to speculate that Edwards' inspiration for this film was the commercial failure of *Darling Lili* (1970), one of the last great works of classical American cinema but a film out of its time. Edwards had even then wanted to establish Andrews as a star for sophisticated material, not forever bound by the image which *Mary Poppins* (1964) and *The Sound of Music* (1965) had established for her (and it appears that with *Victor/Victoria* in 1982 he has at last succeeded). *Darling Lili* lies somewhere in between the first version of *Night Wind* (the fictional film in *S.O.B.*) and the revised version. Neither manifestation of the musical number from *Night Wind* seems as though it would actually appeal to Edwards (although the second, erotic manifestation possesses a certain aestheticism which in another context he might regard seriously). In effect, the world Edwards describes in *S.O.B.* is a world in which an artist could not make a satisfactory film.

The final quarter of *S.O.B.* describes a long wake for the deceased producer by his three best friends (William Holden, Robert Preston, and Robert Webber), who drunkenly switch bodies in order to bury their former companion at sea. This is the least successful part of the film, failing to be hilarious in the manner of its first half and lacking the provocative aspects of the second part. The diminished creative energy which overtakes the film is strangely appropriate, however, in view of the despair over contemporary cinema implicit in every frame of the total work. This despair extends to the cold-blooded world in which the contemporary cinema exists, a world in which the warm gesture of the three friends at the film's end provides little solace. Edwards has the style and temperament to let the emotions of a film breathe through a cold façade, but the caustic wit which informs *S.O.B.* reveals a cynicism of which he was probably free prior to the *Darling Lili* debacle.

Billy Wilder's position is analogous to that of Edwards, and the underrated *Buddy Buddy* is an even more vitriolic film than *S.O.B.* An older director than Edwards, Wilder had known even greater success earlier in his career and has long been an acknowledged master of the cinema. Coincidentally, he also saw the release of his most personal and classically graceful work in 1970, *The Private Life of Sherlock Holmes*, and, like *Darling Lili*, the costly film was both a commercial and critical failure. In the postclassical era, the cynicism associated with earlier Wilder films had worn away to reveal a tender heart; but, daunted by the lack of appreciation for the warm works of his maturity, the writer-director has revealed in *Buddy Buddy* a cynicism surpassing anything found in his earlier works. As a hired gunman, Walter Matthau brilliantly incarnates this cynicism, and the complementary romanticism of the Jack Lemmon character is made to seem foolish and pathetic. All of the scenes involving these two characters alone are scathingly humorous (this is the third film in which Wilder has demonstrated a matchless appreciation of the contrast between the personalities of these two actors). Unfortunately, Wilder becomes a bit carried away by his scorn for the modern world, and the middle part of the film satirizes a sex clinic too baldly to be successful. Elsewhere, his wit is surer. The artist whose own favorite director is Ernst Lubitsch (fondly recalled in a waltz sequence in Wilder's previous film *Fedora*, 1979) slyly names the intended victim of the assassin Rudy "Disco" Gambola.

It is not surprising that an older director who began his career in the best days of Hollywood would feel out of place in the mainstream of 1981 cinema, masking his despair with cynicism. Revealingly, however, some of the best young directors articulate a vision even bleaker than that of Edwards or Wilder. This is especially discernable in the 1981 films of Walter Hill (*Southern Comfort*) and John Carpenter (*Escape from New York*). *Southern Comfort*, much the more successful of the two, relates a fairly familiar story of a group of National Guardsmen lost in the bayous of Louisiana. An absurd conflict with the local inhabitants comes close to claiming the lives of all of the men. Hill realizes the chillingly violent story with the calm and dispassionate style which has characterized all of his previous work. His films tend to be abstract, populated by characters whose purpose is to enact rituals created by the director rather than to emerge as complex people. *Southern Comfort* is one of the only 1981 films to have a persistent color scheme, gray and muted. It is a stylized work in the best sense, achieving a choreographic grace in the staging and editing of its powerful climax which suggests that Hill may be one of the few real artists of cinema of his generation. If Hill merits admiration, however, this does not make a film such as *Southern Comfort* any less disquieting. Hill's abstraction of genre elements and character types in *Southern Comfort* results in a profound emptiness, a negation of the richness of human emotion and experience. Hill strips away from his world everything but the most primitive impulses and actions. He is only able to impose artistic order through the contemplation of spiritual death.

John Carpenter treats *Escape from New York* with less consistent intensity but concludes with an image more nihilistic than any to be found in the works of Hill. The Carpenter film is set in the future, when the island of Manhattan has become a penal colony, and a disillusioned hero of dubious charm (Kurt Russell) must infiltrate this violent world and rescue the kidnaped President of the United States (Donald Pleasence). A number of characters assisting the hero are killed in the process, but the President and the hero's superior (Lee Van Cleef) are only interested in the playing of a tape vital to the success of a world peace conference. When the tape begins to blare through speakers beneath the night sky, it is discovered that the hero has switched the vital tape with one of 1940's big band music played continually by a cab driver (Ernest Borgnine) killed in the course of the escape. The final brief tracking shot shows the hero limping away and tearing the tape out of the switched cassette. The hero's effort to protect the last vestiges of his integrity is an admirable existential act and makes the conclusion of an uneven film very dramatically satisfying. At the same time, Carpenter's treatment of the final image does not suggest a restoration of moral order to an insane world. On the contrary, the methodical tape-pulling of the limping man registers as an embrace of desolation. The traces of emotion with which the image are invested seem to drain away in the same moment they appear.

Although *Escape from New York* only sporadically fulfills the promise of its imaginative concept, this chilling final moment is perhaps the most brilliant single image in a 1981 American film. Carpenter's film, coupled with Hill's, suggests a level of despair in the American cinema not felt before. This has subsequently been confirmed in 1982 by Carpenter's finest film to date, *The Thing*, in which the tendency to empty the frames of emotion at the same time that it appears prevails throughout the work and in which the concept of humanity infected and destroyed by a virulent organism endlessly re-creating itself in man's own image, is treated without a trace of misplaced sentiment. Carpenter's earlier films (beginning with *Dark Star*, a 1974 science-fiction horror entry which playfully suggests the subject of *The Thing* but does not aspire to the same intensity) did not have this maturity and were less obviously modern. The gravitation to solitude of his characters (notably the introverted and mildly repressed baby-sitter played by Jamie Lee Curtis in the 1978 *Halloween*; the lighthouse disc jockey, Stevie Wayne, played by Adrienne Barbeau in *The Fog*, 1980; and, of course, the loner hero of *Escape from New York*) had no clear meaning. One of the reasons for this is that Carpenter, like Hill, represented himself as a neoclassicist. Both directors possess and have demonstrated in their work an affectionate appreciation for classical directors such as Howard Hawks, John Ford, and Alfred Hitchcock. Hill's early films (the first being *Hard Times* in 1975) were not disfigured by sentimental and incidental references to these directors as Carpenter's were, but Hill's artistic aloofness was less ingratiating than Carpenter's lack of pretension.

Retrospectively, it is evident that both of these directors are temperamental opposites of the directors they admire. They may have learned valuable lessons in technique from Hawks and Hitchcock, but the visions of the world their recent films reveal are devoid of the positive values celebrated in classical cinema. *The Thing* illustrates this strikingly, as its tone and dramatic thrust are a world away from the Howard Hawks film (*The Thing from Another World*, 1951) based on the same material. For Carpenter and Hill, the annihilating violence so prevalent and so often gratuitous in the contemporary American cinema is a meaningful element which completes their dark romantic visions.

The level of despair embraced by Carpenter and Hill and acknowledged in the Wilder and Edwards films is relevant to the entire spectrum of 1981 American cinema. The comic strip/fantasy films and mindless comedies which dominate the list of top grossers are works which exist to suppress this level of despair. Their success suggests that a retreat into a world of childish make-believe fulfills the needs of both filmmakers and audiences. More disturbingly, contemporary life is most persistently depicted in the seemingly endless cycle of callous low-budget horror films (the release of the amusingly titled *Friday the 13th, Part III* in 1982 confirms that the market for such films is as depressingly healthy as ever). The genre's resurgence of popularity is largely attributable to the great success of *Halloween*, ironically so in view of the integrity of Carpenter's personal vision. At its most characteristic, the contemporary horror film exploits a crude and graphic delineation of psychotic acts of violence, most often directed against women. The social and psychological implications of this are alarming enough, but the life-denying artistic texture which results is often accompanied by a manipulation of traditional narrative elements so perverse that the effect is completely demoralizing.

This tendency is most pronounced in the 1981 thriller *Blow Out*. The artistic irresponsibility of Brian DePalma, the director of this film, is especially irritating because he is endowed with a superficial stylistic talent beyond that of most purveyors of shock and horror. On a facile level, *Blow Out* is a film not without a certain elegance, but DePalma's contempt for characterization ultimately assures its hollowness. In the film, John Travolta plays a sound engineer who labors on cheap horror films. One night, he inadvertently records evidence of a murder subsequently concealed by a conspiracy. Being a decent human being, he attempts to bring the conspiracy to light, and in the process falls in love with a girl (Nancy Allen) who is more or less innocently linked to the crime. In the course of the film's climax, the girl is murdered and her death cries are recorded by a device the hero has been using to monitor her movements. Naturally, the hero is filled with remorse that in spite of his best professional efforts, he was unable to reach her in time to save her life. During the course of the film, however, there has been a running gag. The cheap horror film to which the hero is assigned is lacking an effective scream for a shower murder sequence. The actress playing the victim is an inept screamer, and so are the girls brought in to dub the scream. The final sequence finds the scream successfully dubbed *with the death cries of the girl the hero loved*! He sits in the screening room passively assenting that the scream is a good one, then puts his fingers to his ears as the completed scene is projected once again.

Perhaps DePalma could not see beyond the clever irony of this ending, but that does not make it any the less insidious. What he has done is nothing less than to destroy his protagonist as a credible human being. The character is initially established as a sensible and healthy individual who is very professional but properly skeptical about the value of the films on which he works. Nothing in the film suggests that he is so obsessive about motion-picture sound that he would callously exploit the death screams of the woman he loved, and his contradictory behavior after he has done so is even less comprehensible. The irreparable violence DePalma inflicts on the characterization is all the more regrettable because Travolta's performance is an excellent one; his convincing naturalistic style brings to the contrived events a needed sense of reality until the character collapses into grotesqueness. The ultimate shallowness of *Blow Out* is aggravated by DePalma's little parodies of horror films (specifically the illusory opening of the film, which turns out to be the film-within-a-film). The film-within-a-film is clearly intended to be a cheap hack effort, but it does not seem substantially different either in style or content from one of DePalma's own films. There is no indication that DePalma is capable of anything more than isolated flourishes unrelated to a thoughtful overall structure. Even the flourishes are overly derivative of Alfred Hitchcock, and they call attention to the vast differences between a classical master such as Hitchcock and a decadent disciple such as DePalma.

A director such as DePalma approaches Hitchcock as the creator of virtuoso set pieces such as the shower murder in *Psycho* (1960), although it is generally agreed that none of the numerous imitations of that particular sequence by DePalma and others have surpassed the Hitchcock original. The true extent of Hitchcock's virtuosity, however, is overlooked by his current imitators. The consummate formal mastery of Hitchcock is even more pronounced in the sequence in *Psycho* which precedes the shower murder, a sequence which does not find even the weakest echoes in recent synthetic thrillers. In that sequence, Marion Crane (Janet Leigh), the basically decent fugitive, and Norman Bates (Anthony Perkins), the likable but troubled motel manager, share a late meal and converse in the motel office. The interchange which occurs precisely crystallizes the emotional thrust of the film and beautifully elaborates both characters. A daring shift of narrative interest is successfully achieved in the process, as previously the film has been experienced entirely from Marion's point of view and Norman has just been introduced. Following this sequence, Marion will be abruptly murdered and the audience's sympathy must be refocused on Norman. In the motel office sequence, this transfer is already occurring. Hitchcock scrupulously divides his shots between the two characters, crosscutting between them so that each will rule the frames in which he or she appears. Marion is framed against a fairly neutral background in straightforward compositions which confirm her potential stability. Norman is framed against an ominous background of stuffed birds and is continually photographed from either a slightly high or slightly low camera angle. The gestures, postures, and vocal inflections of the two players are at once natural and informed by the same deliberation given to the camera angles and the editing. Crucially, the substance of the conversation is not only very serious but relevant to all of the preceding and following action. Hitchcock's attention is directed to a structure which consistently integrates all of the elements of the work. He does not need to violate his characters to achieve an effect, and his matchless technique does not require showy displays.

The motel office sequence is characteristic of the quiet virtuosity which distinguishes the American cinema in its classical years. It is retrospectively apparent that the most enduring and expressive moments of eighty years of cinema are often stylistically subtle. A classical director can eloquently convey the full force of his sensibility in a simple scene involving two characters. For the concluding reel of *The Awful Truth* (1937), Leo McCarey composed an enchanting sequence of romantic comedy with two adept players (Cary Grant and Irene Dunne), two bedrooms, a door, and a clock. In *Notorious* (1946), Hitchcock realized a celebrated love scene of timeless appeal simply by having Ingrid Bergman and Cary Grant exchange kisses in close-up as they walk across a room. The emotionally charged scene in Frank Capra's *It's a Wonderful Life* (1946) in which George (James Stewart) realizes he loves Mary (Donna Reed) occurs in a single fixed composition as she speaks on the telephone with a would-be suitor. The broodingly nostalgic "Have Yourself a Merry Little Christmas" is sung by Judy Garland in Vincente Minnelli's *Meet Me in St. Louis* (1944) as she and Margaret O'Brien sit by a window. The reunion in death of Mrs. Muir (Gene Tierney) and the Ghost (Rex Harrison) in Joseph L. Mankiewicz' *The Ghost and Mrs. Muir* (1947) is realized in only a few images which magically and movingly restore the heroine's youthful beauty and poetically suggest eternity without altering the realistic interior of the house. These examples are not randomly evoked. They are all universally loved passages in acknowledged masterpieces of the classical American cinema. In each instance, the director has demonstrated a complete command of the medium. The duration of the shots, the placement of the camera, and an appreciation of the qualities of the individual actors combine to produce an ineffable effect which is in actuality the result of great artistic discernment.

On another level, these sequences attest the greater maturity of American cinema in the classical years. They are sequences which in every case affirm human relationships and emotions. Although they are artificial reflections of life, they are imbued with an understanding of life's most profound realities. By contrast, the dissipation which presently pervades the American cinema on a formal level is accompanied by a dissipation of this appeal to the mature heart and mind. In 1981, only the generally overlooked final meeting between Jacqueline Bisset and Candice Bergen in *Rich and Famous* is likely to be treasured in the future as a sequence possessing an emotional resonance equivalent to those found in the classic sequences discussed above. It is surely not incidental that this sequence is the work of an aging classical director. Such moments are likely to become increasingly rare in mainstream American cinema. The passion of a true modernist such as John Carpenter, however artistically valid and expressive, exists in striking contrast to the passion of George Cukor. It is a passion born in the paranoid contemplation of a world apparently stripped of positive human experience.

The spiritual poverty which pervades the current American cinema, infecting films both good and bad, is partly attributable to the increasing domination of an impersonal technology. "State of the Art" is an unfortunate term heard more and more often in describing the conditions for the making of a given film. Regrettably, as this technology has become more sophisticated, the craftsmanship which distinguishes the films of the classical era has diminished.

Indifferent cinematography, muddy sound, careless lab work, and waste of film are the rule. The last-named fault is especially serious as it reveals a tendency to self-absorption on the part of filmmakers. In the classical era, a screenplay was constructed in such a way as to give a clear idea of the realized film, on the level of story and structure if not tone and texture. As a result, the director properly devoted most of his attention to nuance and detail within the on-the-set realization of the film.

In current cinema, filmmakers shoot excessive amounts of footage so that they can spend months in the editing room playing with the film. The relatively impersonal act of editing now tends to play a greater part in the creation of a film than the actual production. Formerly, editing was valuable because of the subtle but crucial role it played in completing the style of a film. When the manipulation of the film becomes more important than what is created on the set, this is no longer true. Young filmmakers and students of film are often amazed when they learn of the close ratio between film shot and film used for an average John Ford film, yet Ford's films are generally among the most beautifully edited because he had the relationship of shots in his mind while he was shooting. Though few directors could claim an equal talent for this, most classicists at least shared the intention. Modern filmmakers customarily lack both the skill and the ability. More seriously, the greater ease which directors of the present generation often feel in the editing room rather than on the set is symptomatic of the evasion of human reality which exists on another level in their realized works.

The American cinema is in a state of irreversible decline which cannot be wished away, but this is not a cause for undue pessimism. It is inevitable and natural that change will affect the conditions of artistic creation, and for this reason the death of all great epochs of art is assured. It is equally true that all artistic media continue to produce individually meritorious works even under the least favorable conditions. It is likely that the best American films of the present and future will lie increasingly outside the mainstream. Rather than pallid imitations of the great films of Hollywood's past, these films will be fresh new works perhaps influenced by the more deliberate formalism of European models. There certainly remains a richness of subject matter indigenous to America which remains to be explored.

An overview of 1981 suggests that the effect-oriented fantasy film is the most commercially viable work for theatrical exhibition and likely to remain so. The artist who wishes to create more intimate and human works, however, will always find a way to do so if he searches hard enough for it. The year 1982 has already seen the appearance of a superb equivalent to a feature-length film, John Dorr's *Dorothy and Alan at Norma Place*, made on *videotape*. This was the only way that Dorr could afford to make his serious study of the complex and troubled relationship between celebrated author Dorothy Parker (Strawn Bovee) and her homosexual husband Alan Campbell (George

Lafleur). There is an inevitable rawness in the look of the tape which is not associated with film, but all of the essentials of brilliant film direction are there—an imaginative structuring of the story's emotional flow, thoughtful compositions, adept staging, attention to shot duration, and professional performances exhibiting great skill. The work's limitations are entirely superficial, and its virtues suggest that stories dealing with nuances of human relationships can still be articulated, even if at a necessarily humble level. Perhaps it is in this manner that an American cinema deserving of admiration will continue to endure.

Blake Lucas

MODERN CINEMA AND SILENT CINEMA

The opening precredit sequence of *They Live by Night* (1949) is an especially touching instance of the debt that modern filmmakers owe to the silent cinema. A black and white image, warmly lit, presents in medium close-up a couple (Farley Granger and Cathy O'Donnell) embracing while a tender melody (actually the folk song "I Know Where I'm Going") plays on the sound track. Over the image, an introduction to the narrative is written, one line at a time: "This boy and this girl were never properly introduced . . . to the world we live in . . . to tell their story." When the last line appears the couple turns and looks directly into the camera, as if regarding the audience. Nothing about the couple has been explicitly related. The written line evokes a poignant fatalism, but it is more suggestive than descriptive. The images, however, reveal a great deal more; immediately, the boy and girl are identified as lovers, and the romanticism of the lighting seems to place them in a private world of their own devising. The wistful music poeticizes that world. When the couple turns to the camera, however, the music becomes more starkly dramatic. The expressions of the girl and boy complete the artistic thought. In those last moments of the opening image, they seem bewildered, frightened, resentful, vulnerable, and lost all at once.

If the scene is broken down into its various elements, it will be readily evident that it could conceivably exist in this form in a silent film. Silent-film titles frequently were written over the images, and the later works of the silent era often had synchronized music tracks which would have permitted the use of the folk melody, essential to the mood of the scene. Crucially, the images of the couple compellingly convey both their immersion in a private world of love and their alienation from the cold and hostile world which exists outside of their relationship. It is not the intention of the film to sustain this mood, although the haunting evocation of the silent cinema that the scene achieves is echoed in the final image by a slow and heartbreaking fadeout on the face of O'Donnell. The couple's gaze into the camera transforms the innocence of early cinema into self-consciousness of modern cinema. The credit sequence further ruptures the initial tone, which properly attaches itself to later scenes, among which the opening chronologically belongs. The credits occur over an innovative helicopter shot, and the first third of the narrative gains much of its effectiveness from a sensitive use of sound and tough but lyrical dialogue (beautifully written by Charles Schnee and Nicholas Ray). During this third of the film, there is no theme music (and only occasional source music). The musical score resumes subtly but tellingly in the first actual love scene between the boy and girl.

The relationship of this film to cinema's silent past is therefore oblique but profound, part of a complex aesthetic structure relatively unsubmissive to the stylistic conventions of the film's own era. *They Live by Night* was the first film directed by Ray, who not surprisingly is identifiable as both a classicist and a modernist. The lesson to be learned from this example is a valuable one. The essence of cinema is not something which exists in phases, each phase obscuring or obliterating its predecessor. Of course, the history of cinema demonstrates technical evolution; unfortunately, such evolution tends to be regarded in one of two reductive ways: either early cinema is considered primitive and outdated, or modern cinema is considered a corruption of cinema in its pristine state. There *are* old films which seem sadly dated, and there are new films which seem aesthetically decadent; the best films, however, cross over from one era to another, forward and backward in time, transcending both changing technology and aesthetic fashion.

This balanced critical view is directly attributable to a group of filmmakers associated with what is commonly considered one of the freshest periods in the history of cinema, the French "New Wave." Writing in the pages of a magazine called *Cahiers du Cinéma*, Jean-Luc Godard, François Truffaut, Eric Rohmer, Jacques Rivette, Claude Chabrol, and others intelligently rediscovered the enduring formal qualities of their chosen medium. The films they subsequently made beginning in the late 1950's and continuing into the 1960's were daring not because they offered a totally new kind of cinema but because they used tradition in a new way. Previously, historical currents had tended to push the medium in alleged new directions, although that description was never really accurate. Neorealism, for example, attributed to the postwar Italian cinema, had many precedents, such as the silent D. W. Griffith film *Isn't Life Wonderful?* (1925) and the sound film *Toni* (1935) of Jean Renoir. Symbolism and surrealism had reached their height in the work of, respectively, German expressionism and the early experimental films of Luis Buñuel, nurtured in each instance by the silent cinema. The French New Wave perceived the cinema as a continually flowing spring of recurring artistic strategies which are either perennially fruitful, available for creative rediscovery in succeeding generations, or are merely negligible, the passing fads of a given era.

The greatest directors had always developed in stylistic directions natural to them, often simplifying and refining their approach in maturity and disdaining bravura effects. As an example, the mobility of the camera was established very early in film history. The 1920's are distinguished by camera movements as elaborate as the imaginations of creative directors and cinematographers, and the 1930's, after some initial discord over what the camera was physically capable of in relation to the sound recording, demonstrate the same cinematographic fluency. Yasijuro Ozu, a great Japanese director who began his career in the silent period, moved the camera with great vitality and buoyancy in his early films, seemingly confirming what other directorial styles also suggest, that a moving camera is an integral part of film style. As Ozu matured, however, he moved the camera less and less, developing a style which consisted of very quiet compositions and highly sophisticated but minimally dramatic editing. In his masterly final work, *An Autumn Afternoon* (1962), there is not a single camera movement. Far from indicating that Ozu was old-fashioned or capable of only a modest style, the static camerawork of this film actually reveals that Ozu had become extremely selective with regard to a multitude of cinematic possibilities and had deliberately elected to express himself within an aesthetic imitation of his own choosing.

In recent years, Chantal Akerman—a young Belgian director critically regarded as an extreme modernist and sometimes as an avant-garde filmmaker—has, like Ozu, made a film, *Jeanne Dielman, 23 Quai du Commerce, 1080 Bruxelles* (1976), in which the camera never moves. Moreover, in the Akerman film the shots tend to be very long in duration and to consist of minimal action. *Jeanne Dielman, 23 Quai du Commerce, 1080 Bruxelles* runs counter to almost every contemporary notion of cinematic virtuosity, but more than most films it is a tour de force, not least because its stable shots of lengthy duration tell a very suspenseful story with a minimum of dialogue. In the entire three-hour-and-fifteen-minute film, there are no more than twenty minutes of spoken dialogue, all of which is banal and undramatic. Not only are camera movement and elaborate editing techniques stripped away from the film, but also its images are tangibly reminiscent of the silent film.

Ozu and Akerman are only two directors—significantly of different generations and cultural backgrounds as well as different sexes—who have understood that a filmmaker does not need to avail himself or herself of every cinematic resource and technique in order to make a beautiful and expressive film. What the members of the French New Wave recognized as they sat in the Cinématheque Française watching old films was that early filmmakers also made aesthetic choices, and that even if certain technical limitations presented themselves, the stylistic equivalent for the missing element could be found. For example, Josef von Sternberg's sound films demonstrate a love of dialogue delivered in a mocking or dispassionate manner (*Thunderbolt*, 1929; *Morocco*, 1930; *Blonde Venus*, 1932; and *The Shanghai Gesture*, 1941, among others). In his silent films, Sternberg could not have made use of this stylized dialogue delivery even if he had already thought of it as a potential stylistic element. The temperamental idiosyncracy which eventually resulted in this approach was already evident in his artistic personality, however, and he discovered ways to express it in silent-film terms. *Underworld* (1927) and *The Docks of New York* (1928) are inhabited by prototypical Sternberg characters whose ambivalent demeanor and resistance to sincere exchanges of feeling are expressed physically. The silent and sound films of this director display precisely the same style and sensibility.

Another director, F. W. Murnau, who met with a tragic accidental death during the early years of sound, has customarily been regarded as an artist whose work, confined to silent films, is of merely historical interest. Indeed, his last film (*Tabu*, 1931) was realized with a silent visual style at a time when sound had become a seeming imperative. Retrospectively, however, Murnau has been rediscovered as a director aesthetically relevant to the sound film. *Sunrise* (1927) and *Tabu*, in common with other late silent films, have synchronized sound tracks, largely dominated by music but also incorporating sound effects which have a precise effect on the experience of watching the film. All that is missing is dialogue, and in the Murnau films, its absence is qualified by the relative naturalness of the narrative treatment. The relationships and conflicts of these films are so clearly articulated within the individual images that the muteness of the actors seems almost incidental. The French resurrected Murnau as a central figure of cinema, not specifically for his silent films but because his approach exemplified the spatial and temporal integrity associated with long take styles of the sound era. If Murnau had lived, he would have made sound films, presumably without any sacrifice or compromise of his formal ideals.

Murnau was only one director who blurred the cinematic differences between generations. The discerning young Parisian film lovers drew inspiration from earlier filmmakers such as D. W. Griffith and Louis Feuillade as well. In the New Wave films of the 1960's, a passionate distillation of the fundamentals of cinema coexisted with a contemporary ambience which aggressively undermined the stolid traditions of the complacently literary French cinema of the previous generation. Cinematography and sound recording, especially in the films of Jean-Luc Godard, were sometimes celebrated as bringing a raw and spontaneous impression of reality to cinema, when in actuality the director was at times striving to re-create in personal terms the look and sound of much earlier films. Godard demonstrated that much of the elegance and technical refinement which the cinema had acquired over the years was irrelevant to artistic expressiveness. The natural light of early silent films made out of doors appealed to him, as did the awkwardly raw but creatively employed sound of the more adventurous early sound films. In his films, as well as those of Truffaut and other young directors, neglected or forgotten devices such as wipes, irises, and fades in and out *within* shots had a beguiling place.

In *Paris Nous Appartient* (1961, *Paris Belongs to Us*), Jacques Rivette tells the story of a frightening and mysterious conspiracy which affects the lives of a group of contemporary Parisians. His visual description of the film's world is very realistic. Drab and cheerless black and white images, drained of any trace of glamour or apparent artifice, characterize the film. The premise, however, is inspired by the paranoid fantasies devised by Fritz Lang and Louis Feuillade in the silent era. Lang's Dr. Mabuse and Feuillade's Fantomas were brilliant super criminals metaphorically resurrected by Rivette to serve a contemporary moral perspective. Rivette's characters seem to be drained of hope and will by forces beyond their comprehension. Rivette is suggesting that in an arbitrary and meaningless universe, evil has precisely the same effect on the passive individual as lack of faith. Like his characters, Rivette's narrative drifts uneasily, wary of resolution. Lang and Feuillade shared Rivette's impulses and honored the prevailing melodramatic conventions of theii era only superficially. What is explicit in Rivette's vision is implicit in theirs. When Rivette's characters screen a sequence from Lang's *Metropolis* (1927), they seem to be witnessing an evocation of their own oppression.

Rivette often seems to be an unusually difficult and demanding film stylist, impatient with readily comprehensible modes of film narrative. In this context, his affinity for early filmmakers is extremely revealing. The mute and cold gray images of a Feuillade and the hallucinatory worlds of a Lang predated the tame and tired literalness, readily settled for by too many timid filmmakers, against which Rivette rebels. The formal and narrative daring of other modern French filmmakers also has antecedents in early cinema. The boldly poetic Georges Franju creates films of an uncompromising personal nature, including those associated with popular genres such as the horror film *Les Yeux Sans Visage* (1959). Curiously, when Franju remade *Judex* in 1963 as a homage to Feuillade's 1916 serial of the same name, he seemed more conventional and prosaic than the director who inspired him. In the same way, Alain Resnais' masterly explorations of time and memory are always formally challenging and often richly ambiguous (*Last Year at Marienbad*, 1962), but the simpler interpolations of memory images and fantasies which adorn the films of D. W. Griffith (*Broken Blossoms*, 1919) more magically evoke the subjective life.

Past and present approaches to cinema are mutually illuminating. If earlier films, especially those made in the silent era, sometimes seem to have the advantage of a simultaneous purity of effect and spontaneity of invention, they reciprocate by providing a potential language which later films may draw upon unexpectedly and tellingly. Sound films have traditionally relied heavily on dialogue, for no other reason than narrative expediency, but there are celebrated instances in mainstream commercial cinema of directors abandoning the written word in key scenes and rediscovering unadorned visual storytelling. One example occurs in *Waterloo Bridge* (1940), directed by Mervyn LeRoy. A central love scene between Vivian Leigh and Robert Taylor is set in a nightclub, and LeRoy decided on the set that the dialogue exchanges which were to be delivered as the couple danced would be less expressive of their developing romance than the more believable silences he substituted. In a similar manner, Vincente Minnelli brooded over a scene of a newlywed soldier and his wife (Robert Walker and Judy Garland) having a farewell breakfast following their only night together in *The Clock* (1945). In place of a banal conversation, Minnelli worked out a scene in which the characters eloquently communicate intense emotions by looks and gestures. Sound films are not dependent on purely visual exposition, and such moments are executed with a precision of effect that is rarely the foremost consideration in a silent film, which cannot hold visual power in reserve.

The value of the silent moment is most consistently pronounced in the films of John Ford. Instructively, it is not his silent films which distinguish him as a supreme visual artist. His sound films have a natural and unmannered narrative flow which enhances the often vital nonverbal moments he creates with such apparent ease. The sequence in *The Searchers* (1956) in which Martha Edwards (Dorothy Jordan) caresses the coat of her husband's brother, an admission of suppressed love inadvertently witnessed by an outsider (Ward Bond), is a famous example. In *The Quiet Man* (1952), the introduction of Sean Thornton (John Wayne) to Mary Kate Danaher (Maureen O'Hara), a moment which vividly conveys their mutual attraction, occurs when he sees her herding sheep in a beautiful green landscape. Not a word is spoken, and a single prolonged glance backward by Mary Kate as she slowly departs in an extreme low angle shot establishes her as an uncommonly endearing heroine before the audience even knows who she is. Much of the lyrical quality of the spontaneous Sunday morning "date" of Wyatt Earp (Henry Fonda) and Clementine Carter (Cathy Downs) in *My Darling Clementine* (1946) derives from lengthy pauses and hesitations in which the two characters interact without speaking. A series of eloquently mute images of home and family in *How Green Was My Valley* (1941) are rendered with a vitality and immediacy which instills the accompanying nostalgic narration of the protagonist with a tangible sense of a lost past. Key emotional moments such as these abound in Ford's films, illuminating relationships and narrative shifts with a delicacy and clarity which never seem portentous or overstudied. The visual gifts of a John Ford exist for the sake of his films, not to support any given film theory. He makes no effort to conceal the cinema's lack of purity, and in consequence, his work bears no allegiance to any historical moment of cinema.

If the cinema is to be self-renewing, it must be *more* conscious of fundamental aesthetic strategies which are not indigenous to "traditional" or "modern" films, and *less* conscious of "state-of-the-art" technology. The relationship between silent and sound films persuasively attests this fact. The modern aspects of a Griffith film are as pronounced as the traditional aspects of a Godard film. The achievement of a harmonious balance between montage (editing) and *mise-en-scène* (composition) and respect for the mutually supportive and complementary contributions of image and sound remain the foremost formal considerations of the filmmaker. The arbitrary consignment to history of unfashionable cinematic approaches is refuted by the best contemporary films.

Blake Lucas

SELECTED FILM BOOKS OF 1981

In 1981, students of film were absorbing two masterworks published in 1980: Ronald Haver's *David O. Selznick's Hollywood* (New York: Alfred A. Knopf, 1980) and Aldo Bernardini's *Cinema Muto Italiano 1896-1904* (Rome and Bari: Editori Laterza, 1980). Both rank among the most visually beautiful film-history books every produced, yet these are no mere coffee-table books. Beneath the gloss of both volumes lies evidence of prodigious research and meticulous attention to detail.

Haver could, if the case rested solely upon the evidence of this book, be mistaken for David O. Selznick himself since *David O. Selznick's Hollywood* strongly resembles one of the producer's own films. It has, in fact, been termed a history of Hollywood as Selznick might have written it. Though Haver has presented knowledgeable and evenhanded appraisals of almost fifty films in significant detail, the text and, particularly, the illustrations so accurately recapture the color, flair, and glamour of the man himself that many scholars and historians will overlook the wealth of insight and detail which makes this considerably more than just another Hollywood picture book. *Gone with the Wind* (1939) is obviously given its share of attention but material on that film is readily available in other sources. More impressive, perhaps, is the amount of material presented on Selznick's less famous films. Production facts, historical information, and "behind the scenes" episodes not only provide considerable insight into these achievements but also into the man who was David O. Selznick.

The lavish physical appearance of the book owes much to the flair and imagination of its designer, Thomas Ingalls, who packed it with an impressive array of well-chosen and highly appropriate photographs and illustrations. The design not only complements the text but also, through its very showmanship, adds a dimension of personality that is ordinarily absent from most biographical and scholarly works.

Equally visually impressive but, in many respects, covering more ground is Volume I of Aldo Bernardini's *Cinema Muto Italiano*, an extremely specific, town-by-town history of the development of the Italian cinema during the critical years of 1896-1904. The early Italian film industry has been traditionally considered to have derived almost exclusively from that of the French, who performed most of the early experiments with primitive photographic technology. Once a market developed, the Italians simply imported the hardware as well as a number of French technicians (primarily from the Pathé company), and a remarkably sophisticated industry was born. The uniquely Italian achievements would not occur until 1905-1913, with the development of the singularly Italian film forms of realism and the historical spectacle.

Bernardini, however, puts the early years in perspective. Beginning with a complete overview of the period from 1896 to 1914 (1905-1914 will be treated in more detail in the forthcoming Volume II), he goes on to fill in the social and cultural background of the early years of Italian cinema. Against this atmosphere, he traces the impact of the Edison Kinetoscope and the Lumière Cinématographe on a region-by-region basis, taking the readers along with the French and Italian exhibitors and distributors in their early wanderings through the world of the "cinema ambulante." By 1904, a highly developed system of film theaters had developed throughout the country, anticipating the release of the first Italian feature film in 1905.

Although Bernardini relies heavily and obviously on such general histories as Georges Sadoul's *Histoire Generale du Cinéma* (Paris: Editions du Sevil, 1947), much of his material is new. He provides in minute detail the history of each small town's reception of the new technology of film, tracing the step-by-step evolution of a sideshow exhibit into a major industry which significantly influenced the direction of world cinema. There is little doubt that Bernardini has compiled the definitive history of the Italian silent cinema.

The production of a good, all-encompassing mainstream history of film along the lines of the aforementioned *Histoire Generale du Cinéma* is at least as difficult as the highly focused efforts of Haver and Bernardini, as witnessed by the less than satisfactory efforts in recent years by film historians such as John Fell, Gerald Mast, and Jack Ellis. Thus, the 1981 publication of David Cook's *A History of Narrative Film* (New York: W. W. Norton and Company, 1981) is a remarkable achievement. It is quite simply the best general history of narrative film that has been published in many years. The 720-page volume, the product of eight years of extremely thorough research, provides a remarkably comprehensive overview of the history of the cinema. Whereas most such histories seem dated by the time they are published, Cook's work should remain current for a number of years. A major reason for this is the book's elaborate footnotes and special sections that, among other things, mention individuals who have yet to reach their creative zenith, while other sections chronicle the directions of various national cinemas in some detail.

In the main, however, *A History of Narrative Film* deals with the major figures and issues in the history of film. Cook has chosen to go into impressive detail on the major figures and trends of any given period (offering, for example, in-depth treatments of Sergei Eisenstein and Vsevolod Pudovkin and the various nuances of montage) with briefer discussions of the subluminaries. Although this approach might step on the toes of scholars who may find their highly specialized fields of interest slighted (documentary and experimental works, for example, with the exception of the Kuleshov Workshop, are virtually ignored), Cook's judgments appear to be evenhanded and substantiated by other sources.

While the index could be improved in future editions, particularly in its listing of individual film titles, the lengthy articles, footnotes, and massive compilations of detail more than offset this fault. The book's twelve hundred illustrations, including entire sequences of shots in many cases, complement the text in a manner reflecting an unusual sensitivity of judgment for a historical work and complete the overall impression of sound scholarship.

Other notable film histories of a more or less general nature include the second edition of David Robinson's *The History of World Cinema* (New York: Stein and Day, 1981), which covers a great deal of material but lacks the depth of Cook's history. Nevertheless, Robinson presents an impressive array of data and should be considered a worthwhile introduction to the history of cinema.

The year 1981 also marked the introduction of the paperback edition of Ephraim Katz's *The International Film Encyclopedia* (London: Macmillan, 1981). This less expensive paperback edition constitutes a long-awaited boon for film students and movie buffs alike since it is the most informative, comprehensive, and meticulously researched single-volume encyclopedia of films and filmmaking in the English language. In hardcover, it was a must for libraries; now it is a must for anyone with more than a passing interest in film.

Michael T. Isenberg's *War on Film: The American Cinema and World War I, 1914-1941* (East Brunswick, New Jersey: Fairleigh Dickinson University Press, 1981) is a popular study of the attitudes of the American people as expressed in motion pictures. *Australian Film 1900-1977* (1977, by Andrew Pike) is a film-by-film history of Australian film up to 1977. Since Australia's cinema, like that of Germany, is one of the few in the world on the ascendence, this is an extremely valuable volume. It also constitutes almost a national filmography in many respects. *Langfilm i Sverige 1940-1949* (1949, edited by Bertil Wredlund and Rolf Lindfors), is a seemingly definitive treatment of all films, regardless of country of origin, that were released in Sweden in the 1940's. This is similar to Wredlund's *Filmarsbaken 1979* (Stockholm: Proprias, 1980), which offers synopses and credits for all films released in Sweden during 1979 and which appears to be an ongoing project. Anthony Slide and Edward Wagenknecht's *Fifty Great American Silent Films 1912-1920* (New York: Dover Publications, 1980) is an economical but enlightening and surprisingly comprehensive treatment of fifty early silent films by two universally acclaimed specialists in the early cinema. *In a Glamorous Fashion: The Fabulous Years of Hollywood Costume Design* by W. Robert La Vine (New York: Charles Scribner's Sons, 1981) is a long overdue history of costume. Finally, Roger Dooley's *From Scarface to Scarlett: American Film in the 1930's* (New York: Harcourt Brace Jovanovich, 1981) is a history of the decade's films with the emphasis on nostalgia rather than scholarly insight.

It is usually feast or famine where books dealing with the Hollywood musical are concerned, and 1981 provided a banquet of materials. In a year in which the last vestiges of the musical had all but disappeared, with the exception of the satirical *Pennies from Heaven*, a wave of nostalgia swept over film buffs in the form of four studies of the genre: *The Hollywood Musical* by Ethan Mordden (New York: St. Martin's Press, 1981); *Genre: The Musical* (London: Routledge and Kegan Paul, 1981, edited by Rick Altman); Clive Hirschorn's *The Hollywood Musical* (New York: Crown, 1981); and Ted Sennett's *Hollywood Musicals* (New York: Harry N. Abrams, 1981). This last volume is a large, coffee-table book with a price tag approaching that of Ron Haver's *David O. Selznick's Hollywood* and is comparable to it in the remarkably high quality of its illustrations and full-color reproductions. Unfortunately, the supporting text is weak and a reader might be wise to purchase Ted Sennett's book to supplement textually Hirschorn's lavish pictures. Sennett devotes long paragraphs to fairly detailed discussions of 1,344 musicals, arranged by year of release. He also provides cross-indexing by titles, songs, performers, composers, and lyricists. Together, the two books make a beautiful and informative reference set for musical buffs.

Equally factual and certainly less expensive than Sennett's book is Ethan Mordden's *The Hollywood Musical.* Although encyclopedic in scope, its articles are concise and are oriented to the "behind-the-scenes," technical aspects of the musical. The primary strength of the work is its vast accumulation of facts, details, and odd bits of information, possibly the largest one-volume compilation in recent years. Unfortunately, however, the range and frequency of Mordden's recent publications, including *A Guide to Orchestral Music: The Handbook for Non-Musicians* (New York: Oxford University Press, 1980); *The Splendid Art of Opera* (New Jersey: Methuen, 1980); and *The American Theatre* (New York: Oxford University Press, 1981), hint at the presence of a staff of compilers. Perhaps this accounts for the fact that *The Hollywood Musical* offers little insight into specific musicals or, in fact, into the phenomena of the filmed musical itself. As an encyclopedia of facts, it provides an excellent introduction to the Hollywood musical for the nonscholar, but for serious students of the art, it provides little intellectual nourishment.

More insightful and innovative is *Genre: The Musical*, edited by Rick Altman. While it is fundamentally an introductory reader, many of the essays—notably those by Alan Williams, Richard Dyer, and Jane Feuer—delve into thematic areas not covered by other books on the subject. Other articles vary in the quality of their scholarship but most offer insights into themes and meanings and are less concerned with technical aspects. A bibliography by Jane Feuer maintains this emphasis and leads to lengthier, more specialized treatments of topics similar to those discussed in *Genre: The Musical.*

The musical genre is given further treatment in Thomas Schatz's *Hollywood Film Genres* (New York: Random House, 1981). In fact, every major genre is given its due in the book. More important, however, Schatz has provided an introduction for the nonexpert on what constitutes a genre and why the Hollywood studios have historically relied upon these structured films. He then recounts the conventions of the genre and their social significance. This is followed by a discussion of each major genre from the gangster film to screwball comedy. Although his treatment is perhaps not as penetrating as advanced film students might wish, his work is a superb textbook for those who wish to comprehend the nuts and bolts of formula films that are too often taken for granted. It is one of the most interesting books of 1981 and in many respects is long overdue.

A traditionally overpopulated area in film criticism is the realm of biographical or critical studies of individual film artists. With material ranging from Guido Oldrini's masterful study of Charles Chaplin, *Il Realismo di Chaplin* (Rome: Laterza and Figli, 1981) to *Loving Lucy* by Bart Andrews and Thomas J. Watson (London: Robson Books, 1981), 1981 was no exception.

Between these extremes, however, several studies of individual artists are noteworthy if only for their relative rarity. The first of these is a rather complex and not easily usable work by Dudley and Paul Andrew, *Kenji Mizoguchi: A Guide to References and Resources* (Boston: G. K. Hall, 1981). It is definitely not an introductory text, presupposing as it does the reader's grasp of somewhat obscure technical terms and historical movements. It has been designed for the specialist who has discovered that previous Mizoguchi scholarship has been fundamentally chaotic. The Andrews walk a tightrope above this critical pandemonium and maintain a relatively high degree of objectivity, even when they attempt to interpret the director's troublesome thematic treatment of women by noting (or perhaps creating) a distinction between his depiction of women in his period pieces and in his modern dramas. Discussion of the director and of individual films is supplemented by a comprehensive bibliography and an equally strong filmography. Though many users will be disappointed by the absence of illustrated material and footnotes, it can be argued that anyone who has waded through the morass of earlier works on the director will be well pleased with the ready access to materials provided here.

Another significant work of 1981 surveys the career of director Blake Edwards. Edwards has been significantly undervalued for much of his career, due in part to his association with screen comedies such as Pink Panther films. In the 1980's, however, Edwards is beginning to receive recognition as a director of some depth and complexity. Peter Lehman and William Lehr in their book *Blake Edwards* (Athens: Ohio University Press, 1981) imply that this has been true all along, citing such underrated films as *Gunn* (1967), *The Party* (1968), and *Darling Lili* (1970) to make their points.

Although Lehman and Lehr may have overrated *Darling Lili*, *Gunn* and *The Party* have been cult favorites for a number of years and one is tempted to add 1981's *S.O.B.* and 1982's *Victor/Victoria* as more recent examples of Edwards' particular genius. Lehman and Lehr suggest that Edwards establishes a delicate tension between comic and dramatic elements in any given film. He then adds a fundamental deception in characterization (*Victor/Victoria*) or the milieu (*The Party*) which distorts reality and creates a basic uncertainty among the protagonists concerning their basic identities. The resulting complications, like those in William Shakespeare's comedies, are completely unpredictable while still remaining true to character and situation.

Another interesting study of an individual director with wide implications as well is *Film and Dreams: An Approach to Bergman* (South Salem, New York: Redgrave, 1981, edited by Vlada Petric), a provocative treatment of a subject that is gaining more attention in film criticism. Resulting from a 1978 conference at Harvard, the book brings together essays by specialists including Marsha Kinder, Stanley Cavell, and Vlada Petric.

The implications of a relationship between dreams and film are profound for both scholars and filmmakers. A dream seemingly consists of random or at best loosely ordered images expressed by the brain which somehow selects them from a mass of subjective experiences and perceptions. The dream itself is then almost immediately revised by the dreamer upon waking. It is this final process that most closely resembles the process of making a film. Even a dreamworker such as Luis Buñuel revises his dream images to fit some type of narrative structure (whether traditional or not). Presumably, if the film's images are potent, the members of the audience will store these revised dreams in their minds, where they will again become disembodied until they are reshaped as part of a new dreamer's design. Very little concerning the relationship between film and dreams has been established beyond question, but *Film and Dreams* suggests directions for future studies which may eventually shed light upon the entire spectrum of relationships between dreams and the creative process.

The books reviewed in this survey represent only a miniscule portion of the literature of cinema produced in 1981, and many deserving works could not be mentioned. Film scholarship continues to grow at an increasing rate, and the 1980's promise to be a rich decade for film lovers of every variety.

Stephen L. Hanson

FILMS
OF
1981

ABSENCE OF MALICE

Production: Sydney Pollack for Colmubia
Direction: Sydney Pollack
Screenplay: Kurt Leudtke
Cinematography: Owen Roizman
Editing: Sheldon Kahn
Art direction: Terence Marsh
Music: Dave Grusin
MPAA rating: PG
Running time: 116 minutes

Principal characters:
Michael Gallagher .... Paul Newman
Megan Carter .... Sally Field
Elliot Rosen .... Bob Balaban
Teresa Perrone .... Melinda Dillon
Waddell .... Barry Primus
Malderone .... Luther Adler
McAdam .... Josef Sommer
Wells .... Wilford Brimley
Quinn .... Don Hood
Davidek .... John Harkins

Film treatments of newspaper reporters have traditionally stereotyped them in the mold of Hildy Johnson in *The Front Page* (1931); tough, brash, energetic men—and occasionally, as in *His Girl Friday* (1940) and *Meet John Doe* (1941), women—who chain smoke, talk fast, and sometimes risk their lives to get the big story while in the process solving a crime that has baffled the police. Recently, however, this image has changed. *All the President's Men* (1976), based on Carl Bernstein and Bob Woodward's exposé of the Watergate story, celebrated the journalist as hero, a diligent, dedicated seeker of truth whose labors toppled a corrupt presidency. In *The China Syndrome* (1979), a television reporter portrayed by Jane Fonda unearthed a cover-up at a nuclear power plant, and the popular television series "Lou Grant" consistently depicted the feisty journalist as an investigator and revealer of the facts.

Absence of Malice (1981), however, is the antithesis of all of these earlier treatments of the "Fourth Estate." Its reporter-heroine is an aggressive bumbler who destroys the life of an innocent man by performing her job unprofessionally, in a manner akin to that of an overzealous high-school sophomore tackling her initial assignment for the school newspaper.

Megan Carter (Sally Field) is a bright, detached, ambitious investigative reporter for the *Miami Standard* (a daily newspaper), who is assigned to cover the disappearance of Diaz, a local longshoreman's union leader not unlike Jimmy Hoffa. Elliot Rosen (Bob Balaban), the government investigator, believes that Michael Gallagher (Paul Newman), a wholesale liquor dealer who happens to be the son of a deceased racketeer and nephew of a prominent gangster, Malderone (Luther Adler), must have—or can obtain—information on the crime. Rosen believes that Gallagher, whose father had, in fact, reared him to be honest and law-abiding, can be pressured into assisting the investigation, so he has his staff prepare a file on Gallagher. Rosen then decides to manipulate Megan, and while she is in his office for an interview, he conveniently leaves the room with the dossier in plain sight on his desk. Although there is no hard information on Gallagher, the gullible Megan assumes that the file's mere existence implicates Gallagher. Without first checking with him for his side of the story, she writes a front-page article naming him as a prime suspect in the case.

Megan is subsequently confronted at her desk by an outraged Gallagher, who would like to set the record straight. Yet, instead of using Gallagher's story, Megan nervously spills coffee all over herself and then retreats to a meeting with the paper's lawyer, Davidek (John Harkins), who counsels her not to worry if her piece is factual: "as a matter of law, truth is irrelevant," providing there is "absence of malice," and Gallagher will be unable to win a judgment if he chooses to sue. On this point the paper is libel-free, as Megan has written the "truth" as she knows it, but the insinuations in her story are enough to label Gallagher guilty in the eyes of the community. Gallagher is loyal to his relatives, with no intention of becoming a stool pigeon, and he demands that Megan tell him her source. She, of course, has no intention of talking, but she pursues an acquaintance with him anyway, hoping to tape any information that he might be willing to offer. He invites her to his cabin cruiser, and attempts unsuccessfully to uncover her sources. Eventually, a romance develops between them—instigated by Megan.

Meanwhile, Gallagher's world falls apart. His business is hit by a longshoreman's strike, prompting Teresa Perrone (Melinda Dillon), a scared, repressed Catholic school teacher and Gallagher's platonic, lifelong friend, to take action. She is his alibi since they were together in Atlanta on the day that the labor leader disappeared. When she confides this information to Megan, she is certain of the exact date because Gallagher had accompanied her there to obtain an abortion. It is for this reason that Gallagher is unwilling to use her to clear himself. He knows that she will lose her job if the abortion is made public. Teresa is obviously upset and pleads for anonymity, but Megan, unconcerned with the possible effect on the teacher, chides her into going on the record with the story. The reporter now believes that Gallagher is blameless, and rushes back to her office to write a story in which she identifies Teresa by name and mentions the abortion. As a result, Teresa kills herself.

Megan is shaken, and begins to have doubts concerning her actions. When she visits Gallagher, they have an angry confrontation, and she finally reveals her source. Gallagher now seeks revenge, and concocts a plot to embarrass Rosen and his superior, Quinn (Don Hood), the politically ambitious district attorney. He covertly offers Quinn information about the Diaz disappearance, and then makes it appear as if he is donating money to the district attorney's campaign fund. Rosen uses illegal wiretaps to check on Quinn, and Megan reveals in her paper that the investigator is examining the activities of the district attorney. She learns this from Waddell (Barry Primus), a former boyfriend and government contact, and confirms it first with Gallagher.

Wells (Wilford Brimley), a Justice Department investigator, arrives from Washington and confronts all the involved parties with their errors and lies. Rosen and Quinn lose their jobs and Megan's paper must finally print the full story, complete with the details of their reporter's gullibility and sexual involvement with Gallagher. Her career is ruined, and Gallagher sails out of Miami. The film leaves the impression that perhaps they will meet again.

During the months prior to the release of *Absence of Malice*, the news media received a significant amount of adverse attention. Janet Cooke, a *Washington Post* reporter was required to return her Pulitzer Prize after admitting that she had concocted the piece that won her the honor, the story of an eight-year-old heroin addict. That same paper subsequently printed, and then apologized for, a gossip-column item suggesting that Jimmy Carter had bugged Blair House while he was president. Michael Daly, a columnist for the *New York Daily News*, resigned when he was accused of using aliases and of novelizing the facts in a piece written while he was in Ireland. Carol Burnett won a highly publicized lawsuit against *The National Enquirer*, which had run an item several years earlier claiming that she had been drunk and rowdy in a restaurant. Thus, while immediately after Watergate, the media could do no wrong, in 1981, the press's credibility had been given a crushing blow. When the film opened, the *Wall Street Journal*, *The New York Times*, *Columbia Journalism Review*, and scores of other publications printed opinions on the merits of *Absence of Malice* as a representative example of press ethics. Nat Hentoff, in the *Village Voice*, even wrote four columns dealing with both the film and its critics. Perhaps many in the audience, whose knowledge of the workings of newspapers ended at the corner newsstand, perceived Megan Carter as typical of her profession, the norm rather than the exception.

The fact is that *Absence of Malice* is rife with falsehoods about the vast majority of reporters and editors. Megan Carter is an investigative reporter who consistently refuses to investigate. First, she does not attempt to quote Gallagher in her original story. Next, when he confronts her, the reporter does all that she can to avoid allowing the man an opportunity to reply, when any professional journalist would, and should, gladly quote a major suspect in a headline-making criminal investigation. Megan also callously betrays the confidence of Teresa Perrone, which results in the woman's suicide; she seems never to have heard the phrase "off the record." She does not even bother to call Gallagher or to check the facts of the alibi; a simple check of hotel or airline reservations would suffice. She subsequently betrays one of her sources to Gallagher, yet all the while, McAdam (Josef Sommer), Megan's editor, urges her on and prints her stories. She is eventually blamed for the resulting fiasco, while he goes completely unpunished. Finally, Megan sleeps with Gallagher—and confirms her third story with him as his lover. Would a male reporter—not a member of the "weaker sex"—even succumb to the charms of his "story"? *Absence of Malice* might well be studied by aspiring journalists, who could then write term papers detailing Megan Carter's professional gaffes and breaches of ethics. While the film does make some salient points concerning the issue of journalistic responsibility, Megan as a real-life journalist is lacking in credibility.

As a film, however, the thirteen-million-dollar production, is still an absorbing, diverting drama, with a well-written (if artificial) script by Kurt Leudtke, former executive editor of *The Detroit Free Press* and reporter at the *Miami Herald*, where the film was partially shot. There is slick, fast-paced direction by Sydney Pollack, whose previous film *The Electric Horseman* (1979), featured Jane Fonda as a ruthless television reporter outsmarted by Robert Redford before she could break a story. *Absence of Malice* is, of course, not the first film to depict journalists as less than heroic. For example, in 1931's *Five Star Final* and 1951's *Ace in the Hole* (also known as *The Big Carnival*), ambitious writers wreck lives and selfishly toy with the news. In the main, however, film reporters have been good guys.

Paul Newman is at his best in a role that he has played throughout his career: the macho, alienated loner of films ranging from *Somebody Up There Likes Me* (1956) and *The Hustler* (1961) through *Fort Apache, the Bronx*, released several months before *Absence of Malice*. Though older and smarter, Newman's Michael Gallagher—a role originally slated for Al Pacino, and conceived as a streetwise Italian—is as tough as his Rocky Graziano or Eddie Felson. He deservedly received an Academy Award nomination for his work here, his first since *Cool Hand Luke* in 1967, though he ultimately lost to Henry Fonda in *On Golden Pond*.

Field is adequate as Megan Carter yet she performs well below the level of intensity exhibited in her Oscar and Emmy-winning performances in, respectively, *Norma Rae* (1979) and *Sybil* (1976). Wilford Brimley, who first came to attention as Jack Lemmon's friend and coworker in the nuclear power plant in *The China Syndrome*, dominates the film in his brief appearance as the sociable but no-nonsense Wells. Bob Balaban is effectively sinister as Rosen. In 1981, he also played a lawyer in both *Prince of the City* and *Whose*

Life Is It Anyway? Melinda Dillon as Teresa Perrone is particularly moving in the unforgettable scenes just before she commits suicide, when she scampers across the lawns near her house and pathetically tries to snatch up the morning papers that will publicize her abortion. Dillon had previously worked with Paul Newman in *Slap Shot* (1977) and *The Shadow Box* (1980), which was directed by the actor for television. She earned a Best Supporting Actress Oscar nomination for her performance, losing to Maureen Stapleton for *Reds*.

Absence of Malice received primarily favorable reviews—for its entertainment value if not for its reliability—and did moderately well at the box office, earning almost eleven million dollars after nineteen weeks on *Variety*'s list of top-grossing films. The manner in which it depicts journalistic ethics should not be taken as gospel—the film could easily be retitled *Absence of Credibility*—but it is still an engrossing, entertaining, well-acted drama.

Rob Edelman

Reviews

The Hollywood Reporter. November 17, 1981, p. 3.
Los Angeles Times. November 20, 1981, VI, p. 1.
The New York Times. November 19, 1981, III, p. 21.
The New York Times. November 22, 1981, II, p. 17.
The New Yorker. LVII, January 4, 1982, pp. 83-85.
Newsweek. XCIX, November 23, 1981, p. 125.
Saturday Review. VIII, November, 1981, p. 57.
Time. CXVIII, November 23, 1981, p. 98.

AMERICAN POP

Production: Ralph Bakshi and Martin Ransohoff for Columbia
Direction: Ralph Bakshi
Screenplay: Ronnie Kern
Animation direction: Ralph Bakshi
Editing: David Ramirez
Music: Lee Holdridge
MPAA rating: R
Running time: 95 minutes

Voices of principal characters:
Tony/Pete .... Ron Thompson
Frankie .... Marya Small
Louie .... Jerry Holland
Bella .... Lisa Jane Persky
Zalmie .... Jeffrey Lippa
Eva Tanguay .... Roz Kelly
Crisco .... Frank De Kova
Benny .... Richard Singer
Hannele .... Elsa Raven
Nicky Palumbo .... Ben Frommer

American Pop is a chronicle of American popular culture from the first decade of the century to the present, structured around the lives of four generations of musicians. It is the saga of one family, and of a love for music that is sometimes unknowingly but always clearly and decisively passed from one generation to the next. It is the personalized creation of Ralph Bakshi, producer of *Fritz the Cat* (1972), *Heavy Traffic* (1973), and *The Lord of the Rings* (1978), one of the most innovative animators since Walt Disney.

The story begins in Russia in 1905, when Zalmie Bolinski, the son of a rabbi, is five years old. Zalmie's father, Jaacov, is killed by the Cossacks while praying, and he and his mother flee from pogroms instigated by the Czar and go to the United States. Bakshi himself, born in 1939 in Brooklyn, was the son of poor Russian-Jewish immigrants.

The story then takes one of its many flash-forwards: Zalmie, now a young man, finds a job in a burlesque house on New York's Bowery. When his mother dies in the Triangle Shirtwaist Factory fire, he gets work in Minsky's with the help of his mentor, Louie. There Zalmie meets Bella, a showgirl. She becomes pregnant, they marry, and soon after have a son named Benny.

Several years later, after Zalmie has become involved with the Mafia, Bella is inadvertently killed in a gang war. The next major sequence occurs just before World War II, when Benny has grown to manhood. He is a pianist and the only white member in a black band. His father pleads with him to marry the daughter of mobster Nicky Palumbo, a union that will guarantee Zalmie's status with the racketeers. Benny agrees, and the wedding takes place, but the war is about to begin, so Benny enlists. While he is in the army in Europe, he discovers a piano in a bombed-out building, and sits down to play "As Time Goes By." A German soldier soon comes on the scene though, and he switches to "Lili Marlene." The soldier thanks him in German, and then shoots him dead. By this time his son Tony has been born.

By now Zalmie has spent eight years in Jacksonville State Prison. He decides to testify against his former associates, and his grandson, growing up in suburban Long Island, sees him "sing" on television. The 1950's have arrived, and because Tony is restless, he steals a car, and begins an odyssey across the United States. He has a one-night stand with a pretty, blond truckstop waitress in Kansas. Although Tony is unaware that she has become pregnant, she gives birth to his son (Benny's grandson, and Zalmie's great-grandson), whom she names Pete.

Tony arrives in North Beach, San Francisco. Now a derelict, he is taken in by Frankie, a young hippie who is part Janis Joplin, part Grace Slick, and composes music for her acid rock band. Tony and Frankie live through Vietnam, Kent State, and the Chicago riots. Her group becomes phenomenally successful, but they are now drug addicts, a result of the pressures of their success.

When the band is on tour with Jimi Hendrix, they go to Kansas, and a boy calling himself "Little Pete" arrives backstage. Tony is shocked to learn that Pete is his illegitimate son, but they continue on together. Frankie eventually dies as a result of her habit, and Tony and Pete find themselves in New York City. Pete hustles to support his father's heroin addiction, with Tony soon disappearing to pawn the boy's guitar.

Pete is visited by a black man, who gives him the pawn ticket and a package of drugs. The son then changes into a pusher, but earns a fat record contract when allowed a chance to show off his own musical abilities. Pete has become the true descendant of Zalmie, whose dreams for stardom were never realized. He becomes a Punk rock superstar, performing in stadiums for thousands.

American Pop is haunted by the ghosts of George M. Cohan, Scott Joplin, Jack Kerouac, Janis Joplin, George Gershwin, Jim Morrison, and Sam Cooke. The sound track is a potpourri of American musical classics, from pop to jazz to rock to folk—and more. They are effectively adapted by Lee Holdridge, and include, most prominently, "Sweet Georgia Brown," "Blue Suede Shoes," "Give My Regards to Broadway," "Mona Lisa," "Swanee," "Our Love Is Here to Stay," "California Dreamin'," and "Look for the Silver Lining," among many others.

American Pop is not, however, a sentimental stroll down memory lane. While the film does celebrate American music, it also paints a dark, cynical picture of several ruined, wasted lives that are uniquely American. Zalmie, Benny, Tony, and Pete are all angry young men. The first three are failures, casualties of the respective ills of crime, war, and drugs. Zalmie gains his "place" in America via his mob association; his grandson becomes victimized by the drugs he and his cohorts have pushed and, ironically, at the finale, his great-grandson's "success" is heroin-related. Pete is unlike his predecessors in that he has been able to channel his rage into stardom as an interpreter of the style of music that is popular in his day—in this case, Punk rock. Pete's stardom is tainted, however, another bitterly ironic comment on American society.

The one major flaw of *American Pop* is that its scope is too all-encompassing. Bakshi and screenwriter Ronnie Kern never explain why the characters are attracted to music, and, in only ninety-five minutes, they over-ambitiously attempt to cover seven decades of musical styles and tastes. The film's ambition, in fact, is often its undoing. Images representing characters and eras usually do not go beyond superficial stereotypes—mobsters with machine guns blazing during Prohibition, for example, or a Beat poet frantically reciting Allen Ginsberg's "Howl" thirty years later.

The particulars of each period need to be more fleshed out. *American Pop* could—and perhaps should—have been an eighteen-hour film, not one that runs a bit over an hour-and-a-half. Also, Bakshi's treatment—or, rather, dismissal—of the women in his men's lives is embarrassing. They are all romanticized whores or virgin goddesses who seem to exist solely to bear the next son, and then are killed off or conveniently disappear.

Still, individual segments of the film are unforgettable. Most memorably, Tony woos his waitress on the edge of the Kansas cornfields to the legendary, tragic Sam Cooke's rendition of "You Send Me," one of the greatest songs of the 1950's. The sequence in which Benny is senselessly killed while poignantly playing on the piano—a small beautiful moment in the middle of the devastation of war—is particularly moving and shocking.

American Pop may be flawed, but it is still a feast for the ears—and eyes. It might best be described as an "illustrated film," for the method of animation which Bakshi used here is based on live-action footage, which serves as a basis for the drawing. He first used this "rotoscope" technique in *Wizards*, released in 1977, and in the last few years the style has been seen frequently on television. The film is a multimedia extravaganza of this "animated real life" interspersed with still photos, pencil sketches, and documentary footage. Bakshi's images are lush, and his characters display real emotion. There is so much detail in each setting, and in each frame, that more than one viewing is essential to appreciate fully the craftsmanship. Bakshi's sense of style and aesthetics have made him something of a cynical, raunchy, streetwise Walt Disney of the 1970's and 1980's.

American Pop received mixed reviews: some critics thought it energetic and brilliant, while others stressed its superficial approach to its subject, comparing it unfavorably with Bakshi's earlier efforts. The film did not fare well at the box office, and placed a disappointing ninety-fifth on *Variety*'s list of 1981's film rentals, earning merely $2,953,000. Whether his efforts fail, as with the overlong *The Lord of the Rings*, succeed smashingly, as did the brilliant *Heavy Traffic*, an ode to New York City street life, or achieve a modest success, as in *American Pop*, the cinema of Ralph Bakshi is certainly unique.

Betti Stone

Reviews

The Hollywood Reporter. February 9, 1981, p. 3.
Los Angeles Times. February 13, 1981, VI, p. 1.
The New York Times. February 13, 1981, III, p. 5.
Newsweek. XCVII, March 16, 1981, p. 94.
Time. CXVII, April 6, 1981, p. 71.
Variety. February 9, 1981, p. 3.

AN AMERICAN WEREWOLF IN LONDON

Production: George Folsey Jr., for Universal
Direction: John Landis
Screenplay: John Landis
Cinematography: Robert Paynter
Editing: Malcolm Campbell
Art direction: Leslie Dilley
Special makeup effects: Rick Baker (AA)
Music: Elmer Bernstein
MPAA rating: R
Running time: 97 minutes

Principal characters:

David Kessler	David Naughton
Alex Price	Jenny Agutter
Jack Goodman	Griffin Dunne
Dr. Hirsch	John Woodvine
Chess Player	Brian Glover
Dart Player	David Schofield
Barmaid	Lila Kaye
Sergeant McManus	Paul Kember
Inspector Villiers	Don McKillop
Mr. Collins	Frank Oz

During 1981, for some strange reason, a plethora of werewolf films came to the screen. One of the best of them, *An American Werewolf in London*—written in 1969—was released at the tail end of the pack, on the heels of *The Howling* and *Wolfen*. John Landis, its writer-director, has said that when he first attempted to sell the project, it was turned down because of its offbeat blend of lycanthropy, humor, and grisly horror. It remained for Landis to establish himself as a director with commercial clout, notably with *Kentucky Fried Movie* (1977) and *National Lampoon's Animal House* (1978), before he could get the go-ahead to film his pet project.

The idea for *An American Werewolf in London* was born when Landis, a one-time studio mail boy, was serving as an errand boy on the 1969 Clint Eastwood film, *Kelly's Heroes*, which was made in Yugoslavia. Because of a scarcity of automobiles in the country, Landis was startled one day, while en route to a new location, to encounter a major traffic jam. After making inquiries, he discovered that the traffic tie-up was caused by the fact that a burial was taking place—in the middle of the road. The deceased had been a rapist, who was shot, and because the local gypsies feared he might return from the dead, they wanted him buried at a site from which there would be no return. "That got me to thinking," Landis has said, "what would I do if suddenly that corpse got up? How would I deal with that?"

Thus, in *An American Werewolf in London*, the main character deals not only with lycanthropy—the transformation of a man into a werewolf and the attendant discomfort that such a being suffers beneath a full moon—but also with recurring visits from a deceased friend who is one of the "living dead."

The film, a merging of contemporary strains and genre tradition, opens to find two young American students, David Kessler (David Naughton) and Jack Goodman (Griffin Dunne), backpacking through Northern England, with an uptempo rendition of "Blue Moon" on the sound track. While traveling across lush, misted moors, the young men brag of their sexual conquests, and tell "knock-knock" jokes. Their very modern manners, including plenty of four-letter words, are in marked contrast to the age-old superstitions that they are about to encounter.

The two find a village and enter a pub, aptly named The Slaughtered Lamb. They seem very much out of place, however, because the clientele consists of dour-faced locals who play chess (Brian Glover) and darts (David Schofield), and stare at the two intruders with obvious dislike. Though a skittish barmaid (Lila Kaye) feigns friendliness, Kessler and Goodman decide to continue their hiking in the night. They leave the pub amidst the warnings, "beware of the moon" and "stay to the road."

They are oblivious to those words, however, and wander across the moors, talking about their strange stopover. Eventually, they become silly, but the giddy mood disappears with the uneasy realization that they are being stalked. The villagers' words come back to them—but now it is too late. There is a frantic thrashing in the bushes, accompanied by fierce animal-like sounds. A furious attack follows, in which rapid-fire editing reveals glimpses of fur, claws, teeth, and ripped flesh.

Three weeks later, an understandably shaken Kessler awakens from a coma in a London hospital. He and Goodman were the apparent victims of an animal attack, in which Goodman was killed. Kessler, who still bears scratches and wounds from the attack, also finds himself plagued with horrible nightmares as well as a lingering disorientation. His memory keeps returning to the strange villagers who were clustered at The Slaughered Lamb. The officers assigned to the case, Sergeant McManus (Paul Kember) and Inspector Villiers (Don McKillop), believe that all evidence points to an animal attack, and sharing their views is Dr. Hirsch (John Woodvine). Meanwhile, nurse Alex Price (Jenny Agutter), who is caring for the confused Kessler, finds herself becoming enamored of the young American, whom she finds "sad but terribly attractive."

Though he responds to Alex's beauty and affection, Kessler cannot escape his mental rumblings and begins to doubt his sanity. Kessler is pushed to the brink when he is "visited" by the deceased Goodman. Sporting the ravages (and freshly bloodied face) of the attack, the ghost of the agitated Goodman wanders about the sanitized hospital room. Explaining that he is finding death extremely dull, he asks an incredulous Kessler, "Have you ever talked to a corpse? It's boring!"

The visits from Goodman continue, with Kessler believing them to be hallucinatory, but Goodman's disgusting physical state—as he begins to decompose—and his insistence that it was a werewolf that attacked them, and that Kessler will ultimately become a werewolf himself, do not improve his mental outlook. A romance with Alex, however, does prove somewhat diverting and upon his release from the hospital, Kessler is invited to stay at her flat. One night, to the background music of Credence Clearwater Revival's "Bad Moon Rising," Kessler watches in horror as his transformation to a werewolf begins. His hands elongate, turn furry, and eject claws. His jaw juts forward, pulling downward, until his nostrils are those of an animal, flaring out from a snoot. And of course, there is the inevitable hair appearing everywhere.

Kessler's condition brings about a series of brutal, inexplicable London murders—including one in which the victim is cruelly stalked in an empty subway station. It also occasionally erupts in comedy, as when Kessler awakens, one morning, in a wolf cage at the zoo. Completely naked, Kessler cautiously runs about the grounds, in search of protective bushes. Spying a child with some balloons, he steals them and runs off, with the balloons precariously held in the obvious place. After later stealing some clothing, Kessler—dressed in a woman's coat and scarf—returns to the flat.

Spurred by Alex's reports of Kessler's ravings, Dr. Hirsch pays a visit to the village on the moors, where he discovers that the supernatural has, indeed, ventured into reality. He hurries back to London, where he hopes to keep Kessler restrained because another full moon is expected that night.

Kessler is, however, already out. Summoned to a pornographic movie theater located in London's Piccadilly Circus, he meets with an anxious Goodman, now in skeletal state (with blackened skin hanging from his face), as well as the "living dead" who are the victims of his forays as a wolf. They have gathered *en masse* to plead their case; for until Kessler himself is killed, they are doomed to wander in limbo.

Their stories, told against the gruntings, groanings, and torrid couplings coming from the X-rated screen, send a distressed Kessler running out of the theater as a werewolf, unleashing pandemonium in the bustling Piccadilly Circus. Pursued by gun-wielding police, he is chased down an alleyway, where, despite the protests of Dr. Hirsch and a hysterical Alex, who appear on the scene, Kessler is riddled with bullets fired by an indifferent officer. It is an ending which cynically clashes with lore given currency by the genre (including the 1941 classic, *The Wolf Man*), which insists that only a loved one can kill a werewolf.

With its decidedly unique treatment of lycanthropy, *An American Werewolf in London* seemed to erect—by its very nature—critical and commercial barriers. Those barriers were made evident by Universal's apparent uncertainty over just how to promote the film. Initial advertisements attempted to capitalize on Landis's comic prowess, proclaiming, "from the director of *Animal House*, a different kind of animal," but comedy fans are not necessarily monster movie buffs. When initial box-office returns proved disappointing, the film's special effects, carried out in strict secrecy during the shoot, were used as an enticement. Photographs of the werewolf, once given "top secret" status, suddenly appeared in ads.

An American Werewolf in London was dismissed by most critics, who balked at its uneasy mixture of humor and horror. Some abhorred the film's gruesome makeup effects, most of which involved Goodman. Nearly all, however, applauded the awesome werewolf transformations, and the film's appealing young performers also fared well. David Naughton, who portrayed Kessler, tackled his role with a natural ease. Prior to his work in this film Naughton was recognizable as the "star" of a highly successful series of television commercials, which featured him singing, dancing, and promoting Dr. Pepper. Griffin Dunne, the nephew of writers John Gregory Dunne and Joan Didion, also performed agreeably as the comically creepy Goodman. British actress, Jenny Agutter, who has been performing in films since childhood, was a refreshing love interest for Kessler.

Not surprisingly, however, considering the film's theme, it was the special makeup effects which gained the greatest recognition. In fact, thirty-year-old Rick Baker, creator and designer of those effects, including the startling werewolf transformation, was the recipient of the industry's first Academy Award for makeup for his work on that film. (The new awards category is the first regular category to be established since 1948.) Baker, who had earlier earned industry recognition when he wore a monster suit as King Kong in the 1976 Dino De Laurentiis remake of the horror classic of the same name, is a former chief lab assistant to famed makeup master Dick Smith, whose achievements include the makeup effects of *The Exorcist* (1973). Baker, who paid tribute to his mentor in his Oscar acceptance speech, has in turn passed on some of his secrets to protégé Rob Bottin, who worked on *The Howling*. At first Baker helped Bottin on the film, but Landis ordered Baker to stop.

As a director, Landis leans toward excessiveness, a trait that is frequently singled out by critics. The Piccadilly Circus sequence, involving the werewolf on the loose, is a case in point. Although the scene lasts only forty-seven seconds, it includes seven collisions of automobiles and buses and six deaths. Two are directly caused by the wolf, while the other four, including a grisly decapitation, are caused by the auto accidents.

Subtlety, however, has never been a Landis trademark. He got his start when he wrote, directed, and starred in *Schlock* (1972), a spoof of monster movies, when he was only twenty-one-years old. The production, made for sixty thousand dollars, remains a popular cult film. His subsequent features—*Kentucky Fried Movie*, *National Lampoon's Animal House*, and *The Blues Brothers* (1980)—carried out Landis' penchant for exaggeration on a large scale, prompting some criticism for his excesses.

Hostile critical reaction brings this explanation from Landis: "I try not to make rules. One of the reasons I think I engender such hostility from the American press is because I'm not easily pegged." Elsewhere, in Europe for example, the Landis film is respectfully regarded, bringing him to say, "One of the things that makes me so cynical is the fact that I'm lionized all over the world and vilified in the States."

With plans eventually to film Mark Twain's *A Connecticut Yankee in King Arthur's Court*, Landis is also producing several projects, including the Universal remake of the 1954 film, *The Creature from the Black Lagoon*.

Pat H. Broeske

Reviews

The Hollywood Reporter. August 17, 1981, p. 3.
Los Angeles Times. August 20, 1981, VI, p. 7.
New York. XIV, September 14, 1981, p. 62.
The New York Times. August 21, 1981, III, p. 12.
Newsweek. XCVIII, September 7, 1981, p. 82.
Variety. August 17, 1981, p. 3.

ARTHUR

Production: Rollins-Joffe-Morra-Brezner for Orion
Direction: Steve Gordon
Screenplay: Steve Gordon
Cinematography: Fred Schuler
Editing: Susan E. Morse
Art direction: Stephen Hendrickson
Music: Burt Bacharach
Song: Burt Bacharach, Carole Bayer Sager, Christopher Cross, and Peter Allen, "Arthur's Theme: Best That You Can Do" (AA)
MPAA rating: PG
Running time: 97 minutes

Principal characters:

Arthur Bach .... Dudley Moore
Linda Marolla .... Liza Minnelli
Mr. Hobson .... John Gielgud (AA)
Susan Johnson .... Jill Eikenberry
Mr. Marolla .... Barney Martin
Arthur's grandmother .... Geraldine Fitzgerald
Gloria .... Anne De Salvo
Uncle Peter .... Maurice Copeland
Aunt Pearl .... Justine Johnson
Arthur's father .... Thomas Barbour

In the mid-teens Charlie Chaplin was able to sustain the role of an alcoholic for an entire ten-minute short. In 1981, Dudley Moore attempted to perform the same feat, not for ten minutes but for almost one hundred minutes. Whether Moore succeeded is questionable. The critics, on the whole, thought he did, and so did the moviegoing public, but posterity might have a very different opinion. Dudley Moore's *Arthur* is in many ways a throwback to the early years of filmmaking; it is a slapstick comedy without the slapstick. While some critics have linked the film to the screwball comedies of the 1930's and the sophisticated comedies of the 1920's, its true affinities lie with the humor of Mack Sennett and Al Christie in the teens. *Arthur* is as artificial as any 1930's screwball comedy, as contrived as many a Hollywood effort by Leo McCarey or Preston Sturges, but above all it is as silly and as slight as the typical two-reel silent comedy.

Dudley Moore, fresh from his phenomenal success in *10* (1979), was cast in the role of Arthur Bach, America's richest and most amiable drunk. Arthur drives around Manhattan in a chauffeured limousine, chuckling hysterically to himself at jokes, some of which he delivers out loud and some of which he keeps to himself. He picks up prostitutes, one of whom, Gloria (Anne De Salvo), he takes to dinner at the Plaza hotel. At the hotel, Arthur bumps into his Uncle Peter and Aunt Pearl (Maurice Copeland and Justine Johnson), to whom he passes off Gloria as the princess of a country which is so small that it costs only eighty-five cents to take a taxi from one end to the other, a country so small (Arthur adds) that they recently had the entire place carpeted.

Arthur and Gloria spend the night together, but in the morning the latter is politely removed from the premises by Hobson, Arthur's very English butler, portrayed by John Gielgud. In an exemplary stage and screen career which has spanned the past fifty years, it is doubtful that any other role of Sir John Gielgud has won for him the universal recognition he has received for his portrayal of Hobson. Certainly, Gielgud has essayed no other part requiring him to use so many four-letter words or make such suggestive comments. Perhaps it is somewhat unfortunate that Gielgud should have received an Academy Award, not to mention various other honors, for a characterization such as this, which requires the actor to play to the lowest common denominator in the audience.

All is not well in Arthur's world, for his family has decided that he should marry a wealthy and boring socialite named Susan Johnson (Jill Eikenberry). If he does not obey, his father (Thomas Barbour) and his grandmother (Geraldine Fitzgerald) warn, he may lose his inheritance of $750 million. In the meantime, Arthur has met, and saved from arrest, a pickpocket named Linda (Liza Minnelli). A relationship is formed between the two, and Arthur even visits Linda's drunken and unemployed father in Queens. Nevertheless, Arthur leaves Linda for a celebration of his engagement to Susan at his parents' Long Island mansion. "Marry her," Hobson advises Arthur. "Poor drunks do not find love, Arthur. Poor drunks have very few teeth. They urinate outdoors. They freeze to death in summer. I can't bear to think of you that way."

Yet it is Hobson who urges Linda to attend the engagement party, and there she and Arthur declare their love for each other. Arthur shows signs of maturity as he visits Hobson lying fatally ill in the hospital (in one of the few subdued moments in the production). On the day of his wedding at New York's St. Bartholomew's Church, Arthur arrives drunk in company with Linda. He is assaulted by Susan's father, but eventually Arthur's grandmother assents to Arthur's marriage to Linda, and the pair drive off together.

Arthur marked the debut of Steve Gordon as a director. He had previously coproduced and written the screenplay for *The One and Only* (1978) and been scriptwriter on a number of television comedy series, including "The Dick Van Dyke Show," "Chico and the Man," "Barney Miller," and "Good Time Harry." Gordon began shooting *Arthur* in June of 1980 at Astoria Studios on Long Island and at various New York locations.

American critics adored *Arthur*. Both Pauline Kael in *The New Yorker* and Richard Schickel in *Time* compared the interplaying of Moore and Gielgud to the P. G. Wodehouse characters of Bertie Wooster and Jeeves, delighting in exchanges such as Arthur's announcing, "I think I'll take a bath," and Hobson's retort, "I'll alert the media." Many critics compared the feature to a 1930's screwball comedy; typical was the judgment in *Variety* (July 15, 1981): "*Arthur* is a sparkling entertainment which attempts, with a large measure of success, to resurrect the amusingly artificial conventions of 1930's screwball romantic comedies."

The critics were unanimous in finding the film at its best when Dudley Moore and John Gielgud were on the screen together, and noted that Liza Minnelli (who has not had a screen success since *Cabaret* in 1972) added little to the film and even brought a touch of boredom to the scenes in which she appeared.

Within the first thirty-three weeks of its release, *Arthur* had grossed more than eighty-five million dollars, and was being hailed as the best screen comedy of 1981. Its theme song sold more than one million copies as a single, and the film was placed on many "ten best" lists, including those of the critics for *The New York Times*, the *Los Angeles Times*, *People*, *US*, and *Associated Press*. It won four Golden Globe awards, including Best Motion Picture—Comedy or Musical—and was nominated for four Academy Awards, winning two, for Best Supporting Actor and Best Original Song. The critical and popular success of *Arthur* proved that in 1981, at least, audiences were still willing to have a good laugh at an alcoholic's befuddled view of life and love.

Anna Kate Sterling

Reviews

The Hollywood Reporter. July 13, 1981, p. 3.
Los Angeles Times. July 17, 1981, VI, p. 1.
The New Republic. CLXXXV, August 15, 1981, p. 27.
The New York Times. July 17, 1981, III, p. 10.
The New Yorker. LVII, July 27, 1981, pp. 78-79.
Newsweek. XCVIII, July 27, 1981, p. 75.
Time. CXVIII, August 3, 1981, p. 67.
Variety. July 13, 1981, p. 3.

ATLANTIC CITY

Production: Denis Heroux for International Cinema Corporation; released by Paramount
Direction: Louis Malle
Screenplay: John Guare
Cinematography: Richard Ciupka
Editing: Suzanne Baron
Art direction: Anne Pritchard
Music: Michel Legrand
MPAA rating: R
Running time: 104 minutes

Principal characters:

Lou .... Burt Lancaster
Sally .... Susan Sarandon
Grace .... Kate Reid
Joseph .... Michel Piccoli
Chrissie .... Hollis McLaren
Dave .... Robert Joy
Fred .... John McCurry
Bus driver .... Harvey Atkin

Atlantic City might best be described as a chamber film; it uses a small cast to generate delicate effects. Even though crime and the underworld form its background and there are three killings on screen, the overall emphasis remains upon well-realized characters and subtle, off-beat human relationships. From what we see on the screen, credit for this achievement should be shared approximately equally by director Louis Malle, screenwriter John Guare, and actors Burt Lancaster and Susan Sarandon, who play the two principal roles.

The action of the film takes place in present-day Atlantic City, New Jersey, with its legal gambling casinos and new buildings, but a large part of the atmosphere of the film is derived from its contrast with the Atlantic City of several decades before, when the buildings that are now being demolished were new and when the city was a thriving resort and center for gangsters. Indeed, the opening sequences set up this contrast, but they do so rather subtly, taking many minutes to establish slowly and carefully the mood and style of the film. We first see a young woman, Sally (Susan Sarandon), cutting lemons and rubbing the juice on her skin while she listens to opera on a cassette recorder. Then we see that she is being watched intently from a nearby window by Lou (Burt Lancaster), an older man with white hair and a mustache. The next sequence shows Dave (Robert Joy) picking up a small parcel in a telephone booth. All of these scenes take place before the opening credits are finished. Immediately after the end of the credits, the huge old Marlborough-Blenheim Hotel is shown as it is being dynamited, collapsing into rubble. This is emblematic of the old Atlantic City giving way to the new, but used at this early stage of the film, it is slightly ambiguous rather than simplistic and obvious.

Lou is a small-time gangster who makes a meager living picking up petty bets for Fred O'Reilly (John McCurry), a black racketeer, and catering to the needs of his downstairs neighbor, Grace (Kate Reid), the widow of a big-time mobster. Kate had originally come to Atlantic City for a Betty Grable look-a-like contest; now she seldom leaves her bed and spends her time and energy thinking of small tasks for Lou to do and worrying about her health and her poodle. Sally, on the other hand, works in an oyster bar while she takes lessons on how to be a casino dealer from Joseph (Michel Piccoli), a Frenchman who tries to teach his pupils continental sophistication as well as casino techniques. Sally's dream is to be one of the first women dealers in Monte Carlo. Thus, Lou, Grace, and Joseph live to a great extent on dreams of the past while Sally lives on dreams of the future.

Lou especially likes to reminisce about the glories of the old Atlantic City, seeking to impress people by mentioning such old-time gangsters as Al Capone and Lucky Luciano, whom he claims to have worked for or to have known. At one point, he tries to tell a young man what he misses about the old Atlantic City. He mentions the rackets, whoring, guns, and killings; then, looking out at the ocean he says, "The Atlantic Ocean was something then. Yes, you should have seen the Atlantic Ocean in those days." Legal gambling in casinos is too wholesome for him. Lou, however, does not often indulge in such prolonged explanations.

The catalyst for the action in *Atlantic City* is the arrival of Sally's husband, Dave, and her sister Chrissie (Hollis MacLaren). Sally is not at all happy to see the husband she detests or her sister, who is quite obviously pregnant with Dave's child. We had glimpsed Dave in an earlier scene, but not until this point do we learn anything about him. He and Chrissie have come to Atlantic City from Saskatchewan by way of Las Vegas and Philadelphia, where they had learned of a mobster's drug transfer point (a telephone booth) and had taken a package of cocaine before the mobsters could get it. Now Dave plans to sell the cocaine (worth thousands of dollars) in Atlantic City.

Louis Malle, the director, has stated that Lou represents the 1940's and Sally the 1980's while Dave and Chrissie represent the 1960's. They certainly do look like stereotypical flower children. Chrissie is obsessed with Eastern religions and reincarnation, and Dave is an obnoxious punk who offends nearly everyone he meets. When he accidentally meets Lou in a bar, Dave enlists his help in selling the cocaine. He manages to get Lou's cooperation by playing up to the old man's ego and his desire for money. He tells him that a man in Las Vegas said that Lou is the man to see, and he also offers two hundred dollars for help in making a drug delivery.

While Lou is making the delivery, however, Dave is killed by the two gangsters who were supposed to get the cocaine in the first place. This event changes the lives of every one of the major characters. Lou now has the four thousand dollars from the drug sale as well as more of the cocaine in his room. He helps Sally with the money and paperwork necessary to have Dave's body sent back to Saskatchewan. Sally appreciates his help and, thinking his manner quite sophisticated, she says, "Teach me stuff." Later they make love, but there is no indication of a long-lasting relationship. Subsequently, Lou is completely devastated when the two gangsters accost him and Sally on the street. He can only watch helplessly as they beat her and then rip open her handbag in search of the drugs. When Sally returns to her apartment, she finds that it has been ransacked, and from Chrissie she learns about the cocaine and realizes that Lou's recent wealth has come from Dave's drugs.

Lou, however, is determined to make up for his inability to protect Sally and sends word to the mob that he has what they want and that they are to leave the women alone. He then tries to leave the city on a bus, but Sally pulls him off the bus with a quick-witted story that she tells the bus driver (Harvey Atkin) and demands the money. They are then once again accosted by the two gangsters, but this time Lou has a gun in his pocket and kills both of them.

Later, saying "I can't believe I did it," Lou drives Sally to an out-of-town motel where they drink champagne and watch the news reports about the killings. Lou is ecstatic that he has protected Sally and made the news. He tells her that he is going to buy every newspaper the next day in order to read about his exploits. Full of his victory, he asks Sally to go to Florida with him so that he can show her off to some of his old cronies. He also reveals that most of his previous boasting was empty; that he had never killed anyone and had not known any of the famous gangsters.

Atlantic City, however, is not a fairy tale. The next morning Sally takes most of the money when she thinks Lou cannot see her and leaves on the pretext that she is only going to get them a pizza. Lou has seen her take the money and graciously lets her go. As she leaves, he lets her know that he is aware of what she is doing. At the film's conclusion he returns to Grace.

Unlike most contemporary films, *Atlantic City* is densely packed with atmosphere, information, and characterization. Each scene contributes something significant to our understanding of the situation or the characters. In no instance, however, does the script make its points too obviously. Both John Guare and Louis Malle are obviously quite talented artists. As Lou, Burt Lancaster gives one of the finest performances of his long and distinguished career. He conveys movingly the aging small-timer who keeps up his dapper appearance and his stories of the old days without ever appearing pathetic. Susan Sarandon, as Sally, is equally convincing in her portrayal of the young woman with plans for her future. She shows both determination and vulnerability.

The virtues of *Atlantic City* were recognized by the critics, by the judges at the Venice Film Festival (who gave it the Golden Lion Award), and by the Motion Picture Academy, which nominated it for Oscars in all the five top categories.

Timothy W. Johnson

Reviews

The Hollywood Reporter. April 9, 1981, p. 3.
Los Angeles Times. April 5, 1981, *Calendar*, p. 29.
The New Republic. CLXXXIV, April 18, 1981, p. 29.
The New York Times. April 3, 1981, III, p. 15.
The New Yorker. LVII, April 6, 1981, p. 154.
Newsweek. XCVII, April 6, 1981, p. 103.
Time. CXVII, April 6, 1981, p. 68.
Variety. September 2, 1981, p. 3.

BEAU PERE

Origin: France
Production: Alain Sarde for Sara Films and Antienne 2; released by ParaFrance
Distribution in U.S.: New Line Cinema
Direction: Bertrand Blier
Screenplay: Bertrand Blier; based on his novel of the same name
Cinematography: Sacha Vierny
Editing: Claudine Merlin
Art direction: Theobald Meurisse
Music: Philippe Sarde; performed by Roger Woodward (piano), Maurice Wander (jazz piano), and Stephane Grappelli (violin)
Running time: 120 minutes

Principal characters:
Remy .... Patrick Dewaere
Marion .... Ariel Besse
Charly .... Maurice Ronet
Martine .... Nicole Garcia
Charlotte .... Nathalie Baye

Bertrand Blier is a French filmmaker who writes and directs from an unabashed male perspective. His world is a fantasy creation inhabited by male characters whose feelings he seems to share on a fundamental level, and his female characters are completely mystifying both to the male protagonists and to Blier himself. Blier's first great success, *Going Places* (1974), is composed of a loose narrative involving two young men played by Gerard Depardieu and Patrick Dewaere, who travel about doing as they please with little regard for social order. They approach their numerous sexual adventures with a cheerful attitude and a desire to please, but their understanding of women does not evolve significantly by the end of the film.

Blier's popularity crested with *Get Out Your Handkerchiefs* (1978), an Academy Award winner for Best Foreign Film, in which Depardieu and Dewaere team up again as two friends who share the former's depressed wife (Carol Laure) as well as a love of Mozart. The wife finally falls in love with a pre-adolescent boy and the two selfless heroes have no choice but to leave her to her happiness. Blier's most outrageous film, however, is *Femmes Fatales* (belatedly released in the United States in 1979, but produced several years earlier), an artistic failure but an especially brave venture in these feminist times. The two male heroes of that film try to escape from women altogether—not surprisingly, as the entire female sex is pictured as frightening, ruthless, and sexually insatiable, lacking any emotional depth. After a series of bizarre adventures, the two men finally fall from the sky into strange surroundings. As it turns out, they are helplessly trapped inside the sexual organs of an enormous woman. Although this concluding scene may not be quite as hilarious as Blier intended, it is at the very least a triumph of art direction and set construction.

Nevertheless, what saves all of these films is Blier's sense of humor. He never takes himself too seriously, and, as a result, his narrow male perceptions seem to be charmingly directed against himself. With the exception of *Femmes Fatales* (1976), his films feature women who are loving and captivating, and the male bewilderment these women inspire is the source of much amusement. *Get Out Your Handkerchiefs* is especially witty. Though ultimately too light to be a great film, it suggested that Blier might become one of the masters of the cinema. He already had the flair, imagination, comic vision, and fidelity to self. All that he lacked was emotional maturity. Now, *Beau Pere* reveals this emotional maturity in full flower. Without abandoning the delightful comic touches and the naïve male romanticism which distinguished his earlier work, Blier treats a genuinely affecting love story with remarkable sensitivity and considerable insight.

Blier's hero is Remy, played by the irresistible Patrick Dewaere, whose melancholy countenance and posture speak volumes about his character from the moment he appears. A failed jazz pianist working in cocktail lounges, Remy is introduced in a stunning opening shot. It begins with a reflection of an elegant supper club crowd against the open piano top and pans to the protagonist, who introduces himself and his situation through an eloquent monologue as he plays the piano and the camera continues to move around him. The artificiality of this opening sequence sets the tone for the film and is not subsequently abandoned. Other characters also speak to the film's audience in the course of the narrative, while additional characters in these scenes continue the actions of the narrative with no acknowledgement of the audience. Blier is the heir to a sophisticated literary tradition which he transposes with admirable facility to the cinema. His writing is as brilliant as his direction, and Remy's initial soliloquy concisely encapsulates everything we need to know about the character. He is disappointed in himself as a musician and suffering the pain of a love affair about to end, but he remains a man of a warm and passionate nature in the face of all adversity.

Remy has been living with Martine (Nicole Garcia), an actress, but her affections have cooled as a result of his professional failures as well as her own (she is reduced to doing brassiere commercials on television). The couple seems perpetually to be without money, and one day when their car is out of gas Remy must push it in order for Martine to get a rolling start and go to her job. At the bottom of the hill the car becomes involved in an accident and Martine is abruptly killed as the hapless Remy looks on. Later that day, Martine's fourteen-year-old daughter Marion (Ariel Besse) comes home from school, and in the course of the evening Remy must break the news of her mother's death to her, which he accomplishes by leaving a note when he goes out to buy groceries. The heartbroken daughter and stepfather are attached to each other and want to continue living together, but Marion's real father, Charly (Maurice Ronet), a nightclub owner who always appears to be in a mild alcoholic stupor, insists that Marion live with him. This arrangement does not work out, though, and Marion moves back in with Remy, whom she adores. The man and girl find solace in each other's company and help each other to adjust to their tragic loss.

Eventually, Marion candidly confesses that she is attracted to Remy and wants him to make love to her. Admirably reticent, he does everything he can to discourage her. Ultimately, however, he returns her love and gives in, very reluctantly at first but ardently as the story progresses. At the same time, he must continue to try to be a father to her (in fact, *beau-père* means stepfather). They both sense that as she grows older, an inevitable separation will occur. This is finally brought about through Remy's infatuation with Charlotte (Nathalie Baye), a mature woman with a child of her own. Charlotte is an accomplished classical pianist, and Remy is so awed by her artistry that he abandons his own vocation as a pianist forever and conceals from her that he has ever been a musician. Marion goes back to her father, and Remy, distraught at losing her, is consoled by Charlotte.

Although the conclusion of the story is touching, it is marred by the final scene, in which Charlotte's young daughter looks on unobserved as Remy and Charlotte begin to make love. Blier seems to be cleverly suggesting that the cycle will repeat itself, as earlier Marion had spoken of her awareness of her mother's pleasure when Martine and Remy made love. Of course, it is unlikely that Charlotte will die in a freak accident as Martine did, and this final display of wit seems gratuitous, especially as Charlotte's daughter is seen for the first time in the last few moments of the film. *Beau Pere* is essentially the tender love story of Remy and Marion, two people who, despite the difference in their ages, genuinely appreciate each other. Their separation is a tragedy. Remy's attachment to Charlotte ends his career as a pianist, which the film has shown to be central to his life. Remy and Marion have nurtured their feelings for each other by surviving a mutual tragedy, the death of Martine, and their romantic feelings have evolved naturally. The relationship is not a shocking one, nastily treated, as in Stanley Kubrick's callous and unpleasant *Lolita* (1962). The mood of *Beau Pere* suggests that Remy and Marion belong together and that their relationship is the richest and the most meaningful that either will ever have.

The unsatisfactory coda is the film's only flaw. The rest of the work is delicately paced and lovingly realized. Remy is Blier's most endearing creation, a gentle and passive man who lives through his relationships with women. It is difficult to blame him for this because the three women in the story are all exceptionally attractive. His failure to be recognized as an artist makes his fate even more poignant. He not only loves music but also plays extremely well. A wonderful tragicomic moment occurs when he is hired to play at a teenage birthday party (at which Marion is inadvertently present) and his playing is drowned out by disco records. Although the narrative situations are experienced from Remy's point of view, Marion is a well-realized female character—a male fantasy, perhaps, but one possessing sincerity, intelligence, depth, and individuality. Blier is so thoughtful in his delineation of Marion's feelings that it is fair to suggest that he is now able to draw creatively on the feminine aspect of his sensibility. He does not exploit Ariel Besse's precocious beauty. The few nude shots are brief and tasteful, and Blier does not need to resort to explicit sex scenes in order to evoke romance effectively.

Blier's intention in *Beau Pere* is to emphasize the intimate and subtle aspects of his narrative. To this end, he necessarily suppresses his ready wit more than in previous films, reserving delightful comic touches for unexpected moments in the story. One such moment occurs when Charly is taking Marion away after Martine's death. Charly's car will not start, and Remy is once again seen pushing a car from the identical camera angle utilized in the scene involving Martine. In scenes which find the lonely Remy seeking consolation at the home of his friends, he is seated in the lowest chair, a hilariously pathetic image. Finally, during the climax of the film, the anguished Remy enters three different rooms in three successive images, calling Marion's name in the first, Martine's in the second, and Charlotte's in the third. The first shot is poignant but the last shot abruptly places the three images in a comic perspective. Blier effortlessly discovers many such moments in the film, and it should be emphasized that they owe a great deal to his fluent visual style.

Style is ultimately a foremost consideration in evaluating *Beau Pere*. Its aesthetic qualities are intimately related to its emotional ones and are the source of more pleasure than can be discerned in almost any other recent film. *Beau Pere* is one of the most beautiful recent uses of the wide screen, forcefully reminiscent of the imaginative treatment brought to some of the early CinemaScope films. In *Beau Pere*, space is perceived as resonant with meaning and does not always need to be filled with action. The characters sometimes inhabit the far sides of the image, allowing Blier to meditate expressively on decor and the stillness of a room. This compositional tendency is at once artistically provocative and natural to the wide screen, and Blier deserves gratitude for restoring it to the cinema.

Additionally, the impeccable taste in music which invariably graces Blier's films is especially significant in *Beau Pere*. Philippe Sarde's score utilizes only three musicians, two pianists (one a jazz specialist) and the celebrated jazz violinist Stephane Grappelli. Sarde's music, particularly the theme introduced in the opening sequence and subjected to various contrasting treatments as the film progresses, conveys the precise nature of Remy's musical gifts as well as supporting the mood of the story. Additionally, Blier takes the trouble to designate explicitly the music that Remy admires. A display on Remy's wall of three classic Riverside albums recorded by the great jazz composer and pianist Thelonious Monk in the 1950's tellingly testifies to Remy's seriousness about music. Finally, there is the happiest interlude of the film, occurring at a point when Remy and Marion have begun to adjust to life without Martine but remain innocent in relation to each other. Together, they play Scott Joplin's lovely "Bethena Waltz" on the piano, hesitantly in the first of two sequences, confidently in the second. Blier enhances this passage with a camera which glides so gracefully around the couple that it is as if he were stylistically caressing time. Unquestionably, he is enamored of this joyous duet as he justly hopes his audience will be.

A sad footnote to the film is the fact that its excellent lead actor, Patrick Dewaere, committed suicide in 1982. It is unfortunate that a young star such as Dewaere with the potential for a long and brilliant career should be unable to cope with the pressures of his life.

Blake Lucas

Reviews

The Hollywood Reporter. January 12, 1982, p. 82.
Los Angeles Times. October 20, 1981, VI, p. 4.
The New Republic. CLXXXV, October 14, 1981, p. 26.
The New York Times. October 9, 1981, p. 20.
Variety. May 27, 1981, p. 18.

BLOW OUT

Production: George Litto for Filmways
Direction: Brian DePalma
Screenplay: Brian DePalma
Cinematography: Vilmos Zsigmond
Editing: Paul Hirsch
Art direction: Paul Sylbert
Music: Pino Donaggio
MPAA rating: R
Running time: 107 minutes

Principal characters:

Jack .... John Travolta
Sally .... Nancy Allen
Burke .... John Lithgow
Manny Karp .... Dennis Franz
Sam .... Peter Boyden
Frank Donohue .... Curt May
Lawrence Henry .... Terrence Currier
George McRyan .... John Hoffmeister

Brian DePalma, the writer and director of *Blow Out*, has become a master manipulator of the audience through the use of such devices as beginning a scene with an ambiguous shot that keeps the audience unsure of what is happening, and the employment of camera angles that call attention to themselves, such as overhead shots. Yet, being able to twist and turn the audience is by no means a necessarily negative quality. The late Alfred Hitchcock, for example, was perhaps the supreme practitioner of that type of filmmaking, and DePalma has an undisguised admiration for him, often using references to Hitchcock's films in his own. Whether or not there is any validity to the accusations of detractors who say that DePalma steals from Hitchcock, the viewer of a DePalma film should expect to be teased, surprised, and occasionally confused or misled, but should also anticipate that, as in the films of his English mentor, the loose ends will be tied up and the confusing events will be explained. DePalma is not deliberately trying to make his films ambiguous; he is merely setting up his big and little surprises.

Blow Out, in fact, begins with a long sequence that is confusing and deceptive—for a few minutes. The audience sees a college dormitory in which the coeds are being stalked by a knife-wielding man. Just as the man pulls back a shower curtain and raises his knife to stab the young woman in the shower, the scene stops and the audience realizes that they have been watching a film within the film. With this film stopped, Jack (John Travolta), a sound technician, and Sam (Peter Boyden), the boss of the company that is producing the film, begin to analyze the footage they have just seen. Sam tells Jack that he does not like the sound of the wind or the sound of the woman screaming in several of the scenes. Jack's subsequent effort to record a new wind sound triggers the rest of the plot and Sam's determination to get a better scream becomes a running joke in the film that has a completely unexpected and quite cynical payoff. Also, the stabbing of a woman in a shower is an obvious reference to the famous scene in Hitchcock's *Psycho* (1960), which was also used to a certain extent in DePalma's *Dressed to Kill* (1980). Some critics have seen this opening sequence as a joke by DePalma in which he is making fun of the idea that all of his films consist of sleazy thefts from Hitchcock.

In any case, the "real" plot of *Blow Out* begins when Jack goes out into the countryside to record wind sounds with his extremely sophisticated equipment. As he is doing so, he sees a car veer off a bridge and fall into the river. He jumps into the water and swims to the car, where he sees that a young woman is still alive inside. With the aid of a large stone, he smashes a window of the car and rescues the woman, Sally (Nancy Allen). Later, at the hospital, Jack discovers that no one is interested in hearing his story because it turns out that George McRyan (John Hoffmeister), the governor of the state and a probable presidential candidate was killed in the crash. In fact, an aide of McRyan's, Lawrence Henry (Terrence Currier), tells Jack to forget the whole incident, saying that to publicize the fact that McRyan was with a young woman when he died would only cause more sadness to his grief stricken family. He encourages Jack to take Sally out the back door of the hospital and not to mention to anyone that he was at the scene of the crash.

Jack agrees to the plan until later, when he listens to the tape recording he was making when the car crashed. On the tape he hears what he believes is a gunshot that occurred just before the car's tire blew out, causing the "accident." The audience gradually discovers the true story of the events leading up to McRyan's death. It seems that Manny Karp (Dennis Franz), a small-time photographer, and Sally have been making money through a rather shady business, luring men into compromising situations which are photographed by Manny for the use of his clients in divorce proceedings, blackmail, or anything else the client may desire. In this particular case, they were hired by someone who wanted to destroy McRyan's chances to be president. Sally admits that she had little difficulty in getting McRyan to take her to the secluded spot where Manny was waiting with his camera. None of the parties, however, expected an accident. When the car went off the bridge, Manny photographed it but quickly left the scene when he saw Jack dive into the river. He subsequently sold the pictures to a news magazine.

Although Jack learns most of the story of McRyan's death from Sally, he does not realize that a mysterious character named Burke (John Lithgow), who was working for the people who wanted to stop McRyan, exceeded his authority when he shot out a tire on McRyan's car. Determined to keep the true story from surfacing, Burke tries to kill Sally, but instead murders someone who resembles her. After this mistake, he decides to kill several young women so that when he kills Sally it will seem a part of a series of similar killings and will not be connected to the McRyan case. He also has removed the tire with the bullet hole in it from McRyan's car.

Meanwhile, Jack has cleverly combined Manny's pictures with his tape to produce a sound film of the wreck that he believes will prove his case. The detectives, however, will not take his story seriously, partly because he had once caused the death (revealed in a flashback) of an undercover policeman by equipping him with a hidden microphone to record a number of incriminating statements from some underworld characters. When the policeman began to sweat, however, the battery burned him and the hoodlums discovered the microphone and killed the policeman.

By this point in the film, the parallels between *Blow Out* and some earlier films and political events are becoming obvious. There are the self-evident suggestions of John F. Kennedy's assassination and particularly of Edward Kennedy's automobile accident at Chappaquiddick Bridge as well as some less explicit actions reminiscent of those surrounding the Watergate scandal. Other motifs resemble such films as *Blow-Up* (1966), in which a photographer tries to find evidence of a murder by enlarging photographs; *The Conversation* (1974), which details the story of a surveillance expert who makes and analyzes tape recordings; and the many Hitchcock films in which an innocent person is endangered because of some knowledge that he or she has accidentally gained. These parallels do not necessarily make *Blow Out* a better film, however, because the political allusions are so superficial that they do not enrich our understanding of either the real events or those in the film. Most of the parallels to other films unintentionally emphasize the fact that *Blow Out* is not as well made as the films from which it has borrowed.

The last part of the film evolves into a contest among four people. A television newsman, Frank Donohue (Curt May), learns of Jack's story and its supporting evidence and wants to air his charges. Burke, on the other hand, wants to silence both Jack and Sally and destory their evidence, but although the two know that someone wants their story suppressed, they are not aware of the danger in which they have placed themselves. The climax comes during a Liberty Day celebration in Philadelphia, the city in which the film is set. Burke, pretending to be the newsman, has arranged for Sally to meet him and give him the evidence. When Jack discovers this, he suspects that something is amiss and equips her with a microphone before following her to the meeting place. Burke, however, takes her away on a subway car so quickly that Jack cannot catch up with her, and he has to drive madly through the city to reach their destination. His wild drive is more incredible than exciting, as he drives through police lines, fire lines, groups of people, and even crashes his vehicle but still somehow manages to reach Sally. When he does arrive, however, it is too late. As he runs toward her, he hears her screams and finds Burke about to stab her. He quickly kills Burke but then realizes that Burke has already killed her. This whole sequence is played with a huge American flag in the background and is intermittently illuminated by fireworks, a grisly reminder of a beautifully romantic scene in Hitchcock's *To Catch a Thief* (1956).

Although the film seems to end with Jack beside Sally's body and the fireworks display in the background, a few extra scenes tell us that the true cause of McRyan's death was never discovered and that Jack, though he looks anguished when he hears it, has used his recording of Sally's last moments for the scream in the film-within-the-film with which *Blow Out* began, entitled *Co-ed Frenzy*. This conclusion is indeed a "ghastly irony," as *Newsweek* termed it, and it makes the viewer feel either emotionally jolted or cruelly tricked.

DePalma's direction is flashy throughout, and the acting is generally good, although John Travolta as Jack does not show quite enough emotional range, and the character of Sally, as played by DePalma's wife Nancy Allen, frequently seems too vapid and silly.

Sharon Wiseman

Reviews

The Hollywood Reporter. July 22, 1981, p. 3.
Los Angeles Times. July 24, 1981, VI, p. 1.
The New Republic. CLXXXV, August 22-29, 1981, pp. 22-23.
The New York Times. July 24, 1981, III, p. 6.
The New Yorker. LVII, July 27, 1981, p. 74.
Newsweek. XCVIII, July 27, 1981, p. 74.
Time. CXVIII, July 27, 1981, p. 62.
Variety. July 22, 1981, p. 3.

BODY HEAT

Production: Fred T. Gallo for Warner Bros.
Direction: Lawrence Kasdan
Screenplay: Lawrence Kasdan
Cinematography: Richard H. Kline
Editing: Carol Littleton
Art direction: Bill Kenney
Music: John Barry
MPAA rating: R
Running time: 118 minutes

Principal characters:

Ned Racine	William Hurt
Matty Walker	Kathleen Turner
Edmund Walker	Richard Crenna
Peter Lowenstein	Ted Danson
Oscar Grace	J. A. Preston
Teddy Lewis	Mickey Rourke
Mary Ann	Kim Zimmer

Body Heat is a contemporary *film noir* in which a romantic triangle unfolds against the backdrop of the sweltering Florida sun. Set in the present-day, fictional community of Miranda Beach, where the principals bathe in ice cubes, ask for double orders of iced tea, and wipe at endless streams of perspiration, the film slowly develops a tale of adultery, murder, and deception. Because of its theme and its richly atmospheric look—expressed in shadowy nuances of venetian blinds, palm fronds, and incessant cigarette smoke, all seen in suggestive lighting—*Body Heat* has been widely compared to *film noir* works of the 1940's such as *Double Indemnity* (1944) and *The Postman Always Rings Twice* (1946).

One of the most critically acclaimed films of 1981, *Body Heat* marked an auspicious directorial debut for Lawrence Kasdan, who also authored the film's original screenplay. The story of a small-time lawyer who conspires with a sultry beauty to murder her husband, *Body Heat* is so erotic that many critics wondered how it failed to receive the industry's much-dreaded X-rating, yet its steamy sexual imagery, which includes extensive nudity, sensual couplings, and exceedingly frank dialogue, is crucial to the progress of a torrid plot with a multitude of clever twists.

Throughout the film, the atmosphere of heat (and sexuality) is pervasive. As *Body Heat* opens, a lawyer, Ned Racine (William Hurt), who is renowned for his shyster-type legal tricks and for his sexual prowess as well, looks silently out a window at a fire in the distance. "My history is burning up out there," he muses. The burning building brings back his memories of a turbulent childhood. Racine's life is about to take a new and exciting direction, however; he meets Matty Walker (Kathleen Turner) and is immediately captivated by her blatant sensuality. Their chance meeting is accompanied by verbal sparring, laced with double entendres in which words are foreplay for the physical passion that will follow.

Their initial sexual encounter occurs the night that Racine wanders into a darkened bar and discovers Matty, for whom he has been searching since their first meeting. Taking her hand, he is startled to find that she is hot to the touch. "My temperature runs a couple of degrees high—around 100," Matty casually explains in a not too subtle reference to the film's title. Learning that Matty's husband is away, Racine follows her home to her imposing mansion. There, Matty allows him to come upstairs and view her collection of wind chimes, which hang over the balcony outside her bedroom. Afterward, she abruptly makes Racine leave, but he is unable to do so. After pacing back and forth in front of the house, peering through locked transoms and the small aperture in the bolted door, he picks up a lawn chair and boldly tosses it through a window. Matty is waiting expectantly by the staircase. In the first of many love scenes between the two, Racine and Matty urgently make love on the floor.

As their relationship continues, Matty begins to reveal information about her absent husband, Edmund (Richard Crenna). Calling him "small and mean and weak," she laments, "When I think about it, I wish he'd die. . . ." Yet, when Racine hears these words, and wonders himself about the possibility of murder, she demurs. "Don't talk about it," she admonishes, "Talk is dangerous. Sometimes it makes things happen. It makes them real." The seed has been planted, however, and Racine, prompted by Matty's unhappiness and lust, as well as his own greed for Edmund's wealth, cannot banish the thought from his mind. Eventually, the lovers concoct a plot to murder the unsuspecting husband. The scenes preceding the murder attempt and the act itself are a shrewd, pulsating blend of vivid images established through concise editing. Racine, who drives to Miami in order to establish a "cover," rents another car for use during the murder, but in doing so is momentarily surprised when a fully dressed and made-up clown drives by. Its painted-on smile seems to leer at the conspirator and his deceit.

The murder itself takes place at night, at the Walker mansion. Racine simply clubs Edmund on the head, killing him instantly. The lovers then put the body in the trunk of a car, to be transported to a derelict, beach-area building owned by the victim. Because of a thick fog, however, and a preponderance of eerie happenings—such as branches brushing against the car's windshield and problems with traffic, Racine's driving is erratic. Heightening the mood also is the scene's music. Elsewhere haunting and rather languid (reminiscent of the dreamy score for *Chinatown*, 1974), the John Barry music quickens its pace here, even employing slight "shriek" sounds (like those used in the *Psycho*, 1959, sound track) and this effective use of music, combined with the rapid-fire editing of the scene, creates a tense, hurried sensation. Once the scene finally ends, with a subdued Racine telling Matty they must not meet for awhile, sensations of guilt are beginning to manifest themselves.

When Edmund's body is ultimately discovered in the burned-out rubble of the building which Racine had set on fire through the use of a timer device, it is presumed that he was killed during an attempt at arson for the insurance money. Complications emerge, however, when it is revealed that Edmund's will was altered shortly before his death. Racine was, in fact, the lawyer who handled the changes. At least, his signature is on the new documents. In actuality, though, Matty made the alterations—so that she would inherit all of the estate (previously, Edmund's young niece was to have shared in the fortune).

Somewhat shaken by Matty's forgery, and concerned that it might make them look suspicious, Racine is nevertheless soothed by his lover's promise that the wealth will now be all theirs. Meanwhile, Racine's friends are growing concerned about his relationship with the young widow, whom they view as "poison." Peter Lowenstein (Ted Danson), who is serving as prosecuting attorney on the Edmund Walker case, tells Racine that he suspects Matty, and local police officer Oscar Grace (J. A. Preston) warns Racine to steer clear of her, saying, "You've messed up before and you'll mess up again. It's your nature." On another occasion he tells Racine that his sexual entanglements have been "small time. . . . This might not be. . . ."

There is, of course, irony in Oscar's words, since Matty is the embodiment of the predatory and sexually overpowering *femmes fatales* of the *films noir*. Like earlier characterizations by Veronica Lake, Lizabeth Scott, Barbara Stanwyck, and Jane Greer, Kathleen Turner's Matty is a devious manipulator. Upon first meeting Racine, she surmises, "You're not too smart. I like that in a man." Though offered as a brisk aside, her words grow in meaning as evidence mounts, pointing to Racine's involvement in Edmund's murder. Racine learns from Lowenstein that he has been a dupe. The prosecutor reveals, among other things, that on the night of the murder there were repeated (unanswered) telephone calls placed to Racine's Miami hotel room. The fact that Racine did not answer indicates that he was not there and destroys his cover. Also, the glasses worn by Edmund on the night of the murder, which were not found on the body, are now being offered to the police—as a clue—from an anonymous source.

Racine, who is growing increasingly nervous, is caught completely off-guard when he encounters a legal acquaintance during a Miami business trip. Racine's colleague says that he had told Matty Walker about the Miranda Beach attorney nearly a year earlier. It now looks as if their entire relationship had been prearranged, for the sake of instigating him to commit the murder. Racine confronts Matty with his belief during a late night meeting at the Walker estate. She admits it, but also insists that she has fallen in love with Racine. Racine has learned, however, through a former client of his named Teddy Lewis (Mickey Rourke)—who earlier had helped him to rig the explosive device used in Walker's building—that Matty has rigged a similar device, which she placed in a boathouse that he was expected to enter during a subsequent search for the murdered man's missing glasses. Refusing to accommodate her, however, he instead pulls a gun and forces her to walk toward the boathouse.

Matty obeys, and finally disappears into the distance and, seemingly, into the boathouse. The resulting explosion is followed by a scene which finds Racine in prison. It is an ironic moment as Racine, lying atop his cell bunk, opens his eyes and exclaims—to no one but himself—"she's alive." During a visit from Oscar, one of those who believed him guilty, Racine puts together the pieces of Matty's complex puzzle. Though the body of Matty Walker was identified, by dental charts, following the boathouse explosion, that was not the Matty that Racine knew. To a disbelieving Oscar, Racine recounts his chance meeting with an old school chum of Matty's, a blond named Mary Ann (Kim Zimmer). Matty had explained that Mary Ann had dropped by for a visit. But what if, he ponders, Matty was really using her name—and life—and the real Matty learned of it, and responded with a blackmail threat. In retaliation, "Matty" killed her—placing the body in the boathouse which was, initially, to have also contained Racine's body. Oscar thinks Racine's rantings are incredulous, but later, in his cell, Racine receives a package in the mail. It is the yearbook he has requested from Matty's high school. After thumbing through its pages, Racine finds the girl who was then known as Matty Tyler, the girl who was introduced to him as Mary Ann. He then turns to the photo of Mary Ann Simpson, and finds a smiling photo of "Matty." Her class nickname, the yearbook reveals, was "The Vamp." Her ambition was "to be rich and live in an exotic land." After Racine smiles wryly, the scene shifts to a foreign shore. Matty, basking in the sun, has achieved her ambition. Seated next to her, a handsome male admirer remarks "it is hot." She shows no emotion as the film comes to a close.

With its study of obsessive love, in which Racine joins characters played by the likes of Zachary Scott, Fred MacMurray, and Cornel Wilde, *Body Heat* stands as an invigorating mystery peopled with colorful, intriguing characters. While it can be argued that the character known as Matty is never fully unveiled and that the viewer cannot understand all of her motivations, it is also true that within the total framework of *Body Heat*, even faint peripheral characters are subtly but completely realized. Peter Lowenstein, for example, is not merely Racine's friend and colleague. As scene after scene reveals, even when he is only in the background, his character, bit by bit, becomes fully delineated. He, in fact, aspires to become another Fred Astaire. In a parking lot, following the climactic legal meeting regarding the altered will, Lowenstein is seen doing sprightly dance steps and when he later approaches Racine to let him know he is a suspect in the murder, he is first glimpsed dancing beneath the glaring light off a pier. These subtle touches add complexity to what might easily have been a stock character.

Given such well-written characterizations, the performances in *Body Heat* are superlative. William Hurt and Kathleen Turner, cast as the lovers, achieved considerable notice. A stage actor prior to starring in Ken Russell's *Altered States* (1980), Hurt also appeared in the convoluted mystery *Eyewitness* (1981), followed by *Body Heat*. With his blond good looks, he is among the young actors credited with renewing the popularity of the so-called "WASP-hero," a figure contrasting with some of the more ethnic-oriented roles portrayed by actors such as Dustin Hoffman, Al Pacino, and even Robert De Niro. The smoky-voiced Turner, a newcomer to motion pictures, reportedly got the role of Matty primarily because of the fact that the nudity and the sex scenes frightened "name" actresses away. She came to the role after appearing for twenty months on the daytime soap opera, *The Doctors*, in which she portrayed Nora Aldrich. In making the jump from daytime television to *Body Heat*, she helped direct attention to the many fine performers at work in soap operas, as well as to the many famous veterans of the medium already working on the large screen. Among them are Academy Award winners Ellen Burstyn and Patty Duke Astin. Richard Crenna, who portrayed Matty's husband, the ruthless businessman Edmund Walker, is also a veteran television actor. He is best known for his work on two long-running series, "The Real McCoys" and "Our Miss Brooks," and another, "Slattery's People," which established his dramatic prowess.

Hailed by most critics as one of the year's most thoughtful works, especially when compared to the preponderance of science fiction and to other special effects-laden products, *Body Heat* was considered to be a scintillating first effort for writer-director Lawrence Kasdan. Although *Body Heat* is heavily indebted to *film noir*, and despite its all-consuming preoccupation with imagery (it seems that air conditioning has yet to appear in heat-drenched Miranda Beach), it is an exquisitely plotted mystery. Kasdan came to the project after compiling a number of impressive writing credits in 1980 and 1981. Following the untimely death of Leigh Brackett, who was writing the script for *The Empire Strikes Back* (1980), Kasdan—a one-time advertising man—was hired to complete the project, which was based on a story by producer George Lucas. He also wrote *Raiders of the Lost Ark* (1981) and the romantic comedy *Continental Divide* (1981), which starred the late John Belushi. Despite these other impressive credits, it is with the sensual and stylish *Body Heat* that the thirty-two-year-old Kasdan has gained prominence, even though the commercially popular, critically acclaimed work was ignored by the year's Academy Award nominations.

Pat H. Broeske

Reviews

The Hollywood Reporter. August 17, 1981, p. 10.
Los Angeles Times. August 28, 1981, VI, p. 5.
The New York Times. August 28, 1981, III, p. 14.
The New York Times. October 25, 1981, II, p. 15.
The New Yorker. LVII, November 9, 1981, pp. 182-184.
Newsweek. XCVIII, August 31, 1981, p. 36.
Saturday Review. VIII, September, 1981, p. 49.
Time. CXVIII, August 24, 1981, p. 62.
Variety. August 17, 1981, p. 3.

BUDDY BUDDY

Production: Jay Weston for Metro-Goldwyn-Mayer; released by United Artists
Direction: Billy Wilder
Screenplay: Billy Wilder and I. A. L. Diamond; based on the play and film *A Pain in the A--* by Francis Veber
Cinematography: Harry Stradling, Jr.
Editing: Argyle Nelson
Art direction: Daniel A. Lomino
Music: Lalo Schifrin
MPAA rating: R
Running time: 98 minutes

Principal characters:

Victor Clooney	Jack Lemmon
Trabucco	Walter Matthau
Celia Clooney	Paula Prentiss
Dr. Hugo Zuckerbrot	Klaus Kinski
Captain Hubris	Dana Elcar
Eddie, the Bellhop	Miles Chapin
Receptionist	Joan Shawlee

Buddy Buddy was the first film to be made by writer-director Billy Wilder in more than three years. Although Wilder was a prolific worker in the 1940's and 1950's, when some of his best films were made, the director has made only eight films in the last twenty years. Wilder's age has much to do with this; he was born in 1906. Yet, despite his years, the recent films which he has written and directed, including *The Front Page* (1974) and *Fedora* (1978), show no indication that age has softened his caustic wit or mellowed his view of life. Although some of Wilder's more recent films have been unsuccessful financially and have received mixed reviews, aficionados of his work have found them superior to most other films being released today.

When *Buddy Buddy* was released, it received generally unfavorable reviews and disappeared quickly from general release. Some critics, such as Vincent Canby, praised the film lavishly, but many found *Buddy Buddy* tedious and unimaginative. The pace of the film is slow by current standards, but serious filmgoers are willing to accommodate themselves to the demands of a director who has something to say. Even such audiences found *Buddy Buddy* disappointing, a superficial film which suffers all the more in comparison to Wilder's best work.

The plot of the film is slow to develop after a rather violent beginning. In the opening sequence, a mailman (Walter Matthau) delivers some mail, including a package to a man standing just outside his house. As the mailman casually walks away, the package explodes and the man is killed. Because Matthau is such a popular actor and because he usually plays a sardonic, crusty-but-lovable antihero, the audience finds it difficult to believe that he is indeed a murderer. This playing against type certainly contributed to the film's failure at the box office. Matthau can play rogues or shysters, but the public apparently did not want to see him as a totally amoral professional killer.

The killing turns out to be gang-related; the audience learns that three men are due to turn state's evidence at a hearing and Matthau has been hired to kill them. The film never specifies who has hired him, or exactly what the witnesses will reveal, but that is unimportant. Matthau kills the next witness by poisoning a bottle of milk which is delivered to the man's doorstep just as the police have arrived to protect him. Then Matthau drives to Riverside, California, where the final witness is due to testify, protected by extremely tight security.

On the way to Riverside, the killer, who later identifies himself as Trabucco, stops at a gas station and runs into Victor Clooney (Jack Lemmon), who explains that he has just been throwing up, out of anxiety over his separation from his wife. Trabucco coldly dismisses the man and continues on to his destination. When he arrives in Riverside, he checks into the Ramona Hotel, directly across from the Riverside courthouse, and proceeds to plan his "hit" on the witness. Soon after, Victor arrives at the hotel and orders champagne from the bellhop, Eddie (Miles Chapin). Victor calls his wife to attempt a reconciliation but is rejected once again and decides to kill himself. His suicide attempt is foiled by the weak waterpipe on which he tries to hang himself and by the arrival of Eddie. Trabucco is also involved because his room is next door. This is the beginning of a new friendship on the part of Victor, and a growing resentment on the part of Trabucco.

In the course of the plot, Trabucco is perpetually being forced by Victor into situations which deter him from his appointed course. Celia Clooney (Paula Prentiss), Victor's wife, has, like her husband, worked for a television station, where she was an investigative reporter and he was the station's censor. When she was assigned to do an exposé on a sex clinic run by Dr. Hugo Zuckerbrot (Klaus Kinski), she fell in love with the messianic doctor and left Victor. In one last attempt at a reconciliation (one of several "last attempts"), he drags an unwilling Trabucco with him to the clinic. Celia totally rejects Victor, so in a third effort he feigns another suicide attempt. Instead of being moved, Celia merely allows Dr. Zuckerbrot to sedate Victor. Unfortunately, Zuckerbrot mistakenly sedates Trabucco, who is then unable to perform the "hit."

Out of loyalty to the man whom Victor thinks is his new best friend, he obligingly offers to do the job himself when he discovers Trabucco's problem.

In a plot of complications, Victor misses the witness and kills a policeman standing next to him, but Captain Hubris (Dana Elcar), the officer in charge of the witness' protection, had arranged for the policeman and the witness to change places; thus, the *real* witness has been killed. Trabucco is saved from being killed by the mob for not completing his job, and his only remaining problem is to escape from the police, who know that the shot came from his window.

Trabucco uncharacteristically helps Victor escape with him down a laundry chute and they drive past the police blockade using Trabucco's device of wearing a priest's garb. In an awkward, out-of-character move, Trabucco lets Victor get away to safety while the police ask the "priest" to perform the last rites on the dying witness.

In the next scene, Trabucco is seen on a tropical island sipping a cool drink and watching a sports program on television. He apparently has successfully retired to the island paradise about which he told Victor earlier in the film, and has not a worry in the world. Just then, however, Victor approaches the shore in a totally inadequate boat. He explains to the exasperated Trabucco that the police are after him, not for the killing of the witness, but for blowing up Dr. Zuckerbrot's clinic. Celia, it turns out, ran off with the clinic's receptionist (Joan Shawlee), and Dr. Zuckerbrot left the country. Victor has been going from island to island trying to find Trabucco so they can live in comfort together, forever. As Victor joyfully goes in to lunch with Trabucco's topless maid, the audience sees an ironic parting shot of Matthau giving the fisheye to Lemmon.

Buddy Buddy did not do well at the box office when it opened in December, 1981. Coming during a year in which blockbusters were the norm and sophomoric behavior was popular on the screen, Wilder's sophisticated black comedy could not compete. The situations created by the script allow nothing beyond superficial amusement. As *Time* critic Richard Schickel pointed out, nothing in the story seems to challenge the natural abilities of Matthau and Lemmon. The audience never sympathizes with Trabucco, and rarely does so with the insipid Victor; the audience might even understand why his attractive wife left him, except that she is so unsympathetic herself.

One could say that poor Wilder is better than no Wilder at all, but comparisons to his other films in the same vein, such as *The Fortune Cookie* (1966) or even *Kiss Me Stupid* (1966), make *Buddy Buddy* seem even weaker.

Carl J. Mir

Reviews

The Hollywood Reporter. December 9, 1981, p. 9.
Los Angeles Times. December 11, 1981, VI, p. 1.

The New York Times. December 11, 1981, III, p. 12.
Newsweek. XCVIII, December 14, 1981, p. 124.
Time. CXIX, January 4, 1982, p. 87.
Variety. December 9, 1981, p. 3.

CATTLE ANNIE AND LITTLE BRITCHES

Production: Rupert Hitzig and Alan King; released by Universal
Direction: Lamont Johnson
Screenplay: David Eyre and Robert Ward; based on the novel of the same name by Robert Ward
Cinematography: Larry Pizer
Editing: William Haugse
Art direction: Stan Jolley
Music: Sanh Berti and Tom Slocum
MPAA rating: PG
Running time: 95 minutes

Principal characters:
Bill Doolin .... Burt Lancaster
Annie .... Amanda Plummer
Jenny ....Diane Lane
Tilghman .... Rod Steiger
Bittercreek Newcomb ....John Savage
Engineer .... Michael Conrad

Just when Burt Lancaster's fine, long career (including an Oscar for *Elmer Gantry*, 1960) seemed to be winding down, he delivered three outstanding and memorable performances in little more than three years to reestablish himself as a major actor with a discriminating taste in choosing roles. In 1978 he appeared in *Go Tell the Spartans*, an unjustly neglected film set in Vietnam in 1964. In it he portrays a weary major trying to cope with the conflicting and confusing advice from his superiors as well as the ambition of his underlings and the absurdity of the conduct of the war. In 1981 his portrayal of an aging small-time mobster in *Atlantic City* gained him rave notices from the critics and an Oscar nomination from the Motion Picture Academy. The third of these distinguished performances came in *Cattle Annie and Little Britches*, a minor film made much more interesting by his finely shaded portrayal of a weathered old outlaw.

The premise of *Cattle Annie and Little Britches* is promising. Two girls in 1893 are inspired by their reading of popular Western novels to experience the exciting life depicted in Western fiction. They travel to the West and then have to face up to the difference between reality and the fanciful dime novels. Another theme of the film is the effect of their presence on the outlaw band to which they attach themselves: the outlaws too must deal with the contradictions between their life in print and in fact. Before the girls arrive, they are not even aware that they are also characters in popular stories; now they must decide whether they will, or even can, live up to their images. The other interesting theme, one that has been successfully explored in *Ride the High Country* (1962) as well as many other Westerns, is the fate of individualists, either outlaws or lawmen, as the wild West changes to a society that is no longer so open to them.

The two girls in *Cattle Annie and Little Britches*, which in part is based on a true story, are Annie (Amanda Plummer), who is about sixteen or seventeen years old, and Jenny (Diane Lane), who is somewhat younger than Annie. They decide to go West to see for themselves the romantic life described in dime novels by Ned Buntline. Annie is the more aggressive and outspoken of the two, and is given to speaking in the style of the dime novels, such as, "It's in my mind—like a hot coal." The girls find adventure quickly when the train on which they are sneaking a ride is held up by the famous Doolin-Dalton gang. Even though the hold-up is a comedy of errors in which the gang is able to take only a pig and some baseball equipment, Annie's enthusiasm is undiminished.

Some time later Annie and Jenny join the gang, with Annie showing her usual bravado by downing a glass of whiskey to demonstrate that she is not a "little girl." She expresses her delight at meeting the famous Bill Doolin (Burt Lancaster), and he—both flattered and amused—says, "*Mr.* Doolin to you." It is Doolin also who calls Jenny "Little Britches." Annie also immediately inserts herself into a quarrel between Doolin and Bittercreek Newcomb (John Savage), one of the younger members of the gang. When Bittercreek tells Doolin that their group "used to be a gang, and a good one; now it's just a bunch of bums on the run," Annie boldly states that she agrees with Bittercreek and then tells them all that they should live up to the way they are portrayed in the Buntline novels. This is the first time that they have heard of Buntline, but they are inspired by Annie's stirring words, and—after a spirited baseball game and some frolics in the river—they ride off to rob a bank. Before they reach the bank, however, they are caught in an ambush that results in an old-fashioned gun battle familiar to anyone who has ever seen a Western film. They are saved from death or capture by Annie's quick thinking. She opens a gate to let a herd of cattle into the scene of the action, and in the ensuing confusion the Doolin-Dalton gang is able to escape.

Doolin is liked or even admired by most of the citizens of the towns they go through. Even the engineer (Michael Conrad) of the train that is robbed speaks to him respectfully and seems to be proud to have his train robbed by the famous Doolin-Dalton gang. There is one man, however, who is determined to bring Doolin to justice. He is an old United States Marshal named Tilghman (Rod Steiger), and his introduction into the story adds another promising theme to the film: the rivalry of two long-standing foes who respect each other but are determined to defeat each other. There is a slight romance between Annie and Bittercreek, but not much is done with this thread of the story. Bittercreek tells Annie at the very first that she would make a good outlaw, and the two have two off-screen romantic interludes, but the rest of the time they pay scant attention to each other. There is additionally a sort of romance between Doolin and Jenny, but again, this is little more than an undeveloped conceit.

After the narrow escape from the gun battle, Doolin plans another bank robbery. He is stung by a line from one of Buntline's novels that Annie has with her. The novel says that he is getting old and that Tilghman may be smarter than he is. "I'll show Ned Buntline how my story ends," he thunders. The robbery is successful except that it is momentarily halted when it is discovered that no one brought a sack in which to put the money. The bank manager's trousers are used, but much later as they ride through the rain the gang members discover that all the money has fallen out. Doolin can only laugh.

Doolin is finally caught by Tilghman, but the marshal has to disguise himself as a monk and surround the outlaw when he is bathing in a stream to accomplish the task. As Tilghman takes Doolin to jail, Doolin says, "It's been a grand chase," and Tilghman apologizes when a photographer takes a picture of Doolin in chains. The marshal's victory is short-lived, however. Inspired by Annie's relentless devotion and persistence, the gang blasts open the jail and rescues Doolin. Then the whole group, except for Annie and Jenny, escapes through a pass that they dynamite closed so that they cannot be pursued. At the end of the film, Doolin stands high above them and shouts to the two girls. "May you ride long and hard." End titles then tell us that the two girls spent two years in a reformatory, after which Annie "lived a rich full life in Kansas City" and Jenny became a social worker and a domestic. Doolin died some time later, and Tilghman became a motion-picture director.

Cattle Annie and Little Britches is perhaps best summed up by the words of Pauline Kael in *The New Yorker*: "There is everything here to make a classic comedy-western except a script to give the potentially rich material shape and a dramatic center." The script is quite good in parts but lacks the overall direction that is needed. Indeed, it is unfortunate that a promising situation and several noteworthy acting performances are weakened by the flaws in the screenplay. Amanda Plummer, the daughter of Tammy Grimes and Christopher Plummer, gives a strong, almost too intense, portrayal of Annie. Rod Steiger as Marshal Tilghman is effectively restrained, and John Savage as Bittercreek Newcomb is engaging. Burt Lancaster's performance, however, is by far the best aspect of the film. In the early scenes he is often shown in long-shots, and with his bearded, weathered face he is almost unrecognizable as Lancaster except for his distinctive, expressive voice. As the film progresses, he has more close-ups and his face is equally expressive. The viewer is glad to see the performance and wishes it graced a more worthy vehicle.

Timothy W. Johnson

Reviews

The Hollywood Reporter. April 24, 1981, p. 3.
The New Republic. CLXXXIV, June 6, 1981, p. 26.
The New York Times. May 15, 1981, III, p. 8.
The New Yorker. LVII, June 15, 1981, pp. 135-136.
Variety. April 24, 1981, p. 3.

CHARIOTS OF FIRE

Production: David Puttnam for Allied Stars and Enigma Productions; released by Warner Bros. and the Ladd Company (AA)
Direction: Hugh Hudson
Screenplay: Colin Welland (AA)
Cinematography: David Watkin
Editing: Terry Rawlings
Art direction: Roger Hall
Costume design: Milena Canonero (AA)
Music: Vangelis (AA)
MPAA rating: PG
Running time: 120 minutes

Principal characters:

Harold Abrahams	Ben Cross
Eric Liddell	Ian Charleson
Sam Mussabini	Ian Holm
Aubrey Montague	Nicholas Farrell
Lord Andrew Lindsay	Nigel Havers
Master of Trinity College	Sir John Gielgud
Master of Caius College	Lindsay Anderson
Sybil	Alice Krige
Jackson Scholz	Brad Davis
Charles Paddock	Dennis Christopher
Jenny Liddell	Cheryl Campbell
Prince of Wales	David Yelland

Chariots of Fire, based on actual events, recounts the story of the 1924 British Olympic track team, and in particular, two of its star performers, Eric Liddell (Ian Charleson) and Harold Abrahams (Ben Cross). Running is an obsession for both men, and religion is the spark that ignites their obsession. Eric Liddell runs for his Protestant religion, because when he runs, he feels "His pleasure," the nearness of God. When he runs, his face is transformed: he throws back his head, puts his chin high, flails his arms, and occasionally lifts his eyes skyward as if enjoying a beatific vision as he leads the pack and comes in first. Harold Abrahams, on the other hand, runs because of his Jewish religion. The undercurrent of anti-Semitism that he feels surrounding him in the Anglo-Protestant halls of Cambridge University fuels his rage, and he uses his running skill as a weapon, a means of proving himself worthy of being treated as the equal if not the superior of his detractors.

The film begins in 1978 at the funeral of Harold Abrahams, where the last two members of the 1924 British Olympic track team, Lord Andrew Lindsay

(Nigel Havers) and Aubrey Montague (Nicholas Farrell), recall their halcyon days when they had "hope in our hearts and wings on our heels." Using Montague's letters to his mother as a means of introducing the flashbacks and as a continuity device, the scenes alternate between Harold and Eric. We see Harold and "Monty" meeting on their first day at Cambridge, where Harold quickly attracts attention by becoming the first student in seven hundred years to race around the Great Court at Trinity College before the clock delivers the last stroke at midday. This bravura performance brings him to the attention of the Master of Trinity College (Sir John Gielgud) and the Master of Caius College (Lindsay Anderson). They smugly proclaim the Jewish upstart as "Academically sound, arrogant, defensive to the point of pugnacity, as they invariably are," but with a strong sense of loyalty and duty. It is precisely this condescending, superior attitude that makes Harold run in an effort to beat them all. Harold's father is a Lithuanian Jew who became rich in England, and who desperately wants to make proper Englishmen of his sons, but he has forgotten one thing that Harold cannot forget; that England is Christian and Anglo-Saxon. He feels anti-Semitism every day in ordinary conversation. To prove himself worthy of being an Englishman, he is going to take the bigots on one by one and "run them off their feet."

Scottish missionary Eric Liddell also has his conflicts. While his father urges him to be a "muscular Christian" and to run in "God's name and let the world stand back in wonder," his sister Jenny (Cheryl Campbell) feels that he has a talent for preaching as well as athletic prowess and that it is insulting to God for him to spend so much time on running. She is gratified when Eric tells her that he intends to return to China as a missionary, as he feels that that is part of God's purpose for him. Her joy is tempered, however, when he qualifies this with his intention to do a great deal of running before he goes to China. Eric reasons that God made him fast, and to run is to honor Him; that includes training for and participating in the Olympic games.

Harold's obsession with beating Eric is great, but not so great that he cannot appreciate the other's skill. Watching Eric compete during a Scotland *vs.* France meet, Harold is overwhelmed by his drive. Early in the race, Eric trips and falls completely off the track, but he gets up and comes on strongly from behind to win. Also watching this show of speed and determination is Sam Mussabini (Ian Holm), the best track coach of the time, whom Harold asks to become his personal coach. Harold wants an Olympic medal in the 100-meter race, and to get it he will have to beat Eric.

Eric and Harold finally meet in a match between England and Scotland. When Eric wins the race, Harold goes into a fit of depression from which not even Sybil (Alice Krige), the lovely actress with whom he is in love, can shake him. In losing the race, however, he makes a good enough impression on Sam Mussabini that the coach decides to take him on as a pupil and help him gain the extra speed that he needs to beat Eric. In time, and after a rigorous training program, Harold receives news that he, as well as his friends, Lindsay, Montague, and Stallard, have all made the Olympic team, but so has Eric Liddell.

As the boat carrying the entire British Olympic team leaves for France, Eric is disturbed to learn that the qualifying heats for the 100-meter race are to be run on Sunday. Even though he has devoted the last three years to running and training for the Olympics, he believes that to run on Sunday would be against God's law, and thus he quietly announces his refusal to run. When efforts to get the race changed to another day fall through, the British Olympic committee begins to apply great pressure on him to change his mind. The conflict is quickly and amazingly resolved when Lord Lindsay arrives and says that since he has already won his Olympic medal, a silver in the hurdles, he will let Eric take his place in the 400-meter race on Thursday, so that Eric can still compete. All agree and the crisis is over. On Sunday, as Eric watches the 100-meter heats from the stands, he says that he has regrets but no doubts about his refusal to run that day.

As the races are won and lost, the tension increases as Harold and the two top American runners, Jackson Scholz (Brad Davis) and Charles Paddock (Dennis Christopher), prepare for the 100-meter race. When Harold opens his case, he finds a note and a charm from Mussabini. The coach's father swore by the charm and Mussabini asks Harold to wear it during the race, which he does. The entire 100-meter race, as are all of the film's races, is shot in slow motion and head-on, so the audience cannot tell who is winning the race until Harold breaks the tape first, beating the two Americans who had defeated him earlier in the 200-meter race. Since he is a professional coach, Mussabini cannot be present at the track, so Harold has set him up in an apartment close to the stadium where he can hear the music and see the flagpole from his window. Seeing the British flag raised, he knows that Harold has won, and his emotions overcome him. At first he stands at attention, with his hat over his heart as he watches the flag go up the pole, but he soon gives way to joy and punches out the top of his hat in elation, softly calling Harold "my son." The news of his victory also pleases Sybil, who has promised to be waiting for him when he returns. The Master of Trinity and the Master of Caius are also pleased, proclaiming that they expected nothing but victory from him all along.

Before the running of the 400-meter race, the American coach tells Jackson Scholz that Eric should be easy to beat since he has already run two races, but Scholz is not as sure. He knows that Eric has something to prove, and he passes a note telling him "It says in the old book—He that honors me, I will honor. Good luck." Eric runs and wins the race with Scholz's note clutched in his hand. As he is presented in triumph to the Prince of Wales on the shoulders of his teammates, he sees his once disapproving sister in the stands. The entire team returns to London in triumph.

In the last scene, we return to 1978, and to Montague and Lindsay as they leave the chapel. Monty comments that Harold "did it. He ran them off their feet." Not only that, but he also married Sybil and became a noted barrister and sports figure until his death. Eric Liddell returned to China as a missionary and died there in a Japanese prison camp in 1945.

The film was almost universally well received. The few critics who did complain singled out the synthesized music, too many races shot in slow motion, too much preaching from the Eric Liddell character, and a title that seemed to have nothing to do with the content of the film. (It is taken from a religious poem by William Blake, which is set to music in a hymn well-known to English churchgoers.) Such complaints, however, were definitely in the minority.

Critics were also quick to point out that the first half of the film builds toward a meeting of the two in competition, and when Eric wins, it carries on with Harold's determination to beat him the next time around, which, of course, never occurs. This would seem to be a cinematic *faux pas*, except that such was also the case in real life. It hardly mattered to those who saw the film, for by the time of the Olympics, the characters were so well-developed and likable that the audience happily settled for each of them winning medals in separate races.

The casting is impeccable and the acting is superb throughout, from the principal characters to the smallest speaking role. The use of unknowns in the central roles lent added credibility to their portrayal of Olympic-caliber athletes. There are also many delightful vignettes which not only please the senses but also add to the character development, such as Harold and Sybil flirting delightfully in a restaurant on their first date, and Lord Lindsay practicing his hurdles on the lawn of his estate with glasses of champagne balanced on each hurdle.

Chariots of Fire was the low-budget, Cinderella film of 1981. It won praise for its fine character development, acting, and lush re-creation of upper-class life in the Cambridge of the 1920's, as well as of the 1924 Olympics. Its continually increasing popularity surprised its makers, and it continued to amaze everyone right up to the Academy Awards ceremonies. Nominated in seven categories, including film editing, direction, and best supporting actor for Ian Holm, it took the awards for best original screenplay, music, costume design, and the top prize, for best picture, beating out its high-budget competitors *Reds* and *Raiders of the Lost Ark*, as well as another low-budget jewel, *On Golden Pond*.

The financial success of the film has also had a considerable impact on the film industry. It made more than ninety million dollars in the United States alone, and almost single-handedly revitalized the financially sagging British film industry and renewed public interest. The producers of *Chariots of Fire* seemed to express the new enthusiasm for filmmaking in Britain by joyfully holding up their Oscars at the 1982 Awards ceremony and shouting "The British are coming!"

Ellen Jo Snyder

Reviews

The Hollywood Reporter. August 7, 1981, p. 2.
Los Angeles Times. September 20, 1981, *Calendar*, p. 28.
The New Republic. CLXXXVI, January 27, 1982, p. 24.
The New York Times. September 25, 1981, III, p. 14.
The New Yorker. LVII, October 26, 1981, pp. 176-178.
Newsweek. XCVIII, September 28, 1981, p. 88.
Saturday Review. VIII, September, 1981, pp. 48-49.
Time. CXVIII, September 21, 1981, p. 73.
Variety. August 7, 1981, p. 3.

CITY OF WOMEN (LA CITTÀ DELLE DONNE)

Origin: Italy
Production: Renzo Rossellini for Opera Film-Gaumont; released by Gaumont-New Yorker Films
Direction: Federico Fellini
Screenplay: Federico Fellini, Bernardino Zapponi, and Brunello Rondi
Cinematography: Giueseppe Rotunno
Editing: Ruggero Mastroianni
Art direction: Dante Ferretti
Music: Luis Bacalov
Running time: 138 minutes

Principal characters:

Snaporaz .... Marcello Mastroianni
Dr. Xavier Zuberkock .... Ettore Manni
Elena .... Anna Prucnal
Woman on train .... Bernice Stegers
Motorcyclist .... Jole Silvani
Woman on roller skates .... Donatella Damiani

Federico Fellini's *City of Women* marks the third collaboration between the director and an actor who has been termed, in many quarters, his alter ego—Marcello Mastroianni. While "alter ego" is perhaps too neat a label for one actor among the many utilized by Fellini over the years, the distinctly symbiotic relationship between the two men has already produced two unqualified masterpieces: *La Dolce Vita* (1961) and *8½* (1963). The first film was a meandering journey through a decadent society seemingly on the brink of collapse from the collective rot of its own moral decay, while the second one featured Mastroianni as a director attempting to come to grips with decay of another kind, that of his creative powers and of his youth.

Whether *8½* was as deeply and honestly autobiographical as some critics would have us believe is conjectural, since Fellini has habitually mythologized the events of his life both in and out of films. It is thus tempting to try to categorize neatly *City of Women* as yet another installment in this autobiographical myth that would seem to constitute the Italian director's recent work. The casting of Mastroianni in the title role reinforces that line of reasoning, and, by bringing to mind the actor's earlier relationship with women in *8½*, hints at the idea that this film may, in fact, be a belated attempt on Fellini's part at some kind of a *rapprochement* with the female sex.

City of Women can, however, more realistically be viewed as an egocentric though intelligent attempt at establishing at least a subjective understanding of feminism. Indeed, the subjectivity of the film opened it up to charges of sexism when it opened in Rome. Female members of the cast accused Fellini of "showing the female of the species with disdain and disparagement," a charge that the director countered by stating that *City of Women* was not a statement against women; it was, in fact, simply a picture "about a man." The perceptible sexist overtones might, therefore, be said to evolve from the highly personal, nightmarish fantasies of its protagonist, Snaporaz (Marcello Mastroianni). If this character can be construed on any level, autobiographical or otherwise, to be an extension of the figure represented by Guido in *8½*, he has evolved from a man who formerly could hold women at bay (at least in his fantasies) with the crack of his whip, to one who now hallucinates of castration at the hands of vengeful feminists. Thus, the issue of whether *City of Women* is antiwomen is largely irrelevant, since the film is peopled by characters that have emerged from the baroque recesses of Fellini's psyche, not by real women.

The plot of *City of Women*, like those of all Fellini films, is relatively unimportant since its purpose is to serve primarily as a vehicle for the director's astonishing progression of images, many of which consist of emotional experiments in feeling. The film itself is structured along the lines of an extended dream that weaves alternately in and out of nightmare. It opens symbolically with a shot of a train entering a tunnel—a stock erotic metaphor borrowed from American films. Inside the train, world-weary, middle-aged Snaporaz (Marcello Mastroianni) dozes on his seat opposite a beautiful woman (Bernice Stegers). In his dreams, he fantasizes that the woman smiles seductively at him as she rises to leave the compartment. He, therefore, follows her to a toilet compartment and proceeds to make love to her but is interrupted in the middle of the act when the train stops.

The woman leaves the train and Snaporaz impetuously follows her. After leading him a merry chase through a lyrical countryside (in what suspiciously resembles a Dantean parody), she lures him into a hotel in the middle of nowhere and disappears. The establishment, however, is the site of a conference of feminists and the scenes that follow encompass a melange of seminars in which, among other things, a woman with a pointer renames the parts of the female anatomy; another woman parodies domestic and sexual servitude; and yet another drags in six husbands and discusses enthusiastically the merits of her new marital arrangement. Although Fellini is, in this instance, poking fun at what he considers to be the excesses of the women's movement, the argument soon begins to shift subtly to the women's side as the film progresses.

As the narrative unfolds, the feminists' issues become more complex even as the females themselves begin to appear more seductive. When Snaporaz asks a sexy woman (with an obvious interest in men) what she is doing at such a meeting, she answers "I have my contradictions." Another woman is both a dancer and a revolutionary, and so when Snaporaz asks her why she is a feminist, she replies "How could I not be?"

At this point the film turns, and the second half provides an argument for the feminists' case by examining some of the issues that have sent women shouting into the streets. Snaporaz, aided by a buxom feminist on roller skates (Donatella Damiani), escapes from the conventioneers but is subsequently abducted by an old crone on a motorcycle (Jole Silvani) who seduces him in her mother's cabbage patch. He escapes from her into a car filled with teenage female "Punk rockers." He jumps from the vehicle and is chased by its occupants until he comes upon a fortress-like structure resembling, through its erotic adornments, a museum of masculinity. Its proprietor, Dr. Xavier Zuberkock (Ettore Manni), is giving a large party in celebration of his ten-thousandth sexual conquest, and one of the guests turns out to be Snaporaz's own wife, Elena (Anna Prucnal). Obviously drunk, she harangues him over a variety of his sexual inadequacies. Her charges, although significant in balancing the masculine and feminine viewpoints, are later seemingly undermined, however, by the fact that she disappears with another woman for what appears to be a lesbian dalliance.

At the same time, Dr. Zuberkock and his other party guests are engaging in a series of debaucheries which are apparently intended by Fellini as counterpoint to the earlier excesses of the feminist convention. By the conclusion of the celebration, Snaporez is in bed when suddenly Elena reappears with her face drenched in cold cream and her hair in rollers. She is wailing an aria from *Carmen*. Snaporaz, understandably unnerved by his wife's behavior, takes refuge under the bed, where he is, in the best Fellini fashion, snapped up on a roller coaster ride through the events (particularly those involving his relationship with women) of his past life.

At the end of the ride, he is unceremoniously dumped in a cage and surrounded by the women from the feminist convention. They jeer him with such charges as, "He is guilty of being aloof; self-indulgent; he cannot commit himself to one woman; he can't cook." After suffering as much as he can, Snaporaz climbs a rope leading skyward to a huge balloon which is, in fact, a replica of the buxom woman who had previously rescued him from the convention. As the refugee blissfully floats away, however, he is again victimized when the balloon's real-life counterpart appears, dressed as a terrorist, and shoots him down. He then wakes up and finds himself back on the train in the company of his wife.

Any summation of a Fellini film, however detailed, can only hint at his subtle nuances. Many of these little touches refer back to previous films or are perhaps more accurately extensions or even alternate depictions of stock Fellini characters. Snaporaz's relationship to Guido of *8½* has previously been established, but his wife Elena also bears a not entirely coincidental resemblance to Guido's wife as portrayed by Anouk Aimee in the same film.

Other traditional Fellini motifs, such as that of woman as either virgin or whore, also recur in *City of Women*, although the character of Dr. Zuberkock, whose name is based on a phallic pun and who is easily the most bizarre figure in the film, twists the image a bit to reveal a parallel theme of a masculine whore figure as well. In fact, the entire structure of the film within the borders of the dream is symmetrical. In the first half of the film, the excesses of the women's movement are satirized. In the second half, the flood of masculine "macho" absurdities that undoubtedly instigated the feminist revolution (and its extremes) are parodied as well. Zuberkock's museum of male pleasure is the equivalent of the earlier feminist convention at the hotel.

Yet, for all of its balanced imagery, what actually unfolds before the viewer are two sides of what is essentially a masculine mentality. Regardless of appearances, Fellini is not particularly interested in political or sexual issues here but is instead concerned with the psyche of a man who appreciates women as long as they adhere to his own internalized stereotypes. Like the earlier *8½* with its character of Guido, *City of Women* provides, in Snaporaz, a figure who is little more than a vehicle for Fellini's creative and intellectual obsessions. For example, at the end of *8½* the viewer discovered that the picture he had just seen was, in fact, the process of the film itself being made. Similarly, in *City of Women* the audience watches what the director would have us believe is the artist's attempt at the resolution of his inner sexual conflicts. Yet, whereas *8½* resulted in a cohesive if highly autobiographical and symbolic statement on the creative process, the current film, which should logically provide a progression in its creator's mythic, autobiographical consciousness, is instead merely derived from his previous statements.

City of Women, with its obvious allusions to *Satyricon* (1970), *Amarcord* (1974), *Casanova* (1977), and of course both *Juliet of the Spirits* (1965) and *8½*, can be faulted for a high degree of self-plagiarism. The duplication or echoing of earlier images can be accounted for as a kind of "self-tribute" or, perhaps more realistically, a "self-mockery" based on Fellini's mythical, cinematic autobiography. Yet, there can be little excuse for a creative artist, particularly one with Fellini's wealth of imagination, to repeat not only images but also ideas, attitudes, and postures from his earlier works without altering the perspective to any significant degree.

The maestro still enthralls the viewer with his penchant for arresting new faces, but in this instance he has not supported his choices with sensitive delineations of character, with the grotesque exception of Zuberkock. Thus, what should be a forward-looking film, based upon the possibilities of its subject matter, becomes only a self-satirizing look into an egotistical past. Admitting his own tunnel vision (albeit through unusually rich images), Fellini does not emerge with Snaporaz's train from the tunnel at the end of the film, and the viewer does not experience the sense of revitalization offered by the conclusion of *8½*.

Stephen L. Hanson

Reviews

The Hollywood Reporter. April 10, 1981, p. 37.
Los Angeles Times. May 1, 1981, VI, p. 12.
The New Republic. CLXXXIV, April 4, 1981, p. 26.
The New York Times. April 8, 1981, III, p. 21.
Newsweek. XCVII, April 20, 1981, p. 93.
Time. CXVII, April 20, 1981, p. 84.
Variety. April 11, 1980, p. 3.

CLASH OF THE TITANS

Production: Charles H. Schneer and Ray Harryhausen for Metro-Goldwyn-Mayer; released by United Artists
Direction: Desmond Davis
Screenplay: Beverley Cross
Cinematography: Ted Moore
Editing: Timothy Gee
Art direction: Frank White
Special visual effects: Ray Harryhausen
Music: Laurence Rosenthal
MPAA rating: PG
Running time: 118 minutes

Principal characters:

Zeus .... Laurence Olivier
Perseus .... Harry Hamlin
Hera .... Claire Bloom
Andromeda .... Judi Bowker
Thetis .... Maggie Smith
Ammon .... Burgess Meredith
Aphrodite .... Ursula Andress
Poseidon .... Jack Gwillim
Athena .... Susan Fleetwood
Cassiopeia .... Sian Phillips
Thallo .... Tim Pigott-Smith
Calibos .... Neil McCarthy
Hephaestus .... Pat Roach
The Three Blind Witches .... Flora Robson
Anna Manahan
Freda Jackson
Acrisius .... Donald Houston
Danae .... Vida Taylor

Clash of the Titans is an old-fashioned adventure fantasy, a saga of Greek gods, oracles, witches, and monsters, which has more in common with similar films from the 1950's than with the sword-and-sorcery epics of the 1980's. Its title, for example, would have been ideal for a 1959 Steve Reeves-Joseph E. Levine extravaganza; there is the typical "cast of thousands," and the special effects, by Ray Harryhausen, are obviously fake but still charming, stylistically closer to Harryhausen's work of a quarter century ago than to anything spawned by the imagination of George Lucas or Steven Spielberg. Despite its weaknesses—mainly, a corny, predictable story and a number of bland performances—the film remains entertaining precisely because of its silliness, because it is not slick and sophisticated. *Clash of the Titans* does not look as if it were made by a computer, as many recent films do.

The hero of the story is Perseus (Harry Hamlin), a mortal, who is the illegitimate child of Zeus (Laurence Olivier), the chief deity and father of gods and men. The scenario chronicles Perseus' triumph over a variety of monsters, witches, and animals, sometimes aided, but often hindered, by the whims of the gods as he battles to win the beautiful, virginal Princess Andromeda (Judi Bowker), whose doomed suitors are required to solve impossible riddles.

The gods, endowed with supernatural powers, live on Mount Olympus and are worshiped by the mortals below them. In addition to Zeus, the deities include Thetis, Goddess of the Sea (Maggie Smith); Hera, wife of Zeus, Goddess of Marriage and Maternity (Claire Bloom); and Aphrodite, Goddess of Love (Ursula Andress). As the film opens, they are involved in their favorite activity: quarreling among themselves over the fates of their mortal children, specifically Perseus and Thetis' son Calibos (Neil McCarthy). It seems that Zeus has transformed the handsome Calibos into a rather unattractive beast, and his marriage to Andromeda has thus been canceled. Zeus also decides to destroy the city that has banished Perseus, who has just reached manhood.

Throughout the story Zeus plays with clay figurines, bringing them to life, ordering them to undertake spectacular and dangerous adventures. Perseus is armed with a sword, shield, and helmet that make him invisible, all presents from Zeus. He is aided by Pegasus, the white, winged horse whom he captures from a giant vulture, and Bubo, a magical owl made of golden metal. He battles Calibos, severing one of his hands, and captures a ring on one of his fingers which solves Andromeda's riddle, but the angry Thetis orders Andromeda to be chained to a rock and delivered to the Kraken, a huge sea-dragon, as a human sacrifice.

Ammon (Burgess Meredith), a poet, chronicler of the gods, and Perseus' adviser, tells him to seek help from the Three Stygian Witches (Flora Robson, Anna Manahan, and Freda Jackson), who all share a single eye. He then tangles with Dioskilos, a monstrous two-headed wolf-dog that guards the entrance to the sanctuary of Medusa. In a representative bit of action, Perseus severs one of Dioskilos' heads with his sword, but the animal keeps attacking until finally, Perseus drives the weapon into the animal's body. For his next battle, he takes on the Medusa, with snakes in place of hair, who is so ugly that anyone who sees her face is transformed into stone. While avoiding Medusa's gaze, Perseus severs her neck after a furious battle. After her death, giant crabs and maggots are formed from her blood.

Calibos is killed in a battle, and the Kraken, the mutant offspring of the mating of a Titan and a reptile, emerges out of a violent sea to snatch

Andromeda. Perseus rescues the princess from the Kraken who glances at Medusa's severed head, and turns to stone. Perseus and Andromeda then marry, and live "happily ever after," after having earned their place in the constellation.

The plot of *Clash of the Titans*, originally entitled *Perseus and the Gorgon's Head* and loosely taken from classical mythology, is secondary to Ray Harryhausen's enjoyably quaint visual effects, filmed in "Dynarama" (a name for the Dynamation stop-motion process). Harryhausen began his career as head animator and assistant to Willis O'Brien on *Mighty Joe Young* (1949). He met Charles H. Schneer, with whom he coproduced *Clash of the Titans*, in 1953. Among their films are *It Came from Beneath the Sea* (1955); *The Seventh Voyage of Sinbad* (1958); *Jason and the Argonauts* (1963); *The Golden Voyage of Sinbad* (1974); and *Sinbad and the Eye of the Tiger* (1977). While working all day on *Clash of the Titans*, the prolific Harryhausen was spending his evenings preparing for a new film, to be called *Sinbad Goes to Mars*.

Here, as in all the rest, Harryhausen has not created precision-perfect effects; *Clash of the Titans* is no slick *Star Wars* (1977), or even *2001: A Space Odyssey* (1968). His mattes, miniatures, and models are all clearly illusions, simple and even crude when compared to most other contemporary films which rely mostly on special effects for their entertainment value. Yet Harryhausen's visuals remain pleasing and sometimes even whimsical in their own unique way, particularly his prehistoric-looking creations of diverse sizes, forms, and temperaments. His creatures include a large squawking vulture; Bubo, the cute little owl with spinning eyes (his answer to *Star Wars*' robots, R2-D2 and C-3PO); the winged Pegasus, who glides majestically through the air; and the chilling, menacing Medusa, who terrorizes Perseus in what is easily the film's most exciting sequence. *Clash of the Titans* is vintage Harryhausen, ranking with *It Came from Beneath the Sea* and *The Seventh Voyage of Sinbad* among his best overall efforts.

The performances, direction, and script are unimportant. Classical scholar Beverley Cross's dialogue is mostly silly. Desmond Davis' credits are more impressive as a camera operator on films such as *A Taste of Honey* (1961); *The Loneliness of the Long Distance Runner* (1962); and *Tom Jones* (1963) than as a director. His best films in that capacity are *Girl with Green Eyes* (1962) and *Smashing Time* (1967), both with Rita Tushingham and Lynn Redgrave. His work here, his first directorial credit since *A Nice Girl Like Me* (1969), is unexceptional.

As for the actors, Claire Bloom, Maggie Smith, Ursula Andress, and the other inhabitants of Mount Olympus have little to do. *Clash of the Titans* is perhaps Smith's most anonymous screen appearance. Burgess Meredith is mostly cranky as Ammon, and Flora Robson is sadly unrecognizable in her bit part as one of the witches. Harry Hamlin, cover-boy handsome, should dominate the film as he is seen on screen throughout; however, his presence barely registers. While pre-teenagers may be excited by the monsters and myths in the film, some female members of the audience might appreciate the constant exposure of Hamlin's bare chest. After a promising screen debut as the John Garfield-like boxer in *Movie, Movie* (1978), he has done little to distinguish himself in his subsequent film appearances, which include *King of the Mountain* (1981) and *Making Love* (1982). Judi Bowker, who debuted at age sixteen in Franco Zeffirelli's *Brother Sun, Sister Moon* (1973), is blandly innocent as the lovely Andromeda. Even Laurence Olivier, who effortlessly brings life and energy to the trashiest projects—as evidence by *The Betsy* (1978)—seems to have taken the role of Zeus solely for the pay. His role in *Clash of the Titans* is among the most undistinguished in his exemplary career.

The film was shot on location in Spain (the barren terrain of Gaudix and Antequerra), Italy (the temples of Paestum, the beaches of Palinuro, the ancient amphitheater at Ostia Antica), and Malta. Mount Olympus and other locations were constructed in London's Pinewood Studios. A major publicity campaign costing almost seven million dollars—the production budget was just three million dollars more—was mounted for the film by Metro-Goldwyn-Mayer, with Ray Harryhausen sent on a month-long tour of schools and museums in more than a dozen cities. The reviews were mixed-to-negative, with critics either praising or dismissing Harryhausen's work depending upon their subjective feelings for his brand of special effects. *Clash of the Titans* was ranked nineteenth on *Variety*'s list of 1981's "Big Rental Films," with a gross of $15,632,341. While no box-office bomb, it still performed disappointingly next to such competitive escapist fare as *Raiders of the Lost Ark*, *Superman II*, and *For Your Eyes Only*. All three overwhelmed *Clash of the Titans* in ticket sales.

Nevertheless, *Clash of the Titans* is an enjoyable fantasy-adventure, a representative example of the creativity of its *auteur*, Ray Harryhausen.

Rob Edelman

Reviews

The Hollywood Reporter. June 10, 1981, p. 3.
Los Angeles Times. June 12, 1981, VI, p. 1.
The New York Times. June 12, 1981, III, p. 16.
Newsweek. XCVIII, July 6, 1981, p. 75.
Time. CXVII, June 21, 1981, p. 81.
Variety. June 10, 1981, p. 3.

CONTINENTAL DIVIDE

Production: Bob Larson for Amblin Productions; released by Universal
Direction: Michael Apted
Screenplay: Lawrence Kasdan
Cinematography: John Bailey
Editing: Dennis Virkler
Art direction: Peter Jamison
Music: Michael Small
MPAA rating: PG
Running time: 103 minutes

Principal characters:

Souchak	John Belushi
Nell	Blair Brown
Howard	Allen Goorwitz
Sylvia	Carlin Glynn
Possum	Tony Ganios
Yablonowitz	Val Avery

It is unfortunate that of all the characterizations created by the late John Belushi, the one that will probably linger forever in the minds of filmgoers is his portrayal of the gross undergraduate Bluto Blutarski in *National Lampoon's Animal House* (1978). That film, one of the most financially successful comedies of all time, inspired three network television imitations and established a character that Belushi would continue with minor modifications through Steven Spielberg's disappointing *1941* (1980) and the immensely successful *The Blues Brothers* (1980). Yet in performing on television's satirical series "Saturday Night Live" from 1975 until 1979, the actor established a number of ongoing impersonations incorporating varying degrees of subtlety, ranging from a guttural samurai warrior to former NBC President Fred Silverman to Israeli Prime Minister Menachim Begin. Between these extremes and interspersed with zany impressions of killer bees and the Greek owner of a family-staffed diner were portrayals of relatively normal people caught up in bizarre circumstances. Although these roles were invariably in support of the more flamboyant antics of other members of the "Saturday Night Live" cast, Belushi's performances revealed a restraint and sensitivity that gave evidence of a deeper talent.

Viewers familiar only with *National Lampoon's Animal House* or *The Blues Brothers* were surprised by Belushi's two 1981 efforts *Continental Divide* and *Neighbors*, which attest the fulfillment of this heretofore little-seen sensitivity. *Neighbors* is, on the whole, a disappointing effort, featuring a restrained Belushi reacting to the manic carryings-on of his "Saturday Night Live" partner Dan Aykroyd. *Continental Divide*, however, is a deft, sparkling comedy adroitly directed by Michael Apted, who gained fame with *Coal Miner's Daughter* (1980), and featuring a script by Lawrence Kasdan which evokes memories of Spencer Tracy and Katharine Hepburn (although with some role reversal) in their most contentious portrayals.

Kasdan's highly successful screenplays for *Raiders of the Lost Ark* (1981) and *Body Heat* (1981) are also tributes to classic films of genres of Hollywood's golden period. Indeed, director Steven Spielberg chose Kasdan to write the script of *Raiders of the Lost Ark* after reading his screenplay for *Continental Divide*. Though both films have been open to the charge of simply inserting prefabricated or recycled elements into a particular arrangement to appeal to modern audiences, the meticulous crafting of *Raiders of the Lost Ark* overcomes any deficiencies of imagination it may have and the casting of John Belushi and Blair Brown in *Continental Divide* gives it a contemporary dimension that differentiates it from earlier romantic comedies.

Belushi plays Ernie Souchak, an old-style muckraking Chicago columnist (as opposed to the trendier investigative reporters of the 1970's and 1980's) who makes a career out of exposing corruption in City Hall. His in-depth revelations concerning the activities of one of the aldermen leads that politician to threaten his life with the help of underworld henchmen. Consequently, Howard, his editor (Allen Goorwitz), decides that in order to save Souchak's life, he must take him off the case and send him into hiding until things cool down. An assignment to interview reclusive female ornithologist Nell Porter (Blair Brown) in the Rocky Mountains, where she is performing research on bald eagles, seems the ideal solution.

As it works out, however, the situation is far from ideal. Souchak, a definitive urbanite, hates the outdoor life, and Porter resents the city slicker's intrusion into her simple, well-ordered though rustic existence. The combination produces instant mutual hostility, yet time and proximity work wonders. He develops a growing respect for her dedication to the eagles, and she encourages him to quit smoking after he encounters considerable difficulty in clambering up the slopes after her in her quest for the enormous birds. In short, they fall in love.

The first half of the film spins itself out amidst the rugged beauty of the mountains. The remarkable photography, directed by John Bailey, is punctured by the defensive quips of Belushi as he learns to adjust to the wilds and by the banter he and Brown exchange as two alien beings moving toward each other. The highlight of this portion of the film is perhaps a sequence in which Nell constructs a sled out of rope and ice.

In the second half, Souchak is on firmer ground back in Chicago and it is Nell who is the neophyte learning to cope with the civilized world. She goes to the city because of her love for the newspaperman, but, despite his assurances, she is not optimistic about their future together. "Look! Eagles!" he cries, as he spots a flock of pigeons during one of their walks together. Eventually, she determines to return to the mountains. Despite all of the obstacles to a compatible life together, Souchak realizes that he cannot live without her and pursues her to the train. Though determined to remain on the train for only one short leg of the trip, the reporter succumbs to his feelings for the ornithologist and remains on board. Unlike the traditional Hollywood couples, however, whose differences are simply assumed to be resolved by successful marriages, Souchak and Nell recognize the impossibility of living together because each despises the other's life-style. They marry anyway, determining to be together only when convenient while continuing to live in their accustomed styles.

It admittedly takes an extraordinary pair of actors to portray convincingly a love relationship between characters as diametrically opposed as Ernie Souchak and Nell Porter, yet Belushi and Brown do exactly that. Though working with a strong script by one of the most successful screenwriters of recent years, the actors alone can create chemistry, and the main characters of *Continental Divide* do it well. With less accomplished actors the strange marital relationship which resolves the film would not appear convincing, even in the 1980's, which has witnessed a wide variety of nontraditional relationships.

Michael Apted's direction enhances the fine acting and the solid script. Apted displays a knack for deadpan comedy, which requires a great deal of subtlety and restraint. His pacing is steady and judicious, and it can be surmised that his firm hand was in no small part responsible for Belushi's own admirable restraint and sensitivity in his portrayal of Ernie Souchak.

Although the title *Continental Divide* refers not only to the Rocky Mountains but also to the chasm separating the divergent life-styles of the protagonists, the film successfully balances two extremes and creates a believable portrait of what in less talented hands would fall dangerously close to absurdity. Instead, it is a fitting and beautiful testimony to a side of John Belushi that was too little seen during his life and one that will unfortunately probably be lost in the considerable shadow of Bluto Blutarski and other gross characters who masked an actor of considerable sensitivity and sadly untapped talent.

Thomas A. Hanson

Reviews

The Hollywood Reporter. September 9, 1981, p. 3.
Los Angeles Times. September 18, 1981, VI, p. 1.
The New York Times. September 18, 1981, III, p. 14.

The New Yorker. LVII, November 9, 1981, p. 180.
Newsweek. XCVIII, October 5, 1981, p. 78.
Time. CXVIII, September 14, 1981, p. 90.
Variety. September 8, 1981, p. 3.

CUTTER'S WAY (CUTTER AND BONE)

Production: Paul R. Gurian for Gurian Entertainment; released by United Artists
Direction: Ivan Passer
Screenplay: Jeffrey Alan Fishkin; based on the novel *Cutter and Bone* by Newton Thornburg
Cinematography: Jordan Cronenweth
Editing: Caroline Ferriol
Art direction: Bernard Herzbrun and Hilyard Brown
Sound: Peter Hliddal
Music: Jack Nitzsche
MPAA rating: R
Running time: 105 minutes

Principal characters:

Richard Bone .... Jeff Bridges
Alex Cutter .... John Heard
Maureen (Mo) Cutter .... Lisa Eichorn
J. J. Cord .... Stephen Elliott
George Swanson .... Arthur Rosenberg
Valerie Duran .... Ann Dusenberry
Mrs. Cord .... Patricia Donahue
Woman in hotel .... Nina Van Pallandt

Cutter's Way is one of the relatively few recent American films that have dared to be different, both in style and content. Its resultant commercial fate is therefore instructive. Released early in 1980 under its original (and more appropriate) title *Cutter and Bone*, it played only a few limited engagements, meeting with incomprehension on the part of most critics and failing to find an audience. It was quickly pulled from distribution and given to a releasing company, United Artists Classics, who retitled it *Cutter's Way*. Supported by the enthusiasm of a small band of discerning critics, it reappeared in 1981 and became one of the more respected films of the year, though neither a box-office hit nor an award-winner. Gradually, it has discovered its audience and seems fated to be most appreciated on the revival circuit.

The problems of *Cutter's Way* are easy to understand if the film is placed in the perspective of the somewhat lamentable mainstream cinema of 1981. Large-scale films designed for wide audience appeal, such as *Raiders of the Lost Ark*, tended to do well. It seems to be taken for granted and readily forgiven that such films do not demand a complex response. The same is true of small-scale films such as *On Golden Pond* and *Chariots of Fire*, which exploit a comforting but rather facile humanism. Recent Academy Award winners such as *Kramer vs. Kramer* (1979) and *Ordinary People* (1980) have been careful to foreground their questionable sensitivity to changing social attitudes, and thus have inspired acclaim for mostly superficial reasons. Of course, in varying degrees, all these films are not without merit; but the road presently seems to be more or less closed to adventurous approaches and most particularly to intimate films which do not encourage easy identification with the characters or a clearly defined moral response. It is in this category that *Cutter's Way* belongs. Although somewhat uncomfortable in its relationship to traditional narrative forms and genre conventions, *Cutter's Way* does possess one quality very evident in the classic studio films of the past and much needed today—aesthetic distance. It is stylized but not escapist. The viewer who is used to perceiving films as either comic strips or serious enactments of normal life is likely to be mystified when confronted with such a film. *Cutter's Way* offers its own mysterious world—a world rather remote from conventional experience—and characters who are treated with neither admiration nor contempt but with considerable artistic passion. It is a fascinating film, replete with a haunting visual ambience, superb performances, and quicksilver shifts of tone and mood.

The narrative of *Cutter's Way* comprises two distinct elements, each of which feeds the other. The first element is the relationship between Alex Cutter (John Heard) and Richard Bone (Jeff Bridges). The two men are opposites in every way. Bone, an amiable and easygoing beach bum who lives off his charm, has absolutely no sense of responsibility and no serious convictions. Cutter, a one-eyed Vietnam veteran suffering as well from the loss of both an arm and a leg, is a bitter and unpredictable man given to intense rages and wild flights of fancy. Cutter is the intellectual activist, while Bone is the passive coward. Their friendship is complicated by Bone's uncommitted interest in Alex's alcoholic wife Maureen "Mo" Cutter (Lisa Eichorn). Alex and Mo have a strange marriage, stable but depressing. He seems dependent on her, but often treats her cruelly. Neither is very nurturing to the other, but they are strangely devoted. Their common interest is drinking, which has the effect of numbing her to emotional pain and provoking his episodes of randomly directed hostility. Richard Bone appears not to have a home of his own and needs his ill-defined place in the lives of Alex and Mo. In a sense, the two men complete as well as complement each other. Sadly, neither of them seems to complete Mo, an unusually forlorn woman who conceals her vulnerability with a hard and cynical façade not unlike that of her husband. The psychological intricacies of this unusual triangle are the heart of the film and the source of much of its appeal.

The second element of the narrative is the mystery involving the rape and murder of a teenage girl. The story opens in an unnamed California town (actually Santa Barbara) during Fiesta Days. Richard is leaving the El Encanto

Hotel one evening after a rather melancholy tryst with a wealthy older woman (Nina Van Pallandt) who is not overly impressed with him. His worn-out sports car stalls in an alley and he happens to see another car stop and its occupant place something in a trash can. The next morning, identified as a result of the stalled car which he necessarily abandoned, he is called in by the police, who are investigating the murder of a teenage girl. Although they finally rule him out as a suspect, he is a potential witness—even though he did not see the murderer for more than a moment in the dark. The incident arouses Alex's interest, and during the Fiesta Days parade, Richard's sudden recognition of a man riding a horse and wearing sun glasses sows the seeds of his friend's obsession. The man Richard has identified is J. J. Cord (Stephen Elliott), a powerful oil millionaire, and Alex, seething with hatred of the power structure which he blames for all his misfortunes, is instilled with a desire for vengeance against Cord. Although Richard almost immediately becomes uncertain that Cord actually was the man he saw, Alex is convinced, and plans to blackmail Cord with the ultimate purpose of exposing him. The dead girl's sister, Valerie Duran (Ann Dusenberry), is a willing accomplice and Richard becomes a reluctant one, hoping that Alex will eventually lose interest in the potentially dangerous scheme.

The two narrative threads dovetail as a result of Mo's scornful response to what she considers the excessiveness of Alex's latest paranoid delusion. She begins to feel lost and helpless within the already frustrating conditions of her life with Alex. When Alex and Valerie remain in Los Angeles after Richard has backed out of the scheme, Mo finally gives in and consummates her latent romance with Richard. Unfortunately, Richard remains as fearful as ever of emotional commitment, and after promising Mo that he will stay the night with her, he leaves the house after she has gone to sleep. The next morning, Richard and Alex discover that Mo has died in a fire which has burned the house to the ground. In spite of Richard's hesitant admissions concerning the brief romance, which he believes might have precipitated Mo's suicide, Alex is convinced that Cord has killed Mo in an effort to eliminate Richard. The apathetic Richard is dragged along when Alex crashes an afternoon party which Cord is giving, and the story ends with a bizarre confrontation. Richard and Alex are recognized by Mrs. Cord (Patricia Donahue), who has overheard Alex's crude fantasy of the murder earlier in the story, and Richard is forcibly detained by Cord's men while Alex escapes. Cord is attempting to reason with Richard when Alex comes riding across the lawn on one of Cord's horses, throwing himself through Cord's window and dying in the process. Cord's strange response to this turn of events convinces Richard that he is in fact the murderer, and he shoots Cord with Alex's gun.

The gunshot is heard at the moment the scene fades out, making the conclusion of the film both surprising and ambiguous. Bone, who has not acted decisively elsewhere in the film, seems abruptly to absorb the dead

Cutter's violent energy, willing himself to fire. Cord has not actually revealed himself as the murderer, but the attitude he has assumed and other pieces of information in the film indicate that Bone has correctly identified him. There is another important character in the story, George Swanson (Arthur Rosenberg), a boat salesman who is linked to Cutter and Bone on one hand and Cord on the other. He is friends with the two younger men (it is he who treats them to lunch at the country club where Mrs. Cord overhears Alex's brutal ramblings about the killing—and he who inadvertently supplies the party invitation) and Richard occasionally works for him informally as a salesman. Alex learns that Cord had ruined George's father, prompting the latter's suicide, and had subsequently set up George in business in later years. Throughout the film, George is at the same time fearful for the safety of Alex and Richard and fearful for his own position. Unlike Alex, he is not a paranoid iconoclast, and his tacit acknowledgment of Cord's power and the ruthlessness with which Cord is willing to exercise that power seems to confirm Cord's guilt. Cord's alleged murder of the teenage girl is only one of several ambiguities of the film, however, and if the internal evidence confirms his guilt, it is still possible for the second ambiguity, Mo's death, to be interpreted in a different manner. The tone of the film implies that this is either the tragic accident it initially appears to be or the suicide that Richard believes it to be, rather than the second murder which the grief-stricken Alex too readily insists upon. Alex is a man who easily succumbs to delusion and Cord's guilt in the initial murder seems incidental to Alex's obsessions and meaningful to the central drama of *Cutter's Way* only as a catalyst for the crystallization of the Cutter/Bone symbiosis which occurs in the final image.

The flaw of *Cutter's Way* is that the mystery element—although given equal weight to the relationships between Alex, Richard, and Mo—is always a shade less interesting than those relationships. The mystery is adequately handled and the climactic party and shooting are compelling, but the film ultimately leaves an impression of contriving to resurrect genre conventions which it imbues with insufficient conviction. On the other hand, many contemporary films offer pale and mechanical imitations of classical forms as if they were the real thing, and *Cutter's Way* is to be praised for its deeper purposes at the very least. Jeffrey Alan Fishkin's often witty screenplay offers some incisive dialogue, most memorably Mo's harsh reproach of Alex—"It's like your leg . . . sending messages to your brain only there's nothing there." Alex's status as a crippled Vietnam veteran is not seized upon for any glib social commentary. Although he is articulate about the justified disenchantment caused by the war, he cleverly uses his "broken shell of a man" image to manipulate people. Most happily, the screenplay and the novel from which Fishkin adapted it offer characterizations which bring out all the skill and understanding of director Ivan Passer.

Relatively uncelebrated, Czech-born Passer possesses an intriguingly personal style which seems to thrive on offbeat material. Unlike his contemporary, Milos Forman, who emigrated from Czechoslovakia at about the same time, Passer seems disdainful of the crowd-pleasing instincts which have won such wide attention for Forman's American films (*One Flew Over the Cuckoo's Nest*, 1975, *Hair*, 1978, and *Ragtime*, 1981). Passer is more tough-minded and appreciative of moral ambiguity than Forman as well as being a more skillful *metteur-en-scène* on a scene-to-scene basis. His adeptness with actors is especially evident in the three principal performances. Lisa Eichorn's portrayal of an alcoholic has a subtlety not normally associated with such a characterization, and Passer is careful not to sentimentalize her. As a result, the emotion aroused by Mo's death is honestly earned. John Heard is necessarily intense in his showy role as Cutter, but there is a subtle differentiation between the character's insincere posturing and his real emotions. Passer is very observant of Heard's admirable ability to give a sense of a real man at odd moments in the most theatrical scenes. In the least dramatic of the three leading roles, Jeff Bridges confirms his stature as one of the best and most natural contemporary actors. The charms and weaknesses of Richard Bone are inextricably linked, and Bridges is an actor with the intelligence to appreciate this and the willingness to make such a character seem reflective of his own personality.

Passer never settles for the obvious approach to a scene. For example, a scene of Richard and Mo making love is executed in a single stable close shot and is very quiet, in contrast to the conventions of frenzied editing and ecstatic moans which recently have become common in such scenes. Mo's pleasure is the subtlest and least pronounced aspect of the scene and is less immediately evident than her plaintive weeping. Dramatic confrontations tend to be oblique, although almost every scene is rife with latent conflict. Richard, Alex, and Mo drift about the frames, each of them selfishly protective of his or her own space. As a result, an extremely close three shot in which Richard and Alex almost come to blows over Alex's treatment of Mo is at once unexpected and very dramatically cogent. Passer supports the characterizations by an attention to the Santa Barbara atmosphere so essential to the overall mood of the film. The images and sound of *Cutter's Way* are continually reflective of a desire for both clarity and delicacy. Jordan Cronenweth's lighting is notably vibrant and nuanced. In addition, the sound track subtly alternates the festive mariachi music which defines the film's specific time and place and an unusual zither and glass harmonica score composed by Jack Nitzsche.

From the opening slow-motion credit sequence—in which participants in a fiesta parade gaily glide forth in counterpoint to Nitzsche's melancholy music as the black-and-white image slowly metamorphosizes into vivid color—*Cutter's Way* is a film with a singular aesthetic aura, carefully created and sustained by Passer and his crew. This care and the accompanying rich treatment of character override the relative weakness of the surface narrative. Suggestive of the seriousness and individuality which can still be instilled into mainstream filmmaking, *Cutter's Way* leaves a haunting impression.

Blake Lucas

Reviews

The Hollywood Reporter. March 18, 1981, p. 3.
Los Angeles Times. September 13, 1981, *Calendar*, p. 30.
The New Republic. CLXXXV, August 15, 1981, pp. 26-27.
The New York Times. March 20, 1981, III, p. 6.
Variety. March 18, 1981, p. 3.

DRAGONSLAYER

Production: Hal Barwood for Paramount and Walt Disney Productions
Direction: Matthew Robbins
Screenplay: Hal Barwood and Matthew Robbins
Cinematography: Derek Vanlint
Editing: Tony Lawson
Art direction: Alan Cassie
Photographic effects: Industrial Light & Magic, Inc.
Music: Alex North
MPAA rating: PG
Running time: 108 minutes

Principal characters:
Galen .... Peter MacNicol
Valerian .... Caitlin Clarke
Ulrich .... Ralph Richardson
Tyrian .... John Hallam
Casidorus Rex .... Peter Eyre
Greil .... Albert Salmi
Hodge .... Sydney Bromley
Princess Elspeth .... Chloe Salaman
Simon .... Emrys James

Dragonslayer is a fantasy of sword and sorcery, dragons and death; it is also a retelling of the age-old story of the journey from adolescence to adulthood. A collaborative effort from Paramount and Walt Disney Productions, the critically admired film features some of the most dazzling special effects of the 1980's, particularly a heinous dragon, named Vermithrax Pejorative, created by George Lucas' Industrial Light & Magic, Inc. Brilliantly engineered, at a cost of some four million dollars—approximately one-quarter of the film's budget—Vermithrax is ninety feet in length, with a wingspan of forty feet. The dragon incinerates young virgins, battles with a venerable sorcerer, and spawns hideous dragonlets which feast on human flesh. Truly a denizen of childhood nightmares, the creature was, however, unable to triumph over the "Man of Steel" or the intrepid explorer Indiana Jones, for the summer of 1981 belonged to *Raiders of the Lost Ark* and *Superman II*. *Dragonslayer* was a disappointment at the box office, but it may be vindicated with time, for with its period setting, fantasy theme, and the wonderful Vermithrax, it has an ever-youthful quality. With outlets such as subscription and cable television, the film will continue to find new audiences.

Part of the "sword-and-sorcery" trend popularized by productions such as *Excalibur* (1981) and films of 1982 such as John Milius' *Conan the Barbarian* and the low-budget *Sword and the Sorcerer*, *Dragonslayer* also signifies the growing pains of a former industry giant. Amidst much publicity, the Disney studio has been seeking a return to critical praise and large audiences. Attempting to change with the times, it teamed with Paramount for the Robert Altman-directed *Popeye*, a disappointing but saucy musical of 1980, prior to *Dragonslayer*.

More adult in theme and intensity than most Disney products, *Dragonslayer* is rated PG for a brief glimpse of nudity as well as scenes of violence. It is a film of somber moods; its superlative art direction suggests the twilight of sorcery and the dawn of Christianity. It stands as an auspicious early film for producer Hal Barwood and director Matthew Robbins, who also collaborated on *Dragonslayer*'s script.

The film opens at Castle Cragganmore, where the ancient enchanter Ulrich (Ralph Richardson) has premonitions of an end to the "Dark Ages," and an end to magic. His young apprentice, the eager Galen (Peter MacNicol) cannot comprehend such fears. For him, magic summons up great possibilities. Esteemed as the last remaining sorcerer, Ulrich is later summoned by a disheveled group of travelers, led by a youth named Valerian (Caitlin Clarke), who have come to his gate begging help. Their homes and families, in faraway Urland, have long been ravaged by Vermithrax, the last of the great dragons. Because their king has made a pact with the creature, which means choosing sacrificial virgins by a lottery process, the villagers want to save their daughters. It remains for the renowned Ulrich to bring them salvation.

Although the request is yet another sign of his own cloudy future ("Without sorcerers, there wouldn't be dragons," he tells Galen), Ulrich reluctantly agrees to help. Before he can leave, however, he is challenged by Lord Tyrian (John Hallam), the king's centurion who has been dispatched to halt the sorcerer. In a test of magic, the ancient enchanter fails, meeting his death. It is now up to his apprentice to help the Urlanders. In command of Ulrich's magic amulet, and with the sorcerer's old retainer, Hodge (Sydney Bromley) at his side, Galen begins his journey. Along the way he performs some lighthearted feats—suspending balls in midair, making Hodge's clothing disappear (leaving the spindly little old man in his underwear), and musing over his pending encounter with the dragon. There is also a dark moment, however, when Hodge is killed by Tyrian. Galen makes a blushing discovery about Valerian, when he strips off his clothes and dives into a lake, joining the youth in a swim. Approaching Valerian from underwater, Galen sees that "he" is actually a "she." He sputters and coughs his way to the surface while she makes her way to land and dry clothing. Her feminine form hidden beneath baggy clothing and her dark hair pushed beneath a cap, she later tells Galen that her crafty father reared her in a boy's disguise to save her from the dreaded lottery.

Implored to keep her secret, Galen continues with the band to Urland, where he immediately conjures up a massive landslide which buries the dragon's lair. The village of Swanscombe celebrates the feat with a night of song and dance. It is at this time that Simon the blacksmith (Emrys James) introduces his friends and neighbors to Valerian—his daughter. Shyly wearing her first dress, Valerian stands uncertainly before the villagers, who are shocked by the deception and the new discovery. The moment is made more comfortable when a gallant Galen, the hero of the hour, steps forward to escort her in dance.

Yet Galen's triumph is short-lived, for he is ordered to the castle of King Casidorus (Peter Eyre). Casidorus is angered by the youth's assault on the lair, and he is unimpressed with the simple magic tricks he performs (such as sending a table shaking). Confiscating Galen's amulet, the king orders him imprisoned, but Galen is set free by the beautiful Princess Elspeth (Chloe Salaman), who is growing distressed over her father's fanatical edicts—including the lottery which, she learns, has never included her name.

Galen's escape occurs as earthquakes wrack the country, signaling that Vermithrax still lives. Believing prayer to be a formidable weapon, a Christian monk nears the lair, certain that Vermithrax is Lucifer incarnate. He is immediately incinerated, as the fearsome monster takes flight, soaring above Urland, venting its heated anger. The once-jubilant Galen is now subdued, for the quest to kill the dragon remains. So do attempts to quell the beast's evil. For that reason, the king calls another lottery, and draws his own daughter's name. It is a numbing moment for the king, for without his knowledge, Princess Elspeth rigged the lottery to make certain only she would be called.

Desperate to save his only child, the king returns the amulet to Galen. Armed with the amulet, a special lance forged by Simon, and a shield made of dragon scales, fashioned by Valerian, Galen cautiously enters the cavernous depths of the lair. When the imposing Vermithrax comes up behind him, he spies its reflection in water, then spins around and uses his shield against the dragon's shafts of flames. As the battle continues, the seemingly invincible lance is broken. Galen's spirit is also diminishing, until he recalls mysterious instructions from his mentor. With the help of the amulet, he carries out the curious command—and afterward finds Ulrich standing before him. Not really dead, the old master had saved himself for a final battle. On the highest peak in the country, set against a nighttime sky, the dragon and the sorcerer—the last symbols of a darkened world—carry out a dramatic duel. Galen assists, to his great remorse, for when the murderous Vermithrax at last explodes in a fiery ball, the apprentice's beloved Ulrich also meets his demise.

Ending as darkly as it began, *Dragonslayer* then finds the opportunist king claiming to be the dragon killer. He is hailed as the victor, while a sadly bemused Galen leaves Urland with Valerian, whom he loves. Now a better sorcerer than he had thought, he also knows his magical talents are no longer needed. At the story's end, the symbols of Christianity have replaced those of pagan Britain.

With its setting in sixth century Britain, and art direction drawing upon early Celtic and Anglo-Saxon influences, *Dragonslayer* is an atmospheric adventure filled with intriguing nuances, among them the dawn of a new religious awakening. A film of moody splendor, it is most effective when heralding the presence of the truly terrifying Vermithrax. Not until Galen enters its lair is the creature seen in its entirety. Earlier scenes, photographed to hint at the beast's fearsomeness, reveal an ugly, clawed "paw" and a winding, scaled tail. After such anticipation, the descent into the lair—and the face-to-face confrontation with the dragon—does not disappoint. The creature was designed with such meticulous care and dramatic scope that it is the highlight of the film—whether shown in part, or in whole. Adding to its ominous mystique is its dreaded lair, which spews smokey rumblings. Additionally, the dragon's offspring—ugly little dragonlets—are never treated coyly as "cute" creatures. Rather, they are seen feasting on the flesh of the brave Princess Elspeth. Thus, there are no qualms on the part of the audience when Galen drives his lance through them.

Because of such violence, *Dragonslayer* was among a handful of 1981 films (including *Raiders of the Lost Ark*) which attracted attention for what some critics perceived as a lax rating. Alongside the film's derring-do, the love story between Galen and Valerian is less colorful, though genuinely pleasant. Especially affecting is the scene in which the two declare their love for each other. Valerian is at first concerned that Galen has fallen in love with the Princess (who is later sacrificed), and gives him the dragon-scaled shield. She dared to go into the lair, collecting the scales, because of her love for him. Knowing this, Galen professes his love. With a lottery pending, however, the virginal Valerian still worries for her safety—which caused several critics to suggest that a lovemaking scene would have put such fears to rest.

Aside from a few criticisms directed at the script, as well as several comparisons to *Star Wars* (1977), which also involves a world-weary "sorcerer" of sorts and his eager apprentice (Ben Kenobi and Luke Skywalker), *Dragonslayer* was highly regarded by most critics. Performances by Peter MacNicol and Caitlin Clarke, as Galen and Valerian, were enjoyable, and the distinguished British actor Ralph Richardson, as Ulrich, was an appropriate scene-stealer.

Vermithrax draws upon the Disney tradition. In concept and detailed creation, it is every bit as astounding as the giant squid which was constructed for *20,000 Leagues Under the Sea* (1954). Whereas some Disney dragons are the fat, friendly type, as in *Pete's Dragon* (1977), the studio's disappointing attempt at another *Mary Poppins*, Vermithrax joins the resourceful and cruel school epitomized by the brilliantly animated winged beast of *Sleeping Beauty* (1959), in which the alter ego of the mad Maleficent took dragon form.

A sign of new life for Disney, and another eventful fantasy venture for

Paramount (which has earned large profits with *Star Trek* films), *Dragonslayer* is also a testament to the talents of Barwood and Robbins. Their first film-making venture as producer and director, respectively, was the disappointing comedy *Corvette Summer* (1978), which followed successful scripts for films such as Steven Spielberg's *The Sugarland Express* (1974) and *The Bingo Long Travelling All-Stars and Motor Kings* (1976), a film about a barnstorming black baseball team.

Pat H. Broeske

Reviews

The Hollywood Reporter. June 19, 1981, p. 2.
Los Angeles Times. June 29, 1981, VI, p. 2.
The New York Times. June 26, 1981, III, p. 10.
The New Yorker. LVII, July 13, 1981, pp. 80-81.
Time. CXVIII, July 6, 1981, p. 69.
Variety. June 19, 1981, p. 3.

THE EARTHLING

Origin: Australia
Released: 1980
Released in U.S.: 1981
Production: Elliot Schick and John Strong for Filmways
Direction: Peter Collinson
Screenplay: Lanny Cotler
Cinematography: Don McAlpine
Editing: Frank Morriss
Art direction: Bob Hilditch
Music: Dick De Benedictics
MPAA rating: PG
Running time: 98 minutes

Principal characters:
Patrick Foley .... William Holden
Shawn Daley .... Ricky Schroder
Ross Daley .... Jack Thompson
Bettina Daley .... Olivia Hamnett

The title of *The Earthling* is deceptive. It is not a science-fiction extravaganza in the mold of *Alien* (1980); rather, it is the pleasant, harmless tale of a young boy, stranded in the Australian outback, who learns about survival and ecology from a terminally ill old man. It is adequate family entertainment in an era when it is increasingly difficult to find an inoffensive feature for a Saturday afternoon.

The story centers on only two characters. Crusty, self-centered, world-weary Patrick Foley (William Holden) is a former soldier-of-fortune with a mysterious ailment. He has returned to Australia from the United States to die in the wilderness in which he was reared, leaving the audience to wonder occasionally how such an ill man can hike for days through the mountains. Meanwhile, Shawn Daley (Ricky Schroder), an overprotected ten-year-old boy, is on a camping trip with his parents (Olivia Hamnett and Jack Thompson). Foley and the Daleys meet briefly in a dilapidated gas station. Soon after their brief meeting, Shawn becomes an orphan when the family camper goes off a cliff, killing his parents.

Alone and stranded in a remote area of the bush, Shawn is confronted by an assortment of strange and intimidating creatures: wild dogs, snakes, rats, lizards, and porcupines. He then meets Foley, who has observed the accident. The old man, all too aware that soon he will die, does not have the time or inclination to return Shawn to civilization, so he decides to take the boy to his farm, located in a hidden valley. While on the way, he imparts his knowledge to Shawn so that the boy may later find his way back on his own.

Foley at first growls and sneers at Shawn, treating the boy like excess baggage. Gradually, though, he grows fond of Shawn, yet is unable to express his feelings—a problem that is solved as time allows the boy's companionship to break down his defenses. Foley learns that he needs the boy, and that he also needs friendship and attention. At the same time, he teaches Shawn self-reliance. They sleep under the stars, climb mountains, and hike through the bush. The man catches fish with his bare hands and captures wild animals, shows the boy how to fix an outdoor bed—using soft leaves, under a tall tree—and explains how to determine what types of berries are edible. Naturally Shawn grows to care for his mentor. The finale is predictable but not overly maudlin: Foley dies; Shawn buries him; and then begins the long journey back to civilization.

The key to *The Earthling* is not the ending but the growing relationship between Foley and Shawn, the changes each undergoes, and the effect that adult and child have on each other. The film, shot in the wilderness outside Sydney, benefits mostly from the solid performances of its stars, who play opposite each other quite effectively.

William Holden, in one of his last screen roles, gives an entertaining, thoroughly professional performance. In the latter stages of his career, he specialized in playing cynical, worn-out characters similar to Patrick Foley—all middle-aged versions of Joe Gillis, the penniless scriptwriter in the Billy Wilder/Gloria Swanson classic, *Sunset Boulevard* (1950). He was most effective in this type of characterization in *Network* (1976), which earned him his last Academy Award nomination, and *S.O.B.* (1981), his final screen credit.

Ricky Schroder, who was nine years old when *The Earthling* was filmed, had earlier risen to fame by re-creating Jackie Cooper's role in *The Champ* (1979), opposite Jon Voight and Faye Dunaway. Schroder was a find, a male Margaret O'Brien who could turn his tear ducts on at random and who held his weight among the seasoned professionals with whom he acted. His main competition that year was Justin Henry, so memorable in *Kramer vs. Kramer*. While Henry earned an Academy Award nomination—Schroder did not, but easily could have—he beat his rival in the Golden Globe awards as Best New Male Star of the Year. Unlike Henry, Schroder has continued his film career, appearing in Disney's *The Last Flight of Noah's Ark* (1980); the made-for-television feature, *Little Lord Fauntleroy* (1980), opposite Sir Alec Guinness, in a role played in 1922 by Mary Pickford and 1936 by Freddie Bartholomew; and *An Orchestra Is a Team, Too* (1981), also for television, with Joe Namath. In 1980 he was even signed to star in a planned remake of *Peter Pan*—the first male star to act the role.

Also appearing briefly in *The Earthling* are two of Australia's best-known film actors. Olivia Hamnett, who played Richard Chamberlain's wife in *The Last Wave* (1977), is good as Schroder's mother, and Jack Thompson is equally effective as his father. Thompson, a fine actor with a dynamic screen presence, could be described as the Australian Robert Redford. He won an Australian Best Actor Academy Award and Cannes Film Festival Best Supporting Actor prize for his work in *Breaker Morant* (1980), and recently appeared opposite Ingrid Bergman in *Golda* (1982), a made-for-television movie.

The Earthling's director, Peter Collinson, is known mostly for pretentious, forgettable films such as *The Penthouse* (1967), *The Italian Job* (1969), and *Fright* (1971). His work here is adequate at best; mostly, it is too gimmicky, with one-too-many arty camera angles. Collinson's effort is easily overshadowed by the contribution of veteran Australian cinematographer Don McAlpine. His photography of the stunning scenery and unusual wildlife is appropriately lush, with the flora and fauna of the Australian countryside generously displayed. McAlpine has a strong feel for what he is shooting here. He has worked on some of Australia's top features, including Gillian Armstrong's *My Brilliant Career* (1979) and Bruce Beresford's *Breaker Morant*.

The Earthling, which regrettably received generally negative reviews and a limited release in the United States, had its share of production problems. The film was initially budgeted at $4,500,000. At one point, one of its producers, Elliot Schick, formerly the executive in charge of production at EMI Films who had joined with film packager and financier Stephen W. Sharmat's newly formed International Creative Financing Group, failed to put William Holden's salary in escrow. The project was on the verge of coming to a standstill when enough money was raised to complete the shoot. Holden, who had already unpacked his bags and canceled his trip to the Australian location, then returned to the project.

Money was not, however, the actor's main concern. "It's a story that has seemed very special, something I've really wanted to do," he told columnist Marilyn Beck. Of course the film was completed, but Holden had no way of knowing that, in just two years, he would die, not in the outback which he loved so much, but in his apartment, after bleeding to death from a cut received in a fall.

Rob Edelman

Reviews

The Hollywood Reporter. February 6, 1981, p. 42.
Los Angeles Times. February 13, 1981, VI, p. 8.
The New York Times. February 8, 1981, p. 55.
Variety. July 30, 1980, p. 26.

ESCAPE FROM NEW YORK

Production: Larry Franco and Debra Hill for Avco Embassy
Direction: John Carpenter
Screenplay: John Carpenter and Nick Castle
Cinematography: Dean Cundey
Editing: Todd Ramsay
Art direction: Joe Alves
Music: John Carpenter and Alan Howarth
MPAA rating: R
Running time: 99 minutes

Principal characters:
Snake Plissken ....Kurt Russell
Bob Hauk .... Lee Van Cleff
Cabbie .... Ernest Borgnine
President of the United States ......Donald Pleasence
The Duke of New York ....Issac Hayes
Girl in Chock Full O'Nuts .... Season Hubley
Brain .... Harry Dean Stanton
Maggie ....Adrienne Barbeau

In terms of inventive plot, few 1981 films can match *Escape from New York*, a dark futuristic tale in which Manhattan has become the country's maximum security prison. The year is 1997, the crime rate has risen a staggering 400 percent, and, as a result, prison life affords few options. As the opening narration succinctly reveals, "There are no guards inside the prison. Only prisoners and the world they made." As for prison rules, they are exceedingly simple—and chilling: "Once you go in, you don't come out." In *Escape from New York*, however, one-eyed Snake Plissken (Kurt Russell) must do just that. A former war hero turned master criminal, he has been assigned to rescue the President of the United States, whose plane has crashed within the walled city of New York. At stake is the very future of global peace, because in the President's possession is a tape cassette which must be played at a world summit meeting, to be held in twenty-four hours. For Snake, the mission also carries a life or death sentence; he has been injected with microscopic capsules that carry explosives, and they will detonate within twenty-four hours.

As one of the year's top-grossing films, *Escape from New York* gained much critical attention for its writer-director John Carpenter, who "slashed" his way to notoriety with the milestone horror film, *Halloween* (1978). With its cynical premise, including bleak futuristic overtones, and its New Wave and Punk nuances (evident in costuming and hairstyles), it was especially popular with the so-called "youth market," including science-fiction and horror-genre enthusiasts. Further, the film is full of "camp" elements, including the casting, which finds one-time Disney child star Kurt Russell obliterating his all-American boy image with his portrayal of the surly, unshaven Snake. Delivered in a laconic, clenched-jaw style, the Russell performance purposefully mimics those of Clint Eastwood. In the same satirical vein is the film's casting of Lee Van Cleef, costar of Eastwood's famed "spaghetti" Westerns, as Snake's antagonist, Bob Hauk, the crafty police commissioner.

Directed in Carpenter's terse, no-nonsense mode, *Escape from New York* comes at the screen rapid-fire, with few embellishments. Although tucked between the frames are hints of character development, as well as ideology, it is always action first. Opening with an eerie vista of a nighttime New York skyline—without lights, since there is no electricity within the walls—the film reveals the prison's grim realities as two prisoners, attempting escape by raft, are immediately blown up by a hovering helicopter, which was dispatched by an outside tower. Snake Plissken's (Kurt Russell) arrival at the debarkation center is equally grim. As he is led, handcuffed, down stark hallways, an omnipresent voice from a speaker system matter-of-factly drones, "You now have the option to terminate and be cremated on the premises. . . ."

Snake's processing for departure to prison is interrupted when Air Force One, carrying the President (Donald Pleasence), is hijacked. Before the soldiers of the "National Liberation Front of America" can successfully crash the plane into a New York skyscraper, the President handcuffs his briefcase to his wrist and climbs into a special escape pod which is ejected from the plane before the crash.

Tracing the pod's journey via a computerized scanning system, Police Commissioner Bob Hauk (Lee Van Cleef) quickly boards a helicopter, which lands briefly in Manhattan. There, a zombie-like emissary who sports a bizarre laugh and a disquieting presence (he has a glassy eyed hostility, and a shock of hair which sticks straight up), presents Hauk with the President's severed finger, and the demand that he leave immediately—or the President will be murdered. Hauk has no choice but to return to the debarkation center, where he summons Snake to his office.

The meeting between the two men provides the only clues to Snake's dark personality; it also shows a thread of similarity between the two. Both served in "the wars," and each, in a sense, has the look of a futuristic pirate. The long-haired Snake has a black patch over his left eye; Hauk wears a gold earring through his left ear. It is Snake, however, who is the most intriguing. Once a war hero, he received Purple Hearts for missions in Leningrad and Siberia, and was the youngest man ever to be decorated by the President. Then he turned to crime, finally drawing a life sentence for the robbery of a Federal Reserve Depository. If he appears coolly unruffled by the prospects of prison, Snake does not hide his interest when Hauk proposes a deal. If he will bring the President, and the tape cassette, out of New York within twenty-four hours, he will get a full pardon. To guard against the possibility that Snake will take the escape plane to Canada (and freedom), Hauk has him injected with the deadly capsules. If he succeeds in rescuing the President within the allotted twenty-four hours, the charges can be neutralized with X-rays.

The film's most riveting moments are set within the confines of New York City. Morality is completely gone in Manhattan; criminals and "crazies" rule, and only the strong survive. Thus, as Snake warily makes his way down darkened streets, he is haunted by fleeting shadows and the remnants of a civilization gone mad. Cars have been overturned and set on fire; garbage and graffiti are everywhere; and people brutally prey upon one another. Making his way downstairs in a dilapidated theater, Snake pauses briefly to stare at a woman being gang-raped. Later, in a gutted building that once was a Chock Full O'Nuts coffee shop, he meets a woman (Season Hubley) who is about to offer herself to him—in exchange for transport out of New York. The encounter ends when "crazies" beneath the floorboards pull the screaming woman downwards.

Tracing the President by signals from a special vital signs bracelet which he wears, Snake's nighttime odyssey pits him against the fearsome Duke of New York (Isaac Hayes), undisputed kingpin of the city. The Duke and his followers are holding the President hostage, unaware that any demands they might have will be pointless within twenty-four hours. In carrying out his mission, Snake enlists the aid of several reluctant allies, including Cabbie (Ernest Borgnine), Brain (Harry Dean Stanton), and Maggie (Adrienne Barbeau), who is identified as Brain's "squeeze" and a gift from the Duke.

Before they attempt to spirit the President across the 69th Street Bridge, which has been mined to make escape impossible, Snake goes through a series of adventures. Betrayed by Brain (who later changes sides), he is turned over to the Duke, shot in the leg with an arrow, and beaten unconscious. When he awakens, he is led to a bloody boxing ring where he must do battle, gladiator-style, with a hulking opponent. Their weapons are nail-filled baseball bats, and Snake is able to drive his into his opponent's head, to the delight of the screaming crowd. Once the battle ends, Snake is able to escape to the streets, where he is reunited with Brain and Maggie, who have the petrified President and the good-natured Cabbie in tow. A taxi driver for thirty years (with a penchant for listening to big band sounds on his car's cassette player), Cabbie persistently turns up throughout the film when Snake, whom he admires, needs him most. While crossing the mined bridge, though, Cabbie's car is torn in half, and Cabbie dies instantly, leaving the others to run on foot. When Brain also triggers a mine and meets his death, Maggie reaches for Snake's gun. No longer interested in escape, she stands on the bridge, awaiting the inevitable arrival of the Duke. Yet despite her bullets, he successfully runs her down, and reaches Snake at the wall, just as the President is being pulled to freedom. The two criminals engage in brutal hand-to-hand combat, with Snake getting the worst of it. Just as the Duke is reaching for his gun to finish off his adversary, however, he is shot by a near-hysterical President, screaming from atop the wall. After being pulled to safety, Snake immediately submits to the neutralization of the detonating devices. Afterward, he looks at his watch, which shows only two seconds to spare.

A tired, angry Snake is then approached by Hauk, who has other projects in mind. "We'd make one hell of a team," he tells an incredulous Snake, who walks away without acknowledging the offer. The President, meanwhile, is being made up for a television broadcast, at which he will play the critical cassette which was retrieved by Snake for the summit conference. In the aftermath of the violent rescue mission, Snake wryly observes the transformation of the once-trembling kidnap victim to self-assured bureaucrat. He tries to talk to the President, but is told that air time is approaching. As he trudges dejectedly away, the President steps before the cameras and states "I present this in the hope that our great nations may learn to live in peace." He then inserts the cassette into a player, but instead of stern words about nuclear war, the tape carries only a selection of big band music. In the distance, Snake, who has obviously switched the President's tape with Cabbie's, casually unravels the tape once considered so vital to world peace. On that cynical note, the film comes to an end.

At the time of its release, *Escape from New York* which was budgeted at seven million dollars, was Carpenter's most ambitious project (*Halloween* was filmed for $320,000). Much of the film's striking futuristic look is the result of the shrewd work of art director Joe Alves, who utilized locations in St. Louis, New York, and Los Angeles, as well as miniature sets. As with any science-fiction film, one of the film's highlights is its vision of the future; in the case of *Escape from New York*, that vision entails a look at the World Trade Center (Snake's special escape plane lands on top of it), as well as a crumbling Madison Square Garden, where the gladiator bout is staged.

Escape from New York was actually the first film project to be written by Carpenter since his days at the University of Southern California, where he became involved with *The Resurrection of Bronco Billy* (1970) and the Midnight Circuit favorite, *Dark Star* (1974), but it was not made until Carpenter had established himself as a critically acclaimed genre director, notably with *Halloween* and *The Fog* (1980). When he finally returned to *Escape from New York*, it was with USC friend Nick Castle (who portrayed the Shape, the killer of *Halloween*), as cowriter. Produced by Debra Hill, who has teamed with Carpenter for all of his major projects, the film's cast includes performers who have frequently worked with Carpenter. In fact, Russell followed his portrayal of Snake Plissken with the role of MacReady, the reluctant hero of Carpenter's *The Thing* (1982). Adrienne Barbeau, Mrs. John Carpenter, is invariably in her husband's films.

Like most films by Carpenter, *Escape from New York* has a driving single-mindedness which, along with the feeling that the film's premise was actually more invigorating than its production, caused some critical dismay. The film was mostly praised, however, as was Russell's performance, which borrowed heavily from the smug style of Clint Eastwood's early works.

As for the character of Snake, both Russell and Carpenter feel he is unique among movie antiheroes, because he is never redeemed. That was a conscious understanding between actor and filmmaker, says Russell, who has explained,

> We knew we were taking a chance. After all, if audiences didn't like the character, they wouldn't like the film. . . . Every other movie anti-hero does a turn-around. Not Snake. He never helps a kid, or saves a woman. He's a one-dimensional machine of destruction.

Carpenter himself has said that he made *Escape from New York* in order to present "an extremely black comedy, reflecting my very dim, cynical view of life." That view, he says, usually takes the form of finding people trapped—with evil encircling them. "My feeling," Carpenter explains,

> is that evil never goes away. You never can kill it, you can't destroy it, you can never have a definitive ending to it. . . . What makes the films interesting is the fact that the people trapped in the situations bind together to protect themselves—and win. They try to win, and I think this is the way I see life. The only salvation is to fight against the things that plunge you to self-destruction. . . . It is a fight. So you can take it as a metaphor for life.

Metaphors aside, Carpenter's works also often pay homage—sometimes humorously—to filmmakers who have influenced him. In *Escape from New York*, the Duke's zombie-like messenger is named Romero—a salute to George A. Romero, whose 1968 film, *Night of the Living Dead*, unleashed a plague of zombies. The doctor who injects Snake is named Cronenberg—a nod to Canadian filmmaker David Cronenberg, whose film *Scanners* (1981) involved a number of persons who (like Snake) had been triggered to explode.

With Alan Howarth, the versatile Carpenter also composed the gyrating score for *Escape from New York*. He is now at work on his latest production, *Firestarter* (based on the best-selling novel by horror master Stephen King), following his recent poorly received remake of *The Thing*.

Pat H. Broeske

Reviews

The Hollywood Reporter. June 12, 1981, p. 3.
Los Angeles Times. July 10, 1981, VI, p. 5.

The New York Times. August 2, 1981, II, p. 15.
Newsweek. XCVIII, July 27, 1981, p. 75.
Saturday Review. VIII, August, 1981, p. 61.
Time. CXVIII, July 13, 1981, p. 60.
Variety. June 12, 1981, p. 3.

EVERY MAN FOR HIMSELF (SAUVE QUI PEUT [LA VIE])

Origin: Switzerland
Released: 1979
Released in U.S.: 1981
Production: Alain Sarde and Jean-Luc Godard for Sonimage/Sara Films/Saga Productions
Direction: Jean-Luc Godard
Screenplay: Anne Marie Mieville and Jean-Claude Carriere
Cinematography: William Lubtchansky and Renato Berta
Editing: Anne Marie Mieville and Jean-Luc Godard
Art direction: Romain Goupil
Music: Gabriel Yared
Running time: 87 minutes

Principal characters:

Isabelle Riviere .... Isabelle Huppert
Paul Godard .... Jacques Dutronc
Denise Rimbaud .... Nathalie Baye
First client .... Fred Personne
Second client .... Roland Amstutz
Isabelle's sister .... Anna Baldaccini
Paul's daughter .... Cecile Tanner
Paul's ex-wife .... Paule Muret

Since the release of his first feature film, *Breathless* (1959), French director Jean-Luc Godard has challenged both his audiences and the boundaries of cinema itself. He has captivated, baffled, and sometimes angered filmgoers with his highly personal themes and techniques, and each new Godard picture never fails to generate considerable interest and anticipation. After the violence and upheaval in France in May, 1968, Godard concentrated all his talents toward creating films that were overtly political in content. For the next ten years, the majority of his work was largely inaccessible to all but the most dedicated film scholars, and the relentlessness of his political didacticism alienated many in his former audience. Much of this work was done along experimental lines, often with videotape for French television, further limiting the director's accessibility to a wider audience.

In 1979, however, Godard made a stunning return to the realm of international filmmaking with *Sauve Qui Peut (La Vie)*. The film's English title is *Every Man for Himself*, a phrase which captures perfectly the spirit of the film's action. Godard has called the film his "second first film," and it is indeed a radical break with the ten years of work which preceded it. Gone are the blatant political messages and long character monologues that typified his work from that period. In their place is a freshness and vitality that garnered the film much critical praise when it opened.

Godard's theme in *Every Man for Himself* is, as the title suggests, alienation and isolation. His story follows three characters, two women and a man, as their lives connect, interact, and finally diverge. Each has his or her own method of existing within society, and each method leads eventually to the exclusion of the other two. In Godard's view, it is this alienation which permeates Western society and which leaves each of us ultimately alone in our struggle with life.

The film is set in Switzerland, where Godard himself now lives. Its story is divided into four sections: "The Imaginary," "Fear," "Commerce," and "Music." "The Imaginary" tells the story of Denise Rimbaud (Nathalie Baye), a young woman working for a Swiss television station. Denise longs to leave her life in the city and move to the country, where she hopes to work for a small journal and perhaps write a book. When we first see Denise, she is pedaling a bicycle along a country road. Godard films her using stop-motion photography, and the effect is exhilarating. Each brief freeze frame captures and extends the moment that it records, emphasizing the freedom that Denise experiences on the open country roads. The choice of a bicycle over a car as her means of transportation is deliberate since the car represents the repressive city life she is trying to escape. For Godard, the car is a symbol of modern society which will figure in several of the film's key scenes, just as its absence is important in our introduction to Denise.

The other clue to Denise's search for a happier life is the notebook that she carries with her. Throughout the film, she writes her thoughts and feelings in it. Asked repeatedly if the notes she is making are for a book, she will reply only "It might be someday." What is important for Denise is the act of writing itself—her first step toward reaching the goal she has set for herself.

Denise finds a place to live and telephones her lover, Paul Godard (Jacques Dutronc), telling him that she is planning to rent her apartment in the city when she moves. This begins the second section of the film, "Fear," as we pick up Paul's story. Unlike Denise, Paul is a willing victim of modern society. He has no home of his own, choosing instead to live in a sterile, impersonal hotel. He has left his wife and daughter and has allowed an icy distance to grow between himself and his child. Paul, too, works in television, but he lacks Denise's desire to seek out a less commercial life-style and he is furious at her decision to leave him. Our introduction to Paul comes as he leaves his hotel in the film's opening scene, and later appears before a class discussing the work of writer/director Marguerite Duras. The class has listened to a tape of her voice, and Paul explains that Duras herself refuses to appear. It is here that we first glimpse Paul's spiritual malaise. Commenting on his own work, he tells the class that "I make movies to keep myself busy. If I had the strength, I'd do nothing."

We learn of Paul's relationship with his daughter, Cecile (Cecile Tanner, daughter of Swiss director Alain Tanner) when he picks her up at a sports field. He discusses her with a friend in crudely incestuous terms, and while there is no indication that he has ever acted along these lines, his words are startling nevertheless. Paul and Cecile drive from the sports field to the television station to see Denise. Paul had taken Marguerite Duras to the airport earlier, and Denise, who had planned to work with her on a television show, berates him for his selfishness at not convincing her to stay. Father and daughter then join Paul's ex-wife (Paule Muret) for dinner, where her parents quarrel as Cecile watches and listens. Paul has brought his daughter a present—an assortment of T-shirts in different colors—and he tosses them at her across the table with undisguised hostility when she demands her gift. Later that evening, he meets a prostitute named Isabelle Riviere (Isabelle Huppert) while waiting in line at the movies, and he trades one form of escape for another when he accompanies her back to his hotel.

In its third section, "Commerce," the film picks up the story of Isabelle, and it is here that Godard comes closest to his earlier films. As Isabelle leaves the hotel, she is accosted and threatened by two pimps, who demand fifty percent of her profits. When she returns home, her sister (Anna Baldaccini) is waiting, having come to ask Isabelle for an introduction to the world of prostitution. Isabelle matter-of-factly surveys her figure, vividly describes the type of acts she may be required to perform, then demands fifty percent of her earnings. The profit motive is alive and well in this section of the film as Godard repeats one of his most obsessive themes: the equivalence of capitalism and prostitution. We see Isabelle with two clients; one a man (Fred Personne) who fantasizes that she is his daughter, and the other a businessman (Roland Amstutz) who arranges a bizarre encounter involving himself, his assistant, and two women. He organizes a carefully orchestrated sexual chain reaction which he oversees while taking phone calls. The scene is both shocking and comical in its depiction of the man's ruthless need to dominate those around him.

Throughout the events we witness, Isabelle demonstrates a complete separation between her work and her private feelings. She moves through her day like a sleepwalker, untouched by any of the numerous attempts that are made to humiliate her. She survives her life by removing herself from it, yet she, like Denise, has thoughts of something better. When a friend offers her a job as a drug courier, she accepts and makes plans to find a new apartment. The one she chooses belongs to Denise, making the film's circle complete.

In the final section, "Music," Denise has moved to the country, but we are uncertain if the change has brought her the satisfaction she is seeking; Isabelle is living in Denise's old apartment, but is still a prostitute; and Paul remains in the city. Sudden catastrophe, however, is a staple of Godard's films, and *Every Man for Himself* is no exception. Following a chance encounter with his ex-wife and Cecile, Paul is struck by a car driven by a client of Isabelle's sister. As he lies injured in the street, his former wife turns and pulls her daughter away from the scene, telling her that it has nothing to do with them. The film's final image is of Cecile, walking away from her dying father.

Godard's pessimism regarding the impermanence of human relationships is crystallized in this shot as we see the indifference that is shaping the adult that Cecile will become. For all of the characters in the film, relationships bring pain and hardship. The remote Isabelle is the extreme example of the eventual result of this environment; she chooses to live without emotion altogether. For her, an inhuman aloofness is the only refuge from constant degradation, and she has managed a complete split between her outer life and her inner self. In Paul's case, the reaction is just the opposite. He has allowed himself to become one with the life he leads, and the result is a selfish, thoroughly repellent man. In Denise, we see still another choice. Her efforts are directed toward shaping her outer life to fit her inner feelings, and of the three, she seems to have the best chance at finding some measure of happiness.

The title of the film's last section refers to a running joke which appears throughout the film. As the film's melodious sound track plays, someone on the screen will look up in bewilderment and ask "Where is that music coming from?" As Cecile walks away from her father, she passes an orchestra playing the score in the street. This is but one of Godard's devices to keep his audience constantly aware that they are watching a film. Time and time again he takes us out of the story with the music, the stop-motion photography, and even the character's names. Many of the actors, including Isabelle Huppert, Cecile Tanner, and even one of Isabelle's clients, play characters whose first names are the same as their own. In the case of Paul and Denise, the point is carried even further. Paul, of course, bears the last name of the director himself, and Denise's surname is the same as that of the French poet, Arthur Rimbaud, who, like Denise, left the city in hopes of finding himself. We are not real, these characters seem to tell us; we are only representative figures in a film.

If *Every Man for Himself* is Godard's statement on the condition of modern society, it is also a sign of the filmmaker's own state of mind. Although he has lost none of the vigor with which he has condemned capitalism and consumerism in the past decade, he has broadened his view to include private dreams in the scope of his vision as well. The attempt to reconcile these two areas is the challenge which motivates the film, and Godard explores this challenge with a resurgence of the style and force that infused his earlier films.

Janet E. Lorenz

Reviews

The Hollywood Reporter. October 21, 1980, p. 18.
Los Angeles Times. January 11, 1981, *Calendar*, p. 21.
The New York Times. May 4, 1981, II, p. 13.
The New Yorker. LVI, November 24, 1980, p. 197.
Variety. May 28, 1980, p. 15.

EXCALIBUR

Production: John Boorman for Orion
Direction: John Boorman
Screenplay: John Boorman and Rospo Pallenberg; based on the chronicle *Le Morte d'Arthur* by Sir Thomas Malory
Cinematography: Alex Thomson
Editing: Donn Cambern
Art direction: Anthony Pratt
Music: Trevor Jones
MPAA rating: R
Running time: 140 minutes

Principal characters:

King Arthur .... Nigel Terry
Morgana .... Helen Mirren
Lancelot .... Nicholas Clay
Guinevere .... Cherie Lunghi
Perceval .... Paul Geoffrey
Merlin .... Nicol Williamson
Mordred .... Robert Addie
Uther .... Gabriel Byrne
Igrayne .... Katrine Boorman

After the success of *Star Wars* (1977), it seemed natural that film producers should wish to go back to that period of English mythic history when an Obi-Wan Kenobi figure was called Merlin, Luke Skywalker was King Arthur, and the Force was named Excalibur. Director John Boorman has long had a fascination with the legend of King Arthur; he did a modern version of the story for the BBC in the early 1960's entitled *The Quarry*, and at one point was almost able to arrange financing for a live-action production of J. R. R. Tolkien's *The Lord of the Rings*. Boorman, along with his coscreenwriter Rospo Pallenberg, devised a story which utilized elements from T. H. White's *The Once and Future King* and *The Sword and the Stone*, T. S. Eliot's *The Waste Land*, Jesse L. Weston's *The Grail in Myth and Legend*, John Cooper Powys' *The Romance of Glastonbury*, Sir Thomas Malory's *Le Morte d'Arthur*, the writings of Chrétien de Troyes and Wolfram von Eschenbach, and even Richard Wagner's cycle *The Ring of the Nibelungs*.

The result is a film which is both impressive and muddled. The Dark Ages of English legend are exquisitely photographed by Alex Thomson (who received an Academy Award nomination for his work), with many of the settings appearing somber and foreboding. In trying to re-create the dialogue of mythic characters, Boorman and Pallenberg finished up with lines which are both pretentious and silly, such as Merlin's comment to Morgana: "It's a lonely way, you know, the way of the necromancer." (In *The New Yorker*, Pauline Kael described the dialogue simply as "near-atrocious.") Finally, there are so many characters—characters who, with their dirty faces and armor, look so similar—that one is almost half-way through the film before they are sorted out in one's mind.

Excalibur opens with Uther Pendragon (Gabriel Byrne) promising his necromancer Merlin (Nicol Williamson) that he will end his bloody war with the Duke of Cornwall in return for the magical sword of Excalibur. Upon seeing Igrayne (Katrine Boorman), the Duke's wife, however, Uther persuades Merlin to help him enter the Castle in the guise of the Duke of Cornwall and seduce his bride, while Igrayne's small daughter, Morgana, looks on. Merlin agrees upon the condition that "what issues from your lust must be mine." Nine months later, Merlin returns for Uther's first-born, Arthur, whom he places in the care of a poor knight named Ector.

Before he is killed in an ambush, Uther places Excalibur in a stone, from which, Merlin announces, only a true king can remove it. Eighteen years later, the various knights meet in tournament to decide who shall have the right to release the magical sword. None succeed, but by chance the young Arthur (Nigel Terry) is able to remove the sword. He is proclaimed the boy King and goes forth to unite his kingdom, taking with him Merlin as his guide and counselor. In a clearing beside a waterfall, Arthur meets Lancelot (Nicholas Clay), and the two duel and become comrades. (Interestingly, this sequence was filmed at the famed Powerscourt waterfall just outside Dublin in the Republic of Ireland, and this same estate was used by Sir Laurence Olivier to double for Agincourt in his 1944 film version of *Henry V*.)

Arthur forms the fellowship of the Round Table, whose knights represent the ideals of truth, courage, and purity of heart, and builds the castle of Camelot, a symbol of peace in the land. The knights begin to quarrel among themselves, however, and Morgana (Helen Mirren) adds to the dissent by suggesting that Arthur's Queen Guinevere (Cherie Lunghi) has been unfaithful with Lancelot. To prove his loyalty, Lancelot jousts with King Arthur and is nearly killed in the fight; he goes deep into the forest to bathe his wounds. As he lies naked, Guinevere comes to him, and they consummate the love which they have long resisted. There is something disturbing about the innocent quality of the scene as the naked Lancelot and Guinevere lie together, for their act of love will destroy Camelot. It is curious that Lancelot appears nude in a number of scenes; the contrast between his vulnerable naked body and his resplendent armor is but one of many devices by which Boorman seeks to humanize his legendary characters while retaining a certain mythic resonance. Boorman's Camelot is distinctly shabby, in deliberate contrast to the extravagant images conjured up by that name.

Merlin takes Morgana to the caves beneath Camelot, challenging her to look into the eye of the dragon and despair, but it is Merlin who is trapped in a mist which congeals into diamond hardness around him. In a replay of the sorcerous intercourse she witnessed as a child, Morgana sleeps with Arthur in the guise of Guinevere, and gives birth to a son, Mordred, whom she rears with one purpose, to murder his father and ascend to the throne. A spiritual sickness descends upon the land, and the only solution is to send the knights upon a search for the Holy Grail, the symbol of Christ's suffering upon the Cross. One by one the knights are destroyed through Morgana's witchcraft, until only Sir Perceval remains to solve the riddle and find the sacred chalice. King Arthur leads his knights into battle against Mordred. Merlin is released by Arthur's love and tricks Morgana with a spell that takes away her youth and beauty. Both Arthur and Mordred (Robert Addie) are mortally wounded, and the former instructs Sir Perceval (Paul Geoffrey) to take Excalibur to the Lady of the Lake. Reluctantly Sir Perceval obeys, and a hand rises from the water to remove the magical sword from mankind for all time.

In a perceptive review, *Newsweek* (April 13, 1981) noted that "Boorman is both a romantic and a realist, an idealist and a skeptic, and *Excalibur* is an impressive but uneasy attempt to marry these opposites." It is clear from the beginning of the film that Boorman intends to play against the audience's preconceptions. The brutal, rather exotic pagan world of the opening scenes hardly seems English, and the scruffiness of Boorman's warriors contrasts with traditional images of Arthurian glory. Similarly, Cherie Lunghi as Guinevere is physically quite unlike the familiar images of Arthur's queen. Yet it is not Boorman's intention simply to debunk the Arthurian myth. On the contrary, his treatment of Merlin in particular suggests that he sees his story in mythic terms. Boorman has said that he sees Merlin as "a link between the past—the magic world—and the emerging world of man." As played by Nicol Williamson (who, with Helen Mirren, is the only "name" in the cast), Merlin wears a skull cap with a jewel set in the part covering his forehead, almost like a third eye, and Williamson's acting is an uneasy mix of Shakespearean style and a second-rate gangster in American "B"-pictures. Boorman's intentions to invest his story with something of the "twilight of the gods" are greatly undermined by Williamson's Merlin and are not clearly realized at any point in the film.

Excalibur was originally expected to begin production on October 1, 1979, but shooting did not actually commence until March 31, 1980. Budgeted at ten million dollars, *Excalibur* was filmed in the Republic of Ireland on location and at the National Film Studios of Ireland (of which Boorman was the chairman) in Bray, just outside Dublin. The film was finished in mid-July, 1980, the sixth John Boorman production to be shot wholly or in part in the Republic of Ireland. In the first thirty-eight days of its release in the United States, *Excalibur* grossed twenty-five million dollars and was generally conceded to be the cinema's first major hit of 1981. Although it received no

Academy Awards, *Excalibur* was the recipient of a special award at the 1981 Cannes Film Festival.

Anna Kate Sterling

Reviews

The Hollywood Reporter. April 6, 1981, p. 2.
Los Angeles Times. June 17, 1981, VI, p. 1.
The New York Times. April 10, 1981, III, p. 11.
The New Yorker. LVII, April 20, 1981, p. 146.
Newsweek. XCVII, April 13, 1981, p. 82.
Time. CXVII, April 13, 1981, p. 96.
Variety. April 6, 1981, p. 3.

EYE OF THE NEEDLE

Production: Stephen Friedman for Metro-Goldwyn-Mayer/United Artists
Direction: Richard Marquand
Screenplay: Stanley Mann; based on the novel of the same name by Ken Follett
Cinematography; Alan Hume
Editing: Sean Barton
Art direction: Wilfred Shingleton
Music: Miklos Rozsa
MPAA rating: R
Running time: 111 minutes

Principal characters:

Faber	Donald Sutherland
Lucy	Kate Nelligan
Godliman	Ian Bannen
David	Christopher Cazenove
Billy Parkin	Philip Martin Brown
Tom	Alex McCrindle

Eye of the Needle, based on Ken Follett's 1978 best-selling suspense novel, is both a standard, old-fashioned spy-thriller and a romantic drama centering on a conflict of emotions, predictable material given distinction by excellent performances. Though not without ample intrigue, the film is also a character study of a gentlemanly but ruthless, wily killer, Henry Faber (Donald Sutherland), a Nazi spy, never without his trusty, lethal stiletto. Faber has earned the nickname "needle" because of the manner in which he uses that weapon to kill anyone getting in the way of his work.

The first section of the film is rather difficult to follow because of its seemingly unrelated parallel action. An upper-class, educated German, Faber is first seen in 1940. He has infiltrated the British Army, and is particularly amiable to young Billy Parkin (Philip Martin Brown), a boy approaching manhood. His friendliness is, of course, a façade. Faber murders his nosy landlady when she discovers him transmitting a message to Berlin on a shortwave radio. Percy Godliman (Ian Bannen), a medieval historian in the employ of British intelligence, investigates the crime. Meanwhile, David (Christopher Cazenove), a handsome RAF fighter pilot, and Lucy (Kate Nelligan) marry and race off on their honeymoon. Their car crashes, and, is later apparent, David is paralyzed for life, and his military career is abruptly ended.

A title then informs the audience that four years have passed. Lucy and the bitter, frustrated David are now living in a cottage on Storm Island, a barren, deserted outpost off the coast of England. Lucy looks after her husband and their young son; the only other resident is Tom (Alex McCrindle), the lighthouse keeper. David is more interested in drinking with Tom than in paying attention to his wife.

Over the years, the elusive Faber has still not been caught. At one point he barely eludes Godliman, escaping from a train—but not before killing Billy Parkin, now a soldier, when he is recognized. Faber is perhaps Germany's most successful spy working in Britain.

The Allied invasion of France is nearing, and the spy begins investigating rumors that a large army is planning an attack by way of the Pas de Calais. Faber manages to photograph a phony airbase in eastern England at which all the planes are made of wood. If he can get his evidence back to Hitler, the Germans will be sure that the invasion will occur at Normandy. However, Godliman intercepts the photos, and Faber must somehow find other means to relay the information.

The spy goes to Scotland to meet with a U-boat, but a violent storm forces his boat to land on Storm Island. Lucy takes him in and, despite David's protests, treats him hospitably. The lonely, sexually frustrated Lucy responds to this mysterious stranger, and they begin an affair. Faber murders Tom, contacts the U-boat by radio, and then kills the suspicious David in a fight on a cliffside. Faber pleads with Lucy to trust him—she has a gun, he does not. She prevents him from transmitting the invasion plans, and finally shoots him dead, just after the film's only bit of trite dialogue: "So the war's come down to the two of us."

The plot of *Eye of the Needle* is more closely related to those of the 1940's spy dramas of Fritz Lang than to any similar, contemporary work—with the possible exception of the adaptation of Frederick Forsyth's *The Day of the Jackal* (1973). Stylistically, particularly in the last segment on Storm Island, the film has the flavor of *Masterpiece Theatre*; in fact, Kate Nelligan was appearing on American television as the star of the *Masterpiece Theatre*'s *Thérèse Raquin* around the time of *Eye of the Needle*'s release. Though far from a classic of its genre—British television director Richard Marquand's staging is sometimes awkward, and the finale is overly melodramatic—the film is still an entertaining exercise in mystery and escapism. Its strong points are its performances. Donald Sutherland is calmly, chillingly creepy and sadistic as Faber, who in his evil is similar to the Nazi heavies who have populated scores of melodramas since the early 1940's. Yet Faber is no one-dimensional bad guy. He has his tender side, and he falls in love with the beautiful, desirable Lucy. Sutherland's Faber is a complex character, believably torn between his feelings for a woman—his only concession to humanity—and his duty to Germany.

Sutherland can effectively play comedy, as in *M*A*S*H* (1970), and drama in a variety of genres, as in *Klute* (1971), and *Ordinary People* (1980), yet he has appeared in too many films that have barely been releasable, such as

*S*P*Y*S* (1974), *The Disappearance* (1977), *Nothing Personal* (1979), *Bear Island* (1980), and *Gas* (1981). Henry Faber is one of the actor's better characterizations.

Kate Nelligan, Canadian-born stage and television actress whose film credits include *The Romantic Englishwoman* (1975), *Dracula* (1979), and *Mr. Patman* (1980), is very sensual as the frustrated, vulnerable, but ultimately courageous Lucy. She costarred on Canadian television opposite Donald Sutherland, who is also Canadian, in *Bethune*; given the right roles, she has the talent and screen presence to become a major star. Christopher Cazenove, an actor known mostly for his theater and television work, especially the role of Charles Hazelmere on *The Duchess of Duke Street*, is effectively angry and obstinate as David. His climactic battle-to-the-death with Sutherland is a highlight of the film, and this is his best screen role to date. Ian Bannen is fine as Godliman, even though the character's personality is barely explored in the scenario. Miklos Rozsa's score is particularly stylish, in the romantic manner he has perfected in *Double Indemnity* (1944), *Spellbound* (1945), *A Double Life* (1947), *The Asphalt Jungle* (1950), and many others.

Eye of the Needle, filmed on location in England, Scotland, and on the Isle of Mull, received mixed to negative reviews. It placed a disappointing fifty-fifth on *Variety*'s list of "Big Rental Films of 1981," taking in only $6,661,265 at the box office. Like *The Day of the Jackal*, the film may be predictable: we all know who won World War II, just as we know that Charles de Gaulle was never assassinated. Despite this foreknowledge, however, *Eye of the Needle* provides suspenseful, above average entertainment.

Rob Edelman

Reviews

The Hollywood Reporter. July 21, 1981, p. 3.
Los Angeles Times. July 24, 1981, VI, p. 1.
New York. XIV, August 10, 1981, pp. 56-57.
The New York Times. July 24, 1981, III, p. 10.
Newsweek. XCVIII, August 3, 1981, p. 50.
Saturday Review. VIII, July, 1981, p. 85.
Variety. July 20, 1981, p. 3.

FIRST MONDAY IN OCTOBER

Production: Paul Heller and Martha Scott for Paramount
Direction: Ronald Neame
Screenplay: Jerome Lawrence and Robert E. Lee; based on their play of the same name
Cinematography: Fred J. Koenekamp
Editing: Peter E. Berger
Art direction: Philip M. Jefferies
Music: Ian Fraser
MPAA rating: R
Running time: 99 minutes

Principal characters:
Dan Snow .... Walter Matthau
Ruth Loomis ....Jill Clayburgh
Bill Russell .... Joshua Bryant
Christine Snow ....Jan Sterling

First Monday in October, whose title refers to the traditional opening date of the annual Supreme Court Session, was a successful Broadway play starring Henry Fonda and Eva Marie Saint before its authors, Jerome Lawrence and Robert E. Lee, teamed with director Ronald Neame to turn it into a film. They signed two fine actors, Walter Matthau and Jill Clayburgh, to star in the seriocomic story of the first woman on the Supreme Court and her encounters with a particularly obstreperous male colleague. Although the two justices are poles apart philosophically, they eventually come to a position of respect and friendship.

Ironically, the man who probably did the most to help *First Monday in October* at the box office was ex-actor and President of the United States, Ronald Reagan. In 1981, a few months before the film was scheduled to be released, Reagan appointed Sandra Day O'Connor to be the first female Supreme Court justice. Suddenly life was imitating art, making *First Monday in October* more than merely a political comedy. It was a cinematic gloss on an important bit of current affairs, and although the film's box-office receipts did not equal the producer's expectations, the real life tie-in guaranteed a modest success.

The film opens by establishing the character of justice Dan Snow (Walter Matthau). In a few scenes, the audience learns that Snow is an outdoorsman (he spends his vacations camping in the mountains) and a liberal (he defends free speech and attacks giant multinational corporations). He is also something of a curmudgeon: witty, caustic, and preoccupied with his job—to such an extent that he and his wife Christine (Jan Sterling) have very little in common. The audience is clearly meant to identify Dan Snow with William O. Douglas, the liberal jurist who served on the Supreme Court between 1939 and 1975. Despite Snow's passionately held beliefs, however, he is capable of admiring worthy adversaries. "You don't have to agree with a man in order to respect him," he says at the funeral of one of his conservative colleagues on the court. When the resulting vacancy is filled by the appointment of Ruth Loomis (Jill Clayburgh), a staunch conservative from Orange County, California, Snow is appalled.

In a series of brief expository scenes that parallel the opening of the film, Neame shows the audience Ruth Loomis' background. She is young (at least for a potential Supreme Court justice), athletic, and attractive. She is newly widowed, having been the wife of a prominent attorney, and is being courted by a man named Bill Russell (Joshua Bryant), a friend of her late husband and an attorney for the Omnitech corporation, the target of one of Dan Snow's tirades early in the film. To illustrate Loomis' conservatism and her strength of character, Neame uses excerpts from Loomis' testimony at her Senate confirmation hearings, which reveal that she is also a very articulate defender of her principles. Loomis is as appalled by Snow as he is by her, and their intellectual sparring makes up the bulk of the film.

Two court cases form the battlefield on which Snow and Loomis cross swords. The first is a relatively straightforward censorship case involving a film entitled *The Naked Nymphomaniac*. Loomis advances the traditional conservative viewpoint that society has the right to protect itself from pornography. Snow counters with the equally traditional liberal view that when the Constitution guarantees the right of free expression, it makes no exception for those who are politically or socially unpopular. "It's crap, but it's got the right to be crap," he concludes.

Except for a brief aside involving the breakup of Snow's marriage, the rest of the film revolves around the Omnitech case. It seems that a group of disgruntled stockholders have charged the corporation with suppressing an invention that would supplant the internal combustion engine, but their suit is foundering because the president of Omnitech cannot be located and served with a subpoena. The legal aspects of the case are never satisfactorily explained for an audience of laymen, but that is unimportant, because the issue is handled emotionally rather than intellectually. Snow opposes Omnitech because, as a liberal, he is suspicious of big business. Loomis approves of Omnitech because conservatives favor big business. Aside from this symbolic function, Omnitech serves merely as a plot device through which the filmmakers resolve their story.

Believing that the company's president is dead, Dan Snow works obsessively on the Omnitech case at the expense of his health. At the conclusion of a set-piece scene (paralleling the argument over *The Naked Nymphomaniac*) in which he and Loomis debate the merits of big business, Snow has a coronary.

While Snow is recovering, Loomis decides to play sleuth, using an Omnitech contact of hers to prove to Snow that his suspicions about the company are groundless. Loomis flies to California for the day and when her friend Bill Russell shows Loomis her husband's secret Omnitech files, however, she is astonished to find that Snow has been right all along: Omnitech's president is dead and her late husband had assisted Omnitech in its coverup.

Loomis returns to Washington with the intention of turning her information over to Snow and then resigning. To her surprise, however, Snow vehemently opposes her resignation, even sneaking out of the hospital to offer her a deal: "You don't resign and I won't die." She accepts the proposition and the film ends with the two of them ascending the steps of the Supreme Court building, happily chattering away about all of the upcoming cases upon which they will disagree.

First Monday in October is a pleasant little film, but the fact that it never rises above that level is the fault of the script and of the play on which the script is based. A sense of dispassionate calculation permeates the plot: everything is too pat. After the opening scenes in which Snow and Loomis are introduced, the writers all but abandon any attempt at further character development, and thus the film's protagonists never really come alive. They are obviously more caricature than character, programmed to come up with a clever one-liner or a liberal/conservative platitude at the appropriate moment. Both sides get equal time to make their case, and both cases get made equally well. The film's obsession with balance is frustrating, though, and brings it to the level of a television movie, bland and unchallenging.

Fortunately for the viewer, the professionalism of director Ronald Neame and his cast rescues *First Monday in October* from total innocuousness. Neame, best known for *The Poseidon Adventure* (1974), is a competent director, and he uses enough diverse locations to avoid the overly stagey appearance of a filmed play.

Walter Matthau and Jill Clayburgh are both excellent actors, and they do their best with the characters of Dan Snow and Ruth Loomis. They turn in honest performances, and bring enough charisma to the screen to keep the audience involved despite the script. Nevertheless, they are obviously not challenged by their roles, and it is unlikely that this film will be remembered as one of the highlights of either's career.

First Monday in October, then, is a pleasant but slight film, lifted above a clichéd script by the professionalism of Ronald Neame, Walter Matthau, and Jill Clayburgh—with a little timely help from Ronald Reagan.

Robert Mitchell

Reviews

The Hollywood Reporter. August 17, 1981, p. 2.

Los Angeles Times. August 22, 1981, II, p. 3.
New York. XIV, September 7, 1981, pp. 52-53.
The New York Times. August 21, 1981, III, p. 8.
Newsweek. XCVIII, August 31, 1981, p. 37.
Variety. August 17, 1981, p. 3.

FOR YOUR EYES ONLY

Production: Albert R. Broccoli for United Artists
Direction: John Glen
Screenplay: Richard Maibaum and Michael G. Wilson; based on the characters created by Ian Fleming
Cinematography: Alan Hume
Editing: John Grover
Art direction: Peter Lamont
Music: Bill Conti
MPAA rating: PG
Running time: 127 minutes

Principal characters:

James Bond	Roger Moore
Melina	Carole Bouquet
Columbo	Topol
Bibi	Lynn-Holly Johnson
Kristatos	Julian Glover
Brink	Jill Bennett
The Prime Minister	Janet Brown
Minister of Defense	Geoffrey Keen
Havelock	Jack Hedley

For Your Eyes Only marks the most significant departure in the James Bond series since the second film, *From Russia with Love* (1963). Although the current film's two immediate predecessors, *The Spy Who Loved Me* (1977) and *Moonraker* (1979) were among the most successful films produced in those years—a remarkable feat considering that the series has been running for twenty years and that recent entries have had to compete with *Star Wars* (1977) and *Superman* (1979)—the realization was apparently reached that the gimmicks and special effects had been taken about as far as they could go in *Moonraker*. What seemed innovative in the 1960's became less impressive after the revolution wrought by the technicians of *Star Wars*. Thus, the tone of the new Bond film had to be different.

In *For Your Eyes Only* this new approach is remarkably simple: a well-written, hard-hitting story, eschewing most of the gimmickry in favor of plot development. This shift is further enhanced by more fully developed characters who are given a larger share of the spotlight. Finally, the screenwriters have performed minor surgery on Bond's macho image. The result is a highly entertaining film, another successful metamorphosis of the long-running series.

The traditional James Bond film, after the initial efforts, had evolved largely into a formulaic scissors-and-paste affair highlighting exotic locations and futuristic devices. Whereas the early Sean Connery vehicles functioned in the tradition of the British thriller to a certain extent (some gadgets notwithstanding), they were also following the standards laid down for the spy genre—with one significant exception. Unlike the average film dealing with espionage and political intrigue, which normally features myriad plot twists, double agents, and moral dilemmas, the Bond films were amazingly straightforward, featuring an elemental confrontation between good and evil.

While this mythic confrontation was taken relatively seriously in the first Sean Connery efforts, a new mood was introduced when Roger Moore took over the role. When it became obvious that the new actor could never be hammered into the Connery mold, a new persona was developed which changed the tone of the entire series to one of self-parody. After five films featuring Connery's interpretation of the character, the audience had a number of well-established expectations that could be turned against them to the advantage of the later films. The results have been quite successful and the momentum of the series has thus been maintained.

The fundamental plot formula has not changed, however, with the new interpretation of Bond. A typical film opens with a cataclysmic event that profoundly threatens the world. The villain is usually a madman with vast resources of wealth and technology at his disposal. James Bond is called in and quickly dispatched to an exotic locale, where he becomes the target of numerous assassins. He subsequently becomes involved in several chases and also becomes involved with a *femme fatale*, whom he usually converts (through sexual means) to the side of right. Frequently he is captured by his enemies and threatened with an exotic form of death before escaping and returning in a climactic assault (not always single-handed) that destroys the evildoer's heretofore impregnable fortress.

One film, *From Russia with Love*, deviated from this pattern and concentrated primarily upon Bond's efforts to steal a code machine while eluding the efforts of a trained assassin hired for the sole purpose of killing him. It featured a well-developed story and adhered quite rigidly to patterns and standards established by such masters of the genre as Alfred Hitchcock.

For Your Eyes Only returns to this concept for the most part, although in a slightly parodying fashion. The film begins with a fairly standard sequence in which Bond (Roger Moore) confronts his old enemy Blofel after Blofel tries to have Bond's helicopter destroyed. Using remote control devices, Bond successfully manages to annihilate his archenemy, the man responsible for his wife's death. The scene has some spectacular action, especially the portions showing the helicopter flying through a huge warehouse.

The prologue, however, has nothing to do with the rest of the plot. The bulk of the story concerns Bond's search for a top-secret decoder. The Minister of Defense (Geoffrey Keen, one of the continuing series characters who here supplants the late Bernard Lee as M in the role of Bond's superior) sends Bond looking for the man responsible for the theft. In the meantime, British undercover agent Havelock (Jack Hedley) and his wife are killed on board their oceanography vessel while their daughter Melina (Carole Bouquet, the young French girl from Luis Buñuel's *That Obscure Object of Desire*, 1977) looks on. Melina thus enters the plot in her search for her parents' killer.

Bond's and Melina's paths cross while they are looking for the man responsible for the theft of the decoder and the murder. At a ski resort in the Italian Alps they encounter Kristatos (Julian Glover), a Greek shipping magnate who tells Bond that a former friend, Columbo (Topol), is the man they want. While at the resort, Bond gently turns away Kristatos' protégée Bibi (Lynn-Holly Johnson), a precocious ice-skating star. For the first time in all of the Bond films, the hero turns down an offer to go to bed with an anxious beautiful girl; he does so because she is too young.

The search for Columbo leads Bond and Melina to a Greek island, where Bond finally catches up with Columbo only to learn that Kristatos himself is actually the villain. In the end, after scaling Kristatos' island fortress and surviving a death-ride on an underwater tow line, Bond saves the decoder, kills Kristatos, and inevitably goes to bed with the heroine, only the second sexual encounter in the film, a record in the series.

The new Bond of this film is much softer, less sarcastic, and more in need of help than in previous ventures. He essays glib one-liners with ease, but less so than before. Occasionally he even needs Melina's help. When they are tied together on the tow-line, for example, it is Melina who saves them by recalling where an oxygen tank was left in an underwater excavation site. It seems unlikely that feminist organizations, which have long detested the image of women in the Bond films, will now applaud them, but a definite nod in that direction has been made.

There are some chases in the film—no Bond movie could be made without at least one—but aside from the opening sequence, the most spectacular stunt in the film is a long free fall on a rope set against a high Greek cliff. The simplicity of its execution makes it far superior to a dozen exploding automobiles, and it is reminiscent of the ski-parachute jump in *The Spy Who Loved Me*, considered by some critics to be the greatest single stunt in film history.

For Your Eyes Only finished among the top ten moneymaking pictures of the year, in a year when none of the films in that group earned less than fifty million dollars. By 1981, the James Bond series was the longest and most successful series in cinema history; the producer, Albert R. Broccoli, was rewarded by the Academy of Motion Picture Arts and Sciences with the Irving Thalberg Humanitarian Award. The March, 1982, Oscar ceremonies paid tribute to the series by presenting one of the show's most spectacular musical sequences ever, a lavish, explosion-laden medley of the James Bond music through the years.

Surprising credit for the film's success can also be given to its director, John Glen. A former editor of the Bond films, Glen made his directorial debut with *For Your Eyes Only* and soon after went to work on the next Bond film, *Octopussy* (1983). Glen showed a surprisingly smooth style for a first-time director, due in part, perhaps, to his years as an editor and his knowledge of the series.

The final point of note about *For Your Eyes Only* is the film's epilogue, which bears virtually no relationship to the rest of the film. British impressionist Janet Brown imitates British Prime Minister Margaret Thatcher as she calls Bond to congratulate him on a job well done. Looking somewhat like Mrs. Thatcher and sounding very much like her, Brown portrays the Prime Minister as she talks to Bond on her kitchen extension phone and slaps her husband's hand as he tries to sneak a bite of food. The scene seems totally out of place, but it left audiences, particularly British audiences, laughing, and one of the major assets of the Bond series is that its films always leave its fans happy.

Thomas A. Hanson

Reviews

The Hollywood Reporter. June 24, 1981, p. 7.
Los Angeles Times. June 26, 1981, VI, p. 1.
The New York Times. June 26, 1981, III, p. 8.
Newsweek. XCVII, June 29, 1981, p. 72.
Time. CXVII, June 29, 1981, p. 70.
Variety. June 24, 1981, p. 3.

FORT APACHE, THE BRONX

Production: Martin Richards and Tom Fiorello for David Susskind Productions and Time-Life Films; released by Twentieth Century-Fox
Direction: Daniel Petrie
Screenplay: Heywood Gould; based on the experiences of Thomas Mulhearn and Pete Tessitore
Cinematography: John Alcott
Editing: Rita Roland
Art direction: Ben Edwards
Music: Jonathan Tunick
MPAA rating: R
Running time: 120 minutes

Principal characters:
Murphy .... Paul Newman
Connolly .... Edward Asner
Corelli .... Ken Wahl
Morgan .... Danny Aiello
Isabella .... Rachel Ticotin
Charlotte .... Pam Grier

Based on the experiences of two policemen, Thomas Mulhearn and Pete Tessitore, Daniel Petrie's *Fort Apache, the Bronx* stirred up considerable controversy while it was being filmed in the South Bronx police precinct which served as the model and setting for the story. The residents of "Fort Apache," as the precinct was dubbed by the police, felt that they were unjustly portrayed as lawless, violent, and uncivilized. Yet, when the film opened, most of the controversy died, perhaps because of the power and ultimately optimistic message of the film.

Petrie has had a slow career as a director. He has done many television programs and a number of films, most of which have been undistinguished. The exception was *A Raisin in the Sun* (1961), a highly acclaimed film about a black family in Chicago. His most recent films, such as *The Betsy* (1978), a financially successful yet critically lambasted potboiler, have not added to his reputation. *Fort Apache, the Bronx*, however, does show that he has strengths as a director.

Like the great majority of police-centered films, *Fort Apache, the Bronx* is largely episodic, showing the tedious, everyday work of a cop. In the beginning of the film the audience sees Murphy (Paul Newman), the Mulhearn character, delivering a baby for a young Puerto Rican girl. She lives in an apartment which seems to be inhabited by dozens of other people, a common sight in the South Bronx. Murphy's character is immediately established.

Contrary to the popular image of the hard-bitten cop, Murphy is philosophical and good natured. The other policemen in his precinct, even his partner Corelli (Ken Wahl, as the Tessitore character) cannot understand how he can maintain his attitude while working and even living in the seedy Bronx neighborhood. Murphy likes his job, though, and he likes the people.

There are three main plot lines which make up the bulk of the film. First, Connolly (Edward Asner) is appointed as the new head of the precinct and is immediately disliked by the men, especially Murphy. Connolly is a "by-the-book" man who never bends or compromises, an attitude which Murphy feels is fatal in a precinct such as Fort Apache. The second major section of the plot concerns Murphy's romance with Charlotte (Pam Grier), a young black nurse. Charlotte is a junkie, although she lies to Murphy when he discovers track marks on her arm and claims that she only uses drugs once in a while. "They all do it at the hospital," she claims, "even the doctors." Consistent with his live-and-let-live attitude, Murphy does not interfere with Charlotte's drug habit. They become closer during the course of the film, and Murphy even considers marriage.

The final plot line of the film, the one which eventually brings all the strands of the story together, concerns the death of an innocent boy and girl. During a police shakedown which turns into a minor riot, two policemen go to a rooftop where they think that shots have been fired. When they arrive, they see a young boy and girl together and know that they are uninvolved in the incident, but somehow the policemen panic and one of them shoots and kills the boy. Because he has been in a location where he can see what has been going on, Murphy knows exactly what has happened. Throughout the latter half of the film, Connolly tries to get him to tell the truth and "rat" on his fellow officer. Murphy will not do this, and naturally the girl's story is not believed, so the policeman remains free from any accusation.

Eventually, however, Murphy tells the truth to Connolly. The guilty policeman is a bully who does not deserve loyalty and Murphy gives a deposition implicating him. He wants to resign, feeling that he has committed the ultimate sin for a policeman, turning in another cop. He is also despondent because Charlotte has taken some lethal drugs and dies in the emergency ward of her hospital.

In the last segments of the film, the audience finally has some sympathy for Connolly when he reveals what seems to be the message of the film, and a new goal for the acquiescent Murphy. When he refuses to give in to the demands of a crowd who try to storm the precinct, Connolly tells Murphy that it is not those people whom he wants to please. Rather than bending with the wind—a popular approach in "combat precincts" such as Fort Apache—he wants to show the decent people of the community that there are still standards for them. In one moment, the audience's ideas turn around completely. While in the beginning Connolly seemed hard and almost ludicrous in his by-the-book approach (similar in fact to Henry Fonda's Colonel in John Ford's *Fort Apache*, 1948), at the end the audience realizes that he wants to keep the peace for the honest citizens of the South Bronx, not just "keep the lid on" so the hoods, pimps, and drug dealers will not explode into chaos.

At the end, despite his protests to Corelli that he is through as a cop, Murphy chases one of his favorite hoods, and the film stops with the audience knowing that no matter what happens he is still a cop and a good one.

Fort Apache, the Bronx is a powerful film. The acting, done in a realistic, world-weary manner, is first-rate. Newman, after a film career of almost thirty years, proves again that he is not only a major star but also a dynamic actor. He is perfectly believable as the uneducated, rough-hewn Murphy. He jokes, swears, delivers a baby, and falls in love so naturally that the audience really feels that he is Murphy. In his most powerful scene in the film, when Murphy discovers that Charlotte has died, he cannot stop trying to save her anyway. He screams and tries to "walk" her back to life, but his attempt is fruitless. Whereas he has previously seemed casual, almost flippant, about life, now the depth of his feeling is revealed. Newman's career has had some major ups and downs in the last decade, but his 1981 films, *Fort Apache, the Bronx* and *Absence of Malice*, proved that even at fifty-six, he is still a major box-office star as well as being a fine actor.

The other major parts, although competently performed, all seem like window-dressing for Newman's role. Ken Wahl as Corelli and Pam Grier as Charlotte perform well in their roles, for example, but they are not as well-developed. Asner as the martinet Connolly has a very small part until the end. He is a competent actor, but his close identification with the role of Lou Grant, whom he has portrayed on television in two different series in the last decade, "The Mary Tyler Moore Show" and "Lou Grant," detracts from his effectiveness. Unfortunately, the audience immediately labels him, which lessens the impact of his role.

Fort Apache, the Bronx did extremely well at the box office, and it has done well in its televised showings on cable and in video format. Its violence and language make it too intense for repeated viewings, but it will no doubt continue to be successful on the home video market for some time to come.

Roberta Le Feuvre

Reviews

The Hollywood Reporter. February 6, 1981, p. 3.
Los Angeles Times. February 6, 1981, VI, p. 1.
The New Republic. CLXXXIV, February 21, 1981, p. 24.
The New York Times. February 6, 1981, III, p. 6.

The New Yorker. LVII, February 23, 1981, pp. 101-105.
Newsweek. XCVII, February 16, 1981, p. 81.
Time. CXVII, February 16, 1981, p. 77.
Variety. February 6, 1981, p. 3.

FOSTER DADDY, TORA! (TORAJIRO KAMONE UTA)

Origin: Japan
Released: 1980
Released in U.S.: 1981
Production: Kiyoshi Shimazo for Shochiku Company
Distribution in U.S.: Shochiku Films of America
Direction: Yoji Yamada
Screenplay: Yoji Yamada and Yoshitaka Asama
Cinematography: Tetsuo Takaba
Editing: no listing
Art direction: Mitsuo Idegawa
Music: Naozomi Yamamoto
Running time: 96 minutes

Principal characters:
Tora .... Kiyoshi Atsumi
Sumire .... Ran Ito
Sakura .... Chieko Baisho
Hiroshi, her husband .... Gin Maeda
Tora's uncle .... Masami Shimojo
Tora's aunt .... Chieko Misaki
President .... Hisao Dazai
Temple Priest .... Chishu Ryu
Teacher Hayashi .... Tatsuo Matsumura

Foster Daddy, Tora! (released in Japan in 1980 as *Torajiro Kamone Uta*) is the most recent of the Tora-san films which grew out of a one-season Japanese television series designed around Kiyoshi Atsumi, the actor who plays the protagonist, Tora. After twenty-six successful episodes, writer/director Yoji Yamada finally killed his hero off, but the resulting flood of protests from unhappy viewers persuaded him to revive Tora as a film personality, an event reminiscent of that which led to the development of the *Star Trek* films in the United States. There have been more than twenty films so far and they all follow the same basic formula in which Tora-san returns to his family at an inopportune moment. Frequently the situation develops into a quarrel and Tora leaves again to spend the first ten to twenty minutes of the film wandering aimlessly around Japan before Yamada gets to the actual plot. Additionally, there is always a dream sequence at the beginning in which Tora is a noble loner trying to hide his sordid past from his sister, Sakura (Chieko Baisho), who is searching for her lost brother. A great deal of Tora's character which can only be hinted at in the body of the film is thereby explained in the dreams. Because his role is that of an itinerant peddler, Tora has been unable to help with his sister's upbringing and is not yet—the most recent film to the contrary—in a position to help her and her husband financially. He cannot repay the kindnesses of his aunt and uncle to Sakura, and his inability to fulfill his role as elder brother and uncle causes the tradition-oriented Tora great shame. His lack of education as well as the humiliation that he feels accounts for his argumentative manner. As the series has progressed, however, Tora seems to have matured. As Yamada explains: "At first, we looked down on Tora from an objective point of view—he was merely a well-intentioned fool—but over the course of these films we have come to love him like a brother. His only purpose in life is to bring happiness to others."

Foster Daddy, Tora! begins with a dream sequence, shot in an obviously artificial location in vivid primary colors. As in all the Tora-san films the dream relates to the main story only in that it involves a beautiful young girl in difficulty who is saved by the hero Tora (Kiyoshi Atsumi).

The principal action begins when Tora awakens and proceeds, as usual, on one of his peddling trips. Although the point is thus made that Tora is a street peddler, he carries but one suitcase, containing only his clothes, which seldom vary. He wears a rather gaudy yellow suit with a wide sash in which he keeps his wallet, zoris (sandals), and a conservative hat. He is a stocky, square-faced, pleasant looking man of indeterminate age.

In Hokkaido, Tora decides to visit the grave of an old friend, Tsune, who has died in his absence, and to find it, he has to locate Tsune's daughter, Sumire (Ran Ito). Sumire wants to work in Tokyo and finish high school so Tora brings her home with him to the confectionery store run by his aunt (Chieko Misaki) and uncle (Masami Shimojo) in Katsushika, a lower-class area only a short train ride from the central city. Tora cares for Sumire as though she is his own daughter. He finds a job for her and when, after much difficulty and emotional turmoil, Sumire is accepted at night school, Tora accompanies her to and from the classroom. He stays at the school and prowls around outside the class so much that the teacher invites him to sit in on the lessons. Tora, however, either distracts the students with his stories or falls noisily asleep at the back of the room.

A further commentary on the role of the family in Japanese life is provided by a visit from Sumire's mother. Years before, she had left her husband, who was a drunkard and gambler, and has not seen her daughter since. Although Sumire sends the woman away, Sakura makes her run after her and she finds her mother crying. The two women embrace and Sumire's mother leaves with the words: "Live a happy life."

When Sumire's boyfriend eventually turns up and she spends the night with him, Tora is offended. The couple intends to marry but this does not placate him. Tora's sister, Sakura, tells him that Sumire is grown up and capable of living her own life, but Tora continues to feel betrayed by her behavior and leaves on another peddling trip. On New Year's Day, with everyone at the cake shop celebrating the holiday, a card arrives from Tora wishing them all well and hoping that Sumire will find happiness in her marriage. As Tora stands overlooking a scenic river, he is accosted by one of Sumire's friends from the dried fish factory where she was working when he found her. The woman and her cohorts are on an outing and invite him along on their bus. He is the only man on the excursion, and the film ends as Tora, surrounded by laughing women, rolls off down the highway.

As represented by *Foster Daddy, Tora!*, the protagonist is akin to the character of Shane as played by Alan Ladd, although certainly less intelligent. He bumbles into situations and makes inept but ultimately successful efforts to solve the problems of those around him, and then bumbles out again. He is a do-gooder with no life of his own except that of an itinerant peddler, so it is no wonder that he adopts all of those who come within his purview. The story's main action opens with him giving money to his sister and to her husband, Hiroshi (Gin Maeda), to help them pay off the mortgage on *their* confectionery store. He cannot manage this gracefully, and when they exclaim that it is too much, he takes some of it back, feeling that they look down on him because he is a street vendor. Of course this is not true, and the people that we see in the course of *Foster Daddy, Tora!* demonstrate their affection and esteem for Tora over and over. He is easily offended—clumsy, and emotionally childish, with virtually no social acumen. Yet his heart is in the right place and people are willing to overlook his gaucheries because they see through to the generous, kindly, lonely man hiding behind the gruff façade.

It is typical of Tora's character that the minute he hears of Sumire's predicament, he virtually adopts her and drags her back to live with his relatives. When he is afraid that Sumire will fail her tests, he impulsively tries to bribe her teacher and, as she is too shy to speak during the oral section of her entrance exams, Tora answers for her and has to be ejected from the room. Tora and Sumire literally jump for joy when they learn that she has been accepted.

Although he is essentially an observer of other people's lives, once involved, Tora catapults himself emotionally into their midst and takes over. When he goes to school with Sumire, for example, he brings cookies along to share with the cleaning lady who makes tea for him, an incident which is illustrative of the fact that no one is beneath him. It is wholly within his character that he should leave impulsively on a journey with the women from the fish factory. He is like a child with a limited attention span, easily distracted and easily led—the exact qualities which lead him smoothly from one adventure to the next.

Although *Foster Daddy, Tora!* was successful in Japan, it made little impact in the United States. It was entered into competition for an Oscar for Best Foreign Film in 1981, but failed to get a nomination. Though not a great motion picture, the film is a good example of pleasant entertainment and provides the Western viewer an insight into aspects of Japanese life and customs which are not usually depicted well in American Films about Japan.

Judith M. Kass

Review

Los Angeles Times. May 14, 1981, VI, p. 2.

FOUR FRIENDS

Production: Arthur Penn and Gene Lasko for Filmways
Direction: Arthur Penn
Screenplay: Steven Tesich
Cinematography: Ghislain Cloquet
Editing: Barry Malkin and Marc Laub
Art direction: David Chapman
Music: Elizabeth Swados
MPAA rating: R
Running time: 115 minutes

Principal characters:
Danilo Prozor .... Craig Wasson
Georgia Miles ....Jodi Thelen
Tom Donaldson .... Jim Metzler
David Levine .... Michael Huddleston
Louie Carnahan .... Reed Birney
Adrienne Carnahan .... Julia Murray
Mr. Carnahan .... James Leo Herlihy
Mrs. Carnahan .... Lois Smith
Mr. Prozor .... Miklos Simon
Mrs. Prozor .... Elizabeth Lawrence

Four Friends was director Arthur Penn's first film since *The Missouri Breaks* in 1976, a production, featuring two big-name stars and a large budget, that was not a success, either critically or financially. *Four Friends*, with a small budget and a cast of unknowns, featured a screenplay by Steven Tesich, who had won an Academy Award for another "coming of age in Indiana" film, *Breaking Away*, the previous year. Despite Penn's and Tesich's best efforts, *Four Friends* failed to win a large audience, although it did gain a fair share of critical praise.

The film's title is a bit misleading: there are actually five friends, and the film is primarily about only one of them—Danilo Prozor (Craig Wasson), whose family has immigrated to Indiana from their native Yugoslavia (the country of Tesich's birth as well). We watch Danilo grow from late adolescence to early manhood against a backdrop of the social turbulence of the 1960's. The genius of the film, however, is in its refusal to make its protagonist a conventional 1960's type. Danilo is neither a hawk nor a dove, neither hip nor square. He is a character rather than a caricature.

At the beginning of the film, young Danilo and his mother (Elizabeth Lawrence) are reunited with Mr. Prozor (Miklos Simon) in East Chicago, Indiana, where the father is working in a steel mill. Not at all fazed by this gray industrial setting, Danilo is entranced by everything about his new homeland. His faith in America—in the American dream—is boundless, and grows stronger as he enters adolescence.

After this brief preface, the scene shifts to high school in the early 1960's, where Penn and Tesich introduce Danilo's three friends. Tom Donaldson (Jim Metzler) is the most "American" of the trio, WASP, good-looking, and athletic. David Levine (Michael Huddleston) is his antithesis—chubby, Jewish, and slightly comical. Danilo, Tom, and David share an infatuation with the fourth friend, Georgia Miles (Jodi Thelen). Georgia is a bohemian—a flower child several years ahead of her time. She is an outspoken advocate of free love, and claims to be the reincarnation of the dancer, Isadora Duncan. Georgia's at least theoretical willingness to share her charms equally with her three male friends creates the expected adolescent confusion, particularly in Danilo, who has a much more monogamous view of things. When he rejects a spur-of-the-moment offer to relieve Georgia of her virginity, she takes up with Tom, who has no such scruples.

In addition to Danilo's romantic agonies, he finds himself coming into an increasingly sharp conflict with his father over the issue of college. Mr. Prozor wants Danilo to go to work in the steel mills instead of pursuing his education. For Danilo, the whole issue is tied to his vision of America as a land of limitless opportunity. His father scoffs: "I am tired and I have to go to work. *That* is America." Though the immediate issue is soon resolved—Danilo enrolls at Northwestern—the tension between father and son over the limits of the American dream, and particularly over the "pursuit of happiness," is a recurring subplot in the film.

At college, still brooding about Georgia, Danilo meets the fifth friend, Louie Carnahan (Reed Birney), who is rich, clever, eager for sexual adventure, and suffering from a wasting illness which has crippled and will eventually kill him. Louie is a particularly engaging character, whose one ambition is not to die a virgin.

Georgia, meanwhile, scrambles things further by becoming pregnant by Tom. Danilo is invited to their wedding, and he brings Louie along, but they arrive only to discover that the man Georgia is marrying is the rather sheepish David Levine. Tom, it seems, is not the marrying kind. He has enlisted in the army instead, and will leave for Vietnam shortly after the wedding ceremony. Like all the other young men in the film, Louie Carnahan immediately develops a crush on Georgia.

The web of relationships grows increasingly tangled. Danilo, resolving to put Georgia out of his mind, finds himself attracted to Louie's sister Adrienne (Julia Murray). Their romance blossoms despite the hostility of Adrienne's father (James Leo Herlihy) and the strange attitude of her mother (Lois Smith). Meanwhile Georgia, ever the free spirit, seduces an amazed and delighted Louie. Everything seems to be headed toward a happy ending when the film dramatically shifts to the turbulence of the late 1960's.

The scene in which this abrupt transition takes place is Danilo's wedding. The ceremony is held at the Carnahan mansion, and all of Danilo's friends are there, as are his parents. The wedding goes off very well, until Mr. Carnahan's protracted toast to his daughter and new son-in-law becomes more and more bitter. At the end of his tirade, he pulls out a revolver and shoots Adrienne, Danilo, and himself. Danilo survives, but his faith in himself is shaken. His father's most pessimistic ruminations about life in America seem to have been borne out.

The mood of the film turns temporarily somber. The four friends (Louie having succumbed to his illness while Danilo was still hospitalized from his gunshot wound) scatter, pursuing their lives and dreams. Tom returns to Vietnam; David stays at home, working with his undertaker father; Danilo, a scarred widower, just drifts. Only Georgia seems to have found real happiness. She leaves David and moves to New York City, where thousands of free spirits like her form the burgeoning hippie movement of the late 1960's.

Danilo eventually visits Georgia in New York, but he is bewildered by the hippie/protestor milieu that he finds there. Although he is clearly still in love with Georgia, there is no reconciliation. He continues to drift, settling briefly in rural Pennsylvania and working as a laborer. He is calmed by the tranquillity of life there, and a romance with a local woman begins to blossom.

Just when it appears that his life is back on track, however, Georgia appears. The shallow "revolution for the hell of it" ethos of her big city friends has begun to pall, and now it is Georgia who is in need of spiritual comfort. The resulting liaison is brief and inconclusive—Georgia leaves the next day—but Penn and Tesich are giving us the first clue that Danilo's feelings for Georgia are not totally unreciprocated. Georgia, too, is shown finally something more than a bubbleheaded flower child. Through her pain, she is maturing.

Thus far, the tone of the film has proceeded from enthusiasm to disillusionment. It now turns to reconciliation. Time passes, and Danilo, Georgia, and Tom all find themselves back in East Chicago, older and wiser. Danilo finally makes his peace with his crusty father, who concedes a grudging pride in his son. Georgia finally admits that she has been in love with Danilo all along; her head was full of thoughts of free love, but her heart was monogamous. Tom has brought a Vietnamese wife back from the war, and David has found a nice hometown girl to marry. The film ends with the four friends (plus stray spouses and children) at a bonfire on the beach. The predominant mood is one of gratitude—at having come through so much and having survived intact.

The strengths of the film are in its characterizations, and Penn was probably wise to avoid the potentially distracting presence of big name actors in the film. That established, however, it must be noted that one of the problems with the film concerns the development of Georgia Miles. Even the critics who praised the film cited this difficulty. As written by Tesich and acted by Jodi Thelen, the character of Georgia is neither unusually pretty nor unusually bright, and though she is possessed of a certain loony charm, she is not charismatic. Indeed, it is hardly credible that the four young men (and Danilo in particular) would fall so hard for her. Thelen's performance grows stronger as the film progresses, but the early damage is difficult to undo.

Nevertheless, *Four Friends* succeeds despite the problems centering around Georgia Miles/Jodi Thelen. The script, direction, and acting are superb. Penn gets remarkable performances out of his cast of unknowns; Reed Birney, as Louie Carnahan, and Miklos Simon, as Mr. Prozor, stand out in supporting roles. Still, it is Craig Wasson who sets the tone for the entire film—all openness and enthusiasm at first, then wary, and finally mature and at peace.

In *Four Friends*, Arthur Penn has produced one of the finest films to date about America in the 1960's. He accomplishes this almost by indirection: the central events of the decade—assassinations, war, the protest movements—are referred to in the film only when they have a direct bearing on the lives of the film's characters. Penn and Tesich obviously understand what many less subtle filmmakers do not: that adult audiences, having lived through the 1960's, have not forgotten the experience in the intervening years, and thus can be trusted to supply their own connections between events on the screen and events in recent history. Penn's concentration on character development rather than on attempting to re-create stale newsreel footage provides a refreshing contrast to many films dealing with the 1960's.

In the 1980's, when the American film industry seems increasingly disinterested in the adult audience, Penn's attitude may have been a mistake in terms of marketing strategy. It was not a mistake in terms of art. *Four Friends* is an honest, well-made film that will surely grow in stature as time goes by.

Robert Mitchell

Reviews

The Hollywood Reporter. November 12, 1981, p. 2.
Los Angeles Times. December 11, 1981, VI, p. 1.
The New York Times. December 11, 1981, III, p. 12.
The New Yorker. LVII, January 4, 1982, pp. 80-81.
Newsweek. XCVIII, December 21, 1981, p. 49.
Saturday Review. IX, January, 1982, p. 53.
Time. CXVIII, December 21, 1981, p. 82.
Variety. November 11, 1981, p. 3.

THE FOUR SEASONS

Production: Martin Bregman for Universal
Direction: Alan Alda
Screenplay: Alan Alda
Cinematography: Victor J. Kemper
Editing: Michael Economou
Art direction: Jack Collis
Music: Antonio Vivaldi
MPAA rating: PG
Running time: 107 minutes

Principal characters:
Jack Burroughs .... Alan Alda
Kate Burroughs .... Carol Burnett
Nick Callan .... Len Cariou
Anne Callan .... Sandy Dennis
Claudia Zimmer .... Rita Moreno
Danny Zimmer ....Jack Weston
Ginny Newley (Callan) .... Bess Armstrong
Beth .... Elizabeth Alda
Lisa ....Beatrice Alda

The Four Seasons was one of the first box-office successes of 1981, a somewhat surprising occurrence since the most popular films are usually directed toward a younger audience. *The Four Seasons* is a warm, conventional, and frequently witty comedy about three middle-aged, upper-middle-class couples and their relationships to one another. It offers no deep insights, but according to Alan Alda, the film's writer-director-star, that was not the intention. In an interview he said, "We didn't try to break a lot of new ground," and defined the film simply as "funny and appealing and warm." What the audience sees is a film that employs Vivaldi's "Four Seasons" as a framework in which to examine the relationships of three couples who are close friends. Each section of the film begins with shots appropriate to the season. The first season, spring, begins with the three couples going on a trip to a cottage in the New England countryside.

Jack Burroughs (Alan Alda) is a successful lawyer who is the organizer, manager, and compulsive analyzer of the group and its activities. His wife Kate (Carol Burnett) is an editor for *Fortune* magazine. The other members of the vacation party are Danny Zimmer (Jack Weston), a dentist, hypochondriac, and gourmet cook, and his Italian wife, Claudia (Rita Moreno), an artist; and Nick Callan (Len Cariou), an insurance salesman who likes to refer to himself as an estate planner, and his wife Anne (Sandy Dennis), an amateur photographer. All are apparently affluent, ordinary people who are enjoying their comfortable, long-established marriages and friendships.

At the vacation cottage we learn, however, that Nick is unhappy with his dull, neurotic wife Anne, who talks about nothing but the still lifes of vegetables that she photographs. Nick confides his boredom and unhappiness to Jack, who is disturbed and upset at the implied changes in their relationship. The central conflict in the film is now established, as the others in the group react to Nick's and Anne's divorce and then to Nick's new girl friend.

In the summer, the three couples charter a yacht to cruise around the Virgin Islands. Kate Burroughs and Claudia Zimmer are outraged because Nick has had the effrontery to bring his new girl friend, Ginny (Bess Armstrong), along. Furthermore, their enthusiastic and noisy lovemaking keeps the other couples awake at night. It soon becomes clear that Kate and Claudia are envious of the sexual excitement and ardor displayed by Nick and Ginny. Kate reacts by accusing Jack of having sexual fantasies about Ginny, and relations between all the people on board become considerably strained.

In the autumn, Nick, again accompanied by Ginny, and the Burroughses go off to visit their daughters for Parents' Weekend at a New England college. Though they have no children at the college, the Zimmers naturally accompany their friends. At the inn there is a confrontation with Nick's ex-wife, Anne, who has also come up for the weekend. Anne accuses Kate and Claudia of deserting her after the divorce, and they realize guiltily, that this is true. In fact, Anne has not been invited to any of their parties or vacations because of the presence of Nick and Ginny. Anne's exclusion from the group's activities has been more or less taken for granted.

Everyone's latent frustrations and fears are exhibited during the weekend. Nick has an unsatisfactory talk with his unhappy daughter Lisa (Beatrice Alda); Danny is upset by Claudia's emotional outburst at Ginny and what he considers to be Jack's patronizing attitude toward him; Kate accuses Jack of being indifferent to her needs and secretly jealous of Nick's relationship with young, sexy, blond Ginny. Perhaps Kate's most telling resentment is expressed when she tells Jack that he never wants to go anywhere alone with her.

Winter arrives without any of these conflicts being resolved. Nevertheless, the three couples again go off together on a skiing trip. By now, Danny's fear of illness and death has become even more obsessive and is expressed partly through his concern for preserving the resale value of his new Mercedes Benz. He even forbids Jack and Ginny to eat sandwiches in the back seat because they might get crumbs on the upholstery.

Still resentful of Jack's patronizing, inquisitorial attitude, Danny becomes enraged when his attempt at a serious conversation about death causes the others to laugh at him. Ginny, now married to Nick and pregnant, can no longer take the critical attitude of the others. When Kate condescendingly tells her not to criticize the group's treatment of Danny, Ginny explodes and tells them that they are smug, resentful, unforgiving people, and then stalks off for a long walk in the snow. Nick is concerned but cannot follow her because he has broken his foot, so Danny decides to go to the rescue. Just as he finds her, however, he breaks through some thin ice and begins to sink. Ginny runs back to the cottage for help, and Danny is rescued, but his new Mercedes sinks through the ice. He forgets his own danger and begins worrying about his car as it disappears below the water. In the film's final shot the group trudges slowly back to the cottage, arguing loudly and heatedly among themselves.

The Four Seasons deals with the themes of loneliness, death, and friendship in a direct, straightforward manner by showing the strains imposed on the relationships of three, ordinary, middle-aged couples during the course of the seasons of one year. The acting is quite good and believable, with Carol Burnett giving perhaps the finest performance in a restrained, thoughtful role. Alda's direction is unobtrusive and competent rather than brilliant (this is the first theatrical film that he has directed) but well-adapted to his characters and material. Alan was not, however, the only Alda to contribute to the film. His wife Arlene took the photographs that are seen as Anne's work, and their daughters Beatrice and Elizabeth play the daughters at the college.

In dealing with mid-life rites of passage, *The Four Seasons* is effective because of its sincere, low-key approach to its characters. The film's script is not complex nor does it delve much below the surface, but it does succeed in capturing a certain warm camaraderie among its characters and in directing the audience's attention to the needs that draw people together. It also succeeded in showing that there is an audience for such mature films by finishing among the top ten films at the box office in 1981.

Julia Johnson

Reviews

The Hollywood Reporter. April 6, 1981, p. 3.
Los Angeles Times. May 22, 1981, VI, p. 1.
The New Republic. CLXXXIV, June 13, 1981, p. 25.
The New York Times. May 22, 1981, III, p. 11.
The New York Times. June 14, 1981, II, p. 17.
Newsweek. XCVII, May 25, 1981, p. 74.
Time. CXVII, May 25, 1981, p. 95.
Variety. April 4, 1981, p. 3.

THE FRENCH LIEUTENANT'S WOMAN

Production: Leon Clore for United Artists
Direction: Karel Reisz
Screenplay: Harold Pinter; based on the novel of the same name by John Fowles
Cinematography: Freddie Francis
Editing: John Bloom
Production design: Assheton Gorton
Art direction: Norman Dorme, Terry Pritchard, and Alan Cameron; set decoration, Ann Mollo
Costume design: Tom Rand
Music: Carl Davis
MPAA rating: R
Running time: 127 minutes

Principal characters:

Sarah/Anna	Meryl Streep
Charles/Mike	Jeremy Irons
Sam	Hilton McRae
Mary	Emily Morgan
Mrs. Poulteney	Patience Collier
Ernestina	Lynsey Baxter
Dr. Grogan	Leo McKern

John Fowles's popular and critically celebrated novel *The French Lieutenant's Woman* is a work which long eluded cinematic adaptation. Since its publication in 1969, numerous filmmakers have announced it as a project but have subsequently failed to find a way to transpose it to the screen. The problem lies with the novel's unusual structure. The Victorian tale that it relates is a fairly conventional romance, yet Fowles continually interrupts the narrator in his own voice, reminding the reader of his authorial presence and providing a commentary on the action. In this manner, the story is placed within a contemporary perspective which freshly illuminates it. Fowles also draws attention to the capriciousness of fiction by writing two endings, one happy and the other sad. A film version could ignore the novel's second level and confine itself to a realization of the Victorian story itself, but only at the cost of the very qualities which attracted filmmakers' interest in the first place. There is no precise cinematic equivalent for the structure of the novel, but the adaptation which finally reached the screen in 1981 replaces it with a structure which is arguably just as interesting and is faithful to Fowles's intentions.

The immediate reality which the film imposes is that of a contemporary film production of Fowles's novel. In the opening shot, Anna (Meryl Streep), the leading actress, is introduced as the final touches are applied to her makeup and costume. The film crew is revealed and a take of a scene for the picture begins. Within the same shot, Anna becomes Sarah Woodruff, the title character of the story, and the camera tracks with her as she walks out on the quay of the setting in Lyme, England, where the film crew is shooting on location. It is a truly remarkable opening shot, immediately dispelling the willing suspension of disbelief normally encouraged in the audience. The subsequent realization of the Victorian story is so precisely detailed, however, that it soon becomes as immediate and convincing as the framing story. In fact, the same opening shot which exposes the film's artifice paradoxically achieves a mood, before the first cut, which engenders compelling interest in the character of Sarah. Carl Davis' somber romantic score contributes to this, and so does the visually striking setting. From a formal point of view, however, the key element is the way that Streep walks. She carries herself as a woman confidently willing herself into the past. By the end of the shot, Anna has receded and the dramatic mask of Sarah has taken on life.

Like Meryl Streep, Jeremy Irons plays two characters in *The French Lieutenant's Woman*. He is Mike, the leading man, and Charles Smithson, the male protagonist of the Victorian story. Early in the film, Mike and Anna become lovers. Both are married, but initially neither shows any apparent concern for the consequences of their affair. Interestingly, the film does not encourage a belief that off-screen romance has any discernible effect on their performances as Charles and Sarah. The link between the modern couple and the Victorian couple is of another kind, and does not become apparent until the climactic scenes. Mike and Anna are less richly detailed characters than Charles and Sarah, partly because their story has considerably less space in the film than the one they are enacting. The apparent opacity of these characters is consistently turned to advantage. Their scenes are dramatically vacant until the very last scene, and it is this emptiness which is the film's actual subject.

By contrast to Mike and Anna, Charles and Sarah exist within a long tradition of literary passion. Sarah is a self-defined social outcast, melancholy over her apparent desertion by her lover, the French lieutenant of the title. Charles is a respectable scientist, engaged to a girl of good family, Ernestina (Lynsey Baxter). The patronizing Mrs. Poulteney (Patience Collier) has employed Sarah with a view toward reforming her in conformity with Christian ideals. Sarah, however, is not passive enough to submit to Mrs. Poulteney's strictures. She continues to walk in the hills overlooking the ocean and after several inadvertent meetings, Charles begins to take a sympathetic interest in her which quickly evolves into a barely suppressed love. Dr. Grogan (Leo McKern), a specialist in mental disorder, cautions Charles against pursuing the relationship. Charles persuades himself that he only wishes to help Sarah get away to London, where she believes she can make a new start.

An innocent meeting between the hopelessly attracted Charles and Sarah becomes an embrace, inadvertently witnessed by Ernestina's servant Mary (Emily Morgan) and Charles' servant Sam (Hilton McRae), who keep silent partly out of naïve loyalty and partly to conceal their own affair. Charles and Sarah separate, but after having money sent to her by his lawyer, Charles cannot resist seeking her out. They consummate their love, and Charles learns that Sarah's attachment to the French lieutenant had not in actuality included the sexual union she had earlier claimed. He returns to Lyme and breaks his engagement to Ernestina, arousing the scorn of her family, who humiliate him with a lawsuit. Although it has been Charles' intention to marry Sarah, she has disappeared, and he searches vainly for her among the London prostitutes. Three years later, when they are both in Windemere, she sends for him. She has become a governess and has achieved a personal identity as a mature woman. The tormented self-portraits which she had obsessively drawn in Lyme have become the paintings of a serene artist. She has never stopped loving Charles and the two are at last united.

As all of this occurs, the shooting of the film-within-the-film moves to a conclusion, and the separation of Mike and Anna becomes imminent. Mike loves Anna and does not want to lose her, but her attitude is more ambiguous. Reunited with their respective spouses, the two meet at a party at Mike's house. Their relationship, however, remains unresolved. Mike looks for her at the larger cast party after shooting has concluded, but she has elected to end the affair and Mike can only call out helplessly to her when she drives off with her husband. The two stories are juxtaposed very pointedly in the final reel. The happy ending of the Victorian story immediately precedes the unhappy ending of the modern story. When Mike calls to Anna, he does so from the room used as the last interior set by the film production—the location of Charles and Sarah's reconciliation. Frustrated and defeated, Mike sits on a couch in a brief, discreetly affecting long shot and lights a cigarette—an image replaced by a reprise of the final tranquil image of Charles and Sarah, sailing out of the darkness into the sunlight in a little boat.

The French Lieutenant's Woman invites a provocative interpretation. The two Victorian lovers struggle against a puritanical, repressive world and agonize over their most natural impulses, but this adversity nurtures their passion and their love survives a long separation. By contrast, the two film stars enter into a casual affair quickly and easily, but they are unable to act decisively afterwards. When Charles and Sarah finally make love, their lack of experience is evident. It is over almost before it begins, but the passionate longing of the couple makes the act deeply fulfilling. Mike and Anna, a sophisticated modern couple, can be assumed to enjoy a considerably more nuanced physical relationship but a less meaningful one. A shot of Mike sadly gazing at Anna as she sleeps is suggestive of his alienation within the relationship. He knows that she will never be what he wants her to be, a woman deeply touched by the experience of love. There is no reason for him to expect this of her because he is no less jaded.

Free of guilt, Anna and Mike have no problem other than concealing their involvement from their respective spouses. They do not suffer from their love, and this lack of suffering confronts them with their spiritual emptiness. Mike appears to invest some real emotion in the relationship, but the last shot of him visually nullifies that emotion. If he is different from Anna, it is only to the extent that he wishes he were Charles in real life. Jeremy Irons creates a more subtle differentiation between the two men than exists in Meryl Streep's performance as the two women. Anna is nothing like Sarah and would not want to be, but Mike possesses a serious nature not unlike that of Charles. The revelation of the final scene is that when he looks out the window, it is Sarah's name that he calls, not Anna's. Abandoning this futile longing for passion born of Victorian suppression, the modern hero accepts the desolation born of his emptiness. *The French Lieutenant's Woman* suggests that twentieth century liberation and enlightenment have been won at a severe emotional cost.

Most of the credit for the intelligence of this venturesome adaptation belongs to Harold Pinter. Pinter is not a hack screenwriter but a brilliant literary artist no less accomplished than Fowles. He demonstrates a subtle appreciation of the implications which underlie the novel's structure, and the result is a beautifully constructed screenplay. The modern sequences are distinguished by the kind of elliptical indirection for which Pinter has always shown a special flair, and the Victorian sequences reveal an admirable ear for stylized and often lyrical dialogue derived from a tradition which is not the author's own.

Even a screenplay of this quality can be inadequately realized as a film, however, as is proven by another Victorian subject reflected through a modern sensibility, *The Go-Between* (1971), whose screenplay was also written by Pinter and directed by Joseph Losey. Pinter's collaborator on *The French Lieutenant's Woman* is director Karel Reisz, and one could be forgiven for the low expectations aroused by Reisz's participation. In twenty years, he has arguably failed before now to make a film of genuine merit, although *Morgan* (1968) and *Who'll Stop the Rain?* (1977) have cult followings. Reisz has always had a tendency pretentiously to inflate interesting material, especially *The Gambler* (1974) and *Who'll Stop the Rain?*, and the works which result are unconvincingly portentous.

On the other hand, *The French Lieutenant's Woman* is already pitched at a somewhat abstract level in Pinter's screenplay, and Reisz responds intelligently by treating it with sensitivity and care. His controlled, stately camera movements capture all of the values and dimensions implicit in the material. His transitions between the modern and Victorian episodes are direct and unaffected, and he wisely resists superficial stylistic differences which would disrupt the harmony of the complementary stories. The same muted colors and measured rhythms persist throughout the work. The realization of the Victorian sequences is especially praiseworthy because of the evident difficulty most modern filmmakers have in telling Victorian stories. Modern actors tend to seem anachronistic playing Victorian characters, and that is the reason why even such conscientious works as *Tess* (1980) and *The Go-Between* are unconvincing. *The French Lieutenant's Woman* does not suffer from this failure. All of the players are credible, particularly Jeremy Irons in his role as Charles, and the Victorian atmosphere which other filmmakers have had such difficulty capturing breathes robustly within the frames. The cinematography, costumes, sets, and decor all contribute to the effectiveness of Reisz's *mise-en-scène*.

Divided critical and popular reaction greeted *The French Lieutenant's Woman*. It was nominated for five Academy Awards, but even Harold Pinter's screenplay failed to win. Perhaps the artistic achievement of *The French Lieutenant's Woman* is too subtle for present tastes and will be more appreciated with the passing of time. Its daring formal approach is deserving of profound respect. This adventurous spirit is exactly what the modern cinema most needs.

Blake Lucas

Reviews

The Hollywood Reporter. September 10, 1981, p. 4.
Los Angeles Times. September 13, 1981, *Calendar*, p. 27.
The New York Times. September 18, 1981, III, p. 4.
The New York Times. September 27, 1981, II, p. 17.
The New Yorker. LVII, September 12, 1981, pp. 158-162.
Newsweek. XCVIII, September 21, 1981, p. 96+.
Time. CXVIII, September 7, 1981, pp. 48-50.
Variety. September 10, 1981, p. 3.

GALLIPOLI

Origin: Australia
Released: 1980
Released in U.S.: 1981
Production: Robert Stigwood and Patricia Lovell for Associated R and R Films; released by Roadshow
Distribution in U.S.: Paramount
Direction: Peter Weir
Screenplay: David Williamson
Cinematography: Russell Boyd
Editing: William Anderson
Art direction: Herbert Pinter
Music: Brian May
MPAA rating: PG
Running time: 110 minutes

Principal characters:
Archy .... Mark Lee
Frank Dune ....Mel Gibson
Major Barton .... Bill Hunter
Uncle Jack .... Bill Kerr

Director Peter Weir has been, for several years, the driving force behind what many film critics have termed "the last new wave"—the young Australian film industry. He first came to international attention through a darkly suspenseful small film, *Picnic at Hanging Rock* (1979), featuring some rather bizarre occurrences at a girls' school picnic. Its successor, the highly acclaimed *The Last Wave* (1979), firmly established his reputation as a major new talent, and in 1981 *Gallipoli* won for him a broad international following and became the first Australian film to be released by a major American studio.

Although *Gallipoli* possesses materials of epic potential, it is primarily an intimate story depending upon a visual texture and the establishment of mood to achieve an emotional effect. The film originated in a story written by Weir and was shaped into a sensitive screenplay by writer David Williamson. Its setting is a World War I battle and it centers in particular on the events leading up to a futile stand made by some Australian soldiers against the Turks on the beach of Gallipoli in Turkey.

Yet, this is less a war film than it is a tribute to the spirit of the men who fought the battle. Weir's protagonist, Archy (Mark Lee), a young Australian athlete who leaves his family and the security of his track career to fight for Britain, seems initially to fit the stereotype of the traditional hero. Yet the director holds his young warrior up for scrutiny and, in fact, in many respects reduces him to an abstraction, not only to examine the fundamental nature of heroism but also to question its validity. The battle of Gallipoli, though a noble effort, was a needless massacre of young men in the prime of their lives.

Archy is seventeen when the film opens, and from the outset he is on a track leading to extinction. He is conventional enough at the beginning, being blond, personable, and presumably virtuous like the characters in *Picnic at Hanging Rock* and *The Last Wave*. Though he is one of Australia's fastest runners, he is not one to resist a dare and accepts a foolish challenge to race a man on horseback twenty-four hours before an important race. In doing so, he proves his manhood but injures his feet in the process, jeopardizing his chances in the really important match the following day.

At the match, he strikes up a friendship with a rather cynical competitor named Frank (Mel Gibson). In a sense, the two runners are the antithesis of each other. Archy is idealistic, pure, and noble—a man just waiting for the right cause for which to die. Frank is more worldly-wise and considers heroism something of an exercise in futility. For their own divergent reasons, the two young athletes enlist in the army and eventually come face to face with the battle of Gallipoli.

The two are briefly separated at Perth because Archy is intent on joining the cavalry and Frank cannot ride, but they rejoin each other in Cairo, and the film embarks on a rather lengthy look at the enjoyments of the young troopers in the bazaars of the Middle East. This is followed by some mildly amusing maneuvers in Egypt, and it is thus almost two hours into the film before the young men arrive at Gallipoli. By this time, however, their characters are so well delineated and the audience so emotionally involved with their lives that the impending battle takes on enormous impact. On the evening before the final battle, Archy's commander designates him as a runner to deliver messages between the various units involved in the action. Believing this role to be less heroic than taking part in the fighting, he volunteers the almost equally swift but more fearful Frank to assume the duties of messenger, while he takes part in the noble stand. The more practical Frank is glad to accept the assignment since it obviously enhances his chances of survival in the next day's battle.

By traditional measures of heroism, Archy's decision no doubt seems noble if not particularly wise. Its wisdom becomes even more questionable when a cease-fire message from the British Commander arrives too late to stop the fight. The needless action cost the British Empire 241,000 casualties, of which Australia suffered 26,000 wounded and 7,594 dead out of 60,000 men involved in the campaign. One of these dead men is Archy.

The enormity of the futile stand and the questionable nobility of war itself is brought into brutal focus by Weir, who employs the battle as the climax and devotes the larger part of the film to developing the friendship between the two protagonists. He sensitively establishes their individuality and clearly delineates the characters of the other soldiers with whom they interact. By rendering the men as individual human beings, Weir causes the viewer to care about these soldiers. Thus, a battle little-known in much of the world which occurred in an era long past becomes a real and symbolic epic.

Well aware of the profusion of antiwar films, Weir and his coworkers sought to make their particular statement unique and chillingly effective. The first step was Williamson's script, which emphasizes what is probably a truism—the power of war to unite individuals of widely divergent backgrounds. The process of unification reflected in *Gallipoli*'s script, however, borders almost on team spirit, a fact that allows the characters to overlook differences in values. Historically, Australia's ambivalent feelings toward England are accurately reflected in Frank's initial attitude toward the war. There is simply no reason to get involved. Archy, though, views his participation in the war in much the same manner as he does his involvement in athletics. There is a certain excitement and challenge inherent in it for him, another chance to prove his manhood as he had earlier in the race against the horse. This time, however, he does more than injure his feet in the process. He loses his life. Before that happens, he unfortunately shares his passion and excitement with his comrades, much as an athlete would before a big match.

Weir enhances the power of the script through a collection of beautiful scenes reminiscent of, but without the supernatural overtones of *Picnic at Hanging Rock* and *The Last Wave*. Some of the more memorable images include Major Barton (Bill Hunter) listening to an operatic duet in his tent just before the battle; boats rowing toward the Gallipoli beach bearing awed, nervous faces concentrating on the glow of the war ahead; Archy's uncle (Bill Kerr) reading a book by Rudyard Kipling to sleeping children; and a trek across the formidable landscape of the Australian desert.

Weir, who in his previous films depended almost entirely upon his own resources of imagery, is buttressed in *Gallipoli* not only by Williamson's outstanding script but also by Mel Gibson's impressive performance as Frank. The entire cast, for that matter, is solid and provides meticulously detailed characterizations.

Gallipoli avoids the predictable patterns of most antiwar films, examining the tragic misdirection of natural, straightforward, youthful zest for adventure and of the normal impulses of patriotism.

Diana Lisignoli

Reviews

The Hollywood Reporter. August 10, 1981, p. 8.

Los Angeles Times. August 23, 1981, *Calendar*, p. 32.
The New York Times. August 28, 1981, III, p. 6.
Newsweek. XCVIII, September 7, 1981, p. 82.
Time. CXVIII, September 14, 1981, p. 90.
Variety. August 6, 1981, p. 3.

GHOST STORY

Production: Burt Weissbourd for Universal
Direction: John Irvin
Screenplay: Lawrence D. Cohen; based on the novel of the same name by Peter Straub
Cinematography: Jack Cardiff
Editing: Tom Rolf
Art direction: Norman Newberry
Special effects: Albert Whitlock
Music: Philippe Sarde
MPAA rating: R
Running time: 110 minutes

Principal characters:

Ricky Hawthorne .... Fred Astaire
Dr. John Jaffrey .... Melvyn Douglas
Edward Wanderly .... Douglas Fairbanks, Jr.
Sears James .... John Houseman
Mrs. Hawthorne .... Patricia Neal
Don Wanderly .... Craig Wasson
Eva/Alma .... Alice Krige
Gregory Bate .... Miguel Fernandes
Young Hawthorne .... Tim Choate
Young Jaffrey .... Mark Chamberlin
Young Wanderly .... Kurt Johnson
Young James .... Ken Olin

Although originality of material need not necessarily be a criterion for effective filmmaking, overly familiar material must be handled in innovative ways or explored with unique technical acumen if sheer boredom is to be avoided. Thus, although the action in *Ghost Story* clearly falls within one of the most hackneyed horror-story formulas, one that revolves around a deadly curse of long standing, the producers have utilized several techniques to invest the conventional plot with interest.

The narrative line of the film extends back fifty years, to a time when four young men (Tim Choate, Mark Chamberlin, Kurt Johnson, and Ken Olin) become fascinated with Eva (Alice Krige), a mysterious summer visitor to their hometown in Vermont. Their innocent flirtation leads to a deeper involvement, which results in one of them being granted her sexual favors. His inability to respond satisfactorily generates tension, and at a drunken party he accidentally knocks her down, apparently killing her. His friends join him in concealing the act and drive her car, with her body in it, into a nearby pond. As the car sinks out of sight, however, they see Eva, seemingly alive, trying frantically to escape. Their desultory attempts to rescue her from the now-submerged vehicle prove futile.

The action then flashes forward fifty years in time to a period when the four friends, now grown old, begin to have nightmares. A son of Edward Wanderly (Douglas Fairbanks, Jr.), who has become mayor of the town, dies under suspicious circumstances when he plunges from the window of a New York City skyscraper. His other son, Don (Craig Wasson), falls in love with the beautiful, but unstable Alma (also played by Alice Krige) who is actually a reincarnation of Eva, back from the dead. We learn that she was involved in some way with Don's brother's death as well. Finally, the elder Wanderly dies when he leaps into the icy waters of a Vermont river, and his death, as well as their own recurring nightmares, convinces the surviving friends that something ghostly is interfering in their lives. This knowledge does not save another of their number, Dr. John Jaffrey (Melvyn Douglas), from death, but it does cause the remaining two, Sears James (John Houseman) and Ricky Hawthorne (Fred Astaire), who are both lawyers, to join Don Wanderly in an attempt to exorcise the curse which the older men see as a response to their past crime. Although James dies and Don is injured in the proceedings, Hawthorne lays the ghost to rest when he hoists the car containing Eva's decayed body from the pond.

One approach which the film employs in an effort to lend some originality to this formulaic narrative is that of loading the plot line with some extra twists, which should have added to the mystery and suspense, but which, because of inferior handling, serves only to complicate and obfuscate the development. For example, the avenging ghost in *Ghost Story* enlists the aid of an escaped lunatic, Gregory Bate (Miguel Fernandes), to carry out her revenge. Yet unlike Renfield, the lunatic who serves Dracula in Bram Stoker's novel, Bate ultimately emerges as irrelevant to the unfolding of the plot. Eva does not really need him since she is more than capable of punishing the four men through the use of her own powers, nor is there a clearly developed master-slave relationship between Eva and Bate. One suspects that the presence of the madman is merely designed to satisfy the expectations of contemporary horror-film audiences, who are accustomed to seeing a lunatic as the perpetrator of horror in such films as Alfred Hitchcock's classic *Psycho* (1960) and John Carpenter's more recent *Halloween* (1978). Another twist to the plot line of *Ghost Story* which fails to achieve its desired effect is the attempt to characterize the "Chowder Society," the name which the old men assign to themselves, as a group with a particular interest in the occult. Hawthorne's wife (Patricia Neal) remarks that they spend their time telling "gruesome stories" to one another, and, in fact, an early scene in the film depicts Sears James recounting such a tale. If the old men have occult interests, however, the relationship between those interests and their crime in the past, and Eva's subsequent revenge, is not made clear. Instead of imbuing the formulaic plot with more interest, the introduction of Gregory Bate and the idea of occultism merely clutter the narrative.

Another way in which the film should have risen above its material was through its cast. Four veteran actors, each of them capable of generating interest through their respective performances, appear in central roles. Except for Fred Astaire, however, their actual screen time is minimal. The character played by Douglas Fairbanks, Jr., is killed off during the first third of the film, and the role of Melvyn Douglas, who was performing in his final film, lasts only slightly longer. John Houseman's character, on the other hand, survives almost to the story's conclusion, but he is present on screen only sporadically. Another accomplished performer, Patricia Neal, is also underused as Astaire's wife; she speaks less than ten lines and is on screen for a period lasting less than five minutes. While the rest of the cast, particularly Alice Krige and Craig Wasson, who carry most of the film, are competent, they do not bring with them the cinematic traditions of such veteran actors. Moreover, the sparse appearances of the characters do not allow the audience to gain the sort of identification with them that must occur in horror films if the obligatory murders are to exercise their full effect.

A third possibility for *Ghost Story* to inject new vitality into its conventional plot involves sexual frankness. After all, it was sexual failure that indirectly resulted in Eva's death, and when she returns as Alma, Eva uses her sexuality to entice the Wanderly sons. Yet the only way in which *Ghost Story* handles sexuality differently from other horror films as far back as F. W. Murnau's *Nosferatu* (1922) is that the earlier films were merely suggestive while *Ghost Story* is explicit. Commentators on horror films have frequently noted their covert—and sometimes not so covert—erotic component. Whether making that eroticism explicit represents an innovation significant enough to justify the conventionality of *Ghost Story* in other respects remains arguable.

Finally, horror films often become memorable through the adroit use of special effects. Old ideas can be refurbished and made appealing by means of jarring visual images. For example, a film such as Stanley Kubrick's *The Shining* (1980) vitalized its formulaic plot with such devices as tracking shots through the corridors of the haunted hotel where it is set and visual flashbacks to the tragedies that had occurred there. In this respect as well, however, *Ghost Story* fails to offer anything particularly original. Albert Whitlock, who was responsible for the film's visual special effects, has relied primarily upon such devices as transforming the beautiful, seductive Alma into the skeletal ghost of Eva. The change from Alma's face to a skull, which occurs repeatedly in the film, is a cliché of the horror genre.

Ghost Story represents a failure in a number of respects. It provides no new ideas for the horror-film genre, it clutters its story line with irrelevancies, it fails to utilize a potentially fine cast, and it offers nothing that is particularly stimulating in the way of special effects. Although all makers of horror films must face the temptation to sacrifice quality for easy thrills, *Ghost Story* provides neither quality nor excitement. It must be regarded as a wasted effort for virtually everyone involved, and an especially disappointing one as its appearance was held in such high anticipation by admirers of the principal actors. Predictably, the film did not do well critically or financially, with critics lamenting that so much talent went to waste.

Frances M. Malpezzi
William M. Clements

Reviews

The Hollywood Reporter. December 14, 1981, p. 3.
Los Angeles Times. December 16, 1981, VI, p. 1.
The New York Times. December 16, 1981, III, p. 27.
Time. CXIX, January 4, 1982, p. 87.
Variety. December 14, 1981, p. 3.

THE GREAT MUPPET CAPER

Production: David Lazar and Frank Oz for Universal
Direction: Jim Henson
Screenplay: Tom Patchett, Jay Tarses, Jerry Juhl, and Jack Rose
Cinematography: Oswald Morris
Editing: Ralph Kemplen
Art direction: Harry Lange
Music: Joe Raposo
Choreography: Anita Mann
MPAA rating: G
Running time: 98 minutes

Principal characters:
Lady Holiday .... Diana Rigg
Nicky Holiday .... Charles Grodin
Mr. Tarkanian .... Jack Warden
Man on bench .... Robert Morley
Marla .... Erica Creer
Neville .... John Cleese
Kermit .... Voice of Jim Henson
Miss Piggy .... Voice of Frank Oz
Fozie Bear .... Voice of Frank Oz
Gonzo .... Voice of Dave Goelz
Pops .... Voice of Jerry Nelson

The Great Muppet Caper was the second Jim Henson feature-length film to star the internationally popular Muppets, Kermit the Frog and Miss Piggy. Created in the early 1950's, Kermit became an American sensation when he and dozens of Henson's and Frank Oz's Muppet characters appeared on the public television children's show "Sesame Street" in the late 1960's. After enjoying increasing popularity for several years, Kermit became the star of an internationally syndicated television series called *The Muppet Show*. The series was produced in London, although its production crew was American, and it featured other popular characters which now are worldwide celebrities, Miss Piggy, Fozie Bear, Gonzo, and a score of others. Despite the immense popularity of the show, Henson Associates decided to stop production in 1980 to concentrate solely on feature films and other individual projects. The first film was *The Muppet Movie* (1979), a very successful musical with a Paul Williams score and a number of well-known stars appearing in guest roles.

Their second film, *The Great Muppet Caper*, opened in the summer of 1981 to a very strong box-office showing. Without the added large cast of celebrities featured in *The Muppet Movie*, the story attempted to make the Muppets more human and more versatile.

The opening credits to the film pass by as Kermit, his "identical" twin brother Fozie Bear, and their sidekick Gonzo, whose species is a mystery to all, sail through the sky in a hot air balloon. After a number of wisecracks about the credits, the group crashes into a busy city street (presumably in Chicago or New York), initiating a lavish production number describing the film which the audience will see. During the sequence, the audience, but not "crack investigative reporters" Kermit and Fozie, witnesses Charles Grodin stealing a woman's jewels. The woman turns out to be Lady Holiday (Diana Rigg), the "fashion Queen of London."

The reporters and their photographer, Gonzo, learn about the robbery from their editor on *The Daily Chronicle*, Mr. Tarkanian (Jack Warden, the first of four cameo stars in the film). Tarkanian is furious that their paper's lead story that morning was "Identical Twins Join Chronicle Staff," featuring a smiling photograph of the decidedly unidentical Kermit and Fozie. Tarkanian fires the three, but reluctantly agrees to take them back if, as Kermit suggests, the trio can fly to London (at their own expense) and capture the thief.

The three fly to London in cargo boxes, "9th class," and are thrown out of the plane just over an English pond beside which Robert Morley is seated. Morley suggests the Happiness Hotel as the perfect place for their poverty-ridden stay in London, and the three go there by bus only to be thrown out on the hotel's sidewalk. The ever-mystical Gonzo seems to enjoy the experience; frequently throughout the film he makes references to masochistic tendencies, which seem rather out of place in a film such as this.

Their entry into the Happiness Hotel signals one of the film's most clever numbers, "Welcome Home," in which the various oddities and odd occupants of the hotel are introduced. As Pops, the proprieter, says, succinctly summarizing the ambience of the place, there are three ways to pay: "credit card, travelers checks, or sneak out in the middle of the night."

In the meantime, Lady Holiday is hard at work on her new show and hires Miss Piggy, an overeager erstwhile model, as her new receptionist. While Piggy is in Lady Holiday's office, the designer gives a lengthy monologue describing her ne'er-do-well brother Nicky, who she feels might even steal his sister's famous "Baseball diamond." When the curious Piggy asks why Lady Holiday is saying all this, she replies "plot exposition—it has to go somewhere."

Kermit and Piggy finally meet when Kermit mistakes her for Lady Holiday. It is love at first sight, but Piggy, afraid to admit that she is not Lady Holiday, agrees to meet him that night at the made-up address of her home, 17 Highbrow Street.

That night, preparing for his date, Kermit displays the new acrobatics which camera techniques and special effects made possible for the usually hand-

and-stick-operated Muppets. He jumps, dances, puts his pants on one web-foot at a time, and enchants the audience with the number "Stepping Out with a Star." The song and dance routine, like much of the Henson-produced material, is a paean to old films, in this case *Royal Wedding* (1951), in which Fred Astaire seemingly defied gravity by dancing on the walls and ceiling of his room while singing about his new love.

A virtually unrelated but very clever scene occurs soon after between Neville (John Cleese of the Monty Python Group) and his wife, who happen to live at 17 Highbrow Street. In the manner of an English drawing room comedy, they discuss the weather and their household while casually noticing "a pig" climbing up the house. Cleese is particularly good in his brief role as the stereotype motion-picture Englishman, trying to be unruffled by a pair of animal intruders. The problems of scaling the Muppets with the human actors, particularly a very tall man such as Cleese, were overcome by using small rooms and making him hunch over in pursuit of Kermit and Piggy, who are somewhat larger than their television counterparts.

When Kermit and Piggy, accompanied by Fozie and Gonzo, go to the Super Club suggested by Neville, two other patrons are Lady Holiday and her brother Nicky (Charles Grodin—the man seen earlier disguised in burglar garb). As it develops, Nicky and three of Lady Holiday's models have conspired to steal all her jewels and rob her of a very expensive necklace at the club that night. Kermit, who is enchanted (along with Nicky) by Piggy's dance number "The First Time It Happens," finds out that she has been assuming Lady Holiday's identity when the real Lady Holiday screams that her jewels have been taken.

Gonzo, who had been trying to earn money for their expensive supper by taking photographs of the other diners, takes a picture of the robbery, but his film is ruined when the anxious occupants of the Happiness Hotel burst into the bathroom which he is using as a darkroom.

Kermit and Piggy meet by chance in Hyde Park and reconcile, after which all of the Muppet characters again suspend the audience's disbelief by riding bicycles. A few days later the new fashion show is about to take place, and Nicky and the models plan to blame Piggy for the nightclub robbery by placing the jewels on her. Marla (Erica Creer) accomplishes this by feigning an injury so that Piggy must take her place in the show. During her stint, Piggy fantasizes that she is starring in an Esther Williams style aquacade, replete with synchronized swimming, dancing water, and smoke. When she falls into a fountain, the jewel necklace is planted in her robe and she is arrested.

Kermit and his friends plan to help Piggy when Gonzo discovers that Nicky and the models are the real thieves. Meanwhile, Lady Holiday has given her Baseball diamond to the Mallory Gallery, and Nicky plans to steal it from there. The Muppets, learning of his intentions, decide to catch Nicky in the act.

The Muppets and the thieves plan their strategies in parallel scenes. They meet in a silly but amusing sequence in the Mallory Gallery, where the Muppets play keep-a-way with the Baseball diamond. Piggy saves them all by crashing through the windows on a motorcycle which she just happened to find.

At the end, the thieves are arrested, Kermit, Fozie, and Gonzo get their jobs back, and all the Muppets fly home and again are thrown out of the plane.

Although most reviewers as well as the general public did not like *The Great Muppet Caper* as well as *The Muppet Movie*, the film shows much more sophistication and charm than the earlier work. The art direction and special effects were particularly magnificent. While science-fiction films usually receive the greatest praise in the field of special effects, the simple scenes of Muppets smoothly riding bicycles in Hyde Park represent a tremendous technical accomplishment. Additionally, the original score by Joe Raposo stands up well, and one of his songs, "The First Time," was nominated for an Oscar, losing to "Arthur's Theme" by Christopher Cross, Peter Allen, Burt Bacharach, and Carole Bayer Sager from *Arthur*.

Diana Lisignoli

Reviews

The Hollywood Reporter. June 24, 1981, p. 3.
Los Angeles Times. June 27, 1981, II, p. 4.
The New Republic. CLXXXV, August 1-8, p. 26.
The New York Times. June 26, 1981, III, p. 8.
Newsweek. XCVIII, July 6, 1981, p. 75.
Variety. June 24, 1981, p. 3.

HEARTLAND

Production: Michael Hausman and Beth Ferris for Wilderness Women-Filmhaus
Direction: Richard Pearce
Screenplay: Beth Ferris; based on unpublished sources as well as on *Letters of a Woman Homesteader* and *Letters on an Elk Hunt* by Elinore Stewart
Cinematography: Fred Murphy
Editing: Bill Yahraus
Art direction: Carl Copeland
Music: Charles Gross
Running time: 93 minutes

Principal characters:
Clyde Stewart .... Rip Torn
Elinore Randall Stewart .... Conchata Ferrell
Jack .... Barry Primus
Grandma Landauer .... Lilia Skala
Jerrine .... Megan Folsom
Cattle buyer .... Jerry Hardin

Heartland is an unusual and rewarding film. Made on a small budget with a cast consisting almost entirely of unknown actors, the film is a fine, unsentimental story of a woman's life on a Wyoming ranch in 1910. It is a story of work and survival, two subjects seldom treated in American cinema.

The film begins as Elinore Randall (Conchata Ferrell) and her seven-year-old daughter, Jerrine (Megan Folsom), travel by train to Elinore's new job as a housekeeper on a Wyoming ranch, but we do not learn all these details at once; they are revealed slowly and naturally. There is, however, one title to set the time and location: Burnt Fork, Wyoming, 1910.

Elinore's employer is Clyde Stewart (Rip Torn), a gruff and taciturn Scot. When he meets the train, he immediately gives her a list of groceries and supplies and tells her to get them at the store and be ready to go to the ranch in half an hour. At the ranch he tells her where a few things are, but subsequently speaks only when he is asked a direct question. Having previously lived in the large city of Denver, Elinore now finds herself in a strange, sparsely populated place with no one to talk with except her young daughter.

Because there is little dialogue and the story progresses slowly and often by indirect means, this film is a different sort of viewing experience than that usually provided by the more conventional Hollywood films. *Heartland* requires the viewer to note the things *not* said, the empty spaces of the Wyoming countryside, small changes in relationships, and even the changes in the weather.

Both Elinore and the viewer do pick up some information when Grandma Landauer (Lilia Skala) stops for a visit. She is not especially talkative, but she is friendly and does give Elinore some background, such as the fact that Stewart's wife died three years before. Grandma also warns about the winters, telling Elinore that her own husband froze to death in one of them.

Elinore continues her work during the summer, but her relationship with Stewart remains the same; they speak only of what has to be done and never of personal matters. The hired hand, Jack (Barry Primus), is more friendly toward Elinore and Jerrine than is Stewart, but he, too, is not very talkative and has little in common with them. Occasionally he plays a bit with Jerrine, but most of the time the child is left to find her own amusements. In one instance, after Elinore cooks for the branding crew, Stewart walks over to her and says, "You did all right, Mrs. Randall." This small bit of praise surprises her and she does not know how to respond.

Meanwhile, Elinore has realized that she is tired of always working for someone else, and she decides that she will establish a homestead of her own. This requires paying a filing fee of twelve dollars and living on a 240-acre piece of land for ten years. After she files on a nearby plot, however, Stewart is upset because he expects a full year's work from her since he had paid her way to Wyoming. She replies that she intends to keep working for him. He carefully points out, though, that she cannot possibly make a go of the homestead on the small wage (seven dollars a week) that he pays her. The result of this conversation is that they decide to get married.

Stewart's proposal is, of course, not in the least impassioned, and on their wedding day he is still calling her "Mrs. Randall," but as time passes and winter comes, they grow much closer. When Elinore becomes pregnant, she even evokes some tenderness and concern in her rough-hewn husband. Later, we are almost startled when we hear him call her "Ellie." At the onset of winter, Stewart has decided that the price offered for cattle that year is too low and that he will keep most of his herd and feed them through the cold months in hopes that they will bring a better price the next year. Because there is no money to pay him, Jack leaves to spend the winter in Mexico. At this point, the audience briefly meets the cattle buyer (Jerry Hardin), who is by far the most outgoing and loquacious character in the entire film. His short appearance emphasizes the reserved nature of the rest of the people in *Heartland*.

The dark, cold, and forbidding winter has fully settled in when Elinore's labor begins. She sends Stewart after Grandma Landauer, but he returns covered with snow and nearly frozen to report that she was not there. Elinore has to give birth by herself as her exhausted husband sleeps at the dining table. The new son gives them only a brief period of joy, however, and before many days have passed, he is suffering from convulsions. The new parents have no way of getting help and very little idea of what to do. The child's inevitable death is conveyed by showing Jerrine going to sleep one evening as she watches them caring for him and then showing her waking the next morning and going to the next room where she finds them washing the body for burial—a common ritual for the period.

After the thaw begins, Stewart rides out to check his cattle. He finds many of them dead and begins skinning them to save the only part that he can still sell. As for Elinore, her stoicism is not completely invulnerable. One day as she is hanging out the laundry on the clothesline she suddenly begins screaming for no apparent reason, and some time later when Grandma Landauer is visiting her she breaks down and cries.

Jack comes back and is welcomed by Jerrine, but Stewart is almost overwhelmed by the loss of about half his cattle. He does not talk about this with Elinore until she asks him, but then he tell her he thinks the place is lost. Her reaction is to try to encourage him, explaining that she is his wife and has buried a child on the land, so she is not going to give up. Finally he even makes a small joke. Then he comes to her in the night with an urgent request to help him with a cow that is having trouble giving birth. The two of them have to reach inside the cow and attach ropes to the feet of the calf and then pull it out. They finally succeed and then—as the calf finally begins to breathe—the shot of Elinore and Stewart together freezes. After that there is a final shot of Jerrine walking along as the credits are shown. On that hopeful note the film ends.

Heartland is a true story, based mainly on unpublished letters by Elinore Stewart and the reminiscences of her children. In addition, it was filmed entirely on location (with Montana substituting for Wyoming). The filmmakers and the actors and actresses succeed in conveying both the look and the feelings of that isolated place and time. Conchata Ferrell, who plays Elinore, has said that she regarded it as a once-in-a-lifetime role. "Elinore," Ferrell said, "is a true heroine—just in the way she faced every day of her life. For me, there is something triumphant about that." Ferrell had to learn to drive horses for the role and also actually helped to deliver the calf in the film's final scene. Her acting and her solid physique make her quite convincing in the part. Rip Torn is also effective in conveying the character of Stewart, a man who is not cruel but does not know how to express his feelings.

Richard Pearce, the director, has made documentaries and features for television, but *Heartland* is his first feature film. It was, in fact, made originally as a television production for the Women's Television Workshop to appear on PBS but was deemed to have sufficient theatrical possibilities as well. The film cost well under one million dollars and was almost entirely financed by the National Endowment for the Humanities. It was made in 1979 and received much critical acclaim and several prizes at film festivals. The filmmakers bought the rights from the government to show the film commercially in 1981. Although the film gained much critical praise, it failed to capture a large audience and disappeared from theaters shortly after its release.

Timothy W. Johnson

Reviews

The Hollywood Reporter. October 4, 1981, p. 2.
Los Angeles Times. November 2, 1981, VI, p. 4.
The New York Times. August 23, 1981, p. 65.

HEAVEN'S GATE

Production: Joann Carelli for United Artists
Direction: Michael Cimino
Screenplay: Michael Cimino
Cinematography: Vilmos Zsigmond
Editing: Tom Rolf, William Reynolds, Lisa Fruchtman, and Gerald Greenberg
Art direction: Tambi Larsen, Spencer Deverill, and Maurice Fowler; set decoration, Jim Berkey and Josie MacAvin
Costume design: Allen Highfill
Choreography: Eleanore Fazan
Sound: Darin Knight
Music: David Mansfield
MPAA rating: R
Running time: 145 minutes

Principal characters:
James Averill .... Kris Kristofferson
Nathan D. Champion ....Christopher Walken
Billy Irvine ....John Hurt
Frank Canton .... Sam Waterston
Mr. Eggleston ....Brad Dourif
Ella Watson .... Isabelle Huppert
Reverend Doctor .... Joseph Cotten
John L. Bridges .... Jeff Bridges

Michael Cimino's mercurial career as a screenwriter and director reached a peak with the 1978 release of *The Deer Hunter*, which won Academy Awards for Best Picture and Best Direction. By 1981, however, with the release of his next film, *Heaven's Gate*, he was credited with creating the most expensive failure—thirty-six million dollars—in the history of filmmaking. A 1963 graduate of Yale, Cimino made his screenwriting debut with *Silent Running* (1971, starring Deric Washburn and Steve Bochco), a science-fiction film directed by Douglas Trumbull. He then coauthored (with John Milius) *Magnum Force* (1973), a successful Clint Eastwood "Dirty Harry" film, and the following year he wrote and directed *Thunderbolt and Lightfoot*, again starring Eastwood and Jeff Bridges.

When *Heaven's Gate* was completed, Cimino's early successes seemed to indicate a brilliant future. Cimino attended a New York preview of *Heaven's Gate* held on November 18, 1980, with several United Artists executives and two of the film's principal actors, Kris Kristofferson and Christopher Walken. Before the film began, Cimino was surrounded by numerous sycophants who shook his hand and patted him on the back. Two hours later, however, during the intermission, Cimino and his party were slumped down in their mezzanine seats, with no well-wishers in sight. The following day it was reported that the film was to be pulled from release and reedited at Cimino's request, with Cimino quoted as saying that the pressure of completing the work on time had "clouded my perception of the film."

The 219-minute version was universally lambasted by the critics, who regarded it as an interminable bore and an example of self-indulgence of a magnitude that could destroy the industry. A subsequent 145-minute version was released the following April but the critical reaction was unchanged.

Cimino begins his film with a twenty-minute prologue which depicts the Harvard commencement of 1870, where an incoherent commencement address is delivered by the Reverend Doctor (played by an obviously confused Joseph Cotten). Among the young graduates are James Averill (Kris Kristofferson) and the class orator, Billy Irvine (John Hurt), who also speaks gibberish. Following the ceremonies, the graduates are shown parading on campus to the background music of "The Battle Hymn of the Republic" and later drunkenly celebrating by dancing on the Harvard Green with beautifully gowned young girls to "The Blue Danube Waltz." While the commencement sequence is strikingly filmed and the dance sequence is beautifully choreographed, neither sheds any light whatsoever on the film's rambling plot. Curiously, this expensively made prologue was actually filmed at England's Oxford University.

The film jumps abruptly to the American West of 1890, where Averill has become the Federal Marshal of Johnson County, Wyoming, while Irvine is an alcoholic cattle baron. This sudden transition never explains how Averill became Marshal, but immediately plunges the viewer into the sparse plot around which the movie revolves. It seems that the local cattlemen, headed by Frank Canton (Sam Waterston), have formed the Stock Growers' Association in an effort to maintain control of the county against the large number of poor Eastern European immigrants who are settling there. A mixture of ethnic groups from Bulgaria, Germany, Russia, and the Ukraine, they are accused of rustling stray cattle in order to avoid starvation.

The Stock Growers' Association has compiled a list of 125 settlers whom they wish to have killed and they hire a group of mercenaries led by Nathan D. Champion (Christopher Walken) to do the job. Although the script never explains why, Champion had also been a friend of Averill many years ago.

Among the settlers on the cattlemen's list for extinction is a young madam named Ella Watson (Isabelle Huppert), who runs a house of prostitution called "Hog Ranch." Here, again we are shown another scene with little explication from the script, this one a love triangle involving Ella, Averill, and Champion. From all appearances Ella is really in love with Averill but decides to marry Champion for reasons that are not altogether clear.

Averill elects to take a stand against the murderous intentions of Canton and the Stock Growers' Association and enlists the help of John L. Bridges (Jeff Bridges), a saloon keeper, to organize the settlers to fight for their self-preservation.

It takes more than two hours for the sparse plot to evolve to this point. Champion, next, has a change of heart, and instead of leading the mercenaries against the settlers, he joins Ella and his friend Averill in a lengthy, bloody battle which leaves nearly everyone dead except Averill. This bloodbath takes place with the ill-prepared settlers circling around the mercenaries, who are well-armed with Winchester rifles, in a scene evocative of the work of director Sam Peckinpah at his most excessive.

The final sequence is an epilogue tacked on by Cimino and set in 1900. Produced for a reported three hundred thousand dollars, this epilogue shows an aging Averill aboard a luxurious yacht off the Rhode Island coast wearily remembering the past.

Heaven's Gate is a political interpretation of American history in which Cimino attempts to show the xenophobia of American capitalism and the reverse side of the American Dream, the fatal liability of poverty. The rich will kill for the earth they do not inherit.

The original budget for *Heaven's Gate* was established at $11.6 million, yet, as shooting extended to 156 days with more than 1.5 million feet of film shot, the figure more than tripled. One major reason was that Cimino obsessively demanded a degree of period authenticity for the film which extended to realistic costumes for fifteen hundred extras. Indeed, Cimino sought to give the whole film the look of a nineteenth century photograph, instructing cinematographer Vilmos Zsigmond to film it entirely in an elegiac and often quite beautiful sepia tone. To add further authenticity, Cimino had the immigrants speak in their native languages, translated in subtitles, and the film includes re-creations of an early baseball game, a cock-fight, a lovingly choreographed roller-skating sequence, and similar period touches. Unfortunately, these scenes impede the flow of the action and fail to flesh out any of the principal characters.

The chief problem of the film, though, is the lack of a coherent script. To make matters worse, the dialogue is often lost in a noisy sound track, further marred by an overbearing Dolby sound system. In the truncated version, Cimino shortened the Harvard commencement sequence, reshuffled numerous scenes, and added a voice-over narration by Kris Kristofferson in an effort to explain the plot, yet even these considerable revisions were an exercise in futility.

Cimino had begun the script some ten years earlier. While it is loosely based on a real incident, he does not hesitate to defend the historical misconceptions perpetrated in his interpretation: "I am telling a story that interests me. . . . One uses history in a very free way. After all, you're not trying to rewrite it or reinvent it. You're using it as a context. The specific facts of the incident recounted in a liberal way would be of no interest." Nevertheless, *Heaven's Gate* does distort the facts of the real Johnson County War. In real life Jim Averill was never a federal marshal; he was the local postmaster, with a homestead adjacent to Ella Watson, a lewd, 170-pound woman known as Cattle Kate. They joined forces in rustling cattle, and in 1889, three years *before* the Johnson County War, they were hanged. The actual war, which occurred in 1892, was halted by government cavalry troops, with the result that only two men were killed, not hundreds as depicted by Cimino.

Cimino had revised his original script several times because each time he submitted it to a studio it was rejected. At one point Steve McQueen was interested in portraying Averill, but he changed his mind because he did not wish to place himself in the hands of so inexperienced a director as Cimino.

The revised version, released in April, 1981, received an Academy Award nomination for Art Direction, despite the fact that the best thing about the film was Zsigmond's cinematography. Critics who had found Cimino's *The Deer Hunter* to be a right-wing view of the Vietnam War stated that *Heaven's Gate*, with its liberal, populist point of view, seemed to be Cimino's leftist apology for his earlier film. In any case, the impact of *Heaven's Gate* was such that it most likely will be recalled for its pictorial and budgetary extravagance and not for any philosophical or political message.

Ronald Bowers

Reviews

The Hollywood Reporter. April 24, 1981, p. 4.
Los Angeles Times. April 27, 1981, VI, p. 1.
The New Republic. CLXXXIV, May 16, 1981, pp. 24-25.
New York. XIV, May 11, 1981, p. 64+.
The New York Times. April 24, 1981, III, p. 10.
Newsweek. XCVII, May 4, 1981, p. 44.
Time. CXVII, May 4, 1981, p. 87.
Variety. November 20, 1980, p. 3.

HONKY TONK FREEWAY

Production: Don Boyd and Howard W. Koch, Jr., for EMI
Direction: John Schlesinger
Screenplay: Ed Clinton
Cinematography: John Bailey
Editing: Jim Clark
Art direction: Edwin O'Donovan
Music: George Martin and Elmer Bernstein
MPAA rating: PG
Running time: 107 minutes

Principal characters:
Duane Hansen .... Beau Bridges
Mayor Kirby T. Calo .... William Devane
Carmen Odessa Shelby .... Beverly D'Angelo
Eugene .... George Dzundza
Osvaldo .... Joe Grifasi
Sherm .... Hume Cronyn
Carol .... Jessica Tandy
Hitchhiker .... Daniel Stern
Older nun .... Geraldine Page
Younger nun .... Deborah Rush
Governor .... Jerry Hardin

When *Honky Tonk Freeway* was released, the chief critical reaction was to wonder what had happened to director John Schlesinger. After the highly regarded films *Darling* (1965), *Midnight Cowboy* (1969), and *Sunday Bloody Sunday* (1971), and Oscars for Best Director and Best Picture for *Midnight Cowboy*, critics expected superior films from the British-born Schlesinger. His next three full-length films—*The Day of the Locust* (1975), *Marathon Man* (1976), and *Yanks* (1979)—were received with less enthusiasm than the previous ones, but they were nevertheless regarded as worthwhile films. For *Honky Tonk Freeway*, however, the critical evaluations were scathing: "devoid of any basic human appeal"—*Variety*; "labored, amazingly unfunny"—*Newsweek*; "misanthropic stridency"—*Los Angeles Times*; and "gratuitously insulting"—*The Hollywood Reporter*. Virtually all the reviewers also pointed out that certain elements of the film were good, but they expected much more from Schlesinger.

The film has more than a dozen main characters and another dozen significant supporting ones. It introduces the characters in different parts of the United States and then follows them as they all converge on the town of Ticlaw, Florida. Of the major characters, only Kirby T. Calo (William

Devane) starts out in Ticlaw, and he is its number one citizen. He is both the mayor and the Baptist minister, and owns both the Safari Park and the town's largest hotel. The plot device that brings all the characters together is Ticlaw's desire to have an exit off the freeway that is being built nearby as the film begins. Without an exit, the city will lose its tourist trade, its main source of livelihood. After the mayor unsuccessfully tries persuasion and bribery to get the state to add an exit at Ticlaw, he and some of the other citizens dynamite the freeway and detour the traffic into their town. This happens in the last half of the film and brings together all the various characters who have been driving or hitchhiking toward Florida. *Honky Tonk Freeway* was called an imitation of Robert Altman's *Nashville* (1975), which angered Schlesinger. He pointed out that plots based on the fortuitous gathering of a number of diverse characters go back much further than *Nashville*, with *Grand Hotel* (1932) being a notable early example.

Some of the characters brought together in the film are Carmen Odessa Shelby (Beverly D'Angelo), a waitress from Paducah, Kentucky, who is taking an urn containing her mother's ashes to Florida. Though still in her twenties, she says she has slept with three hundred men and cannot imagine being faithful to only one. The one consistent thing in her life, she says, is the International House of Pancakes. She always chooses a certain booth no matter where she is. Traveling with her after they meet in a café along the road is Duane Hansen (Beau Bridges), a writer of children's books who is currently writing a story called "Ricky, the Carnivorous Pony." The story contains graphic descriptions of the pony munching children's hands.

Introduced to us in New York City are two garbage men, Eugene (George Dzundza) and Osvaldo (Joe Grifasi). They hold up a bank and then head for Florida with the money in a plastic garbage bag. During the hold-up, Osvaldo rebukes Eugene for using abusive language to the teller, and the two also come to the aid of a young actress who cannot cash her unemployment check because she does not have enough money in her account. Eugene points his gun at another teller and orders her to cash the check. On their way to Florida the two pick up an obnoxious hitchhiker (Daniel Stern), who informs them and everyone else he meets that he sells cocaine.

Also driving to Florida are Sherm (Hume Cronyn) and his wife Carol (Jessica Tandy). Sherm is a retired advertising man, and Carol is not, she insists, an alcoholic although she orders five old-fashioneds for lunch. Sherm and Carol, as well as two nuns who are also traveling to Florida, are victimized by car thieves who steal cars but leave the luggage from the cars behind. The older nun (Geraldine Page) must constantly watch the younger (Deborah Rush), who has frequent doubts about her vocation.

While all these characters and several others—including a bus full of Asian-American orphans—are making their way toward Florida, Kirby—as mayor of Ticlaw—continues to try to attract tourists to his town, even though it is now about thirty miles from the nearest freeway exit. He paints most of the town's buildings pink and erects huge billboards by the freeway advertising free gas and a waterskiing elephant. The highway department, however, takes down the signs, which leads Kirby to dynamite the freeway, detouring all traffic into Ticlaw. This happens, of course, at just the time that all the assorted characters we have been following reach the town. They and dozens of other tourists stay the night at Kirby's hotel and Ticlaw is full of activity and more prosperous than ever. The governor (Jerry Hardin) hears about what has happened and thinks the tourists have been taken hostage, but when he arrives in Ticlaw and is given the ten thousand dollars with which Kirby had tried to bribe a highway commissioner, he declares that Ticlaw will get its exit.

The next morning, as all the tourists are leaving, a speeding truck carrying animals bound for Ticlaw's Safari Park crashes through a warning sign and causes a chain reaction that destroys ten to fifteen vehicles. It also frees the animals, and one of the last images of the film shows Sherm and Carol, apparently unhurt, in their upside-down automobile as two lions approach. The very last image is Mayor Kirby riding on the back of the waterskiing elephant.

Schlesinger had never before directed this sort of comedy, which he calls "a romp," and judging by this example, it is probably a form to which he is temperamentally and artistically unsuited. Some of the ideas and some of the scenes are somewhat humorous, but their effect is dissipated by the many scenes that do not work, by the ideas and images that are tired from overuse, by the preponderance of characters and situations that are disagreeable or uninteresting, and by the tastelessness of some of the humor. The bank robbery scene is fairly good, for example, but it is perhaps the fifteenth funny bank robbery to appear on the screen in the last decade or so. The use of the urn containing the ashes of Carmen's mother as a running gag lacks both taste and humor, especially when the hitchhiker thinks the ashes are a drug and inhales some. There is a quiet, memorable scene in which the young nun takes an early morning swim alone in her heavy nightgown, but anything that scene might add to the film is erased by her last scene, when she goes off with a pimp in a flashy car.

Honky Tonk Freeway cost a reported $25 million to make, with some of the money going into blowing up and repairing an actual freeway and painting the town of Mount Dora, Florida, pink and then repainting it in its original colors. The pointless crash at the end also must have been expensive, but—as nearly all the critics agreed—the money and the talents of Schlesinger were wasted. The public apparently agreed, for the film was a dismal flop at the box office.

Schlesinger, however, continued to defend the film. He said that he "wanted to show the indomitability of a small American town . . . even if it means bribery and corruption." He also maintained that he sees the characters as funny, idiosyncratic, and "invested with a certain charm." He stated further that the negative critical reaction proves that the film was accurate and that as a British citizen who had lived in the United States "for fourteen years, on and off," his perceptions were on target.

For most reviewers, the accuracy of Schlesinger's portrait of America was not the issue, and it is to be hoped that *Honky Tonk Freeway* will be merely a short detour in the career of a distinguished director.

Frederick Travers

Reviews

The Hollywood Reporter. August 20, 1981, p. 2.
Los Angeles Times. August 21, 1981, VI, p. 1.
Newsweek. XCVIII, August 31, 1981, p. 36.
Variety. August 21, 1981, p. 3.

THE HOUND OF THE BASKERVILLES

Origin: England
Released: 1978
Released in U.S.: 1981
Production: Michael White, Andrew Braunsberg, and John Goldstone for Michael White Ltd; released by Hemdale
Distribution in U.S.: Tower
Direction: Paul Morrissey
Screenplay: Peter Cook, Dudley Moore, and Paul Morrissey; based on the novel of the same name by Arthur Conan Doyle
Cinematography: Dick Bush and John Wilcox
Editing: Richard Marden and Glenn Hyde
Art direction: Roy Smith
Music: Dudley Moore
MPAA rating: PG
Running time: 84 minutes

Principal characters:

Sherlock Holmes	Peter Cook
Dr. Watson / Mrs. Ada Holmes / Mr. Spiggot	Dudley Moore
Stapleton	Denholm Elliott
Beryl Stapleton	Dana Gillespie
Dr. Mortimer	Terry-Thomas
Arthur Barrymore	Max Wall
Mrs. Barrymore	Irene Handl
Sir Henry Baskerville	Kenneth Williams
Frankland	Hugh Griffith
Mary Frankland	Joan Greenwood
Ethel Seldon	Roy Kinnear
Glynis	Prunella Scales
Policeman	Spike Milligan
Mrs. Tindale	Jessie Matthews
Elder masseuse	Rita Webb

Sir Arthur Conan Doyle's *The Hound of the Baskervilles*, which was first published serially in *The Strand Magazine* in 1901, is probably one of the most filmed of all novels. The most well-known screen versions have been with Eille Norwood as Sherlock Holmes and Hubert Willis as Dr. Watson in 1922; with Carlyle Blackwell as Holmes and Georges Seraft as Watson in 1929; with Robert Rendel as Holmes and Fred Lloyd as Watson in 1932; with

Arthur Wontner as Holmes and Ian Fleming (not the novelist) as Watson in 1937; with Basil Rathbone as Holmes and Nigel Bruce as Watson in 1939; and with Peter Cushing as Holmes and André Morell as Watson in 1959. In addition, there have been other films based on *The Hound of the Baskervilles* in 1914 and 1915 (both starring German actor Alwin Neuss), and in 1920 and 1937. It has been produced at least three times on the stage, beginning in Germany in 1907 with Ferdinand Bonn as Holmes, a successful production which ran for 112 performances; in Spain in 1915 with Sr. Comes as Holmes; and, finally, in Great Britain in 1971 with Tim Preece playing the detective. The novel has also been heard as a radio drama in the United States in 1932 and 1941 and in Great Britain in 1958 and 1961, and again as a BBC television drama in 1968.

It might be supposed, therefore, that there is little new that could be done with *The Hound of the Baskervilles*, but the 1978 British feature, starring comedians Peter Cook and Dudley Moore and directed by Paul Morrissey, indicates that that is far from the truth. As the man responsible for the original stage production of *The Rocky Horror Picture Show*, producer Michael White can certainly be relied upon to put together an unusual cast and, thus, to him must go the credit for the unlikely teaming of Cooke and Moore with Paul Morrissey, the American director best known for the Andy Warhol films, *Lonesome Cowboys* (1968), *Trash* (1970), and *Heat* (1972), as well as *Andy Warhol's Frankenstein* and *Andy Warhol's Dracula*, both released in 1974.

As organized by this team, *The Hound of the Baskervilles* is basically a mixture of British Music Hall humor, Ealing studios-type comedy and *Goon Show* gags. It should be hilariously funny, but for long periods the jokes fall flat and the performers, while seeming to work desperately hard to make the audience laugh, fail dismally. The fault is obviously not that of such professional British laugh-makers as Peter Cook, Dudley Moore, Spike Milligan, and Max Wall, but must rest with director Morrissey, who simply does not understand British humor.

The Hound of the Baskervilles opens at the lodgings of Sherlock Holmes (Peter Cook) and Dr. Watson (Dudley Moore), where the former is first seen in corsets and hairnet before attiring himself in appropriate detective garb to greet three nuns who come to ask his help in retrieving the missing mummified elbow of St. Beryl. The pilgrims are flocking to St. Beryl's shrine, and the nuns beg for Holmes's help for "the flocking pilgrims." Holmes, without too much effort, determines that the relic's disappearance was "almost certainly the work of thieves."

Soon, however, a more important case develops: the mysterious death of Sir Charles Baskerville. Dr. Watson is dispatched to investigate the circumstances while Holmes remains in London. The detective's surrogate meets the new owner of Baskerville Hall, Sir Henry Baskerville (Kenneth Williams)—a somewhat effeminate homosexual given to complaining about his "dicky tummy." Sir Henry is frequently seen knitting and wakes Watson each morning with a simpering cry of "Watty, Watty, wakey, wakey." Watson and Baskerville are shown to their rooms, which are underwater, by the manservant, Arthur Barrymore, played by the superb British Music Hall comedian, Max Wall. Each night Barrymore flashes messages across the moor to his relative Ethel Seldon, an escaped axe-murderer, who is portrayed by Roy Kinnear in drag. The flashing of messages involves Barrymore's flapping the front of his raincoat open and closed.

Meanwhle, back in London, Holmes interviews a one-legged man for the position of runner. "I've got nothing against your right leg, the trouble is neither have you," Holmes tells the poor unfortunate. Holmes visits a massage parlor, reads a volume by S. Freud entitled *Guilt Without Sex*, and then visits his mother (also played by Dudley Moore), who is conducting a fake séance. Also at the séance is a British musical star of the 1920's and 1930's, Jessie Matthews, who seems strangely miscast as Mrs. Tindale in a one-line, two-shot part. Holmes's mother is stereotypically Jewish, calling her son "Sherl."

Back on the moors, Watson meets Frankland (Hugh Griffith) and his Amazonian daughter, Mary, whose bosom flashes "Love me" in neon, and who is portrayed by the marvelously fruity voiced British character actress, Joan Greenwood. Frankland and his daughter are obsessed with a hound "with great oozing eyes and *enormous* private parts" which they believe was involved in the murder of Sir Charles. Watson also meets Stapleton (Denholm Elliott), who breeds chihuahuas. In the most hilarious sequence in the film, the chihuahua which Stapleton is carrying will not stop urinating—over Watson, Stapleton, and everything in sight. The sequence lasts for several minutes, with nonstop urination by the dog, and creates mass hysteria in an audience, so much so that it is difficult to return to the remainder of the plot, which, as devotees of Sherlock Holmes will note, is fairly faithful to the original work.

Holmes comes down to attend an auction of the late Sir Charles' belongings, held to raise money for the Barrymores' unpaid wages, and purchases a mysterious painting, which when displayed correctly proves to be of the infamous hound. That same evening, Seldon is murdered by mistake in place of Sir Henry.

Later, Dr. Watson and Holmes interrupt a dinner party, attended by the Stapletons, the Franklands, and Sir Charles' executor, Dr. Mortimer (Terry-Thomas). In a parody of *The Exorcist* (1973), Mary is possessed by the devil, which leads to a chase across the moor after the hound. It transpires that Dr. Mortimer had murdered Sir Henry and also planned to murder the hound, at whose death Mortimer would have inherited Baskerville Hall. No one inherits the Hall, however; as Mrs. Holmes had predicted at her séance, it is destroyed by a volcano. Barrymore and his wife depart for Kentucky, where they plan to establish a fried chicken empire, and the final shot is of the hound dashing off with Holmes's painting in its mouth.

The plot is as difficult to describe as it was for audiences to understand fully. Some of the absurdities simply are not very funny, such as the parody of *The Exorcist* or the sequence in the massage parlor where Holmes is welcomed by a beautiful, young masseuse and then passed on to an aged, ugly one for a genuine massage. (Rita Webb as the latter is her usual, entertainingly gross self.)

As a result of Dudley Moore's success in *10* (1979) and *Arthur* (1981) as well as Peter Cook's appearance in the American television series, "The Two of Us," *The Hound of the Baskervilles* was at last able to obtain an American release, albeit minimal, some three years after its production. Audience and critical response was, however, poor, and the film played only to limited business at art-house locations.

Anna Kate Sterling

Reviews

Los Angeles Times. July 23, 1981, VI, p. 2.
Variety. November 8, 1978, p. 28.

THE HOWLING

Production: Michael Finell and Jack Conrad for Avco Embassy
Direction: Joe Dante
Screenplay: John Sayles and Terence H. Winkless; based on the novel by Gary Brandner
Cinematography: John Hora
Editing: Mark Goldblatt and Joe Dante
Art direction: Robert A. Burns
Special makeup effects: Rob Bottin
Music: Pino Donagio
MPAA rating: R
Running time: 91 minutes

Principal characters:
Karen White .... Dee Wallace
Dr. George Waggner .... Patrick Macnee
Chris .... Dennis Dugan
William (Bill) Neill .... Christopher Stone
Terry Fisher .... Belinda Balaski
Fred Francis .... Kevin McCarthy
Erle Kenton .... John Carradine
Sam Newfield ....Slim Pickens
Marsha .... Elisabeth Brooks
Eddie .... Robert Picardo
Donna .... Margie Impert
Bookstore owner .... Dick Miller

The Howling has a nerve-shattering impact on audiences because of extraordinary special effects involving the transformation of a man into a werewolf. The sleek production—made for less than one million dollars during a twenty-eight day shooting schedule—is also notable for its humor which sometimes borders on "camp," as well as for its homages to the horror genre (especially werewolf movies) and to sleazy low-budget films. The script cleverly weaves contemporary themes, such as ironic commentary about the state of television news, with genre tradition, including the ageless terror of lycanthropy, under the atmospheric, fast-moving direction of Joe Dante, who also served as coeditor.

With its superlative production values, as well as its black comedy and cult allusions, *The Howling* gained critical accolades, however begrudging, as well as commercial success. Full appreciation of this film, however, warrants some knowledge of its resourceful filmmakers. Dante, for example, got his start working with Roger Corman and Corman's New World Pictures. As director of *Piranha* (1978), Dante milked a meager storyline similar to *Jaws* (1975) for all the broad humor it would allow, including plenty of suspenseful beach sequences. As cowriter of the original story for *Rock 'N Roll High School* (1979), now popular as a midnight cult film, he proved himself an effective satirist (in this instance, of high school mores—as well as of the New Wave). Earlier, as head of the trailer department at New World, Dante created major ad campaigns—previews of coming attractions—for a number of exploitation films, including *Deathrace 2000* (1975) and *Jackson County Jail* (1976). Thus, he developed an extremely fluid editing style and a shrewd estimation of visual manipulation. Dante was also the codirector of *Hollywood Boulevard*, a fifty-thousand-dollar production made in 1976 that is packed with "in-jokes" about the films of Roger Corman, which have themselves come to symbolize clever, low-budget filmmaking.

Credit for the succinct and shrewd script of *The Howling*, by Terence H. Winkless and John Sayles, has gone largely to Sayles, himself an ingratiating presence in low-budget filmmaking. In addition to writing blatantly exploitative works such as *Alligator* (1980), in which alligators invade a big city, and *Battle Beyond the Stars* (1980), a merging of *Star Wars* (1977) and *The Seven Samurai* (1954), Sayles has written and directed the highly praised *Return of the Secaucus Seven* (1980).

The Howling's witty words and crackerjack direction are complemented by the superlative special effects created by Rob Bottin, who was then only twenty-one. A one-time apprentice to Academy Award-winning special effects designer Rick Baker, Bottin worked on the famous cantina sequence for *Star Wars*. His work has also embraced the low-budget genre, ranging from the popular *Rock 'N Roll High School*, for which he designed giant rats, to the obscure *The Incredible Melting Man* (1978). It was his work in *The Howling* that catapulted him to fame, resulting in his commission to create the awesome, visually disgusting monster of John Carpenter's *The Thing* (1982). That creature, which many critics have labeled as the ultimate "gross-out" movie monster, has brought Bottin much notoriety.

Given this combination of filmmaking talent, as well as a capable cast ranging from familiar television faces to venerable character actors, it is no wonder that *The Howling* was a successful film.

Opening with blood-red title credits that "slash" their way through a black background, *The Howling* shows a distorted television picture, as well as scenes inside a television studio, which immediately establish a contemporary setting. There is a quick look at a prominent pop psychologist named Dr. George Waggner (Patrick Macnee), who tells his audience that "repression is the father of neurosis," and "We should never try to deny the beast, the animal in us." Still another scene finds a television news announcer delivering a dramatic reading, but when the camera pulls back, it is revealed that he is practicing his lines in front of a mirror in the station men's room. He will shortly go on the air as a member of the *Update News* team.

Another *Update News* team member is on an investigative assignment. She is petite blond Karen White (Dee Wallace), who has been receiving telephone calls from a man who may be responsibe for a series of violent crimes in the city. Wearing a hidden "bug," so that the police and her co-workers will know where she is, Karen has been directed to a telephone booth where the killer has said he will contact her. Because Karen is so apprehensive about the call, she does not notice that the phone booth is emblazoned with a "happy face" sticker, a sardonic symbol which recurs throughout the film. She is also unaware that her bug is not transmitting properly, and she makes her way to the garish street of porno theaters and adult bookstores to which the killer has directed her without police surveillance. After taking a seat in the claustrophobic peep-show booth in a porno shop, also marked with a "happy face" sticker, she is startled to find that her caller is standing behind her. Warning her to look straight ahead, he places coins in the slot, and forces her to watch a gruesome film which shows a woman being sexually assaulted by several men. According to Eddie (Robert Picardo), the murder suspect, the film's actress is enjoying the act. After taunting her with the threat, "I'm going to light up your whole body, Karen," he orders her to turn around and face him.

Karen obeys, and one of the film's pivotal scenes follows. What she initially sees are muted glimpses of Eddie's features—long, straggly hair and coarse, unshaven face, but because of the light that streams from the projection booth, she is unable immediately to discern facial details. Then, through Karen's wide and terrified eyes, the film's audience can detect that something awesome is happening within the booth. The scene then cuts to outside the arcade booth where police officers have at last tracked down the reporter. Because of her hysterical screams and the sounds of violence, a rookie pulls his gun and fires into the booth. Eddie is killed, and a dazed Karen—splattered with his blood—is led sobbing from the booth, unable to recall precisely what happened.

Following this grisly episode, *The Howling* embarks on two parallel stories which sometimes interwine and ultimately form a cohesive story of werewolves attempting to integrate themselves into the civilized world. The story begins to unravel when Karen's co-workers, Chris (Dennis Dugan) and Terry (Belinda Balaski), reporters who are romantically involved, make their way to the Skid Row neighborhood where Eddie lived. Once inside his room, the two are almost speechless with fright. Agreeing that "he could design the Marquis de Sade coloring book," they examine piles of bizarre refuse, "art," and walls that have been plastered with grim newspaper accounts of Eddie's murder spree. More puzzling are drawings, apparently done by him, including an angry self-portrait that shows an animal-like Eddie, as well as a pleasant seascape.

Karen, meanwhile, is having difficulties at home and on the job. Her husband Bill (Christopher Stone), a professional athlete now in the health spa business, is understanding, but urges her to seek professional help. After she blanks out on the news set, just as she is to deliver her eyewitness account of her meeting with "Eddie the Mangler" (which causes her boss, played by Kevin McCarthy, to boom, "We're going to make ratings history"), she has a session with Dr. Waggner, who wants her to visit his Northern California retreat, called The Colony.

On the way there, Karen tells Bill, "I hope these people aren't too weird," and in a darkly brilliant piece of editing, the next scene finds veteran character actor John Carradine as Erle Kenton letting loose a wild call in the night. The gnarled and hunched Carradine, seemingly fighting an urge to bay at the moon, is one of the residents at The Colony. Karen and Bill are clearly out of place in the group, but of course, as the film's audience has come to suspect, Karen and Bill are also unique because they are humans—in the midst of a werewolf community.

Proving those suspicions are scenes of traditional terror, as well as campy nuances. During a Colony therapy session, for example, a likable young woman tells Karen that she has sought all manner of help (including est, Transcendental Meditation, Scientology—even primal screaming), musing, "I figure another five years of hard work, and maybe I'll be a human being." Another Colony resident, the blatantly erotic Marsha (Elisabeth Brooks), is less anxious to find her humanity. With her penchant for wearing leather, necklaces made of animal teeth, and a haunting expression, she seems to embody primitive urges.

Just as Karen and Bill are enduring the discomfort of The Colony (where Bill is the only vegetarian), Chris and Terry are called to the city morgue. Eddie's body has disappeared from its stainless steel body drawer (the interior bears fierce imprints, as though something tried to force exit). The strange discovery sends them leafing through books on the occult in a bookstore where the owner (played by Dick Miller, familiar to fans of Roger Corman's films) casually says of werewolves, "Silver bullets or fire. That's the only way to get rid of the damned things. They're worse than cock-a-roaches."

Later, Chris and Terry are in bed watching television when the 1941 film *The Wolf Man* airs. Just after the scene in which the old gypsy woman laments, "Whosoever is bitten by a werewolf and lives, becomes a werewolf himself," they receive a phone call from Karen, who says that Bill has been bitten by a wolf. The superstitious ramblings about lycanthropy are no longer amusing—at least to Chris and Terry. For audiences of *The Howling*, though, they encompass a range of moods.

Especially ambiguous is the nighttime sexual encounter between Bill (after he has been bitten) and Marsha. With a flickering campfire providing dramatic lighting, the naked pair begin as humans, embracing and kissing. As their lovemaking reaches ecstasy, however, Bill begins the metamorphosis into a werewolf. As he develops fangs and hair, and grimaces upward, the lovers become increasingly animal-like with each other, even appearing to salivate. The sequence ends with a shot of two wolves howling at the moon.

Though impressive, these special effects are later topped by a much more excruciating and detailed transformation involving Eddie, who was presumed dead (but of course, had escaped from the morgue; "death," after all, had not come by fire or silver bullets). The sequence occurs when Karen encounters Eddie in Dr. Waggner's office at The Colony. It is a most uneasy reunion, as Eddie harangues her for the earlier betrayal, and insists, "I want to give you a piece of my mind." The words have a literal meaning—for Eddie reaches to his forehead, which bears bullet marks, and pushes inward through the wound. His flesh gives way, allowing him to grasp a handful of slushy substance which he grimly hands to Karen. This is but a prelude to Eddie's transformation, as his cheekbones and forehead begin to throb, his chest heaves and expands (shredding his clothing), and his jaw begins to protrude. Giving Karen a wicked smile, he holds up his hand, allowing her to watch as claws sprout from bloodied nails. When the change is complete, a massive wolf, standing upright, moves menacingly toward her. Karen is able to escape only after she throws a vial of acid into his face.

With the help of Chris, who arrives at The Colony with the obligatory, lethal, silver bullets, Karen is able to escape. Terry is killed, however, in a vivid, bone-crunching sequence, and Karen herself suffers a bite in a bloody melee that precedes the escape. At this time, all The Colony's occupants have gathered inside a barn, where they turn on Dr. Waggner. All are werewolves whose lives he has been attempting to "rechannel." With the chant "humans are our prey," they converge on their leader—who seems to welcome death. It is at this point that all begin to take on wolf form—and that Chris and Karen bolt the barn door, and set fire to the structure. In a tersely edited montage there are rapid-fire glimpses of claws, flames, transformation, fur, and death. The creatures' screams, combined with the imagery, accentuate their relentless will to survive.

The experience is later the subject of a special newscast delivered by Karen, who is scheduled to report on the bizarre fire at The Colony, and the death of the noted psychologist. She deviates from the script, though, and instead rambles—to the surprise of her colleagues—about a plague from which some have no escape. Stressing that she has "proof," Karen then begins to transform. Unlike those of earlier scary scenes, this metamorphosis is sad, even pathetic. Watching in horror as her fangs and facial hair appear, Karen's "snout" quivers, and a tear runs down her cheek. Chris, who knew of her plans for the newscast, watches from the control booth, and finally raises the rifle, which he aims at the teary werewolf.

Karen's tragic plea for understanding of the crimes at hand and the plight of the victims is lost in the pandemonium on the set. Meanwhile, the viewers, it seems, have lost the ability to discern reality from fantasy. Several youngsters, watching the newcast as they eat their dinner casually squeal, "Wow, the news lady's turning into a werewolf!" Another viewer merely flips the dial. Seated at the counter of a bar, another muses, "the things they do with special effects these days." His comment is infused with further irony when the cook at the bar hollers out to a customer, inquiring how they want their burger cooked. The camera then moves, and finds Marsha—who obviously escaped the barn-burning. Smugly, she answers, "Rare."

The Howling is a werewolf film with intense social commentary which also applauds the horror genre and low-budget filmmaking in a variety of ways. Forrest J. Ackerman, well known to genre fans as editor of the magazine *Famous Monsters of Filmland*, is seen browsing in the occult bookstore. The character of Dr. George Waggner is named after the director of the 1941 film, *The Wolf Man*. Kenneth Tobey, who managed to survive the monster's assault in the 1951 version of *The Thing from Another World* is seen as a law officer. Scriptwriter Sayles is a morgue attendant, and Corman has a cameo as a man who wants to use the phone, just as Karen receives her call. The casting of Elisabeth Brooks, who bears a striking resemblance to so-called "scream queen" Barbara Steele, is another bright ploy. There are countless moments—some blatant, others extremely subtle—that recognize the lore of the wolf. In addition to watching *The Wolf Man* on television, Chris sits through a *Three Little Pigs* cartoon—just as the Big Bad Wolf makes his house-crashing entrance. The Allen Ginsberg book *Howl* is briefly seen on Chris's desk, and Bill is seen reading a copy of *You Can't Go Home Again,* by Thomas Wolfe.

In addition to its penchant for bright, minute detail, *The Howling* is well-acted, especially by Dee Wallace as the tormented newscaster. An actress with a warm and likable demeanor, she earlier portrayed the lonely bar-hopper in *10* (1979), and is the mother in *E.T. . . . The Extra-Terrestrial* (1982). Patrick Macnee, who is known for his television role of John Steed on the popular British series, *The Avengers*, gives a deliciously civil demeanor to the strange Dr. Waggner. Christopher Stone, who appears frequently on television, is quite engaging as Karen's husband-turned-werewolf. (Shortly after the filming of *The Howling*, Wallace and Stone married in real life.) There are also spirited performances from John Carradine and Slim Pickens, as country sheriff Sam Newfield. Both seem to be having great fun when they begin their furry transformations.

Amplifying the impact of this enjoyable werewolf film is the cinematography of John Hora, who has done award-winning television commercials, as well as the haunting score by Pino Donaggio, who has done the music for numerous thrillers, including *Don't Look Now* (1973), and the Brian DePalma films, *Carrie* (1977) and *Dressed to Kill* (1979).

Pat H. Broeske

Reviews

The Hollywood Reporter. January 30, 1981, p. 3.
Los Angeles Times. April 15, 1981, VI, p. 4.
The New York Times. March 13, 1981, III, p. 10.
The New Yorker. LVII, May 8, 1981, pp. 164-167.
Time. CXVII, April 20, 1981, p. 85.
Variety. January 27, 1981, p. 3.

I SENT A LETTER TO MY LOVE (CHÈRE INCONNUE)

Origin: France
Released: 1980
Released in U.S.: 1981
Production: Lise Fayolles and Giorgio Silvagni for Cineproduction; released by Gaumont
Distribution in U.S.: Atlantic Releasing
Direction: Moshe Mizrahi
Screenplay: Moshe Mizrahi and Gerard Brach; based on the novel of the same name by Bernice Rubens
Cinematography: Ghislain Cloquet
Editing: Francoise Bonnot
Art direction: Michael Anania
Music: Philippe Sarde
Running time: 102 minuites

Principal characters:
Louise .... Simone Signoret
Gilles .... Jean Rochefort
Yvette .... Delphine Seyrig

After their success together as, respectively, director and star of *Madame Rosa* (which won the 1977 Academy Award for Best Foreign Film), it was not surprising that Moshe Mizrahi and Simone Signoret should team up again—this time for an apparently simple yet relatively complex story of love and hate, filmed in France as *Chère Inconnue* and based on a British novel from which is taken the American release title, *I Sent a Letter to My Love*. The film began shooting on location in Brittany (substituting for Wales in the novel) in November, 1979, and was completed in plenty of time for a Paris opening in April, 1980, representing France as its official entry at the Cannes Film Festival.

I Sent a Letter to My Love is the story of an aging brother and sister, Louise (Simone Signoret) and Gilles (Jean Rochefort); he is disabled and she takes care of him at their parents' old home by the sea. One gets the impression that Louise has given up whatever love there might have been in her life for the sake of her brother, and one also senses that there is an undercurrent of hatred in her relationship with Gilles. At one point, it is obvious that Louise considers murdering her brother by pushing him and his wheelchair off a clifftop. Louise's life seems destined to consist of pushing her brother around in his wheelchair while he looks through his telescope at the Atlantic Ocean and preparing coffee and omelets for him to spill deliberately over himself, as if to prove that slovenliness and disablement are related. The only other person who is in any way a part of their lives is Yvette (Delphine Seyrig), whose looks are beginning to fade with age. Yvette works in a local bakery and is romantically attracted to Gilles; each day she brings fresh bread, and on each visit she forgets to wipe her feet before entering Louise's kitchen. Life has taken on a routine drabness which seemingly nothing will change.

Out of a sense of loneliness and frustration (and a concern that Gilles may suddenly die and she will be hopelessly alone), Louise places an advertisement in the personal column of a local newspaper, asking to meet "a refined gentleman." To her surprise, the only respondent is her brother, who writes, "My legs are paralyzed, but my heart is free and I know how to love." Louise realizes that her brother is also lonely, crying out for love and affection, and she continues the correspondence, assuming the name of Beatrice Deschamps. Some of the most touching scenes occur at the local post office, where Louise and other women, living out fantasies, stand in line each day waiting for and hoping that there might be letters for them. Some have stood in line each day for years, each day leaving empty-handed. To all, these letters to and from their loves offer the only rays of happiness in their drab lives.

In time, of course, Gilles demands to meet Beatrice Deschamps, and Louise is forced to hire a local actress for a disastrous afternoon tea together at their home. That meeting, coupled with the letters, gives Gilles a new lease on life, and he becomes more playful—in an amorous fashion—towards Yvette, eventually asking her to marry him. A plan initially devised by Louise to release her from loneliness has worked itself out so that Gilles has been released from his dependence on Louise, and now she must remain forever alone. On the day of the wedding, Gilles finds the identification card which Louise had altered from her own name to that of Beatrice Deschamps in order to collect the mail from the post office, and Gilles realizes the deception which has taken place. The film ends with the marriage service in the local church, where Gilles, just before taking his marriage vows, turns and stares at his sister, his look perhaps revealing too much to her.

The film is somewhat enigmatic as to whether Gilles was aware of Louise's deception from the start. As one critic has pointed out, Louise makes no effort to disguise her handwriting, and, presumably, Gilles would have recognized it. It is even possible within the film's context that perhaps both Louise and Gilles were using the correspondence to make incestuous love to each other, through the written words expressing an affection and a desire which could not be spoken or displayed physically.

There is no question that *I Sent a Letter to My Love* is a slow-moving film, with the camera carefully recording the landscape of the countryside and the town, the quiet simplicity of the house, and the conscious play-acting of the three principals. *I Sent a Letter to My Love* is very much a performers' film. It relies on the abilities of its players, and Simone Signoret, Jean Rochefort, and Delphine Seyrig do not let their director down. Each is playing an uncharacteristic role, and each gives a performance hardly predictable from their previous film parts.

Here Signoret happily shows her age, not as a Madame Rosa-type but as a simply dressed, down-to-earth "ordinary" woman who suddenly discovers her ability to love and be loved. She has come a long way from the attractive young actress who won an Academy Award for Best Actress in 1959 for her performance in *Room at the Top*. "After 40 years in movies, Signoret has the sturdy, pouched, life-lined charm of an old duffel bag," wrote Richard Corliss in *Time* (August 10, 1981); "She is a marvellous behavioral actress. Smiles and tears are easy enough, but no one is better than Signoret at sitting still, daring life to try and impress her." Similarly Delphine Seyrig gives a surprisingly original performance as the simpleminded and plain Yvette, far removed from her roles as director Alain Resnais' favorite actress in *Last Year at Marienbad* (1961) and *Muriel* (1963). Nor should Jean Rochefort's performance be overlooked; from the good-looking leading man of French films of the 1950's and 1960's, he has developed into a character actor of considerable potential, a potential unrealized in most of his more recent features. As Vincent Canby noted in *The New York Times* (May 3, 1981), "It's unlikely casting, and it works beautifully."

Moshe Mizrahi was born in Egypt of Jewish parents in 1941, and, after fighting in the war for Israeli independence, he became a journalist. Mizrahi came to France in 1958 as an assistant director for French television, and directed his first feature-length production, *Le Client de la Morte Saison*, in 1969. Aside from *Madame Rosa*, Mizrahi is best known to American audiences for two films, both of which were nominated for Academy Awards for Best Foreign Film, *I Love You, Rosa* (1972) and *The House of Chelouche Street* (1973).

I Sent a Letter to My Love was received with mixed reactions by the American critics, some of whom found it overly saccharine, while others noted that its plot was a little too simplistic and obvious. *Variety* (May 21, 1980), reviewing the film on its French release, sounded the most negative view, commenting, "Insensitive direction and unconvincing performances ruin an interesting dramatic idea." Similarly *Rolling Stone* (July 9, 1981) noted, "There's something phony about Mizrahi's films: his compassion comes too easily, partly because he turns his lead characters into people who are supposed to be more 'human' than anyone else around them." Of the major critics, Vincent Canby of *The New York Times* was the most enthusiastic, writing, "It's a comedy of blithe spirit and uncommon sense."

Anthony Slide

Reviews

The Hollywood Reporter. May 4, 1981, p. 4.
The New Republic. CLXXXIV, May 30, 1981, pp. 22-23.
The New York Times. May 3, 1981, p. 71.
Saturday Review. VIII, May, 1981, p. 76.
Time. CXVIII, August 10, 1981, pp. 60-61.
Variety. May 21, 1980, p. 16.
Variety. April 29, 1981, p. 22.

IMPROPER CHANNELS

Production: Alfred Pariser and Morrie Ruvinsky for Crown International
Direction: Eric Till
Screenplay: Morrie Ruvinsky, Ian Sutherland, and Adam Arkin
Cinematography: Anthony Richmond
Editing: Thom Noble
Art direction: Nicky Dalton and Charles Dunlop
Music: Micky Erbe and Maribeth Solomon
MPAA rating: PG
Running time: 92 minutes

Principal characters:

Jeffrey Martley .... Alan Arkin
Diana Martley .... Mariette Hartley
Nancy Martley .... Sarah Stevens
Gloria Washburn .... Monica Parker
Harold Clevish .... Harry Ditson
Dr. Arpenthaler .... Tony Rosato

Throughout his stage and screen career, Alan Arkin has revealed an astonishing ability to submerge himself in the roles of extremely intense comic characters. It was during his period with the Second City improvisational troupe in Chicago that Arkin honed the approach that has come to be identified with him so closely. By Arkin's own account, in a 1966 interview with Roberta Brandes Gratz in the *New York Post*, when he went to Second City, he did not know or understand how to be funny or to develop a character. After months of hard work, experimentation, and exposure to other troupe members, however, Arkin began to add one character after another to his repertoire. His method now, as then, is to study a role so thoroughly that he all but becomes that character. In another interview, Arkin told Bernard Weinraub, "I find myself looking at clothes that the character would wear and not me. I can't take my mind off the character. I . . . find myself falling into a thought pattern not my own, a speech pattern not my own." An example of Arkin's strenuous dedication to his different roles is his preparation when given the part of the Russian leader of a landing party in *The Russians Are Coming, The Russians Are Coming* (1966). Arkin studied the Russian language a full three months before even beginning rehearsals. He was convinced that the Russian character could not be accurately portrayed unless the actor thoroughly examined every element that might compose the personality and attitudes of such a character and made them his own. It is with this unusual thoroughness that Arkin has approached the shaping of each of his comic characters over the years.

From his early stage days, when he played the star-struck David Holovitz in *Enter Laughing*, through his interpretation of Yossarian in Mike Nichols' *Catch-22* (1970) to the later starring role in *Freebie and the Bean* (1974), Arkin has made a specialty of projecting the condition of hysteria. The characters he plays usually respond to a frustrating situation in a manner bordering on the maniacal. This has been the case in most of his films, particularly when the character is not at all in control of his destiny and is being victimized by hostile forces. This maniacal response has developed into an Arkin trademark, and it is unusual to find him in a role in which he does not employ it, at least to some extent.

Improper Channels represents somewhat of a departure for Arkin and it is an interesting and significant film for other reasons as well. Arkin plays Jeffrey Martley, an architect living in a large, unnamed city, who has been experimenting with a trial separation from his wife, Diana (Mariette Hartley). The reason for the trial separation is not made clear, but that is a peripheral consideration at the film's outset. The plot of *Improper Channels* is generated from an innocent accident during an outing taken by Martley and his young daughter Nancy (Sarah Stevens). As the two are motoring along the street, Martley stops his truck suddenly to avoid striking a child; Nancy is thrown forward against the dashboard of the truck. She receives a slight injury so Martley takes her to the emergency room of a large hospital. At the hospital, Martley is confronted by an incompetent typist who is there to handle the emergency room paperwork for each case, which is voluminous. While Martley is suffering through this bureaucratic quagmire, a zealot of a social worker named Gloria Washburn (Monica Parker) decides that Nancy is the victim of child abuse by her father. One sign of child abuse is that parent and child offer differing accounts of how an injury occurred, and, in this case, Martley did not want his wife to know that Nancy was not wearing a seatbelt. His story, as overheard by Washburn, varies from Nancy's account, so Washburn mistakenly concludes that Martley is a child-abuser. Washburn's conviction becomes more deeply entrenched when she takes Nancy away, confronts Martley, and accuses him of child abuse. His reaction is the well-known Arkin hysteria, during which he strikes a policeman before escaping the hospital.

Martley returns home and tells his nightmarish story to Diana, who explodes into a rage at the thought of losing her daughter. This is a scene that requires, and receives, superb acting by Mariette Hartley. Diana cannot conceive of her husband returning home without Nancy in tow, and she is not only angry but also frightened by the situation. While Diana is seeking the aid of an attorney, Washburn is transferring Nancy to a county orphanage for safekeeping. Washburn has consulted with another bureaucratic zealot named Harold Clevish (Harry Ditson) to retrieve personal information on Martley through the use of a government computer. The information dredged up by the computer includes the fact that Martley was once arrested for indecent exposure. While the exposure charge was only the result of an innocuous college prank, it is enough to continue the chain of events that has Nancy going to the orphanage, and Martley losing his credit rating and his job. To make matters worse, the Martleys are not told which orphanage has their child.

The Martleys are confronted by further frustrations and complications during much of the remainder of the film. Yet it is these same problems that serve to reunite them, since there is a common enemy and common cause, that of rescuing their daughter from the grasp of the unfeeling, clumsy government. Following the eventual rescue of Nancy, and a "brother" whom they adopt from the orphanage, the Martleys exact revenge upon the government and its computer in the riotous conclusion of the film.

While *Improper Channels* places Arkin in familiar territory, a victim of implacable outside forces, it is notable that his hysteria is not only under control but is also balanced by a calm, logical approach to his crisis. In almost each instance that would normally elicit his hysterical response, Arkin seems to get control and retreat a little. This technique underlines the realism of the film, which, after all, has an extremely frightening and emotional subject. In fact, the film strikes an unusual balance between a trenchant satire on big oppressive government on the one hand, and a rather terrifying realism on the other. The story would have made little or no impact had Arkin and the director, Eric Till, treated it as strictly comic. While the tension between the two elements makes the film unique and keeps the viewer interested, it is Arkin's ability to regulate the intensity of humor and fear from one scene to the next that provides the necessary cohesiveness throughout the film.

Operating as a satire, *Improper Channels* is effective because of the universality of frustration in dealing with bureaucracy. The ending of the film in which Martley reprograms a massive computer system, has great appeal because it depicts the little man fighting back and taking his revenge for all the grief suffered at the hands of the government. Other objects of satire are computers that seem to play too large a part in controlling the lives of people, social workers who exceed their responsibilities, and orphanages that view children as commodities. While the degree of satire is something less than ruthless, it is still pointed enough to provoke a strong sympathetic response from the viewer. Anyone who has had to contend with insensitive government agencies will readily respond to the plight of the Martleys.

Underlying the film's satire is the genuine fear that no one in the modern world has command over his own existence. No matter how each of us feels, some small random incident can cause our downfall and initiate an unraveling of all our hopes. Between satirical moments, *Improper Channels* aims a spotlight on the fragility of the orderliness of modern life. The film forces the viewer to take a sober look at his own situation and draw frightening parallels with that of the Martleys. The treatment of this theme, through the child abduction element, would normally have resulted in a highly melancholy film. The injection of satire changes the overall tone of the production, and because of the balance maintained between satire and realism, *Improper Channels* finally offers a positive message to the audience. The rousing ending is too preposterous to meld with the action that has preceded it; it is a sudden break with the satire/realism balance and almost approaches slapstick. This kind of a finale is most welcome to the viewer, however, since the safety of the daughter is guaranteed and the considerable tension is gone from the film. The closing scenes are received by the viewer as a sort of reward for having suffered with the Martleys during a time of profound distress.

Although the film has the look of a made-for-television movie, it is effective in the theater. It was produced by a Canadian company and did only moderate business, even for a small-budget film. Its merits, however, should be appreciated by a wider audience on its television appearances.

Thomas A. Hanson

Reviews

The Hollywood Reporter. April 24, 1981, p. 3.
The New York Times. May 22, 1981, III, p. 10.
Variety. April 22, 1981, p. 3.
Variety. September 21, 1981, p. 3.

LILI MARLEEN

Origin: Germany
Production: Luggi Waldleitner for Roxy Film, CIP/Rialto Film
Direction: Rainer Werner Fassbinder
Screenplay: Manfred Purzer, Joshua Sinclair, and Rainer Werner Fassbinder; based on the novel *Der Himmel Hat Viele Farben* by Lale Andersen
Cinematography: Xaver Schwarzenberger
Editing: Franz Walsch and Julian Lorenz
Art direction: Rolf Zehetbauer
Music: Peer Raben
Song: Norbert Schultze, "Lili Marleen"
Running time: 120 minutes

Principal characters:
Willie Bunterberg .... Hanna Schygulla
Robert Mendelsson .... Giancarlo Giannini
David Mendelsson .... Mel Ferrer
Hans Henkel .... Karl Heinz von Hassel
von Strehlow .... Erik Schumann
Tascher .... Hark Bohm
Aaron .... Gottfried John
Anna Lederer .... Karin Baal
Miriam .... Christine Kaufmann

Lili Marleen is somewhat of a stylistic enigma, even among the films of Rainer Werner Fassbinder, which are all noted for their radical style. Attempting to tell the story of the woman who popularized the famous song "Lili Marleen," the universal favorite of World War II, the director has made a film that is a cross between an anti-Nazi melodrama and a Douglas Sirk woman's film. Fassbinder was influenced by the Hollywood melodrama of the 1940's and 1950's as is evident in his excessive use of mirrors, his punctuation of the narrative with sentimental music, and similar devices, as well as in his preference for stock melodramatic characters such as the woman who must cope for herself. In *Lili Marleen*, however, his handling of these conventions, which lend a distinctive ironic tone to many of his films, is uncertain. It is as if Fassbinder himself could not decide whether he wanted to poke fun at his heroine Willie Bunterberg (Hanna Schygulla) or make a serious statement about the power of love and the far-reaching effect of a song. The major portion of the film is set in Munich and Berlin from 1938 until the war's end. Fassbinder's Nazis are buffoons rather than dangerous men; indeed, the character of a strong, determined protector of Jews, David Mendelsson (Mel Ferrer), comes off as far more ruthless than any of the Nazis. This odd contrast blunts the moral thrust of the picture and makes one wonder just what Fassbinder was attempting.

The film is loosely based on the autobiographical novel *Der Himmel Hat Viele Farben* by Lale Andersen. A cabaret singer in Germany during the war, her hit record of "Lili Marleen" captured the imagination of fighting troops on both sides of the struggle. Americans, French, Germans, and British all took the song to heart, and guns were supposedly laid down when the song was played over the radio on the battlefield. With this excellent premise, Fassbinder cast Hanna Schygulla as a struggling singer in love with a Swiss Jew, who finds herself caught in Germany during the war with a hit song that gains her the protection of Adolf Hitler himself. Her lover Robert is played by Giancarlo Giannini, bringing his usual sad, almost pathetic appeal to the role. Set in a Munich still influenced by German expressionism, the film veers between making a serious statement and trivializing the events that it depicts. It becomes (in Hanna Schygulla's own words) "a Nazi fairy tale," with many beautiful costume changes, lavish sets, and scenes of Nazi variety shows—all aglow in a beautiful Technicolor wash. *Lili Marleen* was Fassbinder's attempt to make a commercial hit and to gain an international audience, which his previous film, *The Marriage of Maria Braun* (1979), did not quite achieve. In this he succeeded, for the film was popular, but the critics were puzzled and so were some members of the audience.

Lili Marleen opens in Zurich, 1938, where Robert Mendelsson, a wealthy and talented Swiss Jewish musician, is in love with Willie, a German cabaret singer. Robert disappears frequently to make "secret business trips" to Germany, and Willie wants to know the nature of these mysterious journeys. Eventually Robert takes Willie to Munich, and there she learns that he works for his father, David Mendelsson, an influential lawyer and leader of a Jewish relief organization. Robert is smuggling funds out of Switzerland into Germany to help Jews escape from the Nazis. Strongly disapproving of his son's love for Willie, David Mendelsson uses his position to prevent Willie from returning to Switzerland, and she and David part. When Robert makes another trip for his father to Munich and sees Willie, however, it is obvious that their love remains unchanged. After war breaks out, it becomes impossible for them to see each other, so Willie goes to Berlin to find a way to support herself. By chance, a song that she records is broadcast by the Armed Forces Radio Network Belgrade to German troops holding out at the North Cape, in the Sahara, the Pyrenees, and the Russian steppes. The song, "Lili Marleen," which tells of lovers who must stand before the barracks and separate, takes hold of the soldiers' hearts. At the same time, the Allied forces on the Western front hear the song and adopt it as their own. When the Nazi leaders realize the weakening effect of "Lili Marleen," it is too late, for the song has already become a musical icon for soldiers on all fronts. Willie becomes a celebrated singer. She lives in a mansion in Berlin, receives vast amounts of fan mail, and even has an audience with Hitler. In the middle of the war, Robert comes to Berlin and he and Willie have a joyful reunion in a small pension. Robert is followed and arrested on his way back to Switzerland, and is tortured in his cell by hearing Willie's recording of "Lili Marleen" played to him day and night.

Willie, who has established contact with Robert's friends, makes a dangerous mission to Poland and, while performing on the Polish front, gathers photographic evidence of what is happening in the concentration camps. When David Mendelsson threatens the Nazi authorities with publication of the photographs, he is able to secure the release of Robert and other Jewish victims and smuggle them out of Germany. Willie becomes a suspect of the Nazis and attempts suicide. Robert, thinking that her suicide was successful, issues a false statement that "Lili Marleen" had died in a concentration camp. The Nazi propaganda machine denies the report of her death, however, and persuades her to perform again, guaranteeing her safety. Willie survives the remainder of the war hidden on an island. When the war ends, Willie returns to Zurich to see Robert, now a famous conductor. There, in the wings of the Concert Hall, she meets Miriam (Christine Kaufmann), the woman whom Robert married when he believed that Willie was dead. The film ends as Robert triumphantly finishes conducting his first symphony while Willie slinks out into the night.

The film was a huge commercial success in West Germany, grossing as much as *The Tin Drum* (1980), the most successful German movie of the postwar era. As mentioned previously, critics were unsure of its intent, but that did not keep people away. Hanna Schygulla at last seemed poised on the brink of international stardom, but thus far, it has eluded her. It is indeed ironic that two years after his first popular film, Fassbinder died tragically, leaving behind a prolific output of strong individual films (including two not yet released in the United States). His was a bizarre talent. His pictures, which often dealt with the underside of German life, were often esoteric yet strangely accessible. *Lili Marleen* represents "mainstream" Fassbinder, and if it is not a perfectly realized work, it contains some of his most interesting ideas. Garish in tone, it is a perplexing look at Nazi society and a testament to the strength of one woman.

Joan Cohen

Reviews

The Hollywood Reporter. July 14, 1981, p. 10.
Los Angeles Times. July 29, 1981, VI, p. 1.
The New York Times. July 10, 1981, III, p. 15.
The New York Times. August 2, 1981, II, p. 15.

Newsweek. XCVIII, August 10, 1981, p. 69.
Time. CXVIII, July 13, 1981, p. 59.
Variety. February 6, 1981, p. 10.

LOULOU

Origin: France
Released: 1980
Released in U.S.: 1981
Production: Klaus Hellwig and Yves Gasser for Gaumont/Action Films
Direction: Maurice Pialat
Screenplay: Arlette Langmann and Maurice Pialat; based on an original screen story by Arlette Langmann
Cinematography: Pierre William Glenn and Jacques Loiseleux
Editing: Yann Dedet and Sophia Coussein
Art direction: Max Berto
Music: Philippe Sarde
Running time: 105 minutes

Principal characters:

Nelly	Isabelle Huppert
Loulou	Gérard Depardieu
André	Guy Marchand
Michel	Humbert Balsan
Rémy	Bernard Tronczak
Pierrot	Christian Boucher
Dominique	Frédérique Cerbonnet

Loulou is a strange mixture of a film, combining elements emblematic of the coolness of the *nouvelle vague* with the very personal cinema of French filmmaker Claude Chabrol. Its director, Maurice Pialat, known for his extremely naturalistic style, has made a statement in this film about French youth, about class, and about sexual obsession.

Loulou is probably Pialat's most conventional film, in that it employs well-known actors and has a traditional narrative structure. Pialat's background was in French television, and he made his first feature film *Nous ne viellirons pas ensemble/We Won't Grow Old Together* (1972), only after a decade in that medium. His initial effort was shot in a *cinéma vérité* style employing a cast of nonprofessionals. It set the tone for his subsequent pictures, all of which are excruciatingly realistic, dealing with the rather simple concerns of lower- and middle-class Frenchmen. This makes Pialat somewhat of an anomaly in a national cinema which usually concerns itself with politics and ideas.

Yet *Loulou*, in spite of its blend of styles, also projects a gritty realism as if a social worker had gone into the streets of Paris and photographed the different types of young people that exist there. Both middle-class upwardly mobile young professionals and bored, working-class layabouts are portrayed, with little attempt at making judgments as to which life-style is the most desirable. In fact, one of the most endearing qualities of all of Pialat's films is the manner in which the camera tells the story without moralizing and without any hint of condemnation. In *Loulou* one notices that the characters always seem to be teetering on the edge of boredom, even when their lives are changing in a sensational way.

The film also carries an underlying statement about the quality of urban life in today's France. With unemployment high and opportunities for unskilled young people practically nonexistent, the temptation to sit in bars and cafés, becoming increasingly self-centered, is almost irresistable. The boredom that must set in from such a life can lead to petty crime or outbursts of violence, both of which are experienced by the film's title character and his friends. On the other hand, the middle-class aspirations of Nelly, the movie's heroine, with her sporadic reading and dull job, lead to the same restlessness. She, too, feels that nothing will change. Beer versus books and talk versus sex—these are the twin poles of *Loulou*.

In the very beginning of the film, the audience is introduced to Louis, known as "Loulou" (Gérard Depardieu), a tall, good-looking man whose primary occupation in life seems to be pleasing women. He is approached by a recent lover, a beautiful girl named Dominique (Frédérique Cerbonnet), who complains that he has not paid her enough attention lately. When Loulou suggests that they go dancing, she refuses, claiming that he will only dance with other girls. At this point, the other main character in the film enters. Nelly (played impassively by Isabelle Huppert, never known for her wide range of emotions), is bored with her life as the mistress of André (Guy Marchand), who runs the advertising firm for which she works. Nelly and André wind up in the same dance hall where Loulou has gone. He immediately spots Nelly and tries to win her attention. After a quarrel with André, Nelly dances with Loulou and goes with him to his shabby room, intending to spend the night. He excites her tremendously but there is guilt mixed with her pleasure since she has never been away from André for a whole night before. After she returns to André's beautiful apartment, Nelly and André again argue, and she decides to move in with Loulou. At this point, her life changes from a secure, ordered bourgeois existence to one of cheap hotel rooms, drinking bouts, and glorious nights of love. She quits her job at André's agency and seems exhilarated with her new life with Loulou, who, as she tells André, "never stops." In fact, all through the film, Loulou is treated sympathetically by the other characters. His neighbors adore his carefree, amusing ways; he exhibits real compassion for his ex-girl friends, and he seems to have a true regard for Nelly. Although he is shiftless, lazy, and uneducated, his appeal is apparent. Gérard Depardieu is perfectly cast, for he plays Loulou very much as a type—a young man with no ambition, but one who genuinely cares for his pals as well as his women. As the film progresses, Nelly experiences some ambivalence about Loulou's life-style and even takes back her job at André's firm for a time. André's jealousy proves too much for her, though, and she again stops working for him.

André is an interesting character. He is truly in love with Nelly, and at one point pathetically tries to get her back by affecting a leather jacket similar to the one Loulou wears. When Nelly is with André, she lapses back into her essentially middle-class ways; for example, they speak of going to the latest art exhibit at the Palace of Fine Arts. Huppert's Nelly seems to shed class like a second skin—she seems almost sluttish with Loulou but is demure with André.

After a passage of time, there are signs of trouble between Nelly and Loulou. She is nervous when he and his friends rob a warehouse and steal some stereo equipment. Nelly is also puzzled when an ex-con friend of Loulou arrives to stay at the flat she has rented for them. When Nelly finds herself pregnant with Loulou's child, she decides to have the baby. Her brother comes to visit, and when he asks Loulou how he expects to support his new family, Loulou replies that he will find a job after the baby is born. Events culminate when Loulou and Nelly go to the country to spend the day with Loulou's family. Loulou's sister is married to an extremely jealous man, who brandishes a rifle at a friend of Loulou whom he suspects of having designs on his wife. Nelly is somewhat shocked at this violent behavior, and reacts by aborting the baby. This act saddens and shocks Loulou, who feels that Nelly betrayed him by not trusting that he would support her after the child's birth. Loulou's combination of boyishness and sexuality wins out in the end, however, for after a drunken, desparing evening in his local bar, the last shot in the film shows Loulou and Nelly walking back to their flat arm in arm—Loulou staggering with Nelly supporting him, perhaps a portent for their future.

Although filled with fairly explicit scenes of Nelly and Loulou making love, *Loulou* is not an extremely erotic film. Its subject seems to be Nelly's sexual obsession with Loulou, but in fact Pialat is more deeply preoccupied with his sympathetic chronicle of the underprivileged class. He paints Loulou not as a taker but as a giver, even though outwardly he accepts Nelly's money and support in a casual fashion. Loulou's anguish at the abortion implies that Nelly has been the more hedonistic partner. She takes Loulou on because he makes her feel good while Loulou is capable of genuine feeling.

Depardieu and Huppert have never seemed more French; even Huppert's expressionless mode of acting serves her well; she is the modern Parisian with all that implies.

The film received mixed reviews, with some critics especially negative about Depardieu and Huppert. It did little business in the United States, where it lasted for only a short time.

Joan L. Cohen

Reviews

The Hollywood Reporter. October 16, 1980, p. 34.
Los Angeles Times. March 19, 1981, VI, p. 7.
The New York Times. October 8, 1980, III, p. 20.
Time. CXVI, October 20, 1980, p. 94.
Variety. May 28, 1980, p. 15.

MAN OF IRON (CZIEWIEK Z ZELAZA)

Origin: Poland
Production: Polish Corporation for Film Production Zespoly Filmowe, Unit "X" for United Artists Classics
Direction: Andrzej Wajda
Screenplay: Aleksander Scibor-Rylski
Cinematography: Edward Klosinski and Janusz Kalicinski
Editing: Halina Prugarowa
Art direction: Allan Starski
Music: Andrzej Korzynski
Running time: 140 minutes

Principal characters:
Maciej Tomezyk/
Mateusz Birkut .... Jerzy Radziwilowicz
Agnieszka Tomezyk .... Krystyna Janda
Winkiel .... Marian Opania
Anna's mother .... Irena Byrska
Anna Hulewicz .... Wieslawa Kosmalska
Dzidek .... Boguslaw Linda
Captain Wirski .... Andrzej Seweryn
Lech Walesa .... Himself
Anna Walentynowicz .... Herself

A number of recent Polish films have depicted the struggle of individualism against conformity and honesty against corruption in contemporary Poland; ultimately, they are indictments of the repressive policies of the Polish state. Among these films are Krzysztof Kieslowski's *Camera Buff* (1979); Krzysztof Zanussi's *Camouflage* (1976), *The Constant Factor* (1980), and *Contract* (1980); and Andrzej Wajda's compelling *Man of Marble* (1977) and its sequel, *Man of Iron* (1981). In fact, Lech Walesa, the head of Solidarity, the Polish workers' independent trade union and *Time* magazine's "Man of the Year," appears briefly in the latter—along with Anna Walentynowicz, the worker whose firing helped to precipitate the strike chronicled in the film.

Man of Iron presupposes familiarity with the plot of *Man of Marble*. In the earlier film, Agniezska (Krystyna Janda), a passionate, aggressively determined young woman, retraces the life of one Mateusz Birkut for a television film. Birkut (Jerzy Radziwilowicz), a bricklayer, had been lionized a quarter of a century earlier in a documentary as one of the worker-heroes of a nation emerging from World War II. The documentary was a blatant piece of propaganda about a strong young Stakhanovite (model worker) and his "ideological struggle for a better future." Birkut posed for a larger-than-life statue cast in his image, which served as a symbol, an icon; according to the state, all art must be political, conforming to the dictates of Socialist Realism.

As Agnieszka investigates, however, she learns the truth about Birkut's life. He was really a shy man, an innocent idealist used by others to attain power and prestige. He never learned, or wished to learn, how to play the game. Of course, what Agnieszka has uncovered is too politically controversial to be shown on television. Her film is successfully shelved by the authorities—but not before she traces Birkut's son to Gdansk, a seaport city that in 1970 was the scene of a massive worker strike and resulting violence. She also learns that the subject of her film is no longer alive.

Man of Iron opens in August, 1980, when the workers at the Gdansk shipyards have gone out on strike. Winkiel (or Winkel, played by Marian Opania), a shy, alcoholic Warsaw news reporter, is sent to Gdansk to infiltrate the shipyard and fake a story discrediting Maciej Tomezyk (also played by Jerzy Radziwilowicz), the workers' leader. Winkiel gains access to, and credibility with, the workers through Dzidek (Boguslaw Linda), an acquaintance who is a former classmate of Tomezyk. The journalist also learns the story of Birkut—who was Tomezyk's father and who declined to assist his son, then a student, during the demonstrations for political reform twelve years earlier. Winkiel learns that Birkut had in fact been killed in 1970 during the breaking of the strike that Tomezyk, in retaliation, had refused to support. Birkut died at the hands of security police and was buried in an unmarked grave.

With the assistance of Mrs. Hulewicz (Irena Byrska) and her daughter Anna (Wieslawa Kosmalska), who is involved in the current strike, Winkiel discovers that Birkut's grave has mysteriously disappeared. He also visits Agnieszka (again played by Krystyna Janda), who is now Tomezyk's wife. (Lech Walesa is seen as a witness at their Catholic wedding ceremony.) Agnieszka, in prison because she supports the strike, tells Winkiel that she was prevented from completing her film on Birkut and that she later fell in love with his son. She gave up her cinema career, became a wife and mother, and has been active as a union organizer.

Tomezyk's efforts to organize his coworkers finally result in his firing, and Winkiel, whose consciousness has been raised, is no longer willing to spy. He refuses to give his report to Wirski (Andrzej Seweryn), a captain of the secret police, and enters the shipyard to join the strikers with a pass given him by Anna. He observes the historic signing of an agreement by Vice Premier Jagielski and Lech Walesa allowing for the establishment of Solidarity and the workers' demands to become official policy. At the ceremony, Agnieszka and Tomezyk are reunited. Dzidek then tells Winkiel that his real reason for coming on the scene is known. Outside the yard, meanwhile, it is hinted that the agreement may not be binding. It is, after all, "only a piece of paper." In reality, of course, in December, 1981, the Polish government declared martial law throughout the country in an effort to crush Solidarity, and the union has since been outlawed.

Man of Marble does not reveal how Birkut actually died. The film's ending, in which this was explained, was cut by the censors. Thankfully, this problem is rectified in *Man of Iron*. There was a liberalization of censorship in Poland before the latter film was produced, and Wajda was quoted as saying that he could never have made *Man of Iron* otherwise.

The film is almost as good as its predecessor; occasionally, the narrative becomes a bit choppy, but *Man of Iron* is still a superior example of filmmaking and storytelling, as Wajda successfully builds and holds his audience's curiosity. It is both a celebration of the role of the filmmaker as a speaker of truth and an indictment of a repressive system which seeks to control art for its own ends, rewrites history to conceal its crimes and shortcomings, and denies fundamental rights to the workers, who are supposed to be the final authority in a Socialist state.

Man of Iron includes documentary footage from the Polish Film Archive as well as sequences from Andrjez Chodakowski and Andrzej Zajaczkowski's *Robotnicy '80* (*Workers '80*) and Ireneusz Engler and Leon Kotowski's *Sierpien* (*September*). These are carefully woven into the scenario and assist immeasurably in giving *Man of Iron*, which was completed in less than eight months, a sense of immediacy and a for-the-record feeling. It connects the Poland of the 1950's with Poland today as it links the lives of Mateusz Birkut and Maciej Tomezyk, father and son. It is also the story of Winkiel, an essentially weak man who is changed by the people he meets and the events occurring around him—and finally by the moral decision he makes. It is a fascinating glimpse of life inside Poland and of the frustrations of artists and workers who dare question the policy of the state while demanding justice and democracy. Ultimately, though, it is a celebration of Solidarity and a record of the union's establishment.

Throughout his career Andrzej Wajda has focused on the reality behind political mythology, a reality rife with destroyed lives. Among his best films, in addition to *Man of Marble* and *Man of Iron*, are *Kanal* (1957); *Ashes and Diamonds* (1958); *Everything for Sale* (1968); *Land of Promise* (1974); and *The Young Girls of Wilko* (1979). *Man of Iron* received critical acclaim both in the United States and Europe; it earned a Cannes Golden Palm, a slot on the New York Film Festival's closing night program, and a Best Foreign Film Academy Award nomination.

A day before the implementation of martial law, Film Polski notified the Motion Picture Academy of Arts and Sciences that it desired to change the official Polish entry in the Oscar competition from Wojciech Marczewski's *Creeps* to *Man of Iron*. The Polish Ministry of Culture had resisted the change because of *Man of Iron*'s subject matter, but the change was made allegedly because of the film's greater commercial potential. The Polish government later requested withdrawal of the film from the competition, but the Academy refused, declaring that the nominations had already been announced and screenings for voting members had commenced. While sentiment dictated a victory for *Man of Iron*, the film surprisingly lost to Istvan Szabo's *Mephisto*, also featuring Krystyna Janda, a fine actress who has recently been highly visible to Western audiences. Other nominees were *The Boat Is Full*, *Muddy River*, and *Three Brothers*.

Man of Iron totalled $312,785 in box-office earnings after ten weeks on *Variety*'s survey of "50 Top-Grossing Films," a respectable figure for a foreign-made, subtitled feature. In Poland, though, the film was immensely popular and packed the theaters—before martial law.

Rob Edelman

Reviews

The Hollywood Reporter. November 2, 1981, p. 3.
Los Angeles Times. February 14, 1982, *Calendar*, p. 29.
The New Republic. CLXXXV, December 23, 1981, p. 24.
The New York Times. October 12, 1981, III, p. 14.
The New Yorker. XIV, December 7, 1981, pp. 157-158.
Newsweek. XCVIII, December 28, 1981, p. 64.
Time. CXIX, January 11, 1982, p. 88.
Variety. May 27, 1981, p. 17.

MAN OF MARBLE (CZLOWIEK Z MARMURU)

Origin: Poland
Released: 1977
Released in U.S.: 1981
Production: Andrzej Wajda for PRF Zespoly Filmowe, Unit "X"; released by Film Polski
Distribution in U.S.: New Yorker Films
Direction: Andrzej Wajda
Screenplay: Aleksander Scibor-Rylski
Cinematography: Edward Klosinski
Editing: Halina Prugarowa
Art direction: Allan Starski
Music: Andrzej Korzynski
Running time: 165 minutes

Principal characters:
Mateusz Birkut .... Jerzy Radziwilowicz
Agnieszka .... Krystyna Janda
Jerzy Burski .... Tadeusz Lomnicki/Jacek Lomnicki
Wincenty Witek .... Michal Tarkowski
Michalak .... Piotr Cieslak
Hanka .... Krystyna Zachwatowicz

Director Andrzej Wajda once said in an interview that "Film can accomplish less than filmmakers want, but much more than the authorities expect." With *Man of Marble*, Wajda speaks directly to his Polish audiences with a film that deals with a subject that had never been discussed openly. Wajda's picture is both a film about filmmaking and a film about the search for truth. The script initially was written by Aleksander Scibor-Rylski in 1962, but was continually rejected by the Polish authorities. Obsessively, Wajda asked permission to film the script, and for fourteen years he was rebuffed. He wanted to tell a story that would be meaningful to the young people of Poland, who had at best a hazy notion of what actually went on in their country in the 1950's. All they knew was that a figure named Stalin had lived, that people mysteriously disappeared from their jobs and their homes, and that many things that occurred during those years were never explained.

Finally, in 1974, the Ministry of Culture approved the making of the film that was to be *Man of Marble*. Under the Gierek government, a period of progressive relaxation allowed artists to practice "self censorship," and formerly sensitive subjects could be treated, albeit gingerly. The script of *Man of Marble* had undergone many changes in the fourteen years since it was first written. The Gdansk riots of 1970 changed the texture of Polish society, and the finished film reflects those contemporary changes, while attempting to answer questions haunting a previous generation.

The film deals with the attempt of a young woman filmmaker, Agnieszka (Krystyna Janda), to try and trace a forgotten Stakhanovite (model worker) hero of the 1950's who mysteriously fell out of favor with the authorities and gradually faded from view. This is indeed strong stuff, except that Wajda is politically canny and does not point a finger at modern Poland. Instead, he saves his condemnation for the methods of the 1950's. The structure of the film is modeled upon that of Orson Welles's *Citizen Kane* (1941), the first film that deeply impressed Wajda. The actual story is pieced together in *Citizen Kane*-like fashion by Agnieska.

As *Man of Marble* opens, Agnieszka, a strong-minded graduate student in the state cinema school, obtains reluctant permission to make a rather controversial television film for her graduating project. She wishes to make a documentary on the bricklayer Mateusz Birkut (Jerzy Radziwilowicz), a forgotten Stakhanovite hero of the 1950's. She interviews people who knew Birkut and looks at some newsreels and propaganda films that feature the bricklayer as a model worker. She eventually finds that Birkut's reputation was launched by a staged record-breaking display of bricklaying in a film about the new steel town of Nowa Huta. The director of that film, Jerzy Burski (Tadeusz Lomnicki/Jacek Lomnicki), has since made a name for himself as a company man who makes films according to the demands of the state. As Agnieszka goes on, she finds that most of Birkut's former associates have become disassociated from the people they once were—they have either "gone soft," become quiet conformists, or, like Birkut's ex-mistress, become pathetic alcoholics. By careful detective work, Agniesza pinpoints Birkut's fall from grace to the year 1952, when he was jailed for four years as a reprisal during a spy trial. He had attempted to clear a colleague of his, Wincenty Witik (Michal Tarkowski), who had been framed by a party spy. Upon his release, Birkut was filmed with his young son on his shoulders casting a vote in the general election—a rehabilitated man, but a shell of his former self. Agnieszka visits Hanka (Krystyna Zachwatowicz), Birkut's mistress, but there the trail stops and she cannot find out what happened to him after the 1950's. She shows her work thus far to the television officials, but the film is rejected for its inconclusiveness. Deprived of her crew, Agnieszka loses heart and goes home to lick her wounds. Her resolute father tells her to go on with her search in the name of truth, whether the end result is a film or not. Inspired by her father, Agnieszka traces Birkut's son to the Gdansk shipyard. From him, she learns that Birkut is dead, and, as the picture ends, she has reluctantly persuaded the young Birkut to accompany her to the studio to complete the film.

Man of Marble had an amazing impact on Polish audiences. When it was first shown in January, 1977, in Wroclaw, the overflow audience rose to their feet when it was over and sang the Polish National Anthem. The film became one of the greatest popular successes in the history of Polish cinema, despite the fact that all reviews were severely curtailed by the Polish censor. Temporarily suppressed in April, 1977, *Man of Marble* had so great an impact that it led to a governmental shake-up and the head of the film industry was dismissed. Wajda felt justified by the public response to his film. His only compromise had been the deletion of the concluding scene upon advice from his allies within the Ministry of Culture. In the missing scene, Agnieszka is with Birkut's son in the Gdansk cemetery. They are looking for his grave, but are unable to find it, which means that the elder Birkut was killed during the 1970 strikes in Gdansk. Wajda felt that the film would not be released with this scene in it, as there was already a faction against him in the ministry. In the sequel to *Man of Marble*, however, the much acclaimed *Man of Iron* (1981), the sequence is restored. The two films together form a complete story. They are amazing documents which show history unfolding, and demonstrate why Wajda is ranked among the world's leading filmmakers. Andrzej Wajda has been making films in Poland since 1954; his films have continually reflected the many changes in his country. In the light of the latest of these changes, one hopes that he can carry on.

Joan L. Cohen

Reviews

Los Angeles Times. April 8, 1981, VI, p. 1.
The New York Times. January 23, 1981, III, p. 16.
Newsweek. XCVII, February 9, 1981, p. 95.
Time. CXVII, March 9, 1981, p. 69.
Variety. June 1, 1977, p. 17.

MEPHISTO

Origin: Hungary
Production: Mafilm-Objektiv Studio, Budapest, Hungary, in cooperation with Manfred Durniok Productions, West Berlin (AA)
Direction: István Szabó
Screenplay: István Szabó and Peter Dobai; based on the novel of the same name by Klaus Mann
Cinematography: Lajos Koltai
Editing: Zsuzsa Zsa Kany
Art direction: no listing
Music: Zdenko Tamassy
Running time: 144 minutes

Principal characters:
Hendrik Höfgen .... Klaus Maria Brandauer
Barbara Bruckner .... Krystyna Janda
Nicoletta von Niebuhr .... Ildikó Bánsági
Juliette Martens .... Karin Boyd
The General .... Rolf Hoppe
Lotte Lindenthal .... Christine Harbort
Hans Miklas .... György Cserhalmi
Professor .... Martin Hellberg

What are the responsibilities of artists to themselves, their audiences, the societies in which they live and create their art? Should an artist, to gain or maintain power and prestige, compromise his art, and himself, by aligning with those currently in political power—even if they are Nazis? What price will that artist pay if he chooses top billing over his own feelings, sacrificing his friends and lovers in the process? Klaus Mann posed these questions in 1936, in his novel *Mephisto*, one of the first and most perceptive exposés of the Nazi mentality and of those who, lacking in character and morality, alter their personalities and preferences to suit the prevailing philosophy that rules their country. Forty-five years later, the book was made into an engrossing, award-winning film, directed by the Hungarian filmmaker István Szabó and magnificently performed by the Austrian stage actor Klaus Maria Brandauer in the title role.

Hendrik Höfgen, the centerpiece of Mann's novel, a character based on the real-life German actor Gustav Gründgens, is the focus and the core of *Mephisto*. The scenario details the rise of Höfgen (Klaus Maria Brandaucr), a talented, ambitious, vain young actor first seen performing in a provincial theater in Hamburg during the 1920's. Höfgen, who acts as much offstage as he does on, lusts for fame and is willing to subordinate everything—his political beliefs, aesthetic standards, and even personal relationships—in his quest for success. He fraternizes with an assortment of individuals who will profoundly affect his life: intellectuals, leftists, artists, and future Nazis.

Höfgen befriends Nicoletta von Niebuhr (Ildikó Bánsági), an actress whose values are not unlike his own. He is also having an intense, masochistic relationship with Juliette Martens (Karin Boyd), a half-caste dancer, but he decides to court the intelligent and pretty Barbara Bruckner (Krystyna Janda), the daughter of a respected liberal professor. They are miles apart socially, and a marriage to Barbara will be a stepping-stone for Höfgen, so he plays the role of an ardent suitor, and they are married.

Rapidly, Höfgen rises from a small-time, small-town actor to a respected member of the State Theater in Berlin. He becomes a welcome, honored guest at left-wing cabarets and in high society drawing rooms. He also performs the role that he was born to play, Mephistopheles in Goethe's *Faust*.

While shooting a film in Budapest, Höfgen learns that the Nazis have taken control of Germany. "The Nazis are in power," he shrugs. "What do I care." His wife's family has taken exile in Paris, however, and he must decide to accompany them or remain and accept the humiliation befalling an actor out of favor because of his leftist contacts. His greed will not allow him to leave Germany nor to relinquish his status.

Lotte Lindenthal (Christine Harbort), the mistress of a powerful, sadistic Nazi general (Rolf Hoppe), yearns to act on the stage with Höfgen, so he decides to use her to gain favor in Nazi circles. His politics and personal relationships now more than ever become subordinate to this role. His "Germanic" performance is hailed, and he becomes a favorite and confidant of the General.

Höfgen is now at his pinnacle, but he must pay for his actions. He must divorce Barbara, who is now working against the Nazis, and break off all ties to his past. He also severs his relationship with Juliette, who is expelled by the General from Germany. He is lonely and isolated and has only Nicoletta, yet he still remains somewhat aloof after marrying her. Then Höfgen is designated by his mentor as director of the State Theater. As a result he believes that he has gained certain influences in the upper echelons of the Nazi hierarchy. He thus attempts—and fails—to save his old left-wing colleagues from the Gestapo. Then in the film's most terrifying and revealing scene, the General turns on the actor for the first time, his friendly demeanor replaced by wrath. "Actor!" the General spits out at Höfgen. The word might easily be "scum."

Höfgen is subsequently selected to give a speech honoring the General at his birthday festivities. The actor plays his part perfectly, but he is finally beginning to realize that he is just a pawn. He has never been more alone than when, at the Olympic Stadium being constructed for the 1936 games, the General forces him to run around the field with spotlights trained on him.

Höfgen is pathetic, but the General is only amused. Höfgen can only ask, naïvely and pitifully, "What do you people want of me? I'm only an actor."

Mephisto was written by Klaus Mann, son of the famed novelist Thomas Mann and fervent anti-Fascist, while in self-imposed exile in Holland. There is a clear parallel between Hendrik Höfgen and Gustav Gründgens, Mann's brother-in-law and former lover, a leftist during the Weimar Republic years who became famous for his performance as Mephistopheles in *Faust*. (In 1960, Gründgens also produced and starred in *Faust*, a movie made for German television.) The actor became a personal friend of Hermann Göring, and thrived during the Third Reich. Mann was thus unable to publish his book in Germany. Even after the war, when Gründgens again became a prominent actor after serving time in prison and producing witnesses to exonerate him from his Third Reich connections, Mann still could not find a publisher. He committed suicide in a Cannes hotel in 1948, possibly because of this failure. He was forty-three years old.

When Gründgens died in 1963 of an overdose of sleeping pills, his adopted son and heir prevented publication of *Mephisto* on grounds that it defamed the actor. Incredibly, the courts concurred, banning the book after a long legal battle that became known as the "duel of the dead." The film's makers, believing it imperative that the story find its audience, labored for almost a decade to bring the property to the screen.

Klaus Maria Brandauer, recognized for his work as a stage actor in Europe but unknown in America, gives a towering, electric, Laurence Olivier-like performance as Hendrik Höfgen. In the words of one critic, "Brandauer firmly established himself as one of the most magnetic performers to have burst onto the cinema screen in ages." While Brandauer is solidly supported by all of his fellow cast members, German actor Rolf Hoppe's portrayal of the General deserves special praise, as does the direction by István Szabó, who stunningly re-creates both the moral and the physical ambience of the period. Szabó's first feature, *The Age of Illusions* (*Almudoźasok Kora*), was released in 1964; other films include *Father* (*Apa*), made two years later, and 1979's *Confidence* (*Bizaloom*), starring Ildikó Bánsági, which was nominated for a Best Foreign Film Academy Award a year later.

Mephisto had its premiere at the 1981 Cannes Film Festival, where it was honored with prizes for Best Screenplay and for Best Male Actor; the following fall, it was also acclaimed at the New York Film Festival. It was named Best Film of the Year by the International Film Guide, and won an Oscar for Best Foreign Film against stiff competition, including Andrzej Wajda's *Man of Iron* and Francesco Rosi's *Three Brothers*.

The film's original source, Klaus Mann's novel, was finally published in West Germany in December, 1981, where it became a best seller.

Rob Edelman

Reviews

Los Angeles Times. March 26, 1982, VI, p. 1.
The New Republic. CLXXXVI, April 7, 1982, pp. 24-26.
The New York Times. September 29, 1981, III, p. 8.
The New Yorker. LVIII, May 17, 1982, pp. 128-132.
Newsweek. XCIX, April 12, 1982, p. 87.
Time. CXIX, May 3, 1982, p. 73.
Variety. March 17, 1982, p. 26.

MODERN ROMANCE

Production: Andrew Scheinman and Martin Shafer for Columbia
Direction: Albert Brooks
Screenplay: Albert Brooks and Monica Johnson
Cinematography: Eric Saarinen
Editing: David Finfer
Art direction: Edward Richardson
Music: Lance Rubin
MPAA rating: R
Running time: 93 minutes

Principal characters:
Robert Cole .... Albert Brooks
Mary Harvard .... Kathryn Harrold
Jay .... Bruno Kirby
David .... James L. Brooks
Ellen .... Jane Hallaren
George Kennedy/Zoron .... Himself
Sporting Goods Salesman .... Bob Einstein
Head Mixer .... Albert Henderson
Music Mixer .... Cliff Einstein
Sound Effects Mixer .... Gene Garvin

Modern Romance tries very hard to be both Woody Allen's *Annie Hall* (1977) and *Manhattan* (1979). Its star, coauthor, and director, Albert Brooks, is very similar in style, if not looks, to Allen: Brooks was a stand-up comedian before venturing into films, and his character here, like Alvy Singer, Isaac Davis, and other Allen alter egos, is a neurotic, infantile *nebbish* hopelessly dependent on women. *Modern Romance* may be lukewarm Woody Allen, but is, at its best, still quite funny and insightful.

The chunky, curly-haired Brooks plays Robert Cole, a Los Angeles-based film editor who, at the outset, meets his girl friend, Mary Harvard (Kathryn Harrold), a bank officer, for dinner. It seems that Robert and Mary have a great sex life, but they argue a lot and do not communicate. Five minutes after they sit down to dinner, they have broken up. Robert initiates the action. "I haven't been feeling good lately," he mutters. "I think it's probably us. . . . This is more serious than you think. . . . I think it's over." He adds that, like Vietnam, their relationship is a no-win situation, and Mary appropriately stalks out of the restaurant. Yet Robert remains obsessed with her. He can think of nothing else but Mary—and winning her back.

Robert, who is editing a low-budget science-fiction film starring George Kennedy (who plays both himself and the role in the film-within-the-film), discusses the situation with Jay (Bruno Kirby), his co-worker and best friend. Jay reassures him, but Robert insists that he is a mess and cannot work, so Jay gives him two quaaludes to calm his nerves.

Robert arrives home, and curses himself for forgetting to turn on his answering machine. He dials for the correct time, and then phones Jay. "Alone's kind of a nice place to be," he says, but he does not believe his words, adding that he feels "horrible, real bad." He then prepares for bed, but he cannot sleep.

The pills begin to take effect and he fumbles with his clock, causing the alarm to go off accidentally. He calls Jay again, to tell him that he loves him. He then thumbs through his Rollidex and calls Ellen (Jane Hallaren). He tells her he has deep feelings for her, yet in reality he cannot remember who she is. Then, he receives a call from Harry, an assistant editor. When Harry refers to Mary as terrific, and asks if it would be rude to ask her out, Robert blows up. He warns Harry not to move into his territory.

Robert visits Mary at home. Jealously, he accuses her of having a date, as if he owns her—or is at least still seeing her. Then, he arrives at Ellen's apartment for their date. He immediately tells her that he has just broken up with someone, that he does not know who she is, and apologetically ends the date.

He next purchases several toys for Mary, leaving them in front of her door and goes home. He tries to call Mary, who is not at home, and decides to drive by her house. The presents are still where he left them. Later, however, when he enters his apartment, he finds Mary's voice on his answering machine. She loved the giraffe that she found waiting for her and wants him to visit her. They spend the night together but Robert still cannot get beyond his hang-ups. As she leaves for work the next morning, he demands that she change her dress because it is too revealing. While shaving, he notices her phone bill—complete with long distance calls made at late hours.

Later, at work, Robert and Jay view the film they are editing. David, their director (James L. Brooks), arrives, and talks about dubbing the sound of George Kennedy's footsteps in a sequence, to get a "metallic feeling." That evening, Robert and Mary attend David's party, where Robert immediately becomes jealous when Mary recognizes two male guests. He meets George Kennedy, and, while the actor tells him an anecdote, he watches Mary nervously.

The next day, Robert, Jay, and three technicians dub in the footsteps, first with sound effects from "The Incredible Hulk," and then by running on concrete. Robert calls Mary at work, and becomes upset when she explains that she may be working late and that their dinner date might have to be canceled. Then, Robert calls a phone number he had found while shaving at Mary's. He also calls Mary back. She has left for the day. He lies to obtain the name of the restaurant to which she has gone with her boss and clients, and then storms in and confronts her. "Why are you the only woman here?" he asks. Appropriately, Mary is angry and embarrassed. They yell. Mary tells him he must learn to trust her, while Robert professes his love.

Subsequently, they go away for the weekend to Robert's "surprise destination" in the mountains. After they arrive, Mary makes a call from a pay phone as Robert looks at her through the window, and watches her laugh. He angrily confronts her about her long distance calls. She curses at him, and runs off. Robert cannot comprehend what he has done wrong. Mary tells him it's over, that their relationship is too painful for her. Robert proposes, however, and Mary says yes. Before the final credits unfold, the audience is informed that Robert and Mary were married three weeks later in Las Vegas. Their divorce came the following month. Now, they are dating—with plans to remarry.

A pair of sequences stand out in *Modern Romance*: the dubbing in of George Kennedy's footsteps ("Heaven's Gate—short version" is the film next scheduled for the editing room); and the long monologue in Robert's apartment after he breaks up with Mary. *Modern Romance* occasionally offers realistic glimpses into the problems and pitfalls of modern relationships. It is the kind of film in which everyone in the audience will see aspects of themselves.

Albert Brooks has acknowledged that the character of Robert Cole is autobiographical, that in his own life he has been obsessive in his relationships. Unlike Woody Allen, however, whose female counterparts are characters with personalities and idiosyncrasies, Brooks allows Mary Harvard to remain a blank. On the surface, she may be a modern, independent career woman with professional responsibilities, but she unbelievably sticks with a man who is looking for just the opposite: a woman who lives for him alone, who would not even dare to converse with another man. Obviously, Mary has hang-ups, but they are never explained. Thus, she is merely a body, a one-dimensional love object off of which Robert plays. It is never exactly clear why Mary puts up with Robert, why she keeps taking him back. As a result, Kathryn Harrold, whose credits include *The Hunter* (1980), *Bogie* (1980, for television, as Lauren Bacall), and *The Pursuit of D. B. Cooper* (1981), hardly has a role to play. The film is mostly an Albert Brooks monologue.

Brooks, son of radio comedian Harry "Parkyakarkus" Einstein, began his career as a stage and television comic, appearing many times with Johnny Carson on the "Tonight Show." Eventually, he ventured into filmmaking. He played a political campaign worker in *Taxi Driver* (1976), and Goldie Hawn's husband, who dies on their wedding night, in *Private Benjamin* (1980). Previously, he had created zany, original films for television's "Saturday Night Live." In one, he interviewed a blind cab driver, who explained, "Damn right I still drive! What should I do, sit home and collect welfare?" In another, he hilariously parodied promotional spots for network television series. Brooks's first feature, *Real Life* (1979), in which he also starred and coscripted, is a parody of the PBS documentary, "An American Family." In it, he satirized a typical American family whose everyday life is covered by a film crew for a year.

Modern Romance, which cost four million dollars to film, received mixed-to-negative reviews. A few critics thought it hilarious; most, though, felt it was funny at best, a disaster at worst. While it broke the house record the weekend after it opened at New York's Cinema II theater, overall it performed rather dismally, placing 118th on *Variety*'s list of "Big Rental Films of 1981." The film earned a paltry $1,333,000.

Rob Edelman

Reviews

The Hollywood Reporter. March 11, 1981, p. 3.
Los Angeles Times. March 21, 1981, II, p. 5.
New York. XIV, March 30, 1981, p. 41.
The New York Times. March 13, 1981, III, p. 1.
Newsweek. XCVII, March 30, 1981, pp. 82-83.
Variety. March 11, 1981, p. 3.

MOMMIE DEAREST

Production: Frank Yablans for Frank Yablans Productions, Inc., in association with Dunaway/O'Neill Associates, Inc., for Paramount
Direction: Frank Perry
Screenplay: Frank Yablans, Tracy Hotchner, and Robert Getchell; based on the book of the same name by Christina Crawford
Cinematography: Paul Lohmann
Editing: Peter E. Berger
Production design: Bill Malley
Art direction: Harold Michelson; set decoration, Richard C. Goddard
Costume design: Irene Sharaff
Music: Henry Mancini
MPAA rating: PG
Running time: 129 minutes

Principal characters:
Joan Crawford .... Faye Dunaway
Christina Crawford (older) .... Diana Scarwid
Christina Crawford (younger) .... Mara Hobel
Christopher Crawford (older) ....Xander Berkeley
Christopher Crawford (younger) ....Jeremy Scott Reinbolt
Greg Savitt ....Steve Forrest
Louis B. Mayer .... Howard Da Silva
Alfred Steele .... Harry Goz
Barbara Bennett ....Jocelyn Brando

In 1978, a year after Joan Crawford died at age seventy-three, her adopted daughter Christina published her autobiography, *Mommie Dearest*. The book is probably the most shocking of the many recent Hollywood memoirs, not only because its revelations were unexpected but also because it dealt with the closeted subject of child abuse.

When Crawford's will was read to her four adopted children, the two oldest children, Christina and Christopher, were denied any inheritance by Joan's cryptic explanation: "It is my intention to make no provision herein for my son Christopher or my daughter Christina for reasons which are well known to them."

Whether an attempt at revenge or psychotherapeutic exorcism, Christina's account of Joan Crawford as a schizophrenic alcoholic and child abuser is devastating. It remained on the best-seller list for forty-two weeks, selling seven hundred thousand copies in hardback and three million in paperback.

Producer Frank Yablans purchased the movie rights for $500,000 and at first Franco Zefferelli was set to direct with Anne Bancroft as star, but Yablans disagreed with Zefferelli's desire to make the film a psychological study of a movie queen and Bancroft failed to approve any of the scripts. After numerous screenplays were rejected, including two versions by Christina herself and one by James Kirkwood (who wrote *A Chorus Line*), Yablans finally wrote his own version with Tracy Hotchner and Robert Getchell. He then signed Frank Perry to direct and Faye Dunaway to star.

Ironically, Joan Crawford had once said that if she had to make a choice, she would select Dunaway to play her on screen, and at another time she had said, "Of all the actresses—to me, only Faye Dunaway has the talent and the class and the courage it takes to make a real star."

Mommie Dearest covers Joan Crawford's life from 1939, the year she adopted newly born Christina, until her death. At the time of Christina's adoption, Crawford was a top star with two divorces behind her (from Douglas Fairbanks, Jr., and Franchot Tone) and was about to enter the low point of her lengthy career.

The film opens with a brilliantly conceived pre-title sequence in which we hear no dialogue and do not see the face of the star. In the bedroom of Crawford's luxurious Brentwood home we see a gloved hand reach out to shut off the alarm clock, which reads four A.M. The hand removes a sleep mask and the montage takes us to her splendidly appointed bathroom, where the actress neurotically scrubs her hands and arms, then immerses her face into a bowl of ice to close the pores in her skin. She picks out a blouse and slacks from meticulously arranged, well-stocked closets, adds a scarf and coat and descends the elegant staircase to her waiting limousine. While being driven to the studio, she glances over her script to *The Ice Follies of 1939* (one of Crawford's *real* flops) and autographs, in her now familiar scrawl, glamorous portraits revealing her face in its elegantly gelid repose. At the studio there is a knock on her dressing room door, a male voice says, "We're ready for you, Miss Crawford," and out steps Faye Dunaway, uncannily made-up to look like Joan Crawford.

The discipline and determination with which this daily ritual is performed reveal more about the personality of Joan Crawford than anything else in *Mommie Dearest*. From this point on what we see are a series of melodramatic highs and lows in the life of a movie star which tell us nothing about the person behind the public image.

Following the credits we meet a divorced Joan Crawford, who, unable to have children because of numerous miscarriages, is seeking to adopt a child. After being refused several times as a single parent, she enlists the aid of her current lover Greg Savitt (Steve Forrest). For legal and time-saving purposes Savitt is a composite of Crawford's third husband Phillip Terry, Clark Gable, and various other men in Crawford's life. Forrest is very convincing in the role.

The child Christina (Mara Hobel) is soon joined by an adopted brother,

Christopher (Jeremy Scott Reinbolt). To the public and the press, they are the lucky, adored, and pampered children of a movie star. Privately, however, both are subjected to Draconian discipline. This is Christina's story, though, and therefore Christopher is only a footnote in the script. It is soon evident that there is a sense of competition between mother and daughter, a veritable love/hate relationship.

There are numerous illustrations of their strained relationship in the film. Following a race in the family swimming pool, a race which the older and stronger Joan obviously wins, Christina is told that "life is unfair"; when the child is found putting on makeup in front of a mirror her blond curls are hacked away with a pair of scissors; and when she refuses to eat a piece of rare steak, Crawford turns the incident into a two-day punishment and upbraids the child by exclaiming. "She negotiates everything like a goddamned Hollywood agent."

Many of the abuses Christina describes in her book occur in the middle of the night when Joan is drunk—thus the term "night raids." One such night raid takes place after Crawford has been fired from M-G-M (a particularly devastating blow to the actress) and culminates with Crawford destroying her prized rose garden and chopping down a tree. When the enraged and seemingly deranged actress screams, "Tina, bring me the ax," the audience responds with macabre laughter, as if they were watching a scene from one of Crawford's films, *What Ever Happened to Baby Jane?* (1962).

The most chilling night raid begins in Christina's bedroom when Joan discovers one of the child's three-hundred-dollar dresses on a wire coat hanger. Joan, with cold cream on her face, looking almost like a ghoul, beats the child with the hanger, then continues the fight in the child's bathroom, hitting her over the head with a can of Old Dutch cleanser.

Perry's maladroit direction turns these night raids into campy horror-film clichés, fails to shed any light on the fact that Joan, herself an abused child, became a child abuser, and further fails to elicit any explanation of the mother-daughter love/hate relationship. Most of all, and this was a major fault of the book as well, we never see the testing, cagey side of Christina. All we see is an adorable, blond, dimpled girl, the standard film child.

As the teenaged Christina (Diana Scarwid) emerges we get more of the same. When at private school, Christina is discovered petting with a teenaged boy, Joan has her brought home and almost strangles her in front of Barbara Bennett, a visiting *Redbook* writer (Jocelyn Brando). The aftermath is two years in a convent school for Christina. Later, when the mature Christina lands a role on the television soap opera, *The Secret Storm*, and is hospitalized for an appendix operation, an inebriated Joan takes over the role without her daughter's knowledge.

Joan's fourth marriage, to Pepsi-Cola executive Alfred Steele (Harry Goz), brings the only stabilizing relationship in Crawford's personal life, and after what appears to Christina as a period of reconciliation with her forceful mother, Joan's death delivers the final blow with the will's "for reasons which are well known to them" Christopher looks at his sister and says, "As usual, she has the last word," and, smiling deceptively, Christina looks into the camera and says, "Does she?"

The film is a hodge-podge of shrill scenes haphazardly pasted together. As David Denby wrote in *New York* magazine, "only the willfully naïve could take *Mommie Dearest* seriously as a study of child abuse."

In addition to the opening, silent montage, only two scenes show any insight and directorial finesse. When Louis B. Mayer (Howard Da Silva) calls Joan into his Culver City office and guilefully tells her she has been slipping at the box office and that she would be better off at another studio, he not only has already decided to terminate her contract but also has already had her belongings removed from her dressing room. In a final power play he refuses her the dignity of escorting her to her car. Joan was circumspect about many aspects of her career (for example, she feigned the flu on the night of the Academy Awards presentation when she was nominated for *Mildred Pierce*, 1945, because she was terrified she would lose) and she always maintained that she *asked* Mayer to release her from her M-G-M contract after eighteen years, but this scene has the ring of truth about it.

The other candid scene takes place at the Pepsi-Cola Board of Directors meeting following Steele's death. Here Dunaway really *becomes* Joan Crawford when she stands up to the ingratiating directors and yells at them not to try and manipulate her because, "This ain't my first time at the rodeo."

Except for the general praise for Dunaway's physical transformation as Crawford (despite the fact that she resembles actress Patricia Neal more than Joan Crawford), reviews of *Mommie Dearest* were mixed. Frank Perry is an inconsistent director who was out of his depth here. Yet the real culprit in the film's failure was simply the fact of too many involvements—from Yablans and the numerous scripts, to a pro-Crawford Dunaway and an anti-Crawford Scarwid, to Christina's husband (David Koontz) and Dunaway's boyfriend (Terry O'Neill) teamed as executive producers.

The most impressive aspect of the film was the sumptuous Art Deco production design by Bill Malley, who worked on *The Exorcist* (1973). Suzy, gossip columnist for the New York *Daily News*, described the sets as "the *Normandie* painted white." No one seemed to notice or care, however, that Crawford's splendid Brentwood mansion was actually decorated in period antiques and *not* Art Deco.

At the very first public screening in New York City—at noon—the audience was verbally in sympathy with Dunaway's Joan Crawford. *Mommie Dearest* has since become something of a cult film. It is revived constantly, has been a best seller on video tape, and florists and card shops now do a thriving "Mommie Dearest" business on Mother's Day. *The New York Times*' critic

Vincent Canby had the prescience to foresee this macabre reaction when he wrote, "*Mommie Dearest* possibly will turn out to be the all-American mother movie of the '80s."

Just weeks before the opening of the picture, Christina Crawford, at age forty-two, suffered a severe stroke from which she has since recovered. When she finally saw the film, she told the press she was "extremely displeased," supposedly because it depicted her mother in too kind a light. She has since published a novel entitled *Black Widow*, the story of "a woman of pure evil."

Ronald Bowers

Reviews

The Hollywood Reporter. September 8, 1981, p. 3.
Los Angeles Times. September 20, 1981, *Calendar*, p. 27.
The New York Times. September 18, 1981, III, p. 15.
The New Yorker. LVII, October 12, 1981, p. 150+.
Time. CXVIII, September 21, 1981, p. 73.
Variety. September 9, 1981, p. 3.

MONTENEGRO (PIGS AND PEARLS)

Origin: Yugoslavia
Production: Bo Jonsson for Viking Film/Smart Egg Pictures/Europa Film
Direction: Dusan Makavejev
Screenplay: Dusan Makavejev
Cinematography: Tomislav Pinter
Editing: Sylvia Ingemarsson
Art direction: Radu Borusescu
Music: Kornell Kovach
Running time: 96 minutes

Principal characters:
Marilyn Jordan .... Susan Anspach
Martin Jordan .... Erland Josephson
Dr. Pazardjian .... Per Oscarsson
Alex Rossignol .... Bora Todorovic
Montenegro .... Svetozar Cvetkovic
Tirke .... Patricia Gelin
Cookie Jordan .... Marianna Jacobi
Grandpa Bill .... John Zacharias
Jimmy Jordan .... Jamie Marsh
Rita Rossignol .... Lisbeth Zachrisson

The volatile relationship between sex and politics is a recurring theme in the films of Yugoslavian director Dusan Makavejev. In his highly acclaimed *WR: Mysteries of the Organism* (1971), Makavejev examines the controversial theories of psychologist Wilhelm Reich, intercutting documentary footage of Reich's followers with a fictional story of the violent love affair between a free-spirited Yugoslavian girl and a Russian ice skater. The little-seen *Sweet Movie*, made in 1974, contrasts the bizarre sexual practices of a wealthy capitalist with the uninhibited sexuality of the members of a commune. Both of these films also draw a correlation between sex and death, another of the director's frequent themes. Clearly, Makavejev is a filmmaker working decidedly outside the commercial mainstream.

With *Montenegro*, his first film in seven years, Makavejev continues his exploration of these ideas. Once again, we find sexual repression linked to social class, and freedom from that repression linked to death. Yet *Montenegro* is far more accessible in its approach than the director's earlier films. Working with a well-known international cast, he has set his story in the realistic world of Swedish suburbia, disguising his radical themes with the subtlety of his technique. It is not until well into the film that he gives the plot a sharp twist, and we find ourselves thrown suddenly into the realm of fanciful surrealism.

At the center of Makavejev's strange story is Marilyn Jordan (Susan Anspach), the American wife of a Swedish businessman. Marilyn leads the life of a well-to-do housewife, dividing her time with equal measures of boredom among housework, luncheons, and children. She is also slowly losing her mind. In a harrowingly funny series of events, we see Marilyn gradually losing her grip on reality. She prepares a Wienerschnitzel dinner for her family, then eats everything herself, sets fire to the bed after she and her husband Martin (Erland Josephson) have made love, and poisons the dog's milk, telling him that the choice between life and death is now up to him. Sensing that his wife is not well, Martin consults Dr. Pazardjian (Per Oscarsson), a psychiatrist so eccentric that he seems a possible candidate for treatment himself. The doctor visits the Jordans for dinner, but his questions to Marilyn are nonsensical and absurd, and she continues her slide into madness.

When Martin leaves for Brazil on business (his twenty-third trip of the year), Marilyn decides at the last minute to accompany him. She races to the airport, where she is detained by security guards when they discover a pair of gardening shears in her bag. They then lead her to a small room, along with a Yugoslavian peasant girl named Tirke (Patricia Gelin), where both are searched and the girl is relieved of a roast pig that she is carrying. Marilyn has missed her plane by the time they are released, and Tirke and her friend Alex (Bora Todorovic) offer her a ride into town. She accepts, a decision which will change her life.

From the moment she climbs into Alex's car, Marilyn enters another world. It is here that the message of the film's subtitle, *Pigs and Pearls*, becomes apparent. Marilyn, elegantly dressed and wearing an ever-present strand of pearls, finds herself surrounded suddenly by members of a culture completely unfamiliar to her. If Marilyn represents the complacent upper classes, then Tirke, Alex, and their friends are Makavejev's depiction of the thousands of immigrants who have flooded into Northern Europe, bringing with them strange customs and life-styles. The clash between these cultures is the film's central concern.

Instead of delivering her to her home, Alex takes Marilyn to the Zanzi Bar, his bizarre café/nightclub where rules are nonexistent and social codes no longer apply. Inside, the club is steamy and dreamlike, with food hanging from the ceiling and a constant stream of immigrants drifting in and out. Marilyn encounters a man who has been stabbed in the head for cheating at cards, who poses cheerfully for a picture on his way to the hospital. She is welcomed to the bar by Alex and his friends, who toast her in their own language, in what the subtitles tell us are graphically sexual terms. Later that night, she awakens to find Alex and his ex-wife, Rita (Lisbeth Zachrisson), making love by firelight on her bed. For Marilyn, accustomed to the sterile, ordered life of the Swedish bourgeoisie, the atmosphere is first astonishing and then liberating.

Among those living at the Zanzi Bar is a young laborer named Montenegro (Svetozar Cvetkovic), whom Marilyn had met earlier at the city zoo. The attraction between them is immediate, and she nurses him after he is injured in a fight. Tirke, with the help of Alex and Rita, is soon transformed from a drab peasant girl into an exotic dancer, and she performs a highly erotic number to the delight of the club's enthusiastic patrons. Then it is Marilyn's turn, and she sings the sweetly seductive "Give Me a Little Kiss," billing herself as "Susie Nashville." Afterwards, she and Montenegro dance and he carries her to his room, where they fight and then make love.

While Marilyn is discovering the delights of freedom at the Zanzi Bar, her family is undergoing several changes of its own. Daughter Cookie (Marianna Jacobi) steps willingly, and hilariously, into her mother's role, and senile Grandpa Bill (John Zacharias) draws a stream of hopeful women to the house when he advertises for a wife. Even the normally staid Martin departs radically from his usual behavior, striking up an exceedingly odd friendship with Dr. Pazardjian. Were Makavejev a more conventional filmmaker, he might have ended his story here, with each member of the Jordan family discovering his or her own form of happiness after Marilyn's unexpected departure. In Makavejev's world, however, social inequality always claims its victim, and when we return to Montenegro's room for the aftermath of his affair with Marilyn, we find that she has murdered him. In the film's startling conclusion, we see her once again with her family (which now seems to include the doctor), serving them fruit around the dinner table. As in all good fairy tales, it appears that they will live happily ever after. A final subtitle, however, informs us that the fruit is poisoned.

The performers in such a film must necessarily walk a fine line between reality and farce. Susan Anspach is perfectly cast as Marilyn, engaging us from the start in spite of her bizarre actions. Anspach is an actress of considerable sweetness and vulnerability, and she uses these qualities effectively. Erland Josephson is well-known for his work in such Ingmar Bergman films as *Scenes from a Marriage* (1973) and *Face to Face* (1976). His performance here, as the perplexed Martin, is filled with nuance and subtlety as he convinces us that he may be the film's one sane character—until his strange friendship with Dr. Pazardjian begins. As the doctor, Per Oscarsson is a delightful combination of professional ego and utter lunacy, never losing his air of smugness no matter how antic his behavior. Montenegro himself, as portrayed by Svetozar Cvetkovic, remains something of an enigma. A shy, quiet man who loves Marilyn from the moment of their first meeting, he enters into their affair with a naïveté that allows him no glimpse of the danger she brings with her.

Perhaps the film's most memorable performance is that of Bora Todorovic as the irrepressible Alex. He makes the Zanzi Bar's owner larger than life yet warmly human. Todorovic satirizes every cliché of the type of bawdy, rough-hewn behavior that so alarms and irritates the upper classes. Yet hand-in-hand with his boisterousness go boundless enthusiasm and an open heart; a combination which proves to be irresistible.

Montenegro is filled with images of the darkest sort of humor, and scene after scene of the film manages to both shock and amuse. For Makavejev, no subject is sacrosanct, and nothing is safe from his biting wit. With the exception of the death of Montenegro, each theme in the film—whether it be sex, violence, or insanity—is undercut by the director's savagely funny tone. Marilyn's encounter with the man who has been stabbed in the head illustrates this quality of Makavejev's work perfectly. It is Marilyn's introduction to the Zanzi Bar, and we experience it from her point of view, taking her reactions as our own. As the man is loaded into the car next to her for the trip to the hospital, and she finds herself conversing with someone who seems relatively unperturbed at having a knife protruding from his forehead, her reaction is initially one of bewilderment and shock. Yet as she realizes that everyone else, including the injured man himself, seems to regard the incident as fairly commonplace, a bemused smile takes the place of her earlier expression of horror. When the entire group stops to pose for photographs before entering the hospital, Marilyn joins in, accepting the fact that the usual rules and reactions are no longer valid. This acceptance is the beginning of the change that the Zanzi Bar will bring about in her.

The change in Marilyn lies at the heart of Makavejev's story. The atmosphere in the Zanzi Bar and the uninhibited high spirits of the people she meets there fill her with delight and wonder, and provide her with a climate of complete freedom and acceptance. The café is her chance to break free of her stifling life with her family and begin to live with total liberation; it is her opportunity to escape the madness that has been gradually closing in on her. The film's central question is whether or not she will, indeed, be able to escape from the traditional social order and make a life for herself outside its confines.

Makavejev answers the question in the film's final scenes. Marilyn is incapable of accepting the freedom that Montenegro and the Zanzi Bar offer her, but she is not able to rejoin her family successfully, either. In Makavejev's universe, she has entered a kind of limbo; too much a part of her class to turn her back on it, yet too much altered by her experiences to return. Montenegro's murder follows the pattern set by *WR: Mysteries of the Organism* and *Sweet Movie*. In both of these films, as in *Montenegro*, a member of the ruling social class is offered liberation through an affair with a lover from the working class. In all three films the affair results in the murder of the lover. Makavejev's message seems clear: the bourgeoisie will victimize the proletariat at every turn, even in matters of love.

The film's closing scene depicts the second part of Marilyn's dilemma. Having found herself too closely tied to her old life to be able to break with it permanently, she returns to her family and what appears, at first, to be a future of domestic happiness. In this case, however, appearances are deceiving. Marilyn has chosen the one freedom remaining to her—that of death—and she has decided to destroy the family that holds her as well.

Janet E. Lorenz

Reviews

The Hollywood Reporter. November 16, 1981, p. 3.
Los Angeles Times. December 24, 1981, V, p. 5.
The New Republic. CLXXXV, November 25, 1981, pp. 23-24.
The New York Times. November 8, 1981, p. 79.
Newsweek. XCVIII, November 16, 1981, p. 119.

MY DINNER WITH ANDRÉ

Origin: France
Production: George W. George and Beverly Karp for André Productions
Direction: Louis Malle
Screenplay: Wallace Shawn and André Gregory
Cinematography: Jeri Sopanen
Editing: Suzanne Baron
Art direction: Stephen McCape
Music: Allen Shawn
Running time: 110 minutes

Principal characters:
Wally .... Wallace Shawn
André .... André Gregory
Waiter .... Jean Lenauer

In the year of such blockbuster hits as *Raiders of the Lost Ark* and *Superman II*, a small, unusual film appeared and received warm praise from the critics as well as a surprisingly enthusiastic reception from the filmgoing public. The film was *My Dinner with André*, and its style was as far removed from the realm of the action/adventure picture as would seem cinematically possible. Directed by French filmmaker Louis Malle (*Murmur of the Heart*, 1971, *Atlantic City*, 1981), and written by its two stars, Wallace Shawn and André Gregory, the film's premise is simple and yet extraordinarily daring: two old friends meet for dinner and talk about their lives. That's all. There are no car chases, no spaceships, no love scenes, and the only other character of note is the elderly waiter who appears periodically to serve them their meal. Clearly, *My Dinner with André* is not an ordinary film.

The prospect of watching such a film may seem intimidating at first, with the thought of two hours spent listening to someone else's dinner-table conversation bringing visions of numbing boredom. Indeed, with the exception of the film's opening and closing moments, its physical action is entirely restricted to a New York restaurant. Yet in the course of those two hours we seem to travel from the forests of Poland to the Sahara Desert, to a bizarre Halloween night in Montauk on Long Island. *My Dinner with André* is witty, lively, fascinating, and, on its own terms, as gripping as any adventure film. Its excitement, however, is the excitement of ideas and its adventures take place in the mind.

The film opens with playwright Wallace Shawn hurrying along the garbage-strewn sidewalks of New York, on his way to meet his friend André Gregory for dinner. We follow Shawn through the city and onto the subway as his voice over narration tells us of his struggles as a writer, his life with his girl friend Debby, and the events that have led to his planned meeting with André. André, we learn, is a respected stage director whose work in experimental theater ended when he entered a period of personal crisis. As Wally approaches the restaurant, he confides his nervousness over the impending dinner and worries that he will find himself unable to cope with André's problems.

André arrives several minutes later and greets Wally warmly, seeming far more at ease than his anxious friend. The two are seated and Wally begins to question André about his life since the time of his withdrawal from the theater. André responds with a description of the strange and at times harrowing personal odyssey that has obsessed him for nearly five years. Wally listens in amazement as his friend recounts a series of bizarre adventures, beginning with an encounter workshop in the forests of Poland. His story encompasses an odd coincidence involving handprints, surrealism, and Antoine de Saint-Exupéry's *The Little Prince*, a trip to the Sahara with a Buddhist monk, a flag inhabited by evil spirits, and a community in Scotland that speaks with animals and trees. He speaks candidly about his precarious emotional state and of the startling hallucinations that have visited him during this period. Through it all, Wally continues to listen and eat, managing only an occasional "Gosh" or "Gee, what happened then?" before André continues his astonishing tale. The mixture of incredulity and skepticism in his expression evokes sympathetic laughter because it mirrors our own reaction to André's experiences. Like Wally, we find ourselves drawn deeper and deeper into the web of André's story, hypnotized by its strangeness even as we shake our heads over André's unquestioning acceptance of everything he describes. André ends his recollections with a vivid description of a simulated premature burial that he underwent one Halloween at Montauk. He ends his story with the wonderfully understated comment: "That was the end. I mean, I began to realize that I just didn't want to do those things anymore."

As Wally is collecting his thoughts, however, André resumes his monologue, suddenly disavowing the worth of any of his experiences and speaking passionately of the growing apathy that grips our society. His feelings of futility while attempting to break through that inertia were the cause of his rejection of the theater, and he tells Wally that he believes that civilization has decayed beyond the point of possible recovery. It is at this point that Wally begins, tentatively, to interject his own ideas, and the film becomes a true conversation. The two friends find themselves in agreement over the state of modern society, despairing over our use of social roles to mask our emotional alienation from one another and our cultural inability to deal openly with death. Their individual reactions to these shared views differ radically, however, with the point of divergence arising over something quite ordinary: Wally's electric blanket. André expounds on the barrier that the blanket raises between Wally and the world's harsh reality, and Wally responds with a sensible "Yes, but I mean, I would *never* give up my electric blanket, André, because New York is cold, our apartment is cold in the winter."

It is on this deceptively simple subject that Wally and André draw their philosophical lines, and the film becomes a spirited discussion of the ways in which the two men deal with their perceptions of the world. André's spiritual journey has been an increasingly anguished search for an alternative to his disillusionment with the theater, and the conclusion that he presents to Wally is that mankind has reached a state of passivity which necessitates a drastic shock to bring it back to life. "I mean, it may very well be," he posits, "that in another ten years people will pay ten thousand dollars in cash to be castrated, just in order to be affected by something." Wally's response is a reaffirmation of his faith in the power of drama and art to reach people, and he describes his own plays as an attempt "to bring myself up against some little bits of reality, and . . . share that with an audience." The simple pleasures of a cup of coffee and *The New York Times* make Wally's day-to-day existence not merely bearable but enjoyable, and he finally confesses to his friend that he finds much of André's quest absurd. For Wally, reality exists on the streets of New York just as clearly as it does in the Sahara or among the tree people of Scotland.

In spite of their differences in outlook, however, both André and Wally return again and again to the same basic theme; the importance of reaching out to others and sharing one's feelings and thoughts with them. Wally speaks frequently of his girl friend Debby, while André's stories are filled with references to his wife and their two children. As the evening progresses, we realize that their conversation has become an example of the kind of communication each is striving for in his own life. The exchange and interweaving of ideas, the points of sudden recognition and passionate disagreement, and the underlying affection and need to understand what colors and shapes their conversation illustrate their ideas even as they are being expressed. The result is exhilarating, both for Wally and André and for the audience.

As the film unfolds, Malle shoots the two men almost entirely in close-up, drawing the viewer into an intimate proximity with them. The boundaries of the screen seem to disappear and we feel as if we are seated at the table, silent but enthralled participants in the conversation. Malle has photographed and assembled the film in such a way that our experience closely follows Wally's. We share his initial astonishment at André's stories as well as his gradual understanding of the motivation behind his friend's search. We "join" the conversation when Wally does and we share in the excitement of both men as the exchange of ideas gathers momentum and feeling, recognizing, finally, that the experience itself has become as important as anything that was said. As we leave the restaurant with Wally in the film's final scene, we follow him on his taxi ride home where, he informs us, "Debby was home from work, and I told her everything about my dinner with André."

The story behind *My Dinner with André* adds to the film's unusual and intriguing effect. The screenplay was derived from a series of actual conversations between Wallace Shawn and André Gregory, which Shawn felt might be developed into an interesting film. The two men are, therefore, playing themselves, although their characters have been altered slightly to heighten the contrasts between them. The film was not improvised, but very carefully scripted and memorized by Shawn and Gregory, making its spontaneous, conversational quality all the more remarkable. The physical contrasts between the two men also add immeasurably to the film's effectiveness. André is tall and thin, with a wry, sophisticated manner, while Wally is short, round, and balding, with a quizzical face and an air of awkward innocence. Malle uses this contrast to great advantage, juxtaposing shots of Wally and André to emphasize the differences in their personalities.

My Dinner with André is an immensely entertaining film, filled with wit and intelligence, but it does not yield its gifts easily. It is also a challenging work, one which requires lively mental participation on the part of its audience. For those willing to meet that challenge, the film will prove to be exciting, compelling, and filled with food for thought for some time to come.

Janet E. Lorenz

Reviews

The Hollywood Reporter. October 13, 1981, p. 10.
Los Angeles Times. November 1, 1981, *Calendar*, p. 28.
The New York Times. October 8, 1981, III, p. 13.
The New Yorker. LVII, January 4, 1982, pp. 81-83.
Newsweek. XCVIII, October 26, 1981, p. 78.
Time. CXVIII, October 26, 1981, p. 78.
Variety. September 18, 1981, p. 3.

NIGHTHAWKS

Production: Martin Poll for Universal
Direction: Bruce Malmuth
Screenplay: David Shaber; based on an original story by David Shaber and Paul Sylbert
Cinematography: James A. Contner
Editing: Christopher Holmes
Art direction: Peter Larkin
Music: Keith Emerson
MPAA rating: R
Running time: 99 minutes

Principal characters:
Deke DaSilva .... Sylvester Stallone
Matthew Fox .... Billy Dee Williams
Wulfgar .... Rutger Hauer
Peter Hartman .... Nigel Davenport
Shakka .... Persis Khambatta
Irene .... Lindsay Wagner

Nighthawks is a story of policemen pitted against international terrorists that finally narrows down to a duel of wits and weapons between two men. The film begins by showing the two on opposite sides of the Atlantic Ocean in completely unrelated actions. It then brings them more and more closely toward their expected, but still surprising, final confrontation at the end.

The opening sequence gives us no hint of the type of film we are about to see. A woman is walking down a dark street at night. Two toughs advance toward her from opposite directions; then they brandish knives and demand her purse. Suddenly we and the would-be muggers discover that the "woman" is Deke DaSilva (Sylverter Stallone), a New York policeman on decoy duty with his partner, Matthew Fox (Billy Dee Williams). The policemen capture the two criminals, but not before DaSilva chases one of them, confronts him, captures his knife, and then beats him senseless. As we watch a long shot of DaSilva dragging the unconscious man away, we hear the policeman reciting the suspect's rights to him.

A title had labeled the first scene "December 31, New York City." Next, another title says "December 31, London." We see a man buying perfume in a department store, but as he talks to the saleswoman, he pushes a package under the counter with his foot. Moments after he leves the store, it explodes. He calmly places a call to the United Press to explain that the bombing was done as a protest against British colonialism.

Thus the introductory scenes set up the antagonists for the drama that is to come. The British police obtain a picture of the bomber, forcing him to have his appearance changed by a plastic surgeon and then to leave Europe. Meanwhile, DaSilva and Fox have been taken off the decoy squad and assigned to a counter-terrorist group that is being assembled because the police are not sufficiently "ruthless" with terrorists. The counter-terrorist group is being trained by Peter Hartman (Nigel Davenport). He stresses that they must learn every possible fact about the terrorists and how they think. DaSilva, however, is not convinced. He resents being taken off the decoy squad and resents having to sit in a classroom and take notes. He does not see any purpose in the training, and in fact has a moral objection to it. He did not, he says, join the police force to kill people. Hartman replies that combating violence requires greater violence and points out that DaSilva killed more than fifty people in Vietnam. DaSilva, however, remains unconvinced. This moral issue seems to be introduced by David Shaber, the scriptwriter, to add an extra bit of plot complication to the film rather than as a serious issue or as a credible development of the personality of the character.

The two antagonists, DaSilva and Wulfgar (Rutger Hauer)—the terrorist—finally come face-to-face when DaSilva and Fox, acting on information that Wulfgar has changed his appearance and likes nightlife, go searching for him. They know he is in New York because he has blown up a building in the financial district (at night) and has threatened to bomb more. When a stewardess who liked discos is murdered, police find a map of the financial district in her apartment; DaSilva and Fox show a picture of the murdered woman to disco owners until they find one she frequented. Inside they find Wulfgar, whom DaSilva recognizes despite his new face. Why this mastermind would go back to a club where he had been with the murdered woman, how DaSilva and Fox could find that club in just one evening, and how DaSilva could recognize the man are unanswerable questions that are largely obscured by the generally fast pacing of the film and the exciting chase that ensues once Wulfgar realizes he has been seen and identified.

Wulfgar leads the two on a chase that leads out the back door of the disco, through the urban landscape, into a subway station and through a subway train. Wulfgar takes a hostage and presents DaSilva with a moral dilemma. Holding the hostage in front of himself, Wulfgar moves briefly into range of DaSilva's pistol. As Fox yells for him to take a shot at Wulfgar, DaSilva hesitates and then does not fire because he might hit the hostage. As a result, Wulfgar is able to escape, slashing Fox's neck viciously as he runs by him. This enrages DaSilva, who vows vengeance on Wulfgar, althogh Fox's wound is found to be serious but not life-threatening. Fox's only comment is that DaSilva "should have took the shot" ataction of the screen time. The main emphasis is on the excitement of the chase through the back streets, the subway stations, and the subway train.

The scene then shifts to a gathering of United Nations representatives that

Wulfgar is expected to attack. DaSilva, Fox, Hartman, and other members of the counter-terrorist group are there, both openly showing themselves and disguised as waiters and other personnel. Wulfgar's accomplice, Shakka (Persis Khambatta), kills Hartman there, but Wulfgar surprises everyone by waiting until after the event, when he and Shakka stop a Roosevelt Island tramway car high over the East River and hold the occupants, including some U.N. delegates, hostage.

Now the action becomes essentially a duel between two men. Wulfgar demands—besides money, a bus to the airport, an airplane at the airport, and freedom for some jaled terrorists—that DaSilva be brought to the car. Wulfgar has already killed one hostage to show that he is serious, but he lets DaSilva take away an infant on the car so that the press will not write that he is "a man without a conscience." He chooses DaSilva because he is the man who chased him before. DaSilva then, of course, has the chance to demonstrate his bravery by being pulled alone up to the car by a cable, knowing that Wulfgar could kill him at any moment.

Wulfgar's plan is to have DaSilva drive the bus to the airport; then Wulfgar can kill him just before he leaves on the airplane. DaSilva, however, has a plan of his own, and just as Wulfgar, Shakka, and the hostges are about to board the bus, he activates a tape recorder that plays Hartman's description of Shakka. In the ensuing confusion, the hostages are saved but Wulfgar escapes alone on the bus. When the bus veers off the road and into the river, we think we have seen the last of Wulfgar. DaSilva, however, is not so easily fooled. He finds that Wulfgar knows the address of his ex-wife, Irene (Lindway Wagner), who had been seen briefly only twice before in the film. Then we see Irene going into her apartment; next Wulfgar arrives, sees the woman through the glass door and silently breaks in. He stealthily moves toward her, but when she turns to face him, it is DaSilva, once again disguised as a female. He removes his wig and the two start at each other. Finally, Wulfgar starts to raise his knife and DaSilva kills him with his pistol.

Nighthawks is a fairly standard action-adventure film which makes good if conventional use of its New York City locations. Probably its strongest point is the quick, exciting pacing of director Bruce Malmuth and editor Christopher Holmes. Since the plot is not designed to survive careful analysis, the fast pace and the many exciting action scenes must carry the viewer's interest, and they do so quite well. Sylvester Stallone in the lead role gives a solid but unspectacular performance. He is well supported by Billy Dee Williams as Fox and the Dutch actor Rutger Hauer as Wulfgar. The film did moderately well at the box office, but once again demonstrated Stallone's inability to transfer to other films his immense popularity in *Rocky* (1976) and its sequels.

Sharon Wiseman

Reviews

The Hollywood Reporter. April 6, 1981, p. 3.
Los Angeles Times. April 9, 1981, VI, p. 1.
The New Republic. CLXXXIV, May 2, 1981, pp. 26-27.
The New York Times. April 10, 1981, III, p. 6.
Newsweek. XCVVII, April 20, 1981, p. 93.
Time. CXVII, May 11, 1981, p. 87.
Variety. April 6, 1981, p. 3.

ON GOLDEN POND

Production: Bruce Gilbert for ITC Films/IPC Films; released by Marble Arch Productions
Direction: Mark Rydell
Screenplay: Ernest Thompson (AA); based on his play of the same name
Cinematography: Billy Williams
Editing: Robert L. Wolfe
Art direction: Stephen Grimes; set decoration, Jane Bogart
Music: Dave Grusin
MPAA rating: PG
Running time: 109 minutes

Principal characters:
Norman Thayer, Jr. .... Henry Fonda (AA)
Ethel Thayer .... Katharine Hepburn (AA)
Chelsea Thayer .... Jane Fonda
Bill Ray .... Dabney Coleman
Billy Ray .... Doug McKeon
Charlie Martin .... William Lanteau

On Golden Pond represents a significant milestone in motion-picture history that goes well beyond the considerable achievements of the film as a work of art. First, it represents a long overdue first Academy Award for Best Actor for Henry Fonda, one of the most accomplished film and stage actors the United States has ever produced. This oversight on the part of the Academy's voting membership would be even more unbelievable if it were not for the fact that a number of outstanding actors and actresses including Barbara Stanwyck, John Barrymore, Richard Burton, and Deborah Kerr, have been similarly overlooked, while other less accomplished actors have had the good fortune to be at the right place at the opportune moment to give the performance of a lifetime and win an Oscar. Harold Russell's Academy Award for Best Supporting Actor in *The Best Years of Our Lives* (1946), his first and only film prior to 1982, is a good example of this. Frank Sinatra managed a similar feat with his work in *From Here to Eternity* in 1953. Thus, while criminal, Fonda's neglect is not as unique as it might seem.

Almost equally surprising is the fact that *On Golden Pond* marks the first appearance together of Fonda and Katharine Hepburn, whose careers span almost parallel courses over the last half century. Even more remarkable is the fact that the two had not even met before the film went into production.

Finally, the film marked the first appearance together of Henry Fonda with his daughter Jane. It was the younger Fonda, in fact, who made the venture possible when she and her business partner, producer Bruce Gilbert, purchased Ernest Thompson's critically acclaimed Broadway play. The two were originally looking for a vehicle that would accommodate the talents of all three acting Fondas, and *On Golden Pond* came close to filling their needs. Unfortunately, there was no viable part for Peter Fonda without extensive rewriting, so the decision was made to go ahead with father and daughter.

The combination of two generations of actors in the principal roles provided an added dimension in that it furnished a basis for comparison between the traditional approach to character delineation practiced by Hepburn and the elder Fonda and the more recent introspective style utilized by Jane Fonda and her costar, Dabney Coleman. Jane has, in fact, developed a rather bold and successful formula in selecting her recent roles. Her production company operates much the same way in her behalf as the old studio system once did for stars such as her father and Katharine Hepburn. It selects compatible vehicles, fashions them to fit her talents, and then shapes them into hits by adding other ingredients of current interest. *Coming Home* (1978), with its Vietnam veteran theme; *China Syndrome* (1979), with its topic of a nuclear accident; and *Nine to Five* (1980), treating the subject of working women, are prime examples of this type of tailored production. Her approach to depicting her characters in these films is very methodical, considering each character's motivation in every scene, a practice requiring many discussions between actors and the director.

Henry Fonda and Katharine Hepburn approached their roles as Norman and Ethel Thayer as they have approached every other role in their long careers. They followed the script without discussion. "If the script is good and you don't get in its way, it will come off okay," Hepburn believes. Both methods are vindicated in *On Golden Pond*; both Fondas and Hepburn were nominated for Academy Awards.

The story of *On Golden Pond* is a simple and yet a universal one. Norman Thayer (Henry Fonda) is under the impression that he is a dying man when he and Ethel (Katharine Hepburn) arrive to celebrate his eightieth birthday and to spend what would seem to be their final summer together at their home on New Hampshire's Golden Pond. He does not pay much attention to the landscape or notice the red of the setting sun as it spreads its colors on the waters of the lake. He also does not notice the cry of the loons, but Ethel does. "They're welcoming us back," she remarks. He pays her little heed; his concerns are internal. Coping with angina and various other physical defects stemming from the process of aging, he hides his vulnerability behind a façade of crusty eccentricity. If it is Ethel's nature always to find the bright side of things, he considers it his duty to look for the dark. Ethel sees through this guise to the fearful man hidden inside and is quietly supportive. "Ethel and Norman represent the kind of couple I admire very much," Hepburn noted during the filming. "They're not quitters. There's no self-pity. They've been in love all these years and she is satisfied to let him be the star of the marriage."

When Norman, at his wife's urging, goes out into the woods to pick strawberries shortly after their arrival at the pond, he becomes disoriented and runs back to the cottage in a panic. He jokes to Charlie Martin (William Lanteau), the local postman, who has just arrived, but later openly admits his fears to Ethel in one of the few instances in the picture when he honestly and without sarcasm confronts his fears of senility and death.

Several days after this occurrence, their daughter Chelsea (Jane Fonda) arrives to help him celebrate his eightieth birthday. She has not been to see her parents for several years, largely because she and her father are estranged for reasons that neither can quite put into words. Instead of kissing hello, they merely begin their battles anew. This time, however, the situation is complicated by the fact that Chelsea is accompanied by her dentist fiancé, Bill (Dabney Coleman), and his thirteen-year-old son Billy (Doug McKeon). Although all of Chelsea's half-hearted attempts to breach her father's defenses fail, Bill manages to win a modicum of respect and grudging affection from Norman by honestly putting him in his place when he begins a game of playing with people's minds.

The fundamental problem of the relationship between Norman and Chelsea is the fact that as a revered and brilliant college professor he has always been allowed the freedom to be caustic in his treatment of the people around him. Chelsea, although almost equally bright, is intimidated by him and, in her equally superficial cynicism, has never been able to cut through her father's gruff veneer to see the love that he holds for her. To Chelsea, Norman appears to be overbearing and unapproachable, and although she is close to her mother, she never has allowed Ethel to use her leverage with Norman to bring the two together. On her part, Ethel has always allowed her love for Norman to take precedence over her relationship with her daughter, so she cannot be, perhaps, as sympathetic as Chelsea would like.

Following the birthday celebration, Chelsea and Bill announce that they would like to take off to Europe for a few weeks, leaving Billy behind in the Thayers' care. Initially, neither Norman nor the boy is particularly pleased with the arrangement, but gradually they develop an affinity for each other. Billy is won over, at first, by the prospect of riding in the Thayers' motorboat and then by learning to fish. Fishing, it seems, is Norman's passion and in his young charge he now has the companion that he never had in the recalcitrant Chelsea.

The old man and the boy draw closer, as the summer progresses, through their attempts to catch Walter, the lake's largest fish. Walter has eluded Norman's hook for several years, and now, with the boy, the frustrated angler makes a crusade out of catching the enormous trout. A crucial sequence in the film occurs during one of these fishing trips, when Norman and Billy go into a dangerous, rock-strewn cove to look for the fish. They fail to find him, but by the time they leave it has become too dark to navigate properly and the boat crashes into a rock. Although the accident is largely Billy's fault, Norman is forgiving and even tender. The two spend several hours in the water, and Norman has sustained a bad gash on the head, but they are rescued by a worried Ethel and Charlie.

The irony of this scene lies in the fact that the audience realizes that Norman was not necessarily the unforgiving parent that Chelsea perceived him to be while she was growing up. She was merely deceived by his gruff exterior. By the same token, through his gentleness with Billy, the audience also realizes that had he shown such tenderness to his daughter through the years, they might have had a better relationship.

Norman recuperates and he and Billy sneak out to go fishing one final time on the last day of the boy's stay. Ethel stops them, however, and makes them promise to stay in the safe waters around the cottage. While they are fishing, Chelsea returns alone and confides to Ethel that she and Bill have been married. Ethel wants Chelsea to inform Norman of her marriage herself instead of relying on her mother. The daughter agrees to do so only after her mother admonishes her for childishly dwelling on the problems of the past.

Meanwhile, Norman and Billy have caught Walter in the close waters, but return him symbolically to live a few more years in the pond. When they return, Chelsea makes an awkward attempt to tell Norman about her marriage and also tells him that she would like to begin a new relationship with him—the kind that fathers and daughters ought to have. Norman is friendly and readily agrees but their relationship does not begin to change until later that afternoon when Chelsea performs a complicated back flip into the lake. This dive had apparently been a major source of contention between the girl and her father in her youth. Norman had been a championship diver when he was in college and possibly had entertained similar aspirations for Chelsea. Despite her father's proddings, the girl was always too frightened to perform a back flip. When Chelsea sees Billy do it, however, and hears her father remark that she had never been able to do such a dive, she goes onto the platform and does an acceptable back flip amid cheers from her family.

Later, when Chelsea and Billy depart, Norman gives his daughter one of his old diving medals. This is one of the closest moments of their lives and the real beginning of a new relationship between the two. After they leave, however, Norman suffers a severe angina attack. Despite the fact that his panicky wife is unable to reach the telephone operator, his medicine takes effect and he recovers. The film closes with the couple looking out at the autumn colors on the lake. Now Norman too can hear the cries of the loons.

With Ernest Thompson's Academy Award-winning script, *On Golden Pond* has much of the character of the play from which he adapted it; this is a film in which words and not action are of the utmost importance. Director Mark Rydell performed a marvelous job of "opening up" the stage-bound aspects to make it more successful as a film than it had been as a Broadway drama. The scenery and the sense of the changing seasons add immeasurably to its success. Rydell, whose career has included a number of films which contain a pivotal relationship between a man and a boy, such as *The Reivers* (1969) and *Cinderella Liberty* (1973), does a remarkable job here in developing the relationship between Norman and Billy. His most challenging assignment, however, directing such individually accomplished performers as the two Fondas and Hepburn, proved to be the strong point of the film. The three actors were all nominated for Academy Awards, with both Katharine Hepburn and Henry Fonda winning. It was Fonda's last opportunity. He died on August 12, 1982.

Following the Awards ceremonies in March, 1982, many cynics felt that a sentimental vote was responsible for the major Oscars for the film (with the possible exception of Rydell's nomination as Best Director, though he did not win). Yet when one looks dispassionately at the film, one cannot deny its simple brilliance. It is a universal story of love and family relationships, and it does not contain complicated topical elements which might date it in years to come. *On Golden Pond* will undoubtedly become a classic, and will long be appreciated for its elemental beauty.

Grant Davidson

Reviews

The Hollywood Reporter. November 13, 1981, p. 3.
Los Angeles Times. November 29, 1981, *Calender*, p. 37.
The New Republic. CLXXXVI, January 20, 1982, p. 26.
The New York Times. December 4, 1981, III, p. 10.
The New York Times. December 13, 1981, III, p. 17.
The New Yorker. LVII, December 7, 1981, p. 198+.
Newsweek. XCVIII, November 30, 1981, p. 105.
Saturday Review. VIII, December, 1981, p. 69.
Time. CXVIII, November 16, 1981, p. 69.
Variety. November 13, 1981, p. 3.

ONLY WHEN I LAUGH

Production: Roger M. Rothstein and Neil Simon for Columbia
Direction: Glenn Jordan
Screenplay: Neil Simon
Cinematography: David M. Walsh
Editing: John Wright
Art direction: Albert Brenner
Music: David Shire
MPAA rating: R
Running time: 120 minutes

Principal characters:
Georgia .... Marsha Mason
Polly .... Kristy McNichol
Toby .... Joan Hackett
Jimmy .... James Coco
David .... David Dukes

Only When I Laugh, the first film produced by Neil Simon, is a love story, yet it develops no male/female relationships in the conventional sense. Instead, it focuses on a trio of friends, all of whom have serious problems, but who sustain one another through shared love. The central member of the trio is actress Georgia Hines (Marsha Mason), a self-described "thirty-eight-year-old ex-wino," who, as the film begins, has just completed a twelve-week drying out period at a Long Island sanatorium. Her relationships with friends Toby (Joan Hackett) and Jimmy (James Coco), with teenaged daughter Polly (Kristy McNichol), and with former lover David (David Dukes) precipitate crises in her newly nonalcoholic life and—in the first two cases—provide the love to cope with those crises.

The title of the film—and of playwright David's newest opus—is the punch line of an old joke: A man is impaled by a spear and, when asked if it hurts, replies, "Only when I laugh." Metaphorically, Georgia, Toby, and Jimmy are impaled by spears, the pain of which they exacerbate through jokes and wisecracks, yet they help each other through love.

Georgia's is the most fully developed case. Although she has successfully taken a "cure" for alcoholism and has promised Toby to be a "good girl" now that she is back in her Manhattan apartment, the temptations to return to drink are overwhelming. To begin with, seventeen-year-old Polly; who has been living with her father and his new wife, wants to move in with her mother. Georgia realizes that having the girl with her will test her ability to handle the responsibility for Polly's welfare and control the alcoholism which had made her an unsuitable guardian in the past. Moreover, Polly is not totally sure of Georgia's love for her and intimates that her mother had not put up much of a struggle for custody during the divorce proceedings. Georgia deals with the pressures of Polly's needs by recalling her alcoholism—her "spear"—through a constant patter of jokes about it. Polly, who is perhaps the most well-adjusted of the film's major characters, responds with love. Even when the pressures from their relationship as well as other sources in Georgia's life bring about a nearly disastrous drinking bout, Polly maintains her love.

Toby and Jimmy have their "spears" too, and her friends' problems compound the pressures Georgia faces. Toby is obsessed with the decay of her youthful beauty and seems perpetually in search of ways to retard that decay. Her insecurities reach a critical point when, on the eve of her fortieth birthday, her husband announces his intention to leave her because he has grown tired of her. Jimmy's problems include compulsive overeating and lack of professional fulfillment. An actor like Georgia, he has spent his career performing in television commercials and with traveling troupes. Shortly after Georgia returns from the sanatorium, he lands the meaty part he has been dreaming of, but one week before opening—on the same day that Toby learns of her husband's plans—he is fired. Like Georgia, both Toby and Jimmy joke about their problems, bitterly laughing at their hurts, and, like her, they are sustained by the love shared by the members of the trio. Yet their needs add to the pressures that Georgia already faces from her sincere desire to defeat her alcohol problem and be a good mother for Polly.

Another pressure on Georgia involves David. Initially she does not want to deal with him at all, fearing the memories of their relationship, which was soured by her drinking problem. When she reluctantly agrees to meet him for lunch, she discovers that coping with memories will be the least of her difficulties in the new relationship with David. He has written a play—entitled *Only When I Laugh*—which deals with their relationship, and he wants her to act the lead role—in other words, to play herself. Impressed by the play's quality, Georgia undertakes the painful task of recapitulating her past. She pushes for a restoration of her former relationship with David as she becomes more and more caught up in the rehearsals for the play, but that hope shatters when she sees David with his new girl friend.

Georgia's realization that she has been supplanted completely in David's affections occurs on the same day that Toby and Jimmy confront their marital and professional crises. Thus, the film's climactic scenes represent psychological nadirs for all three. Georgia, wounded by David's apparent rejection, comes to Toby's apartment to comfort her friend. On the way, she has been sorely tempted to stop at a bar. When Jimmy appears with the news of his lost job, the temptation becomes too much. She begins to guzzle champagne, on hand for a party planned to honor Toby's birthday but which is now cancelled. As Georgia becomes increasingly drunk, Polly and her date arrive, not having been informed of the party's cancellation. Obviously embarrassed by the spectacle she is making of herself, Georgia reacts by drinking more and more until she is incapable of getting home without Jimmy's assistance. The loneliness of her apartment and a lack of cigarettes, though, send her back onto the streets. In a bar, she meets a man who later beats her up. The next morning Polly confronts the hungover and battered Georgia, who orders her daughter to return to her father, who can care for her more competently. Although Polly apparently complies, she lets her mother know that she still loves her. The film ends on a positive note as Georgia comes to understand that despite her weaknesses she will always have the love of her daughter and her friends.

As in most of his films, Neil Simon has used comedy in the manner of major writers of stage comedy—that is, to develop a serious theme. In *Only When I Laugh*, based on his unsuccessful stage play *The Gingerbread Lady* (1970), Simon has been relatively successful. The subject of alcoholism has been a staple in film melodramas such as *The Lost Weekend* (1945) and *Days of Wine and Roses* (1962), but Simon has managed to avoid much of the sentimentality of films such as those by defusing potentially maudlin situations with a wisecrack. For example, as Polly is leaving her mother's apartment at the end of the film, Georgia quips, "When I grow up, I want to be just like you." Thus, instead of allowing the scene to elicit tears of sentiment, Simon invests it with a comic touch that nicely summarizes the mother-daughter relationship. The audience realizes that Polly is indeed more mature than Georgia. Simon also avoids providing easy solutions for his characters' problems. After the film ends, the audience probably realizes that Georgia will continue to struggle against alcoholism—and sometimes lose the struggle, that Toby will continue to deny the inevitability of the aging process, and that Jimmy will never achieve theatrical stardom, but also realizes that each character will survive as long as he or she can rely on the love of the others.

Critical responses to *Only When I Laugh* were largely positive. Singled out for special praise were Simon's screenplay and the acting of the principal players, especially Marsha Mason (Simon's wife) and James Coco. Coco was nominated for an Academy Award for best supporting actor, and critics acknowledged his sensitive, unaffected portrayal of Jimmy's homosexuality. The film generally seems to stand up well against Neil Simon's other work, the most significant flaw being a failure to develop the full potential of the play-within-the-film, a situation fraught with dramatic possibilities. Despite this flaw, the film is a highly entertaining and meaningful comedy.

Frances M. Malpezzi
William M. Clements

Reviews

The Hollywood Reporter. September 15, 1981, p. 3.
Los Angeles Times. September 24, 1981, VI, p. 2.
The New York Times. September 23, 1981, III, p. 23.
Newsweek. XCVIII, September 28, 1981, pp. 87-88.
Time. CXVIII, October 5, 1981, p. 88.
Variety. September 15, 1981, p. 3.

OUTLAND

Production: Richard A. Roth for Warner Bros.
Direction: Peter Hyams
Screenplay: Peter Hyams
Cinematography: Stephen Goldblatt
Editing: Stuart Baird
Production design: Philip Harrison
Art direction: Malcolm Middleton
Special effects: John Stears
Music: Jerry Goldsmith
MPAA rating: R
Running time: 108 minutes

Principal characters:
O'Niel .... Sean Connery
Sheppard .... Peter Boyle
Dr. Marian Lazarus .... Frances Sternhagen
Montone .... James B. Sikking
Carol .... Kika Markham

During the past decade, students of popular culture have pointed out that many of the patterns and forms of popular film and literature cross conventional generic lines. Thus, distinctions between Western and science fiction or between mystery and romance may become blurred as we recognize that a particular science-fiction film, for example, may resemble a particular Western or mystery as much as it does other science-fiction films. Peter Hyams' *Outland* provides an excellent case study of such genre-crossing.

Set on Io, one of the moons of Jupiter, sometime in the near future, *Outland* treats one man's conflict with a perverted management-labor system in a mining industry on the moon. Bill O'Niel (Sean Connery), a federal district marshal newly arrived on the moon, finds himself all alone when his wife Carol (Kika Markham) decides that she has spent too many years in such isolated outposts. Resisting the temptation to accompany his family as they return to more civilized living conditions, O'Niel faces a major crisis when he has to deal with several psychotic miners. Working with a psychologist, Marian Lazarus (Frances Sternhagen), who suspects that something strange has happened to the workers, O'Niel finds that the mining company under the direction of Sheppard (Peter Boyle), its chief agent, has been lacing the miners' rations with amphetamines. The drugs enhance the miners' capacity for work over a period of several months but inevitably plunge them into self-destructive, violent psychoses. With the help of Montone (James B. Sikking), a locally based law enforcement officer, O'Niel sets out to halt the practice.

Montone is murdered before he can offer any real assistance, though, and O'Niel is then left with only the cynical Dr. Lazarus to face the assassins Sheppard has brought in to prevent the marshal from curtailing the unethical operations. As the miners sit drinking and enjoying the erotic entertainment in Io's single nightclub, unwilling to become involved in O'Niel's attempt to help them, the assassins stalk the marshal through the tubes and corridors of the man-made environment of the oxygen-less moon. The film climaxes in a flurry of gunplay as O'Niel and the assassins shoot it out.

Most viewers of *Outland* have pointed out its clearly developed similarities to the classic Western film, *High Noon* (1952), thus suggesting that formulaic patterns in films can easily be transferred from genre to genre. For example, both the science-fiction film and the Western depict the lonely vigil of a law enforcement officer waiting to face assassins who have come expressly to kill him. Both films present the refusals of virtually everyone in the community to help the lawman in the impending showdown. In both films, the central figure is deserted even by his wife—though in the Western she has a last-minute change of heart. Finally, both *Outland* and *High Noon* end with a violent confrontation in which the hero emerges with only slight damage. Thus, the particular Western conventions which underlie *High Noon* are translated easily into a different film genre.

Outland, however, is much more than a mere futuristic reworking of a classic Western film. Peter Hyams has infused the film with a moral universe which resembles that of hard-boiled detective film and fiction such as works by Dashiell Hammett, Raymond Chandler, Mickey Spillane, and Ross Macdonald. In films based on these writers' works—for example, *The Maltese Falcon* (1941), *Murder, My Sweet* (1944), *Kiss Me Deadly* (1955), and *Harper* (1966)—the gallant detectives move through a milieu in which everyone is corrupt in some way. The settings of such films, usually Los Angeles, are replete with the most seamy degradations of the human condition. The ability of the detective, be he Sam Spade, Philip Marlowe, Mike Hammer, or Harper, to maintain his nobility and sense of honor in the immoral world in which he exists is the hallmark of the hard-boiled detective genre. O'Niel is much like the typical protagonists of these films, and *Outland* evinces as much influence from them as from *High Noon*.

The social environment of Io reveals much in the way of moral degradation. For example, the nightclub is a scene of voyeuristic orgies as the drugged miners watch couples in various combinations of male and female copulate to the deafening music. Prostitutes are readily available to the miners, apparently among the perquisites provided by the mining company. The corruption that leads to the administration of the amphetamines taints everyone with any sort of executive power. Even though Montone and the maverick Dr. Lazarus deplore the practice, they have tried to ignore it until O'Niel pricks their consciences. Perhaps the most telling indication of the pervasive corruption involves the failure of the miners to come to O'Niel's assistance. He is clearly fighting for their benefit, while they are concerned only with their immediate pleasures. In a striking departure from the *High Noon* pattern, where Marshal Will Kane's fight was in one sense a personal matter, *Outland* depicts a lonely figure struggling in a cause for others. Such a figure definitely resembles the hard-boiled detective: isolated, altruistic (despite a crusty cynicism), and incorruptible. O'Niel maintains his sense of honor on Io, where such principles are decidedly out of place. He resists the temptation to ignore what is going on, and he stays to fight for something that will bring him no personal gain and in fact results in loneliness when his family leaves him.

It is interesting that Sean Connery has been cast in the role of Bill O'Niel, in that James Bond, the role which Connery originated for the screen, is a character much like the hard-boiled detective. His world may be more glamorous than that of Sam Spade or Philip Marlowe, but it reflects the same moral struggle as theirs. Connery, then, may be drawing on his experience in the Bond role for at least some of his characterization of O'Niel.

The image of the future which Peter Hyams presents in *Outland* involves an extension of what some writers and filmmakers have perceived as qualities of contemporary American life. Io is an industrial enclave where tedious work is the primary activity. The temptation to exploit the workers and to conspire for higher profits is present, and some people in power yield to it. Escapist entertainment compensates the workers for being exploited. Only the rare individual is able to emerge from the socioeconomic morass to exercise his or her personal principles, and it is the presence of such rare individuals that mitigates the film's cynicism. It offers a hero who surmounts the problems around him just as similar heroes in hard-boiled detective and Western films overcome their environments. Its cynical perspective places *Outland* in the tradition of *film noir*, but it offers hope in the bleakness of its vision.

Although reviews of *Outland* were mixed, the film possesses a number of interesting features. To view it as little more than a remake of *High Noon* set in the future, as many critics did, is overly simplistic. The film does indeed draw its plot from that Western, but director-screenwriter Peter Hyams has incorporated so much of the atmosphere of the hard-boiled detective film into *Outland* that his use of the *High Noon* material is truly innovative. Moreover, the film possesses the requisite elements of good science fiction, particularly the effects staged by production designer Philip Harrison and special-effects supervisor John Stears. It has no bug-eyed monsters or chases through the vastness of space, but the advanced technology of Io reveals a comprehensive and carefully planned setting. *Outland* is also technically innovative, as it is one of the first feature films to make extensive, successful use of miniature sets. By a sophisticated technique, the filmmakers were able to combine the action of the players on bare sets with intricate miniature pictures and models. Thus, many of the futuristic sets were not present during the making of the scenes in which they appear to the audience to be present.

Frances M. Malpezzi
William M. Clements

Reviews

The Hollywood Reporter. May 15, 1981, p. 2.
Los Angeles Times. May 21, 1981, VI, p. 1.
The New York Times. May 22, 1981, III, p. 8.
Newsweek. XCVII, June 1, 1981, p. 91.
Time. CXVII, June 1, 1981, p. 91.
Variety. May 15, 1981, p. 3.

PENNIES FROM HEAVEN

Production: Nora Kaye and Herbert Ross for Metro-Goldwyn-Mayer
Direction: Herbert Ross
Screenplay: Dennis Potter
Cinematography: Gordon Willis
Editing: Richard Marks
Art direction: Fred Tuch and Bernie Cutler
Costume Design: Bob Mackie
Choreography: Danny Daniels
Music: Marvin Hamlisch and Billy May
MPAA rating: R
Running time: 108 minutes

Principal characters:
Arthur Parker .... Steve Martin
Eileen ....Bernadette Peters
Joan .... Jessica Harper
Tom ....Christopher Walken
Accordion man .... Vernel Bagneris
Mr. Warner ....John McMartin
Blind girl .... Eliska Krupka

Pennies from Heaven was one of the major box-office failures of 1981. For a variety of reasons, the film was unable to attract sufficient audience support, although it may very well turn out to have been the best film produced in Hollywood in 1981. It is certainly the most exciting, daring, and original work of the year. Like *Cabaret* (1972), *New York, New York* (1977), and *All That Jazz* (1979), *Pennies from Heaven* extends the conventions of the musical genre. Never before has the hero of a musical been executed for murder, nor has the heroine become a prostitute who thoroughly enjoys her work. It is also unprecedented for a musical to feature its entire cast "lip-synching" along with recordings of old songs rather than actually singing the tunes themselves. Thus, though *Pennies from Heaven* pays tribute to the musicals of the 1930's, it is, through the employment of these techniques, also creating an antinostalgic structure that provides a bitter reminder of what the audiences of those old films experienced in their daily lives once they left the darkness of the movie palaces. Thus, the screenplay serves a dual purpose, both re-creating the fantasies of the 1930's and exploring the nightmarish underside of those dreams.

The film begins symbolically with a shot of shiny, billowy clouds and the song "The Clouds Will Soon Roll By," sung by Elsie Carlisle, on the sound track. Then a darker side is revealed as the camera begins to descend into a thunderstorm and torrential rains, which in turn becomes Chicago in 1934. A quick cut reveals Arthur Parker (Steve Martin), a sheet-music salesman whose territory consists of eastern Illinois. He is tired of traveling and attempts to convince his wife Joan (Jessica Harper) to lend him the money that she has inherited from her father to set up a store of his own so that he can stay in Chicago. Joan not only turns him down but also resists his sexual advances. The frustrated Arthur leaves and threatens not to return. He goes to a bank to apply for a loan, but he has no collateral and his application is not approved. Instead of expressing anger, he breaks into the song, "Yes, Yes, My Baby Said Yes, Yes," which then evolves into an elaborate production number reminiscent of the famous "We're in the Money," directed by Busby Berkeley in the *Gold Diggers of 1933*.

Later, out on the road, Arthur picks up a hitchhiker (Vernel Bagneris), who turns out to be an accordionist. In the next town, the hitchhiker sings on the street as Arthur tries to sell his song sheets in a music store, where he meets Eileen Everson (Bernadette Peters), a junior high schoolteacher. Arthur is immediately attracted to her and sings "Did You Ever See a Dream Walking," dubbed with the voice of Bing Crosby.

In school the next day, Eileen reads the fairy tale "Rapunzel" to her students, but when she sees a picture of the prince, she is reminded of Arthur and lapses into a reverie in which her students are transformed into an orchestra, which she leads while singing "Love Is Good for Anything That Ails You." After school, Arthur meets Eileen and offers her a ride home. Somewhat suspicious, Eileen asks if he is married, and Arthur parries the question by asking if he looks like a married man. Later, however, Arthur slips and mentions his wife, which he covers up by saying that she is dead. He finally seduces Eileen by asking her to help ease the pain of his wife's death. When Arthur returns to Chicago, however, Joan is anxiously awaiting him and agrees to let Arthur use her inheritance for his store. He, of course, tells her that he loves her, but in fantasy she catches on and sings "It's a Sin to Tell a Lie," before attempting to stab him with a pair of scissors.

Meanwhile, Eileen is in trouble. By Thanksgiving, she realizes that she is pregnant. Her principal, Mr. Warner (John McMartin), tells her that the school board knows it too, and gives her some money as she leaves the school. In Chicago, Arthur has finally achieved his dream of his own record store, yet business is slow because of the Depression so he decides to go see Eileen. On the way, though, he stops for a cigarette and meets a beautiful blind girl (Eliska Krupka). He offers to escort her but she refuses, and he drives on. While he is visiting Eileen, the blind girl encounters the accordion man and is murdered. Ironically, the police write down Arthur's license number when he drives by on his return to Chicago because he almost hits a pedestrian in the rain.

When Eileen arrives in Chicago to meet Arthur, she goes into a bar and orders a lemonade, but one of the customers, Tom (Christopher Walken), tells the bartender to put some gin in it. He then performs a spectacular striptease while singing "Let's Misbehave." He turns out to be a pimp, and Eileen, depressed at not being able to find Arthur, becomes Lulu, the newest whore in his stable.

Arthur eventually encounters Eileen working in her new profession, and even though she cannot depend on him, she realizes that she still loves him and agrees to stay with him. Arthur says that he wants to live in a world where the songs are real. Eileen replies that "Happy days are here again, eh, Arthur?" Together, they destroy the contents of the record store, and find a room in a cheap hotel. Subsequently, the police interrogate Joan. They tell her where Arthur is, and she innocently tells them of Arthur's behavior when he returned on the night of the murder. Based on this circumstantial evidence they issue a warrant for Arthur's arrest. Ignorant of this development, however, Arthur and Eileen go to see Fred Astaire and Ginger Rogers in the film *Follow the Fleet.* As Astaire and Rogers perform one of the dances, the two spectators go up on stage where they mimic the dancers' movements. Soon they become the pair that they emulate and finish the number surrounded by chorus boys using canes to form symbolic prison bars. As they leave the theater, Arthur hears the newsboy announcing that he is wanted for murder. They attempt to run away, but he is arrested and, after a quick trial, condemned to death. As Arthur dies, he sings "Pennies from Heaven" on the gallows. Thereupon the scene shifts abruptly to a chorus singing "The Glory of Love."

As is evident from this summation of its story, the mood of the film is somber, relieved only by the upbeat, light-hearted musical numbers, a mood undoubtedly similar to that experienced by film audiences of the 1930's. Such musical films as well as songs on the radio brightened for a few moments the grim, depressing years of worldwide economic catastrophe. While not everyone could sing like Bing Crosby or Connie Boswell, all could take some fleeting comfort in the simple optimism of the cheerful songs they heard. Director Herbert Ross and his screenwriter, Dennis Porter, translate these feelings into a bold, innovative musical which contrasts markedly with such staid examples of the genre as *The Wiz* (1977) and *Grease* (1978). "Lip-synching" is not new, but the use of the technique to enhance and comment upon the psychological conditions of the characters is brilliant.

Similarly, the scene in which Arthur and Eileen transform themselves into Fred Astaire and Ginger Rogers is stunningly audacious. The dance sequence embodies what is probably the best routine in all of Astaire and Rogers' collaborations. A story in dance of unlucky gamblers and suicide attempts in Monte Carlo, the couple soon agree to "Face the Music and Dance." That sequence in *Follow the Fleet* (1936) certainly comments on the situation in *Pennies from Heaven*, since Arthur and Eileen will also have to face the music soon. Yet, in the meantime, they become the elegant, graceful lovers moving on the silver screen. Although they are not quite as graceful as Fred and Ginger, Steve Martin and Bernadette Peters are more courageous than Astaire and Rogers, knowing that suffering will follow the dance. Seeing them so vulnerable, one realizes just how good Martin and Peters are in these roles. In this one dance sequence, the film comments on its plot, on the dreams of the 1930's motion-picture audiences, on the differing abilities of actors and dancers performing fifty years apart, and ultimately reminds the viewer that he too is watching a film and creating new fantasies for himself.

Apart from the fact that many of the musical numbers are too short, there is little to criticize in the production. The camerawork of Gordon Willis establishes the somber mood of the narrative through the use of shadows and soft lighting, and the brightly lit fantasy sequences are more enjoyable partly because they relieve the gloomy tone of the realistic scenes. The art directors re-create 1930's paintings by Reginald Marsh and Edward Hopper while Walker Evans photographs also provide an authentic look and feeling to the Depression-era locales. Danny Daniels' choreography and Herbert Ross's direction further evoke the moods of the musicals of the period. These talented artists all contribute to the skillful adaption of Dennis Potter's original screenplay. Steve Martin's good looks of the sort featured in 1930's advertisements of the "Arrow Collar Man" contrast perfectly with the inner state of the heel that he portrays. Jessica Harper's repressed sexuality is the mirror image of Bernadette Peters' exuberant sexuality. Christopher Walken, more familiar in serious dramatic roles, is surprisingly adept in the role of a sleazy pimp. *Pennies from Heaven* is a wonderful film that has gone unrecognized by the audiences of 1981. Its appeal is timeless, however, and someday it will find the audience that it deserves.

Don K Thompson

Reviews

The Hollywood Reporter. December 9, 1981, p. 3.
Los Angeles Times. December 10, 1981, VI, p. 1.
The New Republic. CLXXXVI, January 6-13, 1982, p. 29.
The New York Times. December 11, 1981, III, p. 16.
The New Yorker. LVII, December 21, 1981, pp. 122-126.
Newsweek. XCVIII, December 21, 1981, p. 49.
Time. CXVIII, December 21, 1981, p. 83.
Variety. December 9, 1981, p. 3.

PIXOTE

Origin: Brazil
Production: Sylvia B. Naves for Unifilm/Embrafilme
Direction: Hector Babenco
Screenplay: Hector Babenco and Jorge Duran; based on the novel, *Infancia dos Mortos*, by Jose Louzeiro
Cinematography: Rodolfo Sanches
Editing: Luiz Elias
Art direction: Clovis Bueno
Music: John Neschling
Running time: 127 minutes

Principal characters:

Pixote	Fernando Ramos da Silva
Sueli	Marilia Pera
Lilica	Jorge Juliao
Dito	Gilberto Moura
Diego	Jose Nilson dos Santos
Chico	Edilson Lino
Fumaca	Zenildo Oliveira Santos
Garatao	Claudio Bernardo
Cristal	Tony Tornado
Sapatos Brancos	Jardel Filho
Juiz	Rubens de Falco
Hector Babenco	Himself

Hector Babenco is an exponent of *Cinema Nôvo*, a movement which has sought to create a distinctively Brazilian cinema. Until the 1960's, with the exception of such pioneering filmmakers as Humbert Mauro and Alberto Cavalcanti, Brazilian cinema relied upon American imports and a few native productions which emphasized lighthearted musical themes.

The late 1950's and 1960's, however, saw the emergence of a new breed of politically conscious filmmakers in Brazil. This new breed has included such talented directors as the late Glauber Rocha, Nelson Pereira dos Santos, Carlos Diegues, and now Hector Babenco must be added to the list.

Babenco is a Jewish-Argentinian émigré who left his native country for six years of traveling in Europe before settling in Brazil in 1972. His first feature was *The King of the Night* (1975), which dealt with the relationship between a bourgeois businessman and a free-living prostitute; his second film, *Lucio Flavio* (1977), was a study of a criminal. He then attempted to make a documentary about a concentration-camplike reform school which housed juveniles between the ages of eight and eighteen, but the authoritarian Brazilian regime imposed such censorship that his plans were thwarted. As an alternative, Babenco and Jorge Duran adapted Jose Louzeiro's trenchant novel *Infancia dos Mortos*, which sharply depicted in fictional terms the brutal world of Brazilian slum children.

Babenco's cinematic interpretation of *Infancia dos Mortos*, now entitled *Pixote* (pronounced "Pee-chot"), is so unrelentingly realistic and exact in its verisimilitude, that for American audiences he added a prologue to explain that it was fiction based on fact, not a documentary.

The film opens with the handsome, bearded Babenco standing on a hilltop overlooking São Paulo, Brazil's second largest city and producer of seventy percent of the country's national product. From this vantage point atop the hill, Babenco is able to overlook the slums of São Paulo and says, "There is a folkloric version that people who live in a *favella* [slum] don't work. It's important to know that these men and women work twelve hours a day, and the children are at home alone. The kids in my film are not orphaned or abandoned. There are twenty-eight million children in Brazil—too much!—of which three million *are* abandoned."

The camera pans the makeshift hovels of this urban blight and rests momentarily on the face of ten-year-old Fernando Ramos da Silva standing in front of his home with members of his family. This face belongs to the film's Pixote (loosely translated as Pee-Wee); he, like all the boys in the film, is a real slum urchin, not an actor.

Despite Brazil's large number of children, Brazilian law prevents anyone under eighteen years of age from being prosecuted for criminal acts. Neglected children of working parents as well as those who are homeless and abandoned roam the streets of cities such as São Paulo and Rio de Janeiro, perpetrating crimes from petty theft to murder. Because of their immunity from criminal prosecution, they fall prey to recruitment by older criminals who use them as pawns.

Authorities must resort to periodic "clean-ups" in which scores of children are rounded up by police and incarcerated in poorly equipped detention centers and reform schools. The fictional part of Babenco's film begins with just such a round-up, following the death of a judge who was pushed in front of an automobile while having his pocket picked by a group of street children. The round-up includes Pixote, who has run away from his grandparents because his grandmother, he says, "bugged him." Included in the round-up are Pixote's friends, Lilica (Jorge Juliao), a seventeen-year-old effeminate homosexual; macho Diego (Jose Nilson dos Santos), who is Lilica's current lover; Dito (Gilberto Moura), another macho teenager; and Chico (Edilson Lino), who is similar to Pixote with a quiet repressed temperament.

Pixote, with his innocent contemplative stare, has scabs on his face from street fighting and a cast on his left leg from an unexplained accident. Pixote soon learns the law of this squalid rehabilitation center when he witnesses the rape of a fellow inmate by four toughs: you keep your mouth shut, and one hand washes the other. Babenco painstakingly depicts the futility of any hope of rehabilitation in detention life. The boys play at robberies, teach one another how to react under police interrogation, smoke marijuana, play soccer, indifferently attend school classes, and divide up into "family" units.

In an effort to find the judge's murderer, a brutal police officer collects the suspected group, which includes Pixote, and takes them into the city jail. On the way, two of the boys are murdered; the rest are thrown naked into solitary confinement. Fumaca (Zenildo Oliveira Santos), a prime suspect, does not return to the detention center with the others. Later it is learned that he has died from a beating, after which his body was tossed in the city dump.

This tragedy prompts a sadly ineffective investigation by social workers. Ultimately, the rebellious and accusing Diego is also beaten and dies in the arms of his lover, Lilica. Diego's death spurs the boys to wreck their dormitory, and many of them, including Pixote and his small group, escape through the infirmary's window.

With Diego dead, Dito becomes the leader of the four: Pixote, Lilica, Chico, and Lilica's new "man." They live on the streets picking pockets and snatching purses until Lilica leads them to a former friend, Cristal (Tony Tornado), a cocaine dealer who likes young boys. Because they are under eighteen and immune from the law, they are enticed by Cristal into a drug deal which takes them by train to Rio de Janeiro. The deal is a scam which ends with Chico being killed by a blond go-go dancer, after which an unemotional Pixote stabs the dancer to death.

Their next touch is a pimp who sells them an aging, alcoholic whore named Sueli (Marilia Pera). The only time in the film when Pixote registers shock is when he sees the bloody remains of a fetus in a wastebasket in the bathroom where Sueli has aborted it with a knitting needle.

With Sueli they set up their own scam, robbing her customers, but soon Dito's affections turn from Lilica to the whore and Lilica moves out. When Dito and Pixote, both armed with guns, surprise another of Sueli's clients, Pixote unintentionally kills Dito, then the man. After this, in a very touching scene, Sueli embraces Pixote, holds him, rocks him, becomes his mother, sister, and lover while he suckles on her breast, an image which the *Village Voice*'s Carrie Rickey succinctly described as "the *Pietà* of the antinuclear family." The film ends with Pixote, still only ten years old but three times a killer, nonchalantly walking down a railroad track kicking pebbles with his feet.

Pixote is a galvanizing and corrosive look at the back streets of Brazil. Babenco refuses to sentimentalize or moralize, offering no solutions nor any didactic political excuses. In an interview he has said: "It's the security of family affection that makes a child grow up with joy. I tried to show how you destroy the innocence of a child. I tried through *Pixote* to give them back their innocence."

Pixote opened in New York in April, 1981, as part of the Museum of Modern Art's New Directors/New Films series and was picked up for general release in September. The reviews were unanimously excellent. Vincent Canby, writing in *The New York Times*, proclaimed that "Fernando Ramos da Silva, who plays Pixote, has one of the most eloquent faces ever seen on the screen." Many critics compared the film's impact with that of Vittorio De Sica's *Shoeshine* (1946), Luis Buñuel's *Los Olvidados* (1950), and François Truffaut's *The 400 Blows* (1959).

Pixote was named Best Foreign Film by both the New York Film Critics and the Los Angeles Film Critics and was on *The New York Times*' Ten-Best List; Marilia Pera was named Best Actress by the National Society of Film Critics. Unfortunately, the film was declared ineligible for an Academy Award nomination; to be eligible, a film had to have opened between November 1, 1980, and October 31, 1981, and *Pixote* had premiered in São Paulo in September, 1980, and in Rio de Janeiro in October, 1980.

Ronald Bowers

Reviews

The Hollywood Reporter. September 1, 1981, p. 2.
Los Angeles Times. October 25, 1981, *Calendar*, p. 29.
The New York Times. May 5, 1981, III, p. 6.
The New Yorker. LVII, November 9, 1981, p. 170.
Newsweek. XCVIII, September 28, 1981, p. 88.

THE POSTMAN ALWAYS RINGS TWICE

Production: Charles Mulvehill and Bob Rafelson for Lorimar-Paramount, in association with M-G-M
Direction: Bob Rafelson
Screenplay: David Mamet; based on the novel of the same name by James M. Cain
Cinematography: Sven Nykvist
Editing: Graeme Clifford
Art direction: George Jenkins
Music: Michael Small
MPAA rating: R
Running time: 122 minutes

Principal characters:

Frank Chambers	Jack Nicholson
Cora Papadakis	Jessica Lange
Nick Papadakis	John Colicos
Katz	Michael Lerner
Madge	Angelica Huston
Kennedy	John P. Ryan

James M. Cain's famous (or notorious) novel *The Postman Always Rings Twice* has attracted filmmakers ever since it was published in 1934. The most obvious ingredients of its story of passion between a drifter and the young wife of the owner of a roadside café are sex and murder, but in the novel the causes and consequences of these actions are also explored and given cynical and ironic twists. The novel was first filmed in France in 1939 as *Le Dernier Tournant*, then in Italy in 1942 as *Ossessione*. The latter version was the first film by Luchino Visconti, who was to become one of Italy's top directors. Hollywood filmmakers were ambivalent about the novel; its sensational elements would attract an audience, but gaining approval from the censors of the 1930's and 1940's would be difficult if not impossible. In 1946, however, Metro-Goldwyn-Mayer filmed the novel, with Tay Garnett as the director and Lana Turner and John Garfield as the stars. The film was both popular and memorable, and the notion of remaking it without the constraints of censorship surfaced periodically. Finally, in 1981, *The Postman Always Rings Twice* once more appeared on the screen.

Jack Nicholson had conceived the idea of filming the novel again in the early 1970's but it was nearly a decade before the project was realized. The talent finally gathered for the film included director Bob Rafelson, who had worked with Nicholson on three previous films, most notably *Five Easy Pieces* (1970); screenwriter David Mamet, the prizewinning playwright whose works include *Sexual Perversity in Chicago* (1974) and *American Buffalo* (1977); and cinematographer Sven Nykvist, famous for the many films he photographed for the great Swedish director Ingmar Bergman.

The 1981 film should not, however, be considered a remake of the 1946 version, because the filmmakers—although they knew the earlier film well—went back to Cain's novel as their source. They included parts of the novel that were left out of the earlier version, and they also left out parts of the novel that were included in the M-G-M film.

The film begins with Frank Chambers (Jack Nicholson) hitchhiking to Los Angeles. He stops at a small roadside café and gas station owned by Nick Papadakis (John Colicos), where he gets a free meal by pretending that his wallet was stolen. After seeing Nick's young wife, Cora (Jessica Lange), he accepts Nick's offer of a job at the gas station, setting up the essential situation of the novel and of the film: the young, discontented wife, the older husband, and the outsider. In the novel and the 1946 film, however, Frank is much younger than Nick, but in this version he looks almost as old and is at least as rough and uncouth as Nick. The passion that Cora develops for Frank is thus not as understandable as it is in the earlier film.

In this film the "romance" between Cora and Frank happens almost instantaneously. The first time that Nick is gone from the place, Frank locks the door, puts up the "Closed" sign, and forces himself on Cora. She resists at first, but then she sweeps the bread and dough off the kitchen table and they have sex there. The next time Nick is gone, Frank and Cora pack up and leave for Chicago, but Cora decides that it would never work because Nick would follow them and find them. Finally, they decide to kill him, which is conveyed in the determinedly elliptical style of the film. Cora tells Frank that it will have to be just the two of them, and then she says, "I'm tired of what's right and wrong." When Frank replies, "They hang people for that, Cora," the audience understands that the decision has been made.

The filmmakers made a strange choice at this point in the script. We do not see or hear Frank and Cora plan the murder of Nick; we simply see them attempt to carry out the plan. The 1946 film, although it has its defects, does build up a good deal of tension and suspense as it depicts both the planning of the murder and the attempt to carry it out. In this way the audience anticipates what is going to happen and is aware each time something goes wrong. In the 1981 version the audience never does learn exactly how the murder was supposed to be committed, but does see that something goes wrong, and finally learns that a cat touched a fuse box and put out the lights just as Cora was about to kill Nick. In the ensuing confusion Frank rushes to Nick, causing Nick to think that Frank saved his life. Nick also has no idea that Cora was involved.

Cora resolves to accept the *status quo*, even though she feels trapped, until Nick tells her that he wants them to have a child. Once again she and Frank plan to kill Nick and once again the audience is not told how. This time their plan works; they murder Nick and try to make it appear that he was killed in an automobile accident. The authorities, however, do not believe their story and the two are tried for murder. The legal outcome is quite complicated. Frank signs a complaint against Cora; she then reveals the whole scheme in front of a man she thinks is a court reporter, Kennedy (John P. Ryan). The man, however, is an employee of Katz (Michael Lerner), their lawyer, who then cleverly contrives a way for both of them to go free by making a deal with the two insurance companies involved. The final result is that both insurance companies save money (because a proven murder would activate the "double indemnity" clause in Nick's policy) and Katz gets the ten-thousand dollar insurance payment as his fee. (Incidentally, in the novel and the 1946 film, the lawyer took no fee; he merely had the pleasure of winning a bet with the prosecutor that he could win the case.)

Nick and Cora leave the courthouse free but unhappy. The main benefit they receive is that their notoriety brings a great deal of business to the café. After several misadventures, including Frank having an affair with a lion-tamer named Madge (Anjelica Huston) and Cora finding out about it, the two finally seem to have accommodated to each other and found happiness. They get married and all their troubles and doubts seem to be over. As they drive back to their home, Cora begins kissing Frank, but it is their last moment of happiness. Frank forgets about his driving and causes an accident that kills Cora. The last image of the film shows his hand with the new wedding ring on it holding her hand. He removes his hand and leaves only her cold, bloody hand on the screen.

This is indeed an ironic ending, but the novel and the 1946 film contained a double irony. After the accident Frank is convicted of the murder of Cora. Therefore, he escapes conviction for a murder he did commit only to be executed for one he did not.

Critical reception of *The Postman Always Rings Twice* was lukewarm. Reviewers, even those who did not admire the 1946 film, thought that the 1981 version left out or changed too many essential parts of the novel. The critics also were less than enthusiastic about the casting and the acting, and some pointed out that, despite the early publicity, the film is curiously lacking in eroticism.

Jack Nicholson has said that Jessica Lange, as Cora, made him look sexy, but unfortunately this is seldom true in the important scenes in the film. Indeed, the kindest statement about Nicholson's acting from a major publication was *The Hollywood Reporter*'s remark that he did not "scratch any new acting surfaces," and Pauline Kael in *The New Yorker* wrote, "His performance could have been given by a Nicholson impersonator." Lange does a better job with the material she is given, and the performance of Michael Lerner as the lawyer is possibly the most interesting in the film.

The film is by no means without merit; it simply is not the first-rate film one expected from the talented people who made it.

Timothy W. Johnson

Reviews

The Hollywood Reporter. March 13, 1981, p. 3.
Los Angeles Times. March 20, 1981, VI, p. 1.
The New Republic. CLXXXIV, April 11, 1981, pp. 26-27.
The New York Times. March 20, 1981, III, p. 12.
The New Yorker. LVII, April 6, 1981, p. 160+.
Newsweek. XCVII, March 23, 1981, p. 81.
Time. CXVII, March 23, 1981, pp. 84-85.
Variety. March 13, 1981, p. 3.

PRIEST OF LOVE

Production: Christopher Miles and Andrew Donally for Stanley J. Seeger; released by Filmways
Direction: Christopher Miles
Screenplay: Alan Plater; based on the biography *The Priest of Love* by Harry T. Moore and the writings and letters of D. H. Lawrence
Cinematography: Ted Moore
Editing: Paul Davies
Art direction: Ted Tester and David Brockhurst
Costume design: Anthony Powell
Music: Joseph James
MPAA rating: R
Running time: 125 minutes

Principal characters:

D. H. Lawrence .... Ian McKellen
Frieda Lawrence .... Janet Suzman
Mabel Dodge Luhan .... Ava Gardner
Dorothy Brett .... Penelope Keith
Tony Luhan .... Jorge Rivero
Angelo Ravagli .... Maurizio Merli
Herbert G. Muskett .... John Gielgud
Aldous Huxley .... James Faulkner
John Middleton Murry .... Mike Gwilym
Ada Lawrence .... Marjorie Yates
Maria Huxley .... Wendy Alnutt

Priest of Love is the first feature-length film biography of D. H. Lawrence, and no doubt it will not be the last. The life of David Herbert Lawrence (1885-1930) is rich in opportunity for the filmmaker, not only because of the once controversial nature of his novels such as *Sons and Lovers* (1913), *Women in Love* (1920), and *Lady Chatterley's Lover* (1928), but also because of Lawrence's extravagantly eccentric and bohemian life-style. For his film, director Christopher Miles relied on Lawrence's own writings—his novels and correspondence—and on a biography, *The Priest of Love* by Professor Harry T. Moore, who died shortly after completion of the film.

Miles, who had previously directed the 1970 film of the novelist's *The Virgin and the Gypsy*, had long wanted to film Lawrence's life, and when the opportunity finally availed itself, he went to considerable lengths to ensure accuracy, not only as far as the story line was concerned, but also as to the locations. The film was shot in Oaxaca, Mexico; Nottingham, England; Lake Garda and Florence, Italy (with key scenes being filmed in the Villa Mirenda in Tuscany, where Lawrence wrote *Lady Chatterley's Lover* and at the presses in Florence where the book was first printed); in Cornwall, England (where Lawrence and his wife lived during World War I); in Venice; and in the French Alpes-Maritimes (where Lawrence died). Additional footage was shot in London and at Shepperton Studios, England.

Priest of Love opens in 1915 with the British censor Herbert G. Muskett (John Gielgud) burning *The Rainbow*, and then quickly moves on to 1924, after D. H. Lawrence (Ian McKellen) has been married to Frieda (Janet Suzman) for ten years. The film juxtaposes the present with the past, illustrating the efforts of Muskett to have Lawrence's books and paintings either banned or destroyed; Frieda and Lawrence's acceptance of an invitation from American art patroness, Mabel Dodge Luhan (Ava Gardner), to stay with her and her native American husband, Tony (Jorge Rivero), on their ranch in New Mexico; and the Lawrences' travels with the eccentric English aristocrat, the Honorable Dorothy Brett (Penelope Keith), who Frieda eventually banishes from their company and who eventually sets up a home and studio close to Mabel Dodge Luhan's ranch. Almost out of a sense of duty, while in Italy, Lawrence attempts to spend the night with Dorothy Brett, but leaves in disgust when she tells him that he must explain what is expected from her.

In a flashback to World War I, the audience sees Frieda and Lawrence living in Cornwall, where they are visited by their longtime friend, John Middleton Murry (Mike Gwilym). Lawrence and a muscular young farmhand go swimming in the nude, and as Lawrence gently dries the back of the naked man, they are interrupted by two British soldiers who suspect the Lawrences of being German spies (because of Frieda's German nationality). Much has been made of this sequence, suggesting that it graphically illustrates Lawrence's bisexuality, but this is highly questionable as neither man displays any romantic inclination toward the other, and even had the scene not been interrupted by the soldiers it is doubtful that it would have progressed further. Indeed, Lawrence jokingly tells his wife of what took place and notes that the soldiers presumably interpreted the encounter as a homosexual tryst. (It should also be noted that virtually all the critics seem confused as to where and between whom this meeting took place in the film; some describe it as happening in Italy, while others—including Vincent Canby in *The New York Times*—mistakenly identify Lawrence's companion as John Middleton Murry.)

Priest of Love details the often-violent quarrels between Lawrence and Frieda, one of which—when Frieda breaks all the dishes at an outdoor party—precipitates a hasty departure from Mabel Dodge Luhan's ranch. A visit to Nottingham and to Lawrence's sister, Ada (Marjorie Yates), is a depressing interlude, because Ada's world is not that of her brother and even family ties cannot keep the two close. Eventually Frieda and Lawrence move to Italy, to a villa provided for them by a new patron, Angelo Ravagli (Maurizio Merli), who was to marry Frieda after Lawrence's death. Here Lawrence writes *Lady Chatterley's Lover*, prepares an exhibit of erotic paintings, which are promptly seized in London by Herbert G. Muskett and later deported, and is visited by Aldous Huxley (James Faulkner) and his wife Maria (Wendy Alnutt). After Lawrence's death, Frieda returns to New Mexico, where she is met at the station by Mabel Dodge Luhan and her husband. In the confusion of their meeting, Frieda leaves the urn containing Lawrence's ashes on the station platform. Only after driving some distance does Frieda remember; she stops the car and goes running back. At last, in death, Lawrence is reunited with Mabel Dodge Luhan, Tony, Frieda, and Dorothy Brett, without rancor and without the violent arguments which had marred the lives of the Lawrences and their friends.

Priest of Love is not an easy film to understand or enjoy. Audiences find the flashbacks confusing, as did some of the critics (witness the confusion over the nude bathing sequence). For those willing to sit patiently through what is, admittedly, a somewhat long narrative, though, there are a host of delights. The film is rightly complex, in that it is the intimate story of a complex human being. It is the story of a man who was at all times devoted to his wife, and yet would beat her mercilessly and who felt no compunction at infidelity. One suspects that long and convoluted as the film is, the production has been severely truncated. At a scene in a printing shop in Florence, for example, one senses that the director is attempting to tell us that Lawrence yearns for a romantic involvement with the good-looking, young assistant. The sequence builds up for such a liaison and is then suddenly dropped, and one can only ponder why the young man is introduced and why Lawrence eyes him so.

Priest of Love is a film of exquisite beauty, at times becoming almost a travelogue with its glimpses of the delights of Cornwall and Italy. Through it all, one is aware of performances of stunning vitality. Christopher Miles has claimed that he handpicked his cast not only because of their acting talents, but also for their close resemblances—in looks and emotions—to the characters they portray. By the time *Priest of Love* opened in the United States, Ian McKellen was about to depart from his Tony Award-winning role in Broadway's *Amadeus*, and these two very different projects illustrate the versatility of this British actor, who came to prominence in the 1974 Royal Shakespeare production of *Dr. Faustus*. Also from the Royal Shakespeare Company came Janet Suzman in the role of Frieda, a part she had already played in a one-woman stage production. John Gielgud appears in the very minor role of Herbert G. Muskett, and, good as he may be, the part is not sufficiently important to warrant his participation. Penelope Keith, brilliant as the Honorable Dorothy Brett, is a comedienne best known to American audiences for her role in the BBC/PBS comedy series, "To the Manor Born." She depicts the aristocratic, would-be artistic eccentric to a fine degree. Finally, audiences must also be grateful to Christopher Miles for giving Ava

Gardner probably the only worthwhile screen role she has had in many years. Here she is no longer Ava Gardner, movie star, but Mabel Dodge Luhan personified.

American critics were not kind to *Priest of Love*, and the film fared poorly at the box office. *Variety* commented, "Miles takes a somewhat removed and cool look at his subject, with emphasis on accuracy over emotional involvement making the pic a tough sell beyond its natural art house market." Vincent Canby, writing in *The New York Times*, thought the film "foolish," and noted, "The movie seems to float from one picturesque place to another, like bored, well-heeled tourists." Gary Arnold in *The Washington Post*, however, described *Priest of Love* as "an unprecedented delight . . . I doubt that anyone has ever filmed a more intelligent or satisfying literary bio."

Six of D. H. Lawrence's stories and novels have been filmed, *The Rocking Horse Winner* (1950), *Lady Chatterley's Lover* (1958 and 1981), *The Fox* (1968), *The Virgin and the Gypsy* (1970), *Women in Love* (1970), and *Sons and Lovers* (1980). Although *Priest of Love* is only partially based on Lawrence's writings, it is as much akin to his novels as these six adaptations were.

Anthony Slide

Reviews

The Hollywood Reporter. October 5, 1981, p. 2.
Los Angeles Times. October 16, 1981, VI, p. 2.
The New Republic. CLXXXV, October 21, 1981, pp. 20-21.
The New York Times. October 11, 1981, III, p. 1.
Saturday Review. VIII, October, 1981, p. 60.
Variety. September 30, 1981, p. 3.

PRINCE OF THE CITY

Production: Burtt Harris for Orion Pictures Company and Warner Bros.
Direction: Sidney Lumet
Screenplay: Jay Presson Allen and Sidney Lumet; based on the book of the same name by Robert Daley
Cinematography: Andrzej Bartkowiak
Editing: John J. Fitzstephens
Production design: Tony Walton
Art direction: Edward Pisoni
Music: Paul Chihara
MPAA rating: R
Running time: 167 minutes

Principal characters:

Daniel Ciello	Treat Williams
Gus Levy	Jerry Orbach
Joe Marinaro	Richard Foronjy
Bill Mayo	Don Billett
Dom Bando	Kenny Marino
Gino Mascone	Carmine Caridi
Raf Alvarez	Tony Page
Rick Cappalino	Norman Parker
Brooks Paige	Paul Roebling
Santimassino	Bob Balaban
District Attorney Polito	James Tolkan
Mario Vincente	Steve Inwood
Carla Ciello	Lindsay Crouse

In an interview given in the 1970's, director Sidney Lumet attempted to define his philosophy of filmmaking. He agreed that films should entertain, but, more important, they should compel "the spectator to examine one facet or another of his own conscience." He further explained that with the demise of television drama (Lumet began his career during the "golden age of television") and the high risk Broadway productions, the only avenue open for such dramatic analysis was what he called the "art film."

His twenty-eighth feature film since 1957, *Prince of the City* has been called Lumet's finest achievement to date, and it expresses, with great dramatic intensity, the ambiguity which Lumet finds inherent in all human behavior. The film is a modern Greek tragedy which makes no attempt to show good versus evil in elementary, black-and-white terms, but instead presents the facts in all their complexity and asks the audience to make up its own mind.

The film is based on the book of the same title, published in 1978, by

Robert Daley, former Deputy Police Commissioner for Public Relations of the New York Police Department, and is the story of Robert Leuci, a narcotics detective with the SIU (Special Investigation Unit) during the late 1960's and early 1970's.

For legal purposes the film identifies Leuci as Danny Ciello (Treat Williams) and all real names have been fictionalized, with a few of the book's characters combined into composites. The most important of these characters are Ciello's closest detective partner Gus Levy (Jerry Orbach), assistant district attorney Rick Cappalino (Norman Parker), his colleague Brooks Paige (Paul Roebling), and Santimassino (Bob Balaban), the federal prosecutor. Leuci's wife is called Carla Ciello and is played by Lindsay Crouse.

The SIU was made up of about sixty narcotics detectives who were an elite group of policemen whose special assignments gave them an immunity unique among police officers. Their jurisdiction was city-wide, their widespread use of illegal wiretaps was overlooked, they were allowed to provide their junkie informants with dope, and they were romantically and heroically called "princes of the city."

In early 1971, Danny Ciello, about to turn thirty-one, a handsome, ingratiating prince of the city, is routinely called before the Commission to Investigate Alleged Police Corruption—the Knapp Commission. Ciello is casually interviewed by assistant district attorney Rick Cappalino. The Commission has no evidence against Ciello for any wrongdoing, but Ciello does not know this. As they talk about alleged police corruption, Ciello remarks, "We are easy, aren't we? Cops are easy." Later, when Cappalino invites Ciello home for dinner, the confused Ciello further hints at his inner turmoil when he says, "Rick, what is it? What is it you want to ask me? I didn't do it, whatever it is."

The die has been cast. Cappalino realizes that Ciello's intensity reveals an emotional anxiety which he either refuses or is unable to articulate. Through subsequent friendly interviews with Cappalino and his partner Brooks Paige and with federal prosecutor Santimassino, an intricate plan is outlined by which Ciello will go underground, wired with a tape recording device, as a police informant.

Ciello's motives for his cooperation are never made clear—in the book or the film. It simply seems to be something he feels compelled to do. When he agrees to take on the role of informant, his one ultimatum is that he must never be forced to betray his fellow SIU detectives. At first he revels in his position—"Nobody I care about is gonna get hurt. . . . It's a game; I love it"—but as his role takes him into the world of junkies, dishonest cops, and his Mafioso cousin—a world that he has known well, but *only* as a cop, never as an informant—Ciello's familiar routine becomes a Kafkaesque nightmare.

He is cajoled and manipulated into revealing more and more. His prosecutor friends are promoted, leaving him unprotected; his detective buddies ignore him or suggest that he commit suicide; and the Mafia tries to kill him. He admits to numerous acts of corruption, including skimming off twenty thousand dollars during routine narcotic arrests. There is also the suspicion that, while Ciello himself possibly is not guilty, he knows who in the SIU may have been involved in the disappearance of $73,000,000 worth of drugs confiscated in the famous French Connection case.

Ultimately Ciello barely escapes federal prosecution himself, but his testimony results in the complete disintegration of the SIU. Of some seventy members investigated, fifty-two are indicted (most of them on tax evasion, the easiest charge to substantiate), two commit suicide, two die of heart attacks, and one goes insane. At the end of the film Ciello appears before a class of new recruits, one of whom exclaims, "I don't think I have anything to learn from you," and gets up and walks out of the room. On this final note of ambiguity, Lumet ends his film.

When the film rights to the book were originally purchased in 1978 for $500,000, Brian DePalma was set to direct and playwright David Rabe worked up two script versions. Robert De Niro, John Travolta, and Al Pacino were all considered to play Danny Ciello. When Orion and DePalma disagreed, DePalma was fired and the project was turned over to Sidney Lumet.

It is interesting to note that eight years earlier Lumet had directed *Serpico* with Al Pacino. The films have similarities, and indeed it was Frank Serpico's fight against police corruption which resulted in the formation of the Knapp Commission. Lumet's interpretation of the two stories, however, is quite dissimilar. Serpico was a strong-willed, iconoclastic crusader—and also a true hero—while Leuci was a much more simple man, a cop's cop who had become a policeman because he wanted to make the world a better place in which to live, but who got in over his head and turned informant because he wanted to be on the *right* side. He was neither crusader nor hero. As Lumet explains, "Leuci fell into a classic trap. He knowingly tangled with powerful forces believing he could manipulate and control them. The results were catastrophic."

Lumet correctly calls *Prince of the City* his most complex film, a film which uses many "unknown" actors to weave a rich tapestry of New York life. Lumet drew from long experience in re-creating New York City on film—*The Pawnbroker* (1965), *Serpico* (1973), *Dog Day Afternoon* (1975), and *Network* (1976)—to achieve what critic Andrew Sarris called "the high point of cinematic realism in the New York school of filmmaking."

Despite the large cast and multiple locations, Lumet made the picture for $1,200,000 under the $10,000,000 budget. One of the best decisions he made regarding the film was to cast the relatively unknown Treat Williams as Danny Ciello. When Lumet saw Milo Forman's underrated screen version of *Hair* (1979), he was impressed with Williams' exuberant "dinner-table scene" and liked Williams' "power, innate sweetness and naïveté." In *Prince of the City*, Williams, who is in nearly every scene, brilliantly captures the guilelessness, bravado, courage, and shame of Detective Robert Leuci.

Regrettably *Prince of the City* received only one Academy Award nomination, for Adapted Screenplay, but the New York Film Critics voted Lumet Best Director of the Year.

Robert Leuci remained on the NYPD until 1981 to serve out the twenty years which made him eligible for his pension. To some of his fellow policemen he was a hero, to others a rat. After seeing the film, he commented that "the brass will hate it; the cops will like it. There are no heroes, no easy explanations." He went on to say that "5% of all cops [are] honest, 5% dishonest and 90% go whichever way the wind blows."

This assessment validates Lumet's approach to the film: "To me, he [Leuci] is a hero. To others he is not. The viewer's own perceptions and values will have to suffice."

Ronald Bowers

Reviews

The Hollywood Reporter. August 13, 1981, p. 7.
Los Angeles Times. August 27, 1981, VI, p. 1.
The New Republic. CLXXXV, September 9, 1981, p. 24.
The New York Times. August 19, 1981, III, p. 17.
Newsweek. XCVIII, August 24, 1981, pp. 67-68.
Saturday Review. VIII, August, 1981, p. 60.
Time. CXVIII, August, 17, 1981, p. 68.
Variety. August 10, 1981, p. 3.

QUARTET

Production: Ismail Merchant and Jean Pierre Mahot de la Querantonnais for Merchant Ivory Productions and Lyric International
Direction: James Ivory
Screenplay: Ruth Prawer Jhabvala and James Ivory; based on the novel of the same name by Jean Rhys
Cinematography: Pierre Lhomme
Editing: Humphrey Dixon
Art direction: Jean-Jacques Caziot
Music: Richard Robbins
MPAA rating: R
Running time: 101 minutes

Principal characters:

H. J. Heidler .... Alan Bates
Lois Heidler .... Maggie Smith
Marya Zelli .... Isabelle Adjani
Stephen Zelli .... Anthony Higgins
Théo the pornographer .... Pierre Clementi
Pierre Schlamovitz .... Daniel Mesguich
Mlle. Chardin .... Virginie Thevenet
Mme. Hautchamp .... Susanne Flon
Guy .... Daniel Chatto
Nell .... Armelia McQueen

Paris during the 1920's was the home of expatriates and dilettantes, characterized by rootlessness, hedonism, and above all else, seediness—a reality beneath the bohemian façade. All the decadence and hypocrisy of the era is captured by director James Ivory and his screenwriter Ruth Prawer Jhabvala in *Quartet*, a solid, entertaining drama.

The setting of the film is Montparnasse in 1927. Stephen Zelli (Anthony Higgins), a Polish art dealer, is imprisoned for a year for trafficking in stolen artifacts. His wife Marya (Isabelle Adjani), an aimless, self-absorbed, unsophisticated West Indian chorus girl, had been happy to overlook Stephen's source of income. Now, with no money and no place to go, she allows herself to be taken in by an older English couple, H. J. and Lois Heidler (Alan Bates, Maggie Smith). The Heidlers are wealthy art patrons and are well known in the Montparnasse social scene; Stephen is very much in favor of his wife moving into their guest room.

Marya, however, is uneasy. She is both afraid of and fascinated by the friendly but neurotic H. J. It is not surprising that he soon makes overtures to Marya while the insecure, calculating Lois, knowing that her husband's affairs are short-lived, uses her to keep their failing marriage afloat. Marya is determined to remain faithful to Stephen, whom she regularly visits in jail, but she is finally overwhelmed by H. J., and gives herself to him. At the same time, she still wishes to secure the necessary funds to leave the Heidlers and reestablish her own identity. For this reason, she almost poses for Théo (Pierre Clementi), a photographer-pornographer.

Eventually, Marya fails to make her weekly trip to Stephen, and instead journeys with the Heidlers to the country on a shooting trip. Symbolically, she rides between them in their car, and hardly a word is spoken. On that first evening, she finally becomes completely aware of how she is being manipulated by both H. J. and Lois: the former egotistically wants to sleep with both women; the latter will be amenable to her husband's games, as long as everything remains "proper." Marya does not have the means to separate herself from the Heidlers, though, and is soon ensconced in a hotel as H. J.'s mistress. Later, when he is ready to abandon her, she considers killing herself—the last girl taken in by the Heidlers had in fact committed suicide—and writes a note to H. J. Lois reads the letter and sends a friend to prevent Marya from following through with her intentions.

Stephen is finally released from jail and is facing deportation from France. Marya pleads with H. J. for enough money so that she can be with her husband, but is turned down. She and Stephen are reunited, though, until he discovers that she has been H. J.'s lover. He strikes her, and then leaves with Mlle. Chardin (Virginie Thevenet), the ex-girl friend of Schlamovitz (Daniel Mesguich), his cellmate. As the film ends, it appears that Marya will take up with Schlamovitz.

Quartet, adapted from Jean Rhys's first novel, written in 1928, was based on her affair with Ford Madox Ford, the English writer and editor. Here, he is H. J. Heidler; Ford had previously changed his name from Hueffer. *Quartet* is not merely the story of an older couple's heartless manipulation of a young, innocent woman: it chronicles the empty life-style of the self-indulgent upper classes, obsessed solely with their own concerns. Indeed, if the film were set in the 1980's, H. J. and Lois would be snorting cocaine, attending chic art openings in Soho, and reading their names in the gossip columns.

The Heidlers play with Marya like a toy and discard her when they have no more use for her. As a result, her marriage is irrevocably destroyed and her life almost ends. While she does not die, she does end up desolate, for she has lost everything. On the surface, the Heidlers are a proper, cultured married couple, yet underneath, there is depravity.

James Ivory's direction is effectively detailed, with a stress on the ambience of the period. Meticulously re-created are the colorful streets, smoky bars, and art deco clubs of 1920's Parisian café society. The California-born filmmaker has had a long and productive association with producer Ismail Merchant and screenwriter Ruth Prawer Jhabvala. In 1959, he filmed *The Sword and the Flute*, an analysis of Indian miniature painting, which led to a commission from New York's Asia Society to direct a documentary on the history of Delhi, eventually entitled *The Delhi Way* (1964). While shooting the latter he met Merchant, a native of Bombay, who was seeking a director for the screen adaptation of the German-born Jhabvala's novel, *The Householder* (1963). The result was the formation of Merchant Ivory Productions. Among Ivory's films are: *Shakespeare Wallah* (1965), *The Guru* (1968), *The Wild Party* (1975), *Roseland* (1977), and *The Europeans* (1979).

The performances in *Quartet* are uniformly good. Alan Bates and Maggie Smith each add another excellent characterization to their filmographies. Bates's screen credits are particularly impressive, and include, among others, *The Entertainer* (1960), *A Kind of Loving* (1962), *Georgy Girl* (1965), *King of Hearts* (1966), and *Women in Love* (1970). Among Smith's many roles are four which won Academy Award nominations, in *Othello* (1965), *Travels with My Aunt* (1972), *The Prime of Miss Jean Brody* (1969), and *California Suite* (1978); she won Oscars for the last two.

Isabelle Adjani's most famous performance remains the lead in François Truffaut's *The Story of Adele H* (1976), for which she won a New York Film Critics Best Actress citation and Academy Award nomination. Other films have included *The Tenant* (1976), *The Driver* (1978), and *Nosferatu* (1978). For her work in *Quartet* and Andre Zulowski's *Possession* she earned the Best Actress prize at the 1981 Cannes Film Festival. Anthony Higgins' best-known film is *Raiders of the Lost Ark* (1981), but he has done many other films, including *A Walk with Love and Death* (1969) and *Something for Everyone* (1970). He is now a member of the Royal Shakespeare Company. Finally, Armelia McQueen in the minor role of Nell strikingly performs a pair of songs, accompanied by Luther Henderson and his Orchestra: "509" and "Good Time Lover." She won a Theater World Award for her work on Broadway in *Ain't Misbehavin'*, and was performing the show in Paris when signed for her role in *Quartet*. Although her appearance is brief, as the type of black chanteuse popular during the era, and has no lines, she practically steals the film.

Quartet received mixed reviews: a few reviewers thought the characterizations were too superficial, while others felt the film was rich and realistic in detail. *Quartet* was barely released in the United States. After ten weeks on *Variety*'s list of "50 Top-Grossing Films," it had earned a mere $437,710; also, it was at the bottom of the survey, the last title on the chart. As Archer Winsten wrote in the *New York Post*, *Quartet* "just might be too good to be popular."

Rob Edelman

Reviews

The Hollywood Reporter. October 30, 1981, p. 2.
Los Angeles Times. March 4, 1981, VI, p. 2.
The New Republic. CLXXXV, November 4, 1981, p. 22.
The New York Times. October 25, 1981, p. 62.
Newsweek. XCVIII, November 9, 1981, p. 94.
Saturday Review. VIII, October, 1981, p. 6.
Variety. May 19, 1981, p. 6.

RAGGEDY MAN

Production: Burt Weissbourd and William D. Wittliff for Universal
Direction: Jack Fisk
Screenplay: William D. Wittliff
Cinematography: Ralf Bode
Editing: Edward Warschlika
Art direction: John Lloyd
Music: Jerry Goldsmith
MPAA rating: PG
Running time: 94 minutes

Principal characters:
Nita .... Sissy Spacek
Teddy .... Eric Roberts
Bailey .... Sam Shepard
Calvin .... William Sanderson
Arnold .... Tracey Walter
Rigby .... R. G. Armstrong
Harry .... Henry Thomas
Henry .... Carey Hollis, Jr.
Mr. Calloway .... Ed Geldart
Sheriff .... Bill Thurman

The first thing that the audience notices about *Raggedy Man* is its feel for the truth. Set in the town of Gregory, Texas, during World War II, the film's atmosphere is absolutely authentic. Never blatantly "period," it has an air of reality that few contemporary pictures attain. Sissy Spacek, who had just won an Oscar for her performance in *Coal Miner's Daughter* (1980), is in no small way responsible for this sense of authenticity. As Nita Longley, a strong yet vulnerable woman with a dead-end job, who must rear two children alone, Spacek brings to the film a naturalness and intelligence that cannot be faulted. Spacek and director Jack Fisk are husband and wife and had been looking for a project to launch Fisk as a director for several years. At the same time, screenwriter William D. Wittliff had been developing the script for *Raggedy Man* over a six-year period, with various independent producers taking out options on it. For a time it looked as if Talia Shire would do it for Universal, and later Sally Fields. Neither of these plans worked out, though, so when Universal bought back the script for Sissy Spacek, she and Fisk were delighted, and felt that this was the kind of story for which they had been looking.

Wittliff's screenplay was based in part on memories of his own childhood—

his parents had been divorced and he grew up in a small Texas town during the war while his mother was a telephone operator. Without excessive period art direction, Fisk and his production team re-created Nita's world, primarily a small living room converted to a switchboard office. The bulk of the story takes place in the early 1940's. This is obvious not only because of period ash trays, furnishings, and posters, but also because of the quality of the acting. The reactions of the characters to one another are slightly naïve; it seems a simpler time. The look of the film is bleached out, at times resembling a sepia-toned photo album. A simple story combining elements of the thriller and of the family drama, *Raggedy Man* works within its own terms and is warm without stooping to excessive sentiment, without seeming slight. The casting is near perfect. Eric Roberts, the young sailor who becomes involved with Nita, is both boyish and manly. He is like Nita herself, diffident yet strong enough to try to get what he wants. The two young boys who play Nita's sons are not like most motion-picture children; not excessively precocious, they are at home in the rural Texas setting. Many extras from the town of Gregory were used for the film; at times, their rough, seamed faces recall the photographs of Walker Evans.

The film opens in the town of Edna, Texas, in 1940. Nita Longley (Sissy Spacek), a young wife and mother, is shocked to discover that her husband is involved in an affair with a local floozie. She quickly leaves him, moving her children to another Texas town, Gregory, where she finds a job as a switchboard operator. The story leaps ahead to 1944; Nita is almost a prisoner in the tiny room in her house that doubles as the telephone switchboard office. Because her job is deemed "essential" to the war effort, she can seldom leave her place of work. Nita is very much aware that she is living a dead-end life, both for herself and for her two young sons. In her spare time, she teaches herself typing and constantly pleads with her boss, John Rigby (R. G. Armstrong), for a transfer to a better job. Her children are resentful of the fact that their mother is so tied down, and social life both for the boys and for Nita is non-existent.

Harry (Henry Thomas) and Henry (Carey Hollis, Jr.), Nita's sons, explore the town during their summer vacation from school. They go to the local pool hall, where they run across the Triplett brothers, Calvin (William Sanderson) and Arnold (Tracey Walter), two ex-cons who pump the boys for information about their divorced mother. The Tripletts play a cruel practical joke on young Henry, who tries to get back at them, but before Henry can get a whipping at their hands, the brothers are stopped from hurting him by Bailey (Sam Shepherd), the town's odd-job man, who pushes his lawn mower between the obnoxious men and the boys. Bailey's face is badly scarred—he is known as "raggedy man" by the townfolks, and is reminiscent of the Boo Radley character in *To Kill a Mockingbird* (1962). After a few beers, Calvin and Arnold work up the nerve to ask Nita out for a date. At first tempted, she finally recognizes their base motives and sends them away.

One rainy night a nineteen-year-old sailor named Teddy Roebuck (Eric Roberts) asks Nita if he can use the phone. Although it is after hours and the switchboard is closed, she consents, and overhears Teddy's disturbing news that his sweetheart has married someone else. Teddy leaves, but the storm becomes so intense that he camps out on Nita's front porch, sleeping all night under his coat. The next morning Henry and Harry find him on the porch and strike up a friendship with the sailor, who plays with them all day long. Nita recognizes Teddy's rapport with the boys and is impressed by his basic warmth and innocence, so she consents to let him stay in her house for the remainder of his four-day leave. As the days go by, the boys become more and more attached to Teddy, and so does Nita. A tentative affair begins between Nita and Teddy, one that does not go unobserved by the gossips of the town. Nita is a courageous woman who gladly braves the town's censure for a little happiness in her life. Their idyll is quickly shattered, however, when the Triplett brothers, pressing the boys for news about their mother's current activities, are set upon by Teddy. Teddy receives a severe beating at their hands and returns home to Nita, who scolds him for bringing the boys into the pool hall. Teddy, however, sticks up for the boys. As they argue, Nita senses that something has been lost between them, and she asks Teddy to leave the next morning. As Teddy is packing, the boys hurl accusations at Nita and claim that they now know why their father left her.

Meanwhile, all of the events that have been taking place have been observed by Bailey, the "raggedy man." Fed up with her job, Nita tells her boss that she is going over his head to ask for a transfer. Rigby admits that her job, in fact, is not "frozen," and Nita quits. She buys three tickets to San Antonio, determined to start her life over. That night, though, when their packing is completed, little Harry heads for the outhouse, where a hand fastens the lock, trapping him inside. The two Triplett brothers knock at Nita's door on the pretext of having to use the phone. Once inside, they attempt to rape Nita, and a terrifying scramble ensues with Nita desperately running from room to room. She is saved at the last minute by Bailey, who stabs Arnold Triplett in the back with a sickle. Calvin is also downed, but not before he stabs Bailey in the chest. Nita, who has by now unlocked the outhouse door and is clinging to her sons, runs out onto the porch. There she sees the dead Bailey and realizes that he was her former husband. The next morning Nita and the boys board the bus and leave town.

Critics referred to *Raggedy Man* as "a little movie," and "a delicate movie,' perhaps because of the modesty of its scale when compared to the blockbusters of 1981. Yet it is more than that. As a film that perfectly realizes its own intentions, it is a success. It is indeed rewarding that a project can find realization without a hefty budget of twenty million dollars or more. The performances, the look of the film, and the story mesh together smoothly.

Its mood is right, its tone is convincing, and its underlying philosophy is sound.

Joan L. Cohen

Reviews

The Hollywood Reporter. August 26, 1981, p. 3.
Los Angeles Times. October 16, 1981, VI, p. 1.
The New York Times. September 18, 1981, III, p. 10.
Newsweek. XCVIII, October 5, 1981, p. 78.
Time. CXVIII, September 28, 1981, p. 87.
Variety. August 26, 1981, p. 3.

RAGTIME

Production: Dino De Laurentiis for Paramount
Direction: Milos Forman
Screenplay: Michael Weller; based on the novel of the same name by E. L. Doctorow
Cinematography: Miroslav Ondricek
Editing: Anne V. Coates, Antony Gibbs, and Stanley Warnow
Production design: John Graysmark
Art direction: Patricia Von Brandenstein and Anthony Reading
Music: Randy Newman
Costume design: Anna Hill Johnstone
Choreography: Twyla Tharp
MPAA rating: PG
Running time: 156 minutes

Principal characters:

Rheinlander Waldo .... James Cagney
Younger Brother .... Brad Dourif
Booker T. Washington .... Moses Gunn
Evelyn Nesbit .... Elizabeth McGovern
Willie Conklin .... Kenneth McMillan
Delmas .... Pat O'Brien
Evelyn's dance instructor .... Donald O'Connor
Father .... James Olson
Tateh .... Mandy Patinkin
Coalhouse Walker, Jr. .... Howard E. Rollins
Mother .... Mary Steenburgen
Sarah .... Debbie Allen
Harry Houdini .... Jeff Demunn
Harry K. Thaw .... Robert Joy
Stanford White .... Norman Mailer
Teddy Roosevelt .... Robert Boyd

E. L. Doctorow's best-selling novel *Ragtime* (1975) is an innovative meshing of America's past with America's myth in a whimsical, entertaining, and thought-provoking fashion, a panorama of American life during the early years of the twentieth century. Doctorow's New York City is a melting pot and a haven for refugees from around the world who are seeking the American Dream. The novel combines a warm sense of nostalgia with trenchant social commentary. Doctorow interweaves real-life characters with his own fictional ones, inventing wonderful confrontations between them to develop his view of the success and failure of the American Dream.

Producer Dino De Laurentiis purchased the screen rights for a proposed Filmways release (it was finally released by Paramount) and signed Robert Altman to direct, based on the success of Altman's *Nashville* (1975). Doctorow himself was mentioned as the possible script-writer but Altman hired Joan Tweksbury for the job. Altman intended to make two three-hour films for release in 1978, with the possibility of a ten-hour version for television, and his choices for the roles of Coalhouse and Father were O. J. Simpson and George C. Scott, respectively. Following the failure of Altman's *Buffalo Bill and the Indians* (1976), however, De Laurentiis fired Altman and hired émigré Czech director Milos Forman.

Doctorow had loosely based his novel on the life of ragtime composer Scott Joplin and on Heinrich von Kleist's novella *Michael Kohlhaus* (1808), the story of a sixteenth century German horse-trader who became a revolutionary bandit. The novel has four storylines which blend to express Doctorow's political views and his observation of historical characters. There is the story of the real-life figure Evelyn Nesbit, a beautiful but dim-witted Gibson Girl/ showgirl who was the center of one of the most notorious scandals of the day. A second plotline concerns a middle-class WASP family in New Rochelle; "Father" (the family members' names are never given, suggesting that they are representative types rather than individuals) heads a company which manufactures such symbols of patriotism as American flags and fireworks. A third subplot follows the story of Tateh, a poor Jewish immigrant who works his way from silhouette-maker to motion-picture pioneer. Finally, there is the story of a black ragtime-pianist-turned-revolutionary, Coalhouse Walker, Jr.

For the screen version, Forman chose to emphasize the Coalhouse Walker storyline. In the film's opening, the dapper Coalhouse (Howard E. Rollins) is seen playing his ragtime music while 1981-made but highly convincing black and white silent newsreels show real personalities of the day: Teddy Roosevelt (Robert Boyd), Harry Houdini (Jeff Demunn), and others. In New Rochelle, Father (James Olson), Mother (Mary Steenburgen), and Younger Brother (Brad Dourif) find their serene homelife upset by the discovery of a black baby in their vegetable garden. The baby has been deserted by its mother Sarah (Debbie Allen), a washerwoman. The mother is found but refuses to reveal the father's name. Several weeks later, Coalhouse appears at the house where Sarah is now being cared for by the gentle Mother, driving a spiffy new Model-T Ford; he announces his intentions to marry Sarah and make a proper home for his family.

Before they can be married, however, Coalhouse encounters trouble while driving near the New Rochelle firehouse, and his path is blocked by a fire truck. An altercation ensues in which the racist firemen, headed by the bigoted fire chief Willie Conklin (Kenneth McMillan), destroy Coalhouse's car. When his attempts to seek legal recourse are deemed futile, Coalhouse joins with several black friends and goes on destructive raids of the local firehouses.

Eventually, Sarah dies because of a backfired attempt to see the president, and Coalhouse becomes obsessed with revenge. He is joined by Younger Brother, whose job as a fireworks salesman has also taught him how to make bombs. The band of radicals occupy the prestigious J. P. Morgan Library and threaten to blow it up unless fire chief Willie Conklin is delivered to them. At this point, Police Commissioner Reinlander Waldo (James Cagney) is called in to mediate prior to the film's violent denouement.

Interspersed throughout are glimpses of famous personages such as Booker T. Washington (Moses Gunn) and Teddy Roosevelt. There is also a greatly truncated depiction of Tateh (Mandy Patinkin), the humble Jewish immigrant who becomes a motion-picture director with the aristocratic airs of an Erich Von Stroheim and directs a film starring the infamous Evelyn Nesbit (Elizabeth McGovern). Patinkin, who played Che Guevera in the Broadway production of *Evita*, displays an especially charismatic screen presence but his part was greatly edited. In the book, his rise to film pioneer *and* radical socialist was a pivotal plot line.

The Evelyn Nesbit segment is the most colorful of the film and Forman spared no expense (the film's budget reached thirty-two million dollars) in re-creating, among other things, the opulent roof garden of old Madison Square Garden and the opening night of the revue, *Mamzelle Champagne*, complete with eighteen dancing girls and Donald O'Connor as an aging vaudevillian and dance instructor. It is in this roof garden nightclub that Pittsburgh millionaire playboy Harry K. Thaw (Robert Joy)—Evelyn's jealousy-crazed husband—fires three shots into Evelyn's former lover, prominent period architect Stanford White, played by an elegantly tuxedoed but nevertheless pugnacious Norman Mailer. Forman's penchant for authenticity is evidenced by details such as the bottles of champagne on White's table with labels marked *Moet et Chandon 1898*.

As a whole, *Ragtime* is a confused and rambunctious film which reveals the struggle that screenwriter Michael Weller and director Forman had in squeezing in as much of the novel as they felt they could. Forman states that he had Doctorow's permission to be "footloose and fancy-free" with the book, saying "I wanted to use the novel as a source and create my own version. Just as Doctorow did when he invented the story."

The film not only emphasizes certain plot lines at the expense of others but also completely eliminates such characters as Sigmund Freud, Emiliano Zapata, and Emma Goldman and such important events as Admiral Peary's voyage to the North Pole and the violent Lawrenceville textile strike. The film is full of richly nostalgic vignettes and retains the novel's strong condemnation of racism, but it sorely lacks both the sweep and the power of the book.

The acting throughout is notable, particularly by unknown Howard E. Rollins as Coalhouse and the lovely Elizabeth McGovern as Evelyn Nesbit, both of whom received Academy Award nominations in the supporting categories. Also notable are Mary Steenburgen playing against type as Mother, Kenneth McMillan as Willie Conklin, and Pat O'Brien, who appears briefly as Thaw's lawyer. *Ragtime* saw the return to the screen of the legendary James Cagney as Rheinlander Waldo, after an absence of twenty years. While it was a pleasure to see the mighty Cagney on the screen once again, his part is stretched out and greatly slows the picture down. In fact, nearly all the film's action and its best scenes take place in the first part of the film, and the lengthy library sequence, which almost appears to be another film, greatly slows this long, 156-minute production.

In addition to the two Academy Award nominations for supporting acting, *Ragtime* received nominations for Best Adapted Screenplay, Original Song ("One More Hour"), Original Score, Art Direction, Cinematography, and Costume Design.

Ragtime was the second novel by Doctorow to reach the screen, the first being *Welcome to Hard Times* (1967), an off-beat and poorly received Western starring Henry Fonda and written and directed by Burt Kennedy. As in the case of *Ragtime*, Doctorow's style proved difficult to adapt to the screen.

Ronald Bowers

Reviews

The Hollywood Reporter. November 13, 1981, p. 3.
Los Angeles Times. November 15, 1981, *Calendar*, p. 29.
The New Republic. CLXXXV, December 1, 1981, pp. 24-26.
The New York Times. November 20, 1981, III, p. 10.
The New Yorker. LVII, November 23, 1981, p. 80+.
Newsweek. XCVIII, November 23, 1981, p. 124.
Saturday Review. VIII, December, 1981, p. 66+.
Time. CXVIII, November 23, 1981, p. 97.
Variety. November 13, 1981, p. 3.

RAIDERS OF THE LOST ARK

Production: Frank Marshall for Lucasfilm; released by Paramount
Direction: Steven Spielberg
Screenplay: Lawrence Kasdan; based on an original story by George Lucas and Philip Kaufman
Cinematography: Douglas Slocombe
Editing: Michael Kahn (AA)
Art direction: Norman Reynolds and Leslie Dilley (AA); set decoration, Michael Ford (AA)
Visual effects: Richard Edlund, Kit West, Bruce Nicholson, and Joe Johnston (AA)
Sound: Bill Varney, Steve Maslow, Gregg Landaker, and Roy Charman (AA)
Music: John Williams
MPAA rating: PG
Running time: 118 minutes

Principal characters:
Indiana Jones .... Harrison Ford
Marion Ravenwood .... Karen Allen
Dietrich .... Wolf Kahler
Belloq .... Paul Freeman
Toht .... Ronald Lacey
Sallah .... John Rhys-Davies
Brody .... Denholm Elliott
Gobler .... Anthony Higgins
Satipo .... Alfred Molina
Barranca .... Vic Tablian

Raiders of the Lost Ark begins in a dense Peruvian jungle. To the eight-year-old boy already on the edge of his seat in a theater in Los Angeles or Milwaukee, the scene is rich with mystery and tension, heightened by the chattering of monkeys, the cries of exotic birds, the unidentifiable clicks and hisses of the jungle. To the boy's father and uncle, both in their thirties, these jungle sound effects are rich with nostalgia, so evocative of the old movies and serials they watched on television as children—*Tarzan*, *Ramar of the Jungle*, nameless others—that the men are both moved to turn to each other and smile. The impulse which moves them is the joy of recognition, of recollection which must be shared to be validated, as one baseball fan will say to another: "And do you remember the catch that Clemente made?"

Thus in its opening moments, *Raiders of the Lost Ark* makes a contract with its audience: it promises to deliver an exciting, continuously absorbing story with an unobtrusive subtext which echoes and alludes to earlier films and genre conventions. In the film's opening scenes, the hero's face is not visible. The camera follows his shadow, watches him from behind as a treacherous guide is about to shoot him in the back, and focuses on his whip-wielding hand as he disarms the would-be killer—but still does not show his face. Finally—anticipation gives these opening moments more duration than mere clock-time—he reaches a clearing, and out of the shadows his profile (still not the full face) is etched against the sky. This device is functional, one of many suspense-building elements in the sequence, but it is also a cliché of the action-film genre—Akira Kurosawa used it in the same playful spirit to begin *Yojimbo* (1961)—lovingly re-created by director Steven Spielberg. Other scenes humorously reverse genre conventions, as when the uniform of an unconscious German soldier, appropriated for purposes of disguise, proves to be much too small. Another reversal scene—one which provokes vocal reaction from the audience—features a confrontation between hero Indiana Jones (Harrison Ford) and an Arab giant who twirls his scimitar like a baton. Jones shakes his head, pulls out his pistol, and calmly shoots his opponent.

Raiders of the Lost Ark is not an *intellectually* allusive film. Its echoes and allusions, scattered here and there and by no means continuous, are for the most part evocations of childhood memories, not references to films one has seen as an adult. The huge seaplane which appears briefly early in the film, the map superimposed on the screen with a moving red line charting the flight to Nepal: these marvelously suggestive images can only be called touches of genius, offering one segment of the audience the pleasures of memory and recognition while keeping the rest of the audience hooked, entirely caught up in the action.

It is that relentless, perfectly paced action which keeps the entire audience on the edge of their seats, regardless of age: the film's allusiveness would fall flat without the direct appeal of its storytelling. The story of *Raiders of the Lost Ark* began in the fertile imagination of George Lucas, inspired, he has said, by the Saturday-matinee serials he watched as a boy. Lucas visualized his hero in some detail: a maverick archaeologist whose trademarks—like Zorro's mask, cape, and sword—would be a leather bush hat and an ever-handy bullwhip. Lucas turned the idea over to director Steven Spielberg and screenwriter Lawrence Kasdan (Philip Kaufman, who shares story credit with Lucas, contributed the premise of a search for the lost Ark of the Covenant). The result of this unusual collaboration is a film that combines many of the distinctive virtues of its two moving intelligences, Lucas and Spielberg.

The story begins in 1936. Indiana Jones, a rather mercenary archaeologist, is in the jungles of Peru to raid a tomb. His prize is a golden statuette, protected by a devilish array of booby-traps, including a giant boulder which almost crushes him to death. He escapes with the idol, only to have it taken from him by his old rival Belloq (Paul Freeman). The scene with the boulder is particularly important in establishing the tone of the film. Like a pursuer in a nightmare, the enormous boulder rolls after the fleeing Indy, always just a step behind him. It is clear that trick photography has been employed; the audience is scared to death and laughing at the same time. Thus Spielberg reserves the right, later in the film, to employ obviously unrealistic twists of plot without violating his implicit contract with the audience. These exaggerated violations of the loosely "realistic" conventions of the film never occur unless the plot demands it and do not extend to parody.

The thrill-a-minute opening in the Peruvian jungle is followed by a wonderful change of pace: cut to a classroom in the United States, where Indy—garbed in professorial tweeds and sweater-vest, wearing glasses—is at the blackboard lecturing on archaeology to a class which seems to consist mostly of love-struck young women. The scene which follows is one of the finest in the film. Indy's superior at the university, Brody (Denholm Elliott), and two men from Army intelligence meet with him in the empty classroom to tell him about Hitler's search for the lost Ark of the Covenant. This is the exposition scene, necessary to provide background information and set the plot in motion. Even in good films, such scenes often have a forced quality, a sense of "let's get this over with." Such is not the case here. Spielberg and screenwriter Lawrence Kasdan use the exposition scene to add another dimension to Indy's character, and Harrison Ford responds brilliantly. The audience has seen him as a hard-bitten, resourceful mercenary with just a couple of humanizing touches: a sardonic sense of humor and a fear of snakes. In this scene, however, they see a combination of formidable expertise, knowledge of arcane lore, and sheer boyish enthusiasm for his subject. From this point in the film, Indy is not merely a hero: he is extremely likable. Ford's characterization is brilliant throughout and contributed significantly to the film's great popular success.

From America the action shifts briefly to Nepal, where Marion Ravenwood (Karen Allen), the daughter of Indy's former professor and mentor, has a medallion which will help to locate the Ark. The character of Marion recalls Howard Hawks's "competent women"—she is running a bar in Nepal, and has just won a drinking bout when Indy arrives—as well as more recent feisty heroines such as Lucas' Princess Leia. She welcomes Indy by slugging him on the jaw; she had fallen for him years earlier, taking it seriously, while he regarded her as just another conquest. Nevertheless, they are soon united against a common foe—Nazis also after the medallion—and, following spectacular scenes of mayhem, they fly together to Cairo, near the site of the Nazi excavations in search of the Ark.

Hitler, characterized by the United States Army intelligence agents as "a nut on the occult," hopes to use the Ark—which the Children of Israel carried before them into battle—as a kind of super-weapon. Lost since the destruction of Solomon's temple in Jerusalem in 587 B.C., the Ark is believed to have traveled to the lost Egyptian city of Tanis, where Nazi excavations are proceeding under the direction of Indy's nemesis Belloq. The remainder of the film—its larger part—concerns Indy's successful excavation of the Ark, only to have it captured by the Nazis, who spirit it away by submarine to a remote hidden base. Indy and Marion are nearby, lashed back-to-back to a stake, when Belloq and the Nazis open the Ark. After an anticlimactic moment—they find only sand within—the Ark releases avenging spirits, swirling spectral presences which utterly consume the defilers, melting them down to nothing.

The conclusion of the story—the Ark is stored by Army intelligence in an ordinary packing crate in an immense warehouse full of thousands of such crates, all marked "Top Secret"—suggests that the Ark might reappear in a later film. The lust for godlike power and knowledge, recalling the theme of J. R. R. Tolkien's *The Lord of the Rings*, might easily be dramatized in other settings, perhaps with analogies to atomic power. In any case, a sequel is already under way; whether the Ark will figure in it remains to be seen.

Technically superb, well-made in every way, the film is particularly strong in its characterizations. Harrison Ford's outstanding work is nicely complemented by Karen Allen in a less interesting but well-acted role; among the minor players, Ronald Lacey as a psychopathic Nazi and John Rhys-Davies as Indy's Egyptian friend are memorable.

Because of its enormous box-office success, *Raiders of the Lost Ark* has been the subject of considerable criticism; it has frequently been charged with contributing to the "infantilization" of American cinema. The charge, perhaps understandable given the lamentable dominance of films aimed at the "youth market," is nevertheless absurd. Brilliant, well-made films are always in short supply and should be acknowledged as such whatever their genre.

John Wilson

Reviews

The Hollywood Reporter. June 5, 1981, p. 3.
Los Angeles Times. June 7, 1981, *Calender*, p. 1.
The New Republic. CLXXXV, July 4-11, 1981, pp. 26-27.
The New York Times. June 12, 1981, III, p. 10.
The New Yorker. LVII, June 15, 1981, pp. 132-135.
Newsweek. XCVII, June 15, 1981, pp. 58-61.
Saturday Review. VIII, June, 1981, pp. 12-15.
Time. CXVII, June 15, 1981, pp. 74-76.
Variety. June 5, 1981, p. 3.

REDS

Production: Warren Beatty for Paramount
Direction: Warren Beatty (AA)
Screenplay: Warren Beatty and Trevor Griffiths
Cinematography: Vittorio Storaro (AA)
Editing: Dede Allen and Simon Relph
Art direction: Richard Sylbert
Music: Stephen Sondheim and Dave Grusin
MPAA rating: PG
Running time: 200 minutes

Principal characters:
John Reed .... Warren Beatty
Louise Bryant .... Diane Keaton
Max Eastman .... Edward Herrmann
Grigory Zinoviev .... Jerzy Kosinski
Eugene O'Neill .... Jack Nicholson
Louis Fraina .... Paul Sorvino
Emma Goldman .... Maureen Stapleton (AA)
Floyd Dell .... Max Wright

It became evident very early in its history that Warren Beatty's *Reds*, an ambitious and highly creative work based on the life of John Reed, would have some problems at the box office as well as with critics. Initial reviews drew comparisons with David Lean's *Dr. Zhivago* (1965) instead of Sergei Eisenstein's *October* (1927), a seemingly more suitable choice. Comparisons with *Dr. Zhivago* immediately opened up the film to a wide range of criticisms. Diane Keaton's performance in a romantic role was judged greatly inferior to Julie Christie's. *Reds* was faulted for its lack of warm and sympathetic characters and an epic, sweeping musical score such as that of *Dr. Zhivago*. Finally and perhaps most damaging, critics charged that *Reds*'s heavy political statements detracted from the effectiveness of the love story.

On the other hand, had it initially been measured, as Beatty would no doubt have preferred, against Eisenstein's *October* (also based upon John Reed's book *Ten Days That Shook the World*), *Reds* would still have had serious problems. In this event, the love relationship that constitutes a significant emphasis of the film would be viewed as a serious distraction from the film's political concerns. Thus, while Beatty's film is an outstanding achievement, one which will undoubtedly become increasingly well-regarded in years to come, it is a film with an identity crisis—one that attempts too many things and consequently spreads itself too thin.

Reds's complex screenplay, jointly written by Beatty and British screenwriter Trevor Griffiths, attempts to serve as a biography of the American journalist John Reed, whose book *Ten Days That Shook the World* was a powerful eyewitness account of the 1917 Bolshevik Revolution. According to one account (later disproved), Reed, after his death in 1920 at the age of thirty-three, became the only American to be buried in the Kremlin. He is now known to be only the first of several of his countrymen to achieve that distinction.

Reed's screen biography is a rather complex and ambitious juxtaposition of several different motifs. The film includes an extremely compressed history of the American radical left and its activities in the period 1915-1920, centering primarily on the activities of Big Bill Haywood, the American Socialist Party, and the ultimate birth of the fledgling Communist Party in the United States. Also included, to some degree, are the liberal intellectual gatherings of the era, emphasizing particularly the movements in Provincetown and Greenwich Village.

The love story, concentrating on Reed's stormy relationship with an aspiring feminist named Louise Bryant, is intercut with the political episodes and seemingly reaffirms the power of traditional human relationships to bind people together in spite of mutual flirtations with sexual freedom and the divergence of careers. Yet the most interesting structural device in the film is a series of interviews with thirty-two surviving "witnesses," actual associates and contemporaries of Reed. These aged witnesses, filmed in black and white against stark backgrounds, provide a remarkable contrast to the film's youthful revolutionaries as well as an uncanny sense of authenticity. It must be admitted, however, that the film is weakened by Beatty's unwillingness to identify these commentators, although older filmgoers will recognize among them the faces of Arthur Mayer, George Jessel, Hamilton Fish, Rebecca West, Roger Baldwin, Henry Miller, and Adela Rogers St. John.

While the recollections of these witnesses provide the framework for the episodes of this three-hour-and-fifteen-minute film, it is the powerful acting of Beatty as Reed and Keaton as Bryant that provides the degree of cohesion that the picture achieves. Still, over the relatively lengthy time span of the film the characters wear a little thin, and the viewer regrets that more time was not devoted to the interesting characterizations of Emma Goldman and Eugene O'Neill, portrayed by Maureen Stapleton and Jack Nicholson, respectively.

The "story" of the film concerns John Reed (Warren Beatty), a newspaper reporter from Portland, Oregon. Born into a wealthy family, Reed becomes increasingly radical as a result of his journalistic experiences. When a growing number of mainstream newspapers decline to print his graphic, firsthand reports of police brutality and labor injustices, he takes them to a smaller circulation left-wing magazine which provides a springboard for his involvement in radical politics. He is a willing recruit and, through a rapid series of events, winds up as both an eyewitness and a participant in the Russian Revolution of 1917.

When he subsequently returns to the United States he becomes involved in the political infighting characteristic of the American left of that period. This causes his earlier, almost blind idealism to ebb somewhat. When he again returns to the newly formed Soviet Union over the protests of his wife Louise Bryant (Diane Keaton), he is further disillusioned to discover that a close-knit, dull bureaucracy has assumed dictatorial powers over the country. He realizes that although he is a member of the group called the Comintern, an international federation of Communist parties, his speeches are deliberately mistranslated to bring them totally in line with Marxist dogma. At this point, Reed finally perceives that he has not only been deceived but also that he is, in fact, trapped. On the whole, he has seen the achievement of the revolutionary dream to which he has devoted his life, yet it is nothing like what he envisioned it would be. He cannot find the strength to renounce it and thus render his life meaningless. His dilemma is resolved in his death from typhus at the age of thirty-three.

Reed's relationship with Louise Bryant is not as easy to summarize as are the political aspects of the film, largely because she is not an easy character to define. She comes into conflict with her husband over the amount of time he spends in political activities with ideological compatriots such as Emma Goldman (Maureen Stapleton), Max Eastman (Edward Herrmann), Floyd Dell (Max Wright), and others. At the same time, she also complains because these people do not take her seriously. She is presented in a more sympathetic light in the second half of the film, however, after Reed has been imprisoned in Finland. She secrets herself on a freighter leaving New York for Norway, survives a terrible storm, and finally treks painfully across the icy tundra to be with her man. The snowy scenes are reminiscent of *Dr. Zhivago* but they do not arise logically out of anything that happened in the initial segments of the film and thus form something of an artificial resolution to her conflicts with Reed.

The performances by the principals are more than competent, although Beatty himself probably has gone to the well once too often with the ingratiating, stammering little boy persona which was so much more effective in *Heaven Can Wait* (1978). It is the acting of the supporting group that provides the core of strength in the film: Jack Nicholson as Eugene O'Neill, Maureen Stapleton as Emma Goldman, novelist Jerzy Kosinski as Grigory Zinoviev, and Paul Sorvino as a remarkably restrained Louis Fraina. The strong performances of this group, especially Stapleton's Oscar-winning role, lent validity to Beatty's Academy Award for Best Director of 1981. He is an excellent actor's director who can enhance the performances of seasoned veterans such as Stapleton and Nicholson while at the same time eliciting almost comparable presentations from less experienced actors.

The fundamental weakness of *Reds* is not in execution but rather in the film's divided intentions. Love and politics are in this case uneasy bedfellows. *Reds* is admittedly a better attempt at achieving an epic than an American film has accomplished in a number of years. It is thus disappointing that it could not have achieved the singleness of purpose that would have made it completely successful.

Thomas A. Hanson

Reviews

The Hollywood Reporter. November 30, 1981, p. 3.
Los Angeles Times. December 4, 1981, VI, p. 1.
The New Republic. XVIII, December 16, 1981, pp. 26-27.
The New York Times. December 4, 1981, III, p. 8.
The New Yorker. LVII, December 21, 1981, p. 126.
Newsweek. XCVIII, December 7, 1981, pp. 83-84.
Saturday Review. IX, January, 1982, p. 52.
Time. CXVIII, December 7, 1981, pp. 66-67.
Variety. November 30, 1981, p. 3.

RICH AND FAMOUS

Production: William Allyn for Jacquet-William Allyn; released by Metro-Goldwyn-Mayer through United Artists
Direction: George Cukor
Screenplay: Gerald Ayres; based on the play *Old Acquaintance* by John Van Druten
Cinematography: Don Peterman and Peter Eco
Editing: John F. Burnett
Art direction: Fred Harpman and James A. Taylor
Costume design: Theoni V. Aldrege
Music: Georges Delerue
MPAA rating: R
Running time: 117 minutes

Principal characters:

Liz Hamilton .... Jacqueline Bisset
Merry Noel Blake .... Candice Bergen
Doug Blake .... David Selby
Chris Adams .... Hart Bochner
Jules Levi .... Steven Hill
Debby at age eighteen .... Meg Ryan
Speaker .... Fay Kanin

Rich and Famous is based on a John Van Druten play, *Old Acquaintance*, which in turn was made into a well-known 1943 Warner Bros. film of the same name. It starred Bette Davis and Miriam Hopkins, two actresses known for their considerable tempers and strong wills as well as for their dramatic abilities. The film was a great success. The audience loved the scrapping and snide remarks of the story's two main characters, who are lifelong friends and rivals.

The 1981 George Cukor version of the play follows the same general story line, with some updating to give the film a more modern look and tone. Jacqueline Bisset plays the serious novelist, Bette Davis' role, and Candice Bergen portrays the best-selling trashy novelist originally portrayed by Miriam Hopkins in *Old Acquaintance*. The film spans twenty-two years in the lives of the new old friends, who are seen at four different time periods: 1959, 1965, 1975, and 1981.

In the beginning sequence, which is the shortest, the two main characters are introduced in their darkened Smith College dormitory room. Liz Hamilton (Jacqueline Bisset) is helping her roommate and best friend Merry Noel (Candice Bergen) run away to get married, just before graduation. As the girls walk toward the train station, the audience discovers that Merry is from

Texas and rather flighty. The more serious Liz is her opposite, but there is a definite bond between them, and as Merry gets on the train with her fiancé Doug Blake (David Selby), she gives Liz her most prized possession, a childhood teddy bear. The audience also learns that Merry is eloping with a man whom Liz had met first, although Liz does not seem to mind.

The next sequence begins at the University of California at Los Angeles, where Liz is being introduced to a group of students as the main speaker at a young women's caucus. Merry, wearing a 1960's hairdo and holding hands with a little girl, watches happily as Liz is described as an important author who is soon to publish her second and long-awaited novel. The speaker is one of several "guest stars" in the film, some of whom are unbilled. She is played by Fay Kanin, the President of the Academy of Motion Picture Arts and Sciences, a good friend of Cukor and the sister-in-law of his frequent collaborator, Garson Kanin.

During the course of the 1965 segment, it is revealed that Liz received a national writer's award for her first novel but that she has been suffering from a serious (and almost unbelievable) writer's block for the last several years. Merry is now happily living in Malibu with Doug; they have a beautiful little daughter, and are surrounded by film-star neighbors. While it is obvious that Doug is not happy with life in Malibu and would rather live in Pasadena near his work at Cal Tech, Merry is in her element. After Doug retires, she reveals to Liz that she has been writing a novel for eight months based on the lives of her celebrity friends. In her Southern belle fashion, Merry says that they have problems, "just like the folks down home."

Liz is enraged by the book. It is predictably thoughtless and filled with gossip, but what seems to make Liz the most angry is that Merry was able to finish it quickly and will undoubtedly make lots of money with it. She vents her rage on Merry and they have the first of several screaming fights, ending with Liz throwing up and Merry under the delusion that Liz likes the book.

On her flight back to New York (in first class, which is rather out of character with her supposedly tight financial circumstances), Liz has a sexual tryst with a fellow passenger in the plane's lavatory. It is a ridiculous scene and one which only seems to serve an underlying theme of the film, Liz's sexual frustration. From a feminist point of view, the brilliant, strong-willed Liz looks foolish as she engages in and talks about several disastrous affairs. Her preoccupation with "young flesh," which she too vehemently denies later in the movie, seems rather ridiculous and out of character.

The film next flashes forward to 1975. Merry is a very successful (although not critically) popular writer. She is interviewed and pampered, a role which she thoroughly enjoys. She is unaware, however, that her marriage to Doug, a good man who is beginning to drink, is crumbling. When they are in New York, Doug visits Liz, for whom he has harbored an innocent attraction for years, and tells her that he wants to leave Merry. Merry storms into Liz's apartment and they all fight, but she calms down at the sight of her old teddy bear in Liz's room. A few days later Doug meets Liz in Central Park and wants her to marry him, but she loyally refuses and has already told Merry about their meeting. Doug walks away from both of them and Liz comforts Merry, who is at first hysterical and then thoughtlessly resolute, feeling that losing Doug is merely losing one piece of her full life.

The final segment of the film takes place in December, 1981. Liz has written several "important," critically acclaimed novels. She lives in Connecticut, but she is staying at New York's famed literary mecca, The Algonquin Hotel, for a few weeks during preparations for the National Writers's Award ceremonies. She is one of the judges for the award and she proposes Merry's newest book, *Home Cooking*, as a winner. Merry has now turned to serious writing and the critics have received her book very well, so she has decided to campaign for the award. She is still wrapped up in herself, throwing parties and giving interviews, all with the award in mind.

Liz comes to a crossroads in her life when she meets Chris Adams (Hart Bochner), a twenty-two-year-old journalist with *Rolling Stone* magazine. He wants to interview her, but she is rude and patronizing to him. Later, though, after she goes to bed with an eighteen-year-old whom she picks up, she consents to the interview and they fall in love. Chris wants to marry Liz, but she adamantly refuses. She cannot help expressing her feelings in lofty literary allusions, but she later admits to Merry that her fear is having someone around watching her thighs grow old.

While Liz is going through an emotional upheaval over Chris, Merry's daughter Debby (Meg Ryan) has been involved in a love affair with an eighteen-year-old Puerto Rican poet cum car thief whom her mother detests. Debby seeks Chris's aid when her boyfriend is arrested and spends the night in his hotel room. Although the incident is apparently innocent, Liz, who has decided to marry Chris, changes her mind and sends him away instead. He will be consoled, however, by Debby, whom he has hired as his new assistant.

This all takes place on New Year's Eve, the same day that Liz must tell Merry that she has tied for the National Writer's Award with another woman, a black writer. Merry is furious. She fights with Liz in her car, then later goes to her hotel room to confront her again. (Doug, who has visited Merry for lunch that day, has revealed that he once asked Liz to marry him.) The two women scream insults at each other as they never have before, with Merry accusing Liz of being a "slut," and Liz accusing Merry of wanting only what Liz wants. The fight ends when they battle over the teddy bear and it is ripped apart. The film ends that evening, at midnight, when Merry takes a cab to Liz's Connecticut home and they realize that through everything, they have had each other's friendship.

Rich and Famous is the most recent film by veteran director George Cukor. The eighty-two-year-old Cukor began his film career in 1930 and has continued to make successful motion pictures for more than fifty years. The last decade has not been as active for him as the first four, but *Rich and Famous* proves that he is still a vibrant filmmaker and most deserving of the title of a "woman's director." There are parts that drag in the almost two-hour film, but compared to most contemporary dramas, it flows very well. The theme is contemporary, and the film does not have that old-fashioned look which is often associated with directors of Cukor's generation. He elicits two of the best performances of Bergen's and Bisset's respective careers, although critically the actresses' efforts were better received than the director's.

Cukor's films, especially with Katharine Hepburn, have been regarded by many feminist film critics as among the best about women ever made in the United States. *Adam's Rib* (1949) and *Pat and Mike* (1952) particularly have high reputations as important "women's films." *Rich and Famous* is no *Adam's Rib*, certainly, but it is one of the few films in recent years to have *two* strong roles for women and virtually no strong role for a man. The men, in fact, are shadowy figures, more window dressing than real characters. One of the flaws in the story—and one which harkens back to the earlier film and play on which it was based—is that one wonders why two women such as Merry and Liz would find their love interests so attractive. *Rich and Famous*, more than *Old Acquaintance*, emphasizes the power of sheer physical attraction, for, mentally, Doug and Chris are no match for Merry and Liz.

Bisset and Bergen perform admirably in their roles. Bisset is typically low-keyed in her performance and shines in her long speeches. Bergen, on the other hand, turns in perhaps the best performance of her career with her flighty, bitchy, Southern accented Merry. Although they are opposites in many ways, the two women have a deeply rooted feeling for each other which survives the vicissitudes of their lives. In this sense, *Rich and Famous* is better than the 1943 *Old Acquaintance*, in which Davis and Hopkins were always rivals, and the audience did not appreciate their friendship until the end. In *Rich and Famous*, the two women are genuinely friends, rivalry being only one aspect of that friendship. Merry is flippant, self-centered, and insensitive in many ways, but she is a true friend. For this reason Liz's affection for her is more believable than Davis' loyalty to Hopkins in the earlier work.

The film opened to generally good reviews, especially for the two stars. There were some negative responses, but unfortunately those seemed to be aimed at Cukor, or the overly long story. It was not a spectacular box-office hit, despite early enthusiasm, but it did finish respectably in the black. While not a perfect effort, it certainly stands far above many recent efforts in its realistic portrayal of women in film.

Patricia King Hanson

Reviews

The Hollywood Reporter. October 7, 1981, p. 3.
Los Angeles Times. October 9, 1981, VI, p. 1.
The New Republic. CLXXXV, November 18, 1981, p. 26.
The New York Times. October 9, 1981, III, p. 16.
The New Yorker. LVII, October 26, 1981, p. 178+.
Newsweek. XCVIII, October 12, 1981, p. 98.
Time. CXVIII, October 12, 1981, p. 102.
Variety. October 5, 1981, p. 3.

RICHARD'S THINGS

Production: Mark Shivas for Southern Pictures; presented by Roger Corman; released by New World Pictures
Direction: Anthony Harvey
Screenplay: Frederic Raphael; based on his novel of the same name
Cinematography: Freddie Young
Editing: Lesley Walker
Art direction: Ian Whittaker
Music: Georges Delerue
MPAA rating: R
Running time: 104 minutes

Principal characters:

Kate Morris .... Liv Ullmann
Josie .... Amanda Redman
Peter .... Tim Pigott-Smith
Mrs. Sells .... Elizabeth Spriggs
Mr. Morris .... David Markham
Richard Morris .... Mark Eden
Margaret .... Gwen Taylor
Dr. Mace .... John Vine
Bill .... Michael Maloney
Joanna .... Tracy Childs

Richard's Things is about the temporary insanity that people sometimes go through when someone very close to them has died. It is a macabre story about the loss of love and what happens to the loved ones that are left behind. Part Alfred Hitchcock and part Patricia Highsmith in theme, the film was adapted by Frederic Raphael from his own 1973 novel. The film follows the novel very closely and has a strange, claustrophobic quality to it, as if most of the action was going on inside the head of its heroine, Kate Morris (Liv Ullmann).

The film is essentially the story of a widow who discovers that her dead husband Richard (Mark Eden) was leading a double life, but the film stops just short of soap opera. Its grave implication is that Kate is trying to take over the life of one of the objects that her husband left behind. Since this particular object was his mistress, what follows verges on the pathological, although nothing really terrifying occurs. Liv Ullmann as the unstrung widow of Richard Morris has never looked plainer or more troubled; she appears as if she were still playing in an Ingmar Bergman film. Yet Ullmann is such a consummate actress that at no time does her Kate seem ludicrous, merely severely disturbed. The audience's sympathies are always with Kate, even if she makes them uncomfortable. As Richard's lover Josie (with whom Kate also has an affair), Amanda Redman is pert, vivacious, and a bit vacuous. The two women have shared a man and try unsuccessfully to share a life. This is the stuff that good BBC drama is made of, yet it works amazingly well on the large screen.

The film's producer, Mark Shivas, had wanted to work with Frederic Raphael since their success on British television with *All the Glittering Prizes*. It was the first project of Southern Pictures, a production company formed in 1979 which plans to offer feature films for television screening in Britain, then theatrically for the rest of the world. This is similar to the television funding that started the "New German Cinema" and may be the kind of step needed to revitalize the ailing British film industry. The film was made on location in Maidenhead, England, for a little under two million dollars. It is a film with a small number of players and has the feel of a filmed play rather than a novel. The central conceit—that Kate, the wife of Richard Morris, and Josie, his mistress, are two of the "things" he left behind—makes an interesting problem drama which touches on the many links between lust and violence.

When the film opens, Kate Morris, a woman in her forties who has been married for twenty years, must face life alone after the sudden death of her husband Richard. He has died of a massive coronary while on a job outside London. As she drives the two hours back to London after clearing up the details of his death, she must come to terms with the disturbing news that she has learned. While checking into the hotel near the hospital to which Richard was brought, she sees on the register that Richard had also stayed there the previous night. He had not been alone, though, as he signed the hotel register "Mr. and Mrs. Morris." When Kate goes to Richard's office the next day to talk over the state of his business with his partner, Peter (Tim Pigott-Smith), she sees a young girl leaving the office and learns that Richard often worked with her. As Kate questions Peter further, she has a strong feeling that this was the woman with whom Richard had betrayed her. Arrangements are made for Richard's burial, with Kate's mother, her son Bill (Michael Maloney), and Peter hovering around her, trying to make her adjustment easier. Peter, whose wife Margaret (Gwen Taylor) has just left him for a younger man, attempts to become more than only a family friend, but Kate is not ready to accept his attentions. She is deeply disturbed. It is not Richard's death that is bothering her so much—her rational mind can accept that, but she cannot face her own faltering interpretation of what their married life had been.

Kate becomes obsessed with seeking out the woman with whom Richard had had the affair, not quite knowing what she will say or do when she finds her. The woman, Josie, is hardly more than a girl. Kate goes to her house and tries to tell her what she is feeling. Josie is open and frank, speaking quite honestly about her own relationship with Richard. Josie assures Kate that he always loved his wife, and that her time with him did not impinge upon his marriage. The two women, drawn together by their mutual sense of loss, see more and more of each other and gradually start up a passionate love affair. It is as if both of them are trying to cling vicariously to Richard.

Meanwhile, Kate's friends and family sense that she is not herself, but her public persona rebukes their inquiries and she convinces them that she is handling everything in a most satisfactory manner. Peter continues to press his suit upon Kate, but her thoughts are of Josie. The girl eventually moves into Kate's house and Kate insists that they spend all of their time together. Josie soon sees that Kate wants to control her completely. She will not let her go any more than she will get rid of Richard's clothes or his pipes. Finally, Josie sickens of this closeness and starts to go out, to see old friends. Kate finds this independence impossible to bear and almost reaches the breaking point, but as she matures and comes to realize the consequences of her actions, she sees that she must let Josie go and continue a life for herself that is devoid of Richard and his possessions. The film ends with Kate very much alone, and, at least on the surface, able to carry on.

Because the characters in *Richard's Things* are so properly English, the incipient violence bubbling offscreen is not readily apparent, but as layers of emotional masks are stripped off Kate, there are moments of genuine fear that she might kill Josie for ruining the memory of her life with Richard. Her long marriage is never really explored, and one has the feeling that she and Richard never really talked. The film has a quiet intensity that is both effective and jarring. It was not treated kindly by the critics and had only a limited release in the United States. Its strength lies in the convincing performance by Liv Ullmann and in the realistic dialogue by Frederic Raphael, who, perhaps more than any other contemporary novelist, has his finger on the pulse of the English upper-middle class.

Joan L. Cohen

Reviews

The Hollywood Reporter. June 22, 1981, p. 15.
Los Angeles Times. July 10, 1981, VI, p. 12.
The New Republic. CLXXXIV, June 27, 1981, pp. 26-27.
The New York Times. June 12, 1981, III, p. 18.
The New York Times. June 28, 1981, II, p. 15.
Variety. January 10, 1981, p. 18.

SHARKY'S MACHINE

Production: Hank Moonjean for Orion; released by Warner Bros.
Direction: Burt Reynolds
Screenplay: Gerald Di Pego; based on the novel of the same name by William Diehl
Cinematography: William A. Fraker
Editing: William Gordean
Art direction: Walter Scott Herndon
Music direction: Snuff Garrett
MPAA rating: R
Running time: 119 minutes

Principal characters:

Sharky .... Burt Reynolds
Dominoe .... Rachel Ward
Victor .... Vittorio Gassman
Papa .... Brian Keith
Friscoe .... Charles Durning
Arch .... Bernie Casey
Hotchkins .... Earl Holliman
Billy Score .... Henry Silva

By the end of the 1970's, when he had evolved into a major box-office attraction, Burt Reynolds had adopted the practice of appearing alternately in "good ol' boy" films, which featured broad comedy and lots of car chases, and in less frivolous works that gave him the opportunity to show off his dramatic acting skills. In 1981, his "good ol' boy" film was the inconsequential *Smokey and the Bandit II*; his serious film was *Sharky's Machine* of which he was both star and director.

Sharky's Machine is an atmospheric though by no means humorless film that pits Reynolds as a vice cop against a powerful pimp whose influence extends even as far as a charismatic gubernatorial candidate. The film opens abruptly: a drug bust has gone awry, and Sharky (Burt Reynolds), a detective in the Narcotics Division of the Atlanta police force, chases his quarry through the crowded streets and finally onto a bus. Sharky gets his man, but not before a bystander is wounded. As a result of this incident, Sharky is demoted to the Vice Squad.

The contrast between the businesslike efficiency of the Narcotics Division and the chaos of the Vice Squad is immediately evident. The squad room is overrun with colorful characters—prostitutes, transvestites, and the policemen as well, most of whom have adopted an air of cynicism as their defense against the petty squalor of their surroundings and their lowly status in the law enforcement hierarchy.

The head of the Vice Squad is a dyspeptic man named Friscoe (Charles Durning), who is counting off the days until his retirement. Friscoe's guiding philosophy is "don't make waves." His two best men are Papa (Brian Keith) and Arch (Bernie Casey), good men at the opposite ends of their careers. Papa is an older man with a marvelous record of bravery under fire; laughing and garrulous, he seems to enjoy the strange characters who cross his path in Vice. Arch is younger, a meditative black man who is greatly influenced by Japanese culture—from sushi to Zen. It is this group of men that Sharky will ultimately weld into an effective crime-fighting machine.

The plot is set in motion when Sharky and his team take a book of names from a pimp who has been arrested. Each name has seven letters, and Sharky immediately deduces that they are in fact telephone numbers. The higher-ups in the Police Department authorize wiretaps on six of the numbers; naturally, Sharky is curious about the seventh—"Dominoe"—which, he is informed, is a protected number.

Sharky persuades a friend to tap Dominoe, and he and his team occupy a room in a nearby highrise apartment complex with a good view of the apartment with the Dominoe phone. Dominoe turns out to be a very lovely and very expensive call girl (Rachel Ward), and the phone tap reveals that one of her clients is none other than a popular politician named Hotchkins (Earl Holliman)—hence the police protection of the number. Sharky, Papa, and Arch disregard this supposed protection and continue their surveillance.

At this point, a curious thing happens: Sharky finds himself falling in love with Dominoe. Since the success of the film depends upon the audience's acceptance of this premise, Reynolds and his writer Gerald Di Pego must make a rather unlikely romance appear plausible. They accomplish this by gradually fleshing out Dominoe's character, using information derived from Sharky's phone taps and other sophisticated means of eavesdropping.

Dominoe, it develops, was lured into prostitution at an early age by a Svengali-like pimp named Victor Scorelli (Vittorio Gassman). Furthermore, she is no ordinary hustler. She is both much prettier and much less flashy than the usual prostitutes who parade through the stationhouse. Her only client appears to be Hotchkins, and she is less interested in his money than in setting up housekeeping with him. She is even taking dancing lessons to prepare herself for a new career. In short, she is a damsel (albeit a slightly sullied damsel) in distress, waiting to be rescued from Victor's clutches. Sharky, a lonely, unmarried man in the throes of a professional crisis, falls for her hard.

While Dominoe's identity is being established, the plot moves on in other directions as well. Victor has been using Dominoe to gain influence over Hotchkins, who is on his way to winning the governorship; Dominoe's unprofessional affection for the man is something on which Victor had not bargained. When Victor sees that he can no longer control Dominoe, he orders his brother, an angel dust addict known as Billy Score (Henry Silva), to kill her. Later, when Billy shotguns a girl to death in Dominoe's apartment, everyone—Billy, Victor, Sharky (who is watching, horror-stricken, from his vantage point across the street), and the film's audience—thinks that Dominoe is dead.

Intent upon avenging Dominoe, Sharky whips his motley crew into the efficient machine suggested by the film's title. Then Dominoe herself reappears. As it turns out, she had been away for the weekend; the murder victim had been a friend who was using the apartment for the night.

Although it is hardly love at first sight, Sharky eventually wins Dominoe over. They become lovers, and she identifies the mysterious Victor. Victor, seeing his machinations unravel, plans to leave town, but is murdered instead by his insane brother. The film's denouement is a lengthy pursuit of Billy Score through the stairwells of a skyscraper. In the resultant shootout, Papa is killed, Arch is seriously wounded, and Billy commits suicide just as Sharky is about to shoot him. A closing, happily-ever-after vignette shows Sharky and Dominoe together, watching children at play in a park.

Though eminently watchable, *Sharky's Machine* is far from a perfect film. There are some glitches in the plotting, with a subplot on corruption within the police department alluded to several times but never satisfactorily developed. Portions of the film are far too gory; one expects a certain amount of blood in contemporary cops-and-robbers films, but scenes such as one in which Sharky has a couple of fingers chopped off are entirely gratuitous. Finally, *Sharky's Machine* is a bit derivative, echoing Martin Scorsese's *Taxi Driver* (1976), with its pimps, prostitutes, and political candidate, and Francis Ford Coppola's *The Conversation* (1974) with its electronic eavesdropping. Both of these films, it must be said, made better use of this material than does *Sharky's Machine*.

In a sense, however, such comparisons are irrelevant. Reynolds knows that he is no Scorsese or Coppola, and he does not try to be. His aim is to entertain, and at that he largely succeeds. Reynolds has shown in *Sharky's Machine* that he is capable of putting together a serious film, an issue that remained in doubt after the release of *Gator* (a Southern gothic melodrama from 1976) and *The End* (a lightweight comic exercise from 1978), the first two films that he directed.

The primary strength of *Sharky's Machine*, however, is not its direction but its cast. Reynolds the director gets a good performance from Reynolds the actor, and also from virtually every other actor and actress that appears on camera. Vittorio Gassman and Henry Silva play the bad guys with aplomb. Their styles—Gassman, as Victor, suave and worldly; Silva, as Billy Score, literally jumping out of his skin—contrast nicely. Newcomer Rachel Ward is also fine as Dominoe, the call girl with nesting instincts. Beauty is the *sine qua non* of a part such as this, of course, but despite her resemblance to

Jacqueline Bisset, Ward is no assembly-line starlet. She has a distinctive husky voice, and she works quite well with Reynolds in their scenes together.

Interestingly enough, however, the most effective scenes in *Sharky's Machine* are those involving Reynolds and Brian Keith, Bernie Casey, and Charles Durning, three veteran character actors. A hallmark of Reynolds' best films, both comic and serious, is the sidekick, a friend and foil for Reynolds' lead. In this film, Sharky's team performs that role as a group. The easy camaraderie that develops between these men is the greatest strength of the film. *Sharky's Machine* provides what audiences have come to expect from Burt Reynolds at his best: the cinematic equivalent of "a good read." Although not wildly praised by critics, the film did receive some good notices, with Reynolds' promising direction particularly noted. It also did very well at the box office, helping Reynolds maintain his high position among money-making stars of the 1970's and 1980's.

Robert Mitchell

Reviews

The Hollywood Reporter. December 16, 1981, p. 3.
Los Angeles Times. December 18, 1981, VI, p. 6.
The New York Times. December 18, 1981, III, p. 10.
Newsweek. XCVIII, December 28, 1981, p. 65.
Time. CXXX, January 11, 1982, p. 88.
Variety. December 16, 1981, p. 3.

S.O.B.

Production: Blake Edwards and Tony Adams for Lorimar; released by Paramount
Direction: Blake Edwards
Screenplay: Blake Edwards
Cinematography: Harry Stradling, Jr.
Editing: Ralph E. Winters
Art direction: Roger Maus
Music: Henry Mancini
MPAA rating: R
Running time: 121 minutes

Principal characters:
Sally Miles .... Julie Andrews
Tim Culley .... William Holden
Mavis .... Marisa Berenson
Dick Benson .... Larry Hagman
Felix Farmer .... Richard Mulligan
David Blackman .... Robert Vaughn
Ben Coogan .... Robert Webber
Eva Brown .... Shelley Winters
Dr. Irving Finegarten .... Robert Preston
Gary Murdock .... Stuart Margolin
Polly Reed .... Loretta Swift

In 1964 Julie Andrews won the Academy Award for Best Actress for her role in Walt Disney's *Mary Poppins*, a children's film concerning the adventures of a magical nanny and her two mischievous charges. Admittedly, such children's fare is not the stuff of Oscar-winning performances and several knowledgeable critics (including her two-time costar James Garner in a 1982 television interview) pointed to her somewhat antithetical characterization of a war widow in Paddy Chayefsky's black comedy *The Americanization of Emily* (1964) as a major factor in her nomination since it attested to a talent of considerable range. The general public, however, chose to typecast her as the wholesome if slightly spunky Mary Poppins and flocked to see her in equally sugary roles in such films as *The Sound of Music* (1965) and *Thoroughly Modern Millie* (1967). Her attempts to extend her range as an actress through dramatic roles in *Torn Curtain* (1966), *Star* (1968), and *Darling Lili* (1970) were met with failure at the box office, largely because they came into conflict with her Mary Poppins image. In fact, the last film raised havoc with her fans because it featured Andrews performing a striptease.

Her husband, director Blake Edwards, has been similarly typecast in the minds of the filmgoing public. Although a filmmaker of considerable dramatic talent, exemplified by the excellent *Days of Wine and Roses* (1962), Edwards is primarily known for his considerable achievement in light comedy, embodied in films such as *Breakfast at Tiffany's* (1961), *10* (1980), and the long-running Pink Panther series.

The frustrations of both star and director would seem to have come to a head in *Darling Lili*, when Edwards was deemed self-indulgent and unbankable by many studio executives and a rumor circulated that the film was so dull that it would never reach neighborhood theaters. Ten years later, however, it is the two artists who are having the last laugh; after the phenomenal success of *10*, they can afford to toss a few well-placed barbs at the studio mentality that stifles serious individualized filmmaking. The vehicle for the release of these pent-up frustrations is *S.O.B.* (Hollywood jargon for "Standard Operating Bullshit," as opposed to other epithets which may also come to mind.)

The satiric tone of the film is quickly established in the opening credits, in which a sugary Julie Andrews, wearing doll-clown clothes, frolics amid toys reminiscent of the nursery in *Mary Poppins* while wearing a hat not unlike that of the novice in *The Sound of Music*. This time, though, she is singing "Fare thee well," serving notice that the image of Mary Poppins is finally dead. *S.O.B.* is the highly cynical account of the manner in which a thirty-million-dollar musical flop becomes an overwhelming box-office success through the infusion of an additional ten million dollars and the device of turning it into a pornographic film whose ironic climax goes *Darling Lili* one better, featuring an erotic nursery scene in which Andrews casts off the Mary Poppins image once and for all by baring her breasts for the camera.

The film is primarily the story of director Felix Farmer (Richard Mulligan), who suffers a nervous breakdown as a result of the failure of an overproduced film called *Night Wind*, featuring his wife Sally Miles (Julie Andrews) in the starring role. *Night Wind* is not, however, particularly evocative of *Mary Poppins*, judging from the few scenes of it which are featured in *S.O.B.* After various futile attempts at committing suicide when the film's failure has become evident, Farmer hits upon the idea of reshooting a number of *Night Wind*'s key scenes to transform it into a soft-core pornographic film. The director hopes in the process not only to recoup his losses from the original version but also to regain his wife, who has walked out on him. To make the film a success, however, he must stage a giant production number in which his wife, paralleling Julie Andrews, herself, must shed her well-established virginal image by baring her breasts to the cameras.

After some complications, Sally is persuaded to do the number and the film appears to be a potential success. Yet, a difference of opinion arises between Farmer and the studio over alterations in the release version of the picture. The director attempts to steal the negative of the film but, in the process, is shot and killed by the police.

In a bizarre but hilarious episode, Farmer's drinking buddies, Tim Culley (William Holden), Dr. Irving Finegarten (Robert Preston), and Ben Coogan (Robert Webber), steal his body from the mortuary for one last round of drinks. Curiously, this sequence is reminiscent of an earlier scene in *W. C. Fields and Me* (1977), in which a similar theft took place featuring actor John Barrymore's body being propped up in a chair with a drink in its hand. Other sources are equally convinced that such an occurrence actually took place, involving the body of Errol Flynn. Thus, Edwards is tapping a body of well-established though ghoulish Hollywood folklore in the construction of this scene. At the film's conclusion, Farmer's buddies burn his body and set it adrift at sea in a Viking-style funeral while a substitute body is being laid to rest miles away in a lavish Hollywood rite.

In a large sense, the greatest achievement of *S.O.B.* is that Edwards has managed to depict a personal vision within an industry which cannot afford such individual psychological excursions. For Federico Fellini to perpetrate an *8½* (1963) or François Truffaut to construct a *400 Blows* (1959) is one thing—they have financial arrangements to support their explorations—but for a Hollywood director to pull off a similar accomplishment within a structure obsessed with making enormous profits is quite another. With perhaps the single exception of Bob Fosse's *All That Jazz* (1979), *S.O.B.* is the only such personalized mainstream film to be both a financial and a critical success.

Yet, although Edwards' protagonist Felix Farmer is depicted as a martyr, the director is surprisingly unsympathetic in his treatment of him. Farmer is not sacred. He is a victim, but one who can be as cold and vicious as the Hollywood society with which he is in conflict, as witnessed by his willingness to expose his wife's breasts to the world for the sole purpose of making his film a financial success. To what extent Edwards himself might be considered guilty of the same charge is conjectural, although there is undoubtedly a certain attraction among filmgoers approaching their fortieth birthday at the prospect of seeing "Mary Poppins" bare her breasts. Yet this fact also reveals one of the few major weaknesses of *S.O.B.* Its very act of debunking the Mary Poppins image also serves to date it. The Disney film and its successor *The Sound of Music* are rooted in the 1960's and represent a type of picture that has not been made in years and probably would not be believable today. In this respect, the satire of *S.O.B.* is no longer relevant.

On the other hand, the film's potshots at large-budget Hollywood extravaganzas are uniquely up to date when one remembers the debacles of *The Sorcerer* (1979), *Heaven's Gate* (1981), and, of course, Edwards' own *Darling Lili*. He does not spare himself in his criticism of this mode of filmmaking. Similarly, one receives the impression that a significant number of the actors and actresses in the cast were also quite joyfully satirizing Hollywood characters with whom they were all too familiar. William Holden, for example plays the studio troubleshooter with a zest reminiscent of his role in *Network* (1976), in which he also portrayed a man walking a tightrope between artistry and financial concerns. Robert Preston is convincing as the "shoot from the hip" (with a drug-laden hypodermic needle) show-business doctor, as is Richard Mulligan as the producer-director-writer. Shelley Winters, Stuart Margolin, and Loretta Swift (playing a gossip columnist) are strong in support. Because of these powerful supporting performances, the viewer is not troubled by the lack of a central focus after Farmer's death or by the fact that Julie Andrews is not on the screen for any significant length of time and is primarily reacting to other characters in most of her brief appearances. She does, however, display hints of the fire she flashed in *The Americanization of Emily*, a spirit which fully surfaces in 1982's *Victor/Victoria*, Edwards' third consecutive screen triumph.

S.O.B. is a film that will increase in stature as time goes on. While Edwards will, in the short term, be best remembered for the Pink Panther series and others of its ilk, *S.O.B.* is his comic and cynical *8½* and will yield much more of its richness to future generations of film students.

Stephen L. Hanson

Reviews

The Hollywood Reporter. June 22, 1981, p. 5.
Los Angeles Times. June 28, 1981, *Calendar*, p. 21.
The New Republic. CLXXXV, July 18, 1981, pp. 26-27.
The New York Times. July 1, 1981, III, p. 21.
The New York Times. August 16, 1981, II, p. 20.
Saturday Review. VIII, July, 1981, pp. 84-85.
Variety. June 22, 1981, p. 3.

SOUTHERN COMFORT

Production: David Giler for Twentieth Century-Fox
Direction: Walter Hill
Screenplay: Michael Kane, Walter Hill, and David Giler
Cinematography: Andrew Laszlo
Editing: Freeman Davies
Art direction: John Vallone
Music: Ry Cooder
MPAA rating: R
Running time: 95 minutes

Principal characters:

Spencer .... Keith Carradine
Hardin .... Powers Boothe
Reece .... Fred Ward
Simms .... Franklyn Seales
Cribbs .... T. K. Carter
Stuckey .... Lewis Smith
Casper .... Les Lannom
Poole .... Peter Coyote
Bowden .... Carlos Brown
Trapper .... Brion James

Southern Comfort is both a devastating action film and an unnerving metaphor for the Vietnam experience. Directed by Walter Hill, who has called the film "a moral tale with an ambiguous morality," it is a wrenching story of survival, set in the winter of 1973 in the gloomy Louisiana bayou. The plot is simple yet has far-reaching implications. Nine indifferent National Guardsmen go on maneuvers in the swampland. When they come upon a body of water that is not detailed on their maps, they decide to facilitate their journey by "borrowing" canoes found at a deserted Cajun campsite. (Though they leave a note, in all probability the Cajuns cannot read English.) When the Cajuns return in time to see the Guardsmen leaving with their canoes, they respond with irate yells. Reacting to their anger, one of the Guardsmen—a prankster—jokingly raises his rifle, firing blanks at the Cajuns. This gesture is misunderstood by the Cajuns, who retaliate with real bullets, killing the squadron leader. At this point, *Southern Comfort* becomes a study of men caught up in a bloody, senseless battle. After losing their canoes and their supplies—including the compass—the Guardsmen become the prey of the vengeful Cajuns.

Faced with a cunning enemy who is at home—rather than at odds—with the alien environment, the Guardsmen, once depicted as a group, now break up into disparate personalities. Only the strong and the calm will ultimately survive; a fact that lends dark irony to the film's title. (*Deliverance*, 1972, similar in tone and subject to *Southern Comfort*, also has a smirking irony, since it delivers its adventurers into the hands of evil—not away from it.) Among the men, most of whom are not prepared for the life-or-death struggle, Spencer (Keith Carradine) and Hardin (Powers Boothe) quickly prove dominant. They are also a study in contrasts. Spencer, who works in a bank, is easygoing and able to remain cool in the face of mounting pandemonium. He is also glib and unruffled by the shortcomings of his buddies. As he tells Hardin, there is more to the Southern mentality than moon pies and RC Colas. Hardin, however, has nothing but disdain for the men. A newcomer to the unit, he is a loner whose job as a chemical engineer has returned him, unwillingly, to his Southern roots. As such, he regards his blue-collar acquaintances with smirking disapproval.

Among them is three-stripe sergeant Casper (Les Lannom), a by-the-book military man who is sadly out of step with the no-rules game that ensues. Rifleman Reece (Fred Ward), a hotheaded soldier-of-fortune type, carries live ammunition, even though it is forbidden. He is dangerously out of place with the unit, as is Rifleman Bowden (Carlos Brown), whose authoritarian personality causes a rift with the men. The unit also includes Cribbs (T. K. Carter), who regularly uses marijuana to keep a safe distance from reality, and Simms (Franklyn Seales), a black struggling to overcome the prejudice which threatens his personal life and even his personality.

The unit's men are stalked by the Cajuns until, finally, only Spencer and Hardin are left alive. Bonded by a growing rapport as well as by their all-consuming passion to stay alive, the two men are briefly befriended by a Cajun who directs them to the highway. The men are still being savagely hunted when they at last encounter what appears to be a National Guard truck (in military green) and—presumably—safety. The film ends with freeze frame images of the men, who are weary from a war that saw neither winners or losers. Some critics have felt that the freeze frame is ambiguous, but the director has said that he intended it as a positive ending.

The film's war is based upon the succinct notion that once a man invades another man's territory, and guns are drawn, the battle escalates. A highly manipulative film, *Southern Comfort* draws its horrors not only from the war that develops between men, but also from the eerie surroundings. The environment becomes yet another "adversary" for the Guardsmen.

Though most of the film has a relentless tone, the mood shifts drastically when Spencer and Hardin come upon a celebration in a Cajun village. Though they are clearly out of place, the two men freely move about, enjoying a quick drink and even a dance. The gathering, however, is not without grim realities for them when they watch as a hog is shot, bled, and gutted (graphically detailed for the cameras) during the festivities. The colorful celebration sequence ends in bloodshed when the Cajun trackers appear. Still, the scene gives the film a semblance of humanity; for a brief while, there is a respite from killing, and while the celebrating Cajuns are not welcoming friends, neither are they enemies.

Directed in the economical, high-energy style that Walter Hill developed in earlier efforts such as *The Warriors* (1979), *Southern Comfort* is a triumph of visual imagery. Filmed with all natural light, to evoke the severity of a bleak winter, the film employs muted tones of grays, greens and browns which never dispel the film's somber tone. Director of photography Andrew Laszlo has said that he visualized the film through the eyes of David Douglas Duncan, the noted *Life* magazine war photographer. Laszlo was particularly impressed by one Korean War photograph by Duncan which depicted a "battle-weary Marine who must have been in the fields for weeks and weeks, he looked just totally spent. Because of the grainy quality of the photograph, you could hardly see this man's eyes because of the underexposure of his face which was created by the light above his helmet." Photographs such as this helped dictate the look of the film, Laszlo has said.

With its look at characters within a group dealing with confrontation, *Southern Comfort* is related to Hill's *The Warriors* and *The Long Riders* (1980). That the film also works as a metaphor for war was the quality which displeased the studios when the script was being offered to various studios in 1976. At the time, says Hill, complaints ranged from the fact that the film was "too masculine" (because there are no women's roles), to a belief that the script was an allegory of the war in Vietnam ("a verboten subject at the time," Hill has recalled). A one-time assistant director, Hill began writing scripts—mostly action-oriented—in the early 1970's. He made his directorial debut in 1975 with the Charles Bronson vehicle *Hard Times*, a saga about Depression-era bare-knuckled fighting, which he also coauthored. *The Driver*, a *film noir* melodrama starring Ryan O'Neal, followed in 1978. Hill's next effort was the controversial, near-surrealistic look at gang warfare, *The Warriors*. When violence allegedly broke out at the theaters where the film screened, resulting in three deaths said to have been inspired by the film, it made headlines. It also gave Hill a reputation for films depicting stylized violence. He coproduced the 1979 science-fiction-horror blockbuster, *Alien*, and also wrote and directed *The Long Riders*, a Western that attempts to strip the glossy legend from the lives of the James and Younger brothers.

Interestingly, although *The Long Riders* is Hill's only Western, he has agreed that all of his works are essentially within that genre's mold. Explains Hill, "They tend to be about simple, narrative problems and they tend to have a kind of moral sense behind them." Indeed, though many critics compared *Southern Comfort* to an updating of *The Lost Patrol* (1934), Hill has said that he views his own story as one with Western overtones.

The writer-director has also argued that *Southern Comfort* is primarily an ensemble piece, even though nearly all critics agreed that Keith Carradine and Powers Boothe rapidly took over the film in characterization and delivery. With his surly, sensual presence, Boothe especially received critical plaudits. After extensive experience in the theater, Boothe first made a name for himself when he won a 1980 Emmy award for his portrayal of cult leader Jim Jones in the television movie, *The Guyana Tragedy*. He also attained celebrity status when he was the only performer to take the stage and accept that award, even though there was at that time a highly emotional boycott of the ceremonies within the Hollywood community.

With its all-male cast and war-games saga, and its extremely abrasive dialogue, riddled with four-letter expletives, *Southern Comfort* has the look and sound of the so-called "man's picture." Thematically, though, this film transcends the "macho" mentality. A significant film which made numerous "Ten Best" lists, *Southern Comfort* brings together terse storytelling, evocative cinematic embellishments, and bloodshed for a grim appraisal of men haphazardly courting survival. The film had its inception when Hill directed *Hard Times*, which utilized New Orleans locales—including a colorful picnic fish fry which featured the region's Cajuns. Long interested in their music (which Ry Cooder stunningly creates for the *Southern Comfort* sound track), Hill wanted to work with them again. He has said, "The last thing the movie is supposed to be is some kind of indictment against Cajun folkways. . . . I wanted the Cajuns because their separate culture builds the contrasts better." *Southern Comfort*, which depicts an indigenous group lashing out against "invaders," is a technically superb film with a timely metaphorical message. Not merely a "Vietnam film," it should slowly win the following it deserves.

Pat H. Broeske

Reviews

The Hollywood Reporter. September 25, 1981, p. 3.
Los Angeles Times. September 26, 1981, II, p. 3.
The New York Times. September 25, 1981, III, p. 20.
The New Yorker. LVII, November 23, 1981, pp. 176-178.
Newsweek. XCVIII, October 5, 1981, p. 78.
Variety. September 25, 1981, p. 3.

STRIPES

Production: Ivan Reitman and Dan Goldberg for Columbia
Direction: Ivan Reitman
Screenplay: Len Blum, Dan Goldberg, and Harold Ramis
Cinematography: Bill Butler
Editing: Eva Ruggiero, Michael Luciano, and Harry Keller
Art direction: James Spencer
Music: Elmer Bernstein
MPAA rating: R
Running time: 105 minutes

Principal characters:

John	Bill Murray
Russell	Harold Ramis
Sergeant Hulka	Warren Oates
Stella	P. J. Soles
Louise	Sean Young
Ox	John Candy
Latino recruit	Antone Pagen
Psycho	Conrad Dunn
Cruiser	Lance LeGault

Stripes is a military comedy, a form that, in cinema, dates back at least to Charlie Chaplin's *Shoulder Arms* (1918) and includes films featuring Bob Hope, Jerry Lewis, Laurel and Hardy, and Abbott and Costello, among dozens of other stars. The chance to be funny by introducing disarray, ineptness, or lunacy into the required discipline and order of the military has beckoned comedians for decades. A more recent inspiration for *Stripes* may well have been the great box-office success of *Private Benjamin* (1980), which featured Goldie Hawn as a misfit in the Army.

In addition to its basic premise, *Stripes* also brought together two other elements that promised a successful film. Its star is Bill Murray, who developed a large following as a result of his work on the television show "Saturday Night Live" and subsequently enhanced his popularity in the film *Meatballs* (1980). The film's co-star, and one of the writers of *Stripes*, Harold Ramis, had earlier been one of the cowriters of *Animal House* (1978), another box-office hit. The collaboration of these two talents was productive, and *Stripes* emerged as the fifth-highest grossing film of 1981.

The first section of the film establishes the situation that causes its two protagonists to join the army, since one of the staples of military comedy is the character who does not really belong in the service. That character's conflict with the army's way of doing things provides much of the humor. In

1981, the draft no longer existed, so the writers had to find a reason for the characters to enlist voluntarily. In the beginning of the film, the audience is introduced to John (Bill Murray), ostensibly a taxicab driver, albeit a singularly unambitious and unsuccessful one. He spends most of his time watching television, but when he does drive his taxi, he is inordinately unlucky in his choice of fares. Some of them run away without paying, and one is a dowager with an imperious and impatient manner as well as several impossibly heavy pieces of luggage. John finally responds to her demands by stopping the taxi on a bridge and then throwing away the keys. Before the day is over, however, he has lost his own car as well as his girl friend. When his friend Russell (Harold Ramis) comes to visit him, he is watching a television commercial soliciting enlistments for the Army. He decides that military service is his only chance and even convinces his friend, a none-too-successful teacher of English to foreign students, to enlist with him.

Murray portrays John as incompetent and almost contemptible yet not without a certain charm, a combination that had caused his girl friend to stay with him for six months before leaving him even though she had a long list of perfectly understandable complaints. This dichotomy is essential to the success of the film. If John is portrayed as merely a worthless bum, as the lady in the taxi calls him, virtually nothing that he does in the film will seem funny.

Once John and Russell are immersed in basic training, they must contend with a tough drill sergeant named Hulka (played by veteran character actor Warren Oates, in his last film role). Russell accommodates himself fairly well to the military routine, but John continually comes into conflict with the Sergeant. The conflicts, however, are curiously inconsequential. Hulka is nearly as sympathetic a character as is John, and the audience does not merely applaud one and hate the other.

John and Russell are supported by the usual mix of ethnic types as the other recruits. Few of them have major roles except for Ox (John Candy), the huge young man who joins the Army to lose weight and to learn aggression. Others include a Latino (Antone Pagan), a hostile trainee who informs everyone that he is called Psycho (Conrad Dunn), and a dim-witted recruit (Lance LeGault) who is continually victimized by the others. In addition, there are two female M.P.'s, Stella (P. J. Soles) and Louise (Sean Young), who find John and Russell irresistible. The M.P.'s not only get them out of trouble several times but also join them in their most outrageous escapades.

In a service comedy of this nature, the hero usually achieves some sort of victory over the army or the tough sergeant. *Stripes* is no exception. After almost six weeks of basic training, Sergeant Hulka is knocked out of action by an errant artillery shell and the entire company is subsequently caught in a police raid on a nightclub where Ox is engaged in a furious mud-wrestling contest with a group of seminaked young women. As punishment, the company is told that if it does not perform perfectly the next day at graduation it will have to repeat all of basic training. John gives them a wild pep talk, after which they practice all night. They almost oversleep, but rush to the graduation ceremonies at the last moment to perform a drill exercise that is, in the words of the *Los Angeles Times* reviewer, "so precise in its goofiness that it has to be seen to be disbelieved."

It becomes a victory of sorts for John because the commanding officer is so impressed with their "go-getter" spirit that he assigns the whole company to his top project, the testing of the EM-50 Urban Assault Vehicle. At this point, however, the film loses most of what little momentum it had. The group is sent to Italy, where they see the EM-50, a sort of armored recreation vehicle with a multitude of James Bond inspired features. John and Russell "borrow" the vehicle to visit their girl friends, Stella and Louise, who are now in Germany. The rest of the company sets off to find them before the Army discovers what has happened. The company's truck accidentally goes into Czechoslovakia, however, and all aboard are taken prisoner. John, Russell, and the M.P.'s learn what has happened and rush to the aid of the others in a mad last-minute rescue that employs all of the vehicle's amazing gadgets. The film ends with the major characters returning to the United States, where each one is featured in a newspaper headline or on a magazine cover. One of the M.P.'s, for example, is shown on the cover of *Penthouse*, and John is portrayed on the cover of a *Newsweek*-like magazine with the caption "The New Army: Can America Survive?"

The director of *Stripes*, Ivan Reitman, makes the film unnecessarily diffuse and often shows his lack of knowledge of effective camera placement. Reitman, however, had also directed Murray in *Meatballs* and found that, in this sort of comedy, financial success has nothing to do with artistic nuances. Although the critical reaction to *Stripes* was mixed, the popular reception was so enthusiastic that the film brought in more than forty million dollars.

Sharon Wiseman

Reviews

The Hollywood Reporter. Junc 15, 1981, p. 3.
Los Angeles Times. June 26, 1981, VI, p. 1.
The New York Times. June 26, 1981, III, p. 16.
The New York Times. August 9, 1981, II, p. 20.
The New Yorker. LVII, July 13, 1981, pp. 82-83.
Variety. June 15, 1981, p. 3.

SUPERMAN II

Production: Ilya Salkind and Pierre Spengler for Warner Bros.
Direction: Richard Lester
Screenplay: Mario Puzo, David Newman, and Leslie Newman; based on an original story by Mario Puzo and the comic strip characters by Jerry Siegel and Joe Shuster
Cinematography: Geoffrey Unsworth
Editing: John Victor Smith
Production design: John Barry and Peter Murton
Art direction: Maurice Fowler, Charles Bishop, Terry Ackland-Snow, Norman Reynolds, and Ernest Archer
Music: Hans Wittstadt
MPAA rating: PG
Running time: 127 minutes

Principal characters:

Superman/Clark Kent	Christopher Reeve
Lois Lane	Margot Kidder
Lex Luthor	Gene Hackman
General Zod	Terence Stamp
Perry White	Jackie Cooper
Non	Jack O'Halloran
Ursa	Sarah Douglas
Otis	Ned Beatty
Eve Teschmacher	Valerie Perrine
The President	E. G. Marshall

Superman II ranks with *The Godfather, Part II* (1974) and *The Empire Strikes Back* (1980) as one of the most successful sequels ever made. While not an Academy Award-winner such as *The Godfather, Part II*, it made an almost successful run at becoming the largest grossing film in motion picture history. Only *Star Wars* (1977), *The Empire Strikes Back* (1980), and two recent blockbusters, *Raiders of the Lost Ark* (1981) and 1982's *E.T.: The Extra Terrestrial*, rank ahead of it in popular appeal, a ranking that may be revised again with *Superman II*'s 1982 re-release to pave the way for *Superman III* in the summer of 1983.

Superman II's predecessor, the long-awaited *Superman The Movie*, did not fare well at the hands of film critics, largely because it was pieced together from the work of a succession of screenwriters and production personnel who came and went, leaving their individual imprints on certain segments of the movie. Yet the picture did phenomenally well at the box office, enthralling audiences with a variety of dazzling special effects.

Superman II did not suffer the constraints of having to conform to a legend well-known to every American over the age of six. Homage had already been paid and the sequel was thus free to create a new legend in virtually any direction that it desired. Indeed, some of the directions proved to be rather startling to many of Superman's devoted fans. Whereas the original had concentrated on the character of Superman, its successor attempted to delineate more fully the character of Clark Kent (Christopher Reeve), depicting a fairly believable image of a man caught in an identity crisis. The woman that he loves, Lois Lane (Margot Kidder), is enamored of one side of him, thinking that aspect to be a separate individual. She has, in fact, very little respect for the side of him that she sees every day—in the guise of Clark Kent.

The inevitable result is that the man of steel must violate the conditions of his immortality to fulfill his emotional needs. In revealing himself to Lois Lane and subsequently going to bed with her, he is shorn of his powers much like the biblical Samson at the hands of Delilah. He becomes human and vulnerable. While the idea of Superman losing his virginity might shock purists, there is nothing in the comic books strictly precluding this occurrence.

Up to the midpoint in the film, the newly mortal Superman has no reason to regret his decision. His life soon becomes quickly complicated, however, by the appearance of three super villains who, like himself, have survived the destruction of the planet Krypton. In *Superman The Movie*, General Zod (Terence Stamp), Non (Jack O'Halloran), and Ursa (Sarah Douglas) are imprisoned in an octagonal prismlike structure and left to drift in space for eternity. A hydrogen bomb explosion at the outset of *Superman II* frees them, though, and they descend to the earth with the idea of taking it over.

As if that were not enough, Superman's nemesis, Lex Luthor (Gene Hackman), escapes from prison and joins forces with the malevolent trio, who proceed to capture the President of the United States and take over the White House, leaving a path of destruction in their wake. During all of this, Superman is mysteriously absent and, as a matter of fact, totally oblivious to the situation, concentrating as he is on his affair with Lois Lane. Returning with her, however, from his "fortress of solitude" situated somewhere in the Arctic, he quickly becomes aware of the state of affairs and of his limited physical resources after he is beaten up by a truck driver in a diner.

He returns to the Arctic (no mean feat since he is now human and has to walk) and mysteriously regains his power by some means which the audience never learns. He then arrives in Metropolis, which is in the process of being destroyed by the three supervillains. After a fight that must rank as one of the most destructive in motion picture history, enhanced by almost unbelievable special effects, the "man of steel" flies away feeling lucky to escape with a draw. His three opponents hold Lois Lane hostage, knowing that he must, at some point, reappear to rescue her.

Before this can happen, Lex Luthor, who earlier in the film had accidentally discovered the location of Superman's "fortress of solitude," leads his comrades there. Superman, however, is waiting for them and another special-effect-laden battle occurs, again ending in a draw. The supervillains then play their trump card—Superman's feelings for Lois. By threatening her life they force him to enter a machine that will strip him of his powers. Fortunately, though, he has secretly rewired the machine to transmit its effect outside. Thus, while he watches in complete safety, his enemies are stripped of their unearthly abilities and are easily dispatched by Superman and an angry Lois. As the film concludes, Luthor is again returned to prison and Superman causes Lois to forget his secret identity through some sort of superhypnosis. He has presumably learned his lesson and is resigned to the loneliness of his role as protector of the earth, as there is little hope of Lois loving Clark. In the film's final scene, Superman flies through the sky carrying the American flag and assuring the nation that he is indeed back on the job.

Superman II, despite its occasional loss of credibility, possesses a cohesiveness that its predecessor lacked. It continues the story logically and bridges the gap to its successor, yet it is a self-contained narrative that can stand solidly on its own. It does lack believability in certain scenes, such as when Superman regains his powers after a significant amount of screen time had earlier been expended explaining that once lost, his abilities could never be regained. On the whole, though, its lapses of credibility are not as great as similar ones in *Raiders of the Lost Ark*.

In such films, deficiencies of this nature are overlooked amidst dazzling special effects, plot twists, tongue-in-cheek acting, and firm direction. *Superman II* possesses all of these. Its spectacular battle scenes will probably never be topped for sheer brilliance and execution. The only technically weak scene is one in which the "man of steel" rescues a boy from the torrents of Niagara Falls. It is obviously a superimposition of one film upon another and not a good one at that, but that is the only flaw in a rather sophisticated package.

Christopher Reeve is boyishly marvelous and believable in the role of Superman and gives promise of better performances to come—a potential that is fast becoming realized in his 1982 vehicles, *Monsignor* and *Deathtrap*. Margot Kidder is also perfect as Lois Lane and portrays her with exactly the right blend of vulnerability and cleverness. Yet it is Gene Hackman who almost steals the film from the principals. One might well wonder if he imported his own writer to conceive of one-liners for Lex Luthor. Time after time, he uses the physically superior supervillains for his foils and in doing so points up the pretentiousness and absurdity of their grandiose scheme.

All of these interacting special effects and tongue-in-cheek acting techniques are presided over by that veteran ringmaster, dirctor Richard Lester, who obviously approached the project in the same irreverent spirit which animated his immensely successful *The Three Musketeers* (1974). He is a master of quick plot-shifts and changes in tone from comedy to pathos and back again at a moment's notice. *Superman II* has become, in his hands, a superb entertainment that will stand up to many repeated viewings in the years to come. It maintains the same light demeanor as the later James Bond films and, like them, makes few demands upon its audience. By the time the series is completed, if the other entrants measure up to the high standards established by Lester and his crew, it could be the most phenomenally successful enterprise in the history of film.

Grant Davidson

Reviews

The Hollywood Reporter. December 3, 1980, p. 2.
Los Angeles Times. June 18, 1981, VI, p. 1.
The New York Times. June 19, 1981, III, p. 8.
The New Yorker. LVII, July 13, 1981, pp. 81-82.
Newsweek. XCVII, June 22, 1981, p. 87.
Time. CXVII, June 8, 1981, pp. 74-75.
Variety. December 3, 1980, p. 22.

TAPS

Production: Stanley R. Jaffe and Howard B. Jaffe for Twentieth Century-Fox
Direction: Harold Becker
Screenplay: Darryl Ponicsan and Robert Mark Kamen; based on James Lineberger's adaptation of the novel *Father Sky* by Devery Freeman
Cinematography: Owen Roizman
Editing: Maury Winetrobe
Art direction: Stan Jolley and Alfred Sweeney
Music: Maurice Jarre
MPAA rating: PG
Running time: 118 minutes

Principal characters:

General Harlan Bache .... George C. Scott
Brian Moreland .... Timothy Hutton
Colonel Kerby .... Ronny Cox
David Shawn .... Tom Cruise
Charlie .... Brendan Ward
Master Sergeant Kevin Moreland ..... Wayne Trippett

Bunker Hill Military Academy, the fictional setting of *Taps*, is a 150-year-old institution which has trained young men for participation in all of America's wars in the twentieth century. Despite its venerable tradition, the Academy faces extinction. Its Board of Trustees has decided to sell the grounds to a real estate developer who plans to build condominiums there. Thus are drawn the lines of conflict in the film, which depicts the response of a group of the Academy's students to their school's closing. On one side is a tradition-rich but slightly anachronistic institution; on the other is the prefabricated commercialism of the 1980's. When the cadets take over the Academy and hold the National Guard at bay, the audience assumes that the film comes down on the side of tradition. Yet when we realize that that tradition is embodied in the pompous General Harlan Bache (George C. Scott), headmaster of the Academy, we are not so sure.

Clearly the film's message is not simple. Life at Bunker Hill Military Academy exhibits a number of attractive features. For example, the film's opening scene—perhaps the most effective in *Taps*—depicts a fairly moving ceremony: a roll call of former students who died in combat preceded by a robust singing of "Onward, Christian Soldiers." Such ceremonies, steeped in tradition, seem to be a point of real pride for the cadets, who feel genuine kinship with their deceased predecessors. Also, the Academy's programs seem successful in providing a basis for maturation and education, since several graduating cadets announce plans to attend West Point. Moreover, the camaraderie which develops among cadets from disparate backgrounds provides them with a true sense of belonging. The Academy has much to recommend it.

These positive features are undermined, however—perhaps even demolished—by the hollow militarism of General Bache. A former cadet at the Academy, Bache has been in uniform since he was twelve years old. Fond of quoting Theodore Roosevelt's manly philosophy and displaying a macho disregard for his doctor's injunction against smoking too many cigars, he exhibits what amounts to virtual paranoia in his perception of a military/civilian dichotomy. In particular, he views the military generally—and Bunker Hill Military Academy specifically—as the ultimate citadel of Honor, the one thing that never changes "in a world where Honor is held in contempt." His insistence on the importance of Honor, which he never clearly defines, pervades the world view of the Academy's cadets, and becomes the rallying point in their take-over of the Academy. General Bache is an object of hero worship for many of the cadets, especially Brian Moreland (Timothy Hutton), who has recently been selected as Cadet Major. When Bache announces the Academy's impending sale during commencement exercises, he insists that the action will mean "an end to the heart of us" and emphasizes that the Academy's supporters "must fight to preserve" it. His rhetoric is taken all too literally by Brian, for after Bache accidentally shoots a "townie" during an altercation with the cadets, Brian leads a number of the cadets in a fight to preserve Bache's misguided principles of Honor.

The failure of *Taps* to articulate a clear stance detracts from its effect. Clearly, the Academy has much to recommend it, yet just as clearly, something about the Academy has fostered the attitudes of Bache, who was educated there and who has presumably enjoyed a relatively long tenure as headmaster. What is not clear is whether the film condemns Bache the individual, who mesmerizes impressionable adolescents; his vague, but high-sounding philosophy; or the institution which has provided an environment for the man and his ideas.

Another weakness of *Taps* is the stereotyped characterization of General Bache. He emerges too predictably as a stock militarist with the requisite insecurities to account for his posturings. Scott's portrayal of Bache draws upon his previous work. His performance combines the broad satire of his depiction of Jack D. Ripper in *Dr. Strangelove* (1964) and his more serious characterization in *Patton* (1969). The combination, though, results in a figure who projects no true individuality.

Since General Bache disappears with a heart attack before the film is half finished, the focus of *Taps* is on Cadet Major Brian Moreland. Hutton's role recalls his Academy Award-winning performance in *Ordinary People* (1980). Once again, he is a sensitive young man with misapplied sensitivity. For example, Brian recalls to a fellow cadet how when his mother died, his father, Master Sergeant Kevin Moreland (Wayne Trippett), had allowed him only a short time to cry. The repressed emotions and the need for an understanding father result in Brian's adoration of Bache, which approaches reverence when he is selected as leader of the cadets and will consequently have opportunity for personal interaction with the Academy's headmaster. His worship of the General and wholehearted acceptance of the creed of Honor motivate Brian to lead the take-over of the Academy. The film, though, attempts to portray Brian as a dynamic character, for he does change his mind drastically about Honor when Charlie (Brendan Ward), a young cadet, is killed in some cross fire between the cadets and the National Guard: "Honor doesn't count for shit when you're looking at a dead eight-year-old boy." Although some preparation for Brian's change of attitude is made when several of the cadets desert the cause and when Brian negotiates with Colonel Kerby (Ronny Cox), commander of the National Guard, the film needs to explore Brian's development more thoroughly to ensure its plausibility. In many ways, Brian Moreland is as predictable a character as Bache or as David Shawn (Tom Cruise), the gung-ho cadet who precipitates the film's predictable ending. Hutton's appearance in the film accounts for most of its relative success at the box office, for he apparently has an established coterie of fans among adolescent girls, traditionally an important group of ticket buyers.

Critical response to *Taps* was decidedly negative in the press (although not among the television critics). The film fails to develop its real potential: the lack of clearly defined sides to the conflict could have resulted in a statement about the problematic choice between good and evil; the psychological development of Brian Moreland could have been articulated in a meaningful way; a message about the interrelationships between ego and authority as evidenced in General Bache's behavior could have been presented. *Taps* fails, however, to take full advantage of these possibilities. Neither does it allow a competent cast to extend their characterizations beyond stereotypes. The interesting aspects of *Taps* cannot compensate for its weaknesses.

Frances M. Malpezzi
William M. Clements

Reviews

The Hollywood Reporter. December 9, 1981, p. 8.
Los Angeles Times. December 18, 1981, VI, p. 3.
The New York Times. December 9, 1981, III, p. 28.
Newsweek. XCVIII, December 28, 1981, p. 65.
Time. CXVIII, December 14, 1981, p. 94.
Variety. December 9, 1981, p. 3.

TAXI ZUM KLO
(TAXI TO THE TOILET)

Origin: Germany
Production: Frank Ripploh, Horst Schier, and Laurens Straub; released by International Films, Lts.
Direction: Frank Ripploh
Screenplay: Frank Ripploh
Cinematography: Horst Schier and Johannes Geyer
Editing: Gela-Marina Runne and Mathias von Gunten
Art direction: no listing
Music: Hans Wittstadt
Running time: 92 minutes

Principal characters:
Frank .... Frank Ripploh
Bernd .... Bernd Broaderup

It is a chiché, albeit true, that Hollywood works in cycles. *Star Wars* (1977) generated a plethora of space films, and the success of the bloody and violent shocker *Halloween* (1978) has spawned countless gory imitations. In 1982, several films with a homosexual theme have been released, partly as a result of the financial success of the French-made *La Cage aux Folles* (1979). Most of the films in the cycle have improved on the farcical depiction of the homosexual life-style in that film. The slick, bland characterizations in *Making Love* (1982), the witty and charming humanity of the principles in *Victor/Victoria* (1982), and the matter-of-fact lesbian romance in *Personal Best* (1982) all contrast favorably with the stereotyped drag queen in *La Cage aux Folles*. The most accurate depiction so far of a gay life-style, however, has been made by a German film director, Frank Ripploh. It is no coincidence that *Taxi Zum Klo* is also the first film intended for mainstream theaters to contain explicit scenes of sex between men. Controversial for many reasons, the film is also a funny, endearing, sometimes shocking, and always unblinking portrayal of its all-too-human protagonist.

The film stars Ripploh the writer (who is also the coproducer) in a re-creation of events in his life in the months preceding the making of the film. It begins with a close-up of Ripploh's naked posterior as he rises and begins his preparations for the day. When he accidentally locks himself out of his apartment while still naked, he must wake up his neighbor in order to crawl over her balcony and back into his apartment. After brushing his teeth and solving the minor crisis of no toilet paper, Frank arrives at the school where he teaches. He uses the incident of being locked out to begin the lesson for the day. It is obvious that he is an effective teacher, and that he likes the children as much as they like him. On the way home in the evening, Frank writes the phone number of a gas station attendant he admires on the back of a student's essay. He then goes to a public restroom where he grades papers in one of the stalls while hoping to make sexual contact with other men using the facility.

We next see Frank bowling with other teachers from the school as a voice-over narration identifies the English teacher, the physical-education instructor, and the teachers of math and science. We overhear snippets of conversations, jokes, gossip, and propositions as the scene is intercut with scenes from a heterosexual pornographic film. Frank leaves the bowling alley and goes to a theater, where he meets the shy manager, Bernd (Bernd Broaderup). Frank offers Bernd a ride, which leads to a sexual encounter in Frank's bathtub. The men are interrupted by a hysterical woman who bursts into the apartment pleading to be protected from her angry boyfriend. Bernd calls the feminist helpline while Frank calms the woman. Their first sexual experience has been aborted, but their relationship begins.

In a series of short scenes, we learn that Bernd yearns to leave Berlin and purchase a small farm. He is attracted to a simple bucolic life and is repelled by the unhealthy atmosphere of the city. We then watch Frank conducting a class in anatomy and coping with a parent who attempts to bribe him in order to improve her daughter's grades. On his way home, Frank picks up a very masculine-appearing man dressed in leather. When Bernd arrives home, Frank and the other man are having sex, and Bernd watches in obvious discomfort. Afterward, Frank is upset that Bernd did not join them, and does not understand Bernd's pain. Yet, in a later sequence, as Frank drives to his doctor, he muses about the dilemma of loving Bernd while needing sex with other men. At the doctor's, Frank learns that he has a venereal disease.

Another segment shows Wally, a drag-queen friend, visiting Frank and meeting Bernd for the first time. While Frank tutors a student in the kitchen, Bernd deflects Wally's attempted seduction by showing a sex education film that Frank has brought home from school. The film shows a young boy resisting the advances of a middle-aged man, while in the kitchen Frank firmly refuses the student's subtle attempts to seduce him.

Frank is next hospitalized with hepatitis. In spite of his illness, he leaves the hospital, hires a taxi, and goes from one restroom to another seeking sex. He contacts a man who is interested until he discovers the hospital gown under Frank's street clothes. Back home Frank and Bernd fight over Bernd's desire to have an orderly life and home-cooked meals. Frank resists Bernd's attempts to domesticate him, and insists on his right to come and go as he pleases. Later Frank meets the gas station attendant in a restroom, and they arrange a date. Shortly thereafter Frank visits the English teacher from the school, and as they discuss her furniture and her desire to travel, the scene is intercut with Frank's violent sexual encounter with the attendant.

In the final episode of the film, Frank, dressed as a harem girl in a filmy pink costume, and Bernd, dressed as a sailor, go to a costume ball. Frank dances all night with a stable boy, causing Bernd considerable jealousy and pain, and provokes their final argument in a subway. Bernd leaves to wander through the zoo, where he finds comfort by hugging a lamb. Frank, still in costume, goes to his class, which quickly dissolves in chaos. At home, as he begins to remove his makeup, an ending title tells us that Frank subsequently lost his teaching job, whereupon he began making the film that we have just seen.

Director/writer Ripploh is very careful to establish that his film is about an individual gay male who does not represent all homosexual men, yet most homosexual men living in America or Western Europe will recognize the milieu of Ripploh's film if not the isolated incidents. Most gay men do not participate in sadomasochistic rites or the more bizarre forms of sexual expression enjoyed by Ripploh in the film, but many will know someone who does and most are aware that these practices are a part of the subculture. The point of the film is not to sensationalize them, but rather to emphasize that they are just one facet in the life of a man who must cope with all of the problems that everyone deals with regardless of sexual preference. Unlike other films in the "homosexual cycle," *Taxi Zum Klo*, by openly showing sex between men, gives perspective to the role that it plays in the homosexual life-style. It is very important, but it is not all-encompassing. As aggressively sexual as Ripploh is, he also comes across as an excellent teacher, a creative and talented filmmaker, and a warm and loving person who has no answers to the problems that he poses in the film.

All of the actors in the film are nonprofessionals, mostly friends of the director. Bernd Broaderup, in fact, was Ripploh's real-life lover during the period that the film re-creates. The willingness of Broaderup and the others to trust Ripploh in depicting their lives increases the appeal of the film. While Ripploh does not agree with Broaderup's values concerning domesticity, he respects Broaderup's position and does not condemn him in the film. He can call Bernd a "boring wallflower" in their final argument, and then show the tenderness and sensitivity of his ex-lover in contrast to his own more ruthless behavior. Indeed, it is Ripploh's willingness to expose all of his faults—his warts, acne, and selfishness—as well as his more positive qualities that insures the film's success. Ripploh is saying: "This is how I am—take it or leave it." That we take it is a tribute to his wit, charm, honesty, and talent. The financial and critical success of *Taxi Zum Klo* both in Europe and the United States guarantees that we can anticipate further films from this brilliant and innovative man.

Don K Thompson

Reviews

The Hollywood Reporter. October 2, 1981, p. 42.
Los Angeles Times. October 29, 1981, VI, p. 1.
The New Republic. CLXXXV, October 28, 1981, pp. 24-25.
The New York Times. October 2, 1981, III, p. 12.
Newsweek. XCVIII, October 19, 1981, p. 93.
Time. CXVIII, November 2, 1981, p. 115.
Variety. June 10, 1981, p. 21.

THEY ALL LAUGHED

Production: George Morfogen and Blaine Novak for PSO/Moon Pictures
Direction: Peter Bogdanovich
Screenplay: Peter Bogdanovich
Cinematography: Robby Muller
Editing: Scott Vickrey and William Carruth
Art direction: Kert Lundell
Sound: Ray West, Met Metcalfe, Richard Tyler, and Michael Hilkeney
Music direction: Douglas Dilge
Songs: Eric Kaz, Earle Poole Ball, and Peter Bogdanovich
MPAA rating: PG
Running time: 115 minutes

Principal characters:

Angela Niotes .... Audrey Hepburn
John Russo .... Ben Gazzara
Charles Rutledge .... John Ritter
Christy Miller .... Colleen Camp
Sam (Deborah Wilson) .... Patti Hansen
Dolores Martin ....Dorothy Stratten
Arthur Brodsky .... Blaine Novak
Leon Leondopolous .... George Morfogen
Amy Lester .... Linda MacEwen
José ....Sean Ferrer

They All Laughed has the distinction of being one of the only American films of recent years that is entertaining and romantic in the tradition of past Hollywood classics. Like the earlier masters of romantic comedy, writer-director Peter Bogdanovich knows how to keep the stylistic surface light and charming while bringing needed emotional texture and a warm understanding to the often amusing and sometimes poignant relationships among his appealing array of characters. Unlike some earlier Bogdanovich films, *They All Laughed* is resonant of past cinema in a manner that is never self-conscious or overcalculated. If he at times evokes the wit of Ernst Lubitsch or the generosity of Jean Renoir, it is not as a result of misplaced nostalgia but because of a genuine spiritual affinity. Bogdanovich is attuned to the present world, but he wants it to be a world in which the audience will take pleasure. The result is a fantasy guided by emotional truth.

After seven films, beginning with *Targets* (1968), Bogdanovich had grown little as a filmmaker. Demonstrating a rare capacity for self-criticism, he faced and overcame his most serious artistic faults. Although his talent had been a precocious one, his films owed more to other films than to life. This fault was aggravated by the relative coldness of Bogdanovich's personality, which seemed ill-suited to his transparent homages to directors he admired, men such as John Ford and Howard Hawks whose films are infinitely warmer. The lamentable *Nickelodeon* (1976), the last of his youthful films, was especially dispiriting because its subject was the early days of movies, an era for which Bogdanovich undoubtedly has deep feelings. The straining for effect and transparent lack of real energy in this film gave the impression that Bogdanovich's creative gifts were severely limited and virtually used up. However, his next film, *Saint Jack* (1979), which told the story of a colorful Hong Kong hustler and pimp (played by Ben Gazzara), gave evidence that Bogdanovich himself was aware of his previous limitations. His style became more spontaneous, a free-flowing blend of artifice and naturalism. The complex but delicate approach to image and sound in this film was adventurous without seeming contrived or pseudoclassical. Significantly, references to films of other directors are not to be discerned in either the structure or content of *Saint Jack*. Its likable but rather cool and aloof hero seemed very suited to Bogdanovich's sensibility; the film can be considered his first mature work.

They All Laughed has many of the formal beauties of *Saint Jack*, but it is additionally distinguished by the surprising warmth with which Bogdanovich treats the material. His transparent affection for every character is a long way from the chilly calculation with which human interaction was manufactured in earlier films such as *Paper Moon* (1973). No longer attempting to emulate the styles and feelings of others, Bogdanovich is able to relax and be himself. It is particularly instructive to compare *They All Laughed* with Bogdanovich's earlier *At Long Last Love* (1975), his misguided attempt at a sound-stage musical, because both films are about falling in love. In the earlier film, an interesting stylistic experiment sadly devoid of spontaneity or a sense of reality, Bogdanovich forced his actors and actresses into roles for which they were not well-suited and in which they appeared uncomfortable. The characters and the musical numbers which they performed seemed to be perversely willed into a half-life, existing in fully realized form only in Bogdanovich's imagination. *They All Laughed*, on the other hand, was shot on location in New York City, and the characterizations seem to be hand in glove with the personalities of the performers. Ultimately, the more mature film remains as much a projection of Bogdanovich's reveries about love as its predecessor, but in this instance, those reveries take on tangible life from the first frames.

The film is set in contemporary Manhattan and takes place over a period of a few days. The male protagonists, John Russo (Ben Gazzara), Charles Rutledge (John Ritter), and Arthur Brodsky (Blaine Novak), all work for a detective agency run by Leon Leondopolous (George Morfogen). Their jobs involve shadowing women whose husbands suspect them of infidelity. Russo, a ladies' man, is assigned to follow Angela Niotes (Audrey Hepburn), the wife of a millionaire. There is a sadly ironic twist to Angela's situation. The husband's unfounded suspicions are the result of his own infidelities, but as a result of Angela's interaction with the detectives, she and Russo fall in love and have a brief affair. Both Angela and the divorced Russo have children, whose presence in the film not only deepens the emotional history of the two characters but also provides a more meaningful context for the vision of romance which the film articulates. Russo is also involved with two other women during the course of the film. One, Christy Miller (Colleen Camp), is a successful country-and-western singer whom Russo has already begun to neglect at the outset of the film's action. The other, Deborah Wilson (Patti Hansen), a cab driver whom Russo calls Sam, is a stunning redhead who is infatuated with the detective from the moment they meet in the film's early scenes. Once Russo has seen Angela, however, he is captivated by her and the considerable charms of the two younger women have little effect on him. Although he is delineated as a heart-breaker, he is no less susceptible to the pain of love than the other characters. As he himself says, "When you're in love, no one is a pro."

By contrast to both Russo and the carefree and confidant Arthur, Charles is completely unsure of himself. He is smitten with the girl he is investigating, Dolores Martin (Dorothy Stratten), a beautiful blonde who appears to be involved with José (Sean Ferrer) behind her husband's back. As a result of his romantic yearning for Dolores, Charles is persistently awkward and guileless. Throughout the film, he is continually ill-at-ease and more or less helpless in relation to doors, props, and skating rinks. All of the film's physical comedy is derived from his touching discomfiture. As it turns out, Dolores' involvement with José has been more or less innocent. She falls in love with Charles and the two are married following her divorce. José and Christy fall in love and they marry. Leon continues his affair with his attractive young secretary Amy (Linda MacEwen). Russo must watch as Angela disappears from his life, although Sam is ready to console him at the fade out.

In this film, Bogdanovich set himself the task of interweaving several individual stories which are naturally related but which possess different moods. The development of the Charles-Dolores relationship is disarmingly sweet and innocent at the same time that it takes full advantage of Charles' propensity for comic disaster. The Russo-Angela relationship is developed in a more low-key, straightforwardly romantic and adult tone. Christy moves between these two sets of relationships. An offbeat and often outrageous character who combines a guileless directness with an endearing unpredictability, Christy is supremely confident at the swank country-and-western saloon where she is the featured attraction but often frustrated by her romantic misadventures involving the other characters. In one amusing scene, piqued by Russo's inattentiveness to her feelings, she playfully attempts to seduce the hapless Charles at her apartment. In spite of his uneasiness, he almost succumbs to her charms, but interruptions break the mood and he struggles to regain his composure. Sam turns up at various points of the narrative, an alluring dream girl whose romantic potential is ironically unappreciated by the male characters in the film.

The various threads of the action are individually exciting, but the lack of a clear dramatic center for the story could be a problem. Bogdanovich overcomes this pitfall by fluid camera movements which emphasize the persistent changes and developments within the evolving narrative, permitting it to jump lightly from one set of characters to another. As the story generally involves the detectives following the women, these camera movements are functional and never appear to be merely decorative. It is also natural for one set of characters to pass another set of characters at certain points in the action, permitting transitions which are especially graceful. Bogdanovich also gives both a sense of immediacy and a romantic aura to the film by the continuous flow of music on the sound track, all of it existing within the film's physical world. Records are heard over speakers in hotels and shops as well as on car radios, and "Christy's," a common meeting ground for the characters, allows for the introduction of several excellent original country-and-western songs ("Kentucky Nights" and "One Day Since Yesterday"), authentically and pleasingly performed by Colleen Camp.

Bogdanovich's sound track is as carefully textured as his camera is light-footed. The characters are always on the move but their drifting conversations unfailingly register with absolute clarity, and the subtle insistence on music dear to Bogdanovich's heart does not undermine the reality of the settings into which he introduces it. For example, the lobby of an elegant hotel would probably not be featuring a rare recording of jazz greats Ben Webster and Art Tatum, but the elegance of their playing enhances the mood of the hotel setting more than conventional lobby music would and admirably counterpoints Charles' pathetic attempt to appear relaxed. Similarly, a virtuoso sequence at a skating rink—the physicality of which vividly underscores Charles' vertigo as the bewitching Dolores glides before him in several mesmerizing subjective shots—is supported by a classic Benny Goodman swing number featuring drummer Gene Krupa rather than more conventional and less exciting contemporary disco music.

Bogdanovich's greatest daring is reserved for the performances, which are uniformly excellent. A persistent mood prevails throughout *They All Laughed*, but it is somewhat elusive. Bogdanovich has different requirements for different performers. Patti Hansen, for example, a former model who has not acted before, is required in the role of Sam to express a self-reliance, confidence, and vibrance akin to that of the heroines of Howard Hawks's films. Hansen's own personality seems to be the key to the interpretation, which is supported by only a few aesthetic touches such as the handsome gray cap she wears over her red hair. The controlled comic abandon which distinguishes the performances of Ritter and Camp and the dramatic shading necessary for the interpretations of Gazzara and Hepburn are not aspects of her role. Nevertheless, the camera of Bogdanovich and astute cinematographer Robby Muller observes many subtle moments of great beauty in Hansen's scenes and she leaves a memorable impression.

Camp, in addition to her singing, stands out for her straight-faced readings of many of the film's most memorable lines (speaking of one of her songs, she tells Charles that it is "climbing the charts even as we speak."). John Ritter, an actor whose comic timing is impeccable, performs all of Charles' physical routines with exquisite grace. At the same time, his demanding role requires that he immediately earn and subsequently hold the audience's complete sympathy, and the anguished yearning of Charles for Dolores is made consistently credible and touching as a result of Ritter's skill. As the object of his affection, the late Dorothy Stratten (to whom the film is dedicated and whose murder was blatantly sensationalized by the press) is a perfect match for Ritter. She projects the same innocence that he does and never seems self-conscious of her translucent beauty.

Veterans Gazzara and Hepburn play in a complementary style to that of Ritter and Stratten. Instead of comedy, understated dramatic flair prevails. The relationship between Russo and Angela is less transparently an enchanting fantasy than that of Charles and Dolores, although in a subtle way, it is perhaps *more* of a *cinematic* fantasy. The casting of Hepburn as an older version of the vulnerable modern Cinderella types she memorably incarnated early in her career is more suggestive than anything else of the film's bittersweet romantic core. At one point, after a tryst with Russo, Angela wistfully tells him, "This is where I turn back into a pumpkin." Angela is explicitly presented as a woman who has not known love for a long time, but Hepburn's undiminished attractiveness suggests that this absence of love has deepened her ability to appreciate love. The affair with John Russo reawakens her capacity for love and the film implies that in some sense, the memory of it will sustain her after the fadeout.

It is Russo who is actually the dramatic center of *They All Laughed*. Unlike the seemingly more vulnerable characters, he is the one who ends up brokenhearted. Gazzara's relatively naturalistic acting style in the film's fanciful context is therefore very significant. The lost love which registers on Gazzara's face in the closing credit sequence seems so faithful to life that it infuses the feathery film with a sudden melancholy which is devastatingly effective.

Bogdanovich's conclusion is rendered even more complex by the fact that as much sympathy is generated for Hansen as for Gazzara. Early in the film Sam sleeps with Russo, and although the film is ambiguous as to what occurred, repeated viewings seem to confirm Russo's contention that there was no lovemaking. The conclusion suggests that Sam is as much in love with Russo as he is with Angela, but that she is more resilient and more generous in her feelings. The happy ending enjoyed by other characters in the film supports the notion that *They All Laughed* is essentially a light farce, but it is at the same time a work very serious about attitudes toward love. The relationships Bogdanovich describes are not frivolous. Though contemporary romances are perceived as easily accessible and superficially frivolous, the only brief romance in the film ends as a heartbreaking love affair and two other relationships conclude in a double wedding. Bogdanovich admirably refuses to treat the film as if it were a profound statement about love, but his underlying thought is unmistakable. The world might change, but men and women still want the same things. If they settle for temporary and uncommitted relationships, it is not because they do not yearn for love that is deep and lasting. Bogdanovich's sentiments are not unlike the Frank Sinatra song stylings which adorn the film. They may be old-fashioned, but they wear well.

It is unfortunate that because Bogdanovich decided to distribute the film himself after much disagreement with other companies, the film was not backed by a successful publicity campaign. It did not receive outstanding reviews and has simply languished at the box office.

Blake Lucas

Reviews

The Hollywood Reporter. November 30, 1981, p. 2.
Los Angeles Times. December 17, 1981, VI, p. 1.
The New York Times. November 20, 1981, III, p. 6.
Newsweek. XCVIII, November 30, 1981, pp. 105-106.
Time. CXVIII, November 23, 1981, p. 98.
Variety. August 21, 1981, p. 3.

THIEF

Production: Jerry Bruckheimer and Ronnie Caan for United Artists
Direction: Michael Mann
Screenplay: Michael Mann; based on *The Home Invaders* by Frank Hohimer
Cinematography: Donald Thorin
Editing: Dov Hoenig
Art direction: Mary Dodson
Music: Tangerine Dream
MPAA rating: R
Running time: 122 minutes

Principal characters:

Frank	James Caan
Jessie	Tuesday Weld
Okla	Willie Nelson
Barry	James Belushi
Leo	Robert Prosky
Urizzi	John Santucci
Grossman	Nathan Davis

Thief is several films in one. It is a character study of a man obsessed with a dream; a curious love story; a caper film; an examination of the underworld; and a nihilistic revenge drama. The main question, however, is whether the parts fit together, and further, if they do fit together, what is the sum of all the parts?

The film opens with an evocative scene of a back alley in a city during a nighttime rain. It soon becomes evident that a robbery is taking place and that the car in the alley contains a lookout. Then we see inside where Frank (James Caan) is drilling open a large safe with a sophisticated device. The camera presents the precise process of opening the safe with remarkable attention to detail. It is almost as if the audience is being taught how to use the drilling machine. One element, however, is strangely missing from the depiction of the elaborate crimes in *Thief*: a sense that the thief is in danger of being discovered or caught. Frank seems so proficient that one assumes the theft will be accomplished without a problem. Indeed, there are no close calls and no shots of police or other people who might discover what is happening. This is perhaps deliberate, for as the film progresses the audience learns that theft is the only area of Frank's life that is perfectly smooth. He has problems collecting his share of what is stolen, but he never has a problem during the actual theft.

The second section of the film fills the audience in on more of Frank's life and sets up a long conversation in a coffee shop in which he details his past and explains his dream, the life he would like to live. First, however, the audience learns that he owns an automobile sales lot and a bar. He has some difficulty in getting his money from the burglary seen at the beginning of the film. In the process of getting his payment, Frank meets Leo (Robert Prosky), the head of a crime syndicate. Leo's slightly pudgy face can convey both innocence and world-weary cynicism, but at first Frank sees chiefly the benevolent side. Leo asks Frank to work for him, but Frank prefers to retain his independence.

The next section of the film consists almost entirely of a conversation, almost a monologue, in a coffee shop. Frank has virtually forced Jessie (Tuesday Weld) to come with him and listen to him. Jessie works in another coffee shop where Frank often eats. It is not clear how well he actually knows her, but soon it is clear that he has chosen her to be his wife. He tells her about his life, eleven years of which he has spent in the penitentiary, and his dream. He has cut pictures out of magazines and newspapers and pasted them together in a collage which represents his dream. It includes a big house and a wife and children; she could be the wife, he says. Earlier, as he drove her to the coffee shop, he had told her that he was a thief, and now he explains why. Because prison took eleven years out of his life, he says, he "can't *work* fast enough to catch up and can't *run* fast enough to catch up." Nothing and nobody, he declares, can stop him from making his dream happen.

Jessie is not immediately receptive to his plea, which is presented almost as a demand. Once married to a drug dealer, she likes her now very ordinary and boring life. Besides, she adds, she cannot have children. Frank brushes that objection aside by saying that they can adopt children. Finally he convinces Jessie, and the scene ends with a shot of their hands together on top of the picture of Frank's dream.

The coffee shop scene has not only revealed a great deal about Frank, but it has also set into motion a series of events that will bring Frank's dream and the film to its blazing end. In order to accomplish his goal more quickly, Frank accepts Leo's offer. He thinks that he can pull one big job and then quit crime and live a quiet and happy life with Jessie and the hoped-for children. Leo then begins setting up a job which will earn Frank $830,000, and Frank has told him that he wants to be committed to only that one job.

Besides the assistance in setting up the big theft, Leo also helps Frank in other ways. He provides a big, impressive house, and when Frank finds that he cannot adopt a child because of his criminal record, Leo gets him a baby boy on the black market.

Frank does discover a few drawbacks to working for Leo. His house and car are bugged, and he is accosted by a policeman named Urizzi, who demands that he be paid off to leave Frank alone. (Urizzi is played by John Santucci, one of the real ex-thieves who served as technical advisers for the film.) Because Frank does not like to give any of his money to anyone else, he refuses to pay off the police to make things easy for himself. Later he suffers the consequences when he is picked up by Urizzi, and four policemen beat him nearly senseless. Ultimately, he gains some measure of revenge against the police when he discovers that they are tracing his car on the night of his big job. He takes their radio device off his car and places it on a bus, leaving the police following a bus to Des Moines.

Before the big job, however, Frank and Jessie are happy together, and Frank even arranges to have his old friend Okla (Willie Nelson), the man who taught him all he knows about burglary, released from prison. Okla has found that he has a serious heart disease and does not want to die in prison. By going to the right lawyer (Fredric Stone) with ten thousand dollars, Frank gets Okla released, but he is out only a few hours before he collapses and then dies. Frank also visits another old friend, Grossman (Nathan Davis), to have him construct a special tool to enable him to get into the extra-strong vault that is the target Leo has picked for him.

The planning for and execution of the second big theft in the film is presented in the style and detail usual to a caper film, except that in *Thief* there is nothing lighthearted about it, and, as mentioned before, the usually obligatory suspense concerning the job itself is nearly absent.

Immediately after the conclusion of the job there is a quick cut to Frank with Jessie and the baby on the beach at San Diego. When Frank goes back to Leo to get his $830,000, however, he finds just what he has gotten himself into. Leo gives him only about eighty thousand dollars and tells him that he will continue to work for him. Then Frank goes to his automobile lot, where Leo's men lie in wait for him. They kill Frank's partner Barry (James Belushi); a short time later, Leo tells Frank that Barry's death shows what happens when Frank does not cooperate: "I own you. There is no discussion."

Frank goes home and apparently realizes the futility of his situation. He gives Jessie a large amount of money and tells her to leave with the baby. When she protests that she will stick with him, Frank tells her he is throwing her out. After she leaves with the baby, Frank also drives off, and the house explodes in flames. Then Frank blows up his bar and his automobile lot. He also throws away the picture of his dream. He then goes to Leo's house, kills Leo and two of his men, and walks slowly away as the film ends.

Thief is director Michael Mann's first film after some highly regarded television work, including the made for television movie *The Jericho Mile*, which won an Emmy. His direction of the film gained him critical praise. Andrew Sarris in the *Village Voice* wrote that Mann is "a director to watch very carefully for future reference," and *Newsweek* admired his "meticulous craftsmanship." Indeed, at times the craftsmanship becomes an end in itself, and Mann uses some strange point-of-view shots, such as a shot from inside a vault into which Frank is breaking. There is also far too much background sound, and the background music (by Tangerine Dream) is frequently too loud. When Frank is breaking into the second vault, for example, it is occasionally difficult to tell whether the sound in the background is the music or is an alarm going off somewhere. In other scenes the dialogue is nearly obscured by the rest of the sound.

The acting is generally quite good, with Robert Prosky's Leo standing out; his almost cherubic face expresses a wide range of emotions, and can shift instantly from a smile to a snarl. James Caan as Frank is effective in his demanding but emotionally limited role. *Thief* was quite well-received by the critics but did not fare well at the box office. Perhaps filmgoers were unable to accept the nihilistic ending of the film.

Timothy W. Johnson

Reviews

The Hollywood Reporter. March 20, 1981, p. 178.
Los Angeles Times. March 22, 1981, *Calendar*, p. 1.
The New York Times. March 27, 1981, III, p. 12.
The New Yorker. LVII, May 4, 1981, pp. 158-160.
Newsweek. XCVII, March 30, 1981, p. 82.
Time. CXVII, April 13, 1981, p. 98.
Variety. March 20, 1981, p. 3.

THIS IS ELVIS

Production: Andrew Solt and Malcolm Leo for David L. Wolper; released by Warner Bros.
Direction: Andrew Solt and Malcolm Leo
Screenplay: Andrew Solt and Malcolm Leo
Cinematography: Gil Hubbs
Editing: Bud Friedgen
Art direction: no listing
Music: Walter Scharf (original only)
MPAA rating: PG
Running time: 101 minutes

Principal characters:
Elvis, age 10 .... Paul Boensch III
Elvis, age 18 .... David Scott
Elvis, age 25 .... Dana MacKay
Elvis, age 42 .... Johnny Harra
Gladys Presley .... Debbie Edge
Vernon Presley .... Lawrence Koller
Priscilla Presley .... Rhonda Lyn
Sam Phillips .... Knox Phillips
Bluesman .... Furry Lewis
Joe Esposito .... Himself

Elvis Presley was a major twentieth century entertainment phenomenon, and his untimely death in 1977, at the age of forty-two, did not begin to diminish public interest in his art or in his life. Indeed, in 1981, Presley's name was in the news more often than it had been at any time in the last decade of his life. Most of the news was unpleasant. Rumors of Elvis' serious drug abuse problem were confirmed in a widely publicized trial involving Presley's personal physician, and Albert Goldman's lurid biography, *Elvis*, made headlines with tales of squalid sexual escapades. Presley's personal reputation, if not necessarily his art, was clearly at a low ebb.

Such was the climate in which filmmakers Andrew Solt and Malcolm Leo released *This Is Elvis*, a quasi-documentary which sought not to deny the existence of any of Presley's vices, but rather to render them insignificant by placing them in the context of his accomplishments. They sought and received the blessing and assistance of the Presley estate in producing what stands for now as the authorized film biography of the singer.

The cooperation of Presley's family and of his manager, Colonel Tom Parker, was vital in the making of the film, for it gave Solt and Leo access to a wealth of material hitherto unavailable to anyone outside Presley's immediate circle. Thus the filmmakers were able to use not only the stock movie clips and 1970's vintage concert footage, but also the seldom seen videotapes of early Presley television appearances, and even a few home movies of him and his family.

This material alone could have been the stuff of a fascinating documentary, but a documentary was not precisely what Solt and Leo were after. To flesh out their enterprise into a full-fledged cinematic biography, they wrote a script, hired a cast, and supplemented the film, video, and newsreel clips of the real Elvis with "re-created" versions of the highlights of his life. Some of these scenes were even filmed in black-and-white to blend in smoothly with old newsreel clips. If the result is a bit unsettling—sometimes it is difficult to tell which parts of the film have been restaged, and the audience is forced to take the accuracy of these interpolations on faith—*This Is Elvis* is nevertheless the closest that one is likely to get to a definitive film version of Presley's life for some time to come.

The film opens with a quick shot of a bloated Elvis (Johnny Harra) roaming his Memphis mansion on the eve of his death, after which the audience sees longtime Presley "gofer" Joe Esposito (a consultant to Solt and Leo who plays himself) breaking the news of Elvis' death to Colonel Tom Parker (the film's "technical advisor"). The rest of the film is a long flashback, narrated mostly by Elvis himself, presumably speaking from the grave (the voice is actually that of Ral Donner, who had a few minor Presleyesque hits in the early 1960's, and who does a good job of imitating Presley's gentle, slightly halting drawl).

No film exists of Elvis before 1956, so the highlights of his first two decades had to be restaged. The Presleys are portrayed as a close-knit family a bit down on their luck. Vernon Presley (Lawrence Koller) is usually out of work, and his wife Gladys Presley (Debbie Edge, who bears a remarkable resemblance to the woman she portrays) keeps the family together. Solt and Leo touch on Elvis' musical roots by showing him as a ten-year-old (Paul Boensch III) singing in church, and then staring in rapt wonder as an ancient black bluesman (Furry Lewis) clowns and improvises a rough blues on his guitar. By the time Elvis is eighteen (David Scott), the Presleys have moved to Memphis, and his interest in rhythm and blues music has gotten him noticed by local recording impresario Sam Phillips (Knox Phillips, Sam's son) of Sun Records. After several fruitless attempts, they hit upon the sound that would soon set the world on its ear.

Perhaps naturally, the most exciting moments in Elvis' career—his flash into stardom in 1956 and 1957—provide *This Is Elvis* with its best moments. Solt and Leo go straight to the videotapes that tell the story best: Presley's first appearance on national television on Tommy and Jimmy Dorsey's *Stage Show*, which unleashed "Elvis the Pelvis" on an unsuspecting nation; and then further clips from appearances with Milton Berle, Steve Allen, and the famous appearances on *The Ed Sullivan Show*, in which Sullivan, though he refers to Elvis as a "real decent, fine boy," nonetheless protects his audience from Presley's gyrations by keeping his cameras focused only on Elvis' head and shoulders.

Next, Elvis is drafted—first by Hollywood, and then by the United States Army. We see brief scenes from his first three films, including the outstanding "Jailhouse Rock" production number from the film of the same name.

Elvis' film career is interrupted by two events: his induction into the army (covered by newsreel footage) and the death of his beloved mother (scenes mostly restaged in black-and-white). Once out of the army, Elvis resumes his movie career, grinding out trifles such as *Fun in Acapulco* (1963) and *Paradise Hawaiian Style* (1966) at the rate of two or three a year. Solt and Leo offer a wry commentary on these mid-1960's years by splicing together several of the more ludicrous scenes, set to Elvis' rendition of "Too Much Monkey Business"—one of many instances in which the filmmakers use his songs to great effect as commentary on the screen images.

In a similar manner, the film also covers the other landmarks of Presley's career—his marriage, his 1968 comeback and subsequent return to the concert circuit, his stint as the king of Las Vegas, and the gradual disintegration of his personal and professional life. Solt and Leo face Presley's decline squarely. The clips of Presley's conversations with his cronies get worse as he gets paunchier. Disgruntled former employees call a press conference to publicize their book highlighting Elvis' increasing dependency on pills.

By the film's end, Presley's deterioration is horrifyingly complete. At a concert filmed a few weeks before his death, Elvis struggles to get through "Are You Lonesome Tonight." Sweating profusely, alternately giggling and mumbling, he scrambles the lyrics thoroughly and finally gives up saying "Aw, the hell with it." Incredibly (and with the aid of a lyric sheet) he pulls himself together for one last song: Frank Sinatra's "My Way." The lyrics, in which an aging but still proud man surveys the failures and successes of his life, take on a tremendous poignancy in this context, and make a fitting climax to the film.

As cinema, *This Is Elvis* had three predecessors: *Elvis—That's the Way It Is* (Denis Sanders, 1970), *Elvis on Tour* (Pierre Adidge and Robert Abel, 1973), and *Elvis* (John Carpenter, 1979). The first two films are a part of the official Presley canon, and not very impressive, consisting as they do of virtually interchangeable 1970's concerts, fan interviews, and carefully edited behind-the-scenes glimpses of what was purported to be the "real" Elvis. Solt and Leo used this same material to much greater effect in *This Is Elvis*. They permit us to see a less perfect Elvis—smoking, bantering with his entourage about his sexual exploits, and so forth. Hardly shocking revelations in this day and age, except that, so carefully had Elvis' public image been manipulated by his manager that even a couple of cigarettes and off-color remarks seem genuinely jarring. All of this, of course, is a good deal more realistic than previous Presley documentaries, and it makes Elvis seem a lot more human.

Carpenter's *Elvis*, on the other hand, was a film biography made for television which resisted any impulse to sensationalize its subject. Featuring a strong performance by Kurt Russell in the lead role, *Elvis* was a powerful and dignified film, but much more of a straight biography than *This Is Elvis*. None of the actors in the re-created scenes in *This Is Elvis* particularly stand out, no doubt intentionally. Most were obviously cast for their physical resemblance to Elvis or his parents, and few have more than a line or two of dialogue. They are characters in a staged newsreel, and the offscreen narration, by Ral Donner as Elvis, holds everything together. Solt's and Leo's script provides a believable (if at times superficial) summation of Presley's life as he himself might have told it.

It is in their choice and compilation of the film clips of the real Elvis, however, that the filmmakers did their best work. Prior to *This Is Elvis*, most clips of his concert footage were from the post-1970 era. It must have taken considerable work to unearth and edit the 1956-1960 material that showed Elvis at the height of his powers, but the results were very successful. Had Solt and Leo done no more than this, they would deserve commendation. Yet *This Is Elvis* does more; it ties the whole Presley era together, and stands as far and away the best film to date on this important figure in twentieth century American music and cinema.

Robert Mitchell

Reviews

The Hollywood Reporter. April 6, 1981, p. 3.
Los Angeles Times. May 7, 1981, VI, p. 1.
The New York Times. May 8, 1981, III, p. 18.
The New Yorker. LVII, June 1, 1981, pp. 132-133.
Newsweek. XCVII, May 4, 1981, p. 44.
Variety. April 6, 1981, p. 3.

TIME BANDITS

Origin: England
Released: 1980
Released in U.S.: 1981
Production: George Harrison, Denis O'Brien, and Terry Gilliam for Handmade Films
Distribution in U.S.: Avco Embassy
Direction: Terry Gilliam
Screenplay; Michael Palin and Terry Gilliam
Cinematography: Peter Biziou
Editing: Julian Doyle
Production design: Milly Burns
Art direction: Norman Garwood
Special effects: John Bunker
Costume design: Jim Acheson, with Hazel Coté
Music: George Harrison
MPAA rating: PG
Running time: 110 minutes

Principal characters:

Robin Hood .... John Cleese
King Agamemnon/Fireman .... Sean Connery
Pansy .... Shelley Duvall
Mrs. Ogre .... Katherine Helmond
Napoleon .... Ian Holm
Vincent .... Michael Palin
The Supreme Being .... Ralph Richardson
Ogre .... Peter Vaughan
Evil .... David Warner
Randall .... David Rappaport
Fidgit .... Kenny Baker
Wally .... Jack Purvis
Og .... Mike Edmonds
Strutter .... Malcolm Dixon
Vermin .... Tiny Ross
Kevin .... Craig Warnock

Time Bandits is a mediocre mixture of comedy and fantasy which has, surprisingly, impressed a number of American film critics and done exceedingly well at the box office. It is basically a continuation of the invasion of the feature film field by the British comedy team Monty Python's Flying Circus, who first came to prominence in the 1970's on British television and quickly achieved a cult following in the United States thanks to their series airing on Public televison. The first film to feature the group was *And Now for Something Completely Different* (1972), which comprised reshot routines from the television series. It was followed by *Monty Python and the Holy Grail* (1974) and *Life of Brian* (1979).

Terry Gilliam, the only American in the group—he was born in Minneapolis in 1940—had been responsible for the animated inserts in the television series. His first solo feature as a director was *Jabberwocky* (1977), and *Time Bandits* is his second effort. In this, Gilliam has the support of all of the Monty Python team, with the exceptions of Graham Chapman and Terry Jones, who despite their lack of credit probably contributed something to the humor of the production.

The idea for *Time Bandits* was exclusively Gilliam's, and the production money came from Handmade Films, a company in which he is a partner with former Beatle George Harrison and Harrison's business manager, Denis O'Brien. (Harrison also wrote some songs for the production, but they are almost impossible to identify on the sound track.) A script was ready by January, 1980, and shooting of the film began in Morocco under the working title of *The Film That Dare Not Speak Its Name* in May of the same year. The sequences in Morocco, featuring Sean Connery as Agamemnon, were filmed in a matter of weeks, and the production was subsequently transferred to the Lee International Studios in the London suburb of Wembley, with additonal location shooting taking place in the West Country, Hertfordshire, Gloucestershire, and Essex. The entire production was completed by the late summer of 1980 at a cost of less than five million dollars.

As of August, 1981—almost a year later—*Time Bandits* had not been picked up by an American distributor, and it was not until November that Avco Embassy, the largest of the independent distributors, released the feature to some eight hundred theaters simultaneously. *Time Bandits* proved to be the surprise box-office success of the season, and in the first twenty-four days of its release had grossed twenty-four million dollars. Doubleday quickly published the script as a tie-in with the feature's phenomenal success.

Time Bandits opens in a typical suburban English home, where the parents are preoccupied with the typical junk which passes for programming on television and pay little attention to their son, Kevin (Craig Warnock). One night, following the appearance of a mystical white stallion, which races through his room, six dwarfs—Fidgit (Kenny Baker), Wally (Jack Purvis), Og (Mike Edmonds), Strutter (Malcolm Dixon), Vermin (Tiny Ross) and their leader, Randall (David Rappaport)—enter Kevin's bedroom, as did the stallion, through the wall. They explain that the Supreme Being (Ralph Richardson) has given them the task of patching up the poorer parts of creation—"one thing I can't stand is a mess," explains the Supreme being later. (In an interview, Gilliam noted that the character was named "Supreme Being" to avoid libel suits). The dwarfs have stolen a map showing "time holes" in the universe and plan to use it to steal treasures of the past.

Accompanied by Kevin, who is armed with a polaroid camera, and pursued by the Supreme Being in the form of a glowing white head, the dwarfs first visit Napoleon (Ian Holm), who is busily conquering Italy. After looting Napoleon, the dwarfs and Kevin escape through a convenient time hole to Sherwood Forest, where their loot is promptly stolen by Robin Hood (John Cleese). Cleese is unquestionably the funniest man in the film, and one can only wish that his sequence had been longer. As Robin Hood, Cleese appears to have based his characterization on the present British Royal Family, patronizingly distributing wealth to the poor. "Have you met the poor? Charming people," he says.

After tying two lovers, Vincent (Michael Palin) and Pansy (Shelley Duvall), to a tree (where they suffer the indignity of being left helpless while passers-by steal their clothing), the dwarfs and Kevin move on to the court of King Agamemnon (Sean Connery), where Kevin helps the latter to kill the Minotaur. Agamemnon, to the disgust of his wife, adopts Kevin as his son. However, the dwarfs rob the Minoan court and the group falls through another convenient time hole onto the *Titanic*, where they again meet the doomed lovers, Vincent and Pansy. After demanding "champagne with plenty of ice," the dwarfs depart the sinking ship for the Land of Legends, where they meet an ogre (Peter Vaughan), Mrs. Ogre (Katherine Helmond), and a giant.

The giant transports Kevin and the dwarfs to the Fortress of Ultimate Darkness, the home of Evil (David Warner), who has been watching the adventures of the group and plotting to acquire the map of the time holes, rather as Margaret Hamilton, the Wicked Witch in *The Wizard of Oz* (1939), watched the journeying of Dorothy and her friends in her quest to acquire the ruby slippers. Evil is contemptuous of the Supreme Being; "God isn't so smart, he created forty-one types of parrots and nipples for men. I would have started with lasers, eight o'clock on day one." The Supreme Being then appears, looking like a somewhat disheveled businessman in a three-piece suit. Richardson behaves as if he had just walked off the street and into the studio and is totally oblivious of what is going on around him. When the question as to why he allowed Evil loose in the world is brought up, he mutters, "Something to do with free will, I think."

The stage is set for a fight between the Supreme Being and Evil, which the Supreme Being, after a number of setbacks (involving special effects), wins. Evil is reduced to pieces of matter, and the dwarfs are ordered to clean up the mess. Kevin wakes up in his bed to find the house on fire, but he is rescued by a fireman (Sean Connery). Kevin's parents are totally destroyed by a piece of left-over Evil, harbored in one of their household appliances.

The film has its amusing moments, but, taken as a whole, it does not work. It has few funny lines, and even the basically amusing premise begins to bore after the first hour, so labored is the plot and so undisciplined the humor. Terry Gilliam seems unable to decide whether to rely on special effects, fantasy, or the type of humor better suited to television situation comedy. Some of the players, notably Shelley Duvall and Katherine Helmond, are totally wasted. The dwarfs are boring, disgusting human beings, and it is hard to empathize with them or to sympathize with Kevin's desire to travel along. Morally, the ending is highly questionable. Some children may want to see their parents blown to smithereens, but that hardly justifies a filmmaker showing such a sequence or even remotely suggesting that a child would be better off being taken care of by a fireman who resembles a mythical hero than by his natural parents. Here is an example of the victory of the mythical world over the materialistic.

As *Variety* commented, "When you can count the laughs in a comedy on the fingers of one hand, it isn't so funny." Joy Gould Boyum in *The Wall Street Journal* (November 27, 1981) noted, "Rather than feeling delighted to travel along with this band of Time Bandits, we're more likely to feel robbed of our time." In *Time* Richard Corliss thought that the film was "a nasty fantasy, an antiepic, a revisionist fable," and concluded, "Who can care about six dwarfs when they're all dopey?"

However, many critics—particularly those, such as the reviewers from the *Los Angeles Times*, close to the industry—could not find sufficient superlatives. Vincent Canby in *The New York Times* called the film "a cheerful, irreverent lark." The critic for *Playboy* (February, 1982) thought "Its freshness outweighs its flaws." Filmgoers apparently agreed, although one suspects that many left the theater somewhat bored, very little amused, and feeling robbed not only of almost two hours of their time, but also of up to five dollars of their income, earned in a far from fantasy-filled world.

Anthony Slide

Reviews

The Hollywood Reporter. November 5, 1981, p. 3.
Los Angeles Times. November 6, 1981, VI, p. 9.
The New York Times. November 6, 1981, III, p. 8.
Newsweek. XCVIII, November 9, 1981, p. 92.
Time. CXVIII, November 9, 1981, p. 98.
Variety. July 20, 1981, p. 3.

TRUE CONFESSIONS

Production: Irwin Winkler and Robert Chartoff for Metro-Goldwyn-Mayer; released by United Artists
Direction: Ulu Grosbard
Screenplay: John Gregory Dunne and Joan Didion; based on the novel of the same name by John Gregory Dunne
Cinematography: Owen Roizman
Editing: Lynzee Klingman
Production design: Stephen Grimes
Art direction: W. Stewart Campbell
Music: Georges Delerue
MPAA rating: R
Running time: 110 minutes

Principal characters:
Des Spellacy .... Robert De Niro
Tom Spellacy .... Robert Duvall
Jack Amsterdam .... Charles Durning
Dan T. Campion .... Ed Flanders
Seamus Fargo .... Burgess Meredith
Brenda Samuels .... Rose Gregorio
Cardinal Danaher .... Cyril Cusack
Frank Crotty .... Kenneth McMillan
Mrs. Spellacy .... Jeanette Nolan
Mrs. Fazenda .... Gwen Van Dam
Mr. Fazenda .... Tom Hill

Robert De Niro and Robert Duvall could be considered the Spencer Tracy and Fredric March of the 1980's: two "stars" who are also superb actors. John Gregory Dunne and Joan Didion, husband and wife, have individually and collaboratively created some of the most memorable fiction recently produced in the United States. These four and a number of other talented artists worked on *True Confessions*, a film that neither broke box-office records nor (with a few notable exceptions) received the rave reviews it most assuredly deserved. The story is a moving account of a crime that refuses to be solved and of the troubled, guilt-ridden relationship between two brothers who are involved in that crime. Finally, *True Confessions* is an exposé of hypocrisy in the Catholic Church.

The plot is set in motion when an Irish Catholic homicide detective named Tom Spellacy (Robert Duvall), brother of the Right Reverend Monsignor Desmond Spellacy (Robert De Niro), is assigned to investigate the murder of a prostitute. The year is 1948, the setting Los Angeles, and in the course of the scenario the two brothers become adversaries. The film opens fifteen years after the main action, when white-haired Tom Spellacy visits his ailing brother in a small church located in the desert. They discuss death—Des has a short time to live—their feelings of guilt, and the past. The bulk of the film takes place in a flashback to the 1940's. The career-minded Des is seen celebrating a nuptial mass for the daughter of construction magnate Jack Amsterdam (Charles Durning). Amsterdam is willing to present part of his land development to his Eminence High Cardinal Danaher (Cyril Cusack) for a school, which, the audience discovers, will be necessary to sell the other lots.

Tom, a tough cop who lives in a world of corpses and who used to be on the take, and his partner, Frank Crotty (Kenneth McMillan), are called to a cheap brothel run by Tom's ex-mistress and a former top Hollywood madam, Brenda Samuels (Rose Gregorio). Inside, they find a scared black prostitute and the dead body of a pastor from Redondo Beach, who has succumbed to a heart attack during a sexual encounter with the prostitute. This introduction to Tom's world is followed by a series of seemingly unrelated scenes which subtly sketch the conflicts that the film will develop. Seamus Fargo (Burgess Meredith), an elderly monsignor, feels the church is being run like a business and complains to the Cardinal. Tom visits Des, and they have an uneasy conversation about Amsterdam's morality, their mother (who is in a nursing home), and the pastor who died in the brothel. That evening, the mutilated body of a young woman, Lois Fazenda, a "party girl," is discovered in a vacant lot. Tom and Crotty are assigned to the case, which at first seems routine.

Amsterdam has previously received many building contracts from the church, but the Cardinal informs Des that he wants to reevaluate the builder's relationship with the diocese. Des and Tom meet again, and are arguing about corruption when Amsterdam appears. Tom announces that he used to work for the businessman years before as a bagman during payoffs when Amsterdam was a vice lord. The Fazenda case suddenly receives headline attention, with the newspapers dubbing the girl the "Virgin Tramp," because she was once an innocent hopeful who came to Hollywood from the Midwest to work in films. In all-too-familiar fashion, she ended up a prostitute, and then dead. The detectives are stymied in their investigation, and the uneasy relationship between Tom and Des festers, symbolized by the physical barrier keeping them apart when the detective is in his brother's confessional.

While watching a porno film featuring Lois, Tom and Crotty notice that the prostitute found with the dead pastor appears in the film as well. From the girl, the police learn that Lois "acted" in several movies for someone named Leland K. Standard. Dan T. Campion (Ed Flanders), the diocese's lawyer, questions Des about Tom's investigation of the Fazenda murder. Des in turn tells Campion that the church should not be associating with Amsterdam, yet a dinner honoring him as "Catholic Layman of the Year" is still planned. Meanwhile, Tom and Crotty learn that Leland K. Standard was killed in a car accident on the night Lois Fazenda died, before she was murdered.

Des and Tom visit their mother (Jeanette Nolan) shortly before she dies. She favors the former and admonishes the latter, just as she did when they were youngsters, and the distance between the brothers is further underlined. Cardinal Danaher orders Des to retire Seamus Fargo, who eventually requests relocation to a parish in the desert. Danaher also has recommended Des for the post of Bishop.

Tom meets Lois Fazenda's parents (Tom Hill and Gwen Van Dam) who have traveled to Los Angeles to claim her body. They give him her notebook, in which the detective finds a telephone number, which he traces to Jack Amsterdam. It seems that Amsterdam had called the number fifty-three times. Brenda, who is planning to leave Los Angeles, tells Tom of her belief that the builder is not involved in the murder. She also says that Amsterdam is dying of cancer and wants to be remembered for his involvement with the church, not for his criminal past.

During the church dinner at which Amsterdam is the guest of honor, Des praises him in a speech. Crotty informs Tom that Amsterdam was receiving radiation treatments the night Fazenda died. Des tells the builder that the church must reevaluate his proposal. Later, when Tom makes a sarcastic comment about Lois, and Amsterdam lunges at him, Des pulls his brother to the side.

Several days later, Campion informs Des that they had picked up Fazenda, who had hitched a ride from them one summer day; the monsignor had completely forgotten the incident. The lawyer, however, reveals that he also had an affair with the girl. If uncovered, this would prove embarrassing to the diocese. When the brothers meet again, Tom is cynical and sarcastic, and Des realizes he will be unable to curtail the detective's investigation.

Tom and Crotty uncover evidence further linking Leland K. Standard to the murder; they speculate that perhaps Fazenda died before the porno filmmaker's accident. Tom visits an abandoned army barracks where Standard shot his movies; the site is splattered with Fazenda's dried blood. He also finds a note from Amsterdam, introducing the girl to Standard. When Tom later learns that Brenda has committed suicide after unsuccessfully attempting to obtain money from Amsterdam, he is committed to breaking the construction tycoon.

In the church confessional, Amsterdam angrily warns Des to get Tom off his case, threatening to link the monsignor with Fazenda. Des gives absolution to Amsterdam, but Tom has arrived and has heard their conversation. He is incensed at his brother, and decides to frame Amsterdam for murder—regardless of the consequences for Des. Their relationship is irrevocably broken.

The film then flashes forward to 1963. Tom accepts blame for their separation. Des forgives his brother, and notes that the incident forced him to relearn what ambition and power had made him forget. Des shows Tom Seamus Fargo's grave—and the spot where he would like them both to be buried, side by side.

In *True Confessions*, the Catholic Church hierarchy, as personified by Cardinal Danaher, Jack Amsterdam, and Des Spellacy, is depicted quite differently from Spencer Tracy's Father Flanagan in *Boys' Town* (1938) or Bing Crosby's Father O'Malley and Barry Fitzgerald's Father Fitzgibbon in *Going My Way* (1944). Amsterdam supports the church and is named "Catholic Layman of the Year," yet he used to deal in prostitution. The powerful, shrewd Cardinal in particular is more concerned with raising money and manipulating people like pieces on a chessboard than with saving souls. He is ruthless and unkind: when the outspoken Seamus Fargo comments on the church's twisted priorities, the Cardinal unfeelingly forces the old man into retirement. Des Spellacy, the young, up-and-coming Bishop-to-be, also wheels and deals, losing touch with his true purpose in the church: to serve people.

The real star of *True Confessions* is the dialogue. John Gregory Dunne and Joan Didion have written a trenchant, gutsy script, based on Dunne's best-selling novel (fashioned loosely after Los Angeles' famed 1947 Black Dahlia murder case). Previously, the pair collaborated on scripts for *The Panic in Needle Park* (1971), Al Pacino's first substantial screen role; *Play It As It Lays* (1972), based on Didion's novel; and the second remake of *A Star Is Born* (1976), with Barbra Streisand and Kris Kristofferson.

The performances are hardly less impressive than the script, though. De Niro and Duvall, who both appeared in *The Godfather, Part II* (1974, although they had no scenes together), play off each other beautifully. Their performances are toned down, subtle, and affecting. Particularly in the sequences set in 1963, without so much as a sentence uttered between them, they express warmth, affection and, most tellingly, brotherly love.

De Niro does not act emotionally and even violently as he did in *Mean Streets* (1973), *Taxi Driver* (1976), and *Raging Bull* (1980)—all seething, more typical De Niro characterizations. His work in *True Confessions* is closer in mood to his fine, unusual performance as the dying motion-picture producer in F. Scott Fitzgerald's *The Last Tycoon* (1976). De Niro assiduously prepares for all his screen roles: he learned to play the tenor saxophone for *New York, New York* (1977); drove a cab for *Taxi Driver*; and learned boxing and gained sixty pounds for *Raging Bull*. He studied the ceremony of the Roman Catholic Mass in Latin for *True Confessions*, learning religious protocol until it became second nature. Meanwhile, Duvall's Tom Spellacy is closer in tone to his steady, vulnerable Tom Hagen in *The Godfather* (1972) and *The Godfather, Part II*, than to his macho, overpowering military men in *Apocalypse Now*

(1979) and *The Great Santini* (1980).

In 1980, both stars competed for the Best Actor Academy Award. De Niro was nominated for *Raging Bull*, Duvall for *The Great Satini*, with the former gaining the prize. Both could—and should—have been nominated for *True Confessions*. Perhaps they might have been if the film had received better reviews, but the notices were curiously mixed, although *The New York Times*' Vincent Canby, among others, gave it a smashing review, and named it to his Ten Best List. A larger box-office showing also would have helped; the domestic gross, according to *Variety*, was a piddling $4,394,072, good enough for seventy-ninth place on the list of "Big Rental Films for 1981." The Best Actor Oscar competition was also unusually strong that year: Henry Fonda in *On Golden Pond*; Paul Newman in *Absence of Malice*; Burt Lancaster in *Atlantic City*; Warren Beatty in *Reds*; and Dudley Moore in *Arthur*. Richard Dreyfuss was similarly overlooked for his stellar work in *Whose Life Is It Anyway?*

De Niro and Duvall are solidly supported by a wonderful cast of character actors, notably Rose Gregorio and Kenneth McMillan. Gregorio, a stage performer who appears rarely in film, is excellent as the world-weary Brenda Samuels. Her scenes with Duvall are particularly touching, and this is easily her best screen role to date. McMillan, who starred on Broadway with Duvall in the Ulu Grosbard-directed *American Buffalo*, is rapidly developing into one of motion picture's most recognizable character actors. He appeared in other prominent films released in 1981, most memorably as William Hurt's father in *Eyewitness* and as the racist firefighter in *Ragtime*. In *True Confessions* he is especially fine as Frank Crotty, a cynical cop who is as crooked as he is fat.

Ulu Grosbard, the Belgian-born stage and film director, effectively parallels the worlds and personalities of Tom and Des Spellacy. In 1962, he directed Rose Gregorio, his wife, in the off-Broadway production of *The Days and Nights of Beebee Fenstermaker*; three years later, he directed Robert Duvall in an award-winning production of Arthur Miller's *A View from the Bridge*. Among his films are *The Subject Was Roses* (1968), which he originally directed on the stage, *Who Is Harry Kellerman and Why Is He Saying Those Terrible Things About Me* (1971), starring Dustin Hoffman and featuring Rose Gregorio, and the underrated *Straight Time* (1978), also with Hoffman. More than sixty locations in the Los Angeles area were utilized by Grosbard during shooting, including a number of landmarks such as City Hall, Union Station, and Chinatown, and religious institutions such as Mount Saint Mary's College in Brentwood and St. Joseph's Cathedral in downtown Los Angeles.

True Confessions differs from the majority of current Hollywood products, which depend on car chases, special effects, and other gimmicks seemingly produced to keep audiences awake between trips to the video game arcade in the theater lobby. Its strengths were more prevalent in films made during the time in which the story is set: good old-fashioned character development, first-rate dialogue, and first-rate performances.

Rob Edelman

Reviews

The Hollywood Reporter. September 2, 1981, p. 2.
Los Angeles Times. September 25, 1981, VI, p. 1.
The New Republic. CLXXXV, September 30, 1981, pp. 24-25.
The New York Times. September 25, 1981, III, p. 4.
The New Yorker. LVII, October 26, 1981, pp. 174-176.
Time. CXVIII, October 5, 1981, p. 88.
Variety. September 2, 1981, p. 3.

VICTORY

Production: Freddie Fields for Lorimar; released by Paramount
Direction: John Huston
Assistant direction: Elie Cohn
Screenplay: Evan Jones and Yabo Yablonsky; based on an original screen story by Yabo Yablonsky, Djordje Millcevic, and Jeff Maguire
Cinematography: Gerry Fisher
Editing: Roberto Silvi
Art direction: J. Dennis Washington
Music: Bill Conti
MPAA rating: PG
Running time: 117 minutes

Principal characters:
John Colby .... Michael Caine
Robert Hatch .... Sylvester Stallone
Luis Fernandez .... Pelé
Terry Brady .... Bobby Moore
Major Karl von Steiner .... Max von Sydow
Colonel Waldron .... Daniel Massey

Victory, John Huston's most recent film before making the big-budget spectacular *Annie* (1982), was labeled by most critics as a combination of *The Great Escape* (1963) and *The Longest Yard* (1974). The World War II German prisoner-of-war camp setting could be a duplicate for that of *The Great Escape*, with *Victory*'s soccer game substituting for the football contest in *The Longest Yard*. While not a bad film, *Victory*, leaves one with the distinct impression that one has seen it all before.

Filmgoers who have not seen either of the earlier films, however, will enjoy a reasonably good story, good acting, and a stirring conclusion. Huston has assembled a strong cast headed by Michael Caine, a fine actor who always gives his best, even in some of the poorer films that he has made recently, such as *The Hand* (1980). Sylvester Stallone is the other lead. He plays a less than lovable character, and next to Caine and accomplished costar Max von Sydow, his acting leaves much to be desired. The rest of the cast, notably a number of well-known professional soccer players, is headed by the retired superstar of world soccer, Pelé. *Victory* marked Pelé's acting debut, and he does a tolerable job. Additionally, the film features him in some of the most spectacular soccer action ever filmed.

The story concerns a German prisoner-of-war camp in which Major Karl von Steiner (Max von Sydow), an honorable man who was a member of Germany's prewar World Cup soccer team, takes an interest in the small band of former professional soccer players who are confined to the camp. John Colby (Michael Caine) was apparently a well-known English player, and he coaches the undernourished squad in their games. Luis Fernandez (Pelé) is one of the team's stars, and Robert Hatch (Sylvester Stallone), the only American, is a former college football player who would like to bring some American-style physical contact to the game.

Steiner thinks up the scheme which is the focal point of the story: a soccer (or "football," as the Europeans call it) game between the prisoners and the German officers. The idea seems simple enough at first, but Steiner's superiors decide to turn the affair into a major propaganda tool. Hoping at last to beat the English team, which they had never done before the war, the Germans make a number of concessions to the prisoner team to make the contest more equitable. Steiner, used by the German high command, allows the prisoners on the team more food, better facilities, and other amenities not usual for P.O.W.'s.

Colby, hoping to help as many prisoners as he can, forces Steiner to allow him use of some miserably undernourished Eastern European players who have been prisoners in other camps. The prisoners practice under less than optimum conditions despite token gestures by the Germans, who plan to have the match publicized to show their superiority. They decide to hold the match in a large stadium in Paris and broadcast it so that they can gloat over their inevitable victory.

While coping with the undernourishment and physical debilitation of his team members, Colby also has trouble with his own British officers in the camp. Headed by Colonel Waldron (Daniel Massey), the British want to use the game as a cover for the escape of the prisoners. Their plan is to contact the French resistance and enlist their aid in helping with the escape. In order to do this, they need to get word to the French, something that is accomplished by the reluctant aid of Hatch. An off-beat escape scheme, similar to Steve McQueen's in *The Great Escape*, is used by the reluctant Hatch, who does not want to have to come back to the camp to let the British know what the French plan is. Naturally, like McQueen, Hatch does the right thing and returns to camp.

The escape is planned to take place during the intermission of the game. To the Allied forces, the prisoners seem to be collaborating with the enemy by their passive participation in the game, but to the players it becomes an obsession to win. Amid tight security the prisoners go to the game, still no match for the well-fed German team.

The first half of the game is no contest for the Germans and they easily score. The game footage is some of the best in the picture, and was directed by assistant director Elie Cohn. Even American audiences who are relatively unfamiliar with the game will find it exciting, and indeed the soccer sequences rank with the best sports footage on film. The magnificent Pelé, who seems to defy gravity, has the grace of a ballerina, and he is ably supported by the rest of the professional players in the film.

During the intermission, and over the strenuous opposition of the British senior officers, the men decide to play out the game, no matter what. To them, victory on the field has become more important than escape. The second half turns the game to the prisoners' favor, and, as the German officers become increasingly displeased (except for the sportsmanlike Steiner, who tries to stifle smiles), the prisoners score a tying goal.

The predominantly French crowd filling the stadium becomes wild with excitement. The fans jump to their feet and begin chanting "*Victoire*! *Victoire*!" just as the prisoners score the final and winning goal of the game. Even the German army cannot hold the fans back from rushing onto the field, and the film ends amid the emotional "Marseillaise" while the French surround the prisoner team and rush them out of the stadium.

As a pure sports film, *Victory* receives high marks, but it unfortunately does not fare very well beyond that. The screenplay by Evan Jones and Yabo Yablonsky is fair enough, but Huston's usual taut direction seldom shows through. The best scenes in fact were not even directed by him, but by Cohn. The characters are never developed, and Hatch particularly seems to be little more than a caricature. Stallone's role was not highly regarded by the critics, some of whom felt that he was trying to be a little too much like Rocky on the soccer field.

Perhaps Huston's best contribution to the film was his ability to "open up" the story. Most prisoner-of-war films have a feeling of claustrophobia about them: small rooms, small yards, and innumerable dark escape tunnels. Huston does away with much of that, preferring to show the prisoners on the field and out-of-doors as much as possible. The film was shot entirely on location in Hungary, a common practice in recent years. Yugoslavia, Hungary, Spain, and other more or less out-of-the-way locations are frequently used to cut costs.

Victory did not do particularly well at the box office and was soon available on cable television channels and on video tape. It is the kind of film that will probably do well on television in the future, for it represents a type of adventure film that seems to improve with age. The adventure film without sex, extensive violence, and gadgetry has virtually disappeared in recent years, and an old-fashioned story such as *Victory* may be more popular on the home screen than at the box office.

Huston made few films in the years before *Victory*. Ill-health virtually forced him to retire after his spectacular *The Man Who Would Be King* (1975), which also starred Caine along with Sean Connery. Yet, after *Victory*, the then seventy-five-year-old Huston went on to direct a major project, the film version of the hit Broadway musical *Annie*. As a reward for his life's work as writer, director, and actor, Huston was announced in the fall of 1982 as that year's recipient of the American Film Institute Life Achievement Award. Although *Victory* is hardly his best film, it proves that Huston is still a director of note, even forty years after his first effort, *The Maltese Falcon* (1941).

Betti Stone

Reviews

The Hollywood Reporter. July 20, 1981, p. 4.
Los Angeles Times. July 31, 1981, VI, p. 1.
The New York Times. July 31, 1981, III, p. 6.
Newsweek. XCVIII, August 10, 1981, p. 69.
Time. CXVIII, August 3, 1981, p. 66.
Variety. July 21, 1981, p. 3.

WHOSE LIFE IS IT ANYWAY?

Production: Martin C. Schute and Ray Cooney for Metro-Goldwyn-Mayer
Direction: John Badham
Screenplay: Brian Clark and Reginald Rose; based on the play of the same name by Brian Clark
Cinematography: Mario Tosi
Editing: Frank Morriss
Art direction: Gene Callahan
Music: Arthur B. Rubinstein
MPAA rating: R
Running time: 118 minutes

Principal characters:

Ken Harrison	Richard Dreyfuss
Dr. Michael Emerson	John Cassavetes
Dr. Clare Scott	Christine Lahti
Patty	Janet Eilber
Carter Hill	Bob Balaban
Judge Wyler	Kenneth McMillan
Nurse Rodriguez	Alba Oms
Mary Jo Sadler	Kaki Hunter
Orderly John	Thomas Carter

The "right-to-die" issue—that is, each individual's right to die with dignity instead of being kept alive only through extraordinary mechanical means—provides the core for *Whose Life Is It Anyway?* Conceived first as a British television play and then as a Broadway production starring Tom Conti, then Mary Tyler Moore, the film approaches an extremely complicated medical, legal, and moral question in terms which reduce it to its most simplistic level. A matter which has provoked complex debates among physicians, legal scholars, philosophers, and theologians is treated in the film as little more than a conflict between two strong-willed individuals.

On one side in the conflict is thirty-two-year-old sculptor Ken Harrison (Richard Dreyfuss in the Conti/Moore role), paralyzed from the neck down in an automobile accident. Convinced that his life is no longer worth living, he petitions the Boston hospital where he is being treated to allow him to die. It is explained in the story that once the weekly dialysis treatments which he receives are stopped, he will die within a few days. His request arises partially from self-pity, but primarily from his inability to pursue his work as a sculptor. Apparently he has lived only for his work, though he does have a girl friend, Patty (Janet Eilber), who remains devoted to him until he forbids her to continue her daily visits to the hospital. Harrison rejects suggestions from well-meaning hospital employees such as Dr. Clare Scott (Christine Lahti) that he shift his creativity to a medium such as poetry, where his quadriplegia will be no hindrance. He is single-mindedly devoted to his own art, and he decides that if he cannot sculpt, he will not live at all.

Opposing Harrison's request is Dr. Michael Emerson (John Cassavetes). He is also single-minded in his devotion to his art, that of preserving life. In an early scene in the film, he confronts a group of interns over a recently deceased patient with his perception of death as the ultimate enemy against which all medical professionals are struggling. His antagonism toward death and his belief that Harrison's desire for death arises from natural shock and that he will eventually change his mind make Dr. Emerson the chief adversary whom Harrison and his lawyer, Carter Hill (Bob Balaban), have to face.

The characterization of Dr. Emerson in *Whose Life Is It Anyway?* is one aspect of the film's oversimplification of a complex issue. Despite the fact that he is primarily devoted to saving life and that his explanation of Harrison's death wish seems plausible, Dr. Emerson emerges as a consummate villain. He is arrogant, yelling at nurses and orderlies when they fail to carry out his orders explicitly. He perceives himself in almost messianic terms in his crusade against death. (When the doctor is making rounds, Harrison asks, "Is he going to do it in the normal fashion, or is he going to walk on water?") He refuses to consider the arguments of Hill for Harrison, dismissing the lawyer abruptly. He becomes almost inhuman in his treatment of his patient. For example, he has Harrison injected with a dose of Valium when the sculptor refuses to take the tranquilizer orally. Presenting the doctor in such an unappealing light detracts from the film's potential for seriously treating the question of the right to die. Instead of providing meaningful arguments against his position, it dismisses his viewpoint by making him so unlikable, resulting in an *ad hominem* argument against the right-to-die which unfairly elicits the audience's sympathy for Harrison's viewpoint.

Whose Life Is It Anyway? also oversimplifies the complex right-to-die debate with a less than full exploration of the legal ramifications of Harrison's request. Dr. Emerson and the rest of the hospital staff should be concerned about their own liability in the case of Harrison's death. Even though a hearing presided over by Judge Wyler (Kenneth McMillan) comes out in favor of Harrison's wishes, the problem of ultimate blame when the patient eventually does die is ignored. Moreover, the film simplifies by conveniently omitting a family from Harrison's life. Thus his decision has no real effect on loved ones, since his girl friend has been dismissed much earlier. (Patty's acquiesence without objection to Harrison's ordering her away from the hospital seems highly implausible, given her devoted attendance upon him until that point.) Finally, by ignoring the religious dimension of the issue, the film sidesteps a significant component of this controversy. Perhaps Harrison is not religious, but no attempt to depict his accepting or rejecting religious counsel is made. The absence of thorough depiction of legal, familial, and religious aspects of a decision to die may make for a more clearly developed conflict in the film, but it undermines the film's pretensions to a meaningful handling of a vital personal and social issue.

Another major problem in *Whose Life Is It Anyway?* involves the characterization of Ken Harrison. Very simply, he seems to be having too much fun to want to die. His mind is active, and he engages in a good deal of witty repartee with the sympathetic members of the hospital staff such as Dr. Scott and Nurse Rodriguez (Alba Oms). His rapport is especially good with novice nurse Mary Jo Sadler (Kaki Hunter) and an orderly named John (Thomas Carter). These two, in fact, take Harrison out for an evening of Punk rock music and marijuana. There are admittedly a few attempts to portray the degradation of Harrison's condition in the film. For example, he falls out of bed, spills food that is being fed to him, and is at the mercy of anyone who decides he should be given medication. The film treats such moments only in passing, however, and presents Harrison as an appealing, vital human being who seems to have a lot to live for. Indeed, it is not until very late in the film, when Harrison delivers a speech at the hearing to decide whether he will be allowed to discontinue dialysis, that we learn of the psychological torment he has been experiencing. A definite problem in the characterization is that no real preparation has been made for this revelation. The steps that lead to Harrison's decision for death are not presented. The film seems to suggest that the decision was virtually automatic once Harrison had discovered the extent of his disability and required no real inner debate on his part. Consequently, no realistic arguments for Harrison's request emerge in the film. The audience must accept the rightness of his view because he is, after all, the appealing, attractive, witty protagonist of the film. We are expected to endorse his right to die for the same reason that we are expected to reject Dr. Emerson's opposing position: because of the personality of the proponent of each of the views.

Although it treats a compelling social issue, *Whose Life Is It Anyway?* fails to present the complexities of that issue or to argue convincingly for its own position in the matter. Instead, it reduces the debate to easily presented personality conflicts. It substitutes emotional identification with and rejection of the specific figures involved in the controversy for any serious attempt to articulate opposing views fairly and clearly. The right-to-die problem which this film skims over deserves a much richer and more rewarding forum than that offered in *Whose Life Is It Anyway?*

The trade reviews for the film were generally favorable, but among popular newspapers and magazines, the reaction was mixed. Although the acting was praised, the believability of the film was questioned. Coming out at the end of the year—almost at the Christmas season—provided little impetus for the film's success, and it quickly disappeared from theaters.

Frances M. Malpezzi
William M. Clements

Reviews

The Hollywood Reporter. November 24, 1981, p. 2.
Los Angeles Times. December 4, 1981, VI, p. 1.
The New Republic. CLXXXV, December 30, 1981, pp. 24-25.
The New York Times. December 2, 1981, III, p. 23.
Newsweek. XCVIII, December 14, 1981, pp. 124-125.
Saturday Review. VIII, November, 1981, p. 56.
Time. CXVIII, December 14, 1981, p. 92.
Variety. November 23, 1981, p. 3.

WOLFEN

Production: Rupert Hitzig
Direction: Michael Wadleigh
Screenplay: David Eyre and Michael Wadleigh; based on the novel of the same name by Whitley Strieber
Cinematography: Gerry Fisher
Editing: Chris Lebenzon, Dennis Dolan, Martin Bram, and Marshall M. Borden
Art direction: David Chapman
Music: James Horner
MPAA rating: R
Running time: 114 minutes

Principal characters:
Dewey Wilson .... Albert Finney
Rebecca Neff .... Diane Venora
Eddie Holt .... Edward James Olmos
Whittington ....Gregory Hines
Ferguson ....Tom Noonan
Christopher Vanderveer ....Max M. Brown
Pauline Vanderveer .... Anne Marie Photamo

Wolfen combines imaginative techniques, serious themes, and a thriller-detection plot to produce a film that is powerful and emotionally involving to those viewers who are persuaded to accept for two hours its unusual premise. Other viewers who, because of weaknesses in the film or a preference for more traditional and realistic cinema, are unable or unwilling to accept the terms of *Wolfen*, find it pretentious and foolish. Any evaluation of the film must acknowledge both responses.

The premise of the film is not revealed until near the end, which confuses even its most enthusiastic admirers. Indeed, it is a mystery that both the audience and the principal characters are concerned with unraveling throughout most of the film. The immediate problem for the police and other authorities of New York is the mysterious murder of a millionaire and politician, Christopher Vanderveer (Max M. Brown), along with his wife (Anne Marie Photamo) and bodyguard. From the strangely torn bodies of the victims the police cannot determine the method of the murderers. Because of the inexplicable means of murder and the prominence of Vanderveer, Dewey Wilson (Albert Finney), an ex-detective, is reinstated by the New York Police Department for the case. He is obviously a man who has gotten results for the force in the past, but he also seems to have little use for ordinary police work or ordinary methods. Because the department suspects that terrorists may be responsible for the murders, Rebecca Neff (Diane Venora), a criminal psychologist who specializes in international terrorism, is also assigned to the case.

Adding another layer to the mystery is the discovery of the body of a derelict in the South Bronx who has been killed in exactly the same fashion as the Vanderveers. Rebecca applies to her study of the case not only her knowledge of terrorist techniques but also a large battery of ultrasophisticated audio and video equipment that can analyze such particulars as a suspect's voice timbre and variations of skin temperature. These devices, however, yield no clues and no suspects.

Meanwhile the audience is seeing a few clues that the police do not have, but is given no way to interpret these clues. Many of the events are shown (at least partially) from a viewpoint very near ground level, and many of the images are given an extraordinary look by photographic and electronic effects combined with computerized optical processing similar in effect to what is seen on sophisticated video games. Among the results of this technique are the changing and intensification of colors. The audience begins to sense that it is seeing the world from another viewpoint, but what that viewpoint is remains unknown for most of the film.

Two other characters are involved in the attempt to solve the case. Whittington (Gregory Hines), an assistant coroner who conducts autopsies in an attempt to understand the strange wounds, is a black man who employs jive talk and gallows humor in his work, but also shows a quick intelligence and seemingly limitless energy. He is a nice contrast to Dewey, who has the same intelligence but a much more languid demeanor. The other expert to whom they turn is "Fergie" Ferguson (Tom Noonan), a decidedly eccentric zoologist whose speciality is wolves. Ferguson is called upon because the types of hair that are found on the bodies of the victims are thought to come from wolves. Ferguson believes that animals are superior to humans, and later, when he finds that wolves are suspected of the killings, says, "With all the psychos running around New York, you're trying to pin this rap on an endangered species?" Ferguson is later killed in the same way as the Vanderveers, apparently because he has discovered the key to the murders.

Another possible cause of the murders is introduced through the character of Eddie Holt (Edward James Olmos), a Native American construction worker who talks about the ecological purity of animals and his people. Hints are given that the Native Americans, many of whom work on construction of high-rise buildings, can undergo "shape-shifting" and become animals. A suspicion that the murders were committed by such "temporary" wolves is thus established. Dewey then observes Eddie in a shape-shifting ceremony, but he does not actually turn into a wolf, and that line of thinking is dropped.

What finally emerges as the cause of the killings is a group of super-wolves who are able to hear the blink of an eye and to detect emotions by registering changes in body temperature. This, then, is the explanation for the extraordinary visual and audio effects in the film as well as the camera angles: the audience is seeing the world from the wolves' point of view. Their territory is the South Bronx, where all their victims are found except for the first ones, the Vanderveers. The wolfen left their own ground to kill this particular man because he was planning a development in the South Bronx that would have put new buildings in place of the urban ruins in which they live. At the denouement Wilson and Rebecca are themselves confronted and almost killed in the Vanderveer's empty penthouse, but they survive and the wolves are apparently destroyed.

The director of *Wolfen*, Michael Wadleigh, is best known as the director of *Woodstock* (1970), the documentary of the famous music festival. *Wolfen* is his first fictional feature film; he also collaborated on the screenplay. His direction is occasionally self-indulgent, especially in the overuse of the visual special effects, but he does elicit strong performances from the main actors. The only exception is Diane Venora, whose role is virtually one-dimensional.

Wolfen also marks the return to the screen of Albert Finney, who is most famous for the title role in *Tom Jones* (1963) and who has devoted most of his time to the stage since 1974. His performance is good, but one wishes he had been asked to do more. Playing an American for the first time on the screen, he is credible and effective.

All in all, *Wolfen* is a light fantasy-suspense film with pretensions, enjoyable if not taken too seriously.

Timothy W. Johnson

Reviews

The Hollywood Reporter. July 20, 1981, p. 3.
Los Angeles Times. July 30, 1981, VI, p. 1.
The New Republic. CLXXXV, September 9, 1981, pp. 24-25.
The New York Times. July 24, 1981, III, p. 6.
Newsweek. XCVIII, August 3, 1981, p. 51.
Time. CXVIII, August 3, 1981, p. 67.
Variety. July 20, 1981, p. 3.

THE WOMAN NEXT DOOR (LA FEMME D'A COTE)

Origin: France
Production: Jean-François Lentretien for Les Films du Carrosse/TFI Films Production
Direction: François Truffaut
Screenplay: François Truffaut, Suzanne Schiffman, and Jean Aurel
Cinematography: William Lubtchansky
Editing: Martine Barraqué and Marie-Aimée Debril
Art direction: Jean-Pierre Kohut-Svelko
Music: Georges Delerue
MPAA rating: R
Running time: 106 minutes

Principal characters:
Bernard Coudray .... Gérard Depardieu
Mathilde Bauchard .... Fanny Ardant
Philippe Bauchard .... Henri Garcin
Arlette Coudray .... Michèle Baumgartner
Madame Odile Jouve .... Véronique Silver
Roland Duguet .... Roger Van Hool

After the grand tapestry of *The Last Metro* (1980), with its parade of actors, actresses, Nazis, and resistance fighters, François Truffaut chose to come back with a domestic drama. *The Woman Next Door* deals with ordinary, middle-class people who have interesting jobs, lovely children, and should be leading prosaic, if enriched, lives. They do, until an event occurs that changes everything for them. This event is not a war, a death, nor a sudden change in their life-style; it is simply that the house next door to Bernard and Arlette Coudray, long vacant, suddenly becomes occupied. Another charming middle-class couple with one child moves in—Mathilde and Philippe Bauchard. They should all be good neighbors and exchange recipes. How unfortunate, then, that Bernard and Mathilde were lovers eight years earlier who entered their respective marriages as refugees from that tempestuous affair.

François Truffaut is back in top form as he traces the effect of proximity on these two conventional people. After a series of domestic scenes showing the lives of the two couples, the camera seems to become a participant in their world, with longer and longer tracking shots employed as the audience becomes aware of the passion that Bernard and Mathilde share. Like the principal characters in *Jules and Jim* (1961), they are extremely likable people, with a touch of madness lurking beneath their placid exteriors. Truffaut's direction is careful and assured: this is a subject he has dealt with before—

obsessive passion and pathological feminine psychology. Written directly for the screen by Truffaut and his collaborators, the film also resembles *The Story of Adele H* (1975) in the purity of its passion.

As always, Truffaut's work with actors is impeccable. Gérard Depardieu (who seemingly works more than any other French actor) is solid, tender, yet convincing as a man who harbors demons beneath the surface. As his former love, Fanny Ardant has the advantage of being a new face to filmgoers. Truffaut took Ardant from the French stage, attracted by her "nineteenth century face." He was right; her dark good looks combined with her unfamiliarity give her a sense of mystery. Another important character in the saga of Mathilde and Bernard is Madame Odile Jouve, whose running narration acts as a counterpoint to the film. Mme. Jouve is a middle-aged fading beauty who runs the local tennis club where much of the action in the film takes place. She too was the victim, in her earlier years, of an obsessive love affair. This technique of having the older woman comment on the action does not work entirely—there are times when one wants to tell her to bow out, for her remarks are often points that the audience can figure out for themselves. This flaw does not detract too much from Truffaut's grand design, though. Unlike Claude Chabrol, who has explored style, and Jean-Luc Godard, who has experimented with technique, Truffaut is still interested in telling a good story. He has always had the ability to get at the heart of his characters—one knows what they do for a living, what they eat, and with whom their children play.

The film begins with marine engineer Bernard Coudray (Gérard Depardieu), who lives in a village near Grenoble with his wife Arlette (Michèle Baumgartner) and their small son Thomas. He has never told his wife of his long affair eight years earlier with a young woman named Mathilde (Fanny Ardant). The affair ended badly when the couple found that they could neither live with nor without each other. Bernard therefore is greatly disturbed when the house next door to him is rented by Mathilde and Philippe Bauchard (Henri Garcin), the older man she has since married. At first Bernard stays away from the couple next door, but a chance meeting with Mathilde at the local supermarket stirs up old feelings. When Mathilde suggests that they become merely friends, Bernard agrees.

The village life revolves around the tennis club owned by Mme. Odile Jouve (Véronique Silver), a woman who was crippled twenty years earlier in a suicide attempt brought on when her lover deserted her. Thrown together with Mathilde at the club and at various places in the village, Bernard tries to remain oblivious to her charms, but he cannot stay away from her and persuades her to resume their affair. The lovers start to meet at a small hotel in Grenoble, keeping it from their mates. Mathilde meanwhile has gone back to her career as a children's book illustrator. She meets and starts to work with Roland Duguet (Roger Van Hool), a homosexual publisher and the confidant of Mme. Jouve. As her life becomes fuller and her career flourishes, she breaks off her liaison with Bernard. Bernard, who is unjustly jealous of Roland, keeps after Mathilde to continue the affair, but she fends him off. Bernard becomes more and more desperate, and finally, at a garden party given by the Bauchards, he loses all self-control and publicly beats up Mathilde.

The couple's secret is thus revealed, but their spouses show understanding and forgive them. Philippe takes Mathilde away to North Africa for a holiday and Arlette reveals to Bernard that she is going to have another child. When Mathilde returns from her vacation, she seems to have gotten over her trauma, but while signing copies of her new book at the tennis club, she breaks down and is subsequently hospitalized. She goes into a rapid decline in the hospital and will not be comforted, even when Bernard comes to visit her at the insistence of her husband. At last Mathilde is released, whereupon she and Philippe move away to an apartment in Grenoble. Life seems to go on as usual for Bernard and Arlette, when one night Bernard is awakened by a noise next door. Entering the Bauchard's former house, he sees Mathilde. They make love, and immediately after, she shoots him and then shoots herself.

The film ends abruptly, violently, recalling Catherine's fatal drive at the end of *Jules and Jim*, but there are hints throughout that the two main characters are not as rational as they seem to be. Bernard, although a loving husband and father, has a fierce temper and is given to shouting at his family for very little reason. Mathilde has a curious argument with her publisher about one of the illustrations she is doing. The book is designed to make a point about home safety and the drawing shows a young boy who has badly cut himself. Mathilde draws him lying in a pool of vivid red blood. When the publisher objects, Mathilde is angry. Blood is red, she insists, and it should be terrifying. As their affair proceeds, both Bernard and Mathilde become more and more nervous. The strain of hiding their passion from the world and reviving what was essentially an unhealthy liaison becomes intolerable. Yet much of the film is cool, gentle, and frequently funny, with the tension only gradually mounting, and nothing that has happened before quite prepares the audience for the violent ending.

The Woman Next Door received good notices but, unlike *The Last Metro*, was not a commercial success. Its theme, however, attests the never-ending versatility of François Truffaut.

Joan L. Cohen

Reviews

The Hollywood Reporter. October 20, 1981, p. 2.

Los Angeles Times. November 12, 1981, VI, p. 1.
The New Republic. CLXXXV, December 30, 1981, pp. 24-25.
The New York Times. October 9, 1981, p. 92.
Time. CXVIII, November 2, 1981, p. 115.
Variety. October 1, 1981, p. 3.

ZOOT SUIT

Production: Peter Burrell for Universal
Direction: Luis Valdez
Screenplay: Luis Valdez; based on his play of the same name
Cinematography: David Myers
Editing: Jacqueline Cambas
Art direction: Tom H. John
Music: Daniel Valdez, with Shorty Rogers
MPAA rating: R
Running time: 103 minutes

Principal characters:
Henry Reyna .... Daniel Valdez
El Pachuco .... Edward James Olmos
George .... Charles Aidman
Alice .... Tyne Daly
Judge .... John Anderson
Enrique .... Abel Franco
Joey .... Mike Gomez
Lupe .... Alma Rose Martinez
Della .... Rose Portillo

Although *Zoot Suit* received only limited theatrical screenings, its theme and genesis make it a milestone. *Zoot Suit* is a story of the racism and intolerance that is deeply rooted in the culture of Los Angeles. Based upon an embarrassing slice of history, the story first took artistic form as a 1978 stage play by Luis Valdez, the country's preeminent Chicano playwright. First presented on the stage of the Mark Taper Forum of the Center Theatre Group in Los Angeles, where it opened in August, 1978, *Zoot Suit* became an unqualified hit that ran for nine months. It later moved to Hollywood's Aquarius Theater. That its Broadway debut in 1979 was an immediate flop gave credence to the feeling that *Zoot Suit* was mostly a West Coast phenomenon. Still, the Mark Taper Forum believed in the work enough to back its filming. Photographed entirely at the Aquarius Theater during a fourteen-day period, *Zoot Suit* combined two sets of crews—motion picture and legitimate stage—and was made on a budget of only $2.5 million.

The history of the real-life case on which the work is based is as follows: On August 2, 1942, a Chicano boy was found dead near the Sleepy Lagoon reservoir, a popular Los Angeles-area teen and romantic hangout. Afterward, six hundred Chicanos were arrested and harassed; though there was no substantial evidence against them, twenty-two were tried. Presiding over the trial, which erupted into a mockery of justice, was a judge nicknamed "the hanging judge." A dozen young men were ultimately sentenced to life terms in San Quentin. A defense committee was formed and an appeal was won; the boys were released eighteen months later. Meanwhile, a year after their imprisonment, the so-called "zoot suit riots" broke out on the streets of downtown Los Angeles. The racially-motivated episode was triggered when a group of sailors said they had been beaten by "pachucos" (a slang term referring to Chicano youths in zoot suits, that is, suits which were made from an overabundance of material, as well as Chicanos with gang affiliations). In retaliation, some two hundred sailors from a nearby naval armory hired a convoy of taxis and went to East Los Angeles, where the streets became a battlefield.

Making use of these events, *Zoot Suit* tells the story of Henry Reyna (Daniel Valdez), a young man straddling two cultures. Henry is a zoot suiter and leader of the 38th Street Gang, but he is also about to join the Navy and fight for his country's future. The night before he is to report, however, he becomes embroiled in battle on his own turf. The trouble begins when a dance is crashed by the Downey Club, rivals to the 38th Street group. A fight breaks out, and later that night a boy is found murdered at Sleepy Lagoon. Henry and his boys are among those rounded up, and eventually a dozen of them stand trial.

Presented in highly stylized treatment, *Zoot Suit* merges music, dance, and various time frames—past, present, and moments of fantasy—to tell of Henry's trial. Actually, *Zoot Suit* probes two trials, for in addition to its portrait of social turmoil, the film depicts a young man faced with personal trials. Throughout the production, Henry is advised by a slim and strutting zoot-suited figure named El Pachuco (Edward James Olmos). Wearing a jet-black suit, red shirt, broadly brimmed hat, and a gold-chained cross, he acts as a combination stage manager and one-man Greek chorus. With a snap of his fingers, he makes sequences begin and end. With irony in his voice, he breaks the mood of heightened emotion by telling the viewer, "Hey, *carnal*! Relax! It's just a show!" Mesmerizing and mysterious, El Pachuco is easily the film's most arresting figure. He struts and sings to the raucous "Zoot Suit Boogie," gives slow, calculated meaning to the lyrics of "Marijuana Boogie," and is constantly taunting and tempting Henry. He advises him to pack a switchblade, makes fun of his dreams of entering the military service, and gives crude advice when Henry is struggling with his passions during a romantic interlude with his chaste girl friend, Della (Rose Portillo). What Henry eventually comes to realize, following both his trials, is that the hip and macho El Pachuco is his alter ego, his allegiance to tradition—good and bad. "He's my best friend and my worst enemy—myself," concludes Henry.

Highlighted by a World War II-era tableau, including pompadours and ducktails and a preponderance of big band sounds, many with a Latin beat—*Zoot Suit* is essentially a filmed play, though it is embellished with full sets as well as mastershots and close-ups. The film opens with a unique touch that serves to remind the viewer of the project's stage origins. After a restored 1939 Chevy (with license plate "ZOOTER") pulls up in front of the Aquarius, a "lowrider" and his family hurry into the theater, taking their seats just as the character of El Pachuco swaggers across the stage, introducing the "play." At various points during *Zoot Suit*, the camera seeks out the audience, and El Pachuco even occasionally makes his way among its members. This ploy in particular proved distracting for critics, who argued that it interrupted the story's flow, and was self-indulgent on Valdez's part. There was also much criticism leveled at the numerous Spanish-language phrases (the feeling was that audiences would not understand their meaning).

With its constant shifting in time, its stagey sensibility (when the boys play handball to pass away their time in prison, a chorus of pompadoured girls is on hand to sing their lament), its garish use of costumes and settings, as well as its indictment of white racism, *Zoot Suit* brought quick dismissal from some reviewers. The film's performances, however, did win some praise, especially Olmos' very cool portrayal of the snide El Pachuco, Valdez's likable Henry, and Charles Aidman and Tyne Daly as Henry's defenders. Aidman portrays the People's Lawyer hired to defend Henry and his friends (who are not even allowed the right to have haircuts or change into fresh clothing throughout their trial), and Daly is Alice Bloomfield, representative for the Congress of Industrial Organizations. During the imprisonment, it is Alice who at last breaks through the misconceptions Henry has developed concerning whites. In a particularly moving sequence, the two come to accept each other as human beings, devoid of labels. Henry even develops a romantic attachment to Alice, which she gently refuses.

In keeping with the diverse moods it evokes, *Zoot Suit* closes with Henry's release from prison, and speculations about his future. Drug addiction, murder, and even another prison term are envisioned for him by El Pachuco, yet the production ends on a hopeful note, with Alice seeing a positive future for Henry, his bride Della, and their children, who, she says, will go to college and will come to call themselves "Chicanos."

With its highly specialized theme and unique delivery, *Zoot Suit* did not find mass audiences, yet it was never geared demographically for wide audiences. Instead, it was aimed at admirers of the play, as well as ethnic communities. The very fact that a film of invigorating theme, though limited appeal, found its way to the screen signifies its importance, as well as the much-lauded reputation of its writer-director Luis Valdez. (Daniel Valdez, the film's star—and composer of some of its music—is a younger brother to Luis.)

Perhaps best known as the founder of El Teatro Campesino (Farmworkers Theatre), renown for its support of farmworkers and their causes, Valdez was born in Delano, California, to migrant farmworker parents. He himself was working grape fields at the age of six, yet while traveling from orchard to orchard throughout the state he also developed and fed his interest in theater. Before graduating from San Jose State University in 1964, his first full-length play, *The Shrunken Head of Pancho Villa*, had been produced by the drama department.

Prior to bringing *Zoot Suit* to the screen, Valdez created and wrote the scripts for several Chicano-themed productions for Public Television. He also collaborated with Richard Pryor on the script for the 1977 film, *Which Way Is Up?* Valdez also performed as an actor in that film. Of *Zoot Suit*, his most famous project, he has said, "I'm trying to bridge the gap to a place where all races can meet." When the project finally was put to film and opened at a gala premiere at the Cinerama Dome, he acknowledged, "This started out in the streets of Los Angeles some forty years ago. Now we're in the heart of Hollywood—which seems very appropriate."

Pat H. Broeske

Reviews

Commonweal. CXI, February 26, 1982, p. 111.
The Hollywood Reporter. September 30, 1981, p. 3.
Los Angeles Times. September 30, 1981, VI, p. 1.
The New York Times. January 22, 1982, III, p. 10.
Variety. September 30, 1981, p. 3.

RETROSPECTIVE FILMS

APACHE

Released: 1954
Production: Harold Hecht for Hecht-Lancaster Productions; released by United Artists
Direction: Robert Aldrich
Screenplay: James R. Webb; based on the novel *Bronco Apache* by Paul I. Wellman
Cinematography: Ernest Laszlo
Editing: Alan Crosland, Jr.
Art direction: Nicolai Remisoff
Music: David Raksin
Running time: 91 minutes

Principal characters:

Massai	Burt Lancaster
Nalinle	Jean Peters
Al Sieber	John McIntire
Hondo	Charles Buchinsky (Charles Bronson)
Weddle	John Dehner
Santos	Paul Guilfoyle
Clagg	Ian MacDonald
Lieutenant Colonel Beck	Walter Sande
Dawson	Morris Ankrum
Geronimo	Monte Blue

Indians rarely have been portrayed by Hollywood with any great sensitivity or substance. Usually, they are portrayed as whooping savages who attack innocent settlers, the cavalry, or wagon trains, one-dimensional heavies who are eliminated in the final reel of the film so that the hero and his lady can "settle" the West. Yet, Indians have sometimes been depicted sympathetically, and occasionally they have even been protagonists in films. *Apache* (1954), for example, a gritty, factually based Western adventure featuring Burt Lancaster at his rugged heroic best, presents a sympathetic picture of the proud, misunderstood Indian, reminiscent of Lancaster's role in *Jim Thorpe—All American* (1951), in which he portrayed the famed football hero of the Carlisle Indian School who became an Olympic athlete. In *Apache*, however, the hero, unlike Thorpe, does not suppress his rage or retreat into an alcoholic haze; in fact, he does his share of killing, yet still somehow survives the final credits.

Lancaster portrays the war chief Massai, a "Bronco Apache"—the name that old cowboys employed to refer to the "untamable, unconquerable, unkillable" Indian. Massai is the only Apache warrior to declare an irrevocable hatred for the white man by attempting to break the truce at the very moment that his leader, the legendary Geronimo (Monte Blue), surrenders. He not only shoots down the truce flag with a rifle but also appears willing to die for his honor. Instead, however, he is taken prisoner by Al Sieber (John McIntire), the United States Cavalry's chief scout, and by Hondo (Charles Buchinsky, who soon became known as Charles Bronson), his Indian aide. In the face of this adversity, Massai pledges to Nalinle (Jean Peters), the Indian maiden who loves him, that he will always wage war against his enemy, the white man.

Massai is chained and must go by train with Weddle (John Dehner), a corrupt Indian agent, as he escorts the tribe to St. Augustine, Florida, where Massai will be imprisoned. When the train stops in St. Louis, however, his leg irons are removed because newspaper photographers are coming on board to shoot pictures of Geronimo. A powder flash from one of the cameras causes confusion, allowing Massai to escape. He severs his handcuffs under the train wheel and spends some time in St. Louis, where he is bewildered by such aspects of modern city life as a player piano, a fire wagon, and women wearing bustles.

After stowing away on several different types of conveyances, he reaches Oklahoma, where he spends the winter with Dawson (Morris Ankrum), a reservation Cherokee who plants corn by a new technique developed by the white man. Massai is immediately impressed with the method, even though he abhors its source. Dawson, who has decided to live in peace as a farmer rather than die as a warrior, offers Massai a gift of the corn seed, which the war chief reluctantly accepts.

Massai eventually arrives home, where he has become a legend to the younger Indians. Santos (Paul Guilfoyle), Nalinle's father and the acting chief until Geronimo's return, will do anything in order to maintain the peace, and he fears that Massai's presence will undoubtedly spark an uprising. The old man therefore betrays his daughter's loved one by selling him to Hondo, who is also courting Nalinle, for some liquor. Thus, Massai, again in chains, is scheduled to go back to jail along with two other recently captured renegades. Weddle and an assistant are given the assignment to guard the Indians, but the agent decides to fake an escape attempt and kill his charges in cold blood. Weddle first turns Massai loose, but the Indian foils the intended plot and declares his own war against the white man. During Massai's "war," Weddle and his aide are executed, telephone wires are cut, and a wagon is blown up.

Massai also kidnaps Nalinle, whom he believes assisted Santos, but the girl, with some difficulty, convinces him that she was not involved in a conspiracy with her father, and that she, in fact, still loves him. To pledge their new beginning, they perform their own marriage ceremony, even as they are pursued by Sieber and Hondo. Finally, though, at the outset of winter, the pursuers give up their chase and leave the Apache and his squaw to settle in a high mountain valley.

Spring inevitably arrives, and finds Nalinle pregnant. Although Massai had earlier thrown away Dawson's corn seed, the seed took root, and now his crops are thriving. When Nalinle travels to the mountain trading post for additional seed, Sieber, who is now back on Massai's trail, recognizes her from the trader's description and with the cavalry rides off to capture Massai.

As they approach, the Apache prepares for one last battle, but by this time, Nalinle is in labor. To keep them away from his wife, Massai storms through the soldier's position, but is wounded and must retreat into the corn stalks, where he is followed by Sieber. They fight, but stop when they hear a baby cry. Massai, realizing that he is now a father, refuses to continue the battle and heads back to his cabin. Sieber, in sympathy, decides to leave the couple alone, and he and his men retreat from the mountain. They allow Massai his freedom because his "war" had been declared; he does not have to make restitution for his killings and other crimes, as an individual criminal would, since he is now willing to make peace.

Lancaster, a former circus acrobat, has plenty of opportunity to show off his athletic prowess as Massai, but, apart from that, his performance is far from the best of his career. Massai is, after all, no Sergeant Warden, Elmer Gantry, or Lou the numbers runner. Throughout his career Lancaster has consistently mixed his roles, from parts in prestigious, award-wining films such as *Come Back, Little Sheba* (1952); *From Here to Eternity* (1953); *Elmer Gantry* (1960), for which he won an Academy Award; *Birdman of Alcatraz* (1962); and *Atlantic City* (1981), to run-of-the-mill Westerns and melodramas which merely require a screen presence rather than a performance. Physically well-equipped to play Massai, he also adds definition to the Indian and makes the character appear to be a "real" human being in a state of emotional turmoil. Massai is no stereotyped "redskin" with clipped dialogue.

Jean Peters, perhaps now best remembered for her real-life role as Howard Hughes's wife than for any of her screen performances, is adequate as Nalinle, though the character is primarily a rehash of a similar role she had played opposite Marlon Brando in *Viva Zapata!* (1952). The supporting cast is serviceable, and the appearance of Charles Bronson before he adopted that familiar surname is a treat for his aficionados. Interestingly, *Apache* was the last film in which he was billed as "Buchinsky." (He still is credited under the name Buchinsky in *Vera Cruz*, also released in 1954, but that film was actually made before *Drum Beat*, his first work as "Bronson," though it came out later.) Monte Blue, a silent star by then relegated to supporting parts and "walk ons," is worthy of mention as Geronimo. The character has been played over the years by a variety of both Indian and non-Indian actors, from Chief Thunder Cloud (in 1939's *Geronimo*) and Jay Silverheels (1950's *Broken Arrow*, 1952's *Battle at Apache Pass*, and 1956's *Walk the Proud Land*) to Chuck Connors (1962's *Geronimo!*), but rarely as sympathetically as portrayed by Blue.

Apache is crisply directed by Robert Aldrich, whose best films, in retrospect, are from the 1950's and 1960's and include *Kiss Me Deadly* (1955), the allegorical Mike Hammer mystery; *Attack!* (1956), one of the most underrated war films ever; *What Ever Happened to Baby Jane?* (1962), with Bette Davis and Joan Crawford; and *The Dirty Dozen* (1967), a solid, action-packed war drama. More recently his films have been disappointing at best, among them *Twilight's Last Gleaming* (1977), *The Choirboys* (1977), a serious distortion of Joseph Wambaugh's fine novel which was subsequently repudiated by the author, and *The Frisco Kid* (1979).

Apache was the first production of Hecht-Lancaster, an independent company formed by the actor with producer Harold Hecht. They had seen *World for Ransom* (1954), a neat low-budget drama filmed by Aldrich in ten-and-a-half days, and his work on that film convinced Lancaster and Hecht to sign him for their project. Since Aldrich had wanted to buy, but could not afford, the rights to Paul I. Wellman's novel *Bronco Apache*, the eventual source for Lancaster's film, the director gladly signed on for the Hecht-Lancaster project.

Aldrich soon convinced Lancaster that, at the film's finale, Massai should be shot in the back by the cavalry; however, United Artists, which released the picture, felt that the Indian should remain unharmed. Aldrich took the precaution of filming both endings, but the latter was used in the final print. Hecht, Lancaster, and Aldrich then went on to make *Vera Cruz*. The director also later worked with Bronson (who had a supporting role in *Vera Cruz*) in *Four for Texas* (1963) and *The Dirty Dozen*, and Lancaster in *Ulzana's Raid* (1972) and *Twilight's Last Gleaming*.

Apache, budgeted at $1,240,000, was filmed on location in New Mexico and at Keywest Studios in Hollywood. The reviews were mixed, but it did nicely at the box office, earning $3,250,000—a healthy figure for its year—and ranking twenty-third on *Variety*'s list of "1954 Box Office Champs."

Although it is no *High Noon* (1952) or *Shane* (1953), the film is a serviceable, enjoyable Western of its period, with an enlightening portrayal of an Indian hero. It is frequently revived on television and is worth watching.

Rob Edelman

Reviews

Commonweal. LX, July 30, 1954, p. 413.
The Hollywood Reporter. June 30, 1954, p. 3.
The New York Times. July 10, 1954, p. 7.
Time. LXIV, August 9, 1954, p. 84.
Variety. June 30, 1954, p. 3.

THE BAREFOOT CONTESSA

Released: 1954
Production: Forrest E. Johnston for Figaro Productions; released by United Artists
Direction: Joseph L. Mankiewicz
Screenplay: Joseph L. Mankiewicz
Cinematography: Jack Cardiff
Editing: William Hornbeck
Art direction: Arrigo Equini
Music: Mario Nascimbene
Running time: 128 minutes

Principal characters:
Harry Dawes .... Humphrey Bogart
Maria Vargas .... Ava Gardner
Oscar Muldoon .... Edmond O'Brien (AA)
Alberto Bravano .... Marius Goring
Count Vincenzo Torlato-Favrini .... Rossano Brazzi
Kirk Edwards .... Warren Stevens
Myrna .... Mari Aldon

In 1953 Joseph L. Mankiewicz wrote *The Barefoot Contessa* with Ava Gardner in mind for the lead role of the tragic movie goddess Maria Vargas. It was an excellent script, as one would expect from the man who had received Oscars for his writing and direction of *Letter to Three Wives* in 1949 and *All About Eve* in 1950. Upon reading the script, Gardner felt that it would be her best role if only her studio, M-G-M, would loan her out to United Artists and Mankiewicz for the film. M-G-M had a reputation for driving a hard bargain when loaning out its stars, however; for example, it made Selznick-International release *Gone with the Wind* (1939) through M-G-M in return for Clark Gable's services. United Artists and Mankiewicz could not afford any such expense, though, and for a while it looked as if the project would have to be made with some other actress. Gardner was persistent and difficult, however, and finally forced Metro to pacify her by consenting to the loan-out.

Mankiewicz directed *The Barefoot Contessa* in and around Rome during the winter of 1954 using the gorgeous Technicolor cinematography of Jack Cardiff to its best effect. Humphrey Bogart played her friend and screenwriter, and Italian film star Rossano Brazzi her husband. With all that talent brought together, everyone's expectations were high. Bogart gave one of his best performances. Edmond O'Brien played Oscar Muldoon, the press agent, with such force that he won the Academy Award for Best Supporting Actor.

Gardner threw herself into her part with an abandon that surprised her coworkers.

The Barefoot Contessa was inspired by Vincente Minnelli's *The Bad and the Beautiful* (1952). The film opens with Harry Dawes (Humphrey Bogart), a veteran Hollywood director and screenwriter, standing alone, away from the crowd that has come for the burial of a movie star. There, in an ancient cemetery on the Italian Riviera, a priest performs the ceremony, as a light drizzle falls upon the curious. Among the onlookers, only Harry really knew the star, and the audience is made privy to Dawes's thoughts through a voice-over narration as he begins to tell her story in flashback.

It began three years before, when Harry accompanied a millionaire-turned-filmmaker to Europe on a talent search. The millionaire, Kirk Edwards (Warren Stevens), is an arrogant dictator, but Dawes is forced to hold his tongue and do Edwards' bidding because he needs the money and work. A decade before, Dawes had been a famous director, but liquor had ruined his finances and reputation.

Accompanying Kirk Edwards on his talent search is his press agent, Oscar Muldoon (Edmond O'Brien), and Myrna (Mari Aldon), a beautiful but hard-boiled blond. Edwards visits a cabaret because he has heard about the gorgeous dancer who performs there.

Unfortunately, they have arrived just as the dancer has finished her performance. When he hears that she will neither dance again nor join him for drinks, Edwards arrogantly demands that Oscar fetch the dancer from her dressing room. Oscar returns mopping his brow, and Edwards demands to know where the dancer is. Oscar answers, "She won't come. She's a wildcat."

Irritated by Oscar's failure, Edwards turns to Harry and demands that he bring the dancer to him. Harry, who finds Maria (Ava Gardner) with a young man whom she calls "her cousin," is a bit more successful. Maria agrees to come to Edwards' table, but turns him down coldly when he suggests that she sign a contract with him. Later that night Harry is ruthlessly dispatched by Edwards to make sure that Maria come back to Hollywood with them. Harry finds that Maria lives in a strange home with an almost catatonic father and a screaming, domineering mother. Although Maria at first refuses the offer, she admires Harry's honesty and eventually she does go to Hollywood.

Maria becomes a star under Harry's direction, and they become very close, although only in a platonic sense. Harry seems to be the only one who understands her, even when she continues her practice of picking up young "cousins" with whom she sleeps. Edwards, meanwhile, has continued his sexual pursuit of Maria without any success. One evening, at a party at Maria's home, a South American billionaire named Alberto Bravano (Marius Goring) takes an interest in Maria. She is uninterested in him, however, until Bravano has a verbal fight with Edwards. The Howard Hughes-like Edwards boasts about his honesty and integrity, while Bravano only laughs at him and calls him a pious hypocrite. Edwards becomes enraged and demands that Maria throw Bravano out, but she only replies, "You always pick the wrong time to ask me." She totally rejects Edwards and decides to go away with Bravano, as does Oscar, who finally tells Edwards off. As Edwards leaves, this time with Myrna, she delivers one of the famous lines of the film and a Hollywood truism, "Do you know why I put up with it? I need the money."

The scene switches to the French Riviera and, through Oscar's narration, the audience learns that it is about a year later. To the world, Maria is Bravano's mistress, but in reality she is not, just as she was never Edwards'. Bravano is now tiring of her, although he enjoys the prestige she gives him. One evening when Bravano has lost a great deal of money at the gambling tables, he insults Maria but is interrupted by Count Vincenzo Torlato-Favrini (Rossano Brazzi), who slaps his face. Maria does not know him, but earlier that day she had seen him at a gypsy camp and they had been attracted to each other almost instantly.

Finally, Maria is happy. She marries Vincenzo and becomes his countess, but on their wedding night she receives a shock. Vincenzo gives her a medical report which reveals that during the war he had received injuries which left him physically impotent. She is shattered—her love for Vincenzo has not diminished, but she will never be able to get the sexual fulfillment which she so desperately needs.

Later she tells Harry, who is in Italy making a film, that she has become pregnant by a local boy and will be able to give Vincenzo what he has always wanted, an heir. Vincenzo, however, does not realize the depths of Maria's devotion; he follows her to her lover's apartment and kills them both. In the last scene, which returns to Maria's funeral, the audience sees the grieving Vincenzo being taken away by police.

The Barefoot Contessa did well at the box office, due in large measure to the drawing power of Humphrey Bogart and Ava Gardner, who was then at the peak of her career. Critically it did not do particularly well, although Mankiewicz was nominated for an Oscar for his screenplay and O'Brien won the award for Best Supporting Actor. It is repeated frequently on television, and although it is badly dated, the theme of Maria's sexual frustration seems remarkably contemporary. Perhaps the most significant criticism of the film is that the building up of the story takes far too much screen time and the denouement comes too quickly. The film jumps from sequence to sequence without smooth transitions. This is particularly evident at the end, when Maria's murder comes as a bit of a shock, even though the audience knows at the outset that Maria will die. Perhaps if Vincenzo had not been built up so strongly as a man of great sensitivity and character, his murderous act would have been more believable.

Larry Lee Holland

Reviews

The Hollywood Reporter. September 27, 1954, p. 3.
The New York Times. September 30, 1954, p. 37.
The New Yorker. XXX, October 9, 1954, p. 173.
Newsweek. XLIV, October 4, 1954, pp. 86-87.
Time. LXIV, October 18, 1954, p. 102.
Variety. September 29, 1954, p. 3.

BECKY SHARP

Released: 1935
Production: Kenneth MacGowan for Pioneer
Direction: Rouben Mamoulian
Screenplay: Francis Edward Faragoh; based on the play *Vanity Fair* by Langdon Mitchell and the novel *Vanity Fair* by William Makepeace Thackeray
Cinematography: Ray Rennahan
Editing: Archie Marshek
Art direction: Robert Edmond Jones
Music: Roy Webb
Running time: 85 minutes

Principal characters:

Becky Sharp	Miriam Hopkins
Marquis of Steyne	Sir Cedric Hardwicke
Joseph Sedley	Nigel Bruce
Amelia Sedley	Frances Dee
Rawdon Crawley	Alan Mowbray
George Osborne	G. P. Huntley, Jr.
Sir Pitt Crawley	George Hassell
Pitt Crawley, Jr.	William Stack
William Dobbin	Colin Tapley
Julia Crawley	Alison Skipworth
Duchess of Richmond	Doris Lloyd
Miss Pinkerton	Elspeth Dudgeon

Although it belongs to the early days of film history, *Becky Sharp* is the most recent screen adaptation of William Makepeace Thackeray's novel *Vanity Fair* (published serially in 1847 and 1848) and the only film version to be titled after the heroine of the novel rather than the novel itself. Previous film versions of *Vanity Fair* had been produced in 1911, 1923, and 1932, featuring, respectively, Helen Gardner, Mabel Ballin, and Myrna Loy in the role of Becky.

It is not as an adaptation of *Vanity Fair* (or as a screen version of Langdon Mitchell's play of the Thackeray novel) that *Becky Sharp* holds a prominent position in film history, however, but rather as the first full-length feature film to be shot in the Technicolor three-strip process. Technicolor had introduced a two-color subtractive process with *Toll of the Sea* in 1922, and through the 1920's a number of silent features, such as *The Ten Commandments* (1923), included Technicolor segments. There were also a number of complete two-color Technicolor features, notably *The Wanderer of the Wasteland* (1924), *The Black Pirate* (1926), and *Redskin* (1928). By May, 1932, Technicolor had built its first three-strip color camera, which introduced a new accuracy of color and tone reproduction to color motion pictures, and three-strip Technicolor was to become the film industry standard for color film until 1950, when Eastman Kodak introduced its new color negative/positive film stock. Technicolor prints, as such, ceased to be made after 1975.

The first film to utilize the new three-strip Technicolor process was the Walt Disney animated short, *Flowers and Trees* (1932) and was soon followed by what is generally recognized as the first live action, three-strip Technicolor short, *La Cucaracha* (1934), produced by the newly-formed Pioneer Pictures, established by Meriam C. Cooper and John Hay (Jock) Whitney. Robert Edmond Jones, who was recognized as one of the legitimate stage's finest designers and an authority in the use of color, was responsible for the "look" of *La Cucaracha* while the production was left in the capable hands of Kenneth MacGowan, who was on loan from RKO, where Cooper was under contract. For its first Technicolor feature, *Becky Sharp*, Pioneer again utilized the talents of Jones and MacGowan, and RKO was again signed as distributor for the film.

Lowell Sherman was intended to be the director of *Becky Sharp* and had, in fact, directed some scenes before his untimely death put an end to what had been a brilliant career as both a director and actor. Rouben Mamoulian was then signed to take over the direction, and he, apparently, reshot all of Sherman's original footage. Despite a number of other setbacks, which included the director and his two female stars, Miriam Hopkins and Frances Dee, contracting pneumonia, as well as the loss of one complete reel of negative in a projection room fire, Mamoulian completed the film on schedule and was honored at the 1935 Venice Film Festival before going on to New York to direct the original Broadway production of *Porgy and Bess* later that year.

Becky Sharp opens in Miss Pinkerton's Academy for Young Ladies, as two of the young ladies, Amelia Sedley (Frances Dee) and Becky Sharp (Miriam Hopkins) are about to leave, having reached adulthood. Miss Pinkerton (Elspeth Dudgeon) fawns over Amelia and presents her with a leatherbound copy of Dr. Johnson's *Dictionary*, while presenting a cheaper edition of the same work to Becky, a charity pupil. Becky, however, takes pains to point out to Miss Pinkerton that she has been helpful around the Academy in taking care of the younger girls and (because of her French ancestry) teaching French. Amelia's brother, the plump Joseph Sedley (Nigel Bruce), comes to pick up his sister, and, on learning that Becky has nowhere to go, insists that she come along with them. The opening scene ends with Becky rushing back into the Academy and hurling her copy of the dictionary at Miss Pinkerton, shouting, "Words are but little thanks—yet let this speak volumes!"

During her stay with the Sedleys, Becky hopes in vain for a proposal from Joseph; but his parents pack him off to India, away from temptation. At the same time, Amelia receives proposals from two childhood sweethearts, George Osborne (G. P. Huntly, Jr.) and William Dobbin (Colin Tapley), and accepts that of the former. Becky is forced to accept a position as governess to the children of the elderly Sir Pitt Crawley (George Hassell). Two of Sir Pitt's children are, however, adults: Pitt, Jr., (William Stack), a pious and somewhat bigoted clergyman and his brother, the rakish soldier Rawdon (Alan Mowbray) who takes Becky away to become a companion to his aunt in London. Becky and Rawdon are soon married. The marriage has its ups and downs; both gamble and both are constantly in debt.

With Napoleon's escape from Elba (which Becky describes as "amusing"), Rawdon is ordered to Belgium and takes Becky along with him. We next see Becky at a ball given by the Duchess of Richmond (Doris Lloyd), which is taking place outside a small village named Waterloo. Amelia's husband George dances with Becky and then loses at cards to Rawdon, while Becky meets and becomes infatuated with the Marquis of Steyne (Sir Cedric Hardwicke). Cannon-fire interrupts the celebrations and the men quickly prepare for battle. Suddenly, the ladies flee in their carriages. George asks Becky to elope with him, but she rejects him, telling him to return to Amelia (who suspects Becky of trying to flirt with her husband). As Becky watches the soldiers depart for battle, she comments, "In an hour they'll be dying for their country. Well, I'm dying for my breakfast!" The Marquis of Steyne is on hand to take care of that immediate need.

Following the Battle of Waterloo, at which George is killed, Becky rises in social circles, thanks largely to the patronage of the Marquis of Steyne. When Rawdon's gambling debts force the couple into the position of having to raise five hundred pounds overnight, Becky tries to blackmail Amelia's former suitor William for the money, offering to sell him a letter written to her by George, in which he asks her to elope with him, a letter that William could use to persuade Amelia to forget her dead fiancé and marry him. William, however, turns Becky down. Pitt Crawley is willing to loan her the money, but his hypocrisy sickens Becky and she refuses his offer. Finally, the Marquis of Steyne offers to provide the money in return for Becky's spending the night with him. She agrees, but their assignation is interrupted by the return of Rawdon.

Becky has now lost everything: her husband and her pride as well as her home and possessions, sold to pay off the gambling debts. We next see her performing in a tavern show in Bath, where, under the name of Madame Rebeque, she sings "The Lass with the Delicate Air." She is not well received by the customers of the tavern, but is seen by Joseph Sedley who has returned from India. He and Amelia visit Becky and try to persuade her to return home with them. Becky shows Amelia the letter from George and thus paves the way for her friend's marriage to William. She and Joseph then decide to marry also. Later, however, while Joseph remains hidden, Becky is visited by Pitt Crawley and his wife, who beg her to come with them, stopping en route at the church to pray and listen to a sermon. Pleading fatigue, Becky persuades the two to leave, but not before they have left her with a volume of sermons on morality. In a replay of the opening sequence, Becky leans out of her window, calling after Pitt and his wife, and hurls the book at them, shouting, "Virtue is its own reward."

La Cucaracha is probably one of the dullest shorts ever produced, and, unfortunately, *Becky Sharp* has the same fault. It is slow and tedious, and all it has to recommend it is the color, which is stunningly beautiful and was the result of very careful thought and consideration. As Rouben Mamoulian explained in an interview with *Photoplay* (August, 1935), "We have tried to use color as we use music or any other contributing element to drama. We help to build climaxes with it. After all, Shakespeare knew what he was talking about when he said, 'The play's the thing.'" The use of color in *Becky Sharp* reaches its climax with the Duchess of Richmond's ball, at which the bright colors of the ladies' gowns are juxtaposed against the grays and reds of the soldiers' uniforms and with the darkness of the scene after the approaching battle has broken up the ball. Earlier, another skillful device, the shadow of Napoleon passing before towns and villages, had been used to emphasize the impact that Napoleon was to have on Europe.

For the color, one must give credit to Robert Edmond Jones. For the tediousness of the story and its telling, one must blame Mamoulian. The latter must also accept responsibility for what is surely the worst error in continuity ever perpetrated in the history of the cinema. In the final sequences of *Becky Sharp*, Becky is living in an apartment on the second floor of the building, and yet continually we see people walking backwards and forwards in front of her window!

Fortunately, the players all acquit themselves well. Miriam Hopkins is ideally cast as the leading character, of whom the Marquis of Steyne rightly comments, "There isn't an ounce of sweetness or goodness about you." Sir Cedric Hardwicke is excellent as Steyne, as is Alan Mowbray as Rawdon. Alison Skipworth, though, is miscast as Rawdon's aunt, while Billie Burke is totally wasted in the small role of an outraged member of the aristocracy at the Duchess of Richmond's ball.

Contemporary critics all admired the color, but remained dubious about the story. Typical is this comment from Andre Sennwald in *The New York Times* (June 14, 1935), "Although its faults are too numerous to earn it distinction as a screen drama, . . . it is a momentous event, and it may be that in a few years it will be regarded as the equal in historical importance of the first crude and wretched talking pictures."

For many years, *Becky Sharp* has been unavailable for viewing in its original Technicolor form. The film was reissued in a two-color process known as Cinecolor, and all extant prints are in that format. UCLA Film Archives, however, under the supervision of its preservation officer, Robert Gitt, has been working to restore *Becky Sharp* to its former Technicolor glory, and, by the end of 1982, the feature will once again be available for viewing—in both 35mm and 16mm—in Technicolor.

Anthony Slide

Reviews

The Hollywood Reporter. June 14, 1935, p. 3.
The New Republic. LXXXIII, June 26, 1935, p. 194.
The New York Times. June 14, 1935, p. 27.
The New York Times. June 23, 1935, IX, p. 23.
Newsweek. V, June 22, 1935, pp. 22-23.
Variety. June 19, 1935, p. 6.

THE BRIDGE OF SAN LUIS REY

Released: 1929
Production: Metro-Goldwyn-Mayer
Direction: Charles Brabin
Screenplay: Ruth Cummings and Marian Ainslee; based on Alice D. G. Miller's adaptation of the novel of the same name by Thornton Wilder
Cinematography: Merritt B. Gerstad
Editing: Margaret Booth
Art direction: Cedric Gibbons (AA)
Music: Carli Elinor
Running time: 86 minutes

Principal characters:
La Perichole .... Lily Damita
Uncle Pio .... Ernest Torrence
Pepita .... Raquel Torres
Manuel .... Don Alvarado
Esteban .... Duncan Renaldo
Father Juniper .... Henry B. Walthall
Viceroy .... Michael Vavitch
Marquesa .... Emily Fitzroy
Doña Carla ....Jane Winton
Jaime .... Gordon Thorpe
Captain Alvarado .... Mitchell Lewis
Don Vicente ....Paul Ellis
A nun .... Eugenie Besserer
A townsman .... Tully Marshall

Thornton Wilder's Pulitzer Prize-winning novel, *The Bridge of San Luis Rey*, was first filmed in 1929 by M-G-M as a partial talkie, and like all such hybrids it suffers from problems which it does not entirely overcome. Most partial talkies had problems deciding when to talk and when to be silent, and how to cope with silent stars who dominated the mute sequences but were significantly unimpressive when the sound scenes commenced. The producers of *The Bridge of San Luis Rey*, however, found an easy solution to this problem. The film begins and ends with Father Juniper (Henry B. Walthall) telling the townspeople the story of the lives of the five people killed when the Bridge of San Luis Rey collapsed, and everything between these scenes is silent. Walthall was an accomplished stage actor who had been in films since the American Biograph days and is best known to audiences for his role as "The Little Colonel" in *The Birth of a Nation* (1915). Walthall is not the star of *The Bridge of San Luis Rey*, but he dominates the film—even when he is not on screen—just as he was to do a few years later in the Will Rogers vehicle *Judge Priest* (1933).

The date is July 20, 1714, and the film opens with the collapse of the bridge of San Luis Rey, built by the Incas, blessed by St. Louis, and guarded by the Cathedral of St. Rose of Lima. The bridge was part of the main highway in Peru, and its collapse on the day of the Feast of St. Louis terrifies the townspeople, who see it as an omen of disaster. Led by one of their own citizens (Tully Marshall), they come to Father Juniper for an explanation. Aside from Walthall, the only other speaking role is that of Tully Marshall, another stage actor who had appeared on Broadway in the late 1800's and had long been active in films. The dialogue sequence between the two men, which takes up most of the opening reel of the film, is impressive, with the one (Marshall) questioning and the other (Walthall) explaining and attempting to offer consolation.

As Father Juniper begins his story, the film becomes a silent drama, accompanied by a synchronized music score and sound effects. Although the audience has seen five people fall to their deaths from the bridge, it is not aware of their identities, and is kept in the dark until the end of the priest's story.

Father Juniper tells of the Marquesa (another wonderful characterization by the harsh-featured Emily Fitzroy), an ugly woman who was overly expressive in her love for her beautiful daughter, Doña Clare (Jane Winton), who had married and moved to Spain. The Marquesa asks the local abbess for a pupil to come and live with her as her ward (and, incidentally, to help with the household chores), and the abbess sends Pepita (Raquel Torres). Through Pepita the Marquesa learns of her shortcomings, that she was guilty of the wrong kind of love for her daughter, and decides to change her life.

Meanwhile Pepita has fallen in love with Estaban (Duncan Renaldo), and that purely physical affection convinces her to return to the convent. Estaban and his twin brother, Manuel (Don Alvarado), had been left as infants at the abbess' school. Manuel falls in love with the fiery actress, La Perichole (Lily Damita), for whom he writes letters to her bullfighter lover. He pretends to his brother that he does not care for the actress—for nothing has ever come between the two men—but after she has pushed Manuel down a flight of steps, in a delirium he tells Estaban the truth and then dies. Unable to face life without his brother, Estaban attempts to hang himself, but is cut down in time by Captain Alvarado (Mitchell Lewis), with whom Estaban is to sail around the world.

Finally there is the story of Uncle Pio (Ernest Torrence), who had discovered the young La Perichole when she was singing and dancing in a tavern. He is disturbed about the change in his protégée, and eventually she agrees to allow him to take her small son, Jaime (Gordon Thorpe), and educate him as a gentleman.

In the final reel of *The Bridge of San Luis Rey*, the film again becomes a talkie, and Father Juniper reveals that the five people killed when the bridge collapsed were the Marquesa, Pepita, Estaban, Uncle Pio, and Jaime. Father Juniper explains that all five had known love and through suffering had experienced a deepening of that love. He continues, "There is a land of the living and the land of the dead—and the bridge is love—the only survival, the only meaning."

Those familiar with Wilder's novel will note a number of major plot changes. In the novel, Father Juniper was present at the collapse of the bridge. He then spent his life investigating the circumstances behind the deaths of the five, published a book on the subject which was condemned by the Church, and eventually was burned at the stake for explaining God's way to man a little too fully. One copy of Father Juniper's book had survived, and that had come into the possession of the author of *The Bridge of San Luis Rey*. The novel does not suggest a romance between Pepita and Esteban, and Manuel is not pushed down a flight of stairs by La Perichole, but instead cuts his leg against a piece of jagged metal.

Despite a "Hollywood look" to the players and their costumes, the sets are particularly impressive, notably the bridge and the interior of the cathedral. Cedric Gibbons received the second Academy Award given for Best Art Direction for his work on the production. Henry B. Walthall steals the acting honors for the film, with many of the older players (particularly Tully Marshall, Ernest Torrence, and Emily Fitzroy) coming a close second. The younger players—Lily Damita, Raquel Torres, Don Alvarado, and Duncan Renaldo—resemble too closely Hollywood's idea of what South Americans are like. Damita's best-known film, aside from this, was *The Cock-Eyed World* (1929); she abandoned the screen after her marriage to Errol Flynn, and has remained in quiet retirement. Torres came to fame with a beautiful performance in *White Shadows of the South Seas* (1928); like Damita, her film career was over by the mid-1930's. Don Alvarado specialized in second-string Latin lover roles from the mid-1920's through the 1940's; his major films include *Drums of Love* (1928) and *Rio Rita* (1929). Renaldo began his screen career with M-G-M in 1928, graduating to Western roles in the 1940's, and is best known as the star of the popular television series, "The Cisco Kid."

The Bridge of San Luis Rey was well liked by the critics, many of whom pointed out, correctly, that the film was too intellectual to achieve much of a box-office success and that it simply had too many characters for an audience to be able to follow and enjoy the plot. In *Script* (June 8, 1929), Rob Wagner wrote, "After the noise and turmoil of 'sound effects'; after the rowdy crime and gangster plays; after the blare and bubbles of the Follies show, what a relief to sit through an hour of art! *The Bridge of San Luis Rey* will not be very successful—a woman beside me yawned—for sheer beauty is not good screen material, especially literary and intellectual beauty. . . . " *Variety* (May 22, 1929) called the production, "A profoundly religious story, magnificently screened picture, but not box office." In *The New York Times* (May 20, 1929),

Mordaunt Hall wrote, "Although it has its queer and unconvincing cinematic ideas, it is in many respects a worthy contribution. Its dramatic value is never pulsating, but it succeeds in holding the attention."

The Bridge of San Luis Rey was remade in 1944 by producer Benedict Bogeaus for United Artists release, under the direction of Roland V. Lee, and starring Nazimova, Louis Calhern, Blanche Yurka, and Donald Woods. Two other Thornton Wilder works have been filmed: *Our Town* (1940) and *The Matchmaker* (1958, later the basis for the Broadway musical *Hello, Dolly!*, filmed in 1970).

Anthony Slide

Reviews

Film Daily. April 28, 1929, p. 9.
The New York Times. May 20, 1929, p. 22.
The New York Times. May 26, 1929, IX, p. 7.
Outlook. CLII, June, 1929, p. 235.
Variety. May 22, 1929, p. 3.

COME AND GET IT

Released: 1936
Production: Merritt Hulburd for Samuel Goldwyn; released by United Artists
Direction: Howard Hawks and William Wyler
Screenplay: Jane Murfin and Jules Furthman; based on the novel *Come and Get It* by Edna Ferber
Cinematography: Gregg Toland and Rudolph Maté
Editing: Edward Curtiss
Art direction: Richard Day
Logging Sequence Direction: Richard Rossen
Music: Alfred Newman
Running time: 99 minutes

Principal characters:
Barney Glasgow .... Edward Arnold
Lotta Morgan/Lotta Bostrom .... Frances Farmer
Swan Bostrom .... Walter Brennan (AA)
Richard Glasgow .... Joel McCrea

Films adapted from the novels of Edna Ferber invariably conform to a certain pattern which finds the narrative divided into a two-part structure. In the first half, the characters are young and vigorous and their lives are full of promise. The second half returns to the same characters years later when they are much older and suffering from their mistakes, disappointments, and failures. *Cimarron* (1931 and 1960), *Giant* (1956), and *Ice Palace* (1960) are among the films which follow this structure. They are alike also in that the opening segments are invariably more exciting and intriguing than the closing segments. The stories generally originate on a frontier of some kind, where the characters are facing the challenges of untamed lands. The passage of years, however, causes these rugged settings to disappear, and the characters tend to wind up rich and comfortable in a civilized world. Unfortunately, the characters have become as tired and dull as the world in which they now live and there is a stiff and slow quality to the final portions of the works absent in the more vibrant opening passages. Although *Come and Get It* conforms to the pattern described, it is much more successful than the other films in sustaining interest all the way through the story, but its first half is so rich in exceptional qualities that its ultimate imperfection is uncommonly sad.

The first half of the film is a logging story, set in the Northwest and centering exclusively on three characters—ambitious Barney Glasgow (Edward Arnold), his friend Swan Bostrom (Walter Brennan), and saloon entertainer Lotta Morgan (Frances Farmer). Barney is in charge of a large section of trees to be cut and delivered to the mill and wants to do an exceptionally impressive job. He successfully prevails upon his loggers to do the considerable work required with great skill and speed and rewards them with a bonus and a night on the town. Barney and Swan meet Lotta in a saloon, where they are captivated by her singing of the song "Aura Lee." She joins them at their table, and when a fight breaks out she takes their side. The three are outnumbered, but by hurling tin trays at their opponents they prevail over a roomful of men. Barney and Lotta fall in love, but their brief romance ends when Barney is called away by the mill owner. The mill owner's daughter wants to marry Barney, and he realizes that by responding positively he will rapidly attain the powerful position he seeks. Swan breaks the news to a shocked and heartbroken Lotta, and the closing scene of this portion of the story finds Lotta preparing to marry Swan.

Comprising only about forty-five minutes of film, this little story is a stunning piece of cinema. It displays direction by Howard Hawks that ranks with the best he has ever done. (All accounts confirm that William Wyler's participation in the film was not considerable and was confined to the second half.) With chillingly brilliant economy, Hawks conveys the full force of tragedy. The heartbreaking transience of Hawks's deceptively casual images puts to shame the strenuous virtuosity of most directors. He literally does not waste a frame. As the film opens, Barney suddenly appears and rings the dinner bell for the loggers in his inimitable manner, shouting the film's title in a brief fixed shot which may be instructively compared to the more elaborate treatment of the same image with which Wyler concludes the film. The logging sequences—beautifully filmed by Richard Rossen, a second-unit director long associated with Hawks—are assembled with a rhythmic composure and clarity of purpose which seamlessly integrates images of documentary purity into the narrative structure. The entire logging process is encapsulated in these passages, but Hawks scorns any didactic acknowledgment that this is occurring. When the job is done, he moves on. In a moment which defines Hawks's style as well as any other, Lotta is introduced into the film without any visual or dramatic emphasis. Barney and Swan are standing in front of a gambling table with some other men, and suddenly she appears in the shot, casually mingling with the group. When she sings "Aura Lee," Hawks's judicious use of a brief, romantically styled medium close-up—a soft and delicately lit image worthy of Josef von Sternberg—is sufficient to suggest the moment in which Lotta burns her way into the hearts of Barney and Swan.

The dramatically effective compression of the narrative which Hawks accomplishes by means of pace and visual style is enhanced by the adept playing of Arnold and Brennan (who won the first Best Supporting Actor Academy Award for his performance). The successful casting of these two character actors is an indication of Hawks's gift for credibly treating a completely unconventional romantic triangle. The crucial element which makes Hawks's work so rewarding, however, is the presence of Frances Farmer in the role of Lotta. Even more than Hawks, she is the one who makes *Come and Get It* a special film.

Frances Farmer was an actress of singular skill and rare beauty whose harrowing, tragic life has provided the material for two 1982 films (one of them a television movie adapted from her autobiography *Will There Really Be a Morning?*). *Come and Get It* was her first film and the only good one she ever made. As a result of her unconventional attitudes, an affronted Hollywood subsequently confined her to increasingly inane program pictures which effectively ended her career after a few years. Her rapport with Hawks, however, was exceptional. He stated both at the time and in his later years that she was the best actress he ever worked with, and the two conspired to transform the role of Lotta from that of a meek and passive girl to that of an independent and vibrant one. To this end, the frequent Hawks collaborator Jules Furthman probably contributed a great deal, and his co-credit for the film's screenplay suggests the extent to which Hawks insisted upon revising the screenplay that he had originally been given to shoot. In fact, Farmer had not even been cast as Lotta by Samuel Goldwyn—she had been set for a smaller part in the film—but Hawks was so impressed with her when they met on the set that he put her into the role without seeking Goldwyn's approval.

The efforts of Hawks, Furthman, and Farmer resulted in the first appearance of the archetypal Hawksian heroine so familiar in the director's later films—the openhearted, sexy girl with the low voice and disarming personality who can hold her own in male company. Farmer brings to this archetype an unaffected sweetness and heartrending vulnerability which Hawks wisely never sought to evoke from the actresses he used later; even the alluring Bonnie Lee of the peerless Jean Arthur in Hawks's *Only Angels Have Wings* (1939) does not possess this poignancy. Lotta is significantly the only Hawks heroine who suffers a tragic fate. The character is a singular match for the gifts of the actress.

Between the first and second parts of *Come and Get It* Lotta Morgan dies, and much of the magic of the film dies with her. Rich and unhappily married, Barney falls in love with the daughter of Swan and Lotta—also called Lotta and also played by Farmer, but a much less vivid character than her mother—and attempts to buy her love by giving her things and taking care of her. In true Ferber fashion, he is compensating for the unfulfilling life he brought upon himself by deserting the original Lotta years before. Young Lotta falls in love with Barney's son Richard (Joel McCrea), who returns her affection. During the course of an elaborate party, a potentially violent confrontation occurs between father and son; but young Lotta intervenes on Barney's behalf, reminding Richard that Barney is an old man. Realizing that he has made a fool of himself, Barney watches sadly as the young couple departs to make their own life together.

In all essential details, this second part of the film completes the story. Though physically absent, Lotta Morgan haunts many of the scenes, her loss to Barney tangibly felt through the continued presence of Swan and her second incarnation in the daughter who resembles her. The friendship between Barney and Swan is beautifully delineated in a reunion scene gently infused with melancholy. Barney's ill-concealed regret over his desertion of Lotta and uncomfortable envy aroused by Swan's happy years with her are subtly contrasted with the simple good will of Swan. The pace is discernibly slower, but a more reflective approach seems appropriate to the material. Still, the creative urgency felt in every frame of the first half becomes intermittent. Hawks seems less engaged by the material unless it offers some humor, as in the charming taffy-pulling sequence which initiates the romance between Richard and young Lotta. These two characters are well-realized, but numerous other new characters seem incidental or insufficiently developed.

The change of directors also weakened the film. There is no reason to denigrate Wyler. He stepped in reluctantly, did a professional job, honored Hawks's narrative intentions, and would have preferred for his predecessor to have sole credit. Hawks's revisions of the screenplay had angered Goldwyn, who believed that directors should not write. The imperious producer fired Hawks, and Wyler finished the film. Ironically, the sequence most recognizably his is the very ending that Hawks had devised. Wyler's elegant style for this sequence might have been well-intentioned, but its visual elaborateness contrasts too jarringly with the stylistic directness of Hawks. Dramatic camera angles and portentous staircase shots seem to come out of nowhere, and the echo of the film's opening image of Barney ringing the dinner bell and shouting "Come and get it!" finds Wyler aggressively tracking into a close-up of a too visibly anguished Arnold.

In the final analysis, *Come and Get It* admirably solves the problems of adapting an Edna Ferber novel for the screen. Its narrative has an impressive unity, even if its style does not. There are many beautiful aspects to the production, not the least of which is Alfred Newman's musical score, which beautifully integrates the "Aura Lee" melody with an equally sensitive main theme composed by Newman himself. Of course, it is disappointing that a film would achieve the high level which this one does in its first half and ultimately be less than a masterpiece. Nevertheless, *Come and Get It* is a film to be valued for a glowing stretch of Hawksian artistry and cherished as the single enduring testament of a remarkable actress.

Blake Lucas

Reviews

The Hollywood Reporter. October 27, 1936, p. 3.

The New York Times. November 12, 1936, p. 31.
The New York Times. November 15, 1936, XI, p. 1.
Newsweek. VIII, November 14, 1936, p. 60.
Time. XXVIII, November 16, 1936, p. 37.
Variety. November 18, 1936, p. 12.

COWBOY

Released: 1958
Production: Jullian Blaustein for Columbia
Direction: Delmer Daves
Screenplay: Edmund H. North; based on the novel *My Reminiscences as a Cowboy* by Frank Harris
Cinematography: Charles Lawton, Jr.
Editing: William A. Lyon and Al Clark
Art direction: Cary Odell
Music: George Duning
Running time: 92 minutes

Principal characters:
Tom Reece ....Glenn Ford
Frank Harris ....Jack Lemmon
Doc Bender ....Brian Donlevy
Maria Vidal .... Anna Kashfi
Charlie .... Dick York
Señor Vidal .... Donald Randolph
Mendoza ....Victor Manuel Mendoza
Paul Curtis .... Richard Jaeckel
Joe Copper ....King Donovan
Mr. Fowler ....Vaughn Taylor
Trailhand .... Strother Martin
Manuel Arriega .... Eugene Iglesias

The robust *Cowboy* handles a familiar theme and makes it fresh. Embellished with the usual accoutrements of the genre, such as a shoot-out between cowboys and Indians, a stampede, a barroom brawl, and even a gunfighter, the film nevertheless shatters illusions. As directed by Delmer Daves, a filmmaker who contributed much to the genre with his thought-provoking themes, *Cowboy* dramatically alters Western myths. The main character, for example, is a hardened trail driver with nothing but disdain for horses, cattle, and life on the trail. Cowboys do their work, but for money, not love of the West. Similarly, there is no romance around the campfire—only tired men.

If the 1958 *Cowboy* breaks with convention, however, it is by no means so gritty-real that it becomes dreary. On the contrary, *Cowboy* is witty, fast-paced, and filled with memorable sequences, salty dialogue, and well-defined characters; interestingly, there are no traditional villains, only men of opposing views. Written by Edmund H. North, from the semiautobiographical novel, *My Reminiscences as a Cowboy*, by Frank Harris (better known as the friend and biographer of Oscar Wilde, than for his days as a cowboy), the film takes a new look at trail life through the relationship between a "tenderfoot" and a tough trail boss who are forced into partnership.

Opening with clever titles, in which the names of cast and crew are intermingled with the headlines of an 1872 newspaper, *Cowboy* immediately turns to its principals. Frank Harris (Jack Lemmon), a young clerk, working in an ornate Chicago hotel, is a romantic idealist who is romancing the beautiful Maria Vidal (Anna Kashfi). He has even written love poems for her—but they were intercepted by her stern father, Señor Vidal (Donald Randolph) who says, "Don't think love can find a way. I know all the ways." Harris insists that his motives are honorable, and tells an unimpressed Vidal that he intends to have a solid future in the cattle business.

Meanwhile, Tom Reece (Glenn Ford) and his rowdy cowhands have arrived at the hotel after two months on the trail. Startled that the grimy-looking group would come to the elegant hotel, Harris is rebuked by his gruff boss Mr. Fowler (Vaughn Taylor). As it turns out, Reece and his men are frequent hotel guests following successful trail rides. Moreover, Reece is far from being socially inept. One of the first inquiries he makes at the hotel is, "What's the opera season like this time of year?" That night, Harris gets to talk with him further, when he takes some drinks to Reece's room. Reece is soaking in a hot tub, carrying on a casual conversation with an old friend. As the men chat, with Harris hovering nearby, Reece spies something out of the corner of his eye. Grabbing for his gun, he shoots—killing a cockroach that was climbing the brocade wallpaper. Startled by this act, Harris also jumps a second time—when Reece again pulls the trigger. This time he accidentally shoots a water pipe, which sends water streaming out. "Thought I saw a spider up there," is Reece's only explanation.

Still later that night, Reece finds, to his surprise, that he has run out of money at the gaming tables. Though he had hoped to spend several weeks at the hotel, it looks as if he and his men will have to return to the trail—on another job. This prompts an eager Harris to approach him with a deal. He has $3,800 saved—and would like to buy in, as a partner, on that drive. Anxious for a chance to win back what he has lost, Reece agrees, and indeed, his luck does change, but next morning, when he tries to pay Harris back, Harris refuses. What he wants is for Reece to honor their verbal contract—and to take him along on the cattle drive as a partner. Somewhat angered by Harris' tenacity, Reece has also never before had a partner, but Harris refuses to give in, and so, with his men watching from the sidelines, Reece finds himself honoring his words.

The trail ride is preceded by scenes in which the men prepare for the seven-week journey. There are horses to be broken, supplies to be gathered, and, for Harris, lessons to be learned. Clearly a greenhorn, he does not even know how to put on chaps before climbing atop his first wild horse. For the viewers, these sequences serve as an introduction to Reece's men. Charlie (Dick York) has a reputation as a womanizer. Doc Bender (Brian Donlevy) is an anachronism of the West that Harris has chosen to romanticize. Bender, an aging gunfighter, has come to the drive simply to avoid yet another gunfight. There are also Joe Copper (King Donovan), who once had to eat an Indian; the hot-tempered Paul Curtis (Richard Jaeckel); and Mendoza (Victor Manuel Mendoza), who is Reece's closest ally. It is Mendoza who keeps the sharpest eye on Harris, as he evolves into a cowboy.

That evolution includes, among other things, a bad case of saddle sores, but more important, it tests Harris' beliefs about humanity. For him, a turning point involves the men's cool attitude toward the death of one of their comrades. The trailhand (played by a then-unknown Strother Martin) dies as the result of a cruel practical joke which is triggered when Paul Curtis tosses a snake his way. Inadvertently bitten, the cowhand dies, leaving Harris angered and Reece nonchalant. In fact, standing over the man's gravesite, where he has elected to speak some "last words," Reece surmises that "in the long run, it really doesn't matter" how death comes.

When the men finally reach Mexico, where they are to pick up their cattle, there is considerable jubilation, but at the Vidal hacienda, where Reece and Harris go to get the cattle, Harris finds a heartbreaking surprise—Maria is now married. Reece senses that his partner is shattered by the news. Later, while attending a Mexican fiesta, Maria'a husband Manuel (Eugene Iglesias) displays his prowess at the dangerous "game of the cattle," in which a participant attempts to toss a small rope ring over the horns of a bull. Though the embittered Harris challenges Manuel, Reece wil not allow him to enter the ring. Instead, he challenges the bull—on foot—and successfully rings the bull's horns. That evening, Harris is summoned to a deserted mission by Maria where she tells him that upon her return home from Chicago her father ordered her marriage. When Harris asks, "do you love him?" she responds with a gentle kiss and rides away. Afterward, Harris stops off at a cantina, where he sees that local men are teaming up against Charlie, who is making overtures to the women. Though he tries to help Charlie, Harris is escorted out of the cantina, so he rides furiously back to camp to get help.

Reece and the rest of the men stubbornly refuse to go with Harris, arguing that Charlie got himself into trouble, and must therefore get himself out. Questioning their humanity, Harris derides them, pointing to their oblique attitude about the death on the trail. He is about to return to his horse, to go to Charlie's aid, when Reece starts a fight by hitting him with a crowbar. It is an ugly beginning to a fight which becomes brutal when Reece holds Harris over the campfire. After Harris screams out in pain, he is released; but neither man will forget the violence during the journey home.

Stunned by his own brutality, Reece becomes more caring—more human. In contrast, Harris turns callous and indifferent. Now it is he who is the ultimate cowboy, looking out only for his herd and his own survival. Concerned by this change, Reece makes attempts at friendly conversation, including some sincere condolences over the broken romance, but Harris wants nothing to do with him. Still, Reece continues to show a gentler side. No longer the hardened businessman, at one point he decides to stampede the entire herd into an arroyo, to save Harris from attacking Indians. During the stampede and shooting, Reece takes a bullet in the leg. Harris, however, has no compassion. Instead, he is angry that Reece risked the herd. With Reece injured, Harris now takes command, ordering the men to round up the stampeded cows. After taking a count, he finds the herd is two hundred head short. Those head, he says, were part of Reece's share. When asked by Reece how he arrived at such a calculation, Harris says, "It was easy. I used a crowbar."

No longer the idealist, Harris is also unmoved when Bender hangs himself rather than face a scheduled gunfight. The news comes just as the cattle are being loaded into cars for transport to Chicago. Harris' only concern is that the men continue their work, but Reece and the others are visibly saddened. The humanity of which Harris once spoke is now something they understand. "You haven't gotten tough, you've just gotten miserable," Reece tells Harris. On the train, later that night, the two men reconcile their differences when Reece comes to Harris' aid after he is trapped in a car containing frightened cows. No longer oblivious to pain or death, Reece even offers a sly smile to the still-dazed Harris when he points to a cow, nearly hurt in the melee, and says, "I suppose this one's mine."

Upon arriving in Chicago, Reece and a much subdued Harris are again fifty-fifty partners. Paralleling the beginning of the film, Reece and his men troop into the opulent hotel, where the prim Fowler is startled to see Harris, dusty and triumphant, among them. Reece is also glad to see that Harris' eyes are following a pretty young woman as she makes her way through the lobby. In the film's final sequence, both men are in bathtubs, placed side by side. When a cockroach scrambles up the wall, it is Harris who is quick on the draw. Comrades at last, the two men are laughing when *Cowboy* comes to an end.

Thoughtful and entertaining, *Cowboy* is a rousing Western that is superlatively photographed—especially the sequences involving the bullfight, and inside the moving cattle car—and expertly scored, with George Duning providing the exhilarating music. Presented in Technicolor and VistaVision, *Cowboy* was critically acclaimed, and went on to earn an Academy Award nomination for editing. For Lemmon, who had never before ridden a horse, the film proved an enjoyable departure. It is Ford, however, who gives the film its strongest performance, with his commanding work as the man who finds renewed humanity. *Cowboy* marked the third successful teaming in a Western for the actor and director Daves, following *Jubal* (1955) and *3:10 to Yuma* (1957). In *Jubal* he is a confused cowboy in love with another man's wife; in *3:10 to Yuma* he is an outlaw who comes to respect the farmer who must bring him in. Known mostly for his many Western roles, and some turgid dramas, including the intriguing *Gilda* (1946) with Rita Hayworth, Ford has appeared in more than one hundred films since making his screen debut in 1936; sadly, though his work has never been acknowledged with an Academy Award nomination. Ford is a prime example of a fine, hard-working actor whose easy style and prolific output in good but not spectacular films have brought him money and recognition, but few critical accolades.

Pat H. Broeske

Reviews

The Hollywood Reporter. February 11, 1958, p. 3.
Los Angeles Times. February 9, 1958, V, p. 1.
The New York Times. February 20, 1958, p. 29.
The New Yorker. XXXIV, March 1, 1958, p. 107.
Newsweek. LI, February 17, 1958, p. 106.
Saturday Review. XLI, March 1, 1958, p. 26.
Time. LXXI, February 17, 1958, p. 64.
Variety. February 11, 1958, p. 3.

THE CREATURE FROM THE BLACK LAGOON

Released: 1954
Production: William Alland for Universal-International
Direction: Jack Arnold
Screenplay: Harry Essex and Arthur Ross
Cinematography: William E. Snyder
Editing: Ted J. Kent
Art direction: Bernard Herzbrun
Underwater sequences: James E. Havens
Music: Joseph Gershenson
Running time: 79 minutes

Principal characters:
David Reed .... Richard Carlson
Kay Lawrence .... Julie Adams
Mark Williams .... Richard Denning
Carl Maia .... Antonio Moreno
Lucas .... Nestor Paiva
Edwin Thompson .... Whit Bissell

At the time of its release in 1954, *The Creature from the Black Lagoon* was regarded as "B"-movie fluff, and yet another example of the decade's infatuation with raging monsters, paticularly products of H-bomb terror and forbidding extraterrestrial life forms. Initially released in 3-D, the commercially popular film has aged well with time. Indeed, it has attained significance both as an important horror science-fiction film and as a major contribution within the body of work of producer-director Jack Arnold. An allegorical tale of good versus evil, the film features stunning underwater sequences, and an exceptionally well-designed monster which has come to be considered a "celebrity" in the same vein as such imposing figures as Frankenstein's monster, King Kong, and Dracula. The film's creature, the Gill Man, has the form of a man, embellished with scales and fins. Its fishlike face includes cold, emotionless eyes which attest to its complete amorality; it exists simply as a creature—doing what it must to survive, wherein lies its greatest horror.

Opening with a quotation from Genesis, and a sequence showing the creation of the universe, the black-and-white film then moves to an angry sea—and a glimpse of footprints leading away from it, into the darkness of a forest. The story then flashes ahead—millions of years later—to an expedition in the upper reaches of the Amazon. Carl Maia (Antonio Moreno), a scientist attempting to unlock the mystery of the beginning of time, is startled to discover a web-fingered skeleton protruding from a rocky surface. Certain that the fossil is one of the keys he seeks, he reaches for the skeleton, breaking the fossil hand free. Meanwhile, unknown to Maia, a webbed hand—a living version of that fossil—is reaching menacingly from the water, just feet from where he stands. It is a brief but momentous introduction to the film's principal "character."

Excited by his find, Maia travels upriver to his marine institute, to put together a scientific team to retrieve the rest of the fossil. Accompanied by colleagues from the United States, including Dr. David Reed (Richard Carlson), Mark Williams (Richard Denning), Kay Lawrence (Julie Adams), and Dr. Edwin Thompson (Whit Bissell), Maia returns to his original campsite, where it is discovered that the two Indians who had been left in charge have been savagely murdered—presumably by the area's wild animals. The film's viewers, however, know otherwise—for the webbed hand was seen reaching through the opening of one of the Indian's tents.

Believing that the remainder of Maia's fossil find was carried away by eroding waters, the expedition continues its journey on a riverboat skippered by the superstitious Lucas (Nestor Paiva). As they enter an eerie lagoon, Lucas unreels Indian beliefs about the region, including tales of nine-foot long catfish, Amazonian rats the size of sheep, and a mysterious half man-half fish. It is, of course, the Gill Man, first glimpsed as a shadowy, threatening figure who watches—among camouflaging rocks and dancing plant life—as Reed and Williams survey the river bottom, searching for specimens. He comes into more awesome view when Kay Lawrence dons a striking white bathing suit and plunges into the water for a solitary swim. As Kay enjoys a leisurely and sensuous swim on the water's surface, the creature is matching her strokes—with a threatening masculinity—beneath the surface. Swimming just a short distance from her, he is seen both as lurking beast and as captivated suitor. The sequence—one of the film's most memorable—has acquired a significant reputation for its sexuality. It is the Gill Man's infatuation with Kay that dominates the balance of the story.

Once her provocative swim comes to an end—at the urging of her worried fellow scientists—Kay treads water for a few moments. At this point the monster can no longer control himself, and he reaches upward for her leg. She can apparently feel something brushing against her, and looks downward with concern, but the dark waters reveal nothing, and she climbs aboard the boat. Because he has ventured too near the boat in his quest of the beauty, the Gill Man becomes entangled in an underwater net. The scientists pull it to the surface, but the creature has escaped—leaving a massive hole. Lucas immediately attributes it to the lengendary half man-half fish, which he calls a "demon."

At this point Reed and Williams become rivals. Already the two men are at odds over Kay, because though Reed is her boyfriend, she was apparently once enamored of Williams. Now the two take different courses regarding the mysterious creature. Reed wants to photograph and study it, while Williams is determined to capture it—dead or alive. When the two men return to the waters, Reed takes a camera and Williams is equipped with a speargun. Pursued by the creature, Williams is able to wound it. Later, the Gill Man retaliates by climbing aboard the boat and murdering a crew member. The scientists employ a new mode of attack when they learn about "rotenone," a native poison capable of producing temporary paralysis. Buckets of rotenone are dumped into the lagoon—the surface of which is eventually covered with bobbing fish and, finally, the lifeless form of the monster.

After being pulled aboard and placed into a tank, however, the creature regains consciousness and manages to break free, killing another crew member before returning to the safety of the water. Maintaining that the creature has all the advantages, including native habitat, Reed argues that the expedition should leave the lagoon. Williams disagrees, but is outvoted, and the ship starts to leave. It is unable to exit the lagoon, however, because the inlet has been blocked by the vengeful creature with a huge log. Williams is attempting to dislodge it when the creature attacks, finally killing him. The Gill Man then climbs on the ship and grabs a terrified Kay, whom he takes to his catacomb hiding place. Reed follows, finally coming upon the disquieting, fog-shrouded grotto where Kay's body is draped over a large rock (in the tradition of the day, she has fainted). After rescuing Kay, Reed is challenged by the creature. Just as he is cornered by the Gill Man, Lucas and Maia arrive—with loaded guns. They fire at the monster, wounding him. As Kay is reunited with Reed, the creature returns to his murky lagoon—apparently to die.

In keeping with many of the screen's most popular creatures, the Gill Man was to resurface in *Revenge of the Creature* (1955) and *The Creature Walks Among Us* (1956). Like *The Creature from the Black Lagoon*, *Revenge of the Creature* was also directed by Arnold. In this sequel the Gill Man is captured and taken to a Florida aquarium (at Marineland) for study. There he encounters another beauty (Lori Nelson), whom he also kidnaps as his "bride." With its sunny Florida setting and its many laboratory and aquarium scenes, this sequel is in marked contrast to the original film, which has many dimly lit sequences filled with darting shadows in the jungle and beneath the lagoon. Still, under Arnold's direction, and with its premise of attempts to further understand a mysterious life form, *Revenge of the Creature* is an excellent sequel. Some critics have even argued that it is as good as the original film. *Revenge of the Creature* is famous especially among trivia buffs because it marks Clint Eastwood's first, very brief, screen appearance. Far less memorable is the third *Creature* film, in which the monster is victimized by man. In *The Creature Walks Among Us*, following experimentation, the Gill Man is able to live out of water; the scenes of him pacing back and forth in his chain link cage are pathetic reminders of man's seemingly insatiable need to conquer all foes.

Of the three *Creature* films, only the first was filmed in 3-D. The visual gimmickry that accompanied many early 3-D ventures, such as 1953's *House of Wax*, however, is not prevalent in Arnold's film, with the exception of a handful of scenes in which harpoons, jets of vapor, and the Gill Man lunge at the audience. Otherwise, the film works best as a "flat" production (and in subsequent rereleases, it was shown "flat"). Delivered in a straightforward manner which contrasts effectively with the film's implications of an otherworldy evil, *The Creature from the Black Lagoon*'s hallmark is its remarkable underwater photography. Utilizing an underwater camera devised and operated by Charles C. Welbourne, a camera crew equipped with leaded belts, swim fins, and aqua lungs worked underwater for thirty-two days—some 153 submerged working hours—to carry out the project. Additionally, a dozen electricians, grips, and other technicians were at work below the water's surface. As a result of such attention, the underwater sequences, which were directed by James E. Havens, are a triumph for the film. They create a stirring, primeval world—ruled by the mysterious figure of the Gill Man—which gives the film a special distinction when it journeys beneath the water's surface, into the depths of the lagoon.

With its examination of a creature that may be the only living link with the beginning of time (critics have theorized that the creature may be Lucifer himself) *The Creature from the Black Lagoon* speaks well for thought-provoking genre work. Arnold's signature on the genre also includes the intelligent *It Came from Outer Space* (1953), in which man is asked to reconsider his fears of alien life forms, and the lyrical *The Incredible Shrinking Man* (1957). Although known mostly for his horror and science-fiction offerings, Arnold and producer William Alland also collaborated on nongenre projects such as *The Tattered Dress* (1957), a mystery starring Jeff Chandler; *No Name on the Bullet* (1959), an Audie Murphy Western; and *High School Confidential* (1958), which is now regarded as a "camp" favorite with its story of a high school student who poses as a "narc."

A prolific filmmaker during the 1950's, Arnold has come to be regarded with new esteem. Interestingly, when filmmaker John Landis announced plans to reproduce a new version of *The Creature from the Black Lagoon*, Arnold once again was named to direct the project. It is due for release by Universal in 1983.

Pat H. Broeske

Reviews

Commonweal. LX, May 14, 1954, p. 145.
The Hollywood Reporter. February 9, 1954, p. 9.
The New York Times. May 1, 1954, p. 13.
The New York Times. May 9, 1954, II, p. 1.

DISRAELI

Released: 1929
Production: Warner Bros.
Direction: Alfred E. Green
Screenplay: Julian Josephson; based on the play of the same name by Louis N. Parker
Cinematography: Lee Garmes
Editing: Owen Marks
Art direction: no listing
Music: no listing
Running time: 89 minutes

Principal characters:

Disraeli	George Arliss (AA)
Lady Clarissa Pevensey	Joan Bennett
Lady Mary Beaconsfield	Florence Arliss
Charles, Lord Deeford	Anthony Bushell
Lord Probert	David Torrence
Hugh Myers	Ivan Simpson
Mrs. Agatha Travers	Doris Lloyd
Queen Victoria	Margaret Mann

When Warner Bros. presented George Arliss, a relatively unknown British stage actor, in the title role of *Disraeli*, England's renowned Victorian prime minister, they achieved one of their first real successes in talking pictures. Although he had made his film debut in a version of Ferenc Molnar's *The Devil* in 1921, his theatrical style of acting did not translate easily onto the screen and he failed to impress the critics. Yet, in playing the part of Disraeli, a characterization that he had perfected over a period of time on the American stage, he created a role that turned his career around and made each successive Arliss film more popular than its predecessor. Warner Bros. had projected *The Green Goddess* (1930) to be Arliss' first talking feature, but since *Disraeli* appeared to possess a certain elegance as well as the expected melodrama, the actor, himself, insisted that it be released first, as it was.

Arliss had originally come to Broadway from the English stage as a member of Mrs. Patrick Campbell's company, appearing in such productions as *The Second Mrs. Tanqueray* and *The Notorious Mrs. Ebbsmith*. Impresario David Belasco noticed him and arranged for him to play the Oriental villain in *The Darling of the Gods*, starring Blanche Bates. At the conclusion of its run, he became a member of Mrs. Fiske's Manhattan company and took parts in such plays as *Becky Sharp*, *Leah Kleschna*, *Hedda Gabler*, and *The New York Idea*.

He first acquired star status in the stage production of Molnar's *The Devil*, but when he subsequently appeared in *Disraeli*, commissioned by producer George C. Tyler, he lived the role for five years, bringing so much of himself to it in performances all over the country that people wondered if he would ever be able to separate himself from the role of Queen Victoria's leading statesman. He accomplished this transition with a series of biographical dramas, including *Hamilton*, *Paganini*, and *The Green Goddess*. He also toured America, gaining a national audience with his first Shakespearean venture as Shylock in *The Merchant of Venice*, featuring Peggy Wood as Portia. It was after he completed his tour with that play that Warner Bros. came to him, offering a contract to perform for them in talking pictures.

Warner Bros., however, was taking no risk in presenting him as a star, because he was not a young man. True, some of the earlier silent heroes such as Frank Keenan, H. B. Warner, and the Farnum brothers were not in their youth when they played romantic heroes, but Arliss was sixty-one when he made his first talking film as a star. Everyone knew that Arliss was much older than Disraeli was in the time period of the film, but, in the end, it did not matter. It became a triumph of age over youth when Arliss won the Academy Award as the Best Actor that year over Maurice Chevalier, Ronald Colman, and Lawrence Tibbett.

Disraeli is not a full-scale biography of its subject; rather, it focuses on a specific episode: England's competition with Russia to acquire the Suez Canal. The film begins at a garden party, where Disraeli (George Arliss) is introduced as he looks over the scene on the lawn with his wife, Lady Beaconsfield (Florence Arliss). Theirs has been a long, successful, and very happy marriage, and they are reveling in anticipation of another great triumph for the prime minister—the acquisition of the Suez Canal.

Disraeli is happy to see his protégée, Lady Clarissa Pevensey (Joan Bennett), with the man she loves, Charles, Lord Deeford (Anthony Bushell), and is amused to see that they are talking lightly to Mrs. Agatha Travers (Doris Lloyd), an adventuress known to be in the employ of Russia as a spy. Also with them, however, is Lord Probert (David Torrence) manager of the Bank of England. Probert has refused to grant Disraeli the money to purchase the canal for England, but a rich Jewish banker, Hugh Myers (Ivan Simpson), has agreed to lend the sum required as soon as a shipment of gold arrives from the Argentine. Thus, Disraeli gives Charles Deeford a blank check and dispatches him to Cairo to conclude the deal.

Disraeli, accompanied by his wife and Clarissa, then returns to his estate, Hughenden, where a doctor is summoned to look after Lady Beaconsfield's health. Word gets out, however, that it is Disraeli who is ailing, and he plays along with the misconception to fool Mrs. Travers and her Russian friends. A coded message soon arrives from Deeford indicating that the deal is finally consummated, but before they can celebrate a victory, Myers appears at

Hughenden to announce that the ship bearing the Argentine shipment of gold has been mysteriously sunk at sea. Disraeli is despondent, and Myers faces bankruptcy.

When Probert subsequently arrives, Disraeli makes a bold move: he tells the truth. He had, in fact, drawn a check on Probert's bank, and Russia has brought about the collapse of Myers' bank. Now Probert must sign a paper guaranteeing unlimited credit to Myers through the Bank of England itself. Probert refuses to sign, however, so Disraeli coldly stares down the only man who can save Great Britain, and in a calm and very effective speech, convinces him to lend the money.

As soon as Probert leaves the room, Clarissa, who has been a witness to the scene says, "Mr. Disraeli, thank the Lord you have such power!" Disraeli smiles slyly and says, "I haven't, dear child, but he doesn't know that."

Queen Victoria (Margaret Mann) attends the reception in Downing Street to celebrate the Suez purchase. Disraeli is the hero of the hour, but his heart is sad, because the health of his wife has taken a turn for the worse. When she suddenly appears in the room beside him, smiling, as always, his happiness is complete

The character of Disraeli has since been seen on the screen in *The Prime Minister* (1941), with John Gielgud as Disraeli, and in *The Mudlark* (1950), with Alec Guinness in the part. In the year of its release as a Warner Bros. special, Julian Josephson was nominated by the Academy as Best Writer of the year for *Disraeli*, and the film itself was nominated as one of the five best of the year, losing to *All Quiet on the Western Front*.

Nobody could deny that George Arliss had contributed his own kind of honor to the cinema. The weekly *Variety* reported: "Good taste and general excellence mark this apex picture which should be commercially successful. It deserves to be." Arliss went on to star in a number of other successful films for Warners, including *The Ruling Passion* (1923), *The Green Goddess* (1930), *Old English* (1930), *The Millionaire* (1931), and *The Man Who Played God* (1932, with Bette Davis) before retiring to his native England. His final film was *Dr. Syn* (1937). He died nine years later of a bronchial ailment, on February 5, 1946, at the age of seventy-seven.

DeWitt Bodeen

Reviews

Commonweal. XI, February 5, 1930, p. 399.
The New York Times. October 3, 1929, p. 27.
Variety. October 9, 1929, p. 3.

THE DIVORCEE

Released: 1930
Production: Robert Z. Leonard for Metro-Goldwyn-Mayer
Direction: Robert Z. Leonard
Screenplay: John Meehan; based on Nick Grinde's and Zelda Sears's adaptation of the novel *Ex-Wife* by Ursula Parrott
Cinematography: Norbert Brodine
Editing: Hugh Wynn and Truman K. Wood
Art direction: Cedric Gibbons
Costume design: Adrian
Music: no listing
Running time: 80 minutes

Principal characters:

Jerry .... Norma Shearer (AA)
Ted .... Chester Morris
Paul .... Conrad Nagel
Don .... Robert Montgomery
Helen .... Florence Eldridge
Mary .... Helene Millard
Dorothy .... Helen Johnson

Although the Hays Office, Hollywood's censorship board, had put Ursula Parrott's best-selling novel, *Ex-Wife*, on the condemned list, in 1930 M-G-M production head Irving Thalberg thought that it would be an ideal vehicle for his wife, Norma Shearer. He turned it over to writers Nick Grinde and Zelda Sears for a toning down, and they skillfully tore it apart. When they put it back together again, it had become an entirely new and very impressive story treatment. The *Ex-Wife* title was the first thing to go, in favor of *The Divorcee*, and there was, in fact, so little resemblance to the Parrott novel in the finished product that the story source was not even indicated in the credits. It thus became a class-A vehicle for Shearer, whose portrayals of modern heroines were always noteworthy.

Gowned most becomingly by Adrian, Shearer acted well enough in *The Divorcee* to earn an Academy nomination as Best Actress of the year, which she won, deservedly, over such noteworthy actresses as Greta Garbo, Ruth Chatterton, Nancy Carroll, and Gloria Swanson. It was only the third year of the Academy Awards, and Shearer was also nominated for her performance in another film, *Their Own Desire*, a common practice in the early years of the awards. *The Divorcee* was also one of five nominees for Best Picture, losing to *Cimarron*.

The Divorcee recounts the story of a modern couple, Jerry (Norma Shearer) and Ted (Chester Morris), a writer, whose whole life changed over a weekend when two of their best friends, Paul (Conrad Nagel) and Dorothy (Helen Johnson), were involved in an auto accident in which Dorothy's face was disfigured beyond repair, and Paul subsequently decided to marry her out of pity. Jerry and Ted were so shocked by the accident that they, too, decided to marry and get the best out of life as husband and wife while they could.

Three years later they are celebrating their anniversary when Jerry learns that Ted has been having an affair with an old girl friend. Ted assures his wife that it does not mean a thing, but she is angry and tries to get even by going to bed with Don (Robert Montgomery). She, of course, does not name her partner (much to Don's relief), but Ted is furious and leaves her, going off to Paris on a story assignment. He does not return, and makes no objection when Jerry divorces him, although she has not stopped loving him. He refuses to have anything to do with her, and she is told only that he is drinking heavily in Paris.

In the meantime, Paul goes to her, and assures her that Dorothy would give him his freedom to marry her if he were to ask for it. Jerry knows that Paul is Dorothy's whole life, so she backs away from making any decision involving Paul.

She eventually goes to Paris on a job of her own and lingers there hoping that she will get a chance to see Ted. Then, on New Year's Eve, in a Parisian ballroom, she runs into her husband, who is almost shocked into sobriety by the sight of her. On the dance floor Jerry realizes that she and Ted still love each other, so, after some discussion, they decide to forgive each other and celebrate the New Year with a new marriage.

The Divorcee has class; it is sophisticated, elegant, and perfectly suited to Shearer's talents. It has aged well and her performance still looks good more than fifty years later. As a result of having her career managed by Irving Thalberg, she became one of the biggest stars at M-G-M. When Thalberg presented her as a modern heroine, as he did in her first eight talking films, she was in her element. *The Divorcee* was her fifth talking film, and was certainly her best. Thalberg envisioned her as a star who could play anything, but unfortunately she had her limitations, which were concealed in her best roles. She was embarrassing in *Romeo and Juliet* (1936) and painful in *The Barretts of Wimpole Street* (1934). Thalberg pictured her as an actress of the caliber of stage actress Katharine Cornell, but Shearer was not in that class. Nor was she interesting in turgid Eugene O'Neill dramas such as *Strange Interlude* (1932) or vehicles that more properly suited Lynn Fontanne, such as *Idiot's Delight* (1938). After Thalberg's untimely death in 1936, Shearer, who had at one time been "Mrs. MGM," shortly proved herself an embarrassment to the company, who did not know what to do with her. She retired after a lightweight comedy that was a complete failure, *Her Cardboard Lover* (1942), saying, "I believe a star should leave them laughing—or crying."

She went to Europe, eventually met an attractive ski instructor several years younger than herself, Martin Arrouge, and became his wife. She had had a son and daughter by Thalberg, and thus for at time lived the socially eventful life of a contented woman who is also an ex-movie star. Then physical ailments began to plague her, and she eventually became a permanent and very exclusive resident of the Motion Picture Country House in Woodland Hills, California. She is nearly completely blind, and leads the life of a recluse, not even remembering the days when she was one of the glories of M-G-M.

Shearer had three leading men in *The Divorcee*—Chester Morris, Robert Montgomery, and Conrad Nagel—all of whom are dead now, but who are remembered for the dozens of features which they made for various studios during the 1930's and 1940's. She herself is remembered only for some of her Thalberg-produced films.

Shearer was a well-bred girl from Canada, with perhaps the most aristocratic profile of any of the stars of her time. Historically she is important because her modern films, seen today, stand up well and are admirable frames for her talent, which is still impressive.

DeWitt Bodeen

Reviews

The New York Times. May 10, 1930, p. 25.
Variety. May 14, 1930, p. 3.

DULCY

Released: 1923
Production: Joseph Schenck for Constance Talmadge Film Company; released by First National
Direction: Sidney Franklin
Screenplay: John Emerson, Anita Loos, and C. Gardner Sullivan (continuity); based on the play of the same name by George S. Kaufman and Marc Connelly
Cinematography: Norbert Brodine
Editing: no listing
Art direction: no listing
Music: no listing
Running time: 72 minutes

Principal characters:

Dulcy	Constance Talmadge
Mr. Forbes	Claude Gillingwater
Gordon Smith	Jack Mulhall
Mrs. Forbes	May Wilson
Billy Parker	Johnny Parker
Angela Forbes	Anne Cornwall
Vincent Leach	André Beranger
Schuyler Van Dyke	Gilbert Douglas

In the mid teens, columnist Franklin P. Adams of the *New York Tribune* (who signed himself "F. P. A.") invented a character through which to satirize the mindlessness of the contemporary American woman. For his inspiration he turned to Dulcinea, the heroine of Miguel de Cervantes' *Don Quixote de la Mancha*, and rechristened her "Dulcy." A few years later, George S. Kaufman and Marc Connelly borrowed the character from him and created the play, *Dulcy*, which opened at the Cort Theater, Chicago, on February 20, 1921, and went on to become an enormous success in New York City, where it opened at the Frazee Theater on August 13, 1921. Lynn Fontanne played the main character, Dulcinea Smith, with "a heart of gold but a rubber stamp mind."

While F. P. A. was creating Dulcy, Constance Talmadge was in Hollywood delighting audiences as the comic Mountain Girl in the Babylonian episode of D. W. Griffith's film, *Intolerance* (1916). Talmadge (1899-1973) had followed her better-known sister, Norma, to the Brooklyn-based Vitagraph Studios around 1912 and, by 1915, she had become a minor film star. *Intolerance* assured her of immortality. In 1917, Joseph Schenck, who was married to Norma, created separate production companies for both sisters; in 1919,

Schenck arranged for both actresses' films to be released by the newly formed First National organization and also signed John Emerson and his wife Anita Loos to write a series of comedy features for Constance. It was the team of Emerson and Loos who were responsible for the screenplay of *Dulcy*.

In the slang of the time, the character of Dulcy was termed a "dumbbell." (In fact, so well-known was the "Dulcy" character that for a short time slang terms such as "dumbbell" and "bonehead" went out of use, to be replaced by "dulcy.") In the film, she ruins the chances of her husband Gordon (Jack Mulhall) for advancement in the business world through a series of well-meaning acts of stupidity. She is cute and everything around her exudes this quality to an extreme. In fact, as the authors of the play noted in their introduction, "If there was a telephone Dulcy would have it covered with a cute little doll."

In order to further her husband's business dealings with a client, Mr. Forbes (Claude Gillingwater), Dulcy invites him and his wife (May Wilson) and daughter Angela (Anne Cornwall) to her home for the weekend. Also present are Schuyler Van Dyck (Gilbert Douglas) of *the* Van Dycks and a society playboy named Vincent Leach (André Beranger). Dulcy does everything possible (unwittingly of course) to antagonize Mr. Forbes. Once the party is assembled, he manifests a strong dislike of sports, for example, but Dulcy arranges for him to go riding on a rather uncooperative horse. He also hates swimming; inevitably, Dulcy insists that he both swim and dive; tennis is anathema to Forbes, but play tennis he must, and as a result he turns his ankle. While Forbes is considering ending his business agreement with Gordon as a result of Dulcy's actions, however, he learns that Van Dyck is supposedly planning to finance the venture. Forbes is unwilling to let this happen, and when it transpires that Dulcy's brother Billy (Johnny Parker) has eloped with Forbes's daughter, the poor man is completely entangled and has no alternative but to become a business partner of Dulcy's long-suffering husband. As Dulcy would say, "all's well that ends well" and "every cloud has a silver lining."

Critical response to the film version of *Dulcy* was mixed. *Photoplay* (November, 1923) commented, "All the joy of the characters [on stage] is completely anesthetized, and, in the place of the lovable dumb bell with her platitudes, we are given a grown-up moron. Connie Talmadge works valiantly to save it." *The New York Times* (September 17, 1923), however, announced, "A splendid picture has been made of the stage's *Dulcy*," proclaimed Talmadge's performance to be "charming," and went on to say that it "showed a hitherto almost unrevealed sense for delicate light comedy, and that in a medium, the screen, to wit, that has not in the past been known for its ready welcome to delicate light comedy delineators." *Variety* (September 20, 1923) was as enthusiastic as *The New York Times*, calling it "One of the sweetest, most amusing and continuously delightful high-power low comedies of recent unveiling."

Dulcy's director, Sidney Franklin (1893-1972), had known Constance Talmadge since the two of them were under contract to D. W. Griffith in 1916. He also directed her in *Two Weeks* (1920), *East Is West* (1923), *Her Sister from Paris* (1925), and *The Duchess of Buffalo* (1926), among others. Franklin went on to become an M-G-M producer, responsible for many of the studio's more prestigious productions, including *The Barretts of Wimpole Street* (1934, also director), *The Good Earth* (1937, also director), and *Mrs. Miniver* (1942). Constance Talmadge starred in ten more features after *Dulcy*, and retired from the screen in 1929, an extremely wealthy woman.

Dulcy was remade by M-G-M in 1929 as a vehicle for Marion Davies, and released, in 1930, under the title of *Not So Dumb*. The title character was also used in the 1940 M-G-M feature *Dulcy*, which starred Ann Sothern.

Anna Kate Sterling

Reviews

The New York Times. September 17, 1923, p. 18.
Variety. August 27, 1923, p. 3.

A GUY NAMED JOE

Released: 1943
Production: Everett Riskin for Metro-Goldwyn-Mayer
Direction: Victor Fleming
Screenplay: Dalton Trumbo; based on an original screen story by Charles Sprague, David Boehm, and Frederick H. Brennan
Cinematography: George Folsey and Karl Freund
Editing: Frank Sullivan
Art direction: Cedric Gibbons
Music: Herbert Stothart
Running time: 118 minutes

Principal characters:

Pete Sandidge	Spencer Tracy
Dorinda Durston	Irene Dunne
Ted Randall	Van Johnson
Al Yackey	Ward Bond
"Nails" Kilpatrick	James Gleason
The General	Lionel Barrymore
Dick Rumney	Barry Nelson
"Powerhouse" O'Rourke	Don DeFore

A Guy Named Joe was one of the films which Hollywood produced in the early 1940's as part of their World War II canon. While not strictly speaking a propaganda film in the vein of *Mrs. Miniver* (1942) or *Thirty Seconds over Tokyo* (1944), the war setting and the ill-fated romance of the two main characters created a definite mood which was characteristic of these films. The film's title refers to the nickname given to the average American G.I. during the war, rather than one denoting one of the characters. Ernie Pyle's *The Story of G.I. Joe*, a 1945 film based on Pyle's wartime writings, later immortalized the nickname.

The film begins in England, where Pete Sandidge (Spencer Tracy) is introduced. Pete is a well-known brilliant pilot, but he is also regarded as something of a risk-taking show-off. Pete's girl friend is Dorinda Durston (Irene Dunne), another excellent pilot who flies supplies for the Army. Pete and Dorinda are quick-witted and hot tempered; they have a very intense relationship, but neither likes to admit to the other the depth of their feelings. They bicker and wisecrack constantly and show tenderness only when Dorinda sings "I'll Get By" to Pete over and over at his request.

When Pete is involved in a near-fatal mission which the company commander "Nails" Kilpatrick (James Gleason) feels is foolhardy, Dorinda and Nails conspire to transfer Pete and his buddy Al Yackey (Ward Bond) to a safe post in Northern Scotland. After Pete and Al have been in Scotland for a while and Pete admits to experiencing a feeling of "slow poison," as Al puts it, Dorinda pays them a surprise visit. She immediately has a premonition that Pete will die. That evening, after she begs Pete to return to the United States to become a training instructor because his "number's up," he reluctantly agrees. He cannot keep his promise, though, when an emergency mission comes up and he must fly into combat one more time. Despite the good sense of his initial intention, Pete cannot resist one last opportunity to be a hero, and he is killled when his plane crashes.

Pete's death initiates the second segment of the film. After the plane crash, the audience sees Pete looking very much alive, walking along a bare set with a cloud-covered floor. (The set is virtually a duplicate to the one used for the celestial scenes in *Here Comes Mr. Jordan*, 1941, which, like *A Guy Named Joe*, was produced by Everett Riskin.) Pete, in fact, seems very much alive, but he gets a queer feeling when he runs into Dick Rumney (Barry Nelson), an old buddy who had earlier died in a plane crash. Dick assures Pete that being dead is not so bad, and then takes him to meet their commanding officer, the General (Lionel Barrymore), a Billy Mitchell-type. The General informs Pete that he and Dick will be celestial "copilots" for young fliers who are having difficulty. When the ever-conceited Pete says that he never needed any help himself, the General lets him know that he, like all fliers, had help even if he did not know it. The General also explains that teamwork rather than Pete's "hot dogging" will be important now.

Dick and Pete go to a training camp in the United States, where new recruits Ted Randall (Van Johnson) and "Powerhouse" O'Rourke (Don DeFore) are not making the grade. Ted is a millionaire, and Pete feels disdain for him at first but later learns to like him. In many ways Ted is similar to Pete (Johnson, in fact, resembles the younger Tracy), and he becomes an excellent flier. Some time passes, and Ted and Powerhouse are sent to Australia, where a changed Dorinda reenters the film. She confides in Al, who is also in Australia, that she is lost without Pete. Al tries to help her overcome her grief and takes her to a local nightclub, where she meets Ted. The scene in the nightclub is one of the best in the film. Pete, whose presence is not known consciously by any of the "living" characters, sees Dorinda and goes to her, speaking much more tenderly than he ever did when he was alive. As he speaks, Dorinda stares into space as if somehow she hears or feels what he is saying. The mood is broken, however, when Ted arrives and makes a play for her. She flirts back as a disgusted Pete looks on.

Soon Dorinda and Ted fall in love, although she cannot get over the feeling that there is something almost eerie about Ted. He is so like Pete in many ways, even in little habits such as pulling at his eyebrows, that she feels strange. When Dorinda agrees to marry Ted, Pete, who has been in the background, suddenly shows his jealousy by whispering to Ted during a test flight that Dorinda likes show-offs. Rather than being angry at Ted's resultant theatrics, Dorinda is impressed, and Pete is again disgruntled when Nails, now Ted's commander, gives him a dangerous and extremely important mission. Ted cannot tell Dorinda about the mission, but Dorinda suddenly has second thoughts about her proposed marriage to him and sends him away. When she finds out about his mission, she decides that she will fly it for him and kill herself in the process. Dorinda steals Ted's plane and flies to the Japanese ammunition site which Ted was to have destroyed. She wants to crash, feeling that she can find no happiness without Pete, but Pete is back in the copilot seat and whispers to her tenderly again. This time he convinces her to complete the mission successfully and return to Ted, at last proving his maturity and good judgment. At the end, Dorinda safely returns to the base; after landing her plane, she runs into Ted's arms. They will be fine, and Pete will go on to another flier.

Some of the plot seems rather maudlin, especially the last scenes, but the sensitive portrayals of Tracy and Dunne make it believable. There were many problems during the production of *A Guy Named Joe* which were absolutely undetectable on the screen. Tracy apparently disliked Dunne. Like his fellow M-G-M star Clark Gable, Tracy liked more down-to-earth women than his aristocratic costar. Additionally, the production had to be interrupted for a considerable period of time when Van Johnson was involved in a near-fatal car accident. Tracy was a good friend and mentor to Johnson and reportedly he agreed to be kinder to Dunne if M-G-M executives agreed to resume the production when Johnson was well again.

Screen chemistry is seldom dependent upon real-life relationships, and Tracy and Dunne are great together in the film. Dunne is perhaps more "womanly" than "girlish," as she had been in most previous roles. Her Dorinda is believable as the equal of the maverick Pete. In this sense, her characterization is more liberated than that of many of the contemporary female wartime characters. Dorinda is a flier, one of the best. It is only her sex which prevents her from being a combat pilot, and she rectifies that at the end. She goes back to Ted at the finale, but she has proven herself.

Tracy is typically excellent as Pete. He is cocky and brash as usual, but he also displays an unusual tenderness in many of the scenes. He took top billing over Dunne at that time, the first male star to do so, but it was justified. It was Pete's and Tracy's picture more than that of any others.

The rest of the cast, many of them familiar character actors from the 1940's, are also good. Ward Bond, James Gleason, and Don DeFore all perform up to their usual standards. Van Johnson, though not a great actor, does well in his role. Although he is not Pete, Ted is not a milquetoast, either. The audience does not have to feel that Dorinda has "settled" for Ted simply because Pete has died; he has much to offer on his own. Although in real life Johnson is eighteen years younger than Dunne, the age difference is not glaringly apparent. Dunne looked beautiful well into her fifties. The audience assumes that Pete is much older than Ted, but it is not obvious or significant that Dorinda is older as well.

A Guy Named Joe was one of the top-ten moneymaking films of the 1943-1944 season and was one of the vehicles which catapulted Johnson to major stardom. Because his health made him ineligible to be drafted, he became one of the few "young" stars to emerge during World War II. Tracy and Dunne were still very popular during that time and would continue to be so for some years.

With the recent Hollywood penchant for remaking old films, it is not surprising that *A Guy Named Joe* is scheduled to be remade. It is reportedly one of Steven Spielberg's favorite films, and he plans to do a remake in the near future.

Robert Le Feuvre

Reviews

The Hollywood Reporter. December 24, 1943, p. 3.
Los Angeles Times. March 17, 1944, p. 23.
The New Republic. CX, January 14, 1944, p. 84.
The New York Times. December 24, 1943, p. 17.
The New Yorker. XIX, January 1, 1944, p. 53.
Newsweek. XXIII, January 10, 1944, p. 82.
Time. XLIII, January 10, 1944, p. 92+.

H. M. PULHAM, ESQ.

Released: 1941
Production: Metro-Goldwyn-Mayer
Direction: King Vidor
Screenplay: Elizabeth Hill and King Vidor; based on the novel of the same name by J. P. Marquand
Cinematography: Ray June
Editing: Harold F. Kress
Art direction: Cedric Gibbons
Music: Bronislau Kaper
Running time: 118 minutes

Principal characters:
Marvin Myles ....Hedy Lamarr
Harry Pulham .... Robert Young
Day Motford .... Ruth Hussey
Bill King ....Van Heflin
Pulham, Sr. ....Charles Coburn

Class consciousness is a key thematic element in the films of King Vidor, finding a significant place in works as different in tone and intention as the ambitious social drama *The Crowd* (1927) and the flamboyant Bette Davis melodrama *Beyond the Forest* (1949). In the context of other Vidor films, *H. M. Pulham, Esq.* explores class differences with unusual gentleness. Vidor was characteristically a bold and forceful director, as evidenced by films such as *Hallelujah* (1929) and *The Fountainhead* (1949), but *H. M. Pulham, Esq.* demonstrates that he could be pleasingly subtle and graceful as well. This relatively intimate character study of a proper Bostonian is distinguished by a remarkable complexity, by the honesty and maturity with which it presents adult relationships, and by the dramatic coherence of a story which meaningfully extends over a twenty-five-year period. This gratifying interplay of quiet romantic melodrama and precise evocation of a circumscribed milieu makes *H. M. Pulham, Esq.* a work deserving of renewed appreciation.

At the beginning of the film, Harry Pulham (Robert Young) is introduced in the present (1940) as a middle-aged man whose daily routine is predictable and monotonous. A series of very deliberate shots, accentuated by intentionally repetitive music and comical emphasis on the banal sounds of domestic life, convey the exactness with which Harry repeats the same actions each morning (shower, breakfast, walk to work, and so on). Harry immediately registers as a likable but dull man, and this is part of Vidor's artistic strategy. The audience does not suspect that this man could ever have known passion, suffering, or uncertainty.

Two related events trigger the expression of Pulham's latent emotions. The first event is notification of a class reunion of the Ivy League school which Harry had attended as a young man. The second is a call from Marvin Myles (Hedy Lamarr), who suggests a meeting with Harry. In these early scenes, Robert Young skillfully conveys the surfacing of Harry's long-suppressed attachment to the past. As Harry speaks with Marvin over the telephone, his voice suddenly becomes warmer and his tone more earnest. He does not, however, drop all traces of the reserve which initially characterized him. A clandestine glance at Marvin in a tea room deepens the audience's interest in Pulham's hidden past. A brief shot of Marvin confirms what the audience has suspected, that she is an aging but still beautiful woman, and Pulham's expression makes it clear that he loved her and perhaps still does. He does not have the courage to see her, but he writes her a note explaining that his unwillingness to keep their engagement is the result of his undiminished feeling for her.

Most of Harry's story is subsequently related in flashbacks which begin in 1915 and comprise the bulk of the film. At school he is more conventional than his best friend Bill King (Van Heflin) but less so than many of his classmates. He comes from a very old and conservative family, and his relationship with his father (Charles Coburn) has always been somewhat strained. After graduation, Harry goes to work for an advertising agency in New York and meets Marvin, a very independent and vivacious young woman. Harry and Marvin fall in love and plan to marry, but Harry is called back to Boston as a result of his father's illness. Pulham, Sr. dies and Harry feels responsible for carrying on the family business. Marvin visits him, but she feels out of place in Boston. In the meantime, Bill is also visiting, and he makes such an impression on Harry's former girl friend Kay Motford (Ruth Hussey) that Kay gives up her current fiancé and has a romance with Bill (which he does not take as seriously as she does). Marvin returns to New York and waits for Harry to return to her, but Harry soon comes to feel that his place is in Boston in the family home, overseeing the family business. When he and Marvin meet again, they break up. Then Harry and Kay begin to see each other again. Each is on the rebound from an ill-fated love affair, and their sympathetic regard for each other is enough to prompt their marriage.

As Harry's story indicates, he is the classic case of a man who succumbs to social conditioning rather than follows the dictates of his heart. When the film returns to the present, Harry is clearly overcome with regret for his lost opportunity with Marvin, the woman he has always loved. The climax of the story finds him having a change of heart about seeing her again. He goes to visit her, half intending to renounce his way of life and return to her. Although both Harry and Marvin confess that their feelings toward each other have not changed, they discover that the differences which separated them years before remain meaningful after all. Harry returns home, but there is a twist to the story. Kay has always been willing to offer him the kind of romantic love he had known with Marvin, and he has never appreciated her as a potentially gratifying marriage partner. The film ends with the suggestion that the future will be richer for Harry and Kay.

Harry's emotional progression during the course of the film is psychologically valid and very intelligently treated. The reason he has preserved his romantic love for Marvin over the years is that he had let her go unwillingly when they were young. The couple had broken up even though they were still in love, and Harry subsequently had never resolved in his heart the conflict between love and his instincts for the kind of life which his background and upbringing had virtually predetermined for him. Once Harry is able to make the choice as a mature man, he becomes free to love his wife. This resolution of the character does not necessarily make *H. M. Pulham, Esq.* an optimistic movie. Marvin is easily its most vibrant character, and both she and Harry do seem to have lost much of the happiness they would have had if they had remained together. The melancholy associated with lost love in all classic melodrama is subtly articulated in both the flashback and present scenes. At the same time, the film does not judge Harry too harshly for his subservience to conservative social and family traditions, suggesting instead that certain individuals are most completely themselves when they capitulate to inherited roles. Rugged individualism is the dominant motif in the American cinema, and a protagonist such as Harry Pulham becomes, in that context, a rather daring figure to be offered as a hero. Although *H. M. Pulham, Esq.* has the superficial appearance of a tastefully conventional studio film, it subtly resists prevailing genre conventions and perhaps might best be described as a melodrama of manners.

J. P. Marquand, author of the novel on which the film is based, was not a modern Henry James, but he was a distinctive literary talent, and the film's careful and ironic observation of a somewhat threadbare Boston aristocracy derives from his work. Marquand had a natural affinity for this kind of material, but King Vidor was more commonly associated with stories involving the common man, such as his independent production *Our Daily Bread* (1934). The director's achievement in *H. M. Pulham, Esq.* is all the more notable for this reason. He seems to understand the material perfectly, and he consistently demonstrates a sympathetic understanding of his upper-class hero. Vidor's intelligence is constantly in evidence during extended scenes full of dramatic shading and emotional shifts, especially those dealing with the evolving relationship of Marvin and Harry. Extremely long takes tend to predominate in key scenes, and the relaxed pacing which results enhances the naturalness and spontaneity of the performances and encourages an intimate atmosphere. Not the least of Vidor's accomplishments is the excellent performance he elicits from Hedy Lamarr. Lamarr was a beautiful woman, often made to look foolish by the outrageous roles in which she was cast. As Marvin, she demonstrates that she can be completely natural, and she admirably projects all the dimensions of a woman of considerable depth and intelligence.

Much of the merit of *H. M. Pulham, Esq.* is attributable to fundamentals of directorial skill—understanding of camera placement and editing and ability to work with actors. It should be emphasized, however, that these factors would not compensate for a lack of feeling for the story. On the contrary, Vidor was very interested in the project. He collaborated on the screenplay and appears to have functioned as his own producer. He always spoke fondly of the film, and his positive feelings about it are fully justified on all levels.

Blake Lucas

Reviews

Commonweal. XXXV, January 2, 1942, p. 270.
The Hollywood Reporter. November 13, 1941, p. 3.
The New York Times. December 19, 1941, p. 35.
The New Yorker. XVII, December 20, 1941, p. 90.
Newsweek. XVIII, December 22, 1941, p. 60.
Time. XXXIX, January 5, 1942, p. 66.
Variety. November 13, 1941, p. 3.

HOLIDAY INN

Released: 1942
Production: Mark Sandrich for Paramount
Direction: Mark Sandrich
Screenplay: Claude Binyon; based on Elmer Rice's adaptation of an original idea by Irving Berlin
Cinematography: David Abel
Editing: Ellsworth Hoagland
Art direction: Hans Dreier and Roland Anderson
Costume design: Edith Head
Music: Irving Berlin
Song: Irving Berlin, "White Christmas" (AA)
Running time: 101 minutes

Principal characters:
Jim Hardy .... Bing Crosby
Ted Hanover .... Fred Astaire
Linda Mason .... Marjorie Reynolds
Danny Reed .... Walter Abel
Lila Dixon .... Virginia Dale
Mamie .... Louise Beavers

Bing Crosby's recording of Irving Berlin's "White Christmas" is still the best-selling single record of all time. The song was only one of several Berlin favorites contained in *Holiday Inn*, including "Lazy," "Easter Parade," and "Happy Holidays." The popularity of Crosby and Berlin combined in a film would seem to point to success, but the addition of Fred Astaire virtually assured it, and the film was the fourth highest-grossing picture of the year. Though the story is far from great, the charm of Crosby and Astaire performing Berlin's songs makes the film a delight.

In 1942, Astaire had been away from RKO and his film dancing partner Ginger Rogers for three years. *Holiday Inn* thus provided him with an opportunity for a few routine (for him) dances and one spectacular one, the Fourth of July number. He and Crosby work surprisingly well together and they later appeared in the less successful *Blue Skies* (1946). *Holiday Inn* utilizes both their singing and dancing abilities and allows them each a chance to shine.

The story begins on Christmas Eve, when nightclub performers Jim Hardy (Bing Crosby), Ted Hanover (Fred Astaire), and Lila Dixon (Virginia Dale) are about to begin their last night together as a successful team. Jim and Lila were planning to leave show business and work on a farm, but Lila has changed her mind and wants to stay with Ted, both professionally and personally. Ted's character is established as that of a lovable rat: he unfeelingly dupes Jim Hardy by having a romance with Lila, but he does not come across as cruel; merely roguish and dazzled by Lila.

After losing Lila, Jim goes to his farm, and the audience hears his voice singing "Lazy" while a montage reveals the real life on his farm—hard work—at which the apparently city-born Jim is totally inept. At the end of the sequence Jim collapses, and in the next scene he arrives at Ted's dressing room on the following Christmas Eve, explaining that he has just recuperated from a nervous breakdown. It turns out that Ted has been having his own problems simply trying to keep Lila in gifts. Jim has decided to turn his Connecticut farm into a "Holiday Inn" which will only be open on fifteen holidays a year. He also gives his former manager Danny Reed (Walter Abel) his card, hoping that Danny will pass it on to acts which could be used at Jim's club. Later when Danny goes to a flower shop to buy Lila orchids in Ted's name, he is helped by Linda Mason (Marjorie Reynolds), an aspiring entertainer to whom he gives Ted's card.

Linda goes to Jim's farm on Christmas Day to audition and finds both him and his Inn very attractive. Jim is similarly attracted and sings "White Christmas" to her for the first time. By New Year's the Inn has a successful opening, but Ted shows up drunk after losing Lila to a Texas millionaire and starts to dance with a surprised Linda. They are a great success—even though Ted can barely stand up. The number is cleverly done, with Ted appearing to fall and Linda picking him up. The next morning a jealous Jim does not tell Ted and Danny who Linda is, so they will not lure her away from the Inn, but they instinctively feel that the mysterious dancing partner will turn up on the next holiday, Valentine's Day.

Just before the opening on Valentine's Day, Jim sings Linda a romantic ballad, "Be Careful, It's My Heart," while behind his back Ted comes in and dances to it with her. Ted wants Linda to be his permanent dancing partner and to open with him at the Inn on Washington's Birthday. Despite their success, however, Linda decides to stay with Jim, and Ted decides to hang around at the Inn to change her mind.

On the Fourth of July, Danny tells Ted that two Hollywood scouts will be in the audience to see him and Linda, but Jim overhears and conspires with Lila, who is now back in New York and unattached, to keep Linda away that night. The plan backfires slightly—Linda does not arrive on time, but when she discovers what Jim has done, she is furious. Because Ted has no partner with whom to dance, he improvises a number using some fireworks which he finds near the stage. This is one of Astaire's greatest and most frequently excerpted solo dances. He wears one of the two types of outfit with which he is most closely associated (the other being a top hat, white tie, and tails): light shoes, dark socks, light rolled cuffed pants with a dark scarf tied in place of a belt, light shirt, and ascot. The description sounds a little silly, but on

Astaire it looked perfect, and the contrast between shoes, socks, and rolled pants made it easier for the audience to follow the movements of Astaire's feet—a device also used by Gene Kelly. During the course of the fast-tempoed tap dance, the smoking Ted takes firecrackers and toy torpedoes out of his pocket, lights them, and throws them down in time to the music. Gradually the dance becomes faster and faster as the fireworks go off by themselves as Astaire whirls by. The igniting of fireworks on the dance floor was accomplished by the placement of caps on the stage which were exploded by off-camera control. The near hysteria and violence of the dance at the end is similar to several other well-known Astaire dances, such as the title number from *Top Hat* (1935) and the dancing shoes number from *The Barcleys of Broadway* (1948).

At the end of the dance, Linda shows up just as the Hollywood men are approaching Jim about a film based on Holiday Inn. She is angered and hurt by Jim's behavior, so she agrees to go with Ted to Hollywood to star in the film for which Jim will provide the music. He will not leave the Inn, however, but will send the songs.

On Thanksgiving, a lonely Jim writes Linda a letter congratulating her on her engagement to Ted, which he has read about in a magazine. His housekeeper Mamie (Louise Beavers) convinces him to go after Linda, however, and on the film's third Christmas Eve Jim is happily reunited with Linda on the set of *Holiday Inn*, as a dejected Ted looks on. The finale, on New Year's Eve, shows Linda and Jim happily singing together as Ted and Lila, back together again, dance.

The script of *Holiday Inn*, which was written by Claude Binyon and adapted by Elmer Rice, was based on an original story idea by Irving Berlin, for which he was nominated for an Academy Award. He won an Academy Award in the Best Song category for "White Christmas." The score was written entirely by Berlin, with some new and some old songs—many of which were inspired by the holidays. The competition for Best Musical Score was very strong that year, and *Holiday Inn* did not win in that category, losing to *Yankee Doodle Dandy*.

Holiday Inn has become a Christmas classic in the years since television began showing old motion pictures. Along with such films as *A Christmas Carol* (1938), *It's a Wonderful Life* (1946), and *Miracle on 34th Street* (1947), *Holiday Inn* is certain to show up sometime during the month between Thanksgiving and Christmas. It deservedly receives a large audience each time it is shown, for the magnificent Irving Berlin score, coupled with Bing Crosby's singing and Fred Astaire's dancing, make it a treat worth waiting for each year.

Patricia King Hanson

Reviews

Commonweal. XXXVI, August 14, 1942, p. 400.
The Hollywood Reporter. June 15, 1942, p. 3.
The New York Times. August 5, 1942, p. 16.
Newsweek. XX, August 3, 1942, p. 58.
Time. XL, August 31, 1942, p. 94.
Variety. June 15, 1942, p. 3.

THE LONG GRAY LINE

Released: 1955
Production: Robert Arthur for Columbia
Direction: John Ford
Screenplay: Edward Hope; based on the autobiography *Bringing Up the Brass* by Marty Maher, with Nardi Reeder Campion
Cinematography: Charles Lawton, Jr.
Editing: William A. Lyon
Art direction: Robert Peterson
Music adaptation: George Duning
Running time: 138 minutes

Principal characters:

Martin Maher ....Tyrone Power
Mary O'Donnell .... Maureen O'Hara
Old Martin .... Donald Crisp
Captain Herman J. Koehler ....Ward Bond
Kitty Carter ....Betsy Palmer
Red Sundstrom .... William Leslie
Chuck Dotson .... Phil Carey
Dwight Eisenhower (as a cadet) ..... Harry Carey, Jr.
Dinny Maher .... Sean McClory
Red Sundstrom, Jr. .... Robert Francis

Fifty years in the life of a regular army man serving as an assistant athletics instructor at West Point might seem like thin material for a film running well over two hours. Nevertheless, *The Long Gray Line* is an emotionally rich and beautifully structured motion picture. Under the guiding hand of John Ford, the true story of Martin Maher (Tyrone Power) becomes a tapestry embroidered with all that was finest and most meaningful in the traditional values which were already beginning to fade when the film was made. It is a measure of the work's strength that while few contemporary viewers could be expected to accept readily the military traditions of West Point as a positive way of life, Ford's treatment is so authoritative that the world the film evokes becomes an inspiring one. Ford shows how the very rigidity of the military structure can have the effect of liberating the individual.

Maher's story is related in flashback when he is an old man facing retirement. Unable to comprehend a life apart from his service at West Point, he goes to Washington to speak with the President (obviously Eisenhower, although he is seen only from the back and speaks from off screen), who not incidentally had been a cadet (Harry Carey, Jr.) during Maher's earliest years at the Point. As the aged Maher begins speaking, the world of the century's first decade is visualized and Maher becomes a young Irish immigrant just arriving in America. Marty goes to work at West Point as a waiter, but soon after joins the army and is taken on as an assistant by the Master of the Sword, Captain Koehler (Ward Bond). Marty cannot swim and is an inept boxer, but his game attitude endears him to Koehler and the cadets. Although he does not plan to stay in the army, his reenlistment is assured when a beautiful Irish colleen, Mary O'Donnell (Maureen O'Hara), arrives to work as a cook for Captain Koehler and his wife. Mary does not even speak to Marty until he proposes to her, but the exasperated Maher then learns that this was Koehler's devious plan to provoke his reenlistment. In the course of the story, Marty often threatens to leave the army once his present enlistment is over. In later instances, the circumstances of this decision are more serious and no longer the source of amusement, but he unfailingly returns to his position once he has regained his perspective. Although he seems to be easily influenced by others, Marty is ultimately alone. In his final years, his decision to remain has become completely his own.

After Marty and Mary are married, Mary manages to save enough money to send for Marty's father (Donald Crisp) and younger brother (Sean McClory) in Ireland. Dinny, the younger brother becomes a successful businessman while Old Martin stays with his son at West Point. In the course of performing his duties for Captain Koehler, Marty has a decisive effect on the lives of several cadets. Chuck Dotson (Phil Carey) and Red Sundstrom (William Leslie) are both on the verge of failing in their academic work when Marty takes them in hand, persuading Chuck to give up football for the sake of his military career and finding a pretty tutor, Kitty Carter (Betsy Palmer), for Red. It is implied that Chuck and Red are only two of the many cadets whom Marty influences positively. When Marty and Mary lose their only child at birth and Mary is told she can never have another, Marty goes out and gets drunk. Red, Chuck, and several other cadets break the rules to find him and bring him home. West Point has an honor system which plays an important part in a number of events throughout the film, and the next day Marty witnesses the cadets taking their punishment—hours of silent marching back and forth—for the gesture of friendship they have shown him and Mary.

Red and Kitty are married at the outbreak of World War I, and Kitty has a child in Red's absence. Red does not return, however, and his death—only one of many cadets Marty had known and helped train—prompts Marty to leave West Point to start a new career with the help of his affluent brother. Although Kitty is herself understandably bitter over Red's death, she is the one who convinces Marty to return to West Point. Even in her grief, she can see the larger meaning of Red's life and the need for continuity. Red has been posthumously awarded the Congressional Medal of Honor, which means that his son will automatically be awarded a place at West Point when he is old enough. This conclusion to the first part of the film provokes a complex response. The individuals who have aroused the audience's sympathy gain comfort from affirming the military tradition which the film celebrates, a tradition which has caused them to suffer tragic losses. Ford is characteristically ambivalent in his treatment of this contradiction. Like Marty, he perceives war as wasteful and inglorious. Yet, at the same time, he recognizes what each character in the film comes to recognize—that the destruction of war is the dark side of the coin of military life, inseparable from its continuity of tradition and its codes of honor, duty, and chivalry.

The narrative is picked up about twenty years later when Old Martin has died and James Sundstrom Jr., also called Red (Robert Francis), has grown up and come to West Point. Over the years, Kitty has remained close to Marty and Mary and they have become like second parents to her son. He has a special place in Mary's life—never explicitly verbalized in the film but eloquently attested by Ford's images—as a surrogate for her own lost son. The honor code is once again invoked when young Red informs Marty of his overnight marriage which has since been annulled. World War II has broken out, and if young Red holds to the honor code he will lose his commission. The character of young Red is partially determined by a persistent pattern in Ford's films, in which the sons are never as good as the fathers. A certain sympathy is generated for young Red, however, because he himself understands this. As he explains, his father, like most of the other cadets, had to work and struggle to get into West Point. He, on the other hand, had to do nothing, and his apparent lack of character is the result of a life passively accepted rather than actively sought. The crisis finds Marty once again giving good counsel to a young cadet, against his own wife's feelings; and the result is that Red adheres to the honor code and accepts his expulsion, enlisting in the army as a private and bravely working his way up through the ranks in action.

The years pass. Mary dies and Marty goes on alone, devotedly serving the Point as an old man. He has become the staunchest defender of the traditions at which he had scoffed as a young man, and he is well-appreciated by the young cadets whose fathers he had helped to train years before. In a deeply moving echo of a scene which occurred early in the film (the night Marty's son was born, before he learned of his premature death), the cadets come to visit him on Christmas Eve. Once again, they drink a toast to him and sing the same song heard earlier, an Irish folk song adapted to celebrate Marty Maher by name. Kitty also turns up with young Red, who is home on leave to recover from a battlefield wound. With this scene, set very close in time to the film's present tense, Marty concludes his story. The President cordially sends him on his way with Chuck Dotson, and Marty returns to West Point to find that there is a parade in his honor. As he stands watching the long gray line of marching cadets and hearing the Irish melodies which have become military anthems, his whole life is crystallized, and characters both present

(Kitty and young Red) and long departed (Mary, Old Martin, Red, Captain Koehler) materialize in his inner gaze. The film has quietly but convincingly visualized Martin Maher's life as a significant one, and these final images explicitly proclaim that significance.

The Long Gray Line benefits throughout its considerable length from the skill and care which invariably distinguish the work of John Ford at his best. The subject is one which clearly engaged him on a very deep level. Although Ford was himself a Navy man, the West Point traditions and values were of the kind he knew from his own experience. Additionally, the hero is an Irish immigrant, as was Ford's own father. The long marriage of the central couple, the tragic personal losses, and the persistence of ideals which require faith and self-sacrifice are all elements of the kind which reflect Ford's own beliefs and inspire his most sensitive artistic responses. Further, the passing of time, which necessarily has a tendency to dull the luster of form and ritual in an institution such as West Point, requires and receives the kind of poetic appreciation of which only an artist of Ford's caliber is capable. The director subtly slows the pace and deepens the mood as the film progresses. There is considerable comedy in the first half of the film as Marty bluffs and blusters his way through his early years at the Point, courts a seemingly eccentric Mary, and interacts with his often exasperating father. A passage of twenty years, indicated by nothing more than a single fade, picks up the characters in a quieter mood. A melancholy and elegiac tone begins to prevail and ultimately suffuses the work.

Ford's collaborations with cinematographers were remarkable, and the visual texture and imaginative lighting consistently evident in *The Long Gray Line* owe something to Charles Lawton, Jr., as well as to Ford. Lawton was a very underrated house cameraman for Columbia who was invariably Ford's choice for projects at that studio (*The Last Hurrah*, 1958, and *Two Rode Together*, 1961, in addition to *The Long Gray Line*). A cinematographer working with Ford has the opportunity to create many magical moments, such as the brief evocation of the marriage of Red and Kitty, two silhouettes kissing in a church entryway framed on either side by the harmoniously shadowed interior of the church, the couple then emerging into the sunlight for the single moment of recognition which the audience requires.

Ford pays a great deal of attention to color in *The Long Gray Line*. Vivid colors such as red are not absent, but the emphasis is on a persistent harmony of gray, tan, green, and blue—the natural colors of West Point and the men's uniforms. This selective use of color seems completely natural, but it also has the effect of inducing the quiet and contemplative mood which so impressively and affectingly prevails in the work. Additionally, the use of CinemaScope permits Ford to follow his natural inclination toward long takes. With the kind of long shots which Ford has always preferred—compositions dictated by movement within the frame rather than elaborate tracking and panning—

cuts are often necessitated (and easily effected by Ford) if a grouping of characters is to remain both natural and dramatically expressive. With the additional space which CinemaScope permits, Ford often lingers on a scene from a single angle. The result is the enhanced emotional effect usually associated with longer takes, accentuated under Ford's direction by his appreciation of the subtlest dramatic values in a scene and by the unfailingly endearing and spontaneous playing of his actors.

The last scene between Mary and Marty is a wonderful example. As a result of adept staging in relation to the interior of the rather ordinary Maher house, three camera angles are all that Ford requires to achieve a poignant effect. A two shot finds Marty and Mary arguing about whether she is well enough to go to a parade. The reverse angle of this shot is used for the final image of the sequence, when Marty runs to the background of the frame, discovers that Mary is dead, and kneels at her side. Because of its realistic relationship to the earlier two shot, this angle does not seem contrived, but it does have the devastating artistic effect of almost removing the couple from view, imparting discretion to the treatment of Marty's response to his wife's death and creating the kind of resonance customarily associated with a Ford long shot. The middle of the sequence describes Mary's final moments as she sits alone on the porch listening for the sound of the parade. She dies quietly, and Ford gently underlines the moment by allowing the focus to soften on a curtain in the foreground of the shot. As this description illustrates, a single sequence in a Ford film is likely to be adorned with a number of lovely aesthetic touches. At the same time, he does not permit the narrative reality of the film to be undone by such touches, as indicated by the functional nature and apparent simplicity of the few shots he needs to realize a sequence this rich in emotional dimension.

The works of John Ford are commonly and justly admired for their visual eloquence and (especially in the case of his later films) thematic density. On these levels, *The Long Gray Line* is an exemplary achievement, but the director's artistry extends beyond these considerations. When the specific world which the film describes has receded so far in time that it becomes abstract, as has already occurred with a Ford Western such as *Wagonmaster* (1950), the director's understanding of life will remain and the timeless appeal of the film will be undiminished. It is sometimes said that Ford's sphere of interest is narrow, that he has a predilection for military settings, that he is more attached to the past than the present, that he favors women who are content to be wives and mothers, and so on. All of this may be true, but such preferences never prevent Ford from instilling a character or situation with the fullness of human experience. In *The Long Gray Line*, the two most interesting and well-realized characters are the two principal women, Mary and Kitty. Mary, like Marty, is initially a broadly drawn comic figure. In both cases, Ford's handling of the characters becomes increasingly precise and subtle and his psychological insights emerge unexpectedly and tellingly, especially in the case of Mary. Mary's attachment to West Point—greater than that of her husband up until her death—is rooted in the solace it gives her. Her desire to watch the young cadets on parade is the desire to re-create her dream of her own lost son.

Kitty, on the other hand, is an example of a character who completely transcends her narrative function as the result of the director's appreciation of a very appealing actress. The screenplay provides no distinctive character touches for Kitty, but Ford nevertheless manages to create one of the freshest and most individual women in 1950's cinema, a woman who conforms to neither traditional nor modern stereotypes. Betsy Palmer's performance is easily the standout in the film, but the entire cast is admirable. Power and O'Hara may lack the romantic chemistry of the O'Hara-John Wayne pairings in other Ford films, but this seems appropriate to the quieter relationship of Marty and Mary. Power was not normally an actor of great range, but he creates quite a moving impression in this film. This is not surprising, as Ford characteristically obtains everything he needs from his actors and actresses.

In his maturity, Ford rarely brought less than the full measure of his gifts to a prodigious series of works. The only problem with such a career is that while some films—such as *The Searchers* (1956) and *The Man Who Shot Liberty Valance* (1962)—enjoy sustained critical attention, others tend to be overlooked. *The Long Gray Line* is one of these neglected Ford masterpieces. It is a film that most admirers of Ford know and love, but it is rarely revived and little discussed. Perhaps this is accounted for by its relative mellowness. It is essentially a positive work, not torn by the haunting ambiguities and contradictory emotional pulls of some other Ford films. At the same time, Ford's sense of the remoteness of the film's world from the mainstream of contemporary life seems very acute. In telling the story of Martin Maher, he suggests sadly and persuasively that nostalgia is not the only reason to cast one's gaze upon the past. For Ford, the vanished world of *The Long Gray Line* is guided by values and ideals which we can ill afford to scorn.

Blake Lucas

Reviews

The Hollywood Reporter. February 9, 1955, p. 3.
The New York Times. February 11, 1955, p. 19.
The New Yorker. XXXI, February 19, 1955, p. 122.
Newsweek. XLV, February 14, 1955, p. 74.
Time. LXV, February 21, 1955, p. 82
Variety. February 9, 1955, p. 3.

MELVIN AND HOWARD

Released: 1980
Production: Art Linson and Don Phillips for Linson-Phillips-Demme
Direction: Jonathan Demme
Screenplay: Bo Goldman (AA)
Cinematography: Tak Fujimoto
Editing: Craig McKay
Production design: Toby Rafelson
Art direction: Richard Sawyer
Music: Bruce Langhorne
MPAA rating: R
Running time: 95 minutes

Principal characters:
Melvin Dummar .... Paul LeMat
Howard Hughes .... Jason Robards
Lynda Dummar .... Mary Steenburgen (AA)
Jim Delgado .... Jack Kehoe
Bonnie Dummar .... Pamela Reed
Darcy Dummar .... Elizabeth Cheshire
Wally Williams .... Robert Ridgely
Lawyer .... Rick Lenz

The Melvin of *Melvin and Howard* is Melvin Dummar, the gas station operator who was named as a beneficiary in the disputed "Mormon" will of Howard Hughes, the Howard of the film's title. Dummar claimed that the reason he was named in the will was that he had once found Hughes in the Nevada desert after Hughes had injured himself in a motorcycle accident. Dummar then took Hughes to his Sands Hotel headquarters in Las Vegas, he says. Though one might expect the film to be an examination of the truth of that claim or an exposé of a fraud, it is neither. *Melvin and Howard* is essentially Melvin Dummar's story, and the part he says that Hughes played in it is simply taken at face value.

Dummar, we find, is a member of that often-parodied class that has little money and lives on dreams that come largely from television and advertising. *Melvin and Howard* tells Dummar's story with very little of the caricaturing and exaggeration and none of the condescension that mark most cinematic treatments of such people.

The film begins with a sequence of an old man with unkempt hair and shabby clothes (Jason Robards) riding a motorcycle in the desert. He is obviously enjoying himself until he suddenly takes a spill. We then see Melvin

Dummar (Paul LeMat) driving through the night in his pickup. When he stops to relieve himself, he sees the old man, then helps him up and takes him to his pickup. He says he will take him to a nearby town for treatment by a doctor or nurse, but the old man insists that he will not see anyone and wants to be taken to Las Vegas. Melvin good-naturedly agrees, although he thinks the man is only an old wino. Indeed, we discover as the film continues that Melvin is always good-natured.

During the drive to Las Vegas, the old man says that he is Howard Hughes, but Melvin does not take him seriously. He merely remarks that he believes that people can call themselves anything they want to. Melvin sings "Santa's Souped-Up Sleigh," a song for which he wrote the lyrics and had a mail-order company supply the music, and insists that Hughes sing along with him. Once in Las Vegas, he lets the old man out behind the Sands Hotel, and Howard Hughes is neither seen nor mentioned again until near the end of the film.

We learn more of Melvin's life when we see him go to his home—a small trailer house in the desert. His family consists of his wife Lynda (Mary Steenburgen) and daughter Darcy (Elizabeth Cheshire). Lynda's first words in the film are spoken as she looks out the window in the morning. "Oh, no. Repossessed again," she says as she watches the pickup and a motorcycle being taken away. Lynda takes Darcy and a few possessions and leaves with another man before Melvin wakes up. When that does not work out, she sends Darcy back to Melvin and gets a job dancing in a topless club in Reno.

Melvin cannot accept Lynda's leaving and tries unsuccessfully to get her back. When he goes to the club and tells her she cannot appear there because she is his wife, she protests that she loves to dance. The scene they create causes Lynda's boss to fire her, but she does not go back to Melvin. Finally he divorces her and gives her the papers in another club where she has found work; once again they create a scene. When the manager approaches, Lynda takes off her scanty costume, hands it to him, and walks out the back door completely nude.

Lynda and Melvin, however, are brought back together. When she is pregnant, out of a job, and living with her mother, Lynda telephones him, and he quickly insists that they remarry. Lynda tells him that she has been reading a book called *The Magic of Believing* and indicates that if she believes in him also, maybe he will achieve his goals. "You know, they didn't burn down Rome in one day," he responds.

The Las Vegas wedding is a delightful comic moment. Lynda is hugely pregnant, wearing a bright blue dress and a five-dollar veil they cannot afford, and the ceremony takes place in a cheap wedding chapel to the accompaniment of "The Hawaiian War Chant," the tune Melvin has chosen. Afterwards they go to a casino in their wedding finery.

The second marriage does not bring success to Melvin, although he does get a new job as a milk delivery man and works hard to win the "Milkman of the Month" award and the television set that goes with it. The dairy deducts from his pay the cost of repairs to a truck that blew its engine while Melvin was driving it, and their car is repossessed while Lynda is shopping at a K-mart. Finally, Melvin decides that the way out of their problems is to get Lynda on a television show called *Easy Street* that we have seen the Dummars watching at various times during the film. The host, Wally Williams (Robert Ridgely), is called Mr. Love, and contestants perform and then choose a door to learn what they have won.

Lynda goes on *Easy Street* and tap-dances to "Satisfaction" by the Rolling Stones, a song we have seen her dancing to in the topless club. Her dancing is terrible, but her enthusiasm is apparent and she wins the top prize in the show, ten thousand dollars and some furniture. With part of the winnings they pay a down payment on a forty-five thousand dollar house. (Melvin wanted a more expensive one, but Lynda is finally trying to be practical.) Then, as Lynda is trying to figure out how they can afford the house payments and their other expenses, Melvin drives up in a Cadillac pulling a huge boat behind on a trailer. He has, Lynda tells him, ruined their last chance to catch up financially. Even though he says the purchases are "an investment" and that he has always envied people driving by in big flashy cars, Lynda takes Darcy and the baby and leaves him for good. She even calls Melvin a "loser," and one can see from his reaction that this is the most wounding thing she could have said to him.

At the Christmas party for the employees of the dairy, Melvin's fortunes begin to look up. First he sings a song he has written that puts down Jim Delgado (Jack Kehoe), the dairy's assistant manager who has been his enemy as long as he has worked there. Then Bonnie (Pamela Reed), the dairy's cashier, makes a proposition to him. If he will marry her, they can take over a relative's lease on a gasoline station and make a thousand dollars a month. He thinks a minute, then asks, "Is that net?" and the next moment we see him at the gas station in Willard, Utah.

Life, however, does not seem any easier for Melvin. He seems to be working hard, but he is behind on his payments to the gasoline company. Then he hears on television that Howard Hughes is dead and mentions to Bonnie that he had told her about the old man he had picked up in the desert. A few days later, a strange man stops by his station and leaves an envelope containing the will of Howard Hughes. Melvin takes it to the Mormon headquarters in Salt Lake City and leaves it in an office. Then the word gets out that a will of Howard Hughes has been found and that Melvin Dummar is to receive 156 million dollars.

Soon Melvin and his family are inundated by reporters, television crews, old "friends," and lawyers. At a press conference a questioner tells Melvin that everyone in the country thinks that he is lying and then asks the question every television "reporter" thinks that he or she must ask, "How does that make you feel?"

Later there is a formal hearing in a courtroom, during which Melvin is pressured by lawyers and by the judge, but he can only assure them matter-of-factly that his story is true. Afterwards he tells his lawyer (Rick Lenz) that he has realized ever since he found the will that no one was going to let him have the 156 million or any significant part of it, but that he had the satisfaction of knowing that Howard Hughes had sung a song written by Melvin Dummar. The film then closes with Melvin remembering the ride with Hughes.

As mentioned above, the effect of the film does not depend upon whether the audience believes Melvin's story, and the film does not go out of its way to convince anyone of its truth; it simply presents it as absolutely true, however incredible it may seem, and does nothing to suggest that Melvin invented any part of it. The overall characterization of Melvin, in fact, holds no suggestion that he is the type of person who would (or could) attempt such a hoax. At the very end of the film, titles are seen on the screen telling what each of the main characters is now doing and stating that no will acceptable to the court has been found. Then, after the credits, it states "This picture was filmed entirely on location in California, Nevada, and Utah where the events actually occurred."

The virtues of this excellent small film are numerous. The fact that all the acting performances are outstanding suggests that part of the credit for them belongs to the director, Jonathan Demme. Demme also shows a marvelous sense of place and detail. Dummar's trailer house in a scruffy desert area in which the main features are sand and rusting old vehicles is shown well but not exaggerated and not overemphasized. Perhaps Demme's directorial style could best be characterized as perceptive and restrained. He sees and shows the essentials of his characters without showing that he feels superior to them.

Besides the compelling portrayal of Howard Hughes by Jason Robards, *Melvin and Howard* boasts two other remarkable performances. Paul LeMat, who had worked for Demme before, and appeared in *American Graffiti* (1973), gives us a Melvin Dummar with whom we can sympathize even as we see his impracticality. Mary Steenburgen's Lynda is much like Melvin but finally has less patience and more need for security. Steenburgen received an Academy Award in the supporting actress category for her spirited performance. Incidentally, the real Melvin Dummar has a bit part in the film as a counterman at a bus depot.

The critical reaction to *Melvin and Howard* was both perceptive and enthusiastic. Even *Variety*, which tends to prefer more commercial films, praised it, saying that "it dares to be modest and quietly observant." *Newsweek* said that "it takes on the deeply satisfying glow of a classic folk tale, lovingly told," and *Time* called it "just about as good as American films get." Despite all this praise—and Academy Awards to Steenburgen and to Bo Goldman for the screenplay—the film never found a large audience, but it is likely to be a continuing favorite in revival houses and on cable television.

Frederick Travers

Reviews

The Hollywood Reporter. September 8, 1980, p. 2.
Los Angeles Times. October 23, 1980, VI, p. 1.
The New Republic. CLXXXVII, November 8, 1980, p. 22.
The New York Times. September 26, 1980, III, p. 32.
The New Yorker. LVI, October 13, 1980, p. 174.
Newsweek. XCVI, September 29, 1980, p. 78.
Time. CXVI, October 20, 1980, p. 90.
Variety. September 8, 1980, p. 3.

MY COUSIN RACHEL

Released: 1952
Production: Nunnally Johnson for Twentieth Century-Fox
Direction: Henry Koster
Screenplay: Nunnally Johnson; based on the novel of the same name by Daphne du Maurier
Cinematography: Joseph LaShelle
Editing: Louis Loeffler
Art direction: John De Cuir and Lyle Wheeler
Costume design: Dorothy Jeakins and Charles Le Maire
Music: Frank Waxman
Running time: 98 minutes

Principal characters:

Rachel	Olivia de Havilland
Philip Ashley	Richard Burton
Louise	Audrey Dalton
Nick Kendall	Ronald Squire
Rainaldi	George Dolenz
Ambrose Ashley	John Sutton
Seecombe	Tudor Owens
Reverend Pascoe	J. M. Kerrigan

English novelist Daphne du Maurier's works, many of which have been best sellers, have provided the screen with some of its finest moments of Gothic romance. *Rebecca* (1940) is perhaps the most famous and certainly the best of the screen adaptations of her works. *The Birds* (1963), based on a short story, and *Don't Look Now* (1973) are also highly regarded films adapted from her fiction. Alfred Hitchcock seems to have had a particular affinity for du Maurier's work; he adapted *Rebecca* and *The Birds* very successfully, but was not so fortunate with *Jamaica Inn* (1939).

When Twentieth Century-Fox bought the best-selling *My Cousin Rachel*, the studio wanted George Cukor to direct the picture and Greta Garbo to play the enigmatic heroine. Garbo, having retired a decade before, refused, and Cukor then politely backed out. The novel finally came to the screen with Olivia de Havilland as Rachel and Henry Koster as the director. The film is memorable as Richard Burton's first American film, and he won an Academy Award nomination as Best Actor in a Supporting Role.

The novel was adapted with skill by Nunnally Johnson, who also served as producer of the film. The picture's weakness—the unbelievability of Rachel—was fatal, however. Had Garbo played her, this flaw would have been eliminated, for Garbo could be utterly believable as an adventuress capable of murder, while de Havilland could not. Perhaps, though, there is no star who could play Rachel and do her justice.

My Cousin Rachel has all the brooding quality of du Maurier's novels set in Cornwall. Many of du Maurier's works are set on the beautiful and mysterious Cornish coast, but *My Cousin Rachel*, more than any of the other film adaptations of her novels, seems to capture the flavor of that region, if not the actual locations. It tells the story of Philip Ashley (Richard Burton), who is very fond of his foster father, Ambrose (John Sutton), who has reared him from boyhood. Ambrose goes to Italy to escape the harsh winters that invade the Cornish coast and threaten his health. Shortly thereafter, Philip receives word that Ambrose has married Rachel, a distant cousin.

Philip is at first jealous of her, and then disturbed when it is hinted in Ambrose's letters that his beloved foster father is being slowly poisoned. Philip prepares to go to Italy himself to investigate, but when he arrives, he is stunned by the news of Ambrose's death. Philip vows vengeance upon Rachel, convinced that she poisoned her husband.

He is Ambrose's heir, and he is astonished when he receives word that Rachel, whom he has never met, will be visiting him shortly at the inherited estate which he has made his home. When Rachel (Olivia de Havilland) arrives, Philip is sullen and almost rude to her. She seems to be an enchanting, sincere person, however, and everyone soon falls under her spell. Gradually, Philip finds that he, too, is growing fond of her, and on impulse, he gives her jewelry, money, and finally the house he has inherited from Ambrose. She accepts all his gifts, yet enigmatically refuses to take his proposal of marriage seriously.

Then he begins to be tormented by little idiosyncrasies. He finds the letter he has been searching for, in which Ambrose warned him of Rachel, writing, "She has done for me at last—Rachel, my torment," and becomes violently jealous of her Italian friend Rainaldi (George Dolenz).

Obsessed, Philip grows ill, and Rachel tries to nurse him. He is certain that the medicine she leaves for him is poisoned, and he does not take it, but he survives meningitis through her instructions to the doctors. When Philip recovers, Rachel again rejects his love and decides to return to Italy.

Philip is confident once again that Rachel is a murderess, but on the day of her departure for Italy he finds new proof which seems to exonerate her. He goes to find her, only to be told that she has gone to the shore by a shortcut—a footbridge that is rotting away and is being destroyed. He runs to stop her, but comes upon her lying on the rocky earth, a victim of the fallen bridge. He lifts her up, and she, in agonizing pain, asks him, "Why? Why?"—and then dies. The audience, however, is not sure of her guiltlessness.

The picture's mood is consistently one of dark gloom and suspicion, as it was in du Maurier's *Rebecca*. Accordingly, the part of Rachel calls for a mysteriously seductive actress. The audience should have been exhausted, torn, wanting to believe her, but forced to side with Philip in his doubts of her. De Havilland's bland sweetness makes Philip's suspicions unconvincing.

The picture is handsomely mounted, like everything from Nunnally Johnson's production unit. In addition to Burton's nomination for his supporting role, the production gained Academy Award nominations for cinematography, art direction, set decoration, and costume design.

DeWitt Bodeen

Reviews

Commonweal. LVII, December 26, 1952, p. 308.
The Hollywood Reporter. December 22, 1952, p. 3.
The New York Times. December 26, 1952, p. 20.
The New Yorker. LVIII, January 10, 1953, p. 75.
Newsweek. XL, December 29, 1952, p. 64.
Time. LXI, January 5, 1953, p. 70.
Variety. December 22, 1952, p. 3.

NAPOLEON

Released: 1927
Production: W. Wengoroff and Hugo Stinnes for Westi
Direction: Abel Gance
Screenplay: Abel Gance
Cinematography: Jule Kruger
Editing: Abel Gance
Art direction: no listing
Music: Arthur Honegger
Running time: 240 minutes

Principal characters:
Napoleon Bonaparte .... Albert Dieudonne
Napoleon (younger) .... Vladimir Roudenko
Josephine de Beauharnais .... Gina Manes
Danton .... Alexandre Koubitzky
Marat .... Antonin Artaud
Robespierre .... Edmond Van Daele
Rouget de Lisle .... Harry Krimer
Saint-Just .... Abel Gance
General Hoche .... Pierre Batcheff

Without question, the cinematic event of 1981 was the reappearance of Abel Gance's masterpiece, *Napoleon*. Although first released in 1927, *Napoleon* had been lost to the world in its original form for fifty-four years. A variety of reedited, severely truncated versions had received showings over the years, but the chance of viewing anything resembling Gance's own vision of the film seemed remote indeed. Yet, those who had consigned *Napoleon* to the ranks of the permanently lost classics had not reckoned with the persistence and dedication of film historian Kevin Brownlow.

Brownlow had long been fascinated by Gance and his work; and *Napoleon*, with its tantalizing history of missing footage and ground-breaking special effects, had been of particular interest to him. Over a period of several years, he contacted film archives throughout the world, viewed countless reels in varying stages of disrepair, and, finally, painstakingly reconstructed *Napoleon* in a form remarkably close to Gance's original. Only a few scenes remain missing, including additional three-screen projections like those employed during the film's dazzling closing sequences, but these omissions do not prevent Brownlow's lovingly assembled version from restoring the film's power and breathtaking imagery.

At this point, Francis Ford Coppola, a filmmaker long noted for the power and scope of his own cinematic vision, entered the project. Coppola's interest in films has never been limited to his own work, and his support and financial backing have aided a variety of filmmakers and their projects. It was Coppola who provided the necessary funds for the presentation of *Napoleon*, enabling the film to open in New York's Radio City Music Hall with a sixty-piece orchestra accompanying it. To compose and conduct the film's monumental score, he enlisted the talents of his father, composer Carmine Coppola, and the result is a blend of music and film so precise and so stirring that it adds immeasurably to the film's impact.

Yet, *Napoleon* remains the creation of its director, Abel Gance. Gance was born in Paris in 1889, and, following a brief career as a stage actor, he entered the motion-picture industry as a writer. The dramatic and technical possibilities of motion pictures intrigued him, however, and it was not long before he tried his hand at directing. In such films as *J'Accuse!* (1919), a powerful antiwar statement, and *La Roue* (1921), Gance experimented with camera movement, editing styles, and superimposition, using each technique to enhance the film's story. These films served as a testing ground for Gance's greatest achievement, and it was in *Napoleon* that he put to use his technical expertise and imagination in a manner that stretched the boundaries of filmmaking.

Gance's original plans for *Napoleon* had been to portray Bonaparte's life in a series of films, but lack of money cut short his scheme. Consequently, this *Napoleon*, the only one of the series that he was able to complete, covers Napoleon's life only up to the beginning of his march on Italy. Yet its ability to convey both the sweep of history and the details of human individuality is so great that one cannot help but feel the loss of the added perspective that Gance could have given to Napoleon in decline had the later films been made.

The film is divided into three segments: "The Youth of Napoleon," "Napoleon and the French Revolution," and "The Italian Campaign." The first segment opens with a high-spirited snowball fight among the schoolboys of the Brienne military academy. A young Napoleon (Vladimir Roudenko) is leading the defense of his team, aided by the friendly warnings of the school's scullion, who spots the opposing team putting rocks in their snowballs. Using tactics that he will later employ on real battlefields, Napoleon directs the action as the screen becomes a flurry of flying snow and frantic activity. Gance uses rapid-fire editing to convey the fury of the snow battle, with Napoleon's face filling the screen every fourth frame. Only when the day is won does the young boy allow his serious expression to soften into a slight smile.

Later that day, when the boys are in class for a geography lesson, another side of Napoleon's personality is revealed. A disdainful description of his birthplace, the island of Corsica, leaves him angry and defensive, an outsider among the other boys. That night, two of the boys whom he had defeated in the snowball fight open the door of the cage that holds Napoleon's pet eagle, and the bird escapes. Discovering the empty cage, Napoleon rushes into the dormitory and demands to know who has freed the bird. When no one confesses, he challenges them all and a pillow fight ensues. This scene, which served as the model for the famous pillow fight in Jean Vigo's *Zero for Conduct* (1932), is another remarkable example of Gance's innovative film techniques. As the fight escalates and feathers begin to fly, he divides the screen into nine squares, each containing a different view of the overall scene. The effect is dazzling, and the multiple imagery conveys a far headier sense of the youthful free-for-all than would have been possible with a more conventional shot.

When the fight is halted by the schoolmasters, it is Napoleon who is singled out for punishment and sent off to spend the night alone. Once again, he is set apart from his schoolmates, isolated and different, and he goes in his unhappiness to the place where he had kept his pet eagle. Curling up to sleep on a large cannon near one of the windows, the lonely little boy looks up to see his eagle returning. It swoops in through the window and perches majestically on the cannon, a fierce guardian spirit and a symbol of defiance for the youth who will become France's greatest hero.

Gance uses the film's opening segment to foreshadow the course of Napoleon's later life. The young boy's skill as a military strategist, his pride, his determination, and his sense of isolation are all traits that will appear in Napoleon the man. The eagle, too, will reappear throughout the film, serving both as a manifestation of Napoleon's own proud spirit and as a symbol of the unification of his personal dream with the dreams and hopes of his beloved France. It is clear from the outset that the path to greatness which the Fates have chosen for Napoleon will also lead him to great loneliness and pain.

The film's second segment, "Napoleon and the French Revolution," begins with one of the film's most stirring sequences. It is Paris in 1789, and the government of France is in turmoil as the spirit of the Revolution grows. Anxious crowds gather as the men who will shape the course of French history, Danton (Alexandre Koubitzky), Marat (Antonin Artaud), Robespierre (Edmond Van Daele), and Saint-Just (Abel Gance) argue over political strategies. When a young soldier, Rouget de Lisle (Harry Krimer), appears with a song that he has written, copies are distributed to the crowd. Tentatively at first, then with growing strength, the assembled throng sings "La Marseillaise." Its words capture perfectly the revolutionary fervor that grips the country, and a young army officer tells Lisle that his song will help lead the French people to freedom. The officer is Napoleon Bonaparte (Albert Dieudonne).

Napoleon returns home to Corsica, where he is greeted affectionately by his family. The joy of their reunion is short-lived, however, when he learns that Corsican officials are attempting to turn the island away from France and unite it with England. Napoleon takes them on in a losing political battle and is soon forced to flee from the enemies he has made. Seizing the French flag, which he feels the island no longer deserves to fly, he escapes on horseback to the sea, where taking refuge in a small rowboat, he uses the flag as a sail and evades his pursuers.

A storm overtakes the tiny boat, and the huge waves threaten to capsize it while at the same moment in Paris, the convention is in a state of upheaval as political factions battle one another for control of the government. Gance intercuts the two scenes with startling dramatic results. As Napoleon's boat pitches and rocks on the sea, Gance makes use of subjective camera techniques, swaying and weaving the camera to create the effect of the audience itself being pummeled by the waves. He then continues the effect as he cuts to the convention, sweeping the camera back and forth over the shouting crowd to draw a striking visual parallel between the storm-tossed boat and the feverish emotional pitch of the French political situation. The fate of Napoleon seems to become the fate of France, and when he is rescued by his brothers and the entire family sets sail for France, the eagle appears, perching on the masthead as the ship carries Napoleon toward the mainland.

Several years pass and Napoleon is now a captain in the army on his way to Toulon where the British are staging an invasion. Faced with an incompetent general, Napoleon draws up plans of his own to regain the site, and when a new general replaces the old, Napoleon's courage and skill are finally noticed, and he is given command of the artillery. He stages a vicious attack during a pouring rainstorm, urging his men on through the sheer force of his own personality. Continuing against the general's wishes, he emerges victorious and falls into an exhausted sleep as the eagle once again appears in the sky above him. Upon his return to Paris, however, Napoleon is swept up in the Reign of Terror and is accused of disloyalty by his enemies when he refuses to fight his fellow Frenchmen. He is assigned to a lowly post in the office of Topography where he fills his empty days drawing plans for the military defeat of Italy.

In Paris, Josephine de Beauharnais (Gina Manes), one of the great beauties of the day, is arrested and sent to prison. She narrowly escapes the guillotine when her estranged husband takes her place. As Royalist sympathizers threaten a counterrevolution, Napoleon is called back to Paris and given command of the Parisian forces. He defeats the Royalists in their attempt to regain control of the government, and order is finally restored to France. The Reign of Terror ends, and the remaining prisoners are released, among them Josephine and her lover, General Hoche (Pierre Batcheff). At the gala Bal de Victimes, she and Napoleon, now a well-known figure in Paris, meet and are immediately drawn to each other. Josephine is fascinated by the Corsican's aloofness in the midst of the drunken celebration taking place around them, and her interest is clearly returned. Indeed, when she coyly asks him which weapon he most fears, he responds, "The fan, Madame."

The tone of the film now shifts as Napoleon is seen caught surprisingly off guard by his growing love for Josephine. The forceful, authoritative soldier becomes a shy suitor, ill at ease with the object of his affections. In a series of lighthearted, often comical scenes, Napoleon courts Josephine in a style reminiscent of Charles Chaplin's Little Tramp, made physically awkward by the sight of a pretty girl. He stands nervously beside her, finding himself tongue-tied in her presence, plays blindman's buff with her children as she spirits another lover out of the house, and finally arrives two hours late for their wedding, after forgetting the time as he worked on his plans for the invasion of Italy. Following a hurried ceremony, the two retire to the bedchamber, where veil after veil falls across the camera lens, obscuring the couple's passion in a hazy mist.

Now happily married to Josephine, Napoleon turns his attention to the conquest of Italy, and soon departs to join his troops. Stopping at the Convention Hall on his way, he stands alone in the now-empty chamber and is visited by the ghosts of the great leaders of the Revolution. They urge him to carry the spirit of the Revolution to the rest of the world, and Napoleon swears that he will carry out their wishes.

Upon his arrival at the Italian border, Napoleon addresses the assembled troops and promises to lead them to greatness. As his own zeal infects them, the film enters its final, and most spectacular phase. It is here that Gance makes use of his remarkable Triptych three-screen process, a technique that predates Cinerama by some thirty years. An additional screen appears suddenly on either side of the one already in use, and the film's action is projected across all three. The vastness of the French army and the scope of Napoleon's plans seem to burst forth from the screen as Napoleon, in one breathtaking moment, gallops his horse toward the camera and flashes almost three-dimensionally across the screens. It is a grandstand gesture on both his and Gance's parts, and it captivates the viewer just as thoroughly as it does the French troops.

The army now begins its march on Italy and Gance divides the action among the three screens, sometimes displaying different shots on each screen, sometimes counterpointing the action on the two outer screens. Napoleon's face fills the central screen as the marching troops stream across on either side of him. A revolving globe appears, with Josephine's face superimposed on its surface. The succession of images is exhilarating, combining moments from throughout the film until, at last, each screen takes on one color of the French tricolor flag, and Napoleon and his armies become part of the very fabric of the emblem of France. In the film's final image, the majestic eagle appears, its wings spreading across all three screens as it soars toward the camera carrying the spirit of France within it.

The most striking narrative point in *Napoleon* is the theme of personal destiny that runs throughout the film. The use of the eagle, the recurring intimations of greatness in Napoleon's future, indeed, the sometimes Christ-like effect of his personal magnetism over a hostile crowd, all serve to convey the feeling that Napoleon's course has been charted for him from birth. Again and again, coincidence and fate play a part in Napoleon's life: the friendly scullion at the military academy turns up as the innkeeper in Toulon; Napoleon sees Josephine by chance when she is on her way to consult a fortune-teller, who predicts that one day she will be a queen. The most improbable, and vastly amusing, coincidence occurs as Napoleon and his family sail for France. Their ship is spotted by a young British naval officer who requests permission to sink the small vessel. The officer is Horatio Nelson, and his request is, of course, denied. Gance's use of such fantastic tricks of fate, as well as the considerable artistic license he takes with history, might have proved damaging in the hands of a less talented filmmaker. In Gance's case, however, his fiery vision of Napoleon translates so compellingly to the screen that the viewer finds himself swept along by the director's passion. The notion of Bonaparte as a man somehow irrevocably chosen for the role he must play in history delights viewers with its power and romanticism, and any perception one may have of the flaws of such an idea seems unimportant by comparison. If Gance plays havoc with details, it is because it better enables him to capture the essence of Napoleon and what he has meant to France.

For Gance, the revival of *Napoleon* after fifty-four years proved to be the final vindication of a lifetime spent struggling to see his dreams transferred to the screen. Too ill to attend the New York opening of the film in January, 1981, he heard the thunderous applause which greeted its conclusion by way of a telephone call made from the wings of the theater. The film's enthusiastic reception brought the career of its director to a triumphant close; Gance died ten months later in Paris.

Janet E. Lorenz

This article appeared in *Magill's Survey of Cinema*, Silent Films, 1982.

Reviews

Los Angeles Times. July 16, 1981, VI, p. 1.
The New Republic. CLXXXIV, February 14, 1981, pp. 24-26.
The New York Times. March 4, 1928, IX, p. 6.
The New York Times. February 12, 1929, p. 23.
The New York Times. February 15, 1981, II, p. 13.
The New Yorker. LXVI, February 16, 1981, p.114+.
Newsweek. February 2, 1981, p. 78.
Time. CXVII, February 2, 1981, p. 70.

SLAP SHOT

Released: 1977
Production: Robert J. Wunsch and Stephen Friedman for Universal
Direction: George Roy Hill
Screenplay: Nancy Dowd
Cinematography: Victor J. Kemper
Editing: Dede Allen
Art direction: Henry Bumstead
Music direction: Elmer Bernstein
MPAA rating: R
Running time: 122 minutes

Principal characters:
Reggie Dunlop .... Paul Newman
Ned Braden .... Michael Ontkean
Lily Braden ....Lindsay Crouse
Francine Dunlop ....Jennifer Warren
Suzanne .... Melinda Dillon
Joe McGrath .... Strother Martin
Dave Carlson ....Jerry Houser
Steve Hanson .... Steve Carlson
Jeff Hanson .... Jeff Carlson
Jack Hanson .... David Hanson
Anita McCambridge .... Kathryn Walker

Leslie Fiedler has proposed in his seminal critique of American literature, *Love and Death in the American Novel*, that the archetypal American hero is a man who flees from civilization and from the smothering embraces of women into the wilderness, where he encounters the savage, a confrontation that is ultimately resolved in either violence or a homoerotic male bonding. Fiedler's thesis is equally applicable to American movies, particularly in genres such as the Western and the gangster film, including films as diverse as *Double Indemnity* (1944), *Red River* (1948), *White Heat* (1949), and *The Searchers* (1956).

One contemporary director to whom Fiedler's theory is particularly applicable is George Roy Hill. Hill has directed three films starring Paul Newman which exemplify the idea of man in the wilderness. All three of these films, *Butch Cassidy and the Sundance Kid*, (1969), *The Sting* (1973), and *Slap Shot* (1977), were extremely popular with the public. In the first two films, Robert Redford costarred with Newman, and in these films male bonding took precedence over male-female relationships. In *Slap Shot*, the bonding occurs among members of a hockey team as other elements in Fiedler's universe percolate just below the film's surface hilarity.

Slap Shot follows the comic, even farcical, final season of the Charlestown Chiefs, a minor league hockey team located in a dying mill town in Appalachia. Reggie Dunlop (Paul Newman) is its player-coach, an aging athlete directing a losing team whose mysterious owner is rumored to be dissolving it for a tax write-off. At the same time, Reggie is struggling to achieve a reconciliation with his estranged wife Francine (Jennifer Warren). The star of the team is Ned Braden (Michael Ontkean), a Princeton-educated athlete who truly loves hockey, much to the disgust of his lonely, neglected wife Lily (Lindsay Crouse). When the mill in Charlestown closes down and forces ten thousand potential hockey fans out of work, Reggie is faced with a loss of fans as well as a losing season, so, in desperation, he plants a news item with the local sports reporter stating that a retirement home in Florida is interested in buying the team. When, soon after this, Reggie picks a fight with the goalie on an opposing team, the players' morale rises and causes them to play hard enough accidentally to win the game. In the next game, another fight gets started. Observing the crowd's excitement, Reggie reasons that increased violence is the key to restoring interest in the team and improving its chances of winning.

He brings in the three Hanson brothers ("retards," as Reggie calls them) to play for the Chiefs. The Hansons are "goons" who deliberately start fights and, not coincidentally, excite the fans' blood-lust in the process. Most of the players happily become caught up in the mayhem, but Ned adamantly refuses to engage in the bloodletting. He simply does not believe in violence. In an effort to move Ned to overcome his scruples, Reggie attempts to seduce his bored and unhappy wife. Although Lily leaves Ned and moves in with Reggie, this idea backfires and does not produce the expected effect in Ned.

Because of the fighting, however, the Chiefs finally have a winning season and enter the play-offs for the league championship against the Syracuse team. Just before the game, Reggie meets the elusive owner of the Chiefs in an attempt to resolve the team's future. In spite of the successful season, Anita McCambridge (Kathryn Walker) informs him that she still intends to dissolve the team because of the advantageous tax write-off. Thus, in the locker room before the championship game, Reggie finally tells the team that the Florida deal has been a hoax, and that the team will be broken up regardless of the outcome. He therefore asks the team to play this last game cleanly and to treat hockey as a sport and not as a circus. The team agrees to play by the rules one final time.

The Syracuse team has collected their own goons, however, and at the end of the second period the bloodied Chiefs are losing the game. Joe McGrath, the angry manager of the Chiefs (Strother Martin), informs the team that National Hockey League scouts are in the audience, so the players had better win. The Chiefs return to their blood-and-guts style in the third and final period, and soon the ice is covered by brawling players. Disgusted by the spectacle, Ned skates to the center of the ice and begins to take off his uniform. Encouraged by the fans, Ned strips to the music of "The Stripper" as the Syracuse players protest this "degenerate exhibition." When the Syracuse team threatens the referee with physical abuse, he orders them off the ice and awards the championship to the Chiefs. Ned, now down to his jockstrap, skates by and takes the trophy for the team. At the victory celebration the next day, Reggie learns that Francine is leaving him for good even though he now has a promising coaching job in Minneapolis.

On one level *Slap Shot* is an entertaining satire exposing the more dubious aspects of a notably violent sport. Yet, on another, less obvious level, the film attempts to explore some of the reasons for that violence. All of the women in the film are depicted as neglected and abused—objects that exist only to satisfy the sexual needs of the team, while the men spend most of their time in one another's company playing hockey and drinking. Their most important emotional commitments are to one another and to the team. Meanwhile, ignored by the men, the wives turn to one another, and, in at least one instance, have lesbian affairs. The men are also somewhat aware of homosexuality since many of the curses and insults that they throw at one another comment on their supposed sexual preferences. Subconsciously, at least, the members of the team are aware of the implications of the feelings they have for one another, yet, unable to admit that men are capable of feeling love for one another, they express these emotions in violence, striving to prove that they are, in fact, "real men" and not weak and womanly. Thus their homophobia and misogamy relates directly to Fiedler's equation of love and death. This subtext is present in American war films, prison films, detective stories, and Westerns. In this sense, Hill's three films with Newman are unusual only in that they were immensely popular and financially successful. *Butch Cassidy and the Sundance Kid*, in particular, began a cycle of "buddy" films in which women were of peripheral interest, with the real emotional involvement occurring between two men.

Apart from the ensemble acting and the deftly comic direction of George Roy Hill, the most important contribution to the film is Nancy Dowd's screenplay. Based on her brother's experiences on a third-rate hockey team, Dowd has written a very funny and an exhilaratingly profane movie. Her dialogue captures the way that American men in all-male environments talk, a complex mixture of vulgarity, insult, threat, and affection. It is a world that attracts most men at some time in their lives, but Dowd's screenplay also shows the sobering result of pursuing that life to the exclusion of all else. The very funny sequences mask an indictment of the manner in which the American male turns to violence because he is afraid of love.

Don K Thompson

Reviews

The Hollywood Reporter. February 24, 1977, p. 3.
Los Angeles Times. February 25, 1977, IV, p. 1.
The New Republic. CLXXVI, March 19, 1977, p. 392.
The New York Times. February 26, 1977, p. 11.
The New Yorker. LIII, March 7, 1977, pp. 91-95.
Newsweek. LXXXIX, March 7, 1977, pp. 68-69.
Time. CIX, March 14, 1977, pp. 73-74.
Variety. February 23, 1977, p. 3.

TESS

Released: 1980
Production: Claude Berri for Renn/Burrill Productions
Direction: Roman Polanski
Screenplay: Roman Polanski, Gerard Brach, and John Brownjohn; based on the novel *Tess of the D'Urbervilles* by Thomas Hardy
Cinematography: Geoffrey Unsworth and Ghislain Cloquet (AA)
Editing: Alastair McIntyre and Tom Priestly
Art direction: Jack Stephens (AA)
Music: Philippe Sarde
Costume design: Anthony Powell (AA)
MPAA rating: PG
Running time: 170 minutes

Principal characters:
Tess Durbeyfield .... Nastassia Kinski
Alec d'Urberville .... Leigh Lawson
Angel Clare .... Peter Firth
Mr. Durbeyfield .... John Collin

Before *Tess* was made, its director, Roman Polanski, was known to most of the American filmgoing public for two films and for two events in his private life. The films, *Rosemary's Baby* (1968) and *Chinatown* (1974), were both critical and box-office successes; the private events were the murder of his wife, Sharon Tate, by the Manson "family" in 1969 and his arrest and trial for the rape of a thirteen-year-old girl in 1977, after which he fled the country before completion of his trial. All these combined to produce an association in the public's mind between Polanski and violence and sexuality. When *Tess* was released, therefore, many were surprised to find that it was a restrained and unhurried film in which neither the sex nor the violence was explicitly depicted.

Tess is an adaptation of Thomas Hardy's classic novel *Tess of the D'Urbervilles* (1891). The screenplay, by Polanski, Gerard Brach, and John Brownjohn, is quite faithful to the plot and characters of Hardy's novel as well as to that author's dark view of the human condition. The story is that of Tess Durbeyfield (Nastassia Kinski). Her father (John Collin) is told that the Durbeyfield family is descended from the aristocratic d'Urberville family and then learns of a rich family by that name. Tess is therefore sent off to the d'Urbervilles to claim kinship and financial help, since the Durbeyfields now feel that they should be living better and working less. A reluctant Tess goes to the d'Urberville farm, but she is not welcomed as a lost relative. Indeed, the audience learns that the family had merely bought the name of d'Urberville.

Tess is given a job by Alec (Leigh Lawson), the young master of the house, only because of his personal interest in her. After Alec seduces Tess, she leaves the farm in shame and gives birth to a child, who soon dies. She then goes to work as a dairymaid. At the dairy farm she attracts the notice of Angel Clare (Peter Firth), the son of a minister who is working there to learn farming because he hopes to own a farm. Because she thinks her past has made her unfit for such a man, Tess refuses Angel's attentions and even his proposal of marriage. Finally, she gives in and agrees to marry Angel because of her love for him and because her parents want her to marry advantageously. Because she still has doubts, however, she writes Angel a letter describing her past and slips it under his door, not knowing that it has accidentally slipped under the carpet as well. When he does not change his attitude toward her the next day, she goes ahead with the wedding. The wedding night, however, is a disaster. Tess realizes that Angel has not seen the letter, so she tells him about Alec, expecting to be forgiven. Angel, though he considers himself liberal-minded, cannot forgive her. He says she is not the woman he married and leaves immediately for Brazil.

Tess returns to her life of poverty and drudgery, but then Alec reappears in her life. She again resists him, but grows increasingly discouraged as Angel refuses to answer her letters. Alec has been generous to her and to her family since he has learned about the death of their child, and Tess eventually relents and becomes his mistress. When Angel then returns, Tess feels that she can only eradicate what Alec has done to her life by extreme means. She kills Alec and goes to Angel, who now forgives her of everything, including the murder. The two have only a few days of happiness, however, before the police catch up with them. Tess is captured early in the morning at Stonehenge and taken away to her certain punishment.

Tess was quite well-received by the critics, although there were those who felt that the film was more faithful to the letter of the novel than to its spirit. Stanley Kauffmann, for example, quoted a sentence from the last paragraph of the novel to show what was missing from the film. The sentence, "'Justice' was done, and the President of the Immortals . . . had ended his sport with Tess," came after the execution of Tess and conveys the sense that Tess was merely a plaything of fate, a sense that Kauffmann finds missing from the film.

In the title role, Nastassia Kinski (the daughter of German actor Klaus Kinski) gives a gentle, disciplined performance, and she has the unaffected beauty to make credible Alec and Angel's attraction to her, but her lack of expressiveness, particularly in the lead role in such a long film (nearly three hours) begins to be tedious. The other actors are generally good within the concept of the film, although Peter Firth's Angel Clare is not completely believable. That character, however, is perhaps the weakest in Hardy's novel, and making an audience completely understand Tess's continuing devotion to him is probably too much to expect.

The cinematography, art direction, and costume design all received Academy Awards, and it is easy to see why. The film is made up of beautiful images—from the beginning, when a moving camera captures both the landscape and the people within it, to the end, which shows a misty daybreak at Stonehenge. The drawbacks to this style, however, are that the pace of the film is often slowed to accommodate the splendor of the cinematography, and the beautiful images often conflict with, or do not convey, the subject matter. The cinematographers were Geoffrey Unsworth, who died during the filming, and Ghislain Cloquet, who succeeded him.

Roman Polanski dedicated the film to Sharon Tate, who had first suggested that he film the novel. His direction avoids flashy effects and explicit violence and sexuality. The murder of Alec by Tess, for example, occurs offscreen. This strategy of restraint is generally effective, but it is accompanied by an unnecessarily slow pace. The film could have been considerably shorter without sacrificing its virtues; restraint can become tedium. These criticisms are not, however, meant to imply that Polanski has made a lifeless, too-reverent version of a literary masterpiece, as Hollywood often used to do.

Tess is a good film that is successful in what it tries to do even though it may lack the spark of genius that would be required to make it match the impact of Hardy's novel. It received three awards from the French Academy—Best Picture, Best Director, and Best Cinematography—in addition to its three American Oscars. Not only was *Tess* a success with critics and the Academies, but it was also a hit at the box office, especially after the Oscars were announced.

Frederick Travers

Reviews

The Hollywood Reporter. December 12, 1980, p. 3.
Los Angeles Times. September 5, 1980, VI, p. 1.
The New Republic. CLXXXIV, January 3-10, 1981, pp. 20-21.
The New York Times. December 12, 1980, III, p. 80.
The New York Times. April 5, 1981, II, p. 15.
The New Yorker. LVI, February 2, 1981, pp. 88-89.
Newsweek. XCVI, December 22, 1980, p. 73.
Newsweek. XCVII, February 23, 1981, p. 60.
Time. CXVI, December 22, 1980, p. 73.
Variety. November 8, 1979, p. 3.

THE WAY WE WERE

Released: 1973
Production: Ray Stark for Columbia
Direction: Sydney Pollack
Screenplay: Arthur Laurents; based on his own novel of the same name
Cinematography: Harry Stradling, Jr.
Editing: Margaret Booth
Art direction: Stephen Grimes
Music: Marvin Hamlisch (AA)
Song: Marvin Hamlisch, Allan Bergman, and Marilyn Bergman, "The Way We Were" (AA)
MPAA rating: PG
Running time: 118 minutes

Principal characters:
Katie Morosky .... Barbra Streisand
Hubbell Gardner .... Robert Redford
J. J. .... Bradford Dillman
Carol Ann .... Lois Chiles

The Way We Were, which features Robert Redford and Barbra Streisand, is in many ways an old-fashioned film, a love story that is a vehicle for two stars. In this sense, it is a throwback to the 1930's and 1940's, when films were promoted with such slogans as "Gable's back and Garson's got him." Indeed, the film business has changed so much that *The Way We Were* was virtually the only popular film of the 1970's that had both a top male star and a top female star in it, and even though *The Way We Were* was quite popular, the films in which Redford co-starred with Paul Newman made two to three times more money.

The Way We Were differs from the usual romantic film of the 1930's and 1940's in three important ways. First, the lovers separate and do not get back together at the end of the film. In the romantic films of the past, death was almost the only thing that could separate two lovers forever. Of course there were disagreements and misunderstandings, but all the obstacles were finally overcome so that they were together at the finish, presumably to live happily ever after. At the end of *The Way We Were* the Redford and Streisand characters meet after a separation of several years but then go their separate ways. Second, politics is an important issue in this film. American films before about 1960, seldom dealt with politics and hardly ever in the context of a romance, but in *The Way We Were* the Streisand character's somewhat leftist political beliefs are an important part of her nature and a major point of conflict between the lovers. The political theme is less strong than it is in the novel on which the film is based, but it still is there. The third difference between this film and the conventional romance is that, in the words of Catherine Hiller in *The New York Times*, "For once, the woman is propelled by sexual desire and the man is the passive beauty."

The film opens in New York near the end of World War II. Katie Morosky (Barbra Streisand) is working in a radio studio for the Office of War Information. When Katie's boss's date cannot go out with him one night, he takes Katie instead, to the fashionable nightclub El Morocco. There she sees a handsome man (Robert Redford) in a splendid white uniform sitting at the bar sound asleep. She says his name, Hubbell Gardner, and then walks over and touches his forehead. As she looks at the still sleeping man, a dissolve takes us into a long flashback that starts with both Hubbell and Katie in college in the mid-1930's. Alternating scenes quickly establish Katie's activism and leftist politics and Hubbell's position as a star campus athlete. Katie and Hubbell are not acquaintances at this time but each knows who the other is and they occasionally cross paths. They have only one thing in common, a desire to write. When both take the same writing class, Katie is surprised and also hurt to find that Hubbell is the better writer when the professor reads one of his stories in class. One part of the story sticks in Katie's mind and also shapes the audience's perceptions of Hubbell: "In a way he was like the country he lived in. Everything came too easily to him. But at least he knew it." Later she sees him one night, and he tells her he has sold a story.

Having filled in the background, the film returns to the present. Katie takes the extremely intoxicated Hubbell home with her and begins making coffee. When she finds that Hubbell has pulled off his clothes and gone to sleep in her bed, she gets into bed also, and he makes love to her. The next morning, though, he apparently does not remember it. He comes to use her apartment the next time he is in New York, but only because he cannot find a hotel room. Katie insists that he stay for dinner—she has bought groceries and flowers—and their relationship finally begins.

Once the background is established and the relationship between Hubbell and Katie has begun, the plot of *The Way We Were* develops rather erratically. Sequences may be separated by days or by years, and the viewer is not always sure how much time has elapsed. The main basis for the love between Katie and Hubbell seems to be her admiration for his writing (as well as his looks), but the chief obstacle, one that is never completely overcome, is her passionate belief in her principles. "You push too hard," Hubbell tells her at one point. She is unable to make small talk with his wealthy friends, such as J. J. (Bradford Dillman) and Carol Ann (Lois Chiles). For example, when they are all together the day after President Franklin Roosevelt's death, Katie cannot ignore the coarse jokes about Eleanor Roosevelt. She tells off everyone in the room and, after an argument with Hubbell, she leaves alone.

After a short scene at the radio station when Hubbell returns the key to her apartment, the two stay apart until Katie is unable to stand it. In a histrionic telephone call she asks Hubbell to come to see her only as her best friend. Soon they are married and in Hollywood, where Hubbell is working on a screenplay of his novel, *A Country Made of Ice Cream*. J. J. is the producer of the film and Carol Ann is now his wife. Katie has determined to be more accommodating and she generally gets along with Hubbell and his friends and associates, even though she has always told him that he is too good for Hollywood. There are also some amusing scenes, such as a Hollywood party in which each of the guests is dressed as one of the Marx Brothers.

Before too long, however, political conflicts disrupt their Hollywood idyll. It is the time of the House UnAmerican Activities Committee investigation of Communism in the film industry, and people are being blacklisted if they do not cooperate with the committee. All of this is treated rather lightly by the film, but Katie, who is pregnant, does go to Washington to support some of the dissidents, despite the opposition of Hubbell and his employers. When she returns and Hubbell meets her at the railroad station, an angry crowd denounces her. When one man calls Katie a "commie bitch," Hubbell hits him, but he also argues with Katie, saying the whole issue is not important, that people are more important than principles. Katie does not agree.

Then, rather suddenly, Katie and Hubbell are splitting up. She asks him to stay with her until their baby is born, and he does so and then leaves. In the novel upon which the film is based and in the film as it was originally made, the cause of the split is quite clear and dramatic. A college classmate of Katie tells the Committee that Katie was a Communist during her college days. Katie must either give the Committee the names of her former left-wing associates or Hubbell's career will be damaged or ended. She cannot make that compromise. This sequence was filmed, but after a sneak preview it was removed, leaving the last part of the film somewhat confusing and less dramatic.

In the last sequence of the film, obviously several years later, Katie and Hubbell meet accidentally on the streets of Manhattan. They talk briefly, and we learn that both have remarried, and that Hubbell is writing scripts for television. Hubbell, we see, has completely given up any effort to be a serious writer, but Katie has stayed with her principles. The film ends with a shot of her giving Ban the Bomb leaflets to passersby on the sidewalk.

The Way We Were seems to have tried to make its politics as inoffensive as possible. Indeed, there is a sequence within the film in which Hubbell is forced to agree to changes in his screenplay that he does not like, and the sequence is not flattering to Hubbell. The irony is that the makers of *The Way We Were* did the same thing that they condemn within the film.

The heart of the film, however, is the romance of Katie and Hubbell and the performances of Barbra Streisand and Robert Redford. Streisand, who tends to be overbearing in her acting, is well-controlled in this film, bringing no more shrillness to the role of Katie than is required. Redford is equally good. In one sense he needs only his good looks, since Hubbell is rather shallow, but at the same time he must show enough personality and potential that we can understand Katie's being in love with him for so long, even though she considers him and his associates decadent.

Critical reaction to the film was decidedly mixed, with reviews generally unable even to agree upon what were its strongest and weakest features, but the public, perhaps grateful for a romantic film even if it was not a masterpiece, was enthusiastic about *The Way We Were*. Its box-office returns put it in the top-ten films released in 1973. The film also won two Oscars, both for its music, which added considerably to the romantic quality of the production.

Timothy W. Johnson

Reviews

The Hollywood Reporter. October 3, 1973, p. 3.
Los Angeles Times. October 24, 1973, IV, p. 1.
The New Republic. CLXIX, November 10, 1973, p. 22.
The New York Times. March 24, 1974, II, p. 13.
The New Yorker. XLIX, October 15, 1973, pp. 158-160.
Newsweek. LXXXII, October 22, 1973, p. 126.
Time. CII, October 29, 1973, pp. 95-96.
Variety. September 20, 1973, p. 2.

OBITUARIES

CECILIA AGER (January 23, 1902-April 3, 1981). One of the first major female film critics in the United States, Cecilia Ager served as film critic for two New York newspapers, *PM* and *The Star*, from 1940 through 1949. Ager was also a columnist for *Variety* in the 1920's and 1930's.

JACK ALBERTSON (1907-November 24, 1981). A crusty character actor who received an Academy Award for Best Supporting Actor for his work in *The Subject Was Roses* (1968), Jack Albertson began his screen career in the mid-1940's after many years in vaudeville and burlesque. His films include *Top Banana* (1954), *Never Steal Anything Small* (1959), *How to Murder Your Wife* (1965), and *The Poseidon Adventure* (1972); television viewers know him particularly for his work on the NBC situation comedy "Chico and the Man," which aired from 1976 to 1978.

NORMAN ALLEY (1895- April 1, 1981). Norman Alley was a leading newsreel cameraman, active from 1912 through 1968; he published his autobiography, *I Witness*, in 1941.

GLENN ANDERS (September 1, 1890-October 26, 1981). Described by *The New York Times* as "one of the most durable and dedicated actors of the century," Glenn Anders was featured in three Pulitzer Prize-winning plays: *Hell Bent for Heaven* (1924), *They Knew What They Wanted* (1924), and *Strange Interlude* (1928). His film credits include *Laughter* (1930) and *The Lady from Shanghai* (1948).

NILS ASTHER (January 17, 1897-October 13, 1981). A handsome, dark-haired leading man to female stars such as Marion Davies, Greta Garbo, and Joan Crawford, Swedish-born Nils Asther made his American screen debut in *Topsy and Eva* (1927), featuring his wife-to-be Vivian Duncan. Other films, silent and sound, include *The Cardboard Lover* (1928), *Our Dancing Daughters* (1928), *Wild Orchids* (1929), *The Bitter Tea of General Yen* (1933), and *Abdul the Damned* (1935). His last film was produced in Sweden in 1963.

CHARLES T. BARTON (May 25, 1902-December 5, 1979). A former prop man and assistant director, Charles Barton began his directorial career in 1934 with the Randolph Scott Western, *Wagon Wheels*. He subsequently directed more than sixty features, including nine with Abbott and Costello, and Walt Disney's first live-action comedy, *The Shaggy Dog* (1959). Barton's last film was *Swingin' Along* (1962).

MATTHEW "STYMIE" BEARD (1925-January 5, 1981). The second black child to appear in the Our Gang comedies, Stymie Beard joined the group in 1930 with *Teacher's Pet* and remained a member of the Gang through 1935. He appeared in a number of features in the late 1930's, but a continuing involvement with drugs (leading to a lengthy prison term) effectively ended Beard's screen career until he was able to make a comeback on television in recent years.

CURTIS BERNHARDT (April 15, 1899-February 22, 1981). Charles Higham wrote, "Curtis Bernhardt . . . was one of that gifted group of Jewish expatriate directors who, as refugees from Hitler, so brightly illuminated the Hollywood scene during World War II and after. He exuded a commanding pride, authority and resilience even during the grievous years that followed a crippling stroke."

Curtis or Kurt Bernhardt was born in Worms, Germany, and began acting on the stage while still in his teens. In Berlin, he turned from acting to directing, and his productions sufficiently impressed a film producer to invite Bernhardt to direct his first film, *Qualen der Nacht*, in 1926. He directed Marlene Dietrich in *Three Loves* (1929), Conrad Veidt in a drama of the Napoleonic war, *The Last Company* (1930), and codirected *The Rebel* (1932) with Luis Trenker. While Bernhardt was making *The Tunnel* (1933), a German-French coproduction about the building of a tunnel under the English Channel, Hitler came to power in Germany, and the director was forced to flee, first to France and later to England, where he made *The Beloved Vagabond* (1934), starring Maurice Chevalier and Margaret Lockwood.

In 1940, Curtis Bernhardt was able to come to the United States, where he went to work at Warner Bros., his first feature being *My Love Came Back* (1940), starring Olivia de Havilland. Bernhardt's best-known American features include *Juke Girl* (1942), *Devotion* (1944), *A Stolen Life* (1946, featuring Bette Davis in a dual role), *Possessed* (1947, with Joan Crawford at her most intensely dramatic), and *Payment on Demand* (1951, again with Bette Davis). In the 1950's, Bernhardt was entrusted with the direction of a number of soap opera-type historical melodramas, including *The Merry Widow* (1952), *Miss Sadie Thompson* (1953), and *Beau Brummell* (1954). They were conventional pictures, and Bernhardt did his best with them.

Bernhardt's last film was *Kisses for My President* (1964), after which ill health forced his retirement. Shortly after his death, Bernhardt was honored with a major retrospective at the Berlin Film Festival.

GEORGE BILSON (August 25, 1904-September 23, 1981). Between 1932 and 1937, George Bilson headed the trailer department at Warner Bros., producing a number of fine one-reel featurettes promoting such films as *A Midsummer Night's Dream* (1935). From 1943 through 1953, Bilson was a short-film producer at RKO, responsible for the Leon Errol and Edgar Kennedy series, among others.

HENRY BLANKE (December 30, 1901-May 28, 1981). Henry Blanke's name may not be a familiar one, but the films that he produced at Warner Bros. are: *The Story of Louis Pasteur* (1935), *The Petrified Forest* (1936), *Green Pastures* (1936), *The Adventures of Robin Hood* (1938), *The Old Maid* (1939), *The Sea Hawk* (1940), *The Maltese Falcon* (1941), and dozens of others. He began his career as an assistant to Ernst Lubitsch in Germany and came with the director to the United States; between 1928 and 1930 Blanke handled Warner Bros. film production in Germany before returning to establish the studio's foreign production department in Hollywood. He retired in 1962.

BEULAH BONDI (May 3, 1888-January 11, 1981). Because she so often played elderly women on the screen, in person Beulah Bondi never showed any signs of growing old. As she says, in character, in *Trail of the Lonesome Pine* (1935), "I was born old." One of the greatest character actresses that the screen has known, Bondi never received an Academy Award for Best Supporting Actress, despite being nominated in 1936, the first year such Awards were given, for her role in *The Gorgeous Hussy*. There are many memorable Bondi screen performances: gossipy Emma Jones in *Street Scene* (1931), the frigid Mrs. Davidson in *Rain* (1932), country woman Melissa Tolliver in *Trail of the Lonesome Pine* (1935), the mother who sacrifices everything for her son in *Of Human Hearts* (1938), Mrs. Webb in *Our Town* (1940), the crotchety grandmother in *The Southerner* (1945), and the vindictive Bible-reading mother of *The Track of the Cat* (1954).

Of all her roles, however, the one with which Beulah Bondi is most closely identified is that of Lucy Cooper in Leo McCarey's heartrending 1937 production, *Make Way for Tomorrow*, one of the finest films ever made on dealing with the problems of old age.

Born in Chicago as Beulah Bondy, the actress made her stage debut at the age of nine as Cedric Erroll in *Little Lord Fauntleroy* at the Memorial Opera House in Valparaiso, Indiana. She worked in stock companies for many years before making her Broadway debut, in 1925, in *One of the Family*. It was her 1929 Broadway hit, *Street Scene*, which led to Bondi's going to Hollywood to repeat her role in the 1931 Sam Goldwyn film version, directed by King Vidor. She appeared in sixty-four films between 1931 and 1963, when her last feature, *Tammy and the Doctor*, was released.

In addition to her film work, Bondi gave a memorable performance as Aunt Martha Corinne Walton in two episodes of the popular television series, "The Waltons," one episode seen in 1976 and one in 1977. For that second episode, "The Pony Cart," Bondi received an Emmy Award. Her last public appearance was at the AFI Life Achievement Award Dinner for James Stewart, whose mother she had played in four features and on "The Jimmy Stewart

Show" in 1971.

Richard Boone (June 18, 1916-January 10, 1981). Richard Boone made his stage debut in *Medea* (1947) and his screen debut in *The Halls of Montezuma* (1951). It is not as a film actor in *The Robe* (1953), *The Alamo* (1960), *Rio Conchos* (1964), or *The Kremlin Letter* (1970), however, that Boone is best-known, but as the star of the CBS television series "Have Gun Will Travel" from 1957 to 1963.

Stephen Bosustow (November 6, 1911-July 4, 1981). A Disney animator from 1934, Bosustow founded UPA Pictures in 1945, a major independent animation studio. Nominated for fourteen Academy Awards, he received three Oscars for *Gerald McBoing-Boing* (1950), *When Magoo Flew* (1954), and *Mister Magoo's Puddle Jumper* (1956).

Keefe Brasselle (February 7, 1923-July 7, 1981). Keefe Brasselle made his screen debut in 1944 with *Janie* but is best remembered for his unfortunate casting in the title role of *The Eddie Cantor Story* (1953). A leading man in minor features, Brasselle later turned his attention to television production.

Bernard R. Brown (1899-February 20, 1981). Thanks to his keen sense of self-promotion, Bernard Brown is probably the best-known of sound engineers. His own claims notwithstanding, his contribution to *The Jazz Singer* (1927) was minimal, but he was responsible for the excellent sound quality of Universal features from 1936 onwards.

Hoagy Carmichael (November 22, 1899-December 27, 1981). "If I could have the sensibility of any composer, it would be Hoagy Carmichael," said Carly Simon to *Rolling Stone*. "His ability to combine a complicated thought with a single way of expressing it is like finding an original word to describe a sunset, or redefining very simply the word love." Hoagy Carmichael was one of the great songwriters of the twentieth century, the man responsible for "I Get Along Without You Very Well," "Georgia on My Mind," "Ole Buttermilk Sky," "Lazy Bones," "Up the Lazy River," "The Nearness of You," and, of course, "Stardust." Mitchell Parrish, who wrote the lyrics for the last, noted, "He was the Will Rogers of the music business. He distinctly had the stamp of Americana on him."

In 1946, Carmichael received an Academy Award nomination for Best Song for "Ole Buttermilk Sky" (from *Canyon Passage*), and in 1951 he won that Academy Award for "In the Cool, Cool, Cool of the Evening" (from *Here Comes the Groom*). That, however, was only a small part of Hoagy Carmichael's contribution to the cinema. Despite trying unsuccessfully to gain a foothold in films when he first came to Hollywood in 1929, Carmichael later went on to become an actor of eminence in films such as *To Have and Have Not* (1944), *Johnny Angel* (1945), *Canyon Passage* (1946), *The Best Years of Our Lives* (1946), *Young Man with a Horn* (1950), and *Timberjack* (1955). Usually, he would be seen sitting at a piano with a cigarette dangling from his lips.

Hoagy Carmichael was born in Bloomington, Indiana, had a law degree from Indiana University, and gave up a legal practice to play piano in a band and to become a composer. Eventually he organized his own band in New York and used it to promote his songs. Carmichael began composing for motion pictures in 1936, and continued to do so through the mid-1950's. He also contributed to a number of stage musicals, including *The Show Is On* (1936) and *Alive and Kicking* (1950).

In more recent years, Carmichael was seen occasionally on television and also found time to write two autobiographies, *Stardust Road* (1946) and *Sometimes I Wonder* (1965). Prior to his death from a heart attack in Palm Springs, he had been semi-retired, although he did participate in the poorly received 1981 Los Angeles stage production of *Hoagy, Bix and Wolfgang Beethoven Bunkhaus*.

PADDY CHAYEFSKY (January 29, 1923-August 1, 1981). Bronx-born Paddy Chayefsky was a well-known screenwriter whose career also encompassed the so-called "golden age" of television and the Broadway stage. An outspoken man, Chayefsky once said, "I have sometimes been accused of writing plays about little people. What my critics pretend to mean, I think, is that my plays are literal and earthbound, and that my characters never can achieve any stature beyond immediate recognition."

Paddy Chayefsky wrote his first television play, "Holiday Song," in 1952 for the NBC Playhouse, but his best-known television work is "Marty," which aired on May 24, 1953, on the Goodyear TV Playhouse, with Rod Steiger in the title role. It was filmed in 1955, with Ernest Borgnine in the lead, and gave Chayefsky his first Oscar. Chayefsky also received Academy Awards in 1971 for *The Hospital* and in 1976 for *Network*.

The writer's first involvement with films had come in 1951, when he provided the story for *As Young as You Feel*, but Chayefsky's screen career really took off after "Marty," when he wrote or adapted *The Bachelor Party* (1957), *The Goddess* (1958), *Middle of the Night* (1959), *The Americanization of Emily* (1964), *Paint Your Wagon* (1969), *The Hospital* 919771), *Network* (1976), and *Altered States* (1979). In addition, Chayefsky had a number of plays produced on Broadway, but not usually with any great success.

At Chayefsky's funeral service in New York, he was eulogized by critic and historian Arthur Schlesinger, Jr.:

> No American in recent times had a more exact and stinging satirical gift, but he never

used that gift for purely destructive purposes. He was sardonic, not cynical. He wanted to clear our minds of cant and our souls of hypocrisy. For all his relish in human folly, he never abandoned hope in humanity. His satire, like that of all great satirists, sprang from love—from his instinctive sweet understanding of the inarticulate Martys and Claras of the world, bravely living lives of quiet desperation.

RENÉ CLAIR (November 11, 1898-March 15, 1981). Writing in *Sequence* (Winter, 1948/1949), Gavin Lambert commented, "A few directors create their own worlds. Instead of re-exploring familiar territory and, by imagination and personal vision, illuminating a new aspect, they invent a world which obeys its own rules and people it with characters not to be found elsewhere. One thinks immediately of Clair, Vigo, Chaplin, Disney."

The world created by René Clair was that of a mystical and surrealistic Paris peopled by eccentrics and lovers who illustrated the absurdities of human behavior. This world, which was first seen in Clair's *Paris Qui Dort* (1923, *The Crazy Rat*), in which the entire city is asleep except for a group on top of the Eifel Tower, came to its zenith with *Sous les Toits de Paris* (1939) and *Le Million* (1931), and faded away with *Quatorze Juillet* (1933). Unfortunately, in more recent years, Clair's world and his films have not been appreciated, and at the time of his death, René Clair was a classic French film director who was largely ignored.

René Clair became a film actor in the early 1920's and worked as an assistant to Jacques de Baroncelli before making his debut as a director in 1923. *The Crazy Rat* was well-received by both critics and the public, and Clair followed it with *Entr'acte* (1924; the film has been described as "the one true masterpiece of Dada," and featured a musical score by Eric Satie), *Le Voyage Imaginaire* (1925), and *An Italian Straw Hat* (1927). In the mid-1930's, Clair went to England to direct *The Ghost Goes West* (1935) and *Break the News* (1936), and returned briefly to France before coming to the United States, where he spent World War II. His films here—*The Flame of New Orleans* (1941), *I Married A Witch* (1942), *Forever and a Day* (1943, one episode only), *It Happened Tomorrow* (1944), and *And Then There Were None* (1945)—are pleasant, mild-mannered entertainments, but certainly give little indication that they were the work of a giant of the French film industry.

In 1946, Clair returned to France and directed a few major works, notably *La Silence est d'Or* (1947), starring Maurice Chevalier and released in the United States as *Man About Town*; *Les Belles de Nuit* (1952, *Beauties of the Night*), starring Gérard Philipe; and *Porte des Lilas* (1956). He was the first individual to be elected to the French Academy solely in recognition of achievements in the cinema and for many years served as head of the jury at the Cannes Film Festival. In 1973, Clair produced Gluck's *Orphée et Euydice* at the Paris Opera.

René Clair once explained, "The cinematic art starts with illusion. Why show a door closing, it is enough to hear it slam? What do you need to make a sexy scene? Two bodies and a camera. It is not very difficult. But it is a challenge to show falling in love. Sex and violence are easy. A girl and a gun always succeed. But the great masters, D. W. Griffith and Charlie Chaplin, never needed that combination. I never did either."

GHISLAIN CLOQUET (1928-November 2, 1981). Ghislain Cloquet was a major French cinematographer whose many credits include *Night and Fog* (1955), *Le Feu Follet* (1964), *Au Hazard Balthazar* (1965), *The Young Girls of Rochefort* (1967), *Love and Death* (1975), *I Sent a Letter to My Love* (1981), and *Four Friends* (1981). He won an Academy Award for his work on Roman Polanski's *Tess* (1980).

DENYS COOP (July 20, 1920-August 16, 1981). An assistant cameraman and camera operator on numerous major British films of the 1930's, 1940's, and 1950's, Denys Coop's credits as cinematographer include *A Kind of Loving* (1962), *Billy Liar* (1963), *This Sporting Life* (1963), *One-Way Pendulum* (1965), and *10 Rillington Place* (1970). He received a special Oscar for his contribution to the visual effects of *Superman* (1978).

BOSLEY CROWTHER (July 13, 1905-March 7, 1981). For twenty-seven years, from 1940 through 1967, Bosley Crowther was film critic of *The New York Times* and therefore the most influential film reviewer in the United States. Aside from film reviewing, Crowther served as an executive consultant to Columbia from 1968 through 1973 and also wrote five books: *The Lion's Share* (1957), *Hollywood Rajah* (1960), *The Great Films* (1967), *Vintage Films* (1977), and *Reruns* (1978).

JIM DAVIS (August 26, 1915-April 26, 1981). Best known to millions of television viewers as "Dallas'" Jock Ewing, Jim Davis had been acting in films since the early 1940's, usually in inconsequential roles or in "B" pictures.

BRENDA DE BANZIE (1916)-March 5, 1981). A character actress best known for her portrayal of Phoebe Rice in the stage and screen versions of *The Entertainer* (1957 and 1960, respectively), Brenda De Banzie also appeared in *Hobson's Choice* (1954), *A Kid for Two Farthings* (1955), *Doctor at Sea* (1955), *The 39 Steps* (1959), *The Pink Panther* (1963), and many other films.

MARK DONSKOI (March 12, 1897-March, 1981). Active in the film world since 1925, Mark Donskoi was a major Soviet director and is best known to Western filmgoers for his Maxim Gorki trilogy: *The Childhood of Maxim Gorki* (1938), *On His Own* (1939), and *University of Life* (1941). Donskoi twice received the Order of Lenin for his work.

MELVYN DOUGLAS (April 5, 1901-August 4, 1981). Somehow it is difficult to imagine the film industry without Melvyn Douglas—he was so much a part of it, from his first film, *Tonight or Never* (1931), through his last, *Ghost Story*, released shortly before his death. Along the way, Douglas was nominated for three Academy Awards, and won two—both for Best Supporting Actor—for his roles in *Hud* (1963) and *Being There* (1979).

Melvyn Douglas was born in Macon, Georgia; his father was a Russian-born concert pianist. After working at a variety of jobs, Douglas became an actor with a touring company in the late teens. In 1928, he made his mark on Broadway with *A Free Soul*, and other plays followed rapidly, notably *Tonight or Never* (1930), which also starred Helen Gahagan, whom Douglas married a few years later (she died in 1980). As a result of his performance on stage, Douglas was signed by Samuel Goldwyn for the screen version, in which his costar was Gloria Swanson.

The actor quickly gained a reputation for his intelligent, urbane performances in films such as *As You Desire Me* (1932), *Counsellor-at-Law* (1933), *Theodora Goes Wild* (1936), *Angel* (1937), *That Certain Age* (1938), *Ninotchka* (1939), *A Woman's Face* (1941), and *Mr. Blandings Builds His Dream House* (1948). Between 1931 and 1942, when Douglas went to Washington to become director of the Arts Council of the Office of Civilian Defense, the actor starred in forty-four features.

From the late 1940's onward, Douglas concentrated on his stage career, beginning with the musical revue, *Call Me Mister*, in 1946. Other notable stage performances include *Inherit the Wind* (1955, in which Douglas took over as Clarence Darrow from an ailing Paul Muni), *The Waltz of the Toreadors* (1957), *Juno* (1959, an exciting, yet poorly received musical version of *Juno and the Paycock*), *The Best Man* (1960), and *The First Monday in October* (1975). Melvyn Douglas still found time, however, for some superb performances on film in *Billy Budd* (1962), *Hud* (1963), *I Never Sang for My Father* (1970), *The Tenant* (1976), and *The Seduction of Joe Tynan* (1979).

In an interview with *The New York Times*, Douglas commented, "The years since I got out of my movie contracts have been the most satisfactory years of my life. I have no regrets. What I've done hasn't always been the most admirable, perhaps, but I've been a free soul." A prominent supporter of liberal causes and often, along with his wife, unfairly labeled a Communist, Melvyn Douglas was a founding member of Americans for Democratic Action.

ALLAN DWAN (April 3, 1885-December 21, 1981). As Peter Bogdanovich wrote in his Introduction to *The Last Pioneer* (a 1971 book-length interview with Allan Dwan), "There will never again be a movie career like Allan Dwan's. Over fifty years, he directed at least 400 pictures, and produced, wrote or supervised as many more." Allan Dwan began his career in 1909 and retired in 1958. Shortly before his death, Dwan was the subject of a tribute at the Academy of Motion Picture Arts and Sciences—he never received an Academy Award nomination, let alone an Oscar—and that day, April 25, was declared Allan Dwan Day by Los Angeles Mayor, Tom Bradley.

Allan Dwan was a young electrician installing lights at a Chicago post office when he happened to notice the studios of the Essanay Company across the way. Essanay's cofounder, George K. Spoor, invited him to design some lights for the studio. From Essanay, Dwan went to the independent American Flying A Film Company, where he became a director simply because a director was needed and he was the only person available. The year was 1911, and Dwan directed approximately two hundred short films for the company before joining Universal in 1913. From Universal, Dwan moved to D. W. Griffith's Fine Arts Company, where he first directed Douglas Fairbanks, Sr., in *The Habit of Happiness*, *The Good Bad Man*, *The Half-Breed*, and *Manhattan Madness*, all released in 1916. He was to direct Fairbanks in six more features, notably *A Modern Musketeer* (1917), *Bound for Morocco* (1918), *Robin Hood* (1922), and *The Iron Mask* (1929).

Other stars whom Dwan directed in silent films include Norma Talmadge (*Panthea*, 1917), Marion Davies (*The Dark Star*, 1919), Bebe Daniels (*The Glimpses of the Moon*, 1923), Florence Vidor (*Sea Horses*, 1926), Thomas Meighan (*Tin Gods*, 1926), and Madge Bellamy (*Summer Bachelors*, 1926). Dwan directed Gloria Swanson in eight feature films, the most important of which were *Zaza* (1923) and *Manhandled* (1924).

In 1926, Dwan signed on with William Fox as a director, and remained with Fox (later Twentieth Century-Fox) through the early 1940's. He directed Shirley Temple in *Heidi* (1937) and *Rebecca of Sunnybrook Farm* (1938), Tyrone Power and Loretta Young in *Suez* (1938), Don Ameche and the Ritz Brothers in *The Three Musketeers* (1939), and Jack Oakie and Linda Darnell in *Rise and Shine* (1941). In the 1940's, Dwan was chiefly directing "B"-pictures, although he was responsible for *Sands of Iwo Jima* (1949). He was still very active in the 1950's, directing twenty-one features, including *Cattle Queen of Montana* (1954, with Barbara Stanwyck) and *Tennessee's Partner* (1955, which many critics argue contains Ronald Reagan's best screen performance).

Dwan retired in 1959 after directing *Most Dangerous Man Alive*, which was not released by Columbia until 1961. He lived very simply in retirement, and when asked why he had quit the industry commented, "It was no longer a question of 'Let's get a bunch of people together and make a picture.' It's just a business that I stood as long as I could, and I got out of it when I couldn't stand it any more."

ISOBEL ELSOM (March 16, 1893-January 12, 1981). A British-born, aristocratic supporting actress who began her screen career in England during

World War I, Isobel Elsom appeared in such films as *You Were Never Lovelier* (1942), *Casanova Brown* (1944), *The Ghost and Mrs. Muir* (1947), *The Paradine Case* (1948), *Love Is a Many-Splendored Thing* (1955), and *My Fair Lady* (1964). She starred in both the stage and film versions of *Ladies in Retirement* (1941).

JEAN EUSTACHE (1939-November 4, 1981). Suicide ended the career of Jean Eustache, the strongly independent French film director who made his screen debut with *Bad Company* (1967) and is best known to American audiences for his four-and-a-half hour *The Mother and the Whore* (1973).

MADGE EVANS (July 1, 1909-April 26, 1981). Madge Evans' film career began when she was a child, and between 1915 and 1919 she was featured in more than twenty films. She returned to the screen as a pleasant ingenue in 1931, appearing in *Hallelujah I'm a Bum* (1933), *Dinner at Eight* (1933), *Stand Up and Cheer* (1934), *David Copperfield* (1935), and *Pennies from Heaven* (1936), among many others. After her marriage to playwright Sidney Kingsley, Madge Evans retired from the screen in 1938.

HUGO FRIEDHOFER (May 3, 1902-May 17, 1981). Hugo Friedhofer began his Hollywood career as orchestrator on films such as *Sunnyside Up* (1929). He came to prominence as a composer with his score for *The Adventures of Marco Polo* (1937), and his other credits include *Woman in the Window* (1945), *The Best Years of Our Lives* (1947, for which he won an Oscar), *Joan of Arc* (1948), *An Affair to Remember* (1957), and *The Young Lions* (1958).

KETTI FRINGS (February 28, 1915-February 11, 1981). A prominent novelist, playwright, and Pulitzer Prize-winner (for *Look Homeward, Angel*), Ketti Frings was responsible for the screenplays of *The Accused* (1949), *Come Back, Little Sheba* (1953), *The Shrike* (1955), and *By Love Possessed* (1961), among others.

ABEL GANCE (October 25, 1889-November 10, 1981). "Abel Gance," wrote Penelope Gilliatt in *The New Yorker* (September 6, 1976), "has been to cinema what Picasso was to painting." A passion for literature and the theater led Abel Gance naturally to the cinema, and by 1911 he had formed his own production company. Gance experimented with film technique through films such as *La Folie du Docteur Tube* (1915), which featured distorted camera effects, and *Barberousse* (1916), which included unusual camera movement and editing.

In 1917, Gance had his greatest commercial success to date with *Mater Dolorosa*, a melodrama which assured him of such stature in the French film industry that he was able to place his name, as director, before those of his stars. Two years later, Gance directed his first epic feature, *J'Accuse* (*I Accuse*), a pacifist statement on the waste of war, which he reedited in 1937. *La Roue* (1921), with its use of cross-editing to emphasize the melodrama of a railroad engineer, is said to have had a major influence on Sergei Eisenstein. Jean Cocteau is quoted as saying, "There is cinema before and after *La Roue* as there is painting before and after Picasso."

Gance's greatest achievement came in 1927 with *Napoleon*, in which the director also appeared in the role of Louis Saint-Just. Painstakingly restored by Kevin Brownlow, *Napoleon* proved to be one of the major film successes of 1981, receiving its repremiere at the Radio City Music Hall in New York and at major sites throughout America. Whether the crowds came to cheer the film's new entrepreneur Francis Ford Coppola (whose father, Carmine, produced a new score, replacing that of the distinguished composer, Arthur Honegger), or because they were expected to so do to be part of the "in" crowd, or simply out of respect for the technical virtuosity of Gance's work, will never be known.

The most distinctive feature of *Napoleon* was Gance's use of Polyvision to create a triptych screen. Gance commented, "To make the public enthusiastic, you have to get the same feeling into your camerawork—poetry, exaltation . . . but above all poetry. That is why Polyvision is so important to me. The theme, the story one is telling, is on the central screen. The story is prose, and the wings, the side screens, are poetry."

Gance never again reached the heights of *Napoleon*, and his sound features, which include *Lucrèzia Borgia* (1937), *Un Grande Amour de Beethoven* (1937, *The Life and Loves of Beethoven*), *Le Paradis Perdu* (1939), and *Austerlitz* (1960), failed to achieve the critical or popular success of his silent features. Gance never ceased working; he worked on a revised sound version of *Napoleon* and was actively involved in the writing of a twelve-hour film on the life of Christopher Columbus. Thankfully, he lived long enough to bask in some of the limelight created by the revival of *Napoleon*, and in 1980 received an honorary César (the French equivalent of an Oscar) in recognition of his vast contributions to the French film industry.

GLORIA GRAHAME (November 28, 1925-October 5, 1981). The sulky blond, who won an Academy Award for Best Supporting Actress for her role in *The Bad and the Beautiful* (1952), made her screen debut at M-G-M with *Blonde Fever* in 1944. Her best screen work came in the 1950's with features such as *The Greatest Show on Earth* (1952), *The Good Die Young* (1955), *Cobweb* (1955), *Oklahoma!* (1955), and *The Man Who Never Was* (1956). She was last seen in *Melvin and Howard* (1980).

RON GRAINER (1924-February 21, 1981). A film composer whose credits include *To Sir with Love* (1967), *The Omega Man* (1971), *A Kind of Loving*

(1962), and *The Caretaker* (1963), Ron Grainer was born and trained as a musician in Australia. He was a frequent composer for British television, responsible for the theme music for "Steptoe and Son" and "That Was the Week That Was."

EDMUND GRAINGER (October 1, 1906-July 6, 1981). The son of a former president of both Republic and RKO, Edmund Grainger became a producer in the early 1930's; his credits include *Flying Tigers* (1942), *Wake of the Red Witch* (1948), *Sands of Iwo Jima* (1950), *The French Line* (1954), *Green Mansions* (1959), and *Cimarron* (1960).

SARA HADEN (1899-September 15, 1981). Sara Haden was well-known for her crotchety characterizations, notably as the spinster Aunt Milly in fourteen of the "Andy Hardy" films at M-G-M. Haden made her screen debut in *Spitfire* in 1934, and other films include *Anne of Green Gables* (1934), *Magnificent Obsession* (1935), *Captain January* (1936), *The Shop Around the Corner* (1940), *Woman of the Year* (1942), and *The Bishop's Wife* (1947). "I am mean in a great variety of fashions," she once remarked.

ANN HARDING (August 7, 1902-September 1, 1981). With the advent of the "talkies," a host of Broadway actors and actresses flocked to Hollywood. Studios were eager to sign performers who could "talk," without considering whether the particular performer was able to make the transition from acting on stage to acting on screen. In fact, few Broadway players from that period lasted in Hollywood, but one who did, and one who brought a beauty and a quiet dignity to all her screen roles, was Ann Harding.

Born at Fort Sam Houston, Texas, where her father, an Army captain, was stationed, Ann Harding always had theatrical ambitions. She made her stage debut with the Provincetown Players in 1920, at which time she changed her name from Dorothy Gatley to Ann Harding (the successful presidential candidate that year was Warren G. Harding). The actress first came to prominence on Broadway in *Tarnish* (1923), and for the rest of the decade was a Broadway favorite.

In 1929, Ann Harding was tested by Pathé and immediately signed to a contract, which commenced with *Paris Bound*, in which her leading man was another stage actor, Fredric March. After *Her Private Affair* and *Condemned* (both released in 1929), Harding starred in *Holiday* (1930), based on the Philip Barry play, in which she gives a magnificent performance certainly on a par with, if not superior to, that of Katharine Hepburn in the 1938 remake.

Between 1930 and 1956, when Ann Harding made her last screen appearance, she was seen in more than thirty features, including *The Girl of the Golden West* (1930), *The Conquerors* (1932), *The Animal Kingdom* (1932), *Gallant Lady* (1933), *The Flame Within* (1935), *Peter Ibbetson* (1935), *Mission to Moscow* (1943), *Those Endearing Young Charms* (1945), *It Happened on Fifth Avenue* (1947), *The Magnificent Yankee* (1950), and *The Man in the Gray Flannel Suit* (1956). In the last, Harding's final important screen appearance, she again played opposite Fredric March, as his estranged wife.

Ann Harding never received an Oscar; she was nominated only once for Best Actress, for her role in *Holiday*. After her screen career ended, the actress made a few off-Broadway stage appearances and also did a certain amount of television work before announcing her permanent retirement from professional life in the early 1960's.

ROBERT H. HARRIS (July 15, 1911-November 30, 1981). After more than twenty years on the Broadway stage, Robert H. Harris made his screen debut as a character actor in *Bundle of Joy* (1956). Other film credits prior to his retirement in 1977 include *The Big Caper* (1957), *No Down Payment* (1957), and *Peyton Place* (1957). Long active in television as an actor and director, Harris played Jake on *The Goldbergs* from 1953 through 1954.

RUSSELL HAYDEN (June 12, 1912-June 10, 1981). Russell Hayden made his screen debut as an actor in the mid-1930's as a Western sidekick, a role he continued to portray in films through the 1950's such as *Hopalong Rides Again* (1937), *Sante Fe Marshall* (1940), *Marshall of Gunsmoke* (1944), and *Fast on the Draw* (1950). In more recent years, Hayden was active as a television director, again of Westerns.

EDITH HEAD (October 28, 1898-October 24, 1981). There can be little question that Edith Head was the only costume designer in the film industry whose name was as familiar as those of many of the stars for whom she worked. Not always liked by her colleagues, Edith Head understood the value of publicity and the necessity to keep the front office of the studio as happy as the stars she clothed. "I've been a confirmed fence-sitter. That's why I've been around so long," she once remarked. Edith Head received twenty-five Academy Award nominations for Best Costume Design, and won an astounding eight Oscars, beginning with *The Heiress* in 1949 and ending with *The Sting* in 1973. Of the latter, she noted it was probably the first time that an Oscar for Best Costume Design went to a film without a female star.

Born in Los Angeles, Edith Head studied languages and earned a B.A. from the University of California at Berkeley and an M.A. from Stanford. While teaching French, she began to take courses in art and design, eventually obtaining a position with Paramount in 1923 as an apprentice to Howard Greer. She worked as an assistant at Paramount to Greer and later Travis Banton until, in 1938, she became the studio's head designer. At Paramount, Edith Head was noted for the costumes she designed for the studio's contract stars such as Mae West, Audrey Hepburn, Grace Kelly, and Dorothy Lamour (for whom she designed the actress' famous sarong, first seen in the 1936 *The Jungle Princess*).

Edith Head remained with Paramount through 1967, and among the dozens of films on which she worked are *Poppy* (1936), *The Big Broadcast of 1938* (1938), *Her Jungle Love* (1938), *Beau Geste* (1939), *The Cat and the Canary* (1939), *The Great McGinty* (1940), *The Lady Eve* (1940), *Here Comes Mr. Jordan* (1941), *Sullivan's Travels* (1941), *The Major and the Minor* (1942), *Five Graves to Cairo* (1943), *Double Indemnity* (1944), *The Lost Weekend* (1945), *The Road to Rio* (1947), *The Big Clock* (1947), *The Emperor Waltz* (1948), *Sorry, Wrong Number* (1948), *The Great Gatsby* (1949), *Sunset Boulevard* (1950), *A Place in the Sun* (1951), *Rear Window* (1954), *White Christmas* (1954), and *The Ten Commandments* (1956). At Paramount, Edith Head won Oscars for *The Heiress* (1949), *Samson and Delilah* (1950), *A Place in the Sun* (1951), *Roman Holiday* (1953), and *Sabrina* (1954). In addition, during this period she received an Oscar for *All About Eve* (1950), made on loan-out to Twentieth Century-Fox.

Although she also worked for other studios, from 1967 onward Edith Head was chiefly active at Universal, and she was still under contract to the studio at the time of her death. Head's more recent credits include *The Man Who Shot Liberty Vallance* (1962), *Love with the Proper Stranger* (1963), *Inside Daisy Clover* (1965), *Sweet Charity* (1969), *Airport* (1970), *The Man Who Would Be King* (1975), and *Airport 77* (1977).

For almost thirty years, until his death in 1979, Edith Head was married to art director Wiard Ihnen. She wrote two books, *The Dress Doctor* and *How to Dress for Success*, and appeared as herself in two features, *Lucy Gallant* (1955) and *The Oscar* (1966). Edith Head's last screen credit was for *Dead Men Don't Wear Plaid*; completed shortly before her death, the film was dedicated to her memory.

WANDA HENDRIX (November 3, 1928-February 1, 1981). An actress who never lived up to early expectations, Wanda Hendrix made her screen debut at the age of sixteen in *Confidential Agent* (1945). Other films include *Nora Prentiss* (1947), *Ride the Pink Horse* (1947), *Miss Tatlock's Millions* (1948), *Prince of Foxes* (1949), *Montana Territory* (1952), and *Stage to Thunder Rock* (1964).

DALE HENNESY (died July 20, 1981). A prominent set and production designer, Dale Hennesy was responsible for the interior of the human body in *Fantastic Voyage* (1966, for which he won an Academy Award), the science-fiction sets of *Logan's Run* (1976), and the sets of *King Kong* (1976). His other credits include *Under the Yum Yum Tree* (1963), *Dirty Harry* (1972), and *Young Frankenstein* (1974). Hennesy died while working on *Annie*, for which he designed the one-million-dollar New York Street, the largest permanent set at the Burbank Studios.

WILLIAM HOLDEN (April 17, 1918-November 16, 1981). In 1981, Hollywood lost two major stars still at the peak of their careers, through accidental deaths. Natalie Wood was one of the stars; the other was William Holden, who was found dead in his Santa Monica apartment after having apparently fallen and hit his head while in an alcoholic stupor.

William Holden was one of those competent leading men who could always be relied upon to give a good performance without displaying too much bravado or outrageous histrionics. He was completely natural as the screen-writer picked up by Gloria Swanson in *Sunset Boulevard* (1950), in a role which could easily have degenerated into melodrama. Similarly, he under-played the part of Sefton, a wheeler-dealer prisoner of war in *Stalag 17* (1953), for which he won his first and only Academy Award. Even in *Network* (1976, which brought Holden an Oscar nomination), the actor remained subdued and calm despite what was happening around him.

Born William Franklin Beedle in O'Fallon, Illinois, Holden began acting while attending junior college in Los Angeles. He was spotted by a Paramount talent scout and given a film contract; after minor parts in *Prison Farm* (1938) and *Million Dollar Legs* (1939), Holden became a star with his performance opposite Barbara Stanwyck in *Golden Boy* (1939). He was kept busy through-out the 1940's and 1950's appearing in, among others, *Our Town* (1940), *The Remarkable Andrew* (1942), *Dear Ruth* (1947), *Rachel and the Stranger* (1948), *Born Yesterday* (1951), *Sabrina* (1954), *Picnic* (1956), *The Bridge on the River Kwai* (1957), *The Key* (1958), *The Horse Soldiers* (1959), and *The World of Suzie Wong* (1960).

Holden told an interviewer, "I wanted to travel. I had to go to Japan for *The Bridges at Toko-Ri* (1954), and I found that I enjoyed the location, if not the movie. So I began to choose films because they allowed me to be in certain places at certain times—Hong Kong for *Love Is a Many-Splendored Thing*, England for *The Key*. I only did *The Lion* (1962) because it was filmed in Africa and *The Seventh Dawn* (1964) in Malaya. . . . I did them because I liked the locations." This desire for travel led to Holden's involvement in the preservation of Kenyan wild life.

The actor's career appeared to have fallen into a rut, but it was helped back on the right track by Sam Peckinpah's violent Western, *The Wild Bunch* (1969), and *The Towering Inferno* (1974), despite being a dreadful film, assured Holden of continuing star status. *Network* (1976) further enhanced Holden's reputation.

GEORGE JESSEL (April 3, 1898-May 24, 1981). George Jessel had many careers. He was a vaudevillian, a singer, a comedian, the star of the long-running play, *The Jazz Singer*, a writer, a film star, a film producer, a eulogist, and Toastmaster General of the United States (an honorary title bestowed on him by President Roosevelt). Jessel was noted for the money he raised for the state of Israel, and there is an apocryphal story that after Jessel had delivered a eulogy for James Mason's cat, a sobbing Jack Benny remarked, "I never knew cats were so good to Israel." One of the high points of Jessel's life was his receipt of the 1969 Jean Hersholt Humanitarian Award from the Academy of Motion Picture Arts and Sciences.

In recent years, George Jessel gave the impression of an embittered old man. His right-wing utterances offended many, as did his avowed intent to write a book on *The Crucifixion of Richard M. Nixon*. During a 1971 interview on the "Today" show, he appeared in full military uniform and denounced *The Washington Post* and *The New York Times*, likening them to *Pravda*. An outraged Edwin Newman cut short the interview, and Jessel was no longer welcome to air his views on network television.

Born in the Bronx, George Jessel began his career singing with song slides at local nickelodeons, and later joined Gus Edwards' company of young entertainers. By 1920, Jessel had become a vaudeville headliner, but his greatest success came in 1925 when he opened in New York in Samson Raphaelson's *The Jazz Singer*. Supposedly, Jessel was to have been the star of the Warner Bros. film version, but was replaced by Al Jolson, and, instead, made his talkie-feature debut in a poverty row production entitled *Lucky Boy* (1929), in which he introduced the poular song "My Mother's Eyes."

Jessel appeared in other films, notably *Happy Days* (1930), *Stage Door Canteen* (1943), *Four Jills in a Jeep* (1944), and *The Busy Body* (1967), but his major contribution to the film industry was as a producer, responsible for *The Dolly Sisters* (1945), *I Wonder Who's Kissing Her Now?* (1947), *Nightmare Alley* (1947), *When My Baby Smiles at Me* (1948), *Oh You Beautiful Doll* (1949), *Wait Till the Sun Shines Nellie* (1952), *Tonight We Sing* (1953), and *Beau James* (1957).

At Jessel's funeral, Milton Berle was given the difficult task of eulogizing the celebrated eulogist. In a reference to his reputation for stealing other comedians' material, Berle remarked, "Right now, I have a feeling that somewhere up there, Georgie is saying, 'Milton is doing the eulogy today? Well why not? He's taken everything else from me.'"

ALLYN JOSLYN (July 21, 1901-January 21, 1981). After a lengthy stage career, Joslyn came to films in 1937 with *They Won't Forget*; he was a character comedian at his best in *Only Angels Have Wings* (1939), *The Great McGinty* (1940), *My Sister Eileen* (1942), *The Shocking Miss Pilgrim* (1947), and *Harriet Craig* (1950), among many others.

PATSY KELLY (January 21, 1910-September 24, 1981). In an interview, Patsy Kelly hastened to point out, "I've never been a star. A star is something very rare . . . Gary Cooper, Spencer Tracy, Tallulah Bankhead." Kelly may never have considered herself a star, but she was a very rare commodity in show business, the perfect supporting character comedienne, always ready with a quip or meaningful look. Plump and jovial, she was the perennial foil and confidante to players as varied as Thelma Todd, Marion Davies, Ruby Keeler, and Alice Faye.

Born in Brooklyn of Irish parents, Patsy Kelly began her show-business career as a partner to Frank Fay in vaudeville. She later appeared on stage in revues with Al Jolson, Will Rogers, and Clifton Webb, before producer Hal Roach signed her to play opposite Thelma Todd in a series of two-reel comedy shorts, released between 1933 and 1936. After Thelma Todd's death, Kelly made several more shorts with Pert Kelton and Lyda Roberti, and then moved on to feature films with *Going Hollywood* (1933), in which she supported Marion Davies and Bing Crosby. Patsy Kelly was always "supporting," but her presence assured fans that they were in for a good time.

Between 1933 and 1943, when Kelly retired temporarily from films, she was featured in thirty-one productions, including *Countess of Monte Cristo* (1934), *Transatlantic Merry-Go-Round* (1934), *Go into Your Dance* (1935), *Page Miss Glory* (1935), *Kelly the Second* (1936), *Pigskin Parade* (1936), *Ever Since Eve* (1937), *The Gorilla* (1939), *Topper Returns* (1941), and *Sing Your Worries Away* (1942).

Kelly was also heard on radio and toured with her longtime friend Tallulah Bankhead in *Dear Charles* (1955). In 1960, Kelly returned to films with *Please Don't Eat the Daisies*, followed by *The Crowded Sky* (1960), *The Naked Kiss* (1964), *The Ghost in the Invisible Bikini* (1966), *C'Mon, Let's Live a Little* (1967), and *Rosemary's Baby* (1968). The last was remarkable in that Kelly played a witch.

In 1971, Kelly made a triumphant return to Broadway in *No, No, Nanette*, starring her old friend Ruby Keeler. For her role as the lovable Irish maid, Kelly won a Tony Award; two years later she was again nominated for a Tony for her supporting role in *Irene*, featuring Debbie Reynolds. Kelly's last film appearance was in *The North Avenue Irregulars* (1978), and her last professional appearance was in a 1979 episode of the popular ABC television series, "The Love Boat."

BARRETT C. KIESLING (June 24, 1894-August 20, 1981). One of Hollywood's prominent publicists, Barrett Kiesling joined Famous Players-Lasky in 1920. He was personal publicity director for Cecil B. De Mille between 1924 and 1931, later joining M-G-M until his retirement in 1958. In 1937, Kiesling published *Talking Pictures*.

EDWIN H. KNOPF (November 11, 1899-December 27, 1981). Edwin Knopf came to Hollywood in 1928 as a director with Paramount. He cowrote and supplied the story for the Anna Sten vehicle, *The Wedding Night* (1935), and later became a producer at M-G-M (1940-1957), where his credits include *The Valley of Decision* (1945), *Edward, My Son* (1949), *Lili* (1953), and *The Glass Slipper* (1955).

ROBERT KRASKER (August 21, 1913-August 16, 1981). Born in Australia, Robert Krasker went to England in 1930, working initially as a camera operator. He soon became recognized as one of the country's leading cinematographers; his credits include *Henry V* (1944), *Brief Encounter* (1945), *Odd Man Out* (1947), *Senso* (1954), *El Cid* (1961), *Billy Budd* (1962), and *The Collector* (1965). He received an Academy Award for his work on *The Third Man* (1949).

LOLA LANE (May 21, 1909-June 22, 1981). The first of the Lane Sisters to enter show business, Lola Lane began her screen career with Fox in the late 1920's. An actress of minor talent, Lola Lane appeared in more than thirty features, including *Movietone Follies of 1929* (1929), *Good News* (1930), *Hollywood Hotel* (1938), *Zanzibar* (1940), and *Deadline at Dawn* (1946).

ZARAH LEANDER (March 15, 1907-June 23, 1981). Swedish-born Zarah Leander's good looks and husky voice helped make her one of the Nazi cinema's top stars in the late 1930's with films such as *To New Shores* and *La Habanera*, both directed by Douglas Sirk in 1937. She made a comeback in 1948, and can be heard singing on the sound track of *The Tin Drum* (1979).

BERNARD LEE (January 10, 1908-January 16, 1981). A pleasant character actor, active in British films and on the stage from the late 1920's, Bernard Lee was best known to filmgoers as "M" in the James Bond films. Among Lee's more than eighty films are *Rhodes of Africa* (1936), *Let George Do It* (1940), *The Courtneys of Curzon Street* (1947), *The Third Man* (1949), *Odette* (1950), *Beat the Devil* (1953), *Dunkirk* (1958), *The Angry Silence* (1960), *The Raging Moon* (1970), and *10 Rillington Place* (1970).

LOTTE LENYA (October 18, 1900-November 27, 1981). Austrian-born Lotte Lenya was considered the finest interpreter of the works of her husband Kurt Weill and Berthold Brecht, notably of *Die Dreigroschenoper* (the 1931 film version of which featured her). She retired around 1933, but returned to the stage after her husband's death in 1950, and appeared in four more films: *The Roman Spring of Mrs. Stone* (1961), *From Russia with Love* (1963), *The Appointment* (1968), and *Semi-Tough* (1977).

MARGARET LINDSAY (September 19, 1910-May 8, 1981). Although noted for her British accent—she even borrowed her stage name from a former

British Ambassador—Margaret Lindsay was born in Dubuque, Iowa. She appeared, generally in supporting roles, in more than eighty films, including *Cavalcade* (1933), *Christopher Strong* (1933), *Jezebel* (1938), *The Spoilers* (1942), and *Please Don't Eat the Daisies* (1960).

ANITA LOOS (April 26, 1893-August 18, 1981). Elinor Glyn may have added "It" to the English language, but it was Anita Loos who gave the world the phrase, "Gentlemen Prefer Blondes," an expression as familiar today as it was fifty or more years ago when first introduced. In addition, Loos became not only the first well-known writer for the screen, not only the best-known female screenwriter ever, but also the one screenwriter whose name is as familiar in the 1980's as it was in the 1920's and even before.

The diminutive Anita Loos was born in Mount Shasta, California, and when her newspaperman father ran short of funds he decided to put Anita and her sister on the stage. While still a minor, Loos sold her first film script, *The Earl and the Tomboy*, to the Lubin Company, in March, 1912. The script was never filmed, but the same fate did not await the third script which Loos sold. She received twenty-five dollars for her script of *The New York Hat*, which D. W. Griffith directed in 1912, for the American Biograph Company, with a cast which included Mary Pickford and Lionel Barrymore.

Griffith encouraged the young writer and she moved with him from Biograph to Mutual and eventually to Fine Arts. She claimed to have written the titles for *Intolerance* (1916) but probably contributed only those of a comic nature. While with Griffith, Loos met and married screenwriter-director John Emerson, and together the two wrote the scripts for many Douglas Fairbanks, Sr., films, including *His Picture in the Papers* (1916), *The Half-Breed* (1916), *The Americano* (1917), *Reaching for the Moon* (1917), and *Wild and Wooly* (1917).

Between 1918 and 1920, Loos and Emerson wrote fifteen scripts for stars as varied as Billie Burke (*Let's Get a Divorce*, 1918), George M. Cohan (*Hit-the-Trail Holiday*, 1918), and Norma Talmadge (*The Isles of Conquest*, 1919). The two were particularly associated with Constance Talmadge, writing eleven of her features between 1919 and 1925, including *A Virtuous Vamp* (1919), *Two Weeks* (1920), *Dangerous Business* (1921), *Polly of the Follies* (1922), and *Dulcy* (1923). In 1928, Loos and Emerson adapted Loos's novel, *Gentlemen Prefer Blondes*, for the screen, with Ruth Taylor as the infamous heroine.

The advent of sound did not affect Loos's career. She wrote or adapted *The Struggle* (1931) for D. W. Griffith; *Red-Headed Women* (1932) for Jean Harlow; *San Francisco* (1936) for Clark Gable, Jeanette MacDonald, and Spencer Tracy; *The Women* (1939) for Norma Shearer and Joan Crawford; *Susan and God* (1940) for Joan Crawford; *Blossoms in the Dust* (1941) for Greer Garson; and *I Married an Angel* (1942) for Jeanette MacDonald and Nelson Eddy.

Loos left Hollywood and Metro-Goldwyn-Mayer, where she had worked for ten years, in 1942. Returning to New York, she wrote for the stage *Happy Birthday* (1946), the book for the 1949 musical version of *Gentlemen Prefer Blondes*, and adaptations of Colette's novels of *Gigi* (1952) and *Cheri* (1957). In more recent years, Loos has written interesting but unreliable accounts of her career and of the personalities with whom she was associated in *A Girl Like I* (1966), *Kiss Hollywood Good-By* (1974), *Cast of Thousands* (1977), and *TheTalmadge Girls* (1978). She and John Emerson had written two early volumes on screenwriting: *How to Write Photoplays* and *Breaking into the Movies*.

LOUISE LORRAINE (October 1, 1903-February 2, 1981). Louise Lorraine began her screen career in the late teens in Western shorts and in serials such as *The Adventures of Tarzan* (1921, in which she played Jane). Active through the 1920's and early 1930's, her features include *Up in the Air About Mary* (1922), *The Wild Girl* (1925), *Exit Smiling* (1926), *Baby Mine* (1928), and *Beyond the Law* (1930).

PHILO MCCULLOUGH (1894-June 5, 1981). A prolific film actor of minor parts, Philo McCullough entered films with the Selig Company in 1911, beginning a career which continued through *They Shoot Horses, Don't They?* (1969). Between 1921 and 1930, he appeared in more than sixty features.

FRANK MCHUGH (May 23, 1896-August 11, 1981). "I play a dumb cluck, and there's nothing to it," remarked Frank McHugh once of his career as a veteran character actor with a plump face and a snicker. After a successful Broadway career, McHugh came to films in the late 1920's, appearing in productions as varied as *Footlight Parade* (1933), *A Midsummer Night's Dream* (1935), *The Roaring Twenties* (1939), *Going My Way* (1947), and *There's No Business Like Show Business* (1954).

ENID MARKEY (1890-November 15, 1981). A silent star with a hauntingly expressive face, Enid Markey entered films with producer Thomas H. Ince in the mid-teens. She was Jane in the first Tarzan feature, *Tarzan of the Apes* (1918), but her screen work, which lasted on and off through *The Boston Strangler* (1968), was relatively unimportant when compared with her New York stage career.

GARY MARSH (May 21, 1902-March, 1981). A balding and stout character actor, who often appeared in sinister roles in more than one hundred British films between 1930 and 1968, Gary Marsh may be seen at his best in *When Knights Were Bold* (1936), *Bank Holiday* (1938), *The Four Just Men* (1939), *Let George Do It* (1940), and *Dead of Night* (1945).

JESSIE MATTHEWS (March 11, 1907-August 20, 1981). The name Jessie Matthews evokes an image of a svelte British singer and dancer with an attractive face, despite an almost nonexistent chin, enunciating the lyrics of songs such as "Over My Shoulder" and "Dancing on the Ceiling" very carefully and with an extremely English accent. Although she continued to perform through the 1970's, Matthews was very much a personality of the 1930's, a fond reminder of the golden years of British film musicals.

Born to a working-class London family, Jessie Matthews worked hard as a child at her dancing and elocution lessons before making her stage debut at the age of twelve. In 1923, Matthews appeared in *The Music Box Revue*, and the following year was an understudy to Gertrude Lawrence in *Charlot's Revue*. With the latter, Matthews went to the United States; she took over the lead from Gertrude Lawrence and returned to England a star. Other early Matthews stage successes include *One Damn Thing After Another* (1927), *This Year of Grace* (1928), *Wake Up and Dream* (1929), and *Ever Green* (1930). In the last, a Richard Rodgers-Lorenz Hart musical, produced by C. B. Cochran, Matthews introduced "Dancing on the Ceiling."

As a result of her performance on stage in *Hold My Hand* (1931), Matthews was asked by director Albert de Courville to star in the film, *There Goes the Bride* (she had earlier played minor roles in two silent films and had also starred in a 1930 musical, *Out of the Blue*). In *There Goes the Bride* (1932), Matthews embarked on a screen career which included *The Good Companions* (1933), *Waltzes from Vienna* (1934), *Evergreen* (1934), *First a Girl* (1935, and one source of the current hit *Victor/Victoria*), *It's Love Again* (1936), and *Gangway* (1937).

Matthews was one of the few British film stars of the 1930's to gain any sort of a following in the United States, despite the fact that she never made a film in America. Failing health and marital problems brought an end to Matthews' screen career, but not before she had directed a 1940 short, *Victory Wedding*, starring John Mills. In later years, she returned to the spotlight, playing the title role for six years on the BBC radio program, "Mrs. Dales' Diary." Matthews made a number of appearances on television and in cabaret; she published her autobiography, *Over My Shoulder*, in 1974, and in 1979 appeared in a widely acclaimed one-woman show at the Mayfair Music Hall in Los Angeles.

Tom Thumb (1958) was Matthews last major screen appearance, in which she gave a delightful performance as Tom Thumb's new mother. Her last film was the 1980 unreleased feature, *Second Star on the Right*.

LILLIE MESSENGER (1900-October 27, 1981). A longtime associate of Louis B. Mayer, Lillie Messenger read properties for the head of M-G-M and would "sell" them to him by acting the scripts out dramatically. In later years, she worked as a developer of stories and talent at Universal and RKO before becoming a talent agent in the 1950's.

HUGO MONTENEGRO (1926-February 7, 1981). A composer best known for the theme from *The Good, the Bad and the Ugly* (1966), Hugo Montenegro's other credits include *For a Few Dollars More* (1965), *Hurry Sundown* (1967), and *Lady in Cement* (1968).

ROBERT MONTGOMERY (May 21, 1904-September 27, 1981). There are obvious similarities between the careers of Robert Montgomery and Ronald Reagan. Both were popular Hollywood leading men; both became presidents of the Screen Actors Guild; and both entered politics, although Montgomery's political activity was limited to his being a television coach and later television and radio adviser to President Eisenhower. Montgomery was the first show-business personality to occupy an office in the White House.

Born Henry Montgomery, Jr., in Fishkill Landing, New York, Robert Montgomery wanted initially to become a writer and entered the theater only out of a desire to earn some income as it became obvious that his skills as a writer were not in demand. He appeared in a number of Broadway productions, none of which ran very long, before *Possession* (1928), in which he was seen by a talent scout from Sam Goldwyn Productions, and, as a result, signed for a screen test. The Goldwyn test came to nothing, but Montgomery was hired by M-G-M, where he was to remain from 1929 through 1941. He was a pleasant, tepid leading man in films such as *Private Lives* (1931), *Letty Lynton* (1932), *Night Flight* (1933), *Riptide* (1934), and *The Last of Mrs. Cheney* (1937). Probably his best performance was as Danny in the screen version of Emlyn Williams' *Night Must Fall* (1937). As Montgomery himself put it, "The directors shoved a cocktail shaker in my hands and kept me shaking it for years."

For three terms, beginning in 1935, Montgomery served as President of the Screen Actors Guild, and was largely responsible for the Guild's first contracts; later he helped to expose corruption among Hollywood union leaders. In 1947, Montgomery was elected to a fourth term as SAG President.

After military service during World War II, Montgomery returned to the screen with *They Were Expendable* (1945), which he directed in part after John Ford, the credited director, broke a leg. A number of unimportant features followed, including *Lady in the Lake* (1946, which Montgomery directed), *Ride the Pink Horse* (1947, also directed by Montgomery), *June Bride* (1948), and *Your Witness* (1950). Montgomery's last screen appearance was in *The Gallant Hours* (1960), which he also directed and produced.

In 1950, "Robert Montgomery Presents" was first seen on NBC, and altogether 326 programs were aired, with Montgomery acting as producer, director, host, and sometimes leading player. It was considered one of television's better programs. In later years, Montgomery became a strong critic of network television and an avid supporter of public television. A liberal much of his life, Montgomery became a conservative with his involvement with Eisenhower.

NIGEL PATRICK (May 2, 1913-September 21, 1981). A suave British supporting actor who occasionally turned director (*How to Murder a Rich Uncle*, 1957), Nigel Patrick made his first film, *Mrs. Pym of Scotland Yard*, in 1939, but did not see his film career really take off until the late 1940's. Among his more than forty features are *Trio* (1950), *Pandora and the Flying Dutchman* (1951), *Encore* (1951), *The Pickwick Papers* (1952), *All for Mary* (1955), *League of Gentlemen* (1960), *The Virgin Soldiers* (1969), and *The Mackintosh Man* (1973).

ELEANOR PERRY (1915-March 14, 1981). A prominent screenwriter and feminist, Eleanor Perry began her career with *David and Lisa* (1963), directed by her husband Frank Perry, with whom she worked frequently and from whom she was divorced in 1971. Perry's other credits include *The Swimmer* (1968), *Last Summer* (1969), *Truman Capote's Trilogy* (1969), *Diary of a Mad Housewife* (1970), and *The Man Who Loved Cat Dancing* (1973).

LOTTE REINIGER (June 2, 1899-June, 1981). Lotte Reiniger created and perfected a unique art form with her silhouette films, first produced in Germany in the late teens. Usually working in association with her husband, Carl Koch, she produced dozens of shorts, most of which were based on fairy tales, and was also responsible for *The Adventures of Prince Achmed* (1926), generally considered the first feature-length animated film.

GLAUBER ROCHA (1939-August 23, 1981). The French critic Michel Ciment wrote that "Rocha's talent, recognized by such contrasting directors as Elia Kazan and Luis Buñuel to be among the most vital and original to appear in the last fifteen years, is deeply rooted in a very clear-cut social, indeed mythological environment; his conventions embrace barbaric culture with a clearly detectable African influence; he aims at effecting a change in the audience."

Glauber Rocha became a film director after studying law. He was active as a film critic, and published an essay on Brazilian cinema in 1961 which was to become the manifesto for "Cinema Novo," Brazil's new national cinema movement. Rocha worked as an assistant to Nelson Pereira dos Santos on *Vidas Secas* (1960) before directing his first feature, *Barravento*, which was shown at the New York Film Festival in 1961. He gained worldwide critical attention with *Deus e o Diabo na Terro do Sol* (1964), released in the United States as *Black God, White Devil*.

The director's best-known work is *Antonio das Mortes* (1969), which received the Jury Award at the Cannes Film Festival, and which the *Village Voice* (August 26, 1981) described as "the synthesis of Rocha's career, brilliantly capturing the contradictions of Bahia, Rocha's native province, in all its polyglot, polychrome extravagance. The haunting meetings of landed European *arrivistes* with Africans imported for slavery and the native Indian population are depicted in a surrealistic ritual that owes its iconography as much to African and Indian belief systems as it does to Christianity."

Glauber Rocha left Brazil in 1964 following a right-wing military coup, but returned eventually to his native country, although he left again some ten years later, claiming that Brazil was no place for a revolutionary filmmaker. His other films include *Terra em Transe* (1967, *Land in a Trance*), *O Leao have Sete Cabecas* (1969), *Cabecas Cortadas* (1970), *Historia do Brasil* (1974), and *Claro* (1975).

In 1980, Glauber Rocha completed his last film, *The Age of the Earth*, which depicted four Christ figures: a black, an Indian, a military officer, and a rebel. Rocha described himself as "a poor, alone and sick artist," and became ill with a lung infection while living in Portugal. He returned to Brazil, and a colleague of his commented, "Although Glauber knew how ill he was, he got on a plane and returned to Brazil to die . . . like an elephant."

BORIS SAGAL (1923-May 22, 1981). An accident while directing an NBC television film, "World War III," ended the career of Russian-born Boris Sagal. Sagal had started his career as an actor in the 1950's before directing a number of television series, including "The Defenders"; he made his feature-film debut with *Dime with a Halo* (1963), and alternated between films (*Girl Happy*, 1964, *The Omega Man*, 1971, and others) and television features ("Masada," "A Case of Rape," and so on).

ALFRED SANTELL (September 14, 1895-July 30, 1981). A prolific film director, Alfred Santell entered the film industry with the Lubin Company in the early teens. In 1915, he began directing the comedy series "Ham and Bud" for Kalem and embarked on a career as a director of comedies and light drama which lasted through the late 1940's. Santell's films include *Orchids and Ermine* (1927), *The Patent Leather Kid* (1927), *Rebecca of Sunnybrook Farm* (1932), *Winterset* (1936), *Aloma of the South Seas* (1941), and *Beyond the Blue Horizon* (1942).

JOYCE SELZNICK (February 12, 1928-September 17, 1981). Joyce Selznick was a producer (*Claudine*, 1974), a talent agent, a personal manager, and, above all, a discoverer of stars-to-be, including Tony Curtis, Faye Dunaway, George C. Scott, Brenda Vaccaro, Joan Hackett, Cicely Tyson, Colleen Dewhurst, and Richard Dreyfuss.

JULES C. STEIN (April 26, 1896-April 29, 1981). Jules C. Stein was the man responsible for creating the largest entertainment conglomerate in the world, the mighty Music Corporation of America. He was also a humanitarian who led the fight for a federally funded national eye institute and who founded and financially endowed the Research to Prevent Blindness Organization of New York and the Jules Stein Eye Institute in Los Angeles. In 1976, Stein received the Jean Hersholt Humanitarian Award from the Academy of Motion Picture Arts and Sciences, and that same year gave a million dollars of MCA stock to his alma mater, the University of Chicago. In 1978, Stein was honored as Motion Picture Pioneer of the Year, and, in 1980, along with his colleague, Lew Wasserman, endowed the Motion Picture Country House and Hospital with a two-million-dollar maintenance fund.

Born in South Bend, Indiana, Jules Caesar Stein studied opthalmology at the University of Vienna before taking up residency at Cook County Hospital in Chicago. In 1923, Stein went into private practice, and at the same time became fascinated with show business. He became a part-time band leader and also sent out other small bands to fill engagements locally. In 1924, out of admiration for the mighty Radio Corporation of America, Jules Stein founded his own, at that time tiny, Music Corporation of America, and a year later he left medicine to concentrate on his booking agency.

In 1928, he signed Guy Lombardo, and after booking the orchestra leader into a New York hotel, quickly began booking dance bands for other New York establishments. Lew Wasserman joined the organization in 1936, and soon MCA had signed up a number of Hollywood stars, including Bette Davis, Betty Grable, Jane Wyman, and John Garfield. In 1945, MCA took over the Hayward-Deverich Agency and its clients, including Myrna Loy, Fredric March, Fred Astaire, Ben Hecht, Billy Wilder, and Joshua Logan.

It was estimated that by the mid-1940's MCA represented one-third of all Hollywood stars. In 1946, Lew Wasserman became president of MCA and Stein moved up to chairman of the board, a position which he held until his death. In 1949, MCA formed Revue Productions to produce programs for television, and in 1957 acquired the Paramount library of feature films produced between 1928 and 1948. Two years later, MCA purchased Universal City Studios. By 1962, the company controlled sixty percent of the entertainment industry, and government intervention forced MCA to withdraw from the talent agency field. In addition to the Universal Studios, MCA also controls Decca Records, the Leeds Music Corporation, Columbia Savings and Loan, and has substantial real estate holdings. Until 1954, Jules Stein had sole ownership of MCA.

In an interview with *The New York Times* (July 21, 1963), Jules Stein explained, "I would rather deal with corporate tax problems and the intricacies of corporate structure. I relax that way. We work hard here and we rule with an iron hand. Our competitors do not have our manpower and our knowledge."

KARL STRUSS (November 30, 1886-December 16, 1981). Karl Struss was one of Hollywood's greatest cameramen, noted for the pictorial impact of his work. With Charles Rosher, he received the first Academy Award for Best Cinematography for his magnificent contribution to *Sunrise* (1927), a triumph of silent-film art in which director, cinematographers, set designer, and actors worked together to create a unified whole. Struss never again received an Academy Award, but he did provide filmgoers with some brilliant camerawork, particularly in *Dr. Jekyll and Mr. Hyde* (1932) and *Island of Lost Souls* (1933).

Karl Struss took night classes in photography with Clarence White at Columbia University, and in 1910 had twelve of his photographs exhibited at the International Exhibition of Pictorial Photography, organized by Alfred Stieglitz's Photo-Secession. After military service during World War I, Struss went to Hollywood as a still photographer for Cecil B. De Mille, and soon began working as an assistant to De Mille's cinematographer, Alvin Wyckoff. Struss's first solo credit as a cameraman was on *The Law and the Woman* (1922), directed by Penrhyn Stanlaws.

In 1924, Struss went to Rome with the *Ben-Hur* company and shot almost half of the footage used in the production, although none of the chariot race sequence. Struss did, however, film the sequence depicting the healing of the lepers, and he utilized the photographic technique that he developed there for the transformation sequences in Rouben Mamoulian's production of *Dr. Jekyll and Mr. Hyde*. Between 1928 and 1930, Struss was under contract to D. W. Griffith, for whom he filmed *Drums of Love* (1928), *The Battle of the Sexes* (1928), *The Lady of the Pavements* (1929), and *Abraham Lincoln* (1930). Around that time, he also filmed Mary Pickford in *Coquette* and *The Taming of the Shrew* (both released in 1929), as well as *Lummox*, *Be Yourself* and *One Romantic Night* (all released in 1930).

Struss joined Paramount in 1931 and remained with that company throughout the 1930's, filming, among others, *Murder by the Clock* (1931), *The Sign of the Cross* (1932), *The Story of Temple Drake* (1933), *Belle of the Nineties* (1934), *The Pursuit of Happiness* (1934), *Goin' to Town* (1935), *Sing You Sinners* (1938), and *Thanks for the Memory* (1938). Struss's film career declined, although his work did not, in the 1940's, but he did garner some major credits, including *The Great Dictator* (1940), *Journey into Fear* (1942), *For Whom the Bell Tolls* (1944), and *Heaven Only Knows* (1947). A list of Struss's later credits is rather depressing, including nonentities such as *Tarzan's Savage Fury* (1952) and *The Rawhide Trail* (1958). Between 1959 and 1970, when he retired, Struss was primarily involved in filming television commercials.

RICHARD TALMADGE (December 3, 1896-January 25, 1981). An actor in his own right from the early 1920's through the mid-1930's, Richard Talmadge is probably better remembered as Douglas Fairbanks' stunt double. By the late 1930's, Talmadge had become a second-unit director, and in more recent years his credits included *North to Alaska* (1960), *How the West Was Won* (1962), *Hawaii* (1966), and *Casino Royale* (1967).

NORMAN TAUROG (February 23, 1899-April 7, 1981). Norman Taurog is best remembered for his direction of child stars; so adept did he become at this that he was known to his young performers as Uncle Norman. He received an Academy Award in 1930 for his direction of *Skippy*, which brought Jackie Cooper to stardom, and received an Academy Award nomination in 1938 for his direction of *Boys' Town*, which featured Mickey Rooney. In addition, Taurog directed the Dionne Quintuplets in *Reunion* (1936) and Deanna Durbin in *Mad About Music* (1938). As Taurog said of his young stars, "They just walk on the set and do what I tell them. I love them all."

Born in Chicago, Norman Taurog had been a child actor himself, and appeared in the 1913 New York stage production of *A Good Little Devil*. In the early teens, he made his screen debut as an actor with the IMP Company, working with King Baggot and Florence Lawrence, and he eventually went to Hollywood, where in 1919 he began directing a series of Larry Semon comedies for the Vitagraph Company. He quickly became a prominent director of comedy shorts featuring Lloyd Hamilton, among others.

Taurog directed his first feature-length production, *The Farmer's Daughter*, in 1928, and soon became one of Paramount's leading directors, responsible for *Sooky* (1931), *If I Had a Million* (1932, the W. C. Fields episode only), *We're Not Dressing* (1933), *Mrs. Wiggs of the Cabbage Patch* (1934), *College Rhythm* (1934), and *The Big Broadcast of 1936* (1936). From Paramount, Taurog directed a few productions for other studios, and then moved to M-G-M, where he was to remain for the next thirteen years. At M-G-M, his directional credits include *Young Tom Edison* (1940), *Little Nellie Kelly* (1940), *A Yank at Eton* (1942), *Girl Crazy* (1943), *Words and Music* (1948), and *The Toast of New Orleans* (1950).

In the early 1950's, Taurog returned to Paramount to direct a series of Dean Martin/Jerry Lewis features, including *The Caddy* (1953), *Living It Up* (1954), and *Partners* (1956). He also worked frequently with producer Hal Wallis, directing Elvis Presley in *G.I. Blues* (1960), *Blue Hawaii* (1961), *Girls! Girls! Girls!* (1962), and *It Happened at the World's Fair* (1963). Norman Taurog's last film was *Live a Little, Love a Little* (1968), which also featured Presley.

After his retirement, Taurog taught at U.C.L.A., and, after becoming increasingly blind, became a director of the Braille Institute in Los Angeles. A versatile director, Taurog always emphasized entertainment in his films.

VERA-ELLEN (February 16, 1926-August 30, 1981). After singing and dancing in nightclubs and on Broadway, Vera-Ellen came to films when signed by Sam Goldwyn to star opposite Danny Kaye in *The Wonder Man* (1945) and

The Kid from Brooklyn (1946). Other films include *Words and Music* (1948), *On the Town* (1949), *Happy Go Lucky* (1951), *Call Me Madam* (1953), and *White Christmas* (1954). Her last film was the British *Let's Be Happy* (1957).

GEORGE WALSH (1889-June 13, 1981). The younger brother of director Raoul Walsh began his screen career as an actor in 1914 and soon became noted for virile, active roles in films such as *The Honor System* (1917), *Luck and Pluck* (1919), and *A Manhattan Knight* (1920). Walsh was originally signed to play the title role in *Ben-Hur* (1925), and it is generally supposed that the loss of the role to Ramon Novarro led to the end of his career, although Walsh did appear in small roles in a number of features in the 1930's.

JOHN WARBURTON (June 18, 1899-November, 1981). After performing on the New York stage, Warburton went to Hollywood in 1932 to appear in *Cavalcade* (1933), and stayed to play debonair minor leading men with English accents in productions such as *The White Cliffs of Dover* (1944), and *Saratoga Trunk* (1946).

JACK WARNER (October 24, 1900-May, 1981). One of England's better-known character actors, Jack Warner entered films in 1943 and came to prominence as the murdered policeman in *The Blue Lamp* (1949). For twenty-one years, he starred on television on the BBC series, "Dixon of Dock Green." Other films include *The Captive Heart* (1945), *Holiday Camp* (1947), *Scrooge* (1951), *Albert R.N.* (1953), *The Ladykillers* (1955), and *Jigsaw* (1962).

HARRY WARREN (December 24, 1893-September 22, 1981). A listing of Harry Warren's song credits reads like a history of the best in twentieth century American music. Among the songs which he composed are "You're My Everything" (1931), "Shuffle Off to Buffalo" (1932), "I'll String Along with You" (1934), "I Only Have Eyes for You" (1934), "Lullaby of Broadway" (1935), "September in the Rain" (1937), "Jeepers Creepers" (1938), "Jezebel" (1938), "I've Got a Gal in Kalamazoo" (1942), "You'll Never Know" (1943), "Zing a Little Zong" (1952), "That's Amore" (1953), and hundreds more.

Not only did Warren write the music for all these songs, but he also wrote most of them for Hollywood musicals. If the songs themselves are not impressive enough, his film musicals include *The Laugh Parade* (1931), *42nd Street* (1932), *Gold Diggers of 1933* (1933), *Roman Scandals* (1933), *Dames* (1934), *Gold Diggers of 1935* (1935), *Cain and Mabel* (1936), *Orchestra Wives* (1942), *Diamond Horseshoe* (1945), *Yolanda and the Thief* (1945), *The Harvey Girls* (1945), *An Affair to Remember* (1957), *Cinderfella* (1960), and more than sixty more.

Harry Warren was born Salvatore Guaragna in Brooklyn, New York, and was a self-taught musician. He entered the film industry with the Brooklyn-based Vitagraph Company in the mid-teens, working as an assistant director and musical accompanist for silent stars as they emoted before the camera. In the 1920's, Harry Warren first worked as a song plugger before graduating to composing scores for Broadway hits. His film career began in earnest in the early 1930's. He teamed with Al Dubin to write the scores for some of the best-known of the Warner Bros. musicals of the early 1930's, including *Gold Diggers of 1933* (1933), *Footlight Parade* (1933), *Wonder Bar* (1934), *Dames* (1934), *Go into Your Dance* (1935), *In Caliente* (1935), *Page Miss Glory* (1935), and *Hearts Divided* (1936).

Warren and Al Dubin split up in the late 1930's, when Warren teamed with Mack Gordon to write the music for such Twentieth Century-Fox productions as *Down Argentine Way* (1940), *Sun Valley Serenade* (1941), *Orchestra Wives* (1942), *Sweet Rosie O'Grady* (1943), and *Diamond Horseshoe* (1945). He received eleven Academy Award nominations and three Oscars for Best Song for "Lullaby of Broadway" (1935), "You'll Never Know" (1943) and "On the Atchison, Topeka and the Santa Fe" (1946).

In more recent years, Warren wrote the theme song for the television series "The Legend of Wyatt Earp." He wrote a number of pieces of serious music, notably a Mass, written in 1962 but not given its first performance until 1980. The 1980 stage musical of *42nd Street* further enhanced Warren's reputation as one of the greatest popular composers of this century.

RICHARD WATTS, JR. (January 12, 1898-January 2, 1981). Richard Watts, Jr., was an influential film critic, initially with *The New York Herald* (later *Herald-Tribune*) from 1924 through 1936. He succeeded Percy Hammond as the newspaper's drama critic in 1936, later becoming drama critic for *The New York Post* from 1946 through 1976.

LAZAR WECHSLER (1896-August 8, 1981). Switzerland's leading film producer since the 1920's and founder of Praesens Film, Polish-born Lazar Wechsler argued, "I want Americans to talk about Swiss films the way they do about Swiss watches." His best-known productions are *Marie Louise* (1944), *The Last Chance* (1945), *The Search* (1948), and *Heidi and Peter* (1954).

GRANT WHYTOCK (1894-November 10, 1981). After many years as an editor, working with director Rex Ingram on such classic films as *The Four Horsemen of the Apocalypse* (1921), *Scaramouche* (1923), and *Mare Nostrum* (1926), Grant Whytock became a production associate of Edward Small.

NATALIE WOOD (July 20, 1938-November 29, 1981). The accidental drowning death of Natalie Wood was a major tragedy, robbing the cinema of one of its most enduring and perennially young leading ladies. Sadly, her death came prior to completion of the actress' current film project, *Brainstorm*, which Douglas Trumbull was directing for M-G-M. Natalie Wood's life was very much that of a fairy-tale character who marries (twice) her Prince Charming, in the form of Robert Wagner—the two made a handsome couple—and offered the world an enchanting personality and a durable acting career.

Born in San Francisco, Natalie Wood first appeared in films as an extra in *Happy Land* (1943), filmed in her hometown of Santa Rosa. The director of *Happy Land*, Irving Pichel, was impressed with Wood's work and brought her to Hollywood for a supporting role in *Tomorrow Is Forever* (1945). Wood quickly became one of Hollywood's busiest dramatic child actresses, typifying the average American daughter without the cuteness of the early Shirley Temple or Margaret O'Brien, in films such as *The Bride Wore Boots* (1946), *The Ghost and Mrs. Muir* (1947), *Scudda-Hoo, Scudda-Hay!* (1949), *Father Was a Fullback* (1949), and *No Sad Songs for Me* (1950). She was superb as the child, wise beyond her years, who learns to believe in Santa Claus in *Miracle on 34th Street* (1947).

Wood began the second stage of her career as a teenager in *Rebel Without a Cause* (1955), in which she portrayed James Dean's girl friend. She was nominated for an Academy Award for her performance, and again in *Splendor in the Grass* (1961) and *Love with the Proper Stranger* (1963), but she was never to win an Oscar. (One distinction, if such it be, which Wood did attain was to have the Harvard Lampoon initiate, in her honor, the Natalie Wood Award for the Worst Performance by an Actress.)

After *The Searchers* (1956), *Marjorie Morningstar* (1958), *All the Fine Young Cannibals* (1960), *Splendor in the Grass* (1961), *West Side Story* (1961), and *Gypsy* (1962), Wood entered upon the third and final phase of her screen career with *Bob and Carol and Ted and Alice* (1969), which offered the new, mature Wood in a disappointing sex comedy. Later roles in *Meteor* (1978) and *The Last Married Couple in America* (1980) were equally disappointing.

Natalie Wood grew up as a Hollywood child. Unfortunately, after her death she was the subject of the sort of scandalous gossip which is so much a part of the Hollywood scene.

WILLIAM WYLER (July 1, 1902-July 27, 1981). William Wyler was a major Hollywood director for more than three decades. He was nominated for twelve Academy Awards for Best Direction and won three, one each for *Mrs. Miniver* (1942), *The Best Years of Our Lives* (1946), and *Ben-Hur* (1959). In addition, Wyler received the distinguished Irving G. Thalberg Memorial Award from the Academy in 1965, in recognition of his long career as the producer of many of the films which he directed.

From his native Alsace, the young William Wyler went to Switzerland and then to France before casually meeting Carl Laemmle, the head of Universal, while the latter was on one of his periodic visits to Europe. Laemmle promised Wyler a position at the studio, and the director-to-be eagerly packed his bags and moved to New York, where he began writing publicity for Universal's releases abroad. There, Wyler met Paul Kohner, who was to become the director's agent and longtime friend, and who recalled, "It was a typical Horatio Alger kind of story. He never suffered. It was a continued story of rise and tremendous success."

In 1925, William Wyler became a director, beginning his career with two-reel Westerns before graduating to feature-length Westerns in 1927. It was not until 1928 that Wyler directed his first non-Western feature, *Anybody Here Seen Kelly?*, which starred Bessie Love and Tom Moore. Wyler's first major production at Universal was the 1933 John Barrymore vehicle, *Counsellor-at-Law*; it is still a fine picture, as is Wyler's last film under his Universal contract, *The Good Fairy* (1935), which boasted a script by Preston Sturges based on the Ferenc Molnar play and starred Margaret Sullavan (whom Wyler married in 1934 and divorced in 1936).

From Universal, Wyler went under contract to Sam Goldwyn, where his first film was *These Three* (1936), which—despite censorship problems forcing the elimination of the lesbian theme—remains a superb production thanks to Wyler's direction and the playing of Bonita Granville, whose performance as the spiteful child completely eclipses those of the stars, Joel McCrea, Miriam Hopkins, and Merle Oberon. *These Three* was followed by *Dodsworth* (1936, for which Wyler received his first Academy Award nomination), *Dead End* (1937), *Jezebel* (1938, in which Wyler directed Bette Davis for the first time), and *Wuthering Heights* (1939).

Goldwyn was happy to loan out Wyler to direct Bette Davis at Warner Bros. in *The Letter* (1940) and to M-G-M to direct Greer Garson and Walter Pidgeon in *Mrs. Miniver* (1942). During World War II, Wyler served as a lieutenant colonel in the Army Air Corps, directing two major documentaries, *The Memphis Belle* (1944) and *Thunderbolt* (1945). During the war, Wyler lost the hearing in his right ear and, as a disabled veteran himself, was able to bring personal objectivity to his first postwar production, *The Best Years of Our Lives* (1946), a study of the problems facing returning veterans, featuring Myrna Loy, Fredric March, Dana Andrews, and the disabled Harold Russell.

The Best Years of Our Lives was followed by *The Heiress* (1949), *Detective Story* (1951), *Carrie* (1952), *Roman Holiday* (1953), *Friendly Persuasion* (1956), and *The Big Country* (1958). In 1959, Wyler directed the M-G-M remake of *Ben-Hur* (he had worked as an assistant director on the silent version), which received a record eleven Academy Awards. It would have been a fitting climax to Wyler's career, but the director was not then ready for retirement. He went on to direct a remake of *These Three*, *The Children's Hour* (1962), *The Collector* (1965), *How to Steal a Million* (1966), and *Funny Girl* (1968). Wyler ended his career with a racial drama entitled *The Liberation of L. B. Jones* (1970).

Wyler had planned to direct *40 Carats*, but his doctors advised against strenuous work. Instead, Wyler worked on an autobiography, and traveled around receiving accolades from colleges and film institutions. In 1976, he received the Life Achievement Award from the American Film Institute, and, just prior to his death, Wyler returned from a retrospective of his films at the British Film Institute.

LIST OF AWARDS

Academy Awards

Best Picture: Chariots of Fire (Warner Bros.)
Direction: Warren Beatty (*Reds*)
Actor: Henry Fonda (*On Golden Pond*)
Actress: Katharine Hepburn (*On Golden Pond*)
Supporting Actor: John Gielgud (*Arthur*)
Supporting Actress: Maureen Stapleton (*Reds*)
Original Screenplay: Colin Welland (*Chariots of Fire*)
Adapted Screenplay: Ernest Thompson (*On Golden Pond*)
Cinematography: Vittorio Storaro (*Reds*)
Editing: Michael Kahn (*Raiders of the Lost Ark*)
Art Direction: Norman Reynolds and Leslie Dilley; set decoration, Michael Ford (*Raiders of the Lost Ark*)
Visual Effects: Richard Edlund, Kit West, Bruce Nicholson, and Joe Johnston (*Raiders of the Lost Ark*)
Sound: Bill Varney, Steve Maslow, Gregg Landaker, and Roy Charman (*Raiders of the Lost Ark*)
Makeup: Rick Baker (*An American Werewolf in London*)
Costume Design: Milena Canonero (*Chariots of Fire*)
Original Score: Vangelis (*Chariots of Fire*)
Original Song: "Arthur's Theme: Best That You Can Do" (*Arthur*: music and lyrics, Burt Bacharach, Carole Bayer Sager, Christopher Cross, and Peter Allen)
Foreign-Language Film: Mephisto (Hungary)

Directors Guild of America Award

Director: Warren Beatty (*Reds*)

Writers Guild Awards

Original Drama: Warren Beatty and Trevor Griffiths (*Reds*)
Adapted Drama: Ernest Thompson (*On Golden Pond*)
Original Comedy: Steve Gordon (*Arthur*)
Adapted Comedy: Gerald Ayre (*Rich and Famous*)

New York Film Critics Awards

Best Picture: Reds (Paramount)
Direction: Sidney Lumet (*Prince of the City*)
Actor: Burt Lancaster (*Atlantic City*)
Actress: Glenda Jackson (*Stevie*)
Supporting Actor: John Gielgud (*Arthur*)
Supporting Actress: Mona Washbourne (*Stevie*)

Screenplay: John Guare (*Atlantic City*)
Cinematography: David Watkin (*Chariots of Fire*)
Foreign-Language Film: Pixote (Brazil)

Los Angeles Film Critics Awards
Best Picture: Atlantic City (Paramount)
Direction: Warren Beatty (*Reds*)
Actor: Burt Lancaster (*Atlantic City*)
Actress: Meryl Streep (*The French Lieutenant's Woman*)
Supporting Actor: John Gielgud (*Arthur*)
Supporting Actress: Maureen Stapleton (*Reds*)
Screenplay: John Guare (*Atlantic City*)
Cinematography: Vittorio Storaro (*Reds*)
Music: Randy Newman (*Ragtime*)
Foreign-Language Film: Pixote (Brazil)

National Society of Film Critics Awards
Best Picture: Atlantic City (Paramount)
Direction: Louis Malle (*Atlantic City*)
Actor: Burt Lancaster (*Atlantic City*)
Actress: Marilia Pera (*Pixote*)
Supporting Actor: Robert Preston (*S.O.B.*)
Supporting Actress: Maureen Stapleton (*Reds*)
Screenplay: John Guare (*Atlantic City*)
Cinematography: Gordon Willis (*Pennies from Heaven*)

National Board of Review Awards
Best English-Language Film: Reds (Paramount) and *Chariots of Fire* (Warner Bros.), tie
Direction: Warren Beatty (*Reds*)
Actor: Henry Fonda (*On Golden Pond*)
Actress: Glenda Jackson (*Stevie*)
Supporting Actor: Jack Nicholson (*Reds*)
Supporting Actress: Mona Washbourne (*Stevie*)
Foreign-Language Film: Oblomov (USSR)

The Golden Globe Awards
Best Picture, Drama: On Golden Pond (Universal)
Best Picture, Comedy or Musical: Arthur (Orion)
Direction: Warren Beatty (*Reds*)
Actor, Drama: Henry Fonda (*On Golden Pond*)
Actress, Drama: Meryl Streep (*The French Lieutenant's Woman*)
Actor, Comedy or Musical: Dudley Moore (*Arthur*)

Actress, Comedy or Musical: Bernadette Peters (*Pennies from Heaven*)
Supporting Actor: John Gielgud (*Arthur*)
Supporting Actress: Joan Hackett (*Only When I Laugh*)
Screenplay: Ernest Thompson (*On Golden Pond*)
Original Song: "Arthur's Theme: Best That You Can Do" (*Arthur*: music and lyrics, Burt Bacharach, Carole Bayer Sager, Christopher Cross, and Peter Allen)
Foreign Film: *Chariots of Fire* (England)

Gold Palm Awards (Cannes International Film Festival)
Gold Palm: *L'Homme de Fer* (*Man of Iron*; Andrzej Wajda)
Grand Special Jury Award: *Les Années Lumières* (*Light Years Away*; Alain Tanner)
Actor: Ugo Tognazzi (*La Tragedia di un Uomo Ridicolo*)
Actress: Isabelle Adjani (*Quartet*)
Supporting Actor: Ian Holm (*Chariots of Fire*)
Supporting Actress: Elena Solovei (*Le Groupe Sanguin Zero*)
Screenplay: István Szabó and Peter Dobai (*Mephisto*)
Artistic Contribution: John Boorman (*Excalibur*)

British Academy Awards
Best Picture: *Chariots of Fire* (Warner Bros.)
Direction: Louis Malle (*Atlantic City*)
Actor: Burt Lancaster (*Atlantic City*)
Actress: Meryl Streep (*The French Lieutenant's Woman*)
Supporting Artist: Ian Holm (*Chariots of Fire*)
Screenplay: Bill Forsyth (*Gregory's Girl*)
Cinematography: Ghislain Cloquet and Geoffrey Unsworth (*Tess*)
Editing: Thelma Schoonmaker (*Raging Bull*)
Production Design: Norman Reynolds (*Raiders of the Lost Ark*)
Costume Design: Milena Canonero (*Chariots of Fire*)
Sound: Don Sharp, Ivan Sharrock, and Bill Rowe (*The French Lieutenant's Woman*)
Original Music: Carl Davis (*The French Lieutenant's Woman*)

MAGILL'S CINEMA ANNUAL

1982

TITLE INDEX

DIRECTOR INDEX

DIRECTOR INDEX

SCREENWRITER INDEX

SCREENWRITER INDEX

CINEMATOGRAPHER INDEX

EDITOR INDEX

EDITOR INDEX

ART DIRECTOR INDEX

MUSIC INDEX

PERFORMER INDEX

PERFORMER INDEX

PERFORMER INDEX

PERFORMER INDEX

PERFORMER INDEX

PERFORMER INDEX

SUBJECT INDEX